THE
SUBSTANCE
OF
POLITICS

THE SUBSTANCE OF POLITICS

A. APPADORAI

OXFORD
UNIVERSITY PRESS

OXFORD
UNIVERSITY PRESS

Oxford University Press is a department of the University of Oxford.
It furthers the University's objective of excellence in research, scholarship,
and education by publishing worldwide. Oxford is a registered trademark of
Oxford University Press in the UK and in certain other countries

Published in India by
Oxford University Press
22 Workspace, 2nd Floor, 1/22 Asaf Ali Road, New Delhi 110002, India

First Edition published in 1942
Eleventh edition 1975
Oxford India Paperbacks 2000
31st impression 2025

ISBN-13: 978-0-19-565633-6
ISBN-10: 0-19-565633-4

Printed in India by Manipal Technologies Limited, Manipal

PREFACE TO ELEVENTH EDITION

IN preparing this edition I have not disturbed the fundamental structure of the book. The essential principles of political theory and organization, on which this book is based, remain valid even in our rapidly-changing world. As with previous editions, an effort has again been made to up-date the section on modern constitutions in particular; however, since the revision of the text was completed by July 1974, constitutional changes occurring thereafter are not referred to in this edition. The chapter on Pakistan has been expanded to include a discussion of the 1973 Constitution, and an additional chapter has been written on the 1972 Constitution of Bangladesh. Political changes within societies frequently result in the replacement of one constitution by another. As this book also discusses various forms of political organization in historical prespective, some superceded constitutions of the world continue to be described, for they contain elements worthy of study and are landmarks in the evolution of institutions.

A. A.

NEW DELHI
1 *August* 1974

PREFACE TO FIRST EDITION

THIS book is an attempt to state briefly and simply the essential principles of political theory and organization. It has been written primarily to meet the needs of the undergraduate.

I wish to thank Mr K. Subrahmanyam, Lecturer in English, Loyola College, Madras, for having read the book in manuscript and corrected many errors; Dr Eddy Asirvatham, Reader in Politics, University of Madras, for having read the book and offered helpful suggestions; and Professor Venkatasubrahmanya Iyer of the Law College, Madras, for helpful criticisms of the chapter on India. I need not say that none of them has any responsibility for the opinions expressed.

I also owe a special debt of gratitude to the Oxford University Press for the great care they have devoted to the printing and publishing of the book.

A. A.

MADRAS
8 *November* 1942

CONTENTS

PART ONE : POLITICAL THEORY

PART TWO : POLITICAL ORGANIZATION

BOOK I. HISTORY OF GOVERNMENT

BOOK II. MODERN CONSTITUTIONS

Part One
POLITICAL THEORY

CHAPTER I

FUNDAMENTAL IDEAS

§1 WHAT IS POLITICS?

WHEN we observe the life of men around us, we cannot fail to be struck by two facts : as a rule, every man desires to have his own way, to think and act as he likes ; and at the same time, everyone cannot have his own way, because he lives in society. One man's desires conflict with those of another. The relations of the individual members of society with one another, therefore, need regulation by government. When a body of people is clearly organized as a unit for purposes of government, then it is said to be *politically*[1] organized and may be called a body politic or State—a society politically organized. The essence of such a society is that a group of people called the Government are clothed with authority to make laws and enforce them; they claim obedience from the members of the society whom they govern.

Politics, then, deals with the State or political society, meaning by the term a people organized for law within a definite territory. The subject has two main subdivisions : (*i*) Political theory and (*ii*) Political organization.

Political theory, in the words of Sir Ernest Barker, is primarily concerned with the purpose or purposes which man proposes to himself as a moral being, living in association with other moral beings. It asks : What are the purposes of political organization and what are the best means of realizing them ? The individual wants to realize his best self : to what extent can the State help him in this, his natural endeavour ? What is the nature of the authority of the State ? Has the State, for instance, unlimited power to regulate the thought and activities of individuals or are there limitations to its powers ? Has the individual rights against the State ? The reconciliation of the authority of the State with the liberty of the individual in order to promote social good on the largest possible scale is thus the fundamental problem of political theory. And, since the freedom of the individual is considerably affected by the form of government under which he lives and by the relation of his State to other States, forms of government and inter-State relations are also of great importance to political theory.

[1] The term Politics is derived from the Greek word *polis*, a city-State.

Political theory is thus concerned with the formulation of the ends and limits of State authority. Government is the instrument by means of which the purposes of the State are sought to be realized. A study of Politics should, therefore, naturally include an analysis of government and its working. This is the subject-matter of the second part of our study, viz. political organization. The forms and the working of government have not, however, always been of the same pattern. Thus in ancient India, Greece and Rome, monarchy was the earliest form of government; in Greece and Rome it gave place first to aristocracy and then to democracy. The study of these forms of government, as they arose under particular historical conditions, should obviously form the first part of a study of political organization. The working of modern Governments with their infinite variety comes next. And, finally, from a study of the past and the present, the student will be in a position to formulate, by an inductive process, principles regarding the organization of government, its structure and working. For instance, a study of Governments, past and present, tells us that all power corrupts, and absolute power corrupts absolutely ;[1] therefore power must be a check to power. Such a study helps one not only to understand the principles of governmental organization but also to learn the comparative merits and defects of the different types of Legislature, Executive and Judiciary.

These divisions of the subject are not watertight compartments ; they touch one another at various points as they all centre in the State. Politics may therefore be defined as ' the science concerned with the State and of the conditions essential to its existence and development ' ; or, in the words of Janet, ' that part of social science which treats of the foundations of the State and the principles of government '.

§2 IS POLITICS A SCIENCE?

At the outset of our study we are faced with a crucial question : Is Politics a science at all ?

' Each professor of political science,' writes Barker,[2] ' is apt to feel about the other professors, if not about himself, that they argue from questionable axioms, by a still more questionable process of logic to conclusions that are almost unquestionably wrong. The layman, even more sceptical, is inclined to adopt towards political science the attitude of Mrs Prig to the Mrs Harris so often mentioned by Mrs Gamp : " I don't believe there's no such a subject." '

[1] The phrase is Lord Acton's.
[2] Sir Ernest Barker, *Education for Citizenship*, p. 6.

In similar vein writes Maitland : ' When I see a good set of examination questions headed by the words " Political Science " I regret not the questions but the title.' [1] Why this hesitation ?

We can explain it only if we grasp clearly the meaning of the term ' science '. The classification of facts and the formation upon that basis of absolute judgements, which are consistent and universally valid, sum up the essential aim of modern science. Thus gravitation tends to make things fall to the ground ; two parts of hydrogen and one part of oxygen constitute water : they cannot help themselves. These are exact statements ; physics and chemistry are exact sciences. Classification, general rules based on such classification, and predictability—these are essential to the scientific method.

Let it at once be admitted that Politics is not and cannot be an exact science in the sense that physics and chemistry are. It has too few certainties. Its premises are uncertain ; its conclusions are dubious. On almost every aspect of the subject there are at least two, and often more, views. For instance, that high authority Mill says that ' it is in general a necessary condition of free institutions that the boundaries of Governments should coincide in the main with those of nationalities'. On the contrary, Lord Acton, an equally high authority, holds that the combination of different nations in one State is as necessary a condition of civilized life as the combination of individuals to form society. Again, should there be two chambers to a Legislature ? Laski and Sidgwick differ.[2] Is communal representation in Legislatures and the public services desirable ? Opinions vary. Even on the definition of fundamental terms, such as the State, there is no unanimity.[3] R. M. MacIver differs from Laski.

Politics is not an exact science, like physics and chemistry, because the material with which it deals is incapable of being treated in the same exact way. Physics and chemistry are natural or physical sciences ; they deal with matter. Politics, economics and ethics are social sciences ; they deal with man in society. ' One chemical element is exactly the same all the world over ; any variations in its composition can be tested and explained.' It is difficult to consider problems of man in the same exact way as we consider problems of matter. Social phenomena are perpetually undergoing change and are more difficult to control. The motives which lead men to act, no less than the consequences of their acts, are so complex and variable that it is difficult accurately to determine the one or confidently to predict the other. Consider, for instance, the effects of the planning of economic life in India. The

[1] F. W. Maitland, *Collected Papers*, Vol. III, p. 302.
[2] See below, ch. xxviii.   [3] See ch. i, §7 and ch. iv, §3.

planning of economic life is being attempted in India and the Soviet Union ; while it is too early to assess precisely the results of the experiment in India, it is possible to say that the method of planning under the democratic set-up of India is clearly different from that adopted in the Soviet Union and that the results cannot be identical. Again, in the natural sciences it is possible to experiment with matter in a way impossible in the social sciences. In other words, it is possible artificially to create actual uniformities for the purposes of comparison ; to make, that is to say, out of unlike things, things so alike that valid inferences can be drawn as to their behaviour in like circumstances. Thus, as Graham Wallas pointed out, metallurgy became a science when men could actually take two pieces of copper ore, unlike in shape and appearance and chemical constitution, and extract from them two pieces of copper so nearly alike that they would give the same results when treated in the same way. This power over his material the student of Politics can never possess. He can never create an artificial uniformity in man. ' He cannot after twenty generations of education or breeding render even two human beings sufficiently like each other for him to prophesy with any approach to certainty that they will behave alike under like circumstances.'

That is why a discerning scholar like Lord Bryce was content to compare Politics to a relatively undeveloped and inexact natural science like meteorology, somewhat in the same way as Marshall had earlier compared economics to the science of tides ; in all these subjects the possibility of error in prediction is considerable. Sir Frederick Pollock maintained that there is a science of Politics in the same sense and nearly to the same extent as there is a science of morals. ' Those who deny the existence of a political science, if they mean that there is no body of rules or law from which a prime minister may infallibly learn how to command a majority in Parliament, would be right as to the fact, but would betray a rather inadequate notion of what science is.' Politics, like other social sciences, has a scientific character because the scientific method is applicable to its phenomena, viz. the accumulation of facts, the linking of these together in causal sequences and the generalization from the latter of fundamental principles or laws. It is true that the laboratory method of experiment is difficult with social sciences ; but the whole field of historical facts and the facts of the contemporary world are there for the student to observe, classify, connect, and compare for the formulation of general principles. Take, for instance, the study of revolutions, their causes and cure. The revolutions of history, such as the English Revolution of 1688, the French Revolution of 1789, the Russian Revolution of 1917 and the Chinese Revolution of 1949, are the materials

for the student to study and compare. Aristotle was able by a study
of the revolutions prior to his day (he studied the history of 158
constitutions) to formulate the generalization that the most general
cause of revolutionary movements was the craving of men for
equality ; and their best preventive, the principle of the mean. It
is not only a tribute to the wisdom of Aristotle but to the possibility
of the scientific character of political investigation, that this generalization applies to the revolutions since his day. The larger the
number of facts studied, the wider the area from which these facts
are observed, and the greater the care with which they are studied
in relation to their environment, the greater the possibility of the
precision and value of the generalization obtained. The development of psychology, the scientific use of history and the application
of quantitative methods to political data will enhance the claim
of Politics to be considered a science.[1]

§3 POLITICS AND HISTORY

The subject-matter of Politics is closely related to history,
economics and ethics.

History is a record of past events and movements, their causes
and interrelations. It includes a survey of economic, religious,
intellectual and social developments as well as a study of States,
their growth and organization and their relations with one another.

Politics and history are mutually interdependent. Some facts
of history constitute a part of the groundwork of political science
—those facts which are significant for the study of political ideas
and institutions ; in this sense, historical facts are the raw material
of political science. On the other hand, history gains in significance
and value because of political science. As Lord Acton said, the
science of Politics is the one science that is deposited by the
stream of history like the grains of gold in the sands of a river.
Professor Seeley puts it well when he says political science is the
fruit of history and history is the root of political science. To
illustrate : it is a lesson of history that people who are denied a
share in political power are also denied a share in the benefits of
power ; hence the conclusion of Politics that democracy with all
its defects is the safest form of government. It has been rightly
remarked that Politics is vulgar when not liberalized by history,
and that history fades into mere literature when it loses sight of
its relation to Politics.

But while political science is thus dependent on history for its
material, it must be made clear that history supplies only part of
its material. It has to draw largely on other social sciences such

[1] On this point see G. Wallas, *Human Nature in Politics*, ch. v.

as economics, ethics, psychology, and jurisprudence—and on contemporary observation. Again, all facts of history are not useful to political science. Only those facts which bear directly or indirectly on the study of the State are useful to it. Much of history, like the history of art, of science, of inventions and discoveries, military campaigns, languages, dress, industries and religious controversies, has little, if any, relation to Politics and affords no material for political investigation. To take familiar examples, the Tudor period in English history (1485-1603) is useful to the student of political science as providing data for the study of factors leading to the establishment of absolute monarchy on a popular basis ; but the rebellions and conspiracies of the period, the marriages of Henry VIII, the religious changes and persecutions, and the course of the Spanish Armada are of little value in laying down principles of political organization. Similarly, the Mogul period of Indian history (1526-1761) is of great value in Politics as providing data for the study of factors leading to the establishment (or disruption) of a unified and stable State where the rulers belong to a militant minority alien in faith to the vast bulk of their subjects ; but the rebellions, disputed successions and military campaigns of the period, the development of Mogul art, and the evolution of the historical literature of the time, though indispensable to the student of history, are hardly of any value to the student of Politics. Political science selects facts out of history. In this selective function, the student of Politics is not limited by chronology as the student of history is. The historian has to aim primarily at presenting facts in their chronological order ; the student of political science has to bring together for comparison societies similar in their political characteristics though separated in time. Thus the Governments of the early Greeks, the Romans and the Teutons of Germany present many similar characteristics.

And, finally, with Sidgwick, we may add that while the primary interest of history is concrete, the presentation of facts, the primary interest of Politics is abstract, the formulation of general laws and principles.

'What as students of political science we are primarily concerned to ascertain, is not the structure or functions of government in any particular historical community, but the distinctive characteristics of different forms of government in respect of their structure or their functions ; not the particular processes of political change in (e.g.) Athens or England, but the general laws or tendencies of change exemplified by such particular processes.' [1]

' H. Sidgwick, *The Development of European Polity*, p. 2.

§4 ECONOMICS AND POLITICS

Economics, so runs a classic definition, is a study of mankind in the ordinary business of life ; it examines that part of individual and social action which is most closely connected with the attainment and with the use of the material requisites of well-being. Briefly, it is the science of wealth. Economics touches Politics at more than one point because the production and the distribution of wealth are largely influenced by government, and because the solution of many economic problems must come through political channels. Indeed, so close is the influence of Politics on economic conditions that early writers on economics considered their subject as a branch of Politics and termed it political economy. Taxation, tariff laws, government ownership of public utilities like railways and electricity, and State aid to agriculture and industry are instances where governmental policy clearly affects economic prosperity. Economic conditions in the Soviet Union differ widely from elsewhere because of the socialistic policy of its Government. Indeed many problems of the modern State are essentially economic in character : the adjustment of the claims of capital and labour, the reduction of economic inequality, nationalization, and the achievement of a stable international order.

Secondly, political ideas and institutions are themselves influenced by economic conditions. A good example in the field of ideas is the rise of socialism, which is largely a theory born out of, and advocated with a view to reducing, economic inequality. The influence of economic conditions on political institutions is illustrated by the rise of feudal government in medieval Europe, in which political power and citizenship were based on the holding of land. The rise of democracy in nineteenth-century Europe owes not a little to the Industrial Revolution, the rise of the artisan class and the growth of towns. The nature and functions of the Government of a pastoral people must differ considerably from those of the Governments of agricultural and industrial communities.

§5 POLITICS AND ETHICS

Ethics is a branch of study which investigates the laws of morality and formulates rules of conduct. It deals with the rightness and wrongness of man's conduct and the ideals towards which man is working. What is the basis of moral obligation ? What do we mean by right action ? How are we to distinguish a right action from a wrong one ? These are some of the questions with which ethics concerns itself.

If, as Lord Acton said, the great question for Politics is to discover not what Governments prescribe, but what they ought to prescribe, the connexion between ethics and Politics is clear, for on every political issue the question may be raised whether it is right or wrong. And, if we agree with Fox that what is morally wrong can never be politically right, we may say that Politics is conditioned by ethics. Political theory is concerned with the end of the State, the rights of individuals, the functions of government and the relations of State with State. Every one of these has a moral aspect. The end of the State has been formulated by the greatest political thinkers in terms of moral values. Aristotle, for instance, said that while the State comes into existence for the sake of life, it continues to exist for the sake of *good* life. The rights of individuals which deserve recognition by the State can be defined only in a moral context. The State exists to promote social good on the largest possible scale : if that object is to be achieved, the State has progressively to recognize and embody the fundamental rights of man, political, economic and private ; the basis of these rights is the membership of man in society and the moral order underlying social relations. If the State does not recognize these rights, has the individual the right of non-cooperation and resistance ? The question cannot be answered on the purely political plane. The Government proposes to pass laws prohibiting usury, drink, early marriage and untouchability. Is it right to do so ? Again, the State proposes to consider a treaty with a neighbouring State as a ' scrap of paper '. Is this right ? Can a prince, following Machiavelli's advice, be both fox and lion ?

'A prudent ruler ought not to keep faith,' said Machiavelli, ' when by so doing it would be against his interest, and when the reasons which made him bind himself no longer exist. If men were all good, this precept would not be a good one ; but as they are bad, and would not observe their faith with you, so you are not bound to keep faith with them.'

Is this sound political theory ? Is there a difference between public morality and private morality ? Briefly, in so far as Politics is concerned with questions of ' ought to be ' it has points of contact with ethics.

There is another aspect of their interrelation which needs mention. Laws or the commands of the State are obeyed with a greater readiness if they are in keeping with the moral ideas of the community : if they are far ahead of those ideas, they may be difficult to enforce. At the same time laws may slowly and in the long run modify moral standards by ' civic habituation '.

§6 STATE AND GOVERNMENT

Some essentials of a State have been implied in a preceding discussion. They are : (*i*) a definite territory, (*ii*) population, (*iii*) a Government. We may add a fourth to complete the list, namely, sovereignty. These points need some elaboration.

That a State should have some territory is obvious ; it is obvious, too, that no limit or uniformity can be prescribed in respect of the size of States. It is reckoned that there are some 140 organized States at the present time in the world ; these vary considerably in area from San Marino in Italy with its 24·1 square miles, India with 1,261,411 square miles, the United States of America with 3,553,890, to the Union of Soviet Socialist Republics with 8,598,700.[1] Variety apart, the insistence on a definite territory as an essential of a State is necessary ; for it distinguishes the State from a nomadic tribe. As will be shown later,[2] the distinctive mark of a tribe is kinship. Territoriality is not essential to a tribe but *is* to a State.

As with territory so with population. It is obviously essential, but neither the minimum population necessary to constitute a State nor the optimum can be prescribed. In modern States the variation ranges from about 18,000 people in the State of Andorra in the Pyrenees to more than 700 million in China.

While uniformity in territory or population cannot be expected of States, it is noteworthy that the size of States may be an important factor in determining their fortunes. In ancient Greece, the prevalent type of State was the small city-State which could be taken in at a single view. Some of the city-States like Athens attained a richness and variety of life which many bigger modern country-States might well envy. That is primarily because the smaller the size, the greater the unity and patriotism among the people, and the concentration of energy in promoting social happiness.

'To the size of States,' wrote Aristotle,[3] 'there is a limit, as there is to other things, plants, animals, implements ; for none of these retain their natural power when they are too large or too small, but they either wholly lose their nature, or are spoiled. For example, a ship which is only a span long will not be a ship at all, nor a ship a quarter of a mile long ; yet there may be a ship of a certain size, either too large or too small, which will still be a ship, but bad for sailing. In like manner a State when composed of too

---

[1] The figures are taken from *India* 1973, *The Statesman's Year-Book,* 1971 and 1974, and *Encyclopaedia Britannica.*

[2] See below, ch. ii, §§9-11

[3] *Politics* (Jowett's translations), vii, 4.

few is not as a State ought to be, self-sufficing ; when of too many, though self-sufficing in all mere necessaries, it is a nation and not a State, being almost incapable of constitutional government.'

On the other hand, small States are relatively less secure, as they fall an easy prey to bigger and aggressive States.

Government may be defined as the agency or machinery through which the will of the State is formulated, expressed and realized. Properly speaking, therefore, the term includes the sum total of the legislative, executive and judicial bodies in the State, whether of the central or local government, of all those who are engaged in making, administering and interpreting law.

Government has three departments : the Legislature, the Executive and the Judiciary. The primary function of the Legislature is to make laws ; of the Executive, to carry them out ; and of the Judiciary, to interpret them and decide upon their application in individual cases. A sharp separation of the functions of these three branches is, however, never made in practice and is not desirable either. The Legislature, everywhere, has some degree of control over the Executive and Judiciary, and in some States, as in the United States of America, shares in some executive functions such as the making of treaties and the appointing of senior officers; the Executive has some initiative and considerable influence in the making of law, and exercises certain judicial powers ; judges, as Justice Holmes said, ' do and must make law', and in many States have also the power of sitting in judgement on the work of executive officials.[1] Nevertheless, the distinction between the three departments is well worth making and is well recognized both in theory and practice.

Sovereignty means supremacy, and may be defined as the power of the State to make laws and enforce them with all the means cf coercion it cares to employ. It is the distinctive mark of the State, distinguishing it alike from individuals and associations within the State. It has two aspects, internal and external. Internally, it means the power which the State claims to make and enforce law upon individuals and associations within the area of its jurisdiction. Externally, it means independence of foreign control : Britain refuses to be controlled by France and vice versa. To the extent that some ' States ' are subject to a foreign State or States as India was before 1947 or Germany was after her defeat in 1945, they must be deemed to lack one of the essential features of a real State.

Taking these characteristics into consideration, we may define the State as

[1] For examples of the interrelations of the functions of the Legislature, the Executive and the Judiciary see ch. xxvii—The Separation of Powers.

' a territorial society divided into Government and subjects claiming, within its allotted physical area, a supremacy over all other institutions '.[1]

The distinction between State and Government is worth emphasis. From the preceding discussion, it must be obvious that the Government is a narrower term than the State, being only one part of it. The State includes both the Government and the governed. Government is only the machinery through which the purposes of the State are sought to be realized. Again, sovereignty is a characteristic of the State, not of the Government, though it may be exercised by the Government on behalf of the State. Moreover, the State is relatively more permanent than the Government, as the Government of a State frequently changes.

§7 STATE AND SOCIETY

We must also distinguish the State from Society. Society is an association of human beings and suggests the whole complex of the relations of man to his fellows. It consists of the complicated network of groups and institutions expressing human association. The State is one of the groups, a society, not Society. It is the most important group, but still not identical with Society. There are many groups in Society like the family, the caste, the church and the trade union which do influence social life, but which owe neither their origin nor their inspiration to the State. Again, there are social forces like custom, imitation and competition which the State may protect or modify but certainly does not create ; and ' social motives like friendship or jealousy which establish relationships too intimate and personal to be controlled by the great engine of the State '.

The State is a way of regulating human conduct ; it orders us not to murder ; it punishes us for a violation of its order. It is Society in its political aspect.

The differences between the State and Society may be summarized thus : (*i*) Society is a wider term than the State. It suggests many social relationships which cannot be expressed through the State, e.g. education, religion, agricultural and industrial activities, domestic institutions. The State is concerned only with those social relationships that express themselves through government. (*ii*) The term ' society ' applies to all human communities whether organized or unorganized ; but organization for law is essential to a State.

[1] H. J. Laski, *A Grammar of Politics*, p. 21.

' In the earliest phases, among hunters, fishers, root-diggers, and fruit-gatherers, there have been social groups which knew nothing or almost nothing of the State. Today, there remain simple peoples, such as certain groups of Eskimos, which have no recognizable political organization.' [1]

While the State is not identical with Society, nevertheless it provides the framework of the social order; it holds Society together. It binds individuals to certain uniform rules of behaviour which are essential for a harmonious and ordered social life. On that account, however, we must not exaggerate the importance of the State and assume that the individual in Society will obey no rules unless they are backed by the coercive power of the State. Social tolerance and intolerance support a whole mass of habits and customs which are vital to the well-being of Society, e.g. standards of conduct in private and public life, which are not suitable subjects for legislation. These latter form the province of social morality. As Barker puts it, the area of Society is voluntary co-operation, its energy is goodwill and its method is elasticity, while the area of the State is mechanical action, its energy is force and its method is rigidity.

The distinction we have made between the State and Society is fundamental to a true theory of the State, because it helps the realization of individual freedom. To equate State with Society would justify State interference in all aspects of the life of the individual. That may lead to over-government, a totalitarian view of the State, and the consequent tyranny of State control. That, in fact, is what happened in Germany under Hitler (1933-45) and in Italy under Mussolini (1922-44). That is also what happens in the totalitarian State of the Soviet Union which makes no distinction between the State and Society. Individual freedom suffers.

§8 NATIONALITY AND NATION

The idea of nationality is not easy to define, for there is not one single factor to which it can be traced. It is essentially a sentiment of unity, the resultant of many forces ; community of race and language, geographic unity, community of religion, common political aspirations, and, above all, historical development. The presence or absence of any one or more of these factors does not necessarily imply the presence or the absence of a spirit of nationality. The example of the people of the United States of America shows that race is of doubtful importance ; the Swiss defy the difficulties presented by a variety of languages ; the history of

[1] R. M. MacIver, *The Modern State*, p. 5.

the Jews shows it may be the aspiration towards the recovery of a homeland rather than the possession of one that is important. Nationality is essentially spiritual in character, a sentiment, the will of a people to live together—the *vouloir vivre collectif*. In Laski's words : [1]

' It implies the sense of a special unity which marks off those who share in it from the rest of mankind. That unity is the outcome of a common history, of victories won and traditions created by a corporate effort. There grows up a sense of kinship which binds men into oneness. They recognize their likenesses, and emphasize their difference from other men. Their social heritage becomes distinctively their own, as a man lends his own peculiar character to his house. They come to have an art, a literature, recognizably distinct from that of other nations. So England only could have produced Shakespeare and Dickens ; so we admit that there are qualities in Voltaire and Kant from which they typify the nationalism of France and Germany.'

Nationality may, therefore, be defined as ' a spiritual sentiment or principle arising among a number of people usually of the same race. resident on the same territory, sharing a common language, the same religion, similar history and traditions, common interests, with common political associations, and common ideals of political unity '.[2] The term is also applied to the people who feel the sense of nationality. A portion of mankind may be said to constitute a nationality, if they are united among themselves by common sympathies which do not exist between them and any others—which make them co-operate with each other more willingly than with other people, desire to be under the same Government, and desire that it should be Government by themselves or a portion of themselves exclusively (Mill).

The term ' nation ' is obviously allied to nationality, both being from the same Latin root *natus* meaning birth. Some writers, e.g. Burgess and Leacock, have defined the term in a racial or ethnographical sense. Thus Burgess defines a nation as a population with ethnic unity, inhabiting a territory with geographic unity. Leacock similarly says that it indicates a body of people united by common descent and a common language. In recent times, however, especially since the first world war of 1914-18, the term ' nation ' has had a more distinctively political connotation : it has stood for a people who feel united and have or desire an independent Government. There has been a more pronounced tendency to create States on the principle of self-determination :

[1] *A Grammar of Politics*, pp. 219-20.
[2] R. N. Gilchrist, *Principles of Political Science*, 6th ed., p. 26.

'one nationality, one State'. The definitions given by Bryce and Ramsay Muir, and, stiil more, by R. N. Gilchrist and C. J. H. Hayes, show the recent emphasis on the political aspect.

'A nation is a nationality which has organized itself into a political body either independent or desiring to be independent.' (Bryce)

'A nation is a body of people who feel themselves to be naturally linked together by certain affinities which are so strong and real for them that they can live happily together, are dissatisfied when disunited and cannot tolerate subjection to peoples who do not share these ties.' (Ramsay Muir)

'Nation...is the State *plus* something else ; the State looked at from a certain point of view—viz. that of the unity of the people organized in one State.' (Gilchrist)

'A nationality by acquiring unity and sovereign independence becomes a nation.' (Hayes)

State and notion

The distinction between State and nation must be made carefully. According to our definition, a State exists where there are a territory, a people, a Government and sovereignty ; it may lack the feeling of nationality, or of oneness among the people, and yet remain a State. The classic example is Austria-Hungary before the war of 1914-18 ; it was a State but not a nation. The term 'nation' emphasizes the consciousness of unity among its people, and, according to the older view which we have indicated, a nation need not necessarily be a State. Since 1920, however, there has been a tendency both in theory and in fact to associate Statehood with nationhood, to equate nation with a united people organized in a State.

Is this principle of organizing States on the basis of 'one nation one State' a sound one ? Has every nationality the right to form a State ? It is true that a 'uni-national', as distinguished from a 'multi-national', State has some distinct advantages : it facilitates harmony among its parts and engenders a sense of compromise and tolerance among its people which makes it relatively easy for them to work democratic institutions. That is why Mill insisted that it is in general a necessary condition of free institutions that the boundaries of Governments should coincide in the main with those of nationalities. The sense of belonging together creates a readiness on the part of the members of a State to subordinate their differences to the common good. A political society is, clearly, in an unsatisfactory condition when its members have no consciousness of any bond of unity among them except obedience to a common Government.

There lurks, however, in this coincidence a danger pointed out by Lord Acton, to which too little attention has been given. That danger is that, under such conditions, the majority may be tempted to increase the sphere of political regulation and enforce ways of behaviour which are akin to totalitarianism. Said Acton :[1]

' The presence of different nations under the same sovereignty is similar in its effect to the independence of the Church in the State. It provides against the servility which flourishes under the shadow of a single authority by balancing interests, multiply-ing associations, and giving to the subject the restraint and support of a combined opinion. In the same way it promotes independence by forming definite groups of public opinion and by affording a real source and centre of political sentiments and of notions of duty not derived from the sovereign will. Diversity in the same State is a firm barrier against the intrusion of government beyond the political sphere, which is common to all, into the social depart-ment which escapes legislation.'

Acton held that the combination of different nations in one State is as necessary a condition of civilized life as the combination of individuals to form society. Inferior races make progress by living in political union with races intellectually superior. Exhausted and decaying nations are revived by their contact with a younger vitality. Nations in which the elements of organization and the capacity for government have been lost, either through the de-moralizing influence of despotism or the disintegrating action of democracy, are restored and educated anew under the discipline of a stronger and a less corrupted race. This fertilizing and regene-rating process can only be obtained by living under one Govern-ment. The ' multi-national' view has the merit of drawing attention to the healthy idea that not every people is capable of creating and maintaining a State ; only a people of political capacity, possessing manly qualities, understanding and courage, and able to defend itself, can rightly claim to establish an independent State. Events since 1939 only reinforce the strength of this view. The dissociation of Statehood from nationhood will help to mitigate much disquiet and frustration in the world and help to establish international peace.

SELECT BIBLIOGRAPHY

E. BARKER, *The Study of Political Science and its Relation to Cog-nate Studies,* Cambridge, 1928

G. E. G. CATLIN, *The Science and Method of Politics,* Kegan Paul, 1927

G. E. G. CATLIN, *Systematic Politics*, ch. i-ii, Allen & Unwin, 1962

A. COBBAN, *National Self-Determination*, Oxford, 2nd ed., 1948

M. COWLING, *The Nature and Limits of Political Science*, Cambridge, 1963

J. W. GARNER, *Political Science and Government*, ch. i-vi, American Book Company, 1932

H. J. LASKI, *A Grammar of Politics*, ch. vi, Allen & Unwin, 5th ed., 1952

F. W. MAITLAND, *Collected Papers*, Vol. III, pp. 285-303, Cambridge, 1911

R. MUIR, *Nationalism and Internationalism*, Constable, 1919

J. R. SEELEY, *Introduction to Political Science*, Lectures I and II, Macmillan, 1923

G. WALLAS, *Human Nature in Politics*, Part I, Constable, 4th ed., 1949

R. YOUNG, *Approaches to the Study of Politics*, Sweet & Maxwell, 1959

CHAPTER II

THE ORIGIN OF THE STATE

§1 INTRODUCTORY

AMONG the first questions which political theory raises is : What is the origin of the State ? Have men always lived under some form of political organization ? If they have not, what are the causes that brought about the original establishment of government ?

Political thinkers are not agreed on the answer to this fundamental question, with the result that there are various theories concerning the beginnings of the State : the social contract theory, the divine right theory, the force theory, the patriarchal theory, the matriarchal theory and the evolutionary theory. We shall state these theories, examine the element of truth in them and conclude with what we consider to be the generally accepted explanation.

§2 THE SOCIAL CONTRACT THEORY: ITS EARLY HISTORY

The substance of the social contract theory is this : The State is the result of an agreement entered into by men who originally had no governmental organization. The history of the world is thus divisible into two clear periods : the period before the State was instituted and the period after. In the first period, there being no government, there was no law which could be enforced by a coercive authority. Men lived, it was said, in a state of nature, in which they were subject only to such regulations as nature was supposed to prescribe. But there was no human authority to formulate these rules precisely or to enforce them After some time, they decided to set up a Government. Thereby, they parted with their natural liberty and agreed to obey the laws prescribed by the Government. How men lived in the state of nature without the coercive agency of a Government, why they decided to establish a Government, who were the parties to the contract, and what the terms of that contract were—on these and other details there are differences of opinion among the exponents of the theory. But they agree on its essential idea, viz. that the State is a human creation, the result of a contract.

The idea of a social contract is found in the political treatises both of the East and the West. Kautilya, the minister of Chandragupta Maurya, refers to this in his *Arthasastra*[1] (*c*. 321-300 B.C.): ' People suffering from anarchy, as illustrated by the proverbial tendency of a large fish swallowing a small one, first elected Manu to be their king ; and allotted one-sixth of the grains grown and one-tenth of their merchandise as sovereign dues. Supported by this payment, kings took upon themselves the responsibility of maintaining the safety and security of their subjects.' There is a reference to it in the writings of the Greek thinker Plato (428-347 B.C.). In his work, the *Crito*,[2] Socrates is represented as awaiting calmly the execution of his sentence, even though he considered it unjust, because he would not break his *covenant* with the State by escaping from prison into exile. Again, in the *Republic* Glaucon puts forth the view, in the course of a discussion on justice, that legislation and contracts between man and man originated in a compact of mutual abstinence from injustice.

In political discussions, the theory of social contract became significant during and after the Middle Ages. Two forms of the theory are found in these discussions, viz. the governmental contract and the social contract proper. The first postulates a tacit agreement between the Government and the people ; and the second, the institution of a political society by means of a compact among individuals.

The idea of a governmental contract was largely employed by the defenders of popular liberties in the Middle Ages to resist the claims of rulers to an absolute dominion over their subjects. Thus Manegold, in the eleventh century, developed the idea that a king could be deposed when he had violated the agreement according to which he was chosen :[3]

' No man can make himself emperor or king ; a people sets a man over it to the end that he may rule justly, giving to every man his own, aiding good men and coercing bad ; in short, that he may give justice to all men. If then he violates the *agreement* according to which he was chosen, disturbing and confounding the very things which he was meant to put in order, reason dictates that he absolves the people from their obedience ; especially when he has himself first broken the faith which bound him and the people together.'

By his ' oath at his coronation ' a king was supposed to have made a pact with his people to promote a happy and virtuous life,

---

[1] Bk. I, ch. xiii.
[2] *Socratic Discourses*, ' Everyman's Library ', p. 359, xii.
[3] Quoted by Carlyle in *A History of Mediaeval Political Theory in the West*, Vol. III, p. 164, n. 1.

and if he failed to fulfil his implied pact with his people he ceased to deserve, says St Thomas Aquinas (*c.* 1225-74), that the pact should be kept by the latter. The same note is struck in *The Grounds of Rights Against Tyrants* by Du Plessis-Mornay (1579), *On the Sovereign Power Among the Scots* by Buchanan (1579), and *On Kingship and Education of a King* by Mariana (1599). An important recognition of the theory was the declaration of the Convention Parliament in England in 1688 that James II 'having endeavoured to subvert the constitution by breaking the original contract between king and people' had rendered the throne vacant.

The social contract, as distinguished from the governmental contract, is probably first mentioned in Hooker's *The Laws of Ecclesiastical Polity* (1594-7). Hooker postulates an original state of nature in which men were subject only to the law of nature. In course of time men realized that to remove the grievances which inevitably arose when men associated together, there was no way but 'by growing into composition and agreement amongst themselves, by ordaining some kind of government public, and by yielding themselves subject thereunto'. On the continent, the German writer Althusius used the idea of an original social contract in constructing his political system (1603). We find the compact theory applied in practice by the Pilgrim Fathers on board the *Mayflower* (1620): 'We do solemnly and mutually in the Presence of God and of one another covenant and combine ourselves together into a civil body politic.' Milton in his *Tenure of Kings and Magistrates* (1649) argued that men were born free, and that wrong sprang up through Adam's sin, wherefore to avert their own complete destruction men 'agreed by common league to bind each other from mutual injury, and jointly to defend themselves against any that gave disturbance or opposition to such agreement.

'The power of kings and magistrates is nothing else, but what is only derivative, transferred, and committed to them in trust from the people, to the common good of them all, in whom the power yet remains fundamentally, and cannot be taken from them, without a violation of their natural birthright.'

We shall now consider the theory as developed by its most famous exponents, Hobbes, Locke and Rousseau, during the latter half of the seventeenth century and in the eighteenth.

§3 HOBBES

Hobbes (1588-1679) was an Englishman who lived in the days of the Civil War (1642-51). This fact is significant in explaining the nature of his political thought, for, as will be shown presently, Hobbes was inclined towards absolutism. This inclination was natural at a time when the most important need of his country was a strong Government to maintain law and order.

Hobbes starts his political inquiry (*The Leviathan*, 1651) with an analysis of human nature : man is essentially selfish ; he is moved to action not by his intellect or reason, but by his appetites, desires and passions. Men living without any common power set over them, i.e. in a state of nature, would be 'in that condition which is called Warre ; and such a warre, as is of every man, against every man '—not war in the organized sense but a perpetual struggle of all against all, competition, diffidence and love of glory being the three main causes. Law and justice are absent. The life of man is ' solitary, poor, nasty, brutish and short '.

Hobbes recognizes that even in the primitive natural state, there are in some sense laws of nature. Their essence is self-preservation, ' the liberty each man hath to preserve his own life '. In detail, these laws are : to seek peace and follow it ; to relinquish the right to all things which being retained hinder the peace of mankind ; to ' perform their covenants made '.

The only way to peace is for men to give up so much of their natural rights as are inconsistent with living in peace. A supreme coercive power is instituted. The contracting parties are not the community and the Government, but subject and subject. Every man says to every other :

' I authorize and give up my right of governing myself to this man or this assembly of men (Government) on this condition that thou give up thy right to him and authorize *all* his actions in like manner '

A State is thus created.

Certain consequences follow from the creation of a State in this manner :

1. The Government is sovereign, and the sovereign's power is absolute, for,

(*i*) The sovereign's power is not held ' on condition ' since the sovereign is the result of the pact, not a party to it.

(*ii*) The pact is not revocable at the pleasure of the subjects

(*iii*) Men surrender all their rights to the sovereign.

(*iv*) As the sovereign embodies in himself the wills of all, his actions are virtually their actions, on the principle that ' whosoever acts through his agent, acts through himself '.

(*v*) The anti-social instincts of man are too insistent to be checked except by absolute authority.

Sovereignty is inalienable, for it is essential to civil government that there should be no power in the State strong enough to gainsay the sovereign. For the same reason, sovereignty is indivisible and the sovereign is unpunishable. The sovereign is judge of what is necessary for the peace and defence of his subjects and judge of what doctrines are fit to be taught. He has the right of making rules whereby each subject may know to what personal property he is entitled. He has the right of judicature, of making war and peace, of choosing counsellors, of rewarding, honouring and punishing.

Hobbes is aware that the sovereign thus defined need not necessarily be one man ; sovereignty may be located in an assembly. Yet he prefers monarchy because it has greater consistency and freedom from fluctuation in policy. Also, there are relatively fewer favourites in a monarchy and, above all, there is the maximum identity of public and private interest in that form of government.

2. Law is, in general, not counsel but command.

' Civil law is to every subject those rules which the Commonwealth hath commanded him by word, writing or other sufficient sign of the will to make use of for the distinction of right and wrong.'

3. The liberty of the subject consists in :

(*i*) Those rights which the sovereign has permitted.

(*ii*) Those rights which by the law of nature, of self-preservation, cannot be surrendered. The subject cannot therefore be compelled to kill himself or to abstain from food or medicine ; he is also not bound to accuse himself.

(*iii*) In general the obligation of the subjects to the sovereign lasts no longer than his power to protect them.

(*iv*) As for other liberties, they depend on the silence of the law, the subject being free to do what the sovereign has not prohibited.

Hobbes thus bases an absolute State on ' free ' contract and consent ; the psychological basis of his theory is fear. These ideas of Hobbes have been criticized from several points of view : the theory of social contract is unhistorical, because primitive society rested on status, not on contract ; [1] his view of human nature as essentially selfish cannot be maintained ; he is prepared to believe in a being who is a savage in the state of nature and a saint in the state of contract ; his contention that men surrender almost all their natural rights is an insult to common sense. Again, Hobbes failed to realize that the principle involved in absolute sovereignty is wrong ; for if the sovereign is all-powerful and stands above law the citizen must be prepared to submit to his arbitrary pleasure ; it is possible that this position may prove to be worse than it was prior to the contract. Above all, Hobbes gives us a purely legal view of rights as claims recognized by the State. Such a view is insufficient for political philosophy, for a legal theory of rights will tell us what in fact the character of a State is ; it will not tell

[1] See below, p. 29.

us whether the rights recognized by it are the rights which need recognition, or whether other rights do not deserve legal recognition. It will tell us, for instance, that, until very recently, according to Hindu law polygamy was recognized, and a daughter's right to inherit along with the son was not recognized. There is no good reason why the former should be recognized or the latter should not be recognized.

If, then, it be asked why Hobbes' influence persists, the answer is, as Ivor Brown puts it, he was the first great philosopher of discipline. Those who think about political affairs and the nature of society fall, intellectually and temperamentally, into two main schools. One party believes that the most essential requisites for human welfare in society are law and order ; the other believes in the ultimate value of individual liberty, seeing that if liberty does not exist in and for individuals, it does not exist at all. Those of ' the law and order school ' see in Hobbes the first Englishman to give a complete and logical expression to the doctrine of sovereignty. As Pollock says, ' Hobbes defines legal sovereignty and legal obligation with admirable strength and precision.'

§4 LOCKE

The purpose of Locke (1632-1704) in his *Two Treatises of Government* (1690) was to justify the English Revolution of 1688. James II had been deposed from the throne and William of Orange invited to occupy it. Locke sought, as he said, to ' establish the throne of our great Restorer, our present King William, and make good his title in the consent of the people '.

Locke's argument is somewhat as follows : In the state of nature men are free and equal ; each lives according to his own liking. This freedom, however, is not licence. There is a natural law or the law of reason which commands that no one shall impair the life, the health, the freedom or the possessions of another. It is significant that the law of nature of Locke stresses the freedom and preservation of all men, unlike that of Hobbes which emphasizes self-preservation. There is, however, no common superior to enforce the law of reason ; each individual is obliged to work out his own interpretation. The result is that while the state of nature is not a state of war (as it is in Hobbes' view) it is still ' full of fears and continual dangers ' and man's enjoyment of rights is ' very insecure '. Therefore, the peace among men may be so precarious as not to be easily distinguishable from the anarchy depicted by Hobbes.

The State or political society is instituted by way of remedy for the inconvenience of the state of nature—to avert, not to escape from, a state of war. These inconveniences are threefold : first, the want of an established, settled, known law, received and allowed by common consent to be the standard of right and wrong, and the common measure to decide all controversies ; secondly, the want of a known and disinterested judge, with authority to determine all differences according to the established law ; thirdly, the want of power to back and support the sentence when right and to give it due execution. The State is created by Locke through the medium of a contract in which each individual agrees with every other to give up to the community the natural right of enforcing the law of reason, in order that life, liberty and property may be preserved. Locke, unlike Hobbes, gives the power to the community and not to a Government. The contract, it may be stressed, is also not general, but limited and specific ; for, the natural right of enforcing the law of reason alone is given up : the natural rights of life, liberty and property reserved to the individual limit the just power of the community.

' The legislative power constituted by the consent of the people,[1] becomes the supreme power in the commonwealth, but is not arbitrary. It must be exercised, as it is given, for the good of the subjects. Government is in the nature of a trust and embraces only such powers as were transferred at the time of the change from a state of nature. The Legislature must dispense justice by standing laws and authorized judges ; no man can be deprived of his property without his consent, nor can taxes be levied without the consent of the people or their representatives. Finally, the Legislature cannot transfer its powers to any other person or body. It is but a delegated power from the people, who alone can dispose of it.'[2]

The people, however, can remove or alter the Legislature, when they find that it acts contrary to the trust reposed in it.

If it be asked who, then, is sovereign in Locke's State, the answer is that there is none in Hobbes' sense.[3] The community is supreme ; but its supreme power is latent. Its power does not come into play so long as the Government is acting according to the trust reposed in it ; but when it acts contrary to that trust, the power of the community manifests itself in its right to replace that Government by another. Thus it is integral to Locke's system that the Government may be dissolved while society remains intact. Locke's theory thus results in constitutional or limited government.

[1] This may be considered as the second (implied) contract in Locke's theory. To this contract, the Government is a party ; in Hobbes' theory the Government is not a party to the contract.

[2] *Two Treatises of Government*, ' Everyman's Library ', p. xv.

[3] Professor Carpenter in his introduction to *Two Treatises* notes that the word sovereign does not appear in Locke's book.

In the words of Laski, Locke gave to the theory of consent a permanent place in English politics. While the idea of social contract as an explanation of State origins has been given up, Locke's central idea of ' government resting on the consent of the governed ' is valuable. This means in practice that a Government can continue to rule a people only if it pays heed to their wishes. Government holds power on condition. This conclusion Locke arrived at by distinguishing between the agreement to form a civil society and the agreement within that society to set up some particular Government. If the acts of that Government are contrary to the interests of the community as a whole ' it is possible for them, as Locke saw, to change the Government without destroying the continuity of civil society itself '. Locke's method of arriving at his conclusion may be criticized as being unhistorical ; but he emphasizes the cardinal idea that government is a trust, and the basis of government is consent.

Secondly, Locke's concept of natural rights is of some value. In the sense in which Locke used it, as the rights of the individual anterior to organized society, it is now generally discredited. But, as T. H. Green points out, interpreted in the sense that the nature of man demands certain rights or some conditions of life which at a particular state of civilization are necessary for the fulfilment of his personality, the concept is invaluable.

§5 ROUSSEAU

The social contract theory of Rousseau (1712-78) developed in his *Contrat Social* (1762) is important in two respects : it inspired the French Revolution of 1789 which was a revolt against the despotic French monarchy ; it also supplied the basis of the theory of popular sovereignty.

Man, according to Rousseau, is essentially good and sympathetic ; the state of nature is a period of idyllic happiness, men being free and equal. Soon, however, with the introduction of private property and the growth of numbers, quarrels arise and man is compelled to give up his natural freedom. His problem is ' to find a form of association which protects with the whole common force the person and property of each associate, and in virtue of which every one, while uniting himself to all, . . . remains as free as before '. The problem is solved through a contract and the creation of civil society.

In this contract, every one surrenders to the community (and not to the Government as in Hobbes) all his rights ; the surrender is as complete as in Hobbes. The community therefore becomes sovereign. Its sovereignty is as absolute as that of the Government in Hobbes is. *Prima facie,* there is no need to limit its sovereignty in the interests of the subjects, for the sovereign body, being formed only of the individuals who constitute it, can have no interest contrary to theirs. From the mere fact of its existence, it is always all that it ought to be (since, from the very fact of its institution, all merely private interests are lost in it). On the other hand, the will of the individual may well conflict with that general will of the community which constitutes the sovereign. Hence the social pact necessarily involves a tacit agreement that anyone refusing to conform to the general will shall be forced to do so by the whole body politic, i.e., ' shall be forced to be free ', since the universal conformity to the general will is the guarantee to each individual of freedom from dependence on any other person or persons.

It is interesting to see how, after the contract, the individual remains as free as he was before.

' Since each gives himself up to all, he gives himself up to no one ; and as there is acquired over every associate the same right that is given up by himself, there is gained the equivalent of what is lost, with greater power to preserve what is left.'

Law is an expression of the general will and can be made only in an assembly of the whole people.

Sovereignty can never be alienated, represented or divided. The sovereign, who is a collective being, can be represented only by himself.

The Government is never the same thing as the sovereign. The two are distinguished by their functions, that of the former being executive, that of the latter, legislative. Government is the exercise according to law of the executive power. The Government, contrary to Locke's opinion, is not established by, and therefore is not a party to, the contract. ' There is only one contract in the State,' protests Rousseau, ' and this excludes every other.' The act by which a Government is established is twofold, consisting first of the passing of a law by the sovereign to the effect that there shall be a Government, and secondly of an act in execution of this law by which the governors are appointed.

Rousseau's social contract can be viewed as the fusion of the premises and temper of Hobbes with the conclusions of Locke. The influence of Hobbes upon Rousseau was indeed marked and singular. That the State is the result of a contract entered into by men who originally lived in a state of nature ; that there was only one contract, and to this the Government was not a party ; that individuals surrendered all their rights and, therefore, after making the contract may have only such rights as are allowed to them by law ; that sovereignty is absolute : these elements in his theory clearly recall Hobbes. But, curious as it may seem, Rousseau did not agree with the conclusion of Hobbes, that the Government was absolute ; he made the Government dependent upon the people and thereby accepted, in essentials, the conclusion of Locke. To this conclusion he was led by two elements in his theory in which he differed from Hobbes : he makes the individual surrender his rights not to the ruler but to the community ; he makes a clear difference between the State and the Government. In both these respects he is nearer Locke. At the same time, Rousseau differs from Locke in more ways than one. He postu- lates a complete surrender of rights on the part of the natural man, and thereby makes sovereignty absolute ; in Locke the surrender is partial, and there is no absolute sovereignty. The popular sovereignty in Rousseau is in continual exercise ; the supremacy of the people in Locke is held in reserve and manifests itself only when the Government acts contrary to its trust. There is only one contract, the social pact, in Rousseau ; there are two contracts implied in Locke, to one of which the Government is a party ; and, as Gierke noted, when Rousseau cut off the idea of a governmental compact from the contract theory, he did a revo- lutionary thing ; he made the State absolute.

The importance of Rousseau in political thought has already been indicated. His theory served as the basis for democracy and the justification of revolutions against arbitrary rule. As Sidgwick points out, the revolutionary doctrine rests on two or three simple principles : that men are by nature free and equal, that the rights of government must be based on some compact freely entered into by these equal and independent individuals, and that the nature of the compact is such that the individual becomes part of the sovereign people, which has the inalienable right of deter- mining its own constitution and legislation. These points are all found, for instance, in the Declaration of the Rights of Man (1789), the charter of the French Revolution ; they are taken straight from Rousseau. Rousseau indeed demonstrated once and for all that will, not force, is the basis of the State, that govern- ment depends on the consent of the governed. Rousseau's idea, that the sovereign community was logically the only lawmaker, has had the indirect effect of stimulating direct legislation by the people through the referendum and the initiative.

At the same time, it must be remarked that Rousseau's political analysis is inadequate in one respect. He was scarcely aware of the fact that the unrestricted power of the general will might result in an absolutism scarcely less formidable than that of the older kingdoms and oligarchies. To argue that the general will is always the disinterested will of the community for the common good, and therefore always right, is, as has been well said, to give a phrase where we ask for a solution. There is no guarantee that the will of the community will always turn out to be for the common good. Rousseau himself realized that the line between the general will so defined and the will of all (which is the sum total of particularist and sectional interests) is not easy to draw. Rousseau's sovereign is the people itself gathered in solemn general assembly, without private interest, as a whole ; and therefore incapable of injustice to any members. That Rousseau without reserve makes this identification of the ideal and the actual it would be unjust to say, but that his enthusiasm leads him constantly to minimize the difference is unquestionable.[1]

§6 MERITS AND DEFECTS

(*i*) From the historical point of view, the contract theory of the origin of political authority is untenable, not only because historical records are wanting as to those early times when, if at all, such compacts must have been made, but also because what historical evidence there is, from which by inference primitive conditions may be imagined, is such as to show its impossibility. The theory presupposes individuals as contracting, when the researches of Maine show that the progress of societies has been from status to contract. Contract, according to Maine, is not the beginning but the end of society. The idea of contract postulates that individuals who enter into the contract are free to do things in their own way ; but, says Maine, the evidence of early law and custom shows that primitive men had no such freedom. Primitive society rested not upon contract but upon *status*. In that society, men were born into the station and the part they were to play throughout life. It was not a matter of choice or of voluntary arrangement in what relations men were to stand towards one another as individuals. ' He who is born a slave, let him remain a slave ; the artisan, an artisan ; the priest, a priest '—is the command of the law of status. Merit, aptitude, and individual freedom were allowed to operate only within the sphere of each man's birthright. Under such conditions, the very idea of individuals contracting themselves into civil society seems improbable.

(*ii*) Even granting that an example of an original contract could be found, it cannot necessarily bind the descendants of those who originally entered into the contract.

' I am bound to obey,' said Bentham, ' not because my great-grandfather may be regarded as having made a bargain which

---

[1] See H. J. Tozer in his introduction to *The Social Contract*, pp. 44-69.

he did not really make with the great-grandfather of George III, but simply because rebellion does more harm than good.'

(*iii*) The theory is dangerous in practice, for it is favourable to anarchy. The State and its institutions are regarded as the result of the individual will, and, therefore, it may be argued, they can have no sufficient authority when they contradict this individual will. Burke states this point well in his famous description of the State :

' It ought not to be considered as nothing better than a partnership agreement in a trade of pepper and coffee, calico or tobacco or some other such low concern, to be taken up for a little temporary interest and to be dissolved by the fancy of the parties . . . It is to be looked on with other reverence . . . It is a partnership in all science, a partnership in all art, a partnership in every virtue and in all ·.erfection. As the ends of such a partnership cannot be obtained in many generations, it becomes a partnership not only between those who are living, but between those who are living, those who are dead, and those who are to be born.'

(*iv*) More than one exponent of the theory assumes that men in a state of nature are equal. This assumption is incorrect. It is possible to argue with the German jurist von Haller (1768-1854) that inequality, rather than equality, is natural.

(*v*) The theory is illogical : ' It presupposes such political consciousness in a people who are merely living in a state of nature as could only be possible in individuals who are already within a State.' As Leacock says, they must have known what a Government was before they could make one.

With all its defects, the theory has some merits. It reminds the Government of those human purposes which the State can serve and which alone can justify its existence. As Kant, the German philosopher, said : ' The legislator is under the obligation to order his laws as if they were the outcome of a social contract.' In the form given to it by Locke and Rousseau, the theory brought out the idea that civil society rests not on the consent of the ruler but of the ruled and thus became an important factor in the development of modern democracy.

§7 THE THEORY OF DIVINE ORIGIN

The theory of divine origin, known more familiarly as the theory of the divine right of kings, states three simple propositions : the State has been established by an ordinance of God ; its rulers are divinely appointed ; they are accountable to no authority but God. Thus we are told in the Bible :[1]

---

[1] *Romans*, xiii, 1-2.

'Let every soul be subject unto the higher powers. For there is no power but of God : the powers that be are ordained of God. Whosoever therefore resisteth the power, resisteth the ordinance of God : and they that resist shall receive to themselves damnation.'

Filmer in his *Patriarcha* (1680) argues that Adam was the first king and 'present kings are, or are to be reputed, next heir to him'. In that great epic, the *Mahabharata*, it is recounted[1] that when the world was in a state of nature and anarchy the people approached God and requested him to provide a remedy. 'Without a chief, O Lord,' they said, 'we are perishing. Give us a chief whom we shall worship in concert and who will protect us.' God appointed Manu to rule over them. The essence of the theory, whether held in the East or the West, is not only that God created the State in the sense that all human institutions may be believed to have had their origin in divine creation ; the will of God is supposed to be made known by revelation mediately or immediately to certain persons who are his earthly vice-regents and by them communicated to the people. Obedience to the State becomes a religious as well as a civil duty ; disobedience, sacrilege.

The importance of the theory is primarily historical ; it helped to support the claims of certain rulers, like James I of England, to govern absolutely and without being accountable to their people. Indeed James I even told his Parliament :

'A king can never be monstrously vicious. Even if a king is wicked, it means God has sent him as a punishment for peoples' sins and it is unlawful to shake off the burden which God has laid upon them. Patience, earnest prayer and amendment of their lives are the only lawful means to move God to relieve them of that heavy curse.'

It is interesting, however, to note that in ancient India the divine right theory was not stretched to include the view that the bad as well as the good ruler was the representative of God and as such entitled to unconditional obedience. On the contrary, its implications were explored to justify rebellion against a tyrannical king. The argument is a simple one : a virtuous king is no doubt a *part* of the gods and is entitled to co-operation and obedience ; but the king who is otherwise is a *part* of the demons. Therefore he may be deposed and even slain.[2]

[1] *Santiparvan*, lxvii, cited in U. Ghoshal, *A History of Hindu Political Theories*, p. 175.

[2] The *Mahabharata* and *Sukraniti*, see U. Ghoshal, op. cit., pp. 219, 248-9. Perhaps Narada is an exception, for he alone among Hindu theorists seems to support absolute non-resistance on the part of the people.

As an explanation of the origin of the State, the theory is now generally discredited, because it necessarily involves propositions that are to be accepted as matters of faith rather than of reason. As J. N. Figgis rightly says, if at the present time the theory finds little acceptance, it is because there is a general belief either that reason should reign supreme; or that, if faith, as distinguished from reasoned conviction, be conceded to have a proper place in the life of men, its precepts should relate exclusively to matters spiritual. In spite of the obvious defect of the theory, that it leaves the community at the mercy of a despot, it has the merit that idealistically interpreted it may create in the mass of the people a sense of the value of order and obedience to law, so necessary for the stability of the State—and in the rulers a moral accountability to God for the manner in which they exercise their power.

§8 THE THEORY OF FORCE

In its simplest form, this theory may be stated thus : 'War begat the king.' The State is the result of the subjugation of the weaker by the stronger. Thus Gregory VII wrote in 1080 :

'Which of us is ignorant that kings and lords have had their origin in those who, ignorant of God, by arrogance, rapine, perfidy, slaughter, b every crime with the devil agitating as the prince of the world have contrived to rule over their fellowmen with blind cupidity and intolerable presumption?'

In the eighteenth century, Hume gave expression to similar ideas : 'It is probable,' said he,[1] 'that the first ascendant of one man over multitudes began during a state of war, where the superiority of courage and of genius discovers itself most visibly, where unanimity and concert are most requisite, and where the pernicious effects of disorder are most sensibly felt. The long continuance of that state, an incident common among savage tribes, inured the people to submission.' Jenks[2] is perhaps the best modern exponent of the theory. 'Historically speaking,' says he, 'there is not the slightest difficulty in proving that all political communities of the modern type owe their existence to successful warfare.' His general argument is somewhat as follows :[3] With the increase of population and the consequent pressure on the means of subsistence, there was also an improvement in the art of warfare. Fighting became the work of specialists. A State is founded when a leader, with his band of warriors, gets permanent control of a

[1] D. Hume, *Essays*, V : 'Of the Origin of Government.'
[2] E. Jenks, *A History of Politics*, p. 71.
[3] *A History of Politics*, pp. 74-5.

definite territory of a considerable size. This may occur in one of two ways. The leader, after firmly establishing his position as ruler of his own tribe, extends his authority over neighbouring tribes until he comes to rule over a large territory. This is what seems to have happened in the England of the ninth century, when the so-called tribal kingdoms of the Heptarchy,[1] after fluctuating for many years between the overlordship of the various tribal chiefs, became more or less consolidated by conquest in the time of Egbert (802-39). Much the same thing happened in Scandinavia, where, in the ninth century, 'the innumerable tribes became gradually consolidated, as the result of hard fighting, into the three historic kingdoms of Norway, Denmark and Sweden'. Or a State is founded by successful migrations and conquests. This was the history, in the sixth century A.D., of the foundations of the kingdoms of Lombardy and of Spain. Perhaps the most remarkable instance of this is supplied by the history of the Normans, 'who, in the ninth century, became the ruling power in Russia; in the tenth founded the practically independent Duchy of Normandy; in the eleventh, the new kingdoms of England; and in the twelfth, the kingdom of the Sicilies'.

The new type of community, whether founded by consolidation or by migration and conquest, differed from the tribe in one essential particular: it was *territorial* in character, i.e., all those who lived within the territory of the ruler (and not only those who were related to him by blood) were bound to obey his commands.

By way of criticism it is sufficient to say that while force has been one element in the formation of the State, it is wrong to say that it has been the *sole* factor. As is shown below,[2] the State is the result of the action of various causes—kinship, religion, force and political consciousness.

§9 THE PATRIARCHAL THEORY

This theory has its strongest supporter in Sir Henry Maine (1822-88) who stated it in his books *Ancient Law* (1861) and *Early History of Institutions* (1875). Maine derives his evidence from three sources—from accounts by contemporary observers of civilizations less advanced than their own, from the records which particular races (e.g. the Greeks) have kept of their own history, and from ancient law (e.g. Roman and Hindu).

The theory is as follows: The unit of primitive society was the family, in which descent was traced through males and in which the eldest male parent was absolutely supreme. His power extended

[1] i.e. Northumbria, Mercia, East Anglia, Essex, Kent, Sussex and Wessex.
[2] §11 of this chapter.

to life and death, and was as unqualified over his children and their houses as over his slaves. The single family breaks up into more families, which, all held together under the head of the first family (the chief or patriarch), become the tribe. An aggregation of tribes makes the State.

'The elementary group is the Family, connected by common subjection to the highest male ascendant. The aggregation of Families forms the *gens* or House. The aggregation of Houses makes the Tribe. The aggregation of Tribes constitutes the Commonwealth.'[1]

Briefly, the State is an extension of the family, the head of the State being the father; the people, his children. Maine cites the Patriarchs of the Old Testament, the 'Brotherhoods' of Athens, the *patria potestas* in Rome and the family system in India as evidence in favour of his theory.

It must be emphasized that the patriarchal society which, according to this theory, was the foundation of the modern State, was characterized by three features, viz. male kinship, permanent marriage and paternal authority.[2] It is indeed integral to this theory that members of the patriarchal family should be able to trace their descent through the male. 'Men are counted of kin because they are descended from the same male ancestor.' (Sometimes no doubt this relationship was fictitious rather than real, as when in the absence of heirs the deficiency was made good by adoption.) This in turn means that the system of permanent marriage, i.e. the permanent union of a woman with one man, had come to stay as a social institution. But, as Jenks points out, it must not be assumed that marriage as we understand it—the permanent union of one man with one woman—was a feature of all patriarchal society. On the contrary, polygamy, i.e. the marriage of one man to several women, was quite common. It need not be added, however, that polygamy is no hindrance to the recognition of kinship through the male. Paternal authority means that the male ancestors had well-nigh despotic authority over the group. Thus in early Rome the *patria potestas* (literally the authority of the father) 'extended to all the descendants of a living ancestor, no matter how old they were' and comprised 'even the power of life and death to say nothing of control and chastisement'.

The defect of the theory is that we cannot say that the patriarchal society has been the foundation of later institutions everywhere, or that it has been necessarily the oldest form of

[1] H. S. Maine, *Ancient Law*, 'World's Classics' edition, p. 106.
[2] E. Jenks, op. cit., pp. 15-17.

social organization. For other evidence [1] suggests that in some societies the patriarchal family was a later development from the matriarchal system, in which descent could be traced only through the female on account of the existence of polyandry.

The theory has the merit, however, that as an explanation of the origin of the State it emphasizes one essential element in the making of the State, viz. kinship.

§10 THE MATRIARCHAL THEORY

Among the chief exponents of this theory are McLennan (*Primitive Society*, 1865), Morgan (*Studies in Ancient Society*, 1877) and Jenks (*A History of Politics*, 1900). As distinguished from the patriarchal theory, this theory holds that the primitive group had no common male head, and that kinship among them could be traced only through the woman. Thus, Jenks says,[2] illustrating his proposition from primitive society in Australia :

'The real social unit of the Australians is not the " tribe ", but the *totem group*. . . The totem group is, primarily, a body of persons distinguished by the sign of some natural object, such as an animal or tree, who may not intermarry with one another . . . The Australian may not marry within his totem. " Snake may not marry snake. Emu may not marry emu." That is the first rule of savage social organization. Of its *origin* we have no knowledge ; but there can be little doubt that its *object* was to prevent the marriage of near relations. . . The other side of the rule is equally startling. The savage may not marry within his totem, but he must marry into another totem specially fixed for him. More than this, he not only marries into the specified totem, but he marries the whole of the women of that totem in his own generation.'

Under such a system, it is obvious that as far as there is any recognition of blood-relationship at all, it is through women, and not through men. 'Maternity is a fact, paternity an opinion.' Jenks holds that society organized on such a basis gradually evolved into the family marked by paternal descent (of Maine's description). It is unnecessary to elaborate the stages in this evolution. Briefly they are : men began to take to pastoral occupations ; they domesticated animals ; they recognized the value of women's labour in tending sheep and cattle, and so gradually realized the value of permanently retaining women at home for the purpose ; and thus arose the institution of permanent marriage.

---

[1] See below, §10 of this chapter.
[2] op. cit., p. 9.

'The tribe, instead of the family, is the primary group; in time it breaks into clans; these turn into households, and ultimately into individual members.'

The matriarchal theory is subject to the same criticism as the partiarchal : it is incorrect to regard matriarchal society as the oldest form of social organization everywhere. The truth seems to be that 'there has been a parallel development, but the patriarchal line is thicker and longer'.[1]

§11   THE EVOLUTIONARY THEORY

The theories discussed must, for reasons already stated, be rejected as unsatisfactory. The generally accepted theory is known as the historical or evolutionary theory. It considers the State neither as a divine institution nor as a deliberate human contrivance; it sees the State coming into existence as the result of natural evolution.

'The proposition that the State is a product of history,' says J. W. Burgess, 'means that it is a gradual and continuous development of human society out of a grossly imperfect beginning through crude but improving forms of manifestation towards a perfect and universal organization of mankind.'

The beginnings of government cannot be traced to a particular time or cause; it is the result of various factors, working through ages. These influences are kinship, religion, war and political consciousness.

In early society, kinship was the first and strongest bond; and government, as W. Wilson points out, must have begun in clearly defined family discipline. Such discipline would scarcely be possible among races in which blood-relationship was subject to profound confusion and in which family organization, therefore, had no clear basis of authority on which to rest. In every case, it would seem, the origin of what we should deem worthy of the name of government must have awaited the development of some such definite family as that in which the father was known and known as ruler. Whether or not the patriarchal family was the first form of the family, it must have furnished the first adequate form of government.

Common worship was undoubtedly another element in the welding together of families and tribes. This worship evolved from primitive animism to ancestor-worship. When ancestor-worship became the prevailing form of religion, religion was inseparably linked with kinship for, at the family or communal

[1] M. Ruthnaswamy, *The Making of the State*, p. 18.

altar, the worshipper did homage to the great dead of his family or group and craved protection and guidance. In some tribes we find that the medicine-man or magician, who naturally held a predominant position, acquired or was elevated to the position of kingship. The primitive man had implicit faith in the existence of spirits, the spirits of the dead and the spirit of nature. The medicine-man, professing ability to control them by means of his sorcery, naturally came to be regarded with mysterious awe and acquired unique influence. The founder of the Mexican power, we are told, was a great wizard and sorcerer.

War and migration, we have already seen, were important influences in the origin of the State. The demands of constant warfare often led to the rise of permanent headship. When a tribe was threatened by danger or involved in war, it was driven by necessity to appoint a leader. The continuity of war conduced to the permanence of leadership. Further, war and conquest helped to give the mark of territoriality to the State. In the patriarchal society or tribe, the nexus had been that of blood; but when a leader established his authority over a territory by conquest, over a people with whom he had no blood-relationship, all those who lived in that territory became his subjects. Blood was no longer the essential bond of unity.

And, finally, political consciousness. As Wilson says, in origin government was spontaneous, natural, twin-born with man and the family; Aristotle was simply stating a fact when he said 'man is by nature a political animal'. The need for order and security is an ever-present factor; man knows instinctively that he can develop the best of which he is capable only by some form of political organization. At the beginning, it might well be that the political consciousness was really political unconsciousness; but 'just as the forces of nature operated long before the discovery of the law of gravitation, political organization really rested on the community of mind, unconscious, dimly conscious, or fully conscious of certain moral ends present throughout the whole course of development'.

§12   EARLY KINGSHIP AND PRIESTHOOD

It hardly needs to be reiterated that kingship was the earliest form of government. Early kings were also priests. The connexion between kingship and priesthood may be illustrated both from Greece and Rome. In Greece it was held that just as the domestic hearth had a high priest in the father of the family, the city religion should also have a high priest. This priest of the public hearth bore the name of king. He kept up the fire, offered the sacrifice, pronounced the prayer and presided at the religious repasts. The principal office of a king, says de Coulanges, was to perform religious ceremonies. An ancient king of Sicyon was deposed because, having soiled his hands by a murder, he was no longer in a fit condition to offer the sacrifices. Being no longer fit to be a priest, he could no longer be king. We know from Demosthenes that the ancient kings of Attica themselves performed all the sacrifices that were prescribed by the religion of the city; and from Xenophon, that the kings of Sparta were the chiefs of the Lacedaemonian religion. The Roman king was similarly the guardian of the city hearth and high priest of its religion; as high priest, he represented the community in their dealings with the gods, appointed and controlled members of the religious colleges and punished offences against the gods. As the king was the supreme chief of the religion, and the safety of the city was to depend upon his prayers and sacrifices, it was important to make sure that the king was acceptable to the gods. So kings entered upon their office after a religious ceremonial, and after a flash of lightning or a flight of birds had manifested the approval of the gods. Even till 1946, the Japanese Emperor was the high priest of the national cult of Shinto.

SELECT BIBLIOGRAPHY

J. G. FRAZER, *The Golden Bough*, one-volume edition, Macmillan, 1922

T. HOBBES, *Leviathan*, 'Everyman Library', Dent

E. JENKS, *A History of Politics*, Dent, 1900

J. LOCKE, *Of Civil Government, Two Treatises*, 'Everyman Library', Dent

A. R. LORD, *The Principles of Politics*, ch. ii, Oxford, 1921

R. H. LOWRIE, *Primitive Society*, Routledge, 1920

J. J. ROUSSEAU, *The Social Contract*, 'Everyman Library', Dent

H. SIDGWICK, *The Development of European Polity*, lectures xxiv-xxvi, Macmillan, 1920

C. VEREKER, *The Development of Political Theory*, Hutchinson University Library, 1957

W. W. WILLOUGHBY, *The Ethical Basis of Political Authority*, ch. v-xiv, Macmillan, 1930

CHAPTER III

THE PURPOSE OF THE STATE

§1 DIVERGENT VIEWS

WHAT is the purpose of political organization? There are perhaps as many answers to this question as there are writers on Politics. We shall cite a few, beginning with Aristotle.

To understand Aristotle's thought on the subject, we must start with his proposition that man is by nature a political animal. This means, first, that the social instinct is implanted in all men by nature, and that man can rise to his full stature only through the State. The State, Aristotle tells us, which originated for the sake of life, continues 'for the sake of the best life'. The end of the State is, therefore, ethical. As Newman puts it, the State exists (according to Aristotle) for the sake of that kind of life which is the end of man—not for the increase of its population or wealth or for empire or the extension of its influence. It exists for the exercise of the qualities which make men good husbands, fathers and heads of households, good soldiers and citizens, good men of science and philosophers. When the State by its education and laws, written and unwritten, succeeds in evoking and maintaining in vigorous activity a life rich in noble aims and deeds, then and not till then has it fully attained the end for which it exists. The ideal State is that which adds to adequate material advantages the noblest gifts of intellect and character and the will to live for their exercise in every relation of life, and whose education, institutions and laws are such as to develop these gifts and to call them into play. We may add that good life is life lived according to reason; 'the function of reason in ethics consists in the direction of conduct by a rule, the rule, namely, of the mean'; in politics, reason prescribes co-operation with one's fellow citizens in promoting the welfare of the State.[1]

The ethical end of the State is subordinated to convenience in Locke. His concern is not with the 'good' but with the 'convenient'. 'The great and chief end of men uniting into

[1] The ethical end of the State was well recognized by thinkers in ancient India. The *Mahabharata* thus says that the State should ceaselessly foster righteousness, guide, correct and control the moral life of the people, besides making the earth habitable and comfortable for them. See Beni Prasad, *The State in Ancient India*, p. 98.

commonwealths and putting themselves under government is the preservation of their property'—which is Locke's general name for 'lives, liberties and estates'. In the state of nature, these are not safe owing to the want of a settled known law, a known and indifferent judge, and a common Executive. The better preservation of these natural rights is therefore the purpose of political society; the exercise of power by a Government is conditioned by that purpose. Locke, it will be remembered, does not make his natural man surrender his natural rights even to the community; only the right of enforcing the law of reason is given up. The end of the State, as defined by Locke, is intelligible when it is remembered that the 'provocation' for his *Two Treatises of Civil Government* was the arbitrary exercise of power by the Stuart kings, and that its aim was to justify the principles of the Bill of Rights and the 'Glorious' Revolution of 1688.

Adam Smith (1723-90) in his *Wealth of Nations* (1776)[1] laid down the following proposition: The sovereign has only three duties to attend to : the duty of protecting society from the violence and invasion of other independent societies; secondly, the duty of protecting, as far as possible, every member of society from the injustice or opposition of every other member of it, or the duty of establishing an exact administration of justice; and, thirdly, the duty of erecting and maintaining certain public works and certain public institutions, which it can never be for the interest of any individual, or small number of individuals, to erect and maintain, because the profit yielded would never repay the expense to any individual or small number of individuals, though it might frequently do much more than repay a great society.

The process of the narrowing down of the purpose of the State reaches its culmination in Herbert Spencer (1820-1903). According to him, the State is nothing but a natural institution for preventing one man from infringing the rights of another; it is a joint-stock protection company for mutual assurance.

§2 'THE STATE IS AN END IN ITSELF'

Locke, Adam Smith and Spencer agree that the State is a means to an end, the end being a better life for the individual, whether conceived in ethical terms or not, whether the State is to interfere more or less. The opposite view that the State is an end in itself has had its exponents too, and is perhaps best illustrated by the school of thinkers known as Idealists, especially by Hegel. Hegel's argument is somewhat as follows : Men want to be free; they are free only when they do what their reason recommends.

1 'Everyman Library' edition, Vol. II, pp. 272-3.

Individual reason is not, however, trustworthy, because it is particularistic and moved by temporary and irrelevant considerations. The existence of some entity, whose will is universal and as acceptable to individuals as the voice of reason itself, is necessary. Such an entity is the State. It is a person and has a will of its own. It has ends of its own divorced from, and superior to, those of the individual human beings subjected to its authority. It carries out the dictates of universal reason and is therefore impelled by its own nature and destiny to seek its own perfection. 'The State, being an end in itself, is provided with the maximum of rights over against the individual citizens, whose highest duty it is to be members of the State.'[1] True freedom, therefore, consists in conformity to law; every law is a veritable freedom. The same trend of thought is illustrated in fascism and nazism. Thus :

'The Italian nation is an organization having ends, a life and means superior in power and duration to the single individuals or groups of individuals composing it.'[2]

It is noteworthy that those who claim that the State is an end in itself also take their stand on the idea that the individual is fleeting, the State is everlasting ; the leaves wither, the tree stands. Says the fascist :

'Society is an imperishable organism, whose life extends beyond that of the individuals who are its transitory elements. These are born, grow up, die and are substituted by others, while the social unit always retains its identity and its patrimony of ideas and sentiments, which each generation receives from the past and transmits to the future.'

The individual cannot therefore be considered as the ultimate end of society. Society has its own purposes of preservation, expansion and perfection, and these are distinct from, and superior to, the purposes of the individuals who at any moment compose it. In the carrying out of its own proper ends, society must make use of individuals ; the individual must subordinate his own ends to those of society.

It sounds grandiose to say that the State has ' ends superior to those of the single individuals composing it '. But what are those ends ? Why should the individual subordinate his own ends to those of the State ? No conclusive answer has been given. Answers involving words and phrases like ' universal reason ', ' spirit ', ' idea ', ' real will ' are only evasions of the issue. One suspects that these phrases are only meant to justify the acquisition of

[1] *The Philosophy of Law* (1821).
[2] Article I of the Italian Labour Charter, 21 April 1927.

power and prestige for the State, i.e. for the glory of the ruler, and to commend to the ruled the sacrifice which this necessarily involves for them. The theory is but one way of justifying absolutism. It is founded on assumptions which are contrary to human experience.

'It regards humanity as something more than men,' writes R. M. MacIver; [1] 'nationality as something more than the members of a nation. It suggests that it is possible to work for humanity otherwise than by working for men, to serve nationality otherwise than by serving the members of a nation. In so far as the end and value of society are regarded as other than the ends and values of its members taken as a whole, the latter count for less than before. Not only can we not give meaning and concreteness to such a value, but the postulation of it deprives of actuality the values we actually know.'

No. The formula laid down by Kant is as true now as when it was laid down : The individual is the end and cannot be considered as a means to an end. The State may rightly be considered only as a means to the enrichment of individual personality.

§3 THE GREATEST HAPPINESS OF THE GREATEST NUMBER

An answer, more satisfactory than most of the answers given above, has been provided by the Utilitarian school, of which Jeremy Bentham (1748-1832) and John Stuart Mill (1806-73) are the best-known exponents. Briefly, their point of view is this : All men desire happiness, which may be defined as the surplus of pleasure over pain. Pleasure and pain are therefore the main springs of human action.

'Nature has placed man under the governance of two sovereign masters, pain and pleasure. It is for them alone to point out what we ought to do, as well as to determine what we shall do... We owe to them all our ideas ; we refer to them all our judgements, and all the determinations of our life.' (Bentham) The sources of pleasure and pain are physical (e.g. good scenery), political (e.g. good laws), moral (public opinion) and religious (relations with God). It is the task of the legislator to manipulate these 'sanctions' to promote human happiness, individual and social. In the calculus of happiness, everybody is to count as one and nobody for more than one. To the individual the value of a pleasure or pain taken by itself depends on a number of factors including its duration, intensity, certainty (or uncertainty) and nearness (or remoteness).

[1] *Philosophical Review*, September 1915.

In dealing with a group the number of persons affected is another factor. So it is a matter for hedonistic[1] calculus, summing up pleasures and pains in any particular case and balancing the pleasures against the pains, considering the number of persons affected and seeing whether the law contemplated produces the greatest happiness of the greatest number.

Utilitarianism has been subjected to a number of criticisms. It assumes that the business aspect of human affairs alone governs man's conduct ; it does not seem to appreciate pure disinterestedness, which it ultimately resolves into the pursuit of individual pleasure. Again, a sum of pleasures may be an attractive phrase ; but when it comes to estimates of human happiness or misery, arithmetic in politics is not much more helpful than politics in arithmetic ; for there is no proof that by pursuing the happiness of the greatest number, we shall produce, or help to produce, the greatest happiness. If men were all equal, it would be simple political philosophy, because it is nothing more than simple arithmetic, to conclude that the greater the number of men made happy, the greater the resulting sum of happiness. But men are not equal ; Bentham himself admitted that the dogma of the equality of men was an ' anarchic fallacy '. As men are not equal, and the same pleasure may be felt by different men unequally, it would be difficult to calculate the greatest happiness of the greatest number with any assurance of success.

But in spite of all this criticism, the formula of the greatest happiness of the greatest number still remains valuable in Politics. It supplies a ' slogan ' which gets imprinted in the popular mind and supplies a standard, a touchstone, with which one can judge State actions. The basic idea of Utilitarianism (as distinguished specially from Idealism) is simply this : all actions must be judged by their results, by their fruitfulness in pleasure, and this pleasure must find actual expression in the lives and in the experience of definite individuals. And above all, to use Pollock's metaphor, the formula of the greatest happiness can be made a hook to put in the nostrils of the leviathan (the State), that he may be tamed and harnessed to the chariot of utility. The criterion of utility serves to simplify the problem of Politics. Bentham said, ' let the State act to remove disabilities '; in so doing the rulers would be forwarding the welfare of their subjects. But if the authorities failed in this purpose, they could claim no rights of sanctity. The claims of legality could not stand for a moment against the claims of morality, and the claims of morality were summed up in the happiness of the people.

[1] Hedonism is the doctrine or theory of ethics in which pleasure is regarded as the chief good or the proper end of an action.

' A public judgement of happiness, expediency, well-being, or whatever else we call it, is in the nature of human affairs a rough thing at best ; and there is plenty of work to be done which ought to be done on any possible view of the nature of duty. The main point was to rouse the State to consciousness of its power and its proper business ; and by persistent and confident iteration, Bentham did this effectually.' [1]

§4 A MODERN VIEW

One of the best statements in recent times regarding the purposes of the State is made by Laski in *A Grammar of Politics* : The State is an organization to enable the mass of men to realize social good on the largest possible scale. It exists to enable men, at least potentially, to realize the best that is in themselves. Men can be enabled to realize the ' best that is in themselves ' only if the State provides ' rights '. Rights are those conditions of social life without which no man can seek in general to be himself at his best. They have a content which changes with time and place. They are prior to the State in the sense that, recognized or no, they are that from which its validity derives. Rights are, therefore, the groundwork of the State.

To illustrate : the citizen has a right to work. Society owes the citizen the occasion to perform his function, for to leave him without access to the means of existence is to deprive him of that which makes possible the realization of personality. The right to work involves the right to maintenance in the absence of work. The right to an adequate wage, the right to reasonable hours of labour, and the right to be concerned in the government of industry are other economic rights which are necessary to provide decent conditions of life and work. The citizen has a right to such education as will fit him for the tasks of citizenship.

A group of other rights is necessary to enable the citizen to have a share in the government of his State, itself a necessary condition for the realization of his best self : the right to vote, periodical elections, the right to stand as a candidate for election, equal eligibility to government office (if the necessary qualifications are fulfilled), and freedom of speech, press and association. They enable the citizen to contribute his instructed judgement for the public good, to elect his rulers and call them to account for their conduct in office. They enable him, too, to work with like-minded men for the promotion of these purposes in life which he deems necessary for realizing his own personality.

[1] F. Pollock, *An Introduction to the History of the Science of Politics*, p. 108.

And, finally, a third group of rights which Laski calls *private* is essential. Under this head he includes the right to reasonable access to judicial remedy, freedom of religion and a limited right of property. These are necessary to give the citizen a sense of personal security and freedom of conscience.

These rights, it is hardly necessary to mention, are not absolute rights : the rights of one are limited by the rights of others. They have also to be defined in detail from time to time in relation to social conditions. Moreover, while it is true that the State must give the citizen these conditions, without which he cannot be that best self that he may be, this does not mean the guarantee that his best self will be attained. It means only that the hindrances to its attainment are removed as far as the actions of the State can remove them. But the State must do its duty ; since it exists to enable men to realize their best, it is only by maintaining rights that its end may be attained.

Laski, it ought to be added, is careful to point out that his way of stating the purpose of the State is only a special adaptation of the Benthamite theory to the special needs of our time. It follows Bentham in its insistence that ' social good is the product of co-ordinated intelligence ', and that social good means the avoidance of misery and the attainment of happiness. It differs from the Utilitarian outlook in its rejection of the egoistic nature of the human impulse and of the elaborate calculus of pains and pleasures.

' Our view,' concludes H. J. Laski, ' is rather, first, that individual good cannot, over a long period, be usefully abstracted from the good of other men ; and, second, that the value of reason is to be found in the degree to which it makes possible the future, not less than the immediate, harmony of impulses.'

The view outlined above has the great merit of being simple, realistic, and intelligible. It is broader than the views of Locke and Spencer. It is clearer and safer than the Idealistic view ; clearer because it does not take shelter behind big phrases like ' cosmic reason ' and ' the personality of the State ', and safer because it leaves the judgement of the performance of the State to the average man and woman who are subject to its laws. It is not static, but takes note of changes in time and place. Above all, it makes the individual the end, and the State the means. It puts the State on trial ; for, over any long period, the State can win the allegiance of its citizens only by the efforts it makes to give their rights increasing substance.

§5 POLITICAL OBLIGATION

If now we ask ourselves the question : ' Why do men obey the State ? ' the answer is clear. In rational terms, men obey the State because they stand to gain by doing so. They are conscious that the State has a rational purpose ; that purpose is the promotion of social good on the largest possible scale ; the achievement of that purpose demands their willing co-operation and obedience to laws. But the same view also tells them that, in certain circumstances, they may deem it their duty to withdraw their co-operation and resist the State, viz. when the mischiefs of obedience are greater than the mischiefs of disobedience. They obey the State because, by doing so, they hope to be provided with those conditions of social life which are necessary for the realization of their own per-sonalities ; it is the duty of the State to recognize their rights and give them increasing substance. When there is clear evidence that, over a reasonable period, the State is not doing its duty—in other words, when its actions are not in accordance with its purpose—the individual has a duty to ask himself why he should continue to render obedience. There is a moral right to resist.

The right to resist the State, however, is itself limited by condi-tions, as indeed all rights are. First, the individual must not resist the State if reasonable grounds exist to show that it is seeking to play its part, even though it has not achieved its object as quickly as he might wish. Second, he must have reasonable ground for the belief that the changes he advocates are likely to result in the end he has in view. Third, he must try constitutional methods of agitation before resorting to resistance : for, very often, by them-selves they may be sufficient to gain the objective. Further, resistance can be resorted to only for the vindication of significant issues, as distinguished from minor details of no moment. The gist of these limitations, is that, as Burke said, the right to resist is the medicine of the constitution and not its daily bread. This is a necessary caution because, while the conscientious individual who leads the resistance may often be motivated by the highest moral purpose, he must remember that he may be followed by others less conscientious who may take advantage of the opportu-nity to gain their selfish ends.

This is purely a rational view of the problem of political obliga-tion and, therefore, inadequate. Graham Wallas has taught us that the play of reason in politics is restricted by the strength of emotions and instincts in the mental life. As Laski suggests, the State as it was and is has found the roots of allegiance in all the complex facts of human nature. This nature is a mixture of impulses and reason. The satisfaction of man's primary wants—

food, drink, sex, clothing and shelter—involves associated life :
and associated life implies the necessity of government.

'The activities of a civilized community are too complex and too
manifold to be left to the blind regulation of impulse ; and even if
each man could be relied upon to act consistently in terms of
intelligence, there would be need for a customary standard by
which the society in its organized form agreed to differentiate right
from wrong.' Some obey through fear of the punishments which
disobedience to law involves. Further, men are born in the State ;
obedience to the State becomes with most men a habit, and few
expend the effort to scrutinize its foundations. And those who
reflect on the nature of the State would find it an organization to
enable the mass of men to realize social good—an instrument to
further men's happiness—and would render obedience to it to the
extent it realizes its purpose.

To enable the State to fulfil its purpose, it is endowed with force,
with coercive power. But force is not the essence of the State but
only its criterion. The Government, as the agency of the State, is
vested with coercive power in order to compel obedience to its
laws for the preservation of order and for the common good of the
community. The purpose of force is to prevent individuals and
associations of individuals from taking the law into their own hands
and to insist on a peaceful settlement of their differences. As
A. D. Lindsay puts it, most people usually wish to obey the law.
Everybody has to obey it always. The force of the State is necessary to fill up the margin between ' most people ' and ' everybody ',
between ' usually ' and ' always '. But force, essential as it is, is
not the *basis* of the State. It is assigned to the Government as
upholders of law ; and the law itself must be such as to command
the general consent of the people. This point is well brought out
in Green's famous statement : ' Will, not force, is the basis of the
State.' [1]

SELECT BIBLIOGRAPHY

ARISTOTLE, *Politics*, Bk. I, ' Everyman Library ', Dent
G. E. G. CATLIN, *Systematic Politics*, ch. ix, Allen & Unwin, 1962
W. L. DAVIDSON, *Political Thought in England : Bentham to Mill*,
   ' Home University Library ', Oxford, 1915
R. G. GETTEL, *Political Science*, ch. xxi, Ginn, 1933
H. J. LASKI, *A Grammar of Politics*, ch. i, Allen & Unwin, 5th
   ed., 1952
W. W. WILLOUGHBY, *An Examination of the Nature of the State*,
   ch. xii, Macmillan, 1922
—— , *The Ethical Basis of Political Authority*, ch. xiv-xv,
   Macmillan, 1930

[1] See pp. 57-8 below, for a further explanation of this statement.

CHAPTER IV

SOVEREIGNTY

§1 THE THEORY OF SOVEREIGNTY

SOVEREIGNTY [1] may be defined as the power of the State to make law and enforce the law with all the coercive power it cares to employ. It is

' that characteristic of the State in virtue of which it cannot be legally bound except by its own will or limited by any other power than itself.' [2]

The modern State claims to be sovereign, to be subject to no higher human authority.

The conception of sovereignty was introduced into political theory by the French writer Bodin (1530-96). Defining the State as an aggregation of families and their common possessions ruled by a sovereign power and by reason, he said that in every independent community governed by law there must be some authority, whether residing in one person or several, whereby the laws themselves are established and from which they proceed. And this power being the source of law must be above the law — though not above duty and moral responsibility. Sovereignty is a power supreme over citizens and subjects, itself not bound by the laws. Bodin did not carry his theory to its logical conclusion, suggested by the preceding summary, because he admitted (i) that there were some fundamental laws (e.g. the Salic law of France[3]) which the sovereign could not lawfully abrogate; and (ii) that private property being granted by law of nature and, therefore, inviolable, the sovereign could not tax the subjects without their consent.

Among other writers who developed the theory may be mentioned Grotius (1583-1645), Hobbes, Locke, Rousseau and Bentham. The importance of Grotius in the development of the theory is that he emphasizes *external* sovereignty, i.e. the independence of States from foreign control. Hobbes, as we have seen,

---

[1] The word ' sovereignty ' is derived from the Latin word *superanus* and means ' supremacy '.

[2] *Lehre von den Staatenverbindungen*, p. 34 ; cited by J. W. Garner in his *Introduction to Political Science*, p. 239.

The law excluding females from dynastic succession.

made sovereignty absolute and located it in the ruler, basing his theory on a social contract. Locke did not use the term sovereignty at all ; in so far as there was a supreme power in his State, it lay with the people ; but normally it was latent. Rousseau maintained that sovereignty belonged to the people ; it could be exercised only in an assembly of the whole people. Government was but the executive agent of the general will ; it had no manner of sovereignty. The sovereignty of the people in Rousseau was as unlimited as that of the Government in Hobbes. Bentham agrees that sovereignty is unlimited by law, but it is not morally unlimited ; for, in practice, it is limited by the possibility of resistance, and there are conditions under which resistance is morally justifiable. He urged the necessity for the sovereign to justify his power by useful legislation with the object of promoting the greatest happiness of the greatest number.

§2 AUSTIN'S VIEW

The most familiar statement of the doctrine of sovereignty is a passage by Austin (1790-1859) in his *Province of Jurisprudence Determined* (1832).

'If a determinate human superior, not in the habit of obedience to a like superior, receive habitual obedience from the bulk of a given society, that determinate superior is sovereign in that society, and that society (including the superior) is a society political and independent.' 'Furthermore,' he continued, 'every positive law, or every law simply and strictly so-called, is set, directly or circuitously, by a sovereign person or body to a member or members of the independent political society wherein that person or body is sovereign or supreme.'

The implications of this, the analytical view of sovereignty and law, are threefold : (*i*) in every State, there must be a sovereign and the sovereign's power is unlimited and indivisible ; (*ii*) the sovereign must be clearly located ; and (*iii*) his commands are laws, a law being defined as a command of the State obliging the subject to do, or to refrain from doing, certain acts, failure to obey being visited by a penalty. A legal right, according to this view, is a privilege or exemption enjoyed by a citizen as against any of his fellow-citizens, granted by the sovereign power of the State and upheld by that power, e.g. the right of property. The subject has no legal rights against the State.

Each one of these implications is subject to criticism.

§3 IS SOVEREIGNTY ABSOLUTE AND INDIVISIBLE?

Critics like Laski argue that it would be of lasting benefit to political science if the whole concept of sovereignty were surrendered. The essence of this criticism is a realistic view of the State, as contrasted with the formal and legalistic view of Austin. The State is a useful instrument for promoting social good. It follows that its laws must be obeyed when they are designed to promote that end. It is senseless, however, to urge that the sovereign power of the State must or will be obeyed when the State's acts have no relation to its purpose. Man has a sense of right and wrong.

' Legally an autocratic Tsar may shoot down his subjects before the Winter Palace at Petrograd ; but morally it is condemnation that we utter . . . . There is, therefore, a vast difference between what Dane Pound had admirably called " law in books " and " law in action ".'

It is with the latter that a realistic theory of the State is concerned.

The power which the State can command is never absolute, for (*i*) in every society there are principles or maxims expressly adopted or tacitly accepted, which the sovereign should habitually observe.

(*ii*) In a democratic State, the legal sovereign should bow to the political sovereign.[1] The legal sovereign is that person or body of persons having the power to make law. The political sovereign is that body of persons in the State (the electorate) whose will ultimately prevails because the legal sovereign in making the law is bound to act according to their will. It is possible to find fault with Dicey's analysis, for his attempt to find the *final sovereign* may be a difficult adventure. As John Chipman Gray said, the real rulers of a society are undiscoverable. In Switzerland, till recently, only men had the right to vote, but was their vote uninfluenced by women ? In this case, the political sovereign of Dicey may be shifted further, indeed may not be easily definable.

Further, the conception of a political sovereign as the ultimate sovereign has the defect that the will of the electorate may not be adequately carried out by the legal sovereign ; and where, as in India and Britain, the electorate have no power directly to make or annul laws (through the methods of the referendum and the initiative [2]), the final sovereignty may be partly shared by the legal sovereign.

[1] A. V. Dicey, *Law of the Constitution*, 9th ed., pp. 72-3.
[2] See below, ch. xxx, §8.

Yet Dicey's criticism is valuable in the sense that normally the lawmaking authority must respect public opinion.

(*iii*) Sir Henry Maine urges that Austin's conception of sovereignty is inapplicable to undeveloped communities where custom is a powerful force. The instance which Maine gives[1] in support of his contention is telling. There could be no more perfect embodiment of sovereignty, as conceived by Austin, than Ranjit Singh (king of the Sikhs, 1801-39). He was absolutely despotic. ' Yet I doubt whether once in all his life, he issued a command which Austin would call a law.' The rules which regulated the life of his subjects were derived from their immemorial usages, administered by domestic tribunals in families or village communities. It might be contended that, as the Sikh despot permitted heads of households and village elders to prescribe rules, these rules were his commands and true laws, on the principle that ' what the sovereign permits, he commands '. But if ' Ranjit Singh never did or could have dreamed of changing the civil rules under which his subjects lived ', the case is different. He could not but permit what he commanded !

(*iv*) The State is but one association among several associations, say the pluralists (e.g. Laski, Cole, etc.), and, therefore, it cannot be invested with the unique sovereign power of the community. Indeed, there must be as many sovereigns as there are associations (e.g. the Church, the Federation of Trade Unions, Employers' Associations). The State must limit its activities to those which concern all people alike, e.g. the maintenance of law and order. In matters which concern lesser groups, the State has no business to interfere. R. M. MacIver's definition of the State illustrates this view.

' The State is an *association* which, acting through law as promulgated by a Government endowed to this end with coercive power, maintains within a community territorially demarcated the *universal* external conditions of social order.'[2]

The traditional or monistic theory of sovereignty, says the pluralist, errs in holding that the various non-political associations are created by the State, are dependent for their continued existence upon the will of the State, and exercise only such powers as are conceded to them by the State. It is urged, on the contrary, that associations grow naturally ; that they have a will of their own and possess personality and that the life lived in the group is a very important part in the life of the individual. Thus a trade

---

[1] *Early History of Institutions*, pp. 380-2.
[2] *The Modern State*, p. 22. Italics ours.

union comes into existence not because the State creates it, but because the workers feel that by uniting themselves into an association they are able to secure better wages and other favourable conditions of work, which individually they are unable to secure. Further, the trade union as a body has a will and a policy which may fairly be distinguished from the will and the policy of its individual members. The pluralist contention is that voluntary associations should not be dictated to by the State.

' The majority of a nation is not competent to act for the interests of all in all things, because the interests of the members of a nation are not common in all things. Therefore, besides a national sovereign deciding questions in cases affecting the common interest of the entire nation, there should be particular sovereigns to decide matters, where the special interest of some group is more important than the remoter interest of the majority.'

There are differences among the pluralists, some holding that the State is only *unus inter pares* (one among equals), and, therefore, must have no control at all over other associations ; others that it is *primus inter pares* (the most important among equals), and, therefore, may be vested with the power of co-ordination between associations, and between associations and the State ; into these details we do not enter. The pluralists have rendered a distinct service in that they have shown the danger of attributing absolute sovereignty to the State and the value of allowing initiative to groups ; their error, briefly, is that they are not content to supplement but attempt to supplant the State.

(*v*) Is sovereignty indivisible ? This question has been particularly raised by American writers on Government, because it has special reference to the type of State to which the United States of America belongs, viz. a federation. The essential characteristic of a federal State, as is shown below,[1] is the division of governmental powers between the common Central Government and the Governments of the units which constitute the federation. Hamilton and Madison,[2] therefore, argued that the sovereignty is divided between the states on the one hand and the federal union on the other, so that ' the whole sovereignty consists of a number of partial sovereignties '. On the other hand Calhoun[3] argued that sovereignty is an entire thing ; to divide it is to destroy it. It is the supreme power in a State ; and ' we might just as well speak of half a square or half a triangle as of half a sove-

---

[1] See below, ch. xxvii.
[2] *The Federalist* (Everyman Library), Essays 32 and 39.
[3] *Disquisition on Government*, 1851.

reignty '. The question is not of mere academic interest, because once admit the divisibility of sovereignty and the units in a federation will claim the freedom to secede of their own will from the federation. It is unnecessary to follow the controversy further ; so far as America is concerned, the issue was decided in favour of the indivisibility of sovereignty by the American Civil War (1861-5). It is now settled doctrine that, legally, sovereignty in a federal State is vested in the amending body of the constitution. While governmental powers are divided between two governmental authorities, sovereignty itself is not divided ; it is vested in that body which can change the constitution or fundamental law — which in Austinian terms can be said to obey no like superior but receives habitual obedience from the bulk of a given society.

§4 CAN SOVEREIGNTY BE LOCATED?

The Austinian theory says that the sovereign is a determinate person or body of persons, but it may be doubted whether this is so in every State. In Britain, no doubt, the sovereignty is clearly located in the Queen in Parliament. A bill passed by both Houses of Parliament and assented to by the queen becomes the law of the land and is put into effect by the courts. But in other States the sovereign is not so determinate. For instance, in the United States of America the sovereign, as noticed earlier, is the body which has power to amend the constitution. But to call this body determinate is an abuse of language. The United States is a federal State consisting of fifty ' states '. The powers of government are divided between the Central Government and the state Governments: this division is effected by a constitution. Both the centre and the units can act only in accordance with the terms of the constitution. This constitution can be amended in the following way :

' The Congress, whenever two-thirds of both Houses shall deem it necessary, shall propose amendments to this constitution, or on the application of the Legislatures of two-thirds of the several states, shall call a convention for proposing amendments, which, in either case, shall be valid to all intents and purposes, as part of this constitution, when ratified by the Legislatures of three-fourths of the several states or by conventions in three-fourths thereof, as the one or the other mode of ratification may be proposed by the Congress.' [1]

---

[1] Article V.

An analysis of this Article shows that there are four alternative methods of amending the constitution : first, the Congress by a two-thirds majority may propose an amendment and the Legislatures of three-fourths of the states may ratify it ; second, a convention, called on the application of the Legislatures of two-thirds of the states, may propose an amendment and the Legislatures of three-fourths of the states may ratify it ; third, the Congress by a two-thirds majority may propose an amendment, and conventions in three-fourths of the states may ratify it, and finally, a convention called on the application of the Legislatures of two-thirds of the states may propose an amendment, and conventions in three-fourths of the states may ratify it. A body, which is now one, now another, can hardly be called determinate. Moreover, this body does not normally meet ; it also does not pass ordinary laws. Truly does Laski consider the discovery of the sovereign in a federal State an ' impossible adventure '.

The difficulty of locating the sovereign is not, says Laski, confined to a federal State. Taking the example of Belgium (a unitary State), he shows how it is difficult to locate the sovereign there. For the constitution of Belgium guarantees certain rights to individuals, such as freedom of religion. These rights are alterable by the Belgian Assembly.

' But before the constitution can be altered, the decision of one Assembly must be ratified by a new one, re-chosen by the electorate for that purpose. There is no guarantee not merely that the new chambers will in a sitting, at which two-thirds of the members are present and two-thirds of these vote for the change, ratify the constitutional alteration ; even more, there is no guarantee that the new Assembly will have the same complexion as the old, and it might, as a matter of theory, prove impossible to alter the constitution. In that background either Belgium is not a sovereign State in its internal affairs or its sovereignty resides in the electorate.'

But the electorate is not the legal sovereign, for it cannot pass laws.

§5 LAW AS COMMAND

The third line of criticism is that which directly challenges the claim that the State, or the sovereign within the State, makes law. It is argued that an adequate view of law should take into account the historical and sociological aspects of it as well. The essence of the historical approach to law, e.g. by Sir Henry Maine, may be expressed thus : ' Law grows as the people grow, develops with the people. Law is the result of a varying, progressive, slow and lengthy formation by society rather than of the arbitrary will of a lawgiver.' We may illustrate this position from one of the epoch-making laws in modern India. The Ruler of Travancore decreed in 1936 that all classes of Hindus, irrespective of caste, could be admitted into the State temples. This decree broke a custom which had prevailed in Hindu society for centuries. It is by no means an adequate explanation of this law to say that the Ruler had the power to pass the law and he passed it. We must also take into account those influences which had been, for over half a century, tending to mitigate the rigours of caste ; the contact of India with Western culture and ways of living, and the opportunities which they provided for the freer contacts of men of all classes ; schools and colleges, clubs, buses, trains, etc. ; urban life with its relative freedom from social conventions which prevail in rural areas ; the influence of Christianity and Islam ; the permeation of egalitarian ideas through the study of European political classics and the propaganda carried on against untouchability by Mahatma Gandhi and other farsighted leaders.

The sociological view is illustrated by Léon Duguit[1] and Hugo Krabbe. The obligations involved in law arise not from the fact that they are decreed by any sovereign ; they arise from the conditions of social life. Duguit holds that social solidarity consti-tutes the foundation of law ; stealing and assault are prohibited by law ; if they were permitted, society would not hold together for long, its community of interests, feeling and action would cease to exist. Krabbe holds that law springs from men's sense of right : their sense of right tells men that stealing and assault are wrong, and, therefore, should not be permitted. As explained below,[2] none of these three schools of law, taken by itself, is adequate ; the generally accepted view is that the nature of law can be properly grasped only if the analytical, historical and socio-logical aspects are all taken into consideration. Therefore, the conception of the legal sovereign as the authority creating law is inadequate, as the content of law is never actually ' created '.

§6 A HISTORICAL ANALYSIS

In a historical analysis of the State it may be urged that (*i*) the idea of the omnipotent State grew up in certain circumstances, internal and external, which no longer hold good ; and that (*ii*) the State has not always been omnipotent.

[1] *Law in the Modern State*, 1921.
[2] See ch. v, §1.

(i) Duguit in an admirable analysis points out that internally the notion of State sovereignty grew up in the sixteenth century when, in the main, the State provided police, military, and judicial services ; then its acts appeared simply as unilateral commands. Today, as the result of a complex transformation, due partly to the progress of knowledge, and partly to economic and industrial changes, the business of government has gone beyond the provision of internal security, justice, and of defence against war. It helps industry and agriculture ; provides public instruction and poor-relief ; establishes insurance systems of various kinds — against unemployment, old age and sickness ; and ensures transport. Briefly, the State has become the national housekeeper. Not command but service is the prominent characteristic of the State. The modern State is a social service State, and, therefore, the idea of public service should replace the idea of sovereignty.

Externally, it is argued, the world has become more interdependent since the time when Bodin developed his theory of sovereignty, especially since the Industrial Revolution. Thus Britain and other European countries are much in need of Indian products — cotton, tea, oilseeds, hides and skins, lac, etc. India, in turn, imports textiles, metals, machinery, vehicles, oils, paper and rubber. The full utilization of the world's resources demands co-operation among the nation-States. But, as it is, the existence of sovereign States prevents the maximum co-operation ; it also leads to war. And modern methods of warfare, especially since the discovery of the atomic and hydrogen bombs, have become so destructive in their results that the recurrence of war is likely to destroy civilization itself. Therefore, nations must agree to the principle that in matters which touch more than one nation, they will be bound by the decision arrived at by a common authority, such as the United Nations, in which they will all be represented. Examples of such common matters are territorial boundaries, international migration, armaments, tariffs, the rights of national minorities, international communications and external capital. Some thinkers, like Clarence Streit, even advocate a federation of nations. The meaning of this proposal is that the external sovereignty claimed by States must be restricted in matters affecting all, so that collective security may be established. The theory of sovereignty developed in a self-sufficient age cannot be maintained in a world where the inter-dependence of States is so marked. A more realistic proposal[1] has been made by Grenville Clark and Louis B. Sohn, viz., the establishment of a common authority with defined powers to maintain peace. All other powers

[1] This is discussed in some detail in ch. xi, §7.

would still be reserved to nations ; but in this limited field, the nations would have to forego their sovereignty.

(*ii*) In practice those who attempted to realize in their conduct the substance of sovereignty found themselves sooner or later deprived of it ; witness, for instance, the French Revolution of 1789 and the Russian Revolution of 1917. Indeed, revolutions, in the expressive phrase of Laski, are footnotes to the problem of sovereignty.

§7 A MODIFIED VIEW

The preceding discussion suggests that there are several valid criticisms of Austin's theory : it is not applicable to undeveloped communities, among whom custom is the king of men ; it does not trace out the real, as distinguished from the formal, repository of political power ; it ignores the power of public opinion ; it wrongly attributes absolutism to the sovereign ; it ignores the strength and freedom of voluntary associations ; it forgets that the sovereign is not everywhere a determinate person or body of persons ; it presents an inadequate conception of law ; and, finally, its emphasis on external sovereignty is out of accord with modern conditions. The merit, however, of the theory is that, as a conception of the legal nature of sovereignty, it is clear and logical.

Is it true, then, to say that no theory of sovereignty has been evolved to fit in with all the facts ? We may perhaps accept as final the view of T. H. Green[1] which is here summarized :

In those levels of society in which obedience is habitually rendered by the bulk of society to some determinate superior who is independent of any other superior, the obedience is so rendered because this determinate superior is regarded as expressing or embodying what may properly be called the general will, and is virtually conditional upon the fact that the superior is so regarded. It is by no means an unlimited power of compulsion that the superior exercises, but dependent upon the sovereign conforming to certain convictions on the part of the subjects as to what is for the general interest. The sovereign is able to exercise the ultimate power of getting habitual obedience from the people in virtue of an assent on the part of the people. This assent is not reducible to the fear of the sovereign felt by each individual ; rather it is a common desire to achieve certain purposes, towards which obedience to law contributes.

The Austinians may therefore maintain that a determinate person or body of persons must have sovereign power. Let us

[1] *Principles of Political Obligation*, pp. 96-7.

only remind them that (*i*) the existence of such determinate sovereignty is true only of the thoroughly developed State ; and (*ii*) that they should not suppose that the coercive power which the sovereign exercises is the real determinant of the habitual obedience to that power. That real determinant is the fact that people have a sense of common interests and a common sympathy and a desire for common objects which we call the general will, and which they believe is embodied in the sovereign. 'Will, not force, is the basis of the State.'

SELECT BIBLIOGRAPHY

J. AUSTIN, *Lectures on Jurisprudence*, Murray, 1832

W. J. BROWN (Editor), *The Austinian Theory of Law*, Murray, 1931

J. BRYCE, *Studies in History and Jurisprudence*, Vol. II, pp. 463-555, Oxford, 1901

L. DUGUIT, *Law in the Modern State*, Allen & Unwin, 1921

T. H. GREEN, *Lectures on the Principles of Political Obligation*, pp. 93-141, Longmans, 1921

B. DE JOUVENEL, *Sovereignty*, An Enquiry into the Political Good, Cambridge, 1957

H. KRABBE, *The Modern Idea of the State*, Appleton, 1930

H. J. LASKI, *A Grammar of Politics*, ch. ii, Allen & Unwin, 5th ed., 1952

B. MOORE, *Political Power and Social Theory*, Harvard University Press, 1958

H. S. MAINE, *Lectures on the Early History of Institutions*, Murray, 1914

C. E. MERRIAM and H. E. BARNES (Editors), *A History of Political Theories, Recent Times*, ch. iii, Macmillan, 1924

C. VEREKER, *The Development of Political Theory*, Hutchinson University Library, 1957

P. W. WARD, *Sovereignty*, Routledge, 1928

CHAPTER V

LAW

§1 NATURE OF LAW

WE ordinarily use the term ' law ' to mean a body of rules to guide human action.[1] In any community, there will develop set and customary ways of carrying on social activities, which save time and avoid friction. They form a sort of unwritten code, enforced by parental and religious authority or by the pressure of public opinion. Some of these customs, however, may become so important for general welfare that stronger pressure than social authority or opinion must be brought to bear on those members of the community who act in violation of accepted social standards. Whenever any community, acting through its Government, undertakes to apply such pressure by fixing a penalty for violation, then such customs cease to be purely social and become political. They become the law of the land. They are virtually commands, ordering or prohibiting certain actions, disobedience to which involves a penalty inflicted by the Government. Law may be defined as follows :

' That portion of the established thought and habit which has gained distinct and formal recognition in the shape of uniform rules backed by the authority and power of government.' (Wilson)

' The body of principles recognized or enforced by public and regular tribunals in the administrations of justice.' (Pound)

' The system of rights and obligations which the State enforces.' (Green)

' The body of principles recognized and applied by the State in the administration of justice.' (Salmond)

---

[1] ' Any kind of rule or canon whereby actions are framed ' (Hooker. *Ecclesiastical Polity*). It may be added that this is its use in the social sciences. In the physical sciences it is used in altogether a difference sense, to indicate the abstract idea of the observed relations of natural phenomena, be those relations instances of causation or of mere succession and co-existence. Thus when we talk of the law of gravity, we mean merely that objects do gravitate ; we are here using the term ' law ' to convey to our minds the idea of order and method. See T. Holland, *The Elements of Jurisprudence*, pp. 17, 18.

' The command of a sovereign, containing a common rule of life for his subjects, and obliging them to obedience.' (John Erskine)

The modern theory of law has been the result of three principal lines of thought : the analytical, the historical and the sociological.

(*i*) *The analytical school.* The two essential features of law according to the writers of this school (e.g. Austin) are : (*a*) Law is something made consciously by lawgivers, whether legislative or judicial. A Law is law because it is set by a sovereign political authority. (*b*) Force is of the essence of law ; nothing that lacks an enforcing agency is law : ' The most obvious characteristic of law is that it is coercive ' (Holland). Machiavelli (*The Prince*, 1513) and Bodin (*The Republic*, 1576) held this view. Hobbes' definition of law clearly places its author in the same school. To Austin, law is the general body of rules, commanding general obedience, addressed by the rulers of a political society to its members. Holland elaborates the same view and defines law as a general rule of *external* human action enforced by a sovereign political authority. The emphasis on externality is intended to show that all that legislation can do is to affect the expression in conduct of the will, and not the nature of the will or motive. We may, while generally admitting this, observe that the enforcement of a formal and outward habit of right living may ultimately in some instances lead to an inward and free acceptance of these habits as a moral code.

(*ii*) *The historical school.* One of the primary defects of the analytical school is that their approach to the study of law is not evolutionary ; they regard law as static rather than progressive. The historical school, of which Sir Henry Maine and Savigny are the best known writers, supplies a corrective to this defect. They suggest that law is the result of a varying, progressive, slow and lengthy social process rather than of the arbitrary will of a lawgiver. They grant that the sovereign may be the *formal* source of law, to adopt the expressive phrase of Salmond ; they are rather concerned with the *material* source. Therefore law must be studied in relation to its environment, religious, moral, and economic, and in relation to historical tendencies and events.

(*iii*) *The sociological school.* Krabbe (*The Modern Idea of the State*, 1930) is perhaps the most suggestive writer of this school. His line of thought is best expressed by a quotation from his own work :

' Law is . . . the expression of one of the many judgements of value which we human beings make, by virtue of our dispositions and nature. We subject to our judgement all human conduct, indeed all reality ; and we distinguish as many different kinds of value as we apply different kinds of measure. The recognition or otherwise of these values is not a matter of *choice* ; we cannot be indifferent or not, at will ; our minds react within us, whether we want them to or not, and we feel ourselves subjected, as a consequence of this reaction, to what we call the good, the beautiful and the just. The rule of law likewise is due to human reaction to the sense of justice and is not a matter of external legal authority but an internal human matter.'

Against Krabbe, it may be said : ' You assume the existence of a property of consciousness : are you justified in making this assumption ? Is not your " consciousness of justice " but an " idle name " . . . which in fact but thinly conceals self-interest ? . . . And even if this is not the case, does this so-called sense of justice give us any standard of value, can it produce a standard of value ? Do not such standards vary from century to century, from year to year, from nation to nation, from group to group, indeed from man to man ? ' [1]

Krabbe's answer to this criticism is :

' If the sense of right among the members of a community differs regarding the rules to be obeyed, those rules possess a higher value which a majority of the members are willing to accept as rules of law. It is necessary that there should be a single rule, and if the persons who have a share in the making of law are of equal importance, a choice between the two rules can be made only with reference to the *number* of persons who assent to each. But if the numbers must decide, this leads of itself to the acceptance of the rule approved by the *majority* because the fact that it is accepted by the majority shows that it possesses a higher value than any other rule.' [2]

In conclusion, it is sufficient to note that these three views are complementary to one another : that is to say, an adequate philosophy of law should recognize that while the authority of the political sovereign gives law its formal sanction, the real material content of law is shaped partly by the historical environment in which it grows and partly by the sense of right of the community.

§2 SOURCES OF LAW

In a formal sense, the State is the source of all law, for it is that from which the authority of law proceeds. But in a discussion of the sources of law, we are rather concerned with those remote and immediate causes which explain the content of law and with

[1] R. Kranenburg, *Political Theory*, p. 142.
[2] H. Krabbe, *The Modern Idea of the State*, pp. 74-5.

the organs through which the State either creates law or grants
legal recognition to rules previously unauthoritative. In this sense,
six 'sources' of law are enumerated by Holland, viz. custom,
religion, scientific discussion, adjudication, equity and legislation.

(*i*) *Custom*. Usage is no doubt the earliest form of law-
making. Its essential feature is that it is a generally observed
course of conduct. No one can say exactly when it arose, but we
can hardly doubt that ' it originated generally in the conscious
choice of the more convenient of two acts though sometimes
doubtless in the accidental adoption of one of two different
alternatives ; the choice in either case having been either deliberately or accidentally repeated till it ripened into habit. The best
illustration of the formation of such habitual courses of action is
the mode in which a path is formed across a common. One man
crosses the common in the direction which is suggested either by
the purpose he has in view, or by mere accident. If others follow
in the same track, which they are likely to do after it has once
been trodden, a path is made.' [1] In primitive society, the many
relations of life — of the members of the family towards one
another, of earning and saving and of buying and selling — were
regulated by customary rules. Their sanction was the fear of
public opinion, or some kind of supernatural penalty. We have
it on Maine's authority [2] that if a Celt of Gaul refused to abide
by a Druid's judgement, he was excommunicated, which was
esteemed the heaviest of penalties. The Hindus advised sitting
dharna, which ' consists in sitting at your debtor's door and starving yourself till he pays ' ; if the debtor allowed the creditor to
starve, it was believed, some supernatural penalty would follow.
Later some customs began to be enforced by political authority ;
only then did they become law. The ' common law ' of England
consists mainly of customs accepted by courts of law.

(*ii*) *Religion*. In the primitive community, custom and law
could not be easily separated from religion ; all rules of life had
a religious sanction. The connexion between kingship and
priesthood, which we have noticed earlier, is a further illustration
of the relation between religion and politics. Indeed, as Wilson
points out, the early law of Rome was little more than a body of
technical religious rules, a system of means for obtaining individual rights through the proper carrying out of certain religious
formulas. The personal laws of the Hindus and Muslims, e.g.
laws relating to inheritance and marriage, have obvious points of
contact with **religion**.

[1] Holland, op. cit., pp. 56-8.
[2] *The Early History of Institutions*, pp. 39-40.

(*iii*) *Scientific discussion.* The opinions of learned writers on law have often been accepted as correct law : in England, for instance, the opinions of Coke and Blackstone ; in America, of Story and Kent ; and in India, of Vijnaneswara and Apararka. These opinions do not *ipso facto* become law ; they become such through recognition by courts. ' The commentator, by collecting, comparing, and logically arranging legal principles, customs, decisions, and laws, lays down guiding principles for possible cases. He shows the omissions and deduces principles to govern them.'

(*iv*) *Adjudication.* At all times and in all countries, the judges, especially of the highest courts in the land, are important law-makers. *Prima facie* the judges are to interpret and declare the law ; but in interpreting and declaring laws, they cannot help making new ones. As Justice Holmes said, judges do and must make law.[1] Whether consciously or unconsciously, in interpreting and applying, they mould and expand the law. This judicial law-making is of particular importance in countries like America and India, where Legislatures are bound by the terms of a written constitution, and, therefore, the judge has to decide whether they have overstepped the power allowed to them by the constitution.

We must, however, note a difference between legislative law-making and judicial law-making. As Roscoe Pound points out,[2] the legislative law-maker is laying down a law for the future ; hence the general security does not require him to proceed on predetermined premises or along predetermined lines. He is free to proceed along the lines that seem to him best. On the other hand, the judicial law-maker is not merely making a rule for the future. He is laying down a legal precept which will apply to the transactions of the past as well as of the future. Hence the social interest in general security requires that he should not have the same freedom as the legislative law-maker.

' It requires that instead of finding his premises or his materials of decision where he will, or where expediency appears to him to dictate, he find them in the legal system or by a process recognized by the legal system. It requires that, instead of proceeding along the lines that seem best to him, he proceed along the lines which the legal system prescribes or at least recognizes.'[3] This is a salutary restriction. It serves to hold down the personality of the judge and constrains him to look at cases objectively.

(*v*) *Equity.* This also is judge-made law ; but the difference between adjudication and equity is that the former is an interpretation of the existing laws, whereas the latter is an addition to

---

[1] See below, ch. xviii, §7, for examples.
[2] *Law and Morals*, pp. 47-50.
[3] Roscoe Pound, op. cit.

them. Equity is intended to provide relief where the existing law affords none. Thus in Rome the praetor announced, at the beginning of his year of office, the principles of adjudication which he intended to adopt, and indicated how he proposed to give relief against the rigidity of the established system ; for instance, that ' he would allow less formal processes than had hitherto been permitted to secure rights of property or of contract '. Effect was thus given to contracts which would not be found in the limited list of those recognized by the law. The Lord Chancellor in England similarly applies rules of equity.

(*vi*) *Legislation.* With the growing complexity of modern life, legislation has grown in importance as the main source of new law. In democratic countries laws are made by representative bodies, so that the laws made may truly reflect the popular will.

§3 LAW AND MORALITY

Our discussion of the nature of the State and law has made it clear that law cannot encompass the whole of man's activity, because the State is not identical with society. Law is the body of rules enforced by Government ; its ultimate sanction is force. By its very nature, it can control only external acts ; it cannot enjoin a spirit. There is then a place for morality, as distinct from law, and to this we must now turn.

In discussing the relation between law and morality, following Sidgwick,[1] we must distinguish between ideal morality and positive morality. The appeal of the moral law, considered ideally, is to the individual conscience, to the individual sense of right and wrong, of good and evil. That conscience is largely the expression of custom, social training and religious influence ; but ' as a principle of conduct, it is the " self-legislating " of a responsible person, choosing in the consciousness of his own liberty the means and end of welfare '.[2] But as the variations of such individual morality are considerable, it is difficult to generalize its relations with law. Distinguished from individual morality is *positive morality,* which has been defined as ' the body of rules supported by the prevalent opinion of the community (to which the individual belongs) at any given time '.

The differences between law and positive morality are twofold : (*i*) The violation of law is punished by Government ; of positive morality, by social intolerance. (*ii*) Law is more definite and consistent than positive morality, because there is a definite body to

---

[1] *The Elements of Politics,* ch. xiii.
[2] R. M. MacIver, *The Modern State,* p. 155.

make law and another to interpret it ; positive morality has neither, with the result that there are a number of variations in what is considered right and wrong. To illustrate : Early marriage is now definitely illegal in India ; before it was prohibited by law in 1930 one could not say definitely what the prevailing opinion of the community on the question was.

The great function of positive morality in a well-ordered community is to regulate those spheres of life and conduct which law can hardly affect, e.g. the region of motives, of personal relationships, etc. Social welfare demands the performance by the individual of a number of duties, which, being unsuitable for legal compulsion, must needs be enjoined by positive morality. Thus one must keep one's word and be punctual ; must have no sexual relationship outside marriage ; must show respect to parents and to elders generally ; parents must support their children, give them education and enable them to earn their living ; sons must support parents if the latter are unable to maintain themselves ; these and a thousand and one other rules of conduct which help to make social life harmonious and happy are enforced by the community's disapproval of those who break them and the approval of those who obey them. Similarly, social praise is the chief means of evoking charity ; the support of the poor and the disabled, the endowment of hospitals, educational institutions and the like, by the rich. These matters are all unsuitable for legal action because their effectiveness depends on spontaneity.

Secondly, where positive morality is in agreement with an action contemplated by a Government, it is a useful ally to that Government in the discharge of its duties. It is easier to enforce a law, and the object of the Government is better achieved, when the Government has behind it the support of public opinion. Take, for instance, the disabilities to which the Harijan community in many parts of India is still subject : untouchability, unapproachability, the denial of access to places of worship, etc.; this is a stain on any civilized community. A Government which wants to remove disabilities of this sort will obviously find it easier to achieve its object if it has social opinion on its side. And even where the opposition is mild, it may be worth while for the Government to proceed with its action, for, as Sidgwick remarks,[1] the legislator has, within limits, a valuable power of modifying positive morality. Through the general habit of observing the law and the general recognition of the duty of obeying rules laid down by a legitimate authority, the legislator may obtain a general obedience to rules to which current morality is indifferent

[1] op. cit., p. 208.

or even mindly overse ; and then, by the reaction of habitual conduct on opinion, a moral aversion to the opposite conduct may gradually grow up. The law prohibiting public expressions of untouchability in India is an instance in point. While untouchability is still practised in many parts of India, it is clear that the passing of the law has been most useful in getting social opinion on its side, and it is not wrong to suggest that the passing away of untouchability in India, not only in law but in fact, is only a matter of time. The law prohibiting child marriage in India is another instance. It may be said that the mild opposition to it in the early days has now given way to general acquiescence.

This observation suggests another ; when positive morality is clearly against a law contemplated by the Government, it becomes difficult to enforce it. Perhaps the best illustration of this difficulty in modern times is the failure of the prohibition law in the United States of America. Positive morality was against prohibition ; instead of supporting the law, it helped the law-breakers to break the law with impunity, with the result that the law had to be repealed. Valuable as an ally, when in agreement, positive morality becomes dangerous in opposition.

The question may be raised whether a Government is not to be considered timid if it desists from introducing the reforms which it considers essential for the good of society. The answer is that, as Aristotle says, one should proceed on a balance of considerations. In attempting to enforce an unpopular law, a Government may be doing more harm than good by creating and spreading the habit of disobedience to the law. The total social cost of such an attempt may well be greater than the social gain. Further, the principle laid down above does not prevent the legal prohibition of serious social abuses, for, as Green says,[1] the State has always to enjoin or forbid acts of which the doing, or not doing, *from whatever motive,* is necessary, to the moral end of society. The prohibition of suttee [2] in India is a clear instance of this.

§4 KINDS OF LAW[3]

Laws may be *private* or *public.* ' In so far as the rules of conduct that authoritatively obtain in a political community are devoted to the regulation of interests between individuals as such, they create only private rights and obligations, and the State appears only as their enunciator, and, if need be, their enforcer.'

---

[1] *Principles of Political Obligation,* pp. ix and 37-8.
[2] The immolation of a widow on the funeral pyre of her dead husband.
[3] An exhaustive classification is not attempted here. Our aim is rather to explain certain terms which occur frequently in the text.

These are private laws. 'Those rules that concern either the organization of the State and the allocation and delimitation of the powers of government, or the direct relations between the State and the individual' are termed public laws.

Again, laws may be *municipal* or *international*. Municipal as distinguished from international law is the law of a State which applies only to individuals and associations within the State; international law is the body of rules which determines the conduct of the general body of civilized States in their dealings with one another.

Laws are also classified into *constitutional* and *ordinary*. Constitutional law may be defined as the body of principles which regulates the powers of the Government, the rights of the governed and the relations between the two. To quote W. W. Willoughby,[1] constitutional laws are 'those laws which relate directly to the form of government that is to exist and to the allotment of powers to, and the imposition of limitations upon, the several governmental organs and functionaries'. All other laws are ordinary laws.[2]

SELECT BIBLIOGRPHY

W. J. BROWN (Editor), *The Austinian Theory of Law*, Murray. 1931

L. DUGUIT, *Law in the Modern State*, Allen & Unwin, 1921

T. E. HOLLAND, *The Elements of Jurisprudence*, pp. 14-90, Oxford, 13th ed., 1928

H. KRABBE, *The Modern Idea of the State*, Appleton, 1930

H. S. MAINE, *Ancient Law*, ch. i & v, 'World's Classics' No. 362, Oxford

R. POUND, *Law and Morals*, Oxford, 2nd ed., 1926

H. SIDGWICK, *The Elements of Politics*, ch. xiii, Macmillan, 1908

W. W. WILLOUGHBY, *The Fundamental Concepts of Public Law*, ch. x & xvi, Macmillan, 1931

---

[1] *The Fundamental Concepts of Public Law*, pp. 83-4.

[2] It ought to be added that constitutional laws are public laws; but all public laws are not necessarily constitutional laws. The term 'public law' is wider than constitutional law. See Holland, op. cit., pp. 368-9.

CHAPTER VI

LIBERTY

§1 MEANING OF LIBERTY

THE term ' liberty ' is used in Politics to mean two things, national liberty and individual liberty. The former obviously means the independence of a State from other States. It is with the latter, individual liberty, that we are concerned in this chapter.

In its absolute sense, liberty means ' the faculty of willing and the power of doing what has been willed, without influence from any other source or from without '. A moment's reflection tells us that a liberty of this unlimited character is an impossibility for all at the same time. Neither the presence of the State nor its absence can ensure it. Politics rests on two fundamental facts of human nature : every man likes to have his own way ; at the same time he possesses an instinct for sociability. From this it follows that the maximum freedom that an individual can enjoy is, as the Declaration of the Rights of Man (1789) put it, the power to do everything that does not injure another.

In practice, therefore, an analysis of the modern concept of liberty shows two main ideas :

(*i*) The individual wants to express his personality in thought, word, and act. He demands freedom, i.e. an absence or a lessening of restraint (or restrictions) on his freedom of thought, speech and action both from the Government and from private individuals and associations.

(*ii*) Secondly, freedom implies, paradoxically, the imposition of some limitations with a view (*a*) to securing the equal freedom of all, e.g. the law of libel and criminal law generally, and (*b*) to providing opportunities or conditions of life which will enable men to develop their personalities, e.g. the provision of compulsory education, factory laws, etc.

We may now give some recognized definitions of liberty :

' The opposite of over-government.' (Seeley)

' The absence of restraint upon the existence of those social conditions which in modern civilization are the necessary guarantee of individual happiness.' (Laski, *Liberty in the Modern State*)

' The eager maintenance of that atmosphere in which men

have the opportunity to be their best selves.' (Laski, *A Grammar of Politics*)

'Freedom is not the absence of all restraints but rather the substitution of rational ones for irrational.' (M'Kechnie)

The careful student will notice that the first two of these definitions emphasize the negative (the absence of restraint) and the last two the positive (the presence of opportunity) aspect of liberty. Taken together they emphasize the idea that freedom exists not only in the absence of restraint but also in the presence of opportunity. It is remarkable that those who possess wealth and power think of liberty primarily in terms of absence of restraint ; those who have no secure livelihood and are dependent on others for their existence, i.e. the mass of wage-earners, desire the provision of opportunity to live the good life.

Laski [1] classifies the content of necessary individual liberty under three heads :

(*i*) Private liberty is the opportunity to exercise freedom of choice in those areas of life where the results of one's efforts are mainly personal to oneself, e.g. freedom of religion and personal security.

(*ii*) Political liberty (sometimes also called constitutional liberty) is the right of an individual to take part in the affairs of the State, through the right to vote, the right to stand as candidate for election, and freedom of speech, press and meeting.

(*iii*) Economic liberty is security and the opportunity to find reasonable significance in the earning of one's daily bread, made possible through such rights as the rights to work, to reasonable hours of labour, to an adequate wage and to self-government in industry.

§2 CIVIL LIBERTY: RIGHTS OF CITIZENSHIP

Laski's analysis gives one a general idea of the freedom that is considered desirable ; but the freedoms that he outlines have not always been recognized, or recognized to the same extent, by all States. The sum total of the rights recognized by law and secured by the coercive agency of the State is known as civil liberty. 'Civil liberty consists of the rights and privileges which the State creates and protects for its subjects.' [2] The most important of these rights, recognized in various degrees in different States, are the following.

---

[1] *A Grammar of Politics*, ch. iii and iv.
[2] R. G. Gettell, *Political Science*, p. 148.

(*i*) *The right to life.* The most fundamental of all rights is the right to life, the foundation on which the superstructure of other rights can be built up. In order to safeguard this right, therefore, many States punish attempts at suicide, and impose the maximum penalty of capital punishment on those who attempt to kill others. That there is no *right* to suicide follows from the very nature of 'right', for 'right' is a condition of social life to enable one to develop one's moral personality; suicide annihilates personality.

On the advisability of capital punishment, however, there is no unanimity of opinion. Modern thought is tending to the view that the State will do most to promote regard for the sanctity of life by itself paying regard to that sanctity, i.e. by refusing to take life in any circumstances. Has not Bentham said that the State affects the conduct and actions of its citizens more by the standards governing its own actions than by the penalties it visits upon others? Besides, the risk of injustice with the death penalty is great, because there is the element of finality about it. If a man has been hanged, the subsequent discovery of his innocence cannot avail him; neither judges nor juries are infallible. The imposition of capital punishment takes for granted that a man may be permanently incapable of rights; it may be doubted whether this presumption is one which we are ever entitled to make. Experience has not clearly proved that capital punishment is effective in keeping down the number of murders committed in a community, for, as Roy Calvert states,[1] where the

[1] E. Roy Calvert, *Capital Punishment in the Twentieth Century.* Available information on the list of countries which have *de jure* or *de facto* abolished Capital punishment may be summarized thus: *The countries and territories which have abolished the death penalty* are divided into three categories: first, those in which the death penalty has been abolished by an express constitutional or legislative provision (abolitionist *de jure*); second, those whose positive law (penal code or special statutes) makes provision for the death are passed but in which such sentences are never carried out by virtue of an established custom (abolitionist *de facto*); third, those in which the death penalty is laid down only for offences committed in certain exceptional circumstances and in which capital punishment has, in fact, virtually disappeared (almost completely abolitionist). The date of abolition is given in each case. In cases where the death penalty was reintroduced after having been previously abolished, the date given is that of the final abolition, which is reflected in the existing law.

Abolitionist de jure. Argentina (1922), Australia (Queensland), Austria (1945)—except in the event of the proclamation of a state of emergency. Brazil (1889), Colombo (1910), Costa Rica (1882), Denmark (1930), Dominican Republic (1924), Ecuador (1897), Federal Republic of Germany (1949), Finland (1949), Greenland (1954), Iceland (1940), Italy (1944), Mexico [25 states out of 29 and the federal territory (Constitution, 1931)], Norway (1905), Netherlands (1870), Netherlands Antilles (1957), New Zealand (1961), Portugal (1867), Republic of San Marino (1865), Sweden (1921), Switzerland (1937), U.S.A. six states: Alaska (1957), Delaware (1958), Hawaii (1957), Maine (1887), Minnesota (1911), Wisconsin (1853), Vatican (1971), Uruguay (1907), U.K. (1969), Venezuela (1863).

death penalty has been abolished for all or some crimes, as in Sweden, Holland and Switzerland, there has been a decrease in murders or, at any rate, the homicidal tendency has not increased. These arguments are not conclusive. The case for capital punishment is that the association of the extremest terror with certain actions, such as treasonable outbreaks, murder, etc., may be necessary among certain communities to preserve the possibility of a social life based on the observance of rights.

(*ii*) *The right to work.* This is implicit in the right to live, because, as Laski rightly says, man ' is born into a world where, if rationally organized, he can live only by the sweat of his brow '. The right to work cannot obviously mean the right to particular work ; it can mean no more than the right to be occupied in producing some share of the goods and services necessary for society.[1] Few States outside the Soviet Union, Bulgaria, Czechoslovakia, Rumania, Yugoslavia, Poland and Hungary[2] have recognized the legal right to work ; for, it is argued, its recognition may throw too heavy a burden on society ; society must be able either to provide work for the individual when the individual cannot find it for himself, or maintain him during the period of his unemployment. Unemployment insurance, to which the individual partly contributes, is now finding favour with some States, but there are many States, like India,[3] which have yet to recognize

Abolitionist de facto. Belgium (1867), Liechtenstein (1798), Luxembourg, Vatican City State.

To these countries which are certainly abolitionist *de facto* could be added, to some extent at least, those in which an experiment in abolition appears to be in progress, the last executions having been carried out on the dates indicated below. The exact scope of these experiments is, however debatable. Australia : Victoria (1951), Gautemala (1956), United States of America : Massachusetts (1947), New Hampshire (1939), New Jersey (1959). In the Principality of Monaco, the death penalty is provided for in the Penal Code of 1874, but no sentence of death has ever been passed under that statute.

Almost completely abolitionist. Australia ; New South Wales, where the death penalty is abolished for murder but not for treason or piracy ; it is not, however, applied in fact. United States of America : Michigan (1847), North Dakota (1915), Rhode Island (1852) ; these three states have abolished the death penalty, except in the state of Michigan, for treason, in the state of North Dakota for treason (for which the death sentence is mandatory) and murder in the first degree, and in the state of Rhode Island, for murder committed by a prisoner under sentence of life imprisonment. In Nicaragua the death penalty is applicable only if the crime is committed with one or more aggravating circumstances.

[1] *A Grammar of Politics,* p. 106.

[2] See G. M. Charter, J. C. Ranney and J. H. Hertz, *The Government of the Soviet Union* (World Press, Calcutta, 1954) and S. L. Sharp, *New Constitutions in the Soviet Sphere,* (Foundation for foreign Affairs, 1950).

[3] The new Constitution of India includes the right to work under Directive Principles of State Policy, thus : ' The State shall, within the limits of its economic capacity and development, make effective provision for securing

it. The moral case for the right to work is that, under the conditions of modern industrial system, society may be held partly responsible for chronic unemployment.

(*iii*) *Personal safety and freedom.* Blackstone describes this right as a person's legal and uninterrupted enjoyment of his life, his limbs, his body and his health ; it also means ' the power of locomotion, of changing one's situation or removing one's person to whatever place one's own inclination may direct, without imprisonment or restraint, except by due course of law '. Thus a person may not be assaulted, wounded or imprisoned, except by due process of law. He has a right not to receive injury from any dangerous substance or animal kept by another. In order to secure this, Governments everywhere permit the use of such force as is necessary for self-defence and make slavery illegal. A person unlawfully imprisoned may recover his freedom by means of a writ of habeas corpus. One who is injured by the careless action of another can claim compensation for damages. This right has, according to Holland,[1] two limitations. First, it is limited during the earlier years of life by the right of parents and guardians to chastise and keep in their custody persons of tender age. Secondly, it may be partially waived. Thus a person who engages in a lawful contest of strength waives, by so doing, as against his antagonist, his right not to be assaulted and battered ; a sailor who goes on board ship waives for the voyage his right to direct his own movements.

(*iv*) *The right to reputation.* Holland[2] describes it thus : ' A man has a right as, against the world, to his good name ; that is to say, he has a right that the respect, so far as it is well founded, which others feel for him shall not be diminished ', whether by words (spoken or written) or gestures or pictures. A defamatory statement is therefore made punishable by law, if it can be shown that (*a*) such statement is made in public, (*b*) it is untrue, (*c*) it is not of public importance. ' Statements in the course of judicial proceedings . . . . fair reports of trials, legislative debates or public meetings, fair comments on public men and fair criticisms of literary and artistic productions are privileged.'

(*v*) *Religious freedom.* It is well known that it took centuries for this right to be recognized by law ; prosecution for heresy was common enough in the sixteenth and seventeenth centuries. The right of following one's own religious faith and worship has, how-

the right to work, to education and to public assistance in cases of unemployment, old age, sickness and disablement, and in other cases of undeserved want.'

[1] *The Elements of Jurisprudence*, pp. 170-1.
[2] op. cit., pp. 183-4.

ever, come to be gradually recognized by modern States. The full implications of this right have, paradoxically, been nowhere better stated than in the Weimar Constitution of Germany : [1]

All inhabitants of the Reich enjoy full liberty of faith and of conscience . . .

Civil and political rights and duties are neither dependent upon nor restricted by the practice of religious freedom.

The enjoyment of civil and political rights, as well as admission to official posts, are independent of one's religious creed.

No one is bound to disclose his religious convictions. The authorities have the right to make inquiries as to membership of a religious body only when rights and duties depend upon it or when the collection of statistics ordered by law requires it.

No one may be compelled to take part in any ecclesiastical act or ceremony, or to participate in religious practices or to make use of any religious form of oath.

There is no State Church.

Freedom of association is guaranteed to religious bodies.

Every religious body regulates and administers its affairs independently, within the limits of the laws applicable to all.

The members of the armed forces are guaranteed the necessary free time for the performance of their religious duties.

Religious bodies have the right of entry for religious purposes into the army, hospitals, prisons or other public institutions, so far as is necessary for the conduct of public worship and religious ministrations, but any form of compulsion is forbidden.

The right to freedom of religion is clearly recognized by the Constitution of India ; subject to public order, morality and health, all persons are equally entitled to freedom of conscience and the right freely to profess, practise and propagate religion. Subject to the same conditions, every religious denomination is also entitled to establish and maintain institutions for religious and charitable purposes, to manage its own affairs in matters of religion, to own and acquire movable and immovable property and to administer such property in accordance with law. It should be added that the State has reserved the right to make any law regulating or restricting any economic, financial, political or other secular activity which may be associated with religious practice and to throw open Hindu religious institutions of a public character to all classes and sections of Hindus.

It need hardly be added that religious freedom is subject to the

[1] Articles 135-41.

condition that the exercise of such a right must not disturb the peace.

(*vi*) *Education.* The importance of education is hardly a matter for discussion. It is necessary as an indispensable condition to free individual development, and to fit the individual for the tasks of citizenship. The legal content of this right varies from State to State. In Britain, a parent has the right to demand free education for his children in a public elementary school. ' If there should be no such school within convenient distance, the State, after inquiry, will cause one to be established.' Besides, the State also helps higher education through the provision of funds and an inspecting agency. In India, free elementary education is not a legal right everywhere ; much leeway has yet to be made up if that ideal is to be realized.

(*vii*) *Freedom of speech, public meeting and publication.* This means the right to say or write what one chooses ' provided that this is not blasphemous, obscene, seditious or defamatory of another's reputation ; and the right to attend any lawful public meeting '.[1]

It is hardly necessary to argue in detail the case for freedom of opinion. The main reasons are clear enough ; it is a means of self-protection ; it enables the rulers to become acquainted with the experience and the wants of the ruled ; its denial is not only an assumption of infallibility, but would mean that the ' decisions registered as law reflect not the total needs of the society, but the powerful needs which have been able to make themselves felt at the source of power '. Terror does not alter opinion, it only drives the opinion underground, thereby making it more dangerous. Those who oppose freedom of opinion are losers, because the silenced opinion may contain a portion of truth — after all, in a classic phrase, the heresies of today are the orthodoxies of tomorrow. Finally, a man always learns by having an open mind.

But freedom of opinion means freedom to express one's ideas on general subjects, on themes of public importance, rather than on the character of particular persons. The statements expressed must be true. Where libel takes place, i.e. where opinion is expressed with a malicious intent to injure a person, the person concerned ought to be allowed damages and, if necessary, to demand proper publicity for the apology where the libel is proved. The State also has the right to protection against the kind of public utterance which is bound to result in disorder. Thus the State may take cognizance of incitements to break its laws or defy its authority, for such incitement is more than the expression of

[1] W. D. Aston and P. Jordan. *Citizenship*. pp. 42-3.

opinion. ' The State is entitled to suppress an incitement which itself is an attempt to dethrone the rule of opinion.' But, as Laski rightly points out, no Government is entitled itself to assume that disorder is imminent ; the proof must be offered to an independent Judiciary. And the proof so offered must be evidence that the utterance to which it takes exception was, at the time and in the circumstances in which it was made, definitely calculated to result in a breach of the peace. Its prohibitions, in other words, must not be preventive prohibitions. ' It must not prohibit a meeting before it is held on the ground that the speaker is likely to preach sedition there.' Comments on a case which is *sub judice* may be regulated, as they would interfere with the course of justice. And, finally, published documents should contain the name of the printer and the publisher ; where newspapers publish attacks on a person, they may be compelled to publish gratis a reply from the person concerned.

Freedom of opinion in war-time raises several important issues.[1] It is agreed on all hands, of course, that a citizen must subject himself to greater restrictions in war-time than in normal times in the interests of his country's security and independence ; he cannot, for instance, be allowed to communicate military secrets to the enemy. But has he the right to oppose his nation's entry into and prosecution of the war if he believes honestly that war as such is wrong, or to criticize the Government's conduct of military operation, diplomatic policy, war aims and peace proposals ? All Governments normally take the safe course and limit the expression of opinion to opinion which does not, in their judgement, hinder the prosecution of war, on the ground that it is important above all to present a war-time unity of outlook. It is sufficient to say here that such interference does not always lead to the happiest results and involves a serious invasion of civic rights which can be justified only on the — not always correct — assumption that the Executive is always well-informed and correct and private citizens are always ignorant and wrong.

(*viii*) *The right of association.* There are many voluntary associations in modern times devoted to the promotion of objects in which their members are interested — social, religious and economic. These quite largely determine a man's choice of friends, his career and opportunities. In the expressive words of Laski, they give the individual ' a feeling that he has found himself, a power of self-recognition that is an invaluable factor in the achievement of personal harmony. What, without them, is a

[1] See Laski, *Liberty in the Modern State*, Pelican edition, pp. 116-21, for an able discussion of these issues.

chaotic world, becomes a world ordered by the opportunity to do with others who share an experience akin to his own.' In a previous discussion,[1] we have indicated the claims of the pluralists on behalf of voluntary associations ; it is sufficient here to say that no modern State accepts such wide claims. While it permits a wide (and varying) freedom in the formation of such associations and allows them to exercise large powers, it also prevents such acts by recognized associations as fundamentally contradict its own purposes. Thus while a communist association has the right of spreading the ideals of communism by peaceful persuasion, it cannot attempt actions such as military drill and the purchase of munitions, which show a determination to overthrow the social order by violent means.

(*ix*) *Family rights.* These rights result from the institution of marriage, and include a man's marital right to the society of his wife and vice versa, and the custody and control of his children and to the produce of their labour till they arrive at years of discretion. The marriage tie terminates on the death of one of the parties or their divorce. As to the permissibility of divorce and the grounds on which it ought to be granted, the widest difference prevails among different societies.

(*x*) *Property.* Almost every State outside the Soviet Union recognizes the right to private property.[2] This right is held to include the right to the unhampered use of one's gains, whether land or goods, the right of exclusive use, the right to destroy and the right to alienate by gift or exchange during life, and the right to bequeath. The rationale of the right to property is being widely questioned : without its abolition, equality is declared to be impossible. On the other hand, it has been argued that (*a*) the right to own private property is derived from nature, not from man ; and the State has by no means the right to abolish it but only to control its use ; (*b*) men in general need an incentive to labour : the power to acquire property supplies such an incentive ; (*c*) property is the return made to the individual for effort ; (*d*) it is the nurse of virtues essential to society, such as love of one's family and inventiveness ; and (*e*) historically speaking, progressive societies have been those built upon the regime of private property. The true justification of property is that it is needed

---

[1] See above, pp. 50-1.
[2] A limited right to private property is also recognized in the Soviet Union as may be seen from Article 10 of the constitution : ' The right of personal property of citizens in their income from work and in their savings, in their dwelling house and auxiliary husbandry, in household articles and utensils and in articles for personal use and comfort, as well as the right of inheritance of personal property of citizens, is protected by law.'

for the development of personality.[1]   Rights are those conditions
of social life without which no man can seek in general to be himself at his best. 'And if property must be possessed in order that
a man may be his best self, the existence of such a right is clear.'
(Laski)

At the same time, the right to property, like other rights, has
limitations.   These limitations arise from the twofold aspect of
property, individual and social.

'The right to own private property has been given to man by
nature, or rather by the Creator Himself, both in order that individuals may be able to provide for their own needs and those of
their families, and also that by means of it the goods which the
Creator has destined for the whole human race may truly serve
this purpose.'[2]

It follows from this that men must take into account in this matter
not only their own advantage but also the common good.   To
define in detail the necessary limitations on the right to property
is an important function of government.   Thus all modern States
have laws regulating the transfer of property in order to ensure
that the transfer is made between persons possessing at the time
mature reason, without coercion and without wilful or careless
misrepresentation.   Similarly they regulate inheritance and be-
quests in order to see that reasonable expectations on the part of
the members of a family are not upset and, generally, to see that
the social virtues of thrift and industry are not allowed to decline.

(*xi*) *The right to the general advantages of social life.* By this,
is meant (*a*) the right of a person to the unmolested pursuit of the
occupation by which he gains his living ; (*b*) the free use of public
roads, parks and libraries ; (*c*) the use of the posts, telegraphs
and railways subject to prescribed payments ; (*d*) the right of
resort to law courts in vindication of legal claims ; (*e*) the right
to the use of public dispensaries and hospitals, subject to the
rules ; and, generally, (*f*) the right to avail oneself of those communal advantages which are provided by the modern social service State.

The citizen also has certain duties. Rights are privileges, duties
are obligations. The most general duties are to obey the laws of
the State and pay the taxes. The citizen must refrain from interfering with the rights of other citizens, such as freedom of person
and security, property, reputation, etc. Again he must sit upon
juries when chosen, appear before the courts as a witness when

---

[1] W. S. M'Kechnie, *The State and the Individual*, p. 337.
[2] Papal Encyclical *Quardragesima Anno* (1931).

summoned to give evidence and treat courts of law with proper respect. Where military service is made compulsory by law, it is obvious that the citizen has to serve as a soldier for the prescribed period.

§3 POLITICAL LIBERTY

In addition to these rights, the democratic State also recognizes political liberty, i.e. the right to a share in the Government of the State. As Rousseau wrote,[1] in this type of State, the associates are called collectively a *people,* severally *citizens* as sharing in the sovereign authority and *subjects* as submitting to the laws of the State. A citizen, as Aristotle said, is one who is capable of ruling as well as being ruled. The necessity for this right is argued in detail later ;[2] it is sufficient here to refer to the remark of Laski, that exclusion from power means in the long run exclusion from the benefits of power. The exercise of political power is also a necessary training in social responsibility.

Political liberty involves the following rights :

(*i*) The right to vote ; the normal rule in democratic States is that all adults have the right to vote, subject to the reasonable disqualification of criminals, lunatics and idiots. Some States also deny the right to women.

(*ii*) The right to stand as a candidate for election is a corollary of (*i*). Invariably everyone who is a voter also has the right to stand as a candidate for election ; some States, like the United States of America, however, prescribe a higher age qualification for the representative (21 for a voter and 25 for a member of the House of Representatives) ; in India also a person is qualified to be chosen to the House of the People only if he is not less than 25.

(*iii*) Periodical elections : power cannot be conferred on any body permanently ; the accountability of the Legislature to the electorate necessitates periodical elections.

(*iv*) Equal eligibility for government office, provided the necessary technical or professional qualifications are satisfied.

(*v*) The right to criticize the Government. This is provided by the right of speech, public meeting, publication, and association. The importance of this right is that, especially in a democratic State, the Government must be in touch with public opinion; otherwise the taunt of Rousseau,[3] that the English people are free only during the election of members of Parliament, would be justified. If government must be based on the consent of the

---

[1] *The Social Contract*, bk. I, ch. vi.
[2] See below, ch. x, §3.
[3] ibid, bk. III, ch. xv.

governed, law-making must be the result of free discussion and continuous consent. Political liberty is not safe or complete where the people's voice is taken into account only at election times, or where there are no centres of association other than the political. As Lindsay put it so effectively, in a democracy public opinion, instead of being something expressing itself only at authorized times and only in a choice of representatives, is something always there — always being influenced and influencing — an invisible public meeting of the whole country in perpetual session.

The provision of these rights does not mean that everyone will exercise his share in government. What the law can do is to provide the rights ; it can at no time make sure that the rights will be exercised or exercised for the common good.

§4   SAFEGUARDS OF LIBERTY

The question that now arises for consideration is : How best are we to ensure that these rights are secured to the citizen, so that he may really be free ?

(*i*) Law, as is argued later,[1] is clearly an important condition of liberty. Montesquieu argued,[2] indeed, that it is principally by the nature and proportion of punishments imposed by law that liberty is established or destroyed.

(*ii*) The independence of the Judiciary is essential to freedom. By this is meant that judges must, as far as is humanly possible, be made independent of the Executive in the discharge of their official duties. It must be remembered that judges may be called upon to protect the liberty of individuals from invasion by private individuals and by Government officers. It is obvious that they will not feel free to deal with the latter if, for doing their duty, they are likely to incur the wrath of the Executive, and if, on that account, they are likely to be dismissed or otherwise adversely affected. It is usual, therefore, to provide that the salaries of judges shall not be diminished during their term of office and that they shall not be dismissed by the Executive on their own responsibility. In Great Britain judges may be removed by the Crown only on an address presented by both Houses of Parliament ; in the United States of America a judge may be removed only by impeachment by the lower House before the upper House. In India a judge of the Supreme Court may be removed from office before his term is over if an address by each House of Parliament supported by a majority of the total membership of each House

---

[1] See §5 of this chapter.
[2] *The Spirit of Laws*, bk. XII, ch. ii.

and not less than two-thirds of the members of each House present and voting has been presented to the President for such removal on the ground of proved misbehaviour or incapacity. The salary and allowances of a judge and his rights in respect of leave of absence or pension shall not be varied to his disadvantage after his appointment. As J. Kent has said : ' To give the judges the courage and the firmness to do their duty fearlessly, they ought to be confident of the security of their salaries and station.'

(*iii*) Democracy is a helpful factor. It is a form of government in which political power is with the mass of the people. As John Stuart Mill insisted, its superiority over other forms of government is based on the principle that the rights and interests of every or any person are only secure from being disregarded when the person interested is himself able, and habitually disposed, to stand up for them. But, at the same time, democracy by itself is no automatic guarantee, for democracy involves government by the majority ; and the majority may sometimes tyrannize over the minority. Unless, therefore, the habit of tolerance is widespread in a community, there is no reasonable chance of the widespread enjoyment of liberty.

(*iv*) A healthy development of local self-governing institutions further helps freedom ; for, as Laski truly says, the more widespread the distribution of power in the State, the more decentralized its character, the more likely men are to be zealous for freedom. Maximum satisfaction is at least partly a function of maximum consultation.

(*v*) A declaration of fundamental rights, included as part of a written constitution, is a necessary safeguard. A declaration of rights is a series of rules, generally embodied in a written constitution, setting forth the fundamental civil and political rights of the citizens and imposing certain limitations on the power of the ordinary Government, as a means of securing the enjoyment of those rights. Thus in the constitution of the United States of America the free exercise of religion, freedom of speech and of the Press, the right of the people to assemble, the right to petition, the right to keep and bear arms, the right to be secure in person, houses, papers, etc., against unreasonable searches and seizures, and trial by jury, are inserted in the constitution as fundamental rights. The Weimar Constitution of Germany included, in addition, the equality of sexes in civic rights, the secrecy of correspondence, secret elections, free education, property, freedom of contract, freedom of association and the right of entry of all religious bodies to public institutions. The Constitution of India lists a number of fundamental rights such as right to equality, right to freedom, right against exploitation, right to freedom of religion and right to property.[1]

The value of a declaration of rights as a safeguard of freedom is this : it draws attention to the fact that vigilance is essential in what Cromwell called ' fundamentals ' ; and since these rights can be modified only by a special amending body, as distinguished from the ordinary Legislature, the constitutional declaration of rights is a check on possible excesses by the *ordinary* Government.

(*vi*) Finally, indeed, eternal vigilance is the only sure safeguard of freedom. The knowledge that the citizens are alert and will not meekly submit to unreasonable interference with their rights, and that they will be prepared to fight for them, will help to prevent such interference.

§5 DOES LAW HELP OR HINDER LIBERTY?

What is the relation of law to liberty ? How far can the commands of the State help or hinder the eager maintenance of that atmosphere in which men have the opportunity to be their best selves ? Two opposing answers have been given :

(*i*) Every law is a veritable freedom. Thus Locke :

' Law is, in its true notion, not so much the limitation as the direction of a free and intelligent agent to his true interest ... So that however it may be mistaken, the end of law is not to abolish or restrain but to preserve and enlarge freedom.'

This view, as we have seen, is best typified in the Idealist view of the State and law.

(*ii*) ' The more there is of the one, the less there is of the other ' (Dicey). ' Law is an institution of the most pernicious tendency ' (William Godwin). Spencer called his book *Man versus the State* : this can be explained only on the assumption that he thought that law and liberty were opposed to each other. An extreme instance of this view is to be found in the attitude of the anarchists who would abolish government and law altogether.

These are two extreme views ; and, as often happens, the truth lies between the two. Law is an important condition of liberty in three ways : (*i*) Law protects one's freedom from invasion by others ; from this point of view, law and liberty, far from being opposed to each other, are correlative terms, because, as Hobbes

[1] The rights guaranteed by the Constitution of India are dealt with in ch. xxii, §2.

keenly realized, no individual liberty is safe without the assumption
of a sovereign power to make and enforce law. The criminal code
is an obvious example. (*ii*) By providing certain essentials of
social life, such as education and healthy conditions of life in
factories, law may promote the real liberty of the individual and
enable him to realize his personality. (*iii*) In a special sense, the
fundamental or constitutional law of a State may, as in India and
America, protect the freedom of the individual from invasion by
the Government of the day, by providing some fundamental rights,
which that government is powerless to alter.[1]

But all laws are not necessarily conducive to liberty ; some may
be positively injurious to freedom. It is unreal to contend, as do
the Hegelians, that one who is asked to give up belief in a religion
in which he passionately believes, and to desist from expressing
opinions which he thinks are right and ought to be expressed, is
really free. Hence the question whether law promotes liberty must
be answered on the merits of each case—with the qualification that
in a well-ordered, civilized community, the institution of law
normally helps liberty by preventing individuals and associations
of individuals from ' taking the law into their own hands '. The
existence of a law-enforcing agency helps the liberty of individuals
by denying them the use of force and insisting on a peaceful settlement of their differences. To the extent, moreover, that laws are
passed after wide consultation and are based on the consent of the
people who are affected by them, the sense of freedom is increased.
But there must be continuous vigilance to see that there is no over-
government and excess of laws : for, as Seeley insisted, liberty is
the opposite of over-government. Our aim should be to secure
such a balance ' between the liberty we need and the authority that
is essential as to leave the average man with the clear sense that he
has elbow-room for the continuous expression of his personality '.

§6. THE ORGANIC THEORY

The concept of individual liberty is often connected with a theory
of the State known as the organic (or organismic) theory ; indeed,
supporters of the theory have used it in support of contradictory
ends — of more and less liberty.

The organic theory compares the State to an organism : an
organism is a living structure composed of parts different in kind ;
these parts are complementary to one another. The health of the
organism depends on the healthy discharge by each part of its own
function. Thus the human organism has several parts, such as

[1] See above, §4(*v*).

the eye, the ear, the hand and the leg ; the health of the body depends upon each part performing its specific function. Similarly,
society is an organism, with its several parts closely related to, and
dependent upon, one another. According to the detailed analogy
which one of the exponents of the theory, Spencer, has made,
society has three systems corresponding to the sustaining system,
the distributory system and the regulating system in the human
body. The analogy may be presented thus :

THE PARTS	NATURAL ORGANISM	SOCIAL ORGANISM
The sustaining system	The alimentary canal (mouth, gullet, stomach, intestines)	Manufacturing districts and agricultural areas
The distributory system	Blood vessels (heart, arteries and veins)	Roads, canals, railways, posts, telegraphs
The regulating system	Nerve-motor mechanisms (brain, spinal chord, nerves)	Government

The climax of the comparison is reached when the State is made
a person :

‘ The purpose of the whole constitution is to enable the person
of the State to express and realize its will, which is different from
the individual wills of all individuals, and different from the
sum of them.’ [1]

Further, the State has a masculine character in contrast with the
feminine character of the Church !

Two different conclusions are possible, and indeed have been
drawn from this comparison. First :

‘ As nothing that affects the parts can be indifferent to the
whole, the State is bound by its laws and government to aim
jointly with the citizens at the perfect development of every
individual in the community. Nothing is beyond the proper
sphere of government in pursuing this high end ’ (M’Kechnie).
A truly organic State has an all-embracing sphere. It may refrain
from unwise interference in special cases, but it has the *right* to
interfere in all. This is a logical deduction from the theory, for

[1] J. K. Bluntschli, *The Theory of the State*, pp. 22-3.

the central idea of the theory, as Leacock suggests, is to set aside the contrast between the individual and the State by amalgamating them into one. 'As is the relation of the hand to the body, or the leaf to the tree, so is the relation of man to society. He exists in it, and it in him.' The part, therefore, must be subordinate to, and may be sacrificed for, the welfare of the whole.

The second (and indeed contradictory to the first) conclusion is that arrived at by Spencer, viz. that the State's functions should be limited to the prevention of violence and fraud; the individual should otherwise be left alone. This conclusion Spencer arrived at by distinguishing the natural from the social organism. The natural organism is 'concrete', the social organism 'discrete', i.e. the units of a natural organism are physically contiguous and are fixed in position; they are not so in society. Moreover, in the body of an animal the feeling and the consciousness are confined to a special tissue (viz. the cerebrum or brain); in society, all members are so endowed. It follows that not the happiness of the whole but individual happiness is the purpose of the social organism. This can best be achieved by the Government following the biological law of specific function and confining itself to the function for the performance of which it was evolved, viz. to assure internal and external security.

· A theory which admits of such contradictory conclusions must needs be defective; its first defect is a tendency to carry the comparison between the natural and the social organisms too far. As Barker puts it, society is like an organism, but is not an organism. The differences between the two, which Spencer recognized, are in reality so fundamental that he was able to save the social organism only by cutting it into pieces! Secondly, the theory gives one no clear guidance as to the limits of State activity; for, as we have seen, its exponents arrive at diametrically opposite conclusions. If we accept one of them, there is a danger of sacrificing the individual to the State; if we follow the other, there is all the danger of *laissez-faire*.[1] To say, as M'Kechnie says,[2] that the theory contains the germ of the whole truth of political philosophy and that it is in itself a complete theoretical solution of the problem of the sphere of government is certainly to overshoot the mark.

Yet the theory has some value. It emphasizes the idea that society is something more than an aggregate of individuals loosely

---

[1] See below, ch. viii, §3.
[2] op. cit., pp. 56 and 431.

thrown together without any unifying bond ; its members are dependent upon one another. The welfare of each is involved in the welfare of all. The attainment of the common purpose therefore depends on the proper performance by every citizen of his duties. Properly grasped, the theory may thus be useful in reminding citizens of their social obligations.

SELECT BIBLIOGRAPHY

W. D. Aston and P. Jordan, *Citizenship : Its Rights and Duties*, University Tutorial Press, 5th ed., 1936

E. Barker, *Political Thought in England from Spencer to the Present Day*, ch. iv, ' Home University Library ', Oxford, 1947

J. K. Bluntschli, *The Theory of the State*, pp. 18-23, Oxford, 3rd ed., 1921

G. E. G. Catlin, *Systematic Politics*, ch. iii-iv, Allen & Unwin, 1962

T. E. Holland, *The Elements of Jurisprudence*, pp. 82-358, Oxford, 13th ed., 1928

R. G. Gettell, *Political Science*, ch. x, Ginn, 1933

H. J. Laski, *Liberty in the Modern State*, Penguin Books, 1938

S. Leacock, *Elements of Political Science*, ch. v, Constable, 1933

J. S. Mill, *On Liberty*, ' World's Classics ', No. 170, Oxford

J. R. Seeley, *Introduction to Political Science*, lectures V & VI, Macmillan, 1923

UNESCO, *Capital Punishment*, New York, 1962

C. Vereker, *The Development of Political Theory*, Hutchinson University Library, 1957

CHAPTER VII

EQUALITY

§1 THE MEANING OF EQUALITY

In the Declaration of the Rights of Man (1789) issued by the National Assembly of France during the French Revolution, the following categorical statement is made : ' Men are born, and always continue, free and equal in respect of their rights.' A similar statement is found in the American Declaration of Independence (1776): ' We hold these truths to be self-evident, that all men are created equal . . .

It will be observed that the natural equality of man has been asserted in these documents to be a self-evident truth. But in what sense are men by nature equal ?

The most striking fact about human life is the inequality of men, not their equality. Men are unequal in bodily proportion, physical strength, intellectual abilities, and moral capacity. This inequality springs from two sources, nature and nurture. Men are not born equal ; some babies are born white, some black and very little can be done to alter the colour of either. Provided a child is receiving an adequate diet, it is probably impossible to add an inch, let alone a cubit, to its stature, though a few pounds might be added to its weight by proper nutrition. In point of mental equipment, some are congenitally feeble-minded ; others are not. The effects of physical and social environment enhance or reduce the inequalities present at birth. The statement that all men are equal, is then, as erroneous as that the surface of the earth is level.

Inequalities are inescapable facts. Why then is equality assumed and asserted as the ideal ? Is not the assertion that all men *ought* to be equal as absurd as that the earth ought to be one vast plain ?[1] There are two grounds for the assertion, one historical, the other ethical, which suggest that, after all, the ideal of equality, properly interpreted, is not as absurd as at first sight it would appear to be.

(*i*) It is to the credit of Ritchie to have shown[2] that the ideal

[1] M'Kechnie, *The State and the Individual*. p. 323.
[2] D. G. Ritchie, *Natural Rights*. p. 248.

of equality is an inheritance from the inequalities of ancient societies. It arose from the idea of peerage, an order or caste of nobles who recognized each other as in some respects and for some purposes equal, while asserting their superiority to others. The idea of equality has thus grown out of the idea of privilege ; the same is the case with the idea of freedom. ' Both ideas are the outgrowth of aristocratic and slave-holding communities. It was in *contrast* with the subject and the slave that men first felt themselves equal and free.'

(*ii*) Ethically, men as such are equal in the possession of rationality. This at once separates man from the lower animals and connects him with his fellow men. He has the power of reflecting on his place in the universe, which power, however little developed, exists in germ in every human being. Man is capable of sharing in the same type of mental life as his neighbour, even though he may actually be inferior to that neighbour in his mental and moral stature. It is then the infinite worth of every human soul, its potential membership of a common society, which gives a basis, a meaning, to the ideal of equality. It is this that effectually marks man off from chattel, and even from the highest animal. It is this thought presumably, as MacCunn says,[1] that arises in the religious mind when it is said that all men are equal in the sight of God.

Let us admit, then, that the ideal of equality has some basis. But the more difficult question to answer is : What is its precise content ? To what extent is the ideal capable of being translated into practice, in the laws and in the institution of society ?

(*i*) *Civil equality*. This is perhaps best described as equality before law. Where all the citizens of a State have the same status in the sphere of private law, which concerns the relations between one individual and another, they are said to possess *civil* equality. The recognition of civil equality means that the citizens of a State are treated alike in respect of the control that may be legitimately exercised over them and of the measure of protection which they may be entitled to demand at the hands of a Government. Thus the Weimar Constitution of Germany :[2]

(*a*) All Germans are equal before the law.

(*b*) Men and women have fundamentally the same civic rights and duties.

(*c*) Public legal privileges or disadvantages of birth cr rank shall be abolished.

[1] *Ethics of Citizenship*. p. 4.
[2] Article 109.

The Constitution of India specifically lays down that the State shall not deny to any person equality before the law or the equal protection of the laws ; the State shall not discriminate against any citizen on grounds only of religion, race, caste, sex, place of birth or any of them. No citizen shall, on grounds only of religion, race, caste, sex, place of birth or any of them, be subject to any disability or restriction with regard to access to shops, public restaurants and places of public entertainment, or the use of wells, tanks, bathing ghats, roads and places of public resort maintained out of State funds or dedicated to the use of the general public ; untouchability is abolished and its practice in any form is forbidden.

These points hardly need defence ; justice obviously demands that the courts of a State in dispensing law shall treat all citizens without fear or favour.

(*ii*) *Political equality*. That a measure of equality in the share which the citizens of a State have in their Government is desirable, indeed essential, is now recognized by the best thinkers of the age. The demand for such equality is the basis of democracy, the demand that the system of power be erected upon the similarities and not the differences between men.

' Of the permanence of this demand there can be no doubt ; at the very dawn of political science Aristotle insisted that its denial was the main cause of revolutions. Just as the history of the State can perhaps be most effectively written in terms of the expanding claims of the common man upon the results of its effort, so the development of the realization of equality is the clue to the problem of democracy.'[1]

The merits and defects of democracy are described elsewhere ;[2] here, it is sufficient to remark that the concrete expression of political equality is the conferment on all adult citizens of the right to vote and its corollaries, the right to stand as a candidate for election and equal eligibility for administrative and judicial posts provided the necessary technical qualifications are fulfilled.[3] It need hardly be added that the legal recognition of this minimum political equality does not mean that the effective influence exercised by all citizens is equal. The wiser and the better citizens do exercise greater influence on the Government through the greater and more effective part they play in moulding public

[1] *Encyclopaedia of the Social Science*, Vol. V.
[2] See ch. x, §3.
[3] See also ch. x, §3, in this connexion.

opinion. The rights we have mentioned above ensure but a minimum political equality. They provide a necessary armour for the average man against the abuse of political power by the few, for, theoretically at any rate, as James Mill said, in democracy the rulers being all, the interests of the rulers are the interests of all. They also enable those who are politically minded to play their legitimate part in public life which cannot be closed to those who are fit for it without contracting their life and stunting their development.

(*iii*) *Economic equality*. Economic equality has been interpreted by some writers like Bryce in a literal sense as ' the attempt to expunge all differences in wealth, allotting to every man and woman an equal share in worldly goods '. A reasonable view of equality must dismiss such a conception as being beyond the bounds of practical politics, for, even if we have a clean slate to start with, men's differences in need and capacity are too great to enable equality of wealth to be maintained for any length of time.

' Render possessions ever so equal,' said Hume, ' men's different degrees of art, care, and industry will immediately break that equality. Or if you check these virtues, you reduce society to the most extreme indulgence.'

But it is quite possible and desirable to reduce the excessive inequalities of existing fortunes. Properly interpreted, economic equality therefore means the provision of adequate opportunities for all : the right to work, to adequate wages, to reasonable hours of labour and leisure and to self-government in industry, so that every one may have a fair start in life and the chance to develop the best that he is capable of. It means a minimum equality, equality up to the margin of sufficiency. But it allows differences of income, provided they are capable of explanation in terms of social good. It only urges, to use Laski's phrase,[1] that no man shall be so placed in society that he can overreach his neighbour to the extent which constitutes a denial of the latter's citizenship. Equality, as Laski insists, is not identity of treatment. Fundamentally it implies a certain levelling process.[2] and is in fact largely a problem in proportions. It is such an organization of opportunity that no man's personality suffers frustration to the private benefit of others.[3]

Can the view of equality outlined here be justified ? Let Hume answer :

[1] *A Grammar of Politics*. ch. iv.
[2] ibid.   [3] ibid.

' Wherever we depart from . . . equality,[1] we rob the poor of
more satisfaction than we add to the rich. The rule of equality
is useful and has been shown by history to be not wholly
impracticable.'

By adopting it, we avoid the ugly spectacle of an economic
system in which the luxury of a few is paralleled by the misery
of the many. We shall no more be subject to the reproach of
Matthew Arnold : ' Our inequality materializes our upper class,
vulgarizes our middle class, brutalizes our lower.'

§2 EXTENT OF EQUALITY IN MODERN STATES

Modern States in general recognize civil equality. No man is
above the law, and no man is punishable except according to
law. The equality of citizens before law is secured above all by
judicial impartiality ; this in turn is sought to be secured by the
independence of the Judiciary.[2] There are some apparent exceptions and limitations to equality before law, but, as will be seen
later,[3] the exceptions are generally justified by public considerations. The exceptions are :

(*i*) In some States, like France, there are special courts for
the trial of government servants for mistakes committed in the
discharge of their official duties.

(*ii*) Even in States where there is no regular system of administrative jurisprudence and the ' rule of law ' prevails, as in
Britain, a new type of administrative court has been coming into
existence to meet some felt need.

(*iii*) The State itself, as a collective entity, is not liable in tort,
on the principle that the State itself can do no wrong.[4]

The one great practical limitation to equality before law arises
from disparity in income, which is so marked a feature of modern
economic life. Inequality of wealth reacts on civil equality ; the
richer man is obviously in a better position to meet the expenses
incidental to successful litigation, e.g. engaging competent counsel.
Truly, as Laski says,[5] there seems to be one law for the rich and
another for the poor whenever the preparation of a defence is an
item of importance in the case. It is, however, difficult to see

---

[1] Hume uses the term to mean relative, not absolute, equality.
[2] See above, ch. vi. §4(ii).
[3] See below, ch. xvi, xvii and xxii.
[4] The principle accepted in Britain until recently that the Crown itself
cannot be liable in tort has been modified by the Crown Proceedings Act
of 1947.
[5] *A Grammar of Politics*, pp. 564ff.

how this defect can be removed so long as there are inequalities in the distribution of wealth and so long as better remuneration can command better talent, though obviously it can be mitigated by a reduction in the disparity of incomes.

The exceptions and limitations (both legal and practical) are more marked in the political sphere. Political equality demands adult suffrage, the equal right of all adults to stand as candidates for election and equal eligibility to government office.

(i) In some States women are not given the right to vote. Where adult suffrage prevails, this inequality obviously does not exist. The exclusion of minors, lunatics, and criminals is, clearly, reasonable.

(ii) Plural voting (recognized, for instance, until 1948 in Britain) is another infringement of the principle of political equality. Thus an elector had the right to vote in one constituency as a resident and in another as an occupier of land or business premises ; or an elector might have a second vote as the holder of a university degree. In India under the Government of India Act, 1935, an elector could vote in a territorial constituency, as a member of a recognized Chamber of Commerce and in a university constituency. Plural voting is, however, the exception rather than the rule.

(iii) In India political rights, under the Government of India Act, 1935, were conditional on the possession of a prescribed amount of property, the payment of tax, or the possession of a prescribed educational qualification. One of the main reasons for prescribing such qualifications was the administrative difficulty of managing the large electorate which would result from the introduction of adult suffrage.

(iv) Elsewhere, e.g. South Africa and some of the states in the U.S.A., certain national and racial groups, like people of Indian origin and Negroes, are not given equal political rights with the so-called ‘true’ nationals.

(v) In some States a higher age qualification is prescribed for membership of legislative bodies ; for instance, in the U.S.A., only those who are over 25 years old can stand for election to the House of Representatives ; in India also it is laid down that a person shall not be qualified to be chosen to fill a seat in Parliament unless he is, in the Council of States, not less than thirty years of age, and in the case of a seat in the House of the People not less than twenty-five years of age. This restriction, in so far as it is based on a natural inequality, cannot be considered unjust.

(vi) In Britain the right of hereditary peers to be members of the second chamber is a relic of political privilege ; it may, however, be argued that the second chamber is no longer a purely hereditary one on account of the addition to it of life peers and peeresses under the Life Peerages Act, 1958 and because it has been rendered innocuous by the reduction of its political powers.

The inequalities recognized by law apart, there is one considerable factor which results in the unequal influence exercised by citizens on their Government, viz. money-power in politics.[1] This influence may be traced in (a) the corruption of members of Legislatures, administrative officials and judges ; (b) elections ; and (c) the practice of lobbying, i.e. bringing influence to bear on members of Legislatures to vote for or against a bill. Money-power is especially formidable because it works secretly.

And, finally, economic equality. Here the disparity is most marked. It is true that every State has been attempting in varying degrees, especially by the application of the progressive principle in taxation and by social legislation, to reduce economic inequalities.[2] Nevertheless, great inequalities still continue. For example, it has been calculated that in India (in 1955-56 to 1956-57) 95·3% of households are in the income group Rs 0-3000, 4·5% in the group Rs 3001-25000 and 0·2% in the group Rs 25001 and above[3] ; in Britain, the actual number of incomes in the different income groups is estimated as follows : (1957-58)[4]

£	
200 – 499	9,060,000
500 – 999	539,000
1000 – 1999	144,000
2000 – 3999	42,100
4000 – 5999	4,575
6000 – 8000 +	4,125

In the United States one-tenth of the incomes were below $ 1400 in 1947 to 1960 while the top income-receivers (one-tenth of the income-receivers) received over $ 10,510 per year.[5]

§3 EQUALITY AND LIBERTY

There are two views among political thinkers on the relation between equality and liberty ; one that they are antithetic, the other that they are complementary. Lord Acton may be taken

[1] See, on this point. J. Bryce, *Modern Democratic*, Vol. II. ch. lxix.
[2] See below. pp. 93-4, and the references cited therein.
[3] *Reserve Bank of India Bulletin*, 1926. p. 1360.
[4] Richard M. Titmuss. *Income Distribution and Social Change*.
[5] *Statistical Abstract of the United States*. 1962. p. 329.

as representative of the first. The passion for equality, he says,[1] ' made vain the hope of freedom '. This is true if freedom is interpreted in its absolute sense to mean that every individual shall be free according to his opportunities, to satisfy *without limit* his appetite for wealth and power. Equality is unattainable under conditions of such unrestricted freedom. It is a lesson of history that when the freedom of individuals to do what they please is not checked, the clever and more capable will use their freedom to concentrate all wealth and power in themselves to the misery and oppression of the rest. The achievement of any measure of equality therefore demands ' the deliberate acceptance of social restraints upon individual expansion. It involves the prevention of sensational extremes of wealth and power by public action for the public good '. Hence liberty and equality appear antithetic to each other.

But, realistically considered, ' a large measure of equality, so far from being inimical to liberty, is essential to it,'[2] and vice versa. Freedom is catholic ; it is to be enjoyed by all, not by the few alone. And, whatever else it involves,

' it implies at least, that no man shall be amenable to an authority which is arbitrary in its proceedings, exorbitant in its demands, or incapable of being called to account when it abuses its office for personal advantage.'

. These elements of civil and political freedom have partly been secured by civil and political equality : equality before law, and a certain minimum share for everyone in government. Freedom will have a better content, too, if a measure of economic equality, in the sense which we have indicated earlier, is attained. For there is no denying the fact that the concentration of wealth in the few enables them to put their civil and political freedom to better use than others. Equality in justice is a primary condition for attaining civil freedom ; but as has been pointed out earlier.[3] ' the inability of a poor person to employ a counsel, still more to employ really skilful counsel, is a fatal bar to his obtaining justice '. Similarly, the influence of money in politics makes the share of the poor in government all but a mockery. Civil and political freedom will be more real for the masses if there is less economic inequality. Indeed, ' if liberty means the continuous power of expansion in the human spirit, it is rarely present save

---

[1] *The History of Freedom and other Essays*, pp. 57-8.
[2] R. H. Tawney, *Equality*, p 245.
[3] See above, ch. vii, §2.

in a society of equals. Where there are rich and poor, educated
and uneducated, we find always masters and servants ' (Laski).
That is why Rousseau insisted [1] that liberty cannot exist without
equality.

' Allow neither rich men or beggars ', said he. ' These two
estates, which are naturally inseparable, are equally fatal to the
common good ; from the one come the friends of tyranny, and
from the other tyrants. It is always between them that public
liberty is put up to auction ; the one buys, and the other sells.'

The converse proposition, that a large measure of freedom is
essential to equality, is no less true. For political freedom has
as a matter of fact been used to reduce economic inequalities.
Thus in England, after 1832, social legislation in its manifold
forms — unemployment and health insurance benefits, old-age
pensions, the provision for the treatment of the sick, free education and the increase of amenities in general — has improved the
lot of the common man in terms of vitality and happiness, giving
him a longer life as well as more energy during life. The result
is that the main body of the working classes is absolutely (and
relatively to the propertied classes) a good deal better off in terms
of material well-being than it was a century ago, before the advent
of democracy. And the limit of improvement in the direction of
a greater equalization is not yet reached.[2]

SELECT BIBLIOGRAPHY

H. J. LASKI, *A Grammar of Politics*, pp. 152-65, Allen & Unwin, 5th ed., 1952
— —, *The Dangers of Obedience and other Essays*, pp. 207-37, Harper, 1930
W. S. M'KECHNIE, *The State and the Individual*, ch. xxiii, James MacLehose, 1896
D. G. RITCHIE, *Natural Rights*, ch. xii, Allen & Unwin, 1924
R. H. TAWNEY, *Equality*, Allen & Unwin, 4th ed., 1952
R. M. TITMUSS. *Income Distribution and Social Change*, Allen & Unwin, 1962

[1] *The Social Contract*. p. 46 and n. 1.
[2] See A. Appadorai. *Revision of Democracy*. pp. 15-18.

CHAPTER VIII

THE SPHERE OF THE STATE

§1 ANCIENT AND MEDIEVAL VIEWS

ONE of the most difficult problems which the student of political science has to solve is that of determining (to use the words of Edmund Burke) ' what the State ought to take upon itself to direct by public wisdom, and what it ought to leave, with as little interference as possible, to individual freedom '. In an earlier section, we pointed out that, in our view, there is a distinction between State and Society ; this means that there are limits to State action. This, however, has not always been the view among the peoples of the world. Among the Greeks, for instance, according to Bluntschli, ' the State was all in all. The citizen was nothing except as a member of the State. His whole existence depended on and was subject to the State.' The ancient idea of the State embraced the entire life of man in the community, in religion and law, morals, art, culture and science. Well might Burke's description of the State be applied to it : ' a partnership in all science, a partnership in all art, a partnership in every virtue and in all perfection '. The State's end being the comprehensive one of securing a good life for all citizens, all forms of control calculated to secure that result were considered proper, and no line was drawn between matters political, moral, religious or economic. The State might control trade, prescribe occupations, regulate religion or amusements. To the ancient Greek, the city was at once a State, church and school. In other words, the Greeks made no difference between State and Society.

Sidgwick, however, contests this view.[1] He says that, outside Sparta (and if we put aside the regulation of religious ceremonies and military service) the practical difference between ancient and modern conceptions of the function of government in ordinary civil life and transactions is not very great. He points out that ' when we look through the list of actions, public and private, or the list of officials at Athens, or the offices treated as normal by Aristotle, we find no sign of any excessive réglementation. We

[1] H. Sidgwick. *The Development of European Polity*, ch. xii.

hear of controllers of markets, . . . whose business it was to prevent fraud and disorder, of commissioners of the city . . . who had to prevent private houses from encroaching on the public streets.' But the prevention of fraud, disorder, and encroachment on public streets is one of the elementary functions undertaken by modern Governments. Briefly, ancient Governments were not as omnipotent as they are made out to be.

Perhaps it is better to say, with Barker, that the individual was not regarded as having rights of his own, to be protected as against the State. The mark of the Greek State is rather a desire for the action of the State and an attempt to stretch the lines of its action than any definition or limitation of the scope of its interference.

The Romans adopted the Greek conception of the State with some modifications. They ' left very much to social customs and to the religious nature of man. The Roman family was more free as against the State.' This does not mean that the Roman State was less powerful in theory ; no one could resist the State if it uttered its will. Rather, the Roman State limited itself ; it restricted its own action.

In the Middle Ages, two new forces, the growth of Christianity and the rise of the Teutonic races, brought into prominence a different conception regarding the sphere of the State. It was held ' that the whole religious life of the community, although not altogether withdrawn from the care and influence of the State, was yet essentially independent,' [1] and should be regulated by the Church.

It took some time for the new idea to prevail ; indeed, a struggle had to be waged by the Church against the State to get the idea accepted. The State was now only ' a community of law and politics, no longer also of religion and worship '.

Secondly, only with reluctance does the Teuton submit himself to the sovereignty of the whole body. He ' claims for himself an inborn right which the State must protect, but which it does not create, and for which he is ready to fight against the whole world, even against the authority of his own Government. He rejects strenuously the old idea that the State is all in all.' [2] To him individual freedom is all-important. The rights of the State are thus limited by the rights of the individual as well as by those of the Church.

Thirdly, the Middle Ages were pervaded by the feudal conception. Men became sovereigns by virtue of owning land. The functions of government under such a system were simply the

[1] Bluntschli, *The Theory of the State*, p. 41.
[2] ibid, pp. 43-4.

functions of proprietorship, of command and obedience. Government was for the most part divided out piecemeal among a thousand petty holders. The dispersal of governmental power among a considerable number of persons gradually gave rise to the idea of the rights of individuals against a central authority.

§2   THE EARLY NINETEENTH CENTURY

In the early nineteenth century, the prevalent view was what is generally known as individualism or *laissez-faire* : the sole duty of the Government is to protect the individual from violence or fraud. That Government is best which governs least. As John Stuart Mill put it in his essay *On Liberty* :

' The sole end for which mankind are warranted, individually or collectively, in interfering with the liberty of action of any of their number, is self protection. . . The only purpose for which power can be rightfully exercised over any member of a civilized community, against his will, is to prevent harm to others. His own good, either physical or moral, is not a sufficient warrant . . . The only part of the conduct of any one, for which he is amendable to society, is that which concerns others. In the part which merely concerns himself, his independence is, of right, absolute. Over himself, over his own body and mind, the individual is sovereign.'

According to this theory, the following functions of government alone would be proper : (*i*) to secure to the individual the right of personal security including security of health and reputation, the right to private property together with the right of freely transferring property by gift, sale or bequest and the right to fulfilment of contracts freely entered into ; and (*ii*) to protect the individual from foreign aggression. Briefly, the State was to be ' negative ' or ' police ' State.

Such important functions undertaken by modern States as the provision of education, poor-relief, and unemployment insurance, the regulation of public health, and aid to agriculture and industry, which in fact make the modern State a social service State, were considered improper. The theory was justified on psychological, economic and biological grounds.

The psychological argument is a simple one : individuals may be expected in the long run to discover and aim at their own interest better than a Government can do it for them. Self-help is the best help.

On economic grounds, it pays to let the individual alone. The individual requires a steady supply of good commodities and services at a cheap price. This requirement is best satisfied under conditions of free competition ; for the consumers, seeking their own interest, will create an effective demand for commodities and services ; producers, seeking their own interest, will meet this demand. Competition among consumers and producers will keep prices at a reasonable level and ensure quality.

From the biological point of view, the fittest will, and ought alone to, survive. That is the natural law. Besides, the health of the social, as of the natural, organism depends on the observance of the law of specific function — that every part should do that function for the performance of which it has been intended by nature. Government ' is a joint-stock company for mutual assurance ' ; its natural function is to hinder hindrances. Its interference in any other aspect of life is unnatural and socially harmful.

Laissez-faire was popular in England approximately from 1750 to 1850. This popularity was due partly to the failure of the older policy of mercantilism and partly to the Industrial Revolution. Mercantilism meant wellnigh complete Government control over trade, commerce and industry. By 1780, with the loss of the American Colonies, this policy had become discredited. The tremendous leap forward in industry as a result of the introduction of mechanical power and the factory system did away with the necessity for the subsidies and protective measures of mercantilism. It was now felt that non-interference by Government in industry and trade would enable the leaders of industry to take the maximum advantage of the new inventions, and lead to an enormous increase in national wealth. The Government, by a series of laws, therefore relaxed its control over trade and industry :

1784–6   The reduction of tariff duties.
1796   Relaxation of Navigation Laws in favour of the United States of America.
1813   The trade to India was thrown open.
1846   Repeal of the Corn Laws.
1849   Repeal of the Navigation Laws.

The *immediate* result of *laissez-faire* was that it led to an enormous expansion in trade and industry, and, indeed, seemed to justify its adoption.

§3 THE PASSING OF LAISSEZ-FAIRE

In the long run, however, *laissez-faire* proved disastrous to the community ; its social cost outweighed its economic gains. Long hours of labour, inadequate wages, overcrowded factories, and insanitary arrangements — these were the lot to which the workman had to submit. ' I have worked till 12 p.m., last summer ; we began at 6. I told book-keeper I did not like to work so late ; he said I must. We took our breakfast and tea as we could, a bite and a run, sometimes not able to eat it from its being so covered with dust.' Such is the recorded evidence [1] of one of the factory workers of those days. Children too were overworked.

' The parent who would endeavour to realize the life of a factory child in 1832,' writes Walpole,[2] ' should try to imagine his own little boy or girl — eight or nine years of age— working in a factory. He should try to recollect that it would be his duty to rouse the child on a cold winter's morning at five that it might be at its work at six ; that, day after day, week after week, month after month, it would be forced to rise at the same hour ; that with two short intervals of half an hour each, it would be kept to its dull empoyment for thirteen hours every day ; that during the whole of that time it would be breathing a dusty, unwholesome atmosphere, rarely able to relieve its limbs by sitting down.'

This social misery was directly due to certain unforeseen but inherent defects in the policy of non-interference. That policy, in Joad's analysis, wrongly assumes that each individual is equally farsighted and has an equal capacity for knowing what he wants, that each individual possesses an equal power of obtaining what he wants and has an equal freedom of choice under free competition, and that the satisfaction of the wants of all individuals is identical with the well-being of the community. Briefly it forgot two elementary propositions :

(i) Free competition can lead to the best social advantage only where there is approximate equality of bargaining power. As it was, ' free competition ' was free in name only ; the employers with their immense resources could in effect get their terms accepted by the starving wage-earners ; for the latter, the freedom to reject the terms offered meant little more than the freedom to perish. It is the duty of society to moralize competition.

(ii) Social organization can supply a much needed corrective to the ignorance and self-interest of individuals. In Joad's

---

[1] Quoted by F. R. Worts in *Modern Industrial History*, p. 77.
[2] Sir Spencer Walpole, *History of England*, Vol. III, p. 201, cited by F. R. Worts, op. cit., p. 79.

expressive phrase, economic action is ' blind ' ; that is to say, the economic activities of individuals, concerned as they are with individual ends, often lead to results which are willed neither by society nor by any individual. To cite an example : if there is a rumour that a bank is in difficulties, depositors are anxious to withdraw their money, there is a run on the bank and the bank fails—a result, 'which nobody wants, is nevertheless due to what everybody has individually willed '. Society, through its Government, can regulate economic action in the interest of social good. It can supply knowledge and foresight to mitigate the hardships of blind action and promote social welfare. Two examples in point are : (a) the salutary effect produced by the social organization of agricultural marketing in India. Government has helped to put the farmer in possession of better value for his goods by timely intervention ; (b) the prevention of widespread starvation by enforcement of rationing in many parts of India in rice and wheat in the post-war years. Rationing clearly helped the equitable distribution of these commodities at fair prices.

Gradually, every State began to realize the folly inherent in *laissez-faire* and to assume greater responsibilities, particularly in the economic field. Factory Acts, Mines Acts, Trade Board Acts, Shop Hours Acts and similar laws were passed. Thus *laissez-faire* passed away.

While *laissez-faire* is clearly a fallacious theory, its merits should not be ignored. It teaches the wholesome lesson, so necessary as a set-off to current totalitarian ideas, that too much Government help (maternalism) and too much State regulation (paternalism) are bad. It teaches the value of self-help and reliance : to kill individual initiative is, as the saying goes, to kill the goose that alone can lay golden eggs. Social action, while achieving social ends, should encourage individual initiative, because it is a great social asset.

§4 THE PRESENT DAY

While there is general agreement in rejecting the conception of *laissez-faire*, such agreement is wanting in deciding on the positive limits of political control. One view is the socialistic one, which is discussed later.[1] Another is the totalitarian conception of the State : ' Nothing beyond the State, nothing against the State, nothing outside the State.' This, however, is an extreme view, which is considered in general to be inimical to liberty.

[1] ch. ix, §§1-6.

More generally, it is agreed that it is the State's duty to promote the greatest happiness of the greatest number. The State is an organization to promote social good on the largest possible scale. And in attempting to achieve this purpose, the tendency is for Governments to make themselves more and more conspicuous, especially by the planning of economic life.

(*i*) *Personal security.* Admittedly Government aims, first, at assuring to the individual personal security, and protecting the whole State from foreign aggression. To achieve this aim, it defines and punishes crime, administers justice, maintains the police and the fighting forces, and conducts dealings with foreign States.

(*ii*) *Property.* It protects the right to private property, together with the right to the free transference of property by gift, sale or bequest : it also enforces the right to fulfil contracts freely entered into.

(*iii*) *Political rights and duties.* It determines the political rights and duties of citizens, passes laws to regulate voting and delimits constituencies.

(*iv*) *Education.* There is a tendency to enforce compulsory elementary education and to supervise and aid secondary and higher education.

(*v*) *The family.* The family is a natural institution required by the needs of man. It may well be said to be the nursery of the State, as the moral and intellectual training of individuals in society very much depends on it. The modern State exercises a certain control over its exterior aspect, generally insisting on conformity to the prevailing type of marital union, prescribing limits of kinship within which marriage is prohibited, regulating divorce and making rules regarding inheritance. A few States encourage marriages by providing financial aid ; some insist on certain health and age requirements as conditions of marriage ; some (e.g. India) encourage family planning and the use of birth control appliances to limit the growth in population ; nearly all States have regulations to ensure the protection and care of children and to safeguard wives against non-maintenance and other economic consequences of desertion, and generally provide institutions to meet those cases where the family fails in its task of rearing its young. There is a tendency for the State to take over by the provision of hospitals, old-age pensions, insurance schemes and by free compulsory education, the obligations which formerly fell upon the kin.

(*vi*) *Industry.* The tendency towards increased State interference is particularly manifested in industry. This interference is effected with a view to protect (a) the home manufacturer, (b) the worker, (c) the consumer, and (d) the investor.

(a) State help to industry in the form of protective duties is generally advocated and given. First, it is argued, as against the Ricardian theory, that every State should have a certain amount of economic independence or self-sufficiency, especially in times of war. Secondly, there is the infant industry argument ; the natural resources and circumstances of a country may be such that while the initial cost of starting and establishing certain industries may, in the face of foreign competition, be great, such industries, once established with State protection, may well be able to stand foreign competition. The story of discriminating protection in India, particularly as applied to the iron and steel industry, is a clear instance of this. Thirdly, it is believed, whatever economists may say, that protection will partly solve the problem of unemployment in the short run. Protection apart, where sufficien capital is not available from private sources, the Government, for instance in India, gives financial assistance for the development of important industries either by granting loans on special terms or by participating in equity capital. The steel and textile machinery industries are among those which have received such assistance from the Government of India. Further a National Productivity Council has been set up to inculcate productivity consciousness in the country and apply the latest techniques of increasing productivity in industry.

(b) The State's attitude towards industrial labour is no longer one of individualism. The Factory Acts contain provisions for fire escapes, the fencing of machinery, ventilation, etc.; they regulate hours of labour for men, women and children, besides prescribing rest intervals and holidays and fixing the minimum age for children to enter factories. Similarly, various Acts regulate the conditions of employment in mines. The laws regulating trade unions and trade disputes, the system of compulsory insurance and old-age pensions and Workmen's Compensation Acts, now operative in various countries, further demonstrate the solicitude of Governments for the welfare of labour.

To illustrate : In India the Factories Act of 1948, as at present amended, prescribes a daily limit of 9, and a weekly limit of 48, hours of labour in factories. The maximum hours of work for children are 4½ per day. Rest intervals and a weekly holiday are prescribed. Further, every worker is entitled to leave with wages after twelve month's continuous service at the following rate : adults — one day for every 20 days of work, subject to a minimum of 10 days ; children — one day for every 15 days of work, subject to a minimum of 14 days. Necessary conditions with regard to ventilation, light, temperature, sanitation and safety are also insisted on. In some states, e.g. Madras, special Maternity Benefit Acts have been passed to provide leave of absence (with a wage or allowance) to women for some months before and after confinement. The Workmen's Compensation Act (1933), the Payment of Wages Act (1936) and the Industrial Employment Standing Orders Act (1946) are other important laws ; the first regulates the compensation to be paid by employers for certain kinds of injury, occupational disease, or death arising from employment ; the second defines the periods of wage payment and deductions from wages ; and the last requires the larger employers to frame standing orders defining the conditions of employment and get them ratified by the appropriate Government authority. Further, under the Industries (Development and Regulation) Act, 1951, all industrial undertakings are required to be licensed ; 162 industries are within the scope of the Act. The Government are authorized to examine the working of any undertaking, to issue directions to it and to take over the control if this be deemed necessary. A Central Advisory Council has been set up consisting of representatives of industry, labour, consumers and primary producers, and 16 Developmental Councils have been instituted for individual industries.[1]

(c) To protect the consumer, the State interferes with competitive prices. The old idea that prices should be left altogether to the play of free competition among buyers and sellers has been found to be productive of serious injustice to the buyer due to the increasing prevalence of monopoly. The State therefore regulates trusts and cartels, fixes standards of weights and measures, passes anti-adulteration laws and encourages the consumers' co-operative movement. In war-time, Governments everywhere passed laws to prevent profiteering and the hoarding of essential commodities like rice, and even introduced, where necessary, schemes of rationing in order that the available supply of such commodities should be equitably distributed. A special case of the interference of the modern State in regard to prices, as Leacock points out,[2] is seen in legislation concerning railway rates, which are of course prices charged for transportation of persons and freight. The distinctive position which the railways occupy in the industrial world has induced some modern Governments not only to subject them to special regulations, but also, as in India, to own and operate railways. Indeed, opinion is gaining ground that what are known as

[1] *The Statesman's Year-Book.* 1971/1972.
[2] *Elements of Political Science,* p. 375.

key industries and public utilities — for instance, coal-mines, railways, electricity and gas supply — should be nationalized, i.e. owned and worked by the State.[1] The same eagerness to protect the interests of the consumer may be seen in the emphasis on compulsory arbitration in the labour legislation of several countries and particularly India. This rightly stresses the idea that the interests of both capital and labour have to be subordinated to the larger interests of society.

(*d*) To protect the investor, Governments regulate banks and companies.

(*vii*) *Agriculture.* As illustrated below[2] with reference to India, most Governments interfere to protect the tenant from exploitation by the landlord, to help the ryot with cheap credit and marketing facilities and to organize agricultural research. They also construct, as in India, large irrigation works to help the ryot.

(*viii*) *Other functions.* Besides the above-mentioned functions, modern States maintain sanitation and health departments, looking to drainage and hospital relief, aiding the poor and the incapable by maintaining workhouses and institutes for defectives. They also undertake those functions which obviously fall outside the sphere of the individual, such as the control of currency and credit, the postal system, the carrying out of surveys and censuses, and the collection and dissemination of data of various kinds.

(*ix*) *Distribution.* There is, finally, the social control of distribution. The State endeavours to direct wealth into new channels as it is produced by seeing that the daily result of production goes into the pockets of those who have so far been receiving less than they should This is done partly by the regulation of profits and wages, and partly by taxation. The progressive principle of taxation, generally adopted by the modern State, enables it to take wealth from those who have it and transfer it to others either by direct payments (old-age pensions, unemployment allowances, etc.) or by the provision of communal enjoyments (such as free education, free libraries, parks, hospitals, etc.).

To summarize : the modern State is a social service State, a positive State as compared with the police or negative State of the *laissez-faire* conception. It properly intervenes to uphold social standards, to prevent exploitation and manifest injustice, to remove the needless hazards of the economic struggle and to assure and advance the general interest against the carelessness or selfishness of particular groups.

[1] Railways and life insurance have, for instance, been nationalized in India.
[2] §8 in this chapter.

§5 REASONS FOR INCREASED STATE ACTIVITY

The increased activity of the State in modern times may be explained by the following reasons :

(*i*) *The nature of economic life since the Industrial Revolution.* The most outstanding social result of the Industrial Revolution has been the introduction of large-scale production in factories. This, in its turn, has brought about a fundamental change in world economy. For mass production has meant a distance between the producer and the consumer, between the employer and the employed, and between the company-promoter and the investor ; the human element in all these relationships tends to be ignored. The possibilities of fraud and of exploitation are increased, necessitating increased State intervention to protect the weak and the exploited. Again, mass production necessitates wide and ever-expanding markets abroad ; the interdependence between State and State in capital, market, and labour becomes marked, and without the help of the State the industrialist is unable to make the maximum profit. Further, unemployment is implicit in a system where the production is dependent upon the anticipation of a demand which is affected by world factors ; frequent crises are the result ; the State has to attempt to mitigate the social evils of unemployment. The increased activity of the State in economically underdeveloped countries like India is also explained by the urge to raise the living standards of the people by making the optimum use of the country's resources, physical and human ; it is felt that in an underdeveloped economy, State action by planning economic life is essential to achieve the desired result.

(*ii*) *The growth of monopolistic corporations.* The rise of trusts and cartels, which virtually introduces an element of monopoly in trade, increases the necessity for the State to safeguard the interests of the consumer and the worker.

(*iii*) *The failure of laissez-faire. Laissez-faire* has been weighed in the balance and found wanting.

(*iv*) *The political enfranchisement of the working classes.* In the nineteenth century, the vote was extended to larger and larger numbers of people. The political value of the vote was not lost on the enfranchised people ; they naturally returned people to Parliament who were pledged to support all measures calculated to achieve a better distribution of wealth. The formation of the Labour Party in Britain, and similar socialistic parties elsewhere, has given a fillip to State action.

Paradoxically, the failure of democracy and the rise of dictatorship in States like Germany (1933-45) and Italy (1922-43) brought about a similar result in those countries.

(*v*) *The Great Wars.* The wars of 1914-18 and 1939-45 accustomed men to greater State interference in their lives ; the habit of acquiescing in such interference has helped such interference to continue.

(*vi*) *Political theories.* The influence of radical political theories, like socialism and communism, has been pronounced. They point to evils to be remedied and maladjustments in economic life to be adjusted. The Government has necessarily to act to remedy the evils, which are pointed out with obvious sincerity, both within the Legislature and outside, by socialists.

§6 THE STATE AND EDUCATION IN INDIA

Education comes within the sphere of the State because (*i*) Popular education is necessary for the preservation of those conditions of freedom, political and social, which are essential to free individual development. It is necessary to fit the citizen for the tasks of citizenship. Further, the great social problem of our day, the reduction of inequalities, is largely a question of the provision of adequate opportunities, which, again, is largely dependent on education. (*ii*) No machinery less extensive in its power than Government can secure popular education.

There are three possible ways by which the State may ensure to every child the necessary minimum of education. First, it may leave the education of the child to the care of the family. Second, it may command that every child should receive a certain minimum of education as a legal right and compel the family to provide it out of the family funds. Third, it may order that every child should have schooling up to a certain age, and make education free, providing the necessary funds from its revenues. The tendency in modern States is to adopt the third method, for experience has shown that the first two do not achieve the desired result.

In India, compulsory and free elementary education still remains an ideal. It is true that even as early as 1904 the Government of India had gone so far as to ' fully accept the proposition that the active extension of primary education is one of the most important duties of the State '. That they have not succeeded in such extension may be seen from the fact that only 80·3% of the boys and girls of ages 6 to 11 are under

instruction.[1] It is also stated that about 34·1% of the children of
the age-group 11-14 are at school'.[2] Finance is the greatest stumb-
ling-block. The memorandum prepared by the Educational Adviser
to the Government of India in 1944 estimated the cost of a system
of universal, compulsory and free education for all boys and girls
between the ages of 6 and 14 in the area then called Br.tish
India (i.e. excluding Indian States) at Rs. 200 crores a year
In view of the fact, however, that education is a great social
investment, funds must be found and every effort made to attain
the ideal within a measurable period of time. A study of the
education budgets of progressive countries is an eye-opener in this
regard. The educational expenditure per head in England is
£6; there is no good reason why in India it must be as low as
Rs. 3·9.[3]

The first task, then, of the Governments [4] in India is to increase
literacy by the gradual application of the principle of compulsory
and free elementary education; the second is to see that with
lavish expenditure on education is secured an increased return
in educational value. Mere quantitative expansion, in other
words, is not enough; it must be accompanied by the prescription and enforcement of proper standards in respect of staff,
equipment, etc.[5] It is not necessary that the State should directly
run all the schools; the system of grants-in-aid and the provision of an efficient inspecting agency will secure the object.
Where local bodies run the schools, Governments have a particular duty to see that the schools are properly managed.

Somewhat different considerations apply in secondary and
higher education. Secondary education obviously cannot be made
compulsory or free; there are far too many practical difficulties
for such a task to be attempted. The best that the Governments
can do is to make liberal grants-in-aid to schools managed by
private agencies and local bodies and to insist that the money be

---

[1] The proportion of children of the age-group 6-11 attending school
is said to have increased from 62·4 to 80·3% over the decade 1961-71.
India 1973, p. 63.
[2] *India* 1973, p. 63.
[3] Expenditure in 1953-54. Figure supplied by the Ministry of Education.
[4] We say 'Governments' because, under the present constitution, education is largely the concern of state Governments.
[5] The Sargent memorandum (*Post-War Educational Development in
India*, 1944) referred to in the text [and the *Proceedings of the Twenty-
Second Meeting of the Central Advisory Board of Education* (Ministry
of Education, Government of India, 1955)] contain useful suggestions on
this as on other aspects of educational policy.

spent properly.   Higher education is also important as a preparation for political leadership and for administrative duties.
Here the duties of the State in India appear to be to provide
financial help, consistent with its more onerous obligations in
respect of elementary and secondary education ; to lay down the
necessary framework of university bodies, and, having done this,
to allow the universities the largest possible internal freedom ;
and to provide facilities to bona-fide students for research in the
Government record offices.

Finally, there is the important problem of adult education.   Its
magnitude can be seen from the fact that in India according to
the 1971 Census[1], the literacy percentage (excluding age-group,
0-5) was only 29·45 of which the figure for men was 39·45 and
for women 18·70.   Governments could do a lot to wipe out adult
illiteracy by, first, realizing the urgency of the problem ; second,
enlisting the co-operation of non-official agencies ; third, making
liberal grants-in-aid ; and, finally, making available such expert
advice as is necessary.

The Central Government in India performs a useful service
in maintaining a co-ordinating agency in its Central Advisory
Board of Education.   This Board serves to bring educational
experts from various provinces together to compare notes and
consider how best improvements can be effected in the system of
education.   The Government has also constituted an All-India
Council for Elementary Education to advise the Central and
State Governments on all matters relating to elementary education and the Central Board of Secondary Education to conduct
a common all-India higher secondary examination ; it has also
established the University Grants Commission, primarily to consider applications from universities for financial assistance ; the
Commission, it is expected, will also serve as an agency of co-
ordination and maintenance of standards in higher education.

§7   PROHIBITION

The issue of prohibition came to the forefront in Indian
politics after the Congress party secured majorities in the Legislatures of seven provinces in India in the elections of 1937 ; for
among the first social reforms attempted by the Congress
ministries was the introduction of prohibition, i.e. the prevention by law of the manufacture, sale, or use of intoxicants.

---

[1] *India*, 1973. It is also to be noted that the percentage of literacy
varied considerably from state to state—from 60·42% in Kerala to
11·29% in Arunachal Pradesh. See *India* 1973, p. 65.

Madras was the first province to introduce it (1938). In some States, e.g., Andhra Pradesh, Assam, Madhya Pradesh, Karnataka, Orissa, Kerala and Punjab, there is partial prohibition.

Social legislation of this magnitude naturally met with some opposition. The arguments against prohibition may be summarized thus :

(*i*) Prohibition is difficult to enforce. The instance of America which introduced prohibition in 1920 and revoked it in 1933 is a warning. That instance shows indeed not only that it is difficult to enforce, but that it creates a widespread habit of disobedience to law, which offsets any advantage it might otherwise have.

(*ii*) It involves great financial loss, and that in a double sense. Its enforcement is costly, needing as it does an extra police force ; it also means the loss of considerable revenue. The revenue from excise is, next to land revenue, the biggest item in state revenues, and, in view of the urgent need for funds for the nation-building departments, should not be forgone, especially at the present stage of Indian economic development.

(*iii*) It is an unwarranted interference with the freedom of the individual. Man cannot be made moral by Act of Parliament.

(*iv*) It creates unemployment among that section of the population which lives by supplying ' drink ', such as tappers, toddy sellers, etc.

But, in favour of prohibition, it is rightly argued :

(*i*) Drink is an evil both from the individual and social points of view. Alcohol is bad for the health of the individual. Socially it is undesirable because it results in a larger number of crimes and increases the poverty and misery of the masses. Family life is often unhappy not only because womenfolk are beaten by drunken husbands, but the money which ought to be spent in supplying the needs of the family is spent on drink.

(*ii*) In India, prohibition is not difficult to enforce, because the religious sentiment of the country is against drink. The lesson of America does not apply *in toto* to India ; in western countries, unlike India, drink is an integral part of ritual and food.

(*iii*) To make up the loss of revenue resulting from the introduction of prohibition, alternative sources of revenue, such as the sales tax, can be found. Retrenchment also can be resorted to. The experience of the working of prohibition so far does not help the student to arrive at a final judgement. The reports issued by the Madras Government in the early years of its introduction (1938-40), as well as by impartial investigators sent out by universities, showed that prohibition was a great boon to the masses : it resulted in great economic and social improvement. Family life was happier and there was less crime. People ate better and more food ; women and children had better clothing. But from 1940 onwards reports were less optimistic. Cases of breaches of the law were on the increase. The Government in power, therefore, felt that it was difficult to enforce the law and suspended it from 1 January, 1944. The working of prohibition in Madhya Pradesh has also disclosed a number of defects ; indeed, according to a Committee appointed to inquire into its working, prohibition has not succeeded in the State : 'There has been no elimination of the drink evil and even if there is reduction, it is not appreciable. . . . . . Prohibition has opened a hideous underworld where flourish secret drinking, blackmarketing, profiteering and bootlegging on an enormous scale'. In Maharashtra, steps were taken for the modification of the Prohibition law, as it was felt that it was found difficult to enforce the law and law-breakers were increasing in number. It is too early to conclude from these experiments that prohibition cannot succeed in India. The lesson rather is that prohibition, to be successful, requires enforcement for a long time, at least two generations, and demands incessant vigilance on the part of the administration as well as the enthusiastic co-operation of the general public, particularly in detecting law-breakers. The Congress Government in Madras, who are enthusiastic supporters of prohibition, reintroduced it in 1946 in eight districts. The D.M.K. Government which succeeded the Congress Government abolished prohibition for some time but later in 1974 reintroduced it. The Constitution of India has also included among the Directive Principles of State Policy the following : 'The State shall endeavour to bring about prohibition of the consumption except for medicinal purposes of intoxicating drinks and of drugs which are injurious to health.'

§8   THE STATE AND AGRICULTURE IN INDIA

The general principles of State interference which we have laid down earlier apply to agriculture as well, i.e. the State properly intervenes to prevent exploitation and manifest injustice, and by placing the resources of the State at the disposal of the individuals helps to remove the needless hazards of the economic struggle. As the Royal Commission on Agriculture put it concisely, the aim of the Government's agricultural policy must be to help to establish a smiling and happy countryside.

Five main lines of government activity are noticeable in regard to agriculture

(*i*) *The promotion of scientific agriculture.* This is mainly the function of the Departments of Agriculture, acting in co-operation with the Indian Agricultural Research Institute at New Delhi (maintained by the Union Government), the Indian Council of Agricultural Research, and the Veterinary Departments. Their methods are : (*a*) Research, with the object of introducing new crops, manures, implements and methods of cultivation and of improving indigenous types, destroying insects that are a pest to crops, and breeding superior types of livestock. (*b*) Propaganda, with the object of inducing the cultivators to adopt the results of research. This takes several forms : demonstrations at experimental farms, or on the cultivators' own land, lectures, pamphlets, and the distribution of the new varieties of seeds, manures and implements. (*c*) Agricultural education through the establishment of agricultural schools and colleges.

(*ii*) *The organization of rural finance.* In India, as in other countries where small-scale cultivation is practised, the problem of rural indebtedness is a vital one : those who help the agriculturist to get cheap credit for necessary purposes help him to get a better net return from his land. Action is being taken to deal with the problem of rural indebtedness as well as to increase the supply of finance to cultivators. Relief from indebtedness is being provided to the cultivator by (*a*) scaling down old debts either by amicable settlement or compulsorily ; (*b*) by exempting lands and homesteads from attachment ; (*c*) by controlling the nefarious practices of moneylenders ; and (*d*) by fixing the maximum rates of interest that can be charged. The supply of rural finance is being increased (*a*) through the provision of takkavi loans (*b*) by the organization of Co-operative Credit Societies and Land Mortgage Banks. The Co-operative Credit Societies supply short-term credit while Land Mortgage Banks provide long-term credit and through the nationalized Banks, the Banks being instructed to make special provision for helping the small farmer with cheap credit.

The history of the co-operative movement in India starts with the passing of the Co-operative Credit Societies Act of 1904 ; the Act has since been amended in several respects ; several defects have been discovered in the working of the societies and attempts have been made to remove them. In this context it is sufficient to say that the Government in India, in the early stages of the movement, supplied not only the much needed initiative, but also provided an official inspecting agency to direct the movement on right lines and to audit the accounts of societies.

(*iii*) *The protection of the tenant.* A series of Acts have been passed since 1859 in order to protect the tenants against exploitation by the landlord. The general features of this legislation are :[1] (*a*) There is a limit to the enhancement of the rent both as regards the amount and the period which must elapse before rent can be increased. Thus in Bengal enhancement can occur only as a result of agreement and cannot be more than twelve paise in the rupee. (*b*) The tenant cannot be ejected at the will of the landlord for frivolous reasons. (*c*) The occupancy right is hereditary and can only be alienated on certain conditions. (*d*) The payment of rent can be demanded only by instalments. (*e*) Remissions and suspensions of land revenue granted by the Government to landlords must be followed by corresponding concessions to tenants from landlords. (*f*) The right to make improvements on land without enhancement of rent is protected within certain limits.

Moreover, far-reaching agrarian reforms have recently been undertaken in Uttar Pradesh, Bihar and a number of other states. These aim at eliminating intermediaries—zamindars, jagirdars, etc.—between the State and the cultivator. Such reforms are also accompanied by schemes for the transference of ownership rights to cultivators at reasonable prices and for fixing ceilings on the area of land which may be owned by landowners.

(*iv*) *Stepping-up agricultural production.* During the last few years the problem of increasing agricultural production, particularly food crops, has assumed very great importance. A number of Central and State Committees (e.g. the Famine Inquiry Commission, the Sub-Committee of Policy Committee on Forests, Fisheries and Agriculture) have studied the various aspects of the agricultural problem and have made comprehensive recommendations for the reorganization of agriculture on more efficient lines. The immediate problem of stepping-up production is being tackled in three ways. Firstly, the Government are giving financial assistance either by way of loans or by way of grants for the construction of such works as will increase the production of food crops as well as cotton and jute. An idea of the

[1] G. B. Jathar and S. G. Beri, *Indian Economics*, Vol. I, 9th ed., pp. 352-6.

effort being made can be gauged from the fact that for the two years 1949-50 and 1950-51, Rs. 34 crores were placed at the disposal of the Ministry of Food and Agriculture for the Grow More Food schemes. Secondly, the Governments are arranging to supply the means of production (seeds, fertilizers, iron and steel, cement, etc.) to cultivators either on a concessional basis or on a no-profit-no-loss basis. Thirdly, legislative and administrative action is being taken to increase the area under cultivation, conserve farmyard manure and to prepare compost, to construct huge storage dams such as the Bhakra-Nangal dam in the Punjab and develop irrigation channels and to regulate production of non-food crops, etc.

(v) *The organization of marketing.* On account of his chronic indebtedness and need for money, coupled with the lack of storage facilities, the Indian cultivator is normally compelled to sell his produce to middlemen at a time when prices are low. The states have recently begun to encourage the formation of regulated markets and co-operative sale societies with the object of enabling the farmer to realize a better price for his goods. The Government of India have appointed a marketing expert on the staff of the Indian Council of Agricultural Research. Marketing officers have been appointed by state Governments to conduct marketing surveys of the principal crops in the different states. To secure the proper grading of agricultural produce, an Agricultural Produce (Grading and Marketing) Act has been in operation since 1937.

Mention may also be made of the fact that the Government of India's Five-year Plans place special emphasis on the improvement of agriculture and village life ; various steps have been taken in this direction, especially through large river-valley schemes such as the Damodar Valley Project and through the Community Projects and the National Extension Service.

Many other improvements are necessary if the object of promoting a smiling countryside is to be achieved. *The Report of the Royal Commission on Agriculture in India* (1928) is a mine of valuable suggestions in regard to legislation designed to promote the consolidation of holdings, measures to prevent the spread of contagious cattle diseases and for protection against insects and pests, and the re-examination and readjustment of railway freights on fodder, fuel, timber and agricultural implements. *The Report of the Famine Enquiry Commission* (1945), *The First Five-Year Plan,* and *The Second Five-Year Plan* also deal with the improvement of food production, nutrition and the agricultural economy in general. Special aspects of the agricultural economy are dealt with in the reports of the various sub-committees of the policy committees on Agriculture, Forestry and Fisheries. For detailed information the interested student is referred to these documents.

SELECT BIBLIOGRAPHY

V. ANSTEY, *The Economic Development of India*, ch. vii & viii, Longmans, 1936

J. K. BLUNTSCHLI, *The Theory of the State*, Bk. I, ch. iii to vi, Oxford, 3rd ed., 1901

The First Five-Year Plan, Planning Commission, Government of India, New Delhi, 1953

T. H. GREEN, *Lectures on the Principles of Political Obligation*, pp. 154-247, Longmans, 1921

India, A Reference Annual 1963, Compiled by Research and Reference Division, Ministry of Information and Broadcasting, Government of India Publications Division, Government of India, 1963

C. E. M. JOAD, *Introduction to Modern Political Theory*, pp. 24-32, Oxford, 1924

S. LEACOCK, *Elements of Political Science*, Part III, ch. i, Constable, 1933

J. S. MILL, *On Liberty*, 'World's Classics' No. 170, Oxford

Report of the Prohibition Enquiry Committee 1954-55, Planning Commission, Government of India, 1955

H. SIDGWICK, *The Development of European Polity*, lecture XII, Macmillan, 1903

— —, *The Elements of Politics*, ch. iii & iv, Macmillan, 1908

R. H. SOLTAU, *The Economic Functions of the State*, Pitman, 1931

F. G. WILSON, *The Elements of Modern Politics*, ch. xxi, McGraw-Hill, 1936

W. W. WILSON, *The State*, ch. xv & xvi, Heath, 1899

CHAPTER IX

MODERN THEORIES OF THE STATE

§1 SOCIALISM

SOCIALISM may be defined as a theory and a movement aiming at the collective organization of the community in the interests of the mass of the people through the common ownership and collective control of the means of production and exchange. Its essentials, according to Morrison,[1] are that all the great industries and the land should be publicly or collectively owned, and that they should be conducted (in conformity with a national economic plan) for the common good instead of for private benefit. The points need some explanation.

It is important to observe that socialism, as an economic and political theory, originated as a protest against the evils of capitalism. Capitalism may be defined as an economic system in which private persons are permitted (under regulations laid down by the State) to undertake enterprises, providing or borrowing the necessary capital, and taking the profits, if any, after all the costs of the enterprise have been met. Its essentials are the private ownership of the means of production, private enterprise and private profit or unlimited acquisitiveness as a motive in individual life. Experience has shown that capitalism has several defects : (*i*) It results in an unjust distribution of the national wealth, i.e. in *inequality* of wealth, income and opportunity. (*ii*) It results in *insecurity* also. This is a direct consequence of the wage system, which is implicit in capitalism. The wage system, according to G. D. H. Cole,[2] abstracts labour from the labourer, so that the one can be bought and sold without the other. Consequently wages are paid to the wage workers only when it is profitable to the capitalist to employ his labour. The periodical breakdown of the economic system, with its inevitable consequences of unemployment and misery, is the result. (*iii*) The wage system results not only in insecurity, but it makes

---

[1] *An Easy Outline of Modern Socialism*, p. 9, cited by A. C. Pigou in *Socialism versus Capitalism*, pp. 7-8.
[2] G. D. H. Cole, *Self-Government in Industry*, pp. 78-9.

of the worker a ' wage-slave '; for, in return for the wage, he surrenders all control over the organization of production, and all claim upon the product of his labour ; the feeling that he is able to express himself in his work is absent. (*iv*) The price system in a capitalist economy responds not to the real needs of the community but to the demands of those who have money to spend. Therefore production is for profit, not for use. (*v*) Finally, those who ought to be partners in production, viz. the employers and the employed, are, or tend to be, antagonists.

Socialists suggest that all these defects of social organization arise from one root cause, viz. the private ownership of the means of production and the desire for private profit. Therefore they would abolish all forms of private capital—private property in land, natural resources, factories—and with it the incentive to private profit. In place of private capital they would substitute common ownership and control. At the start of the century, as A. C. Pigou points out,[1] socialism was held to include only these two requirements ; but recently, as is evident from the definition by Morrison cited at the beginning of this section, there has been an emphasis on central planning as a third requirement of socialism. It is increasingly felt that the efficient organization of economic life under a system of public ownership of capital demands a central planning machinery to divert the productive activities of society into the most useful channels, and to increase social good to the utmost. There is no doubt that the example of the Soviet Union has had its share of influence in modifying socialist theory in this direction.[2]

Socialists agree on the outline given above ; but they are not all agreed on the ideal society they desire to see realized, nor on the method of attaining it. Broadly speaking, there may be said to be two schools of socialist thought, the revolutionary and the evolutionary. The former (communists and syndicalists) hold that revolution or direct action is the only effective method of bringing into existence the new society ; the latter (collectivists and guild socialists) believe that evolutionary, constitutional methods are not only possible but have more lasting effects. We shall describe these schools of thought in some detail.

---

[1] *Socialism versus Capitalism*, ch. i.

[2] A good example of the earlier notions of socialism referred to by Pigou is provided by F. J. C. Hearnshaw's description of the essentials of socialism as what may be called the six *E's* ; the exaltation of the community above the individual ; the equalization of human conditions ; the elimination of the capitalist ; the expropriation of the landlord ; the extinction of private enterprise ; and the eradication of competition.

§2 COMMUNISM

Karl Marx (1818-83) is generally known as the father of socialism. A German by birth, he early displayed signs of intellectual brilliance and took a keen interest in history, jurisprudence, and philosophy. He became a severe critic of the existing economic and political order and soon had to leave the land of his birth for France, and later, in 1849, for England. There he remained for the remaining thirty-four years of his life, studying and writing. He took part in forming a socialist association called the 'International' in 1864, and 'remained thereafter in every way the dominant personality of the socialist movement'. His main writings are the *Communist Manifesto* (1848), drafted in co-operation with his friend and collaborator Friedrich Engels, the *Critique of Political Economy* (1859), and *Capital* (1867-94). The theory of socialism which he developed is known as communism.

The essential principles of communism are all found in the *Communist Manifesto* issued in 1848 :

(*i*) *The materialistic interpretation of history.* The foundation of communism is the belief that the mode of production in material life determines the general character of the social, political and spiritual processes of life.

' In the social production which men carry on they enter into definite relations that are indispensable and independent of their will ; these relations of production correspond to a definite stage of development of their material powers of production. The sum total of these relations of production constitutes the economic structure of society—the real foundation, on which rise legal and political superstructures and to which correspond definite forms of social consciousness.'

(*ii*) *The class war.* ' Since the establishment of private property, society has been divided into two hostile economic classes. Just as in the ancient world the interest of slave-owners was opposed to that of the slaves, and in medieval Europe the interest of the feudal lords was opposed to that of the serfs, so in our own times, the interest of the capitalist class, which derives its income mainly from the ownership of property, is antagonistic to the interest of the proletariat class, which depends for its livelihood chiefly upon the sale of its labour power.'

(*iii*) *The theory of surplus value.* The primary reason for this antagonism is that the capitalist class, through its ownership and control of the means of production, is able to appropriate the ' surplus value ' which is created by labour and, therefore, ought to go to labour. The surplus value arises because labour power produces values above the cost of tools, raw materials and the cost of its own subsistence. The modern State is but a tool in the hands of the capitalist class to protect it from rebellion by the workers who suffer from this process of exploitation.

(*iv*) *A social revolution* is inevitable because the future development of capitalism will take the form of the concentration of capital in fewer and fewer hands, while, at the same time, there will be ' the ever closer and more elaborate organization of the proletariat '. ' At its climax, the proletariat will arise, overthrow the capitalist class and expropriate them of the means of production.' [1]

(*v*) *The dictatorship of the proletariat.* The dominant class will not, however, give up comfort and power without a severe struggle. ' The Red Terror,' wrote Trotsky, ' is a weapon utilized against a class, doomed to destruction, which does not wish to perish.' This animal, in other words, is naughty ; ' when it is attacked, it defends itself without realizing that its skeleton is needed for a museum of specimens.' To stabilize the results of the revolution, therefore, a dictatorship of the dominant class, viz. the proletariat, will confiscate all private capital, organize labour, compel all to work, centralize credit and finance, establish State factories, concentrate means of transport and speed up production. ' The road to socialism lies through a period of the highest possible intensification of the State.'

(*vi*) Ultimately, the State will wither away. After capitalism is completely destroyed, the State is unnecessary, for there will no longer be any capitalists, for whose protection it now exists. Therefore it will ' wither away '.

' When organizing production anew on the basis of a free and equal association of the producers,' wrote Engels, ' society will banish the whole State-machine to a place which will then be the most proper one for it—the museum of antiquities—side by side with the spinning wheel and the bronze axe.'

(*vii*) The new society will then be organized on the principle, ' from each according to his capacity, to each according to his needs '. Each man will contribute to the social wealth by his labour as much as he can, and will take from it what he needs.

It is not widely known that Marx himself in his later years modified the theory of communism put forward in the Communist Manifesto, admitting the possibility of the workers achiev-

---

[1] See C. E. M. Joad, *Introduction to Modern Political Theory*, pp. 44-5.

ing their socialist goal by peaceful means. At a meeting in Amsterdam in 1872, Marx said : [1]

'We know that the institutions, customs and traditions of the separate countries have to be taken into account ; and we do not deny that there are countries like America and Britain—and if I knew your institutions better, I might add Holland to them—in which the workers can achieve their goal by peaceful means.'

It is significant that this view has now been officially accepted by the Twentieth Congress of the Communist Party at its meeting on 24 February 1956 :

'The Communist Party of the Soviet Union bases itself on Lenin's precept that " all nations will arrive at socialism "—this is inevitable, but not all will do it exactly the same way.

. . . .

'It is quite logical that forms of transition to socialism will become more and more diversified. Moreover, the implementation of these forms need not be associated with civil war under all circumstances.' [2]

Every one of these fundamental principles of communism has been subjected to vigorous criticism by students of economics and politics. The materialistic interpretation of history is a partial view ; accident, great men, religion and geography have all played some part in history. The idea of a class war, denying as it does the possibility of a common civic consciousness, is unduly pessimistic. The labour theory of value, on which is based the notion of surplus value, is an inadequate explanation : other factors, such as the relation of supply to demand and the existence of competition or monopoly, must be taken into account. A social revolution of the kind predicted is not inevitable : recent economic history shows that social thought and foresight have brought about a gradual, and can bring about a further, amelioration of social ills. It is a historical fact that in countries with a high per-capita income (such as the U.S.A., Britain, Sweden, Australia, New Zealand, the Netherlands, Canada and Belgium), communism has not made much headway and communist parties are either non-existent or weak. As a matter of fact, the first socialist revolution did not, as Marx predicted, arise out of the culmination of capitalist development in the West but

[1] Marx and Engels, *Works*, First Russian edition, Vol. XIII, Part II, p. 669.
[2] *For a Lasting Peace, For a People's Democracy*, 2 March 1956, p. 2.

out of the pre-capitalist system in the East. Indeed, the very idea that a revolution is inevitable acts as a stimulus to prevent its coming.

Further, the dictatorship of the proletariat envisaged during the transition period is clearly undesirable. Any form of dictatorship is defective because we have no assurance that the interests of the dictators will always coincide with the interests of the community.

Communists constantly emphasize the evils of the concentration of wealth but they are blind to the evils of the concentration of power. Even if the first dictators are high-minded, we have no assurance that their successors will be. Dictatorship is incapable of voluntary abdication ; the State will not wither away. And finally the communist goal is not possible of realization, for it demands a revolution in human nature. A social ideal which assumes such fundamental change in human nature and habit is by the nature of things incapable of realization.

§3 SYNDICALISM

' Syndicalism ' is derived from *syndicat,* the ordinary French term for labour union, and may be defined as ' that form of social theory which regards the trade union organizations as at once the foundation of the new society and the instrument whereby it is to be brought into being ' (Joad). Its home is France ; its main exponents are Sorel (1847-1922) and Pelloutier (1867-1901).

The syndicalists accept the general socialist position that society is divided into two classes, the capitalist and the proletarit, whose claims are irreconcilable ; that the modern State is a class State dominated by the few capitalists ; that the institution of private capital is the root of all social evils and that the only remedy for them is to substitute collective capital in place of private capital.

Syndicalism differs from communism primarily in the method it advocates for achieving the socialist objective. That method is direct economic action. In contrast to other socialist schools, it stresses the idea that

' the social transformation to be sought by the proletariat must be a self-transformation and that the institutions through which existing society is to be displaced by a new society are institutions that grow out of, and are built up by, the working class through its unaided efforts and in defiance of political authority '.[1]

[1] F. W. Coker, *Recent Political Thought,* p. 234.

The efficient organization of labour unions, by crafts or industries, and of local labour councils is the first step towards syndicalism. The boycott (the refusal to take employment with or purchase articles made by a firm regarded as unfair in its dealings with workers), the label (to indicate work done under union conditions, ' ca' canny ' (the practice of doing a minute quantity of work with scrupulous care), sabotage (e.g. the damaging of plant by workmen), strikes, and, on top, the general strike, are the tactics adopted by syndicalists to achieve their ends. The general strike does not necessarily mean, contrary to what the term appears to denote, a strike of *all* the workers in a country. It is sufficient to have a strike of the workers in the key industries (e.g. electricity, gas, and transport) in order to paralyse economic life to end capitalism.

Regarding the structure of syndicalist society, the syndicalist writers are not clear ; they do not, indeed, consider it worth their while to work out the details of a future organization of society. There will be no political State, as we understand it, which presupposes an organization in which a delegated minority centralizes in its own hands the power of legislation over all matters. Syndicates of workers will control the means of production ; they will only use (not own) such property with the consent of society. They will be connected with the rest of society through local unions of workers and a general confederation of labour. This last will control such national services as railways and the post office. This picture is necessarily incomplete and hazy ; only two features stand out clearly : there will be the producers' control of industry ; the State will disappear.

No criticism of the ideal of syndicalist society is called for, as that ideal has not been clearly stated by the syndicalists themselves. Of their method, the most cogent criticism is that ' a general strike is unnecessary, because a general election is never far off '—for, given the discipline and the unity which are necessary for a successful general strike, the desired end can be achieved gradually, through constitutional methods. Indeed, the chances of success are greater, and the results more lasting, if syndicalists adopt constitutional methods, educate the voters, return representatives to Parliament on the socialist ticket and pass the necessary laws. In a general strike, the working classes are likely to starve before achieving their object ; and failure of a strike may produce reaction against the workers. Further, methods like ca' canny and sabotage are sure to have a vicious effect on the morale of the workers.

§4 COLLECTIVISM

Communism and syndicalism agree in being revolutionary. They advocate ' direct ' action, rejecting the use of indirect parliamentary methods for achieving the socialist objective. Collectivism believes in the efficacy of the democratic method for this purpose. It is defined as that policy or theory which aims at securing *by the action of the central democratic authority* a better distribution, and in due subordination thereto a better production, of wealth than now prevails. Its principles are best explained by reference to the ideals of the English school of collectivism, known as Fabian socialism.[1]

The Fabian society was established in January, 1884. It has counted among its members many distinguished men and women including Bernard Shaw, Sidney and Beatrice Webb, Graham Wallas, H. G. Wells, and Annie Besant. The name of the society is explained by its motto :

' For the right moment you must wait as Fabius did when warring against Hannibal, though many censured his delays ; but when the time comes you must strike hard, as Fabius did, or your waiting will be in vain and fruitless.'

The present social organization discloses several defects ; it assures the happiness and comfort of the few at the expense of the suffering many ; it secures political freedom but maintains economic insecurity and slavery ; there is ' poverty in plenty '. The Fabians therefore aim at the establishment of a society in which equality of opportunity will be assured, and the economic power and privileges of individuals and classes abolished, through the collective ownership and democratic control of the economic resources of the community. But it is no use attempting a sudden and radical transformation. Society must be ' permeated ' with socialistic ideas through lectures, books and pamphlets ; men who believe in them must be returned to Parliament ; and public opinion must urge the adoption of legislative and administrative measures embodying socialistic ideas. To start with, the national minimum of work, leisure, wages, security against unemployment and sickness, provision for old age, self-government in industry, and education must be guaranteed to all. This of course means an extension of the progressive principle in taxation already at work, and the further taxation of inheritances, investment incomes

---

[1] Collectivism is more or less equivalent to State Socialism or Revisionism.

and of unearned increment. The public ownership (national and municipal) of public utilities and natural monopolies must be pressed forward, and ultimately the land and all forms of industrial capital must be nationalized.

' The transfer must be effected gradually, applied at any given time only to such industries as can then be successfully administered by the community, and, though without full compensation, yet with such relief to the expropriated individuals as may seem fair to the representatives of the community in the political department.' [1]

Briefly, the democratic State is the instrument through which the social transformation is accomplished ; the democratic State is also retained in the socialist society in order to be the agent of the community to own capital and regulate production and distribution. Socialism, indeed, is viewed as the next step in democracy.[2]

The distinction between communism and collectivism must now be clear. The former is revolutionary, the latter evolutionary. The former considers that the State, being dominated by the capitalist, is useless as an instrument to abolish capitalism ; the latter, that if the citizens of a democracy will simply make adequate use of the political power they have, they can bring about the social millennium through the State. The former envisages a dictatorship during the transition period ; the latter, a continuous use of democratic methods. The former suggests that the State will finally disappear ; the latter, that State will have added functions.

§5 GUILD SOCIALISM

Guild socialism has been popularized as a theory by some English writers, particularly S. G. Hobson and G. D. H. Cole. It aims at the achievement of socialism with the guild as its foundation. The guild is a trade union modified in two ways : it will be inclusive of all workers in an industry, including the unskilled workers as well as the clerical, technical, and managerial workers who are now largely excluded from trade union

[1] Coker, op. cit., p. 105.
[2] The success of the Labour Party in the General Elections of 1945 and 1950 gave it an opportunity to put its socialist theories into practice, and, among other socialistic measures, it secured the nationalization of the Bank of England, the coal mines and iron and steel ; the Iron and Steel Act of 1953, however, denationalized iron and steel (passed under the Conservative Government).

membership ; and it will be organized to control industry, not merely to secure better conditions of work. The trade unions are the key to the situation in two respects : they will become the guilds of tomorrow, and they are the organizations by means of which the actual transition to socialism is to be accomplished.[1]

The guild socialists recognize with other socialists the evils of the present social organization—poverty, inequality and insecurity. In particular, they stress two defects, the one political, the other economic. From the political point of view, that a Parliament elected from territorial constituencies should exercise a general power of law-making is wrong : no man can represent another—an agriculturist may represent agriculturists ; a lawyer, lawyers ; and a coalminer, coalminers. Functional representation is clearly indicated. Further, the State, being but one association among several associations, can exercise power only in a limited field, i.e. the political ; it should have no concern with other functions which should be left to other organized, functional bodies. From the economic point of view, the most important single defect of the present social organization is the wage system, for, under present conditions, the wage worker in return for his wage surrenders all control over the organization of production and all claim upon the product of his labour. This is clearly inadequate. Economic freedom demands that industry should be administered by all the workers, both manual and intellectual, who carry on the industry.

The structure of the guild socialist society is somewhat as follows : (i) There will be a guild for each industry which will be administered by the guild on behalf of society. (ii) Consumers' councils will co-operate with the bodies of producers to determine costs and prices. (iii) A common Parliament will (according to some authorities) look to the affairs common to all, such as defence and taxation. On this point, however, there is some difference of opinion, some thinkers suggesting a body representing the essential functional associations to regulate such matters. (iv) There will be local regional bodies to look after matters of common interest in the locality.

The methods to be used to achieve this social order are partly the political method of the collectivist, and partly the economic method of the syndicalist.

Guild Socialism as a political theory has this value : it stresses the desirability of producer's participation in the management of the workshop. Its defects are that (i) as a socialist system, it

---

[1] Joad, op. cit., p. 84.

asks too much of human nature ; (*ii*) the functional representation which the theory stresses is open to the objection that it under-estimates the unity of society ; territorial representation with all its defects is a rough device for the expression of the common interest ; (*iii*) it may be unworkable in practice. ' The constitution of the State contemplated, especially in its latest elaboration by Mr Cole, is a complicated nightmare of committees and joint-committees which reminds one of the machinery made by boys out of Meccano ' (Hearnshaw)

§6 AN ESTIMATE OF SOCIALISM

We have described the various schools of socialist thought and are in a position to form an estimate of socialism. Is socialism practicable ? Is it desirable ? How far is it likely to remove the defects of the existing social organization ? It is obviously difficult to give definite answers to these questions. Socialism is still largely theoretical and the only big experiment on which a judgement can be based is not only incomplete, but the available accounts of it vary far too much to be made the basis of correct conclusions.

On one thing there is general agreement : socialism is strong in its critical, if not in its constructive, aspect. It points out clearly the evils of an acquisitive, capitalist society : its inequality, poverty, and insecurity ; the agitation it stirs up reveals maladjustment, and presents a plea for the needy and the weak. It emphasizes the economic foundations of the good life : ' that while civilization may be everything above mere subsistence, the base cannot be neglected '. It exposes the fallacies of unbridled individualism, and suggests that social action can very largely overcome the hazards of a competitive society. It is a significant challenge to our generation to produce an acceptable alternative, if its thesis is considered erroneous.

It is on its constructive side that socialism has had its severest critics. (*i*) It is asked whether socialism is at all practicable as a permanent way of social life. It goes contrary to the well established facts of human nature. Man puts forth his best effort because he knows that the reward of his effort can, in the main, be enjoyed by himself and his family. It is doubtful if he will work for society with the same enthusiasm that he now displays in working for himself. (*ii*) Socialism is another name for slavery. As Spencer put it : ' Each member of the community as an individual would be a slave of the community as a whole.' If all industry and commerce must be managed from a central authority which has to calculate and regulate everything, it follows that all deviations from the appointed and expected routine on which these calculations are based must be strenuously put down. The order of things established by the State must be maintained at all costs, and all opposing individual interests, wishes or aspirations must be remorselessly brushed aside.[1] (*iii*) Socialism must mean the regulation of the laws of supply and demand, a task impossible of fulfilment. No central authority can ever regulate production so as to meet the constantly varying demands of every part of a great nation. (*iv*) State management may be less efficient than private management.

It is significant that academic economists of the standing of Professor Pigou[2] (not a professed socialist) have refused to accept these rather ' old-fashioned ' arguments at their face value. They point out, for instance, that the problem of incentive to work is not so simple as stated above : all work is not unpleasant ; it is possible by the application of science to reduce the number of unpleasant jobs in society ; the latent forces of professional pride, joy in work, and the sport *motif* can be enlisted in the service of society. Again, socialism is not a rigid system : it is possible to manage State-owned industries efficiently and maintain the freedom of the individual through the development of new socialistic techniques, as, for instance, their management through public boards or commissions on a semi-public, semi-commercial basis.

Nevertheless, there is an element of uncertainty and of risk when one leaves well-tried paths of economic and social organization for new ones. Pigou himself therefore prefers accepting for the time being the general structure of capitalism and modifying it with a view to reduce economic inequalities and promote social welfare. There is considerable truth in a remark of M'Kechnie[3] that a true theory of the State must be socialistic and individualistic at once ; and it is a false science which finds place for only one of these. What we need is capitalism transformed so as to combine safeguards for public interest with scope for private ownership and initiative, public supervision to be proportionate to public interest. Economic practice and theory are slowly discovering the outlines of such a system : a central planning machinery with the object of increasing efficiency in production all round ; the nationalization of public utilities and their direction for public ends with adaptable commercial business

---

[1] M'Kechnie, *The State and the Individual*, p. 192.
[2] See his *Socialism versus Capitalism*.
[3] M'Kechnie, op. cit., p. 182.

management through public corporations ; the encouragement of consumers' and producers' co-operation to eliminate middlemen ; the organization of marketing ; the avoidance of large fluctuations in the demand for capital goods through the control of the rate of interest and a wise public works policy ; the development of the Investment Trust for the rational direction of the flow of investment ; the limitation of profits ; minimum and maximum wages ; the organization of the industrial unit in such a way as to secure efficiency as well as freedom ; the collaboration of capital and labour in joint councils and corporations ; income and inheritance taxes. Details apart, the economic basis of a free society should be a basic equality, the differences to be the outcome of genuine variations and explicable in terms of the common good. This will naturally lead to the predominance of the middle class in society, which Aristotle considered the greatest bulwark of stability in the State.

§7 FASCISM

The word ' fascism ' is derived from Latin *fascis,* = ' a group or cluster ' ; it is used of a cluster of plants or branches which grow stronger by being thus bound together. A *fascis* of sticks with an axe in their midst was carried by the Roman lictors before the Roman consuls and represented the authority of the State ; it was from the lictors' *fasces* that the Italian fascists derived their emblem.

The theory of fascism is primarily an Italian product, evolved to justify the fascist movement.[1] The creation of a State of truly sovereign authority which dominates all the forces in the country and which at the same time is in constant contact with the masses, guiding their sentiments, educating them and looking after their interests—this is the central political idea of fascism.

In the words of Mussolini, fascism repudiates (*i*) pacifism, (*ii*) socialism, (*iii*) democracy and (*iv*) individualism.

(*i*) It repudiates pacifism, because that is born of a renunciation of struggle, and is an act of cowardice. Perpetual peace is neither possible nor desirable. ' War is to man what maternity is to woman.'

[1] See below ch. xxiii. The account of fascist philosophy given here is primarily based on Mussolini's own essay, 'The Political and Social Doctrine of Fascism ', translated in *The Political Quarterly*, Vol. IV, 1933, pp. 341 ff. See also, M. Oakeshott, *The Social and Political Doctrines of Contemporary Europe*, ch. IV.

(*ii*) It repudiates socialism, because it believes that the institution of private property strengthens family ties and, if properly regulated, is generally in the interests of the community.

(*iii*) It does not believe in democracy. The majority, simply because it is a majority, has no power to direct human society ; the sum of wills is not the same thing as the general will. The majority is not necessarily more reasonable than the minority. The democratic notion of the equality of man is wrong. Democracy indeed gives power to the masses to decide innumerable issues, about which they cannot possibly have the knowledge required to exeicise a sound judgement ; the masses are led by clever, unscrupulous demagogues who have the gift of the gab. Further, popular government does not tend to throw up an aristocracy of intelligence and character.

In contrast to democracy, fascism believes in the principle that authority is exercised for the sake of the community, but is not derived from the community. The specific sanction of a government is its power ; its ultimate sanction, its reasonableness. The fascist would wholeheartedly subscribe to Carlyle's idea :

' Find in any country the ablest man that exists there, raise him to the supreme place and loyalty, reverence him ; you have a perfect government for that country ; no ballot-box, parliamentary eloquence, voting, constitution building or other machinery whatsoever can improve it a whit. It is the perfect State, the ideal country.' [1]

(*iv*) It repudiates individualism. The business of the State is to govern. The conduct of life cannot be left to the individual choice of the people ; it must, instead, be determined for them by a power which is above them and comprehends them, viz. the State. The State must preside over and direct national activity in every field, and no organization, whether political, moral or economic, can remain outside it. ' All within the State ; none outside the State ; none against the State.' The State is totalitarian. Individuals are transitory elements ; they are born, grow up, die and are replaced by others, while society must be considered an imperishable organism, which always retains its identity and its patrimony of ideas and sentiments which each generation receives from the past and transmits to the future. As the fascist Charter of Labour in Italy put it : ' The Italian nation is an organism having ends, life, and means of action superior to those of the

---

[1] G. H. Sabine, *A History of Political Theory*, p. 764.

separate individuals or groups of individuals which compose it. It is a moral, political, and economic unity that is integrally realized in the fascist State.' The State may, therefore, in principle,

'control every act and every interest of every individual or group, in so far as the good of the nation requires it, and of this the State is itself the sole judge. Except by the permission of the State, there may be neither political parties, trade unions, industrial or commercial associations ; except under the regulation of the State, there may be neither manufacture, business, nor labour ; both work and leisure are within the control of the State ; except under the direction of the State, there may be neither publication nor public meeting ; education, indeed all the ethical, intellectual, and even religious interests of its members are theoretically within the keeping of the nation and the supervision of the State.'

By way of criticism, it is sufficient to say that fascism represents in political theory a view diametrically opposite to the one developed in the foregoing pages. That view, which may be called liberal, is that the ultimate purpose of man is man himself ; the State is a means to the development of individual personality and is not an end in itself. Our aim is, according to the liberal view, to enable the individual to think and express what he likes, to plan his way of life in his own way and to grow to his natural height without dictation from outside, provided he does not interfere with the equal freedom of others and does not exploit the weakness of others for his private advantage. The liberal view stresses freedom ; the fascist view, authority.

SELECT BIBLIOGRAPHY

F. W. COKER, *Recent Political Thought*, Appleton, 1934

G. D. H. COLE, *Guild Socialism Re-stated*, Allen & Unwin, 1921

— —, *Fabian Socialism*, Allen & Unwin, 1943

E. O. GOLOB, *The 'ISMS', A History and Evaluation*, Part III, Harper, New York, 1954

W. GURIAN, *Bolshevism : Theory and Practice*, Sheed & Ward, 1932

R. N. C. HUNT, *Marxism, Past and Present*, London, Bles, 1954

C. E. M. JOAD, *Introduction to Modern Political Theory*, Oxford, 1924

H. W. LAIDLER, *Social-Economic Movements*, Routledge & Kegan Paul, 1949

H. J. LASKI, *Communism*, 'Home University Library', Oxford, 1928

J. R. MACDONALD, *Socialism : Critical and Constructive*, Cassell, 1928

W. S. M'KECHNIE, *The State and the Individual*, ch. xiii, James MacLehose, Glasgow, 1896

M. OAKESHOTT, *The Social and Political Doctrines of Contemporary Europe*, Cambridge, 1939

A. C. PIGOU, *Socialism versus Capitalism*, Macmillan, 1937

G. H. SABINE, *A History of Political Theory*, ch. xxxiv, Harrap, 3rd ed., 1951

CHAPTER X

FORMS OF GOVERNMENT

§1 MONARCHY

THE freedom of the individual, which is the central subject of political inquiry, is considerably affected by the form of government under which he lives : a citizen, for instance, is obviously more free under a democracy than under a dictatorship. The forms of government have, therefore, a place in a discussion of political theory. Among these forms, the earliest has been monarchy, i.e. government by one individual not subject to any legal limitations, ' who does everything according to his own will '.[1] A good king, indeed, as James I said,[2] ' will frame all his actions according to the law ; yet he is not bound thereto but of his good will and for good example to his subjects.' Hereditary monarchy is the normal type, but elective forms are also known, as in ancient India and Rome and in Poland until recent times. In any case, the essence of monarchy is ' the personification of the majesty and sovereignty of the State in an individual '. This means two things: (*i*) the personal elevation of the head of the State, as the individual representative and organ of the supreme power, and (*ii*) the substantial concentration in the monarch of the highest dignity and power of the State.[3]

Two forms of monarchy are usually distinguished, absolute and limited or constitutional. In the former, the monarch is the head of the State both in name and in fact; in the latter only in name. The power of a constitutional monarch is regulated by the constitution. He can promulgate only those laws which are agreed to by the elected Parliament. Similarly, the ' financial arrangements and the granting of taxes are also dependent upon the co-operation and consent of the representative bodies '. In administration, the constitutional king is bound to accept the advice of ministers who are chosen from, and are responsible to, the Parliament. Finally, he ' is bound to respect not only the letter of the constitution,

---

[1] Aristotle, *Politics*, §1287a.
[2] *The True Law of Free Monarchies*. The word ' monarchy ' is from the Greek *monarkhes* (*monos* alone, *arkhein* rule).
[3] Bluntschli, *The Theory of the State*, p. 431.

but also the laws of the State. He can only expect and demand obedience as regulated by the constitution and the laws.'[1] It may, however, be doubted whether such a form of government (e.g. in Britain) is to be counted monarchical at all ;[2] it is much the same in principle as a democratic government, because the substance of power is with the people.

Merits

Monarchy has been defended from time to time on various grounds: the unity and orderliness necessary to every stable political society can best be secured only where supreme authority is vested in a single ruler. The greater the unity within the Government itself, the greater the likelihood of achieving unity among the people.[3] The clearest statement of this idea is in Frederick the Great's Political Testament of 1752: ' A well conducted government must have a system as coherent as a system of philosophy, so that finance, policy and the army are coordinated to the same end, namely, the consolidation of the State and the increase of its power. Such a system can only emanate from a single brain, that of the sovereign '.[4] Monarchy helps to harmonize different interests and presents social strife. Because it best satisfies the criterion of unity, says Rousseau, it is also the most vigorous system.

' The will of the people, the will of the prince, the public force of the State, and the particular force of the Government, all answer to a single motive power ; all the springs of the machine are in the same hands, the whole moves towards the same end ; there are no conflicting movements to cancel one another, and no kind of constitution can be imagined in which a less amount of effort produces a more considerable amount of action.'[5]

Again, monarchy is a natural institution, obedience to a king being as natural as the obedience of a child to its parents. This was the view of Francis Bacon (1561-1626). Filmer in his *Patriarcha* (1680) suggested that the State is but an extension of the family, the king being the father, the people his children.

---

[1] Bluntschli, *The Theory of the State*, p. 437.
[2] See Gilchrist, *Principles of Political Science*, p. 242.
[3] St. Thomas Aquinas (1227-74) in *The Government of Princes*.
[4] G. P. Gooch, *Frederick the Great, the Ruler, the Writer, the Man*, London, 1947, p. 282.
[5] *The Social Contract*, p. 62.

Burke supported monarchy for historical and practical reasons: where hereditary kingship has been in existence for a considerable time, it is unwise and unnecessary to abolish it. The democratic element can be grafted on to it; and nothing will be gained by abolishing it.

Monarchy is best adapted to deal with emergencies, thought Bodin (1530-96), for the monarch need not consult others before deciding on the necessary action. Further, only a monarch can ensure order and none but a monarch can create any sense of unity, especially as contrasted with a democracy: ' In a democracy sovereignty is vested in a majority; and a majority is not only, at best, an ignorant, foolish and emotional mob, but shifts continually and alters from year to year.'

In certain circumstances, the king may well be the protector of the people at large from the tyranny of the few:

' A great population (as in Russia before 1917) scattered over a large territory and struggling against the oppression of great magnates, being unable to organize concerted action over so large a space, may collect all its power into the hands of an individual, and arm him with a sort of iron mace strong enough to crush any or all of the enemies of the people.' [1]

In Germany in the Middle Ages, the Crown ' became what it has been wherever an aristocracy presses upon both [Crown and people], the ally . . . of the people '. [2]

And, finally, it provides the most satisfactory government for those who cannot govern themselves, who ' have not yet developed a high political consciousness and who therefore lack the capacity themselves for participating actively in the management of public affairs. Perhaps no better form could be devised for disciplining uncivilized peoples, leading them out of barbarism and inculcating in them habits of obedience.' [3]

Defects

These arguments assume not only that the monarch is able and hard-working, but also that he deliberately rules for the good of his people. The defects of monarchy primarily arise from the fact that this assumption may not always be justified. Ability, industry and good intentions are not hereditary, and ' history indicates that

[1] Seeley, *Introduction to Political Science*, p. 171.
[2] Bryce, *The Holy Roman Empire*, p. 132.
[3] Garner, *Introduction to Political Science*, p. 207.

for a Louis XIV a country has to pay the price of a Louis XV and Louis XVI '. In the hands of a bad ruler, despotism is the worst form of government, because unified power is mightier for evil, as well as for good, than dispersed power. Further, while the wise and strong king will realize that it is in his interest to keep his people strong and prosperous—for their power, ' being his own, might make him formidable to his neighbours ' [1]—the unwise and weak one may be tempted, in order to maintain his position, to keep them weak, so that they may be unable to resist him.

It is not right, however, for us to judge any form of government by a degraded specimen. The truth is that the utility of particular forms of government is, as Aristotle long ago saw, relative to circumstances. Where one individual is clearly superior to the rest of the community in ability and character, as Aristotle said, or where the people are divided among themselves and are unable to govern themselves, monarchy is indicated. It has, besides, the great advantage, in Bagehot's phrase, of being an intelligible government.

' The mass of mankind understand it, and they hardly understand any other. . . The nature of a constitution, the action of an assembly, the play of parties, the unseen formation of a guiding opinion are complex facts, difficult to know and easy to mistake. But the action of a single will, the fiat of a single mind, are easy ideas : anybody can make them out and no one can ever forget them. . . Royalty is a government in which the attention of the nation is concentrated on one person doing interesting actions. A republic is a government in which that attention is divided between many, who are all doing uninteresting actions. Accordingly, so long as the human heart is strong and the human reason weak, royalty will be strong because it appeals to diffused feeling, and republics weak because they appeal to the understanding.' [2]

§2 ARISTOCRACY

Aristocracy is literally ' government by the best citizens '.[3] A State governed by the best men, upon the most virtuous principles, has alone a right to be called an aristocracy ; [4] its principle, therefore, is virtue : the moral and intellectual superiority of the

[1] Rousseau, op. cit., pp. 62-3.
[2] W. Bagehot, *The English Constitution*, pp. 33-9.
[3] Greek, *aristokratia* (*aristos* best, *kratos* power).
[4] Aristotle, op. cit., §§1293b and 1294a.

ruling class. It follows that the ' essence of aristocracy lies in the respect accorded to the aristocrat by others ; a respect to be enhanced more by deeds than words '. Moreover, in a well-established and effective aristocracy ' the member of the ruling class assumes, but does not explain his superiority. Should he be compelled to justify his power, it will be proof that his position is crumbling.' ' It loses all real vitality,' says Bluntschli,[1] ' when the ruling class degenerates from the qualities which raised it to power, when its character decays, and it becomes weak and vain. It perishes equally, even though its great qualities remain, when the subject classes attain to equal distinction.' The distinction of quality, which ought to characterize an aristocracy, may be expressed through birth (aristocracy of family), culture and education (aristocracy of priests or of scholars), age (aristocracy of elders), military distinction (aristocracy of knights), or property (aristocracy of landowners).[2] The two most successful aristocracies of history are those of Rome during the period from the fourth to the second centuries B.C., and of Britain in the eighteenth century.

In theory, there is much to be said in favour of an aristocratic government. It stresses quality, as against quantity. It gives the community a ruling class, who inherit and bequeath to their posterity high traditions of public service, and who can be trusted to administer public affairs with a complete personal integrity and honour, because they possess a great position independent of politics. It seems to be a natural institution. Even Rousseau thought that ' it is the best and most natural arrangement that the wisest should govern the many, *when it is assured that they will govern for its profit, and not for their own*'.[3] ' It is the ever-lasting privilege of the foolish,' said Carlyle, ' to be governed by the wise.' In a famous passage, he tells us :

' Surely, of all " rights of man ", this right of the ignorant man to be guided by the wiser, to be, gently or forcibly, held in the true course by him, is the indisputablest. Nature herself ordains it from the first ; society struggles towards perfection by enforcing and accomplishing it more and more... In Rome and Athens, as elsewhere, if we look practically, we shall find that it was not by loud voting and debating of many, but by wise insight and ordering of a few that the work was done. So is it ever, so will it ever be.'[4]

Besides, aristocracies are conservative, and an element of conservatism is necessary for the health of the body politic. They

[1] op. cit., pp. 451-2. [2] ibid.
[3] op. cit., bk. III, ch. v ; italics ours.
[4] *Chartism* (1839).

avoid rash political experiments ; they advance by cautious and measured steps. As Montesquieu noted, they have the great virtue of moderation. This moderation is dictated by the need for their security ; they have always to remember that the subject masses are superior in number and physical force, and therefore, an immoderate use of their power may lead to resistance. Above all, aristocracies are conducive to progress : history is a sound aristocrat. The progress of mankind has hitherto been effected, said Maine, ' by the rise and fall of aristocracies, by the formation of one aristocracy within another, or by the succession of one aristocracy to another '. [1]

If every aristocracy answered to its ideal description, it would be the best form of government. But historical reality has little in common with the ideal of political philosophers. It is the tragedy of all aristocracies, says a competent authority, [2] that they have degenerated so quickly into oligarchies ; the attempt to arrest the development of the constitution at the aristocratic stage, and to devise safeguards against its degenerating into an oligarchy, has never succeeded. Aristocracies tend to become constantly smaller and more exclusive.

' The famous aristocracy of Venice is perhaps the best example of this. The almost unrestrained powers, which in the seventh century had been vested in the Doge, were in 1172 limited by the institution of the Great Council, a body of 480 citizens. These, although originally elective, rapidly became a hereditary aristocracy. And out of this there developed a smaller executive council, the *pregadi* or Senate ; and of this six were chosen as direct advisers of the Doge. But in the fourteenth century, owing to the attempts of the people to regain control over the government, the aristocracy sacrificed their own power to the famous institution, the Council of Ten, a body whose criminal jurisdiction was so complete that the real government of the State fell into its hands.' [3]

From exclusiveness to arrogance and pride is an easy step ; the ruling aristocrats ' have often displayed towards the lower classes a harshness and cruelty which have been the more intolerable because accompanied by contempt '. Witness the treatment of the Helots by the Spartans, and the oppression of plebeian debtors by the Roman patricians.

[1] *Popular Government*, p. 42.
[2] E. F. Bowman, *An Introduction to Political Science*, p. 75.
[3] Bowman, op. cit., p. 76.

A second great defect of aristocracy, says Bluntschli, [1] is its excessive rigidity. Society is hardly static. It is the mark of a good Government to adapt itself to changing social and economic conditions. But aristocracies, in the attempt to preserve their power, are unwilling to adapt themselves. Thus the decline of the feudal aristocracy of Europe in the Middle Ages and of the Whig aristocracy of Britain in the eighteenth century has been attributed partly to their inability to adjust themselves to the social and economic changes introduced by the maritime discoveries and the Industrial Revolution respectively.

These defects have in modern times, generally, led to the discrediting of aristocracy, though critics of democracy and particularly the fascists are inclined to sing its praises. The modern view is that aristocracy has a great value as an element in a State rather than as a form of government : every society, whatever its form of government, should arrange its social and political institutions in such a way that the opinions of the best citizens will shape decisions arrived at by the Government.

§3 DEMOCRACY

Democracy may be described as a system of government under which the people exercise the governing power either directly or through representatives periodically elected by themselves. This means that a State may, in political science, be termed a democracy if it provides institutions for the expression and, in the last analysis, the supremacy of the popular will on basic questions of social direction and policy. Other factors, such as economic equality, fraternal feeling and the small size of the State, are desirable and make for its successful working, the optimum of democracy ; political liberty is the indispensable minimum.

The content of political liberty has differed in different countries at different times ; but its essence is the right of every man bound by the decisions of a Government to contribute (whatever is in him to contribute) to the making and remaking of those decisions. Its institutional expressions (in modern *representative* democracies) are : the equal rights of all normal adults to vote and to stand as candidates for election ; periodical elections ; equal eligibility for executive and judicial office (provided the essential qualifications for the performance of these duties are satisfied) ; and freedom of speech, publication, and association. These rights provide the opportunities for political participation,

[1] op. cit., p. 454.

i.e. for choosing rulers and deciding the general lines of their policy ; they enable those who are so minded to devote themselves to political problems as much as they please. The social environment, economic resources, and natural endowments decide the extent to which these legal rights are effectively used ; but even to those who are the least politically minded opportunity is provided by these rights to pass judgement freely and frequently on the work of the political engineers whose decisions affect their lives. There is political equality at a minimum level.

Among the political rights outlined above, stress must be laid on the rights of speech, publication and association. These rights are integral to democracy because they make possible free discussion and the *continuous* participation of the people in the Government, not only at the time of the general elections. Free discussion is necessary because democracy is based on a belief in the value of individual personality. This implies the obligation to respect the other man, to listen to his arguments and to take into account his point of view. Its classical expression is to be found in the saying attributed to Helvetius : ' I detest your opinions, but I will contend to the death for your right to utter them.' The process of law-making should therefore allow full scope for the consideration of different and opposing viewpoints. Those who are adversely affected by a law must feel that their case has been properly heard.

Free discussion, free association and periodical elections ensure another essential of democracy, which it is important to note especially in contrast to dictatorship, viz. the possibility of an alternative Government. Where power is conferred permanently, or where, on account of an atmosphere of fear and coercion, people do not feel free to discuss, vote and displace the existing Government if they want to do so, democracy cannot be said to exist, even though the other political rights enumerated continue to be enjoyed by the people.

Conditions of success

The opportunity for political participation, political equality and the possibility of an alternative Government—these make a State democratic in form. In order, however, that democracy may work successfully, certain additional conditions are necessary. Foremost among these is the widespread habit of tolerance and compromise among the members of a community, a sense of ' give and take '. This is necessary because democracy involves the conception of majority rule, and the acquiescence of the minority in the decision of the majority. If either presses its demands at the expense of the other, democracy becomes difficult to work. Such a temper can exist in a society only if there is a general agreement on fundamentals among the members thereof ; it is difficult to secure if there are deep cleavages concerning their fundamental institutions. It is difficult, for instance, to secure compromise where a strong minority believes passionately that private property is theft, whereas the majority believes in its sanctity. That is why political theory has agreed with Mill that it is in general a necessary condition of free institutions that the boundaries of Governments should coincide in the main with those of nationalities. The sense of belonging together creates a readiness on the part of the members of a State to subordinate their differences to the common good.

There must, secondly, be the provision of adequate opportunities for the individual to develop his personality : access to knowledge, through a · system of State-aided free education, security against unemployment, a minimum wage (which should include provision against sickness and for old age), coupled with fair conditions of work, leisure, and some voice in determining the conditions of work to guard against economic slavery. This implies that vast disparities in the distribution of national wealth should be progressively reduced. The connexion between such a postulate and effective democracy is clear : men languishing in want and living under insecure and deleterious conditions of work can hardly be blamed for not taking that intelligent part in the Government which democracy demands. Great accumulations of wealth also lead to an undue influence of money-power in politics, with all its attendant evils.

Democracy demands from the common man a certain level of ability and character : rational conduct and active participation in the Government ; the intelligent understanding of public affairs ; independent judgement ; tolerance and unselfish devotion to public interest. It is the excellence of individual character that has made Switzerland the envy and pattern of modern democracies.

'Survey the countries of the world,' writes Dubs : 'you may find elsewhere greater political achievements, but assuredly in no country will you meet so many good citizens of independent opinions and sound practical judgement ; nowhere so great a number of public men who succeed in fulfilling their functions in minor spheres with dignity and skill ; nowhere so large a proportion of persons who, outside their daily round, interest themselves so keenly in the welfare and in the difficulties of their fellow citizens.'

To equip the citizen for the performance of his civic duties, education ' in the spirit of the constitution ' is necessary. Free and compulsory education is not sufficient ; it must also be suited to the requirements of democracy. It must help to produce thinking human beings, men and women, who will take an intelligent interest in public affairs, and will be critical of the Government, who will be tolerant of views different from their own, and who will not pervert public power to private interest. If, instead, the educational system produces fear, an uncritical herd instinct, selfishness and indifference to common affairs, the Government will sooner or later be turned into a dictatorship, open or veiled.

And, finally, democracy requires proper organization and leadership. Organization is supplied by parties which, in spite of their admitted defects,[1] are essential to the successful working of representative government.

The difficulty and the importance of leadership in democracy arise from two facts :

(*i*) In the complex society of modern days, on most of the questions which matter in government, a general will—in the sense of a clearly desired end related to the means by which this end may be realized—simply does not exist.

(ii) For most people, government is only a part and, with many, the least important part, of the business of life. Earning a living, family and social calls and amusements occupy a good part of their time and attention.

To rouse such men and women to a sense of their common interest and their public duty ; to think out what are, in a given period, the best interests of the community and the means to achieve them ; to present them in a simple, intelligible and interesting form to the common man and get his general (and continuing) consent to them and to reshape them in the light of altered circumstances are the functions of leaders in a democracy. To perform them successfully certain qualities are demanded ; a will directed to a high purpose clearly visualized and courageously pursued ; the instinct of gauging clearly the needs of the people and the initiative to formulate means of realizing them ; the ability to present issues clearly to the people and to arrive at a fair judgement of the content of public opinion at a given time ; self-reliance, honesty and a sense of respon-

---

[1] See below, ch. xxix.

sibility. To the extent that leaders display these qualities, do
they contribute to the success of democracy.

Defects

The history of democracies shows that these conditions are
rarely fulfilled. In practice democracy is the rule of ignorance.
It pays attention to quantity, not to quality ; votes are counted,
not weighed. A large number of citizens still regard government
as something quite apart from the main business of life, in which
they have no vital concern ; they work and play ; practise the
professions and the arts ; plough, sow, harvest, and sell, and
forget that they are the governors. There is a real danger in
democracy that the citizens may not be sufficiently educated to
appreciate the meaning of the issues which come before them at
elections. They may be misled by class passions or by demagogues ; Sir Henry Maine went so far as to say that democracy can
never represent the rule of the many because, as a rule, the
people merely accept the opinions of their leaders.

Further, it may be argued, modern democracy is capitalistic,
i.e. the political State represents nothing but the rule of a propertied oligarchy—an opinion held particularly by socialists. The
principle and the practice of representation are also faulty. No
man, says Cole, can represent another ; at best one can represent
only a function.[1] As it is, a representative knows enough of
everything to do everything badly, and enough of nothing to do
anything well. Even granting that territorial representation is free
from defects of principle, in practice it rarely achieves the purposes of representation. True representation is secured only if
Parliament represents every element and every interest in the
nation in proportion to its relation to the whole. But Parliament
is rarely ' a mirror of the nation '. Moreover, democracy in
practice is too slow in arriving at a decision as it has to consult
a number of interests ; as Baldwin said, it is always two years
behind dictatorship.

There are some who question the fundamental principles of
democracy, viz. political equality and majority rule. Thus,
according to Voltaire,[2] equality is a myth. ' . . . it is as
impossible for men to be equal as it is impossible for two professors in theology not to be jealous of each other '. According to Burke, decision by a majority is not a law of nature.

[1] See above, p. 124.
[2] *Voltaire's Philosophical Dictionary*, selected and translated by
H. I. Wolfe, London, 1929.

The smaller number may be the stronger force and may have all the reason against the mere impetuous appetite of the majority. There is as little of utility or policy as there is of right in the maxim that the will of a mere majority should be law. The fascists similarly condemn the principle : except, they say, among a body of specially competent judges, the majority has no greater likelihood of having reason on its side than the minority has.

Above all, democracy is a difficult form of government, for the assumptions on which it rests are difficult of fulfilment. It assumes civic capacity on the part of the citizens. This capacity, according to Bryce, involves three qualities : *intelligence, self-control* and *conscience*. The citizen must be able to understand the interests of the community, to subordinate his own will to the general will and must feel his responsibility to the community and be prepared to serve it by voting and by choosing the best men. Bryce, in a classic analysis, points out that in practice these assumptions have not been adequately fulfilled. Instead, *indolence* makes itself felt in the neglect to vote, the neglect to stand as a candidate for election, and the neglect to study and reflect on public questions ; *private self-interest* reveals itself in the buying of votes, in class legislation and in other forms of corruption ; *party spirit* kills independent judgement.

Merits

Democracy, with all its defects, implies a recognition of the duties of government and the rights of the people. It postulates a measure of personal freedom and equal consideration for all classes. As John Stuart Mill said, it is superior to other forms of government because the rights and interests of every person are secure from being disregarded only when the person interested is himself able and habitually disposed to ' stand up ' for them ; and the general prosperity attains a greater height and is more widely diffused in proportion to the amount and variety of the personal energies enlisted in promoting it. The participation in governmental affairs lifts the individual above the narrow circle of his egoism and broadens his interests. It makes him interested in his country and gives him a sense of responsibility.

According to MacIver,[1] in democracy the Government is less dependent on the psychology of power than in other forms of government. Always those who wield power are tempted to

[1] *The Modern State*, p. 229.

extol it, but the more so if that power is unchecked and irresponsible. Democracy makes authority a trust ; the common interest, the common welfare, becomes the sole justification of government.

It is the importance which a democratic system attaches to human personality that makes it valuable. The democratic method is to reach decision by discussion, argument and persuasion. Democracy does not believe in suppression of thought.

And, finally, the standard by which one can measure the merit of a form of government, says Byrce, is the adequacy with which it performs the chief functions of government : the protection from internal and external enemies, the securing of justice, the efficient administration of common affairs. History shows that these functions have been carried out as well by democracies as by any other form of government. If democracy has failed to subdue the clash of capital and labour, to establish peace between nations, and to abolish corruption, it is because no form of government can be expected to accomplish a revolution in human nature. No realistic thinker regards democracy as the ideal form of government ; it is at best the least objectionable form of government that is practicable. ' Things may be bad today, but they were worse yesterday. As Cavour said, however faulty a legislative chamber may be, an nte-chamber is worse. However grave the indictment that may e brought against democracy, its friends can answer, " What etter alternative do you offer ? " '

The truth seems to be that democracy contains within it the eeds of dissolution and decay, as well as of life and progress. It may conceivably lead to the despotism of a collective mediocrity, the negation of freedom, the free play of self-interest, and the deterioration of individual and national character. But under favourable conditions it encourages the intelligence, self-reliance, initiative and social sense of free men by placing the ultimate responsibility for government on the citizens themselves ; it makes authority a trust, and ensures equal consideration for all. Its success depends on the spiritual effort the people put forth and the readjustment of democratic institutions in accordance with changing conditions.

SELECT BIBLIOGRAPHY

A. APPADORAI, *Revision of Democracy,* Oxford, 1940
R. BASSETT, *The Essentials of Parliamentary Democracy,* Macmillan, 1935

J. K. Bluntschli, *The Theory of the State*, bk. VI, Oxford, 3rd ed., 1921

E. F. Bowman, *An Introduction to Political Science*, Pt. I, Methuen, 1931

J. Bryce, *Modern Democracies*, Macmillan, 1923-9

C. D. Burns, *Democracy, Its Defects and Advantages*, Allen & Unwin, 1929

G. E. G. Catlin, *Systematic Politics*, ch. v-vi, Allen & Unwin, 1962

E. Faguet, *The Cult of Incompetence*, Murray, 1911

J. W. Garner, *Introduction to Political Science*, ch. vi, American Book Co., 1910

A. D. Lindsay, *The Essentials of Democracy*, Oxford, 2nd ed., 1935

H. S. Maine, *Popular Government*, John Murray, 1918

J. S. Mill, *Representative Government*, 'World's Classics' No. 170, Oxford, 1912

C. N. Parkinson, *The Evolution of Political Thought*, University of London Press, 1958

E. Simon and Others, *Constructive Democracy*, Allen & Unwin, 1938

CHAPTER XI

INTERNATIONAL RELATIONS

§1 NATIONALISM: MERITS AND DEFECTS

WE have earlier referred to the fact that the freedom of the individual is considerably affected not only by the form of government but also by the relations of his State with other States, and, therefore, these inter-State relations are of great importance to political theory. To this subject we must now turn.

Modern States are sovereign States. They are, therefore, independent in relation to other States. They do not brook interference from other peoples. Further, they are in general organized upon a national basis and unified by national sentiment. Two things, as Renan insisted,[1] go to make up this sentiment.

'One of these lies in the past, the other in the present. The one is the possession in common of a rich heritage of memories ; and the other is actual agreement, the desire to live together, and the will to continue to make the most of the joint inheritance ... To share the glories of the past, and a common will in the present, to have done great deeds together, and to desire to do more—these are the essential conditions of a people's being.'

Modern nationalism is a powerful sentiment ; whether it is good or bad depends upon how we are able to organize and use it for constructive ends. That it has considerable merits is now generally recognized. First, it rescues the world, as Burgess recognized,[2] from the monotony of the universal empire. This is an indispensable condition of political progress. ' We advance politically, as well as individually, by contact, competition and antagonism. The universal empire suppresses all this in its universal reign of peace, which means, in the long run, stagnation and despotism.' Just as the destruction of individuality may destroy genius, so the attempt to make all groups of men exactly alike in their customs or creeds may destroy some special character of endurance or wit, which may be developed even in a small

---

[1] 'What is a Nation ?' in *Modern Political Doctrines*, ed. by A. Zimmern, pp. 202-3.
[2] J. W. Burgess, *Political Science and Constitutional Law*, Vol. I, pp. 38-9.

nation. 'There is some special quality in every group,' says Burns,[1] 'which it would be well for the sake of the whole of humanity to preserve. But this can only be preserved if the group has an opportunity for characteristic development of its own laws and institutions.' Nationalism is but a recognition of the principle that States should vary in their methods of law and government, reflecting in their variety the distinctions of human groups. Not only does each nation gain in its individuality, but humanity as a whole thereby adds to its cultural wealth. 'For the human race is not at its best when every man or every group is a copy of every other. Civilization progresses by differentiation as well as by assimilation of interests and character.'

Secondly, States that are unified by national sentiment are always more stable and their laws are always better obeyed than States that are only held together by subjection to a common authority. Moreover, it is only in national States that the institutions of self-government can ever work properly, because it is only in these States that the people can sympathize with one another sufficiently to be willing to submit to the decisions of a majority. In the words of Burgess : 'The national State solves the problem of the relation of sovereignty to liberty ; so that while it is the most powerful political organization that the world has ever produced, it is still the freest.'[2]

But the great defect of nationalism is that it contains within it the possible source of its own destruction, and, unless carefully guarded against exaggeration, will of itself lead to a disturbance of the equilibrium upon which the diversity of our civilization depends. 'Within the latter half of the nineteenth century, nationalism has been thus exaggerated ; going beyond a healthy desire to express the true native characteristics of a people, it has come, in some quarters, to mean the decrying, as barbarous or decadent, of everything originating outside of the national boundary.'[3] It becomes exclusive. This exclusiveness leads to two evil consequences of the first magnitude.

(*i*) *Economic*. It makes the optimum utilization of the world's economic resources impossible. Ever since the Industrial Revolution, the world has economically been more and more unified. Distance has been reduced. The countries of the world have become more than ever interdependent in respect of capital,

[1] C. D. Burns, *Political Ideals*, p. 179.
[2] op. cit., pp. 38-9.
[3] P. S. Reinsch, *World Politics*, pp. 3-7.

raw materials, skilled labour and markets. Interdependence is a reality ; but, with its trade restrictions and tariffs, its customs and its quotas, the nation-State sets up barriers between itself and its neighbours and thereby prevents the free flow of trade : the result is an imperfect utilization of the world's economic resources. As Joad puts it effectively :

'On the one side — the side of technology, economics and common sense—is a manifest drive to unity ; and on the other— the side of politics, pugnacity and reaction—are the nation-States that impede and obstruct it : on the one hand, the revolution in living caused by the changes in our environment ; on the other, the obsolete divisions of mankind which the State exists to perpetuate : on the one hand, the gradual shrinking in the size of the world ; on the other, the nation-States whom the shrinking has squeezed so closely together that, unless they can be superseded before it is too late, they will grind one another to pieces.' [1]

(*ii*) *Political*. Nationalism has been throughout the modern era the most fruitful cause of wars, divided nations striving for unity, subject nations fighting for freedom, triumphant nations aspiring after domination. It has fostered national arrogance ; each nation looks upon itself as the bearer of the only true civi lization. It has ' almost obliterated the sense that civilization is a collective achievement and common responsibility'. It becomes aggressive and regardless of the rights of other nations, and thus a menace to the peace of the world. This menace, it ought to be added, has assumed alarming proportions in recent times with the increase in the destructiveness of modern warfare.

§2 COLLECTIVE SECURITY

The only remedy is, in Laski's pregnant phrase, to equate nationalism with ' right '. Nations must agree to the principle that, in matters which touch more than one nation, they will be bound by the decision arrived at by a common international body, in which all nations are in some way represented. Such matters are : territorial boundaries, international migration, armaments, tariffs, privileges of national minorities, international communications, foreign capital. Briefly, the external sovereignty claimed by nation-States must be restricted in these matters. There must be the rule of law between nations as there is the rule of law between individuals within each State.

[1] In his Foreword to Duncan and Elizabeth Wilson's *Federation and World Order*, p. xii.

The implications of the rule of law between nations are far-reaching, and can be fully grasped only by contrast with the conception which now rules, viz. the rule of might. Under the present system, or lack of system, when a nation's interests are supposed to conflict with those of another, the nation concerned resorts to war to secure its interests. This necessarily involves the idea of national security, i.e. States which are judges in their own disputes can use war as an instrument of national policy and must try individually or through alliances to be stronger than every other State or group of States. But the world wars of 1914-18 and 1939-45 have been slowly teaching mankind the painful lesson that a system of national security is really impossible for all at the same time, or even for a few for all time. This indeed is inherent in the logic of facts : *every* State or group of States cannot be stronger than *every* other State or group. Might cannot be the basis of right.

What then is the alternative? The answer is the rule of law and collective security. This means three things :

(*i*) States must agree to the principle that, in matters which affect other States besides their own, they will accept the rule of conduct laid down by a common international authority as binding on themselves.

(*ii*) They must agree to renounce the right to settle disputes by making war.

(*iii*) They must ' bind themselves to regard any act of war by any State in breach of this primary obligation as an act of war against themselves and to come to the assistance of the victim of the aggression '.[1]

If every State realizes the truth of these three principles and acts up to them, collective security is assured : the knowledge that an act of war against one is an act of war against all is sufficient inhibition to any possible aggression in violation of international law. There will be the rule of law, not of might ; there will be collective security, which will include national security.

§3 ATTEMPTS AT INTERNATIONAL ORGANIZATION

There are two ways of establishing the rule of law and collective security : the voluntary acceptance of the principle symbolized in a league of sovereign nations and the establishment of

[1] *The Political Quarterly*, Vol. VII, 1936, p. 334.

a super-State. The League of Nations (1919) is an illustration of the first ; Streit's proposal for a federation of democracies gives us some idea of the second.[1]

The idea of establishing some inter-State organization for the prevention of wars can be traced at least as early as the fourteenth century.[2] In his work, *The Recovery of the Holy Land* (*circa* 1305), Pierre Dubois suggested international arbitration and the establishment of an international Judiciary. The letters of Erasmus (1466-1536) mention some schemes for establishing a League of Peace. In the seventeenth century, Grotius (*The Law of War and Peace,* 1625) and his schools formulated some principles which should govern the relations of States towards one another, without, however, suggesting any organization to enforce them. The French writer Abbé de St Pierre in the eighteenth century proposed[3] a federation of nineteen States for the maintenance of peace. Kant, the German philosopher, in his work *On Perpetual Peace* (1795), suggested that something in the nature of a federation between nations for the sole purpose of doing away with war was the only rightful condition of things reconcilable with individual freedom.

The tendency to joint action, as distinguished from theoretical schemes, is noticeable in the Holy Alliance (September 1815) and the Hague Conferences (1899 and 1907).

The Holy Alliance was formed between Russia, Prussia and Austria. The signatories declared their

' fixed resolution both in the administration of their respective States, and in their political relations with every other Government, to take for their sole guide the precepts of that Holy Religion, namely, the precepts of justice, Christian charity and peace, which, far from being applicable only to private concerns, must have an immediate influence on the councils of princes, and guide all their steps, as being the only means of consolidating human institutions and remedying their imperfections. They mutually promise to remain united by the bonds of a true and indissoluble fraternity, and, considering each other as fellow countrymen, they will on all occasions and in all places, lend each other aid and assistance ; and, regarding themselves towards their subjects and armies as fathers of families, they will lead them in

---

[1] See below, §6.
[2] Burns, op. cit., pp. 305-16, gives a convenient summary of ideas and schemes of international organization prior to 1914.
[3] In his work *Projet de traité pour rendre la paix perpétuelle entre les souverains chrétiens* (1713-17).

the same spirit of fraternity with which they are animated, to protect religion, peace and justice.'

Many rulers of Europe, out of deference to the Tsar of Russia, signed the treaty and were duly admitted to the Holy Alliance. The vagueness of its terms and the failure of its signatories to do it more than lip service led to its failure.

The Concert of Europe was a quadruple alliance between Russia, Austria, Prussia and Britain (formed after the close of the Napoleonic wars) by which the participants pledged themselves to maintain the exclusion of the house of Bonaparte from France and further agreed to meet together at agreed periods to discuss their common interests and matters affecting the peace and security of Europe. The Concert was not able to achieve much because, in the words of Fisher, ' the union of the powers was more apparent than real '; differences in points of view began to develop, and by 1822 it became ineffective.

The Hague Conferences were summoned to meet (at the Hague) in 1899 and 1907 on the initiative of the Tsar of Russia to promote peace and disarmament. At the first conference twenty-six States were represented, and at the second forty-four. The mutual suspicion of Germany, Russia and Britain led to the failure of these conferences ; but they resulted in ' the ultimate establishment of an international tribunal at the Hague which contributed to the settlement of many international disputes by arbitration, and led the way to the greater efforts towards international organization made at the end of the Great War '.

§4 THE LEAGUE OF NATIONS

These early attempts at international organization were halfhearted and inadequate. Besides, there was no permanent organization of a political character to bring the nations together to enable them to understand one another's point of view, settle disputes and avert war. The League of Nations was established in 1919 to remove these defects, promote international co-operation and achieve international peace and security.

The essential conceptions underlying the League of Nations Covenant may be analysed under six headings :

(*i*) The causes of war must be removed. Members recognized that this demanded the reduction of national armaments to the lowest point consistent with national safety, and the enforcement by common action of international obligations. They also undertook to respect and to preserve, as against external aggression, the territorial integrity and political independence of members of the League. Treaties between States were also to be registered with the Secretariat of the League, to be published by it as soon as possible, for secret treaties, it was realized, had often encouraged wars.[1]

(*ii*) If a dispute arose between nations, certain procedures were laid down to prevent its leading to war. Any threat of war was declared a common concern of the League; members agreed that any dispute likely to lead to rupture should be submitted to arbitration, to judicial settlement, or to inquiry by the League Council and they agreed never to resort to war until three months after the award by the arbitrators, or the judicial decisions, or the report by the Council. They also agreed that they would not go to war against any State which complied with the award, decision, or the recommendations of the report.[2]

(*iii*) If, in disregard of the obligations accepted, a member resorted to war, provision was made to help those member-States who stood by their promises. Members therefore agreed to subject the covenant-breaking State to

'the severance of all trade or financial relations, the prohibition of all intercourse between their nationals and the nationals of the covenant-breaking State and the preventing of all financial, commercial, or personal intercourse between the nationals of the covenant-breaking State and nationals of any other State, whether a member of the League or not.'

It was the duty of the League Council to 'recommend to the several Governments concerned what effective military, naval or air force the members of the League' were 'severally to contribute to the armed forces to protect the Covenants of the League'.[3]

(*iv*) The organization of peace was as essential as the prevention of war. Members agreed accordingly to secure and maintain fair and humane conditions of labour; to entrust the League with the general supervision of the trade in arms and ammunition with the countries in which the control of this traffic was necessary in the common interest; and to make provision to secure and maintain freedom of communications and of transit and equitable treatment for the commerce of all members of the League.[4]

---

[1] Articles 8, 10 and 18 of the Covenant.   [2] Articles 11-15.
[3] Article 16.   [4] Article 23.

(*v*) The well-being and development of the people of the colonies and territories lost by the Central Powers (in the war of 1914-18) formed a sacred trust of civilization. Therefore, members agreed that the tutelage of such peoples was to be entrusted to advanced nations who were to exercise such tutelage as mandatories on behalf of the League.[1]

(*vi*) Permanent institutions were to be created to carry out the objects of the League. Provision was therefore made to organize an Assembly, a Council, a Secretariat, and a Court of International Justice.[2]

All the members of the League were represented on a footing of complete equality in the Assembly, where they had only one vote and not more than three delegates each. The Assembly was authorized to deal with any matter within the sphere of action of the League or affecting the peace of the world.

The Council was originally to be composed of nine members : five Great Powers as permanent members and four non-permanent States elected by the Assembly. Later the permanent members were reduced to four, and the non-permanent members increased to nine. The idea of this distinction between permanent and non-permanent seats was that 'the great Powers, having world-wide interests and heavy political and other responsibilities, must have permanent seats on the Council', while for other Powers the principle of representation by a few countries, elected from time to time by the Assembly, could be accepted without injustice. The Council met more frequently than the Assembly. More than the Assembly, it was in practice responsible for carrying on the work of the League. It appointed and controlled various committees, appointed the Secretary-General with the permission of a majority of the Assembly, prepared the agenda for the Assembly and was generally authorized, like the Assembly, 'to deal with any matter within the sphere of action of the League or affecting the peace of the world'.

The Secretariat, the permanent organization of the League, was appointed by the Secretary-General with the consent of the Council. It stood in roughly the same relation towards the Council and the Assembly as ministerial departments stand towards their national Governments. It collected material before the actual proceedings, and afterwards carried out the decisions taken. At the same time, it provided the necessary continuity between one meeting of the Council or Assembly and the next. The expenses were met out of contributions made by members of the League.

[1] Article 22.   [2] Article 2-7.

The permanent Court of International Justice, which was set up in 1920-2, and sat at the Hague, had eleven judges and four deputy judges elected for nine years by the Assembly and the Council. It settled such disputes between States as were referred to it and were capable of judicial settlement and gave opinions on matters referred to it by the Council or the Assembly.

There was also an auxiliary to the League, viz. the International Labour Office,[1] which tried to secure and maintain fair and humane conditions of labour for men, women and children.

§5 RECORD OF THE LEAGUE

It is now a definitely established fact that, while the League appreciably succeeded in minor spheres of activity, it clearly failed to achieve its primary purpose of maintaining international peace and security.

That the League had a measure of success in minor spheres deserves to be better known, as such knowledge will prevent the wholesale condemnation of it implied by descriptions such as the 'Geneva Council of Fools' and the 'League of Notions'. Thus (*i*) it helped to settle inter-Statal disputes 'when both parties to a dispute were genuinely attached to peace'. Examples of such settlements are the frontier dispute between Turkey and Iraq (1924-6) and the dispute between Colombia and Peru regarding the Leticia Trapezium (1931-5).[2] (*ii*) It helped, through the Mandate system, to improve the standard of colonial administration. (*iii*) It focused attention on the necessity for the fair treatment of minorities, though it did not always succeed in compelling fair treatment. (*iv*) It administered two territories, viz. the Saar and the City of Danzig, with some success. (*v*) The Permanent Court of International Justice delivered over sixty judgements and opinions. Its reputation for impartiality was so great that more than once a dispute which arose between a powerful State and one far less powerful was settled in the latter's favour; whereupon the powerful State invariably yielded with a good grace. (*vi*) Through the International Labour Office, attempts were made to improve the conditions of labour. (*vii*) It achieved marked success in its efforts at international financial settlement as in its reconstruction scheme in Austria (1921-2). (*viii*) Through its technical and social organizations, it helped

---

[1] This organization still exists as an auxiliary to the United Nations and continues to do good work.

[2] For details of these disputes, refer to *The Aims, Methods and Activity of the League of Nations*, 1935.

to promote international co-operation in economic and social matters. Thus, as a result of conferences in 1921 and 1923 on Communications and Transport, an agreement was arrived at, and ratified by thirty-four States, that all goods transported by rail or inland water-way, whatever their country of origin or destination, should, subject to agreed restrictions, enjoy complete freedom of transit under absolutely equal conditions. The Health Organization set up by the League helped to co-ordinate the efforts of various European Governments to combat the typhus, cholera and smallpox epidemics, and to conduct research work on the prevention of such diseases as malaria and tuberculosis. Through the League Committee on Intellectual Co-operation, attempts were made to assist States in the improvement of their educational service, to promote the disinterested discussion of intellectual subjects and spread the ideals of peace. The prevention of forced labour from developing into virtual slavery, and of traffic in women and children, the promotion of child welfare and the supervision of the drug traffic — these are other aspects of social work which engaged the attention of the League.

But, as we have stated earlier, the League failed to settle disputes between powerful States. Thus in 1931-3 it was unable to settle the Sino-Japanese dispute. In 1931 Japanese troops invaded Manchuria; China appealed to the League; the League appointed a Commission of Inquiry and on its recommendations drew up a report (1933). The Japanese Government did not accept the League proposals, but continued to fight, and later withdrew from the League. Similarly, in 1934-6, the League's advice was not heeded by Italy. Italy invaded Abyssinia in disregard of her international obligations; the League offered a solution which was rejected by Italy. Then, for the first time in history, about fifty States joined, though without success, to apply the 'sanctions' laid down in Article 16 of the League Covenant against Italy, by imposing an embargo on imports to their countries from Italy, and on the export of arms, etc. to Italy. Italy conquered Abyssinia and left the League. The failure to settle these disputes apart, the general weakness of the League lay in its inability to bring about disarmament, in the continuance of secret treaties, in the disregard paid to it in important international agreements like the 'Munich Pact' (1938) and, above all, in the recurrence of a second disastrous world war within twenty-five years. The League formally ceased to exist in 1947.

How can we explain this failure? What were the defects of the League? Some are clear enough : the League was not comprehensive enough, as the United States of America remained

outside it, and, later, Japan, Germany and Italy left it; it was
tied to a vindictive treaty, the Treaty of Versailles, and so was
suspected of being a mere tool in the hands of the 'have' as
distinguished from the 'have-not' powers; secession from the
League was easy; its representatives were sent by the Governments, and were not elected by the people, of the member-States;
the League lacked all sovereign power. The 'failure' of the
League must, however, be mainly attributed to the fact that too
much was expected of it. To expect that the establishment of
the League of Nations would mean the elimination of power
from international relations, and the substitution of discussion for
armies and navies, was but wishful thinking. Power held in reserve
has always played an important part — both before the League
was founded and after — in international politics. The best evi-·
dence of this is the tendency, in the politics of the League, shown
by the minor powers to follow the lead given by the greater.

'The decisions on the application of sanctions against Italy in
1935-6 were, in effect, taken solely by Great Britain and France,
the possessors of effective military and economic power in the
Mediterranean . . . When France was militarily supreme in Europe
in the first years after the War, a number of smaller Powers
grouped themselves under her aegis. When German military
strength eclipsed that of France, most of these Powers made
declarations of neutrality or veered to the side of Germany.'[1]

Power, then, is a fact. The League could have succeeded in its
primary object only if the statesmen in the powerful nations
were prepared to use the power of their States on the side of
the League and Collective Security. But events show clearly that
the statesmen were not prepared for anything of the sort. 'When
the Covenant appeared to require action which might have entailed
practical consequences for the mass of the people, successive
Governments preferred inaction.'[2] The best evidence of this is
the unwillingness of Britain and France to apply 'oil sanctions'
against Italy in 1936. Statesmen preached big things, but did
little. Political hypocrisy reached its zenith. The promoters of
war were preaching peace.

'I cannot recall any time,' Winston Churchill said, 'when the
gap between the kind of words which statesmen used and what
was actually happening in many countries was so great as it is now.'

---

[1] E. H Carr, *The Twenty Years' Crisis*, 1919-39, p. 134.
[2] ibid., p. 22.

Only the ideal of the League remained. In so far as it expressed and embodied the general interest of all nations in the preservation of peace, and made such preservation a collective responsibility in which every nation had to take a more and more effective share, it rendered useful service ; in other words, its merit lay in its potentialities, not in its actual achievements. Any State which wished to avoid war had in the League the means of showing the world the genuineness of its wish. The shortcomings were not so much in the League as in people and their Governments, who, even with the best intentions, were too often held back by timidity, by routine, by prejudice, and could not see where their duty lay or were not prepared to do it.

§6 PROPOSALS FOR A FEDERAL UNION

The failure of the League experiment gave rise to new proposals regarding international organization. Thus Oscar Newfang suggested [1] the conversion of the League of Nations into a world federation with a world Legislature, world Executive and world Court.

Streit [2] contemplated a federal union of fifteen democracies to start with — the United States, Great Britain, five of the dominions (Canada, Australia, New Zealand, South Africa, Eire), France, Belgium, Holland, Switzerland, and the four Scandinavian States (Denmark, Norway, Sweden and Finland), having between them a population of more than 300 millions. These States would hand over to the federal authority certain of their sovereign powers including, in the political field, the raising of armed forces, the conduct of diplomacy and the making of treaties and the decision upon peace and war, and, in the economic field, the regulation of tariffs, currency and immigration. We start with democracies (according to Streit) because the world order is to be based on the principle of freedom, and because common ideals of government among the units would facilitate the smooth working of the federation. Other States might later be admitted if they accepted the ideals of the federal union.

Jennings [3] put in a plea for a federation of Western Europe. To start with, it would include thirteen democracies : France, Germany (democratized), Switzerland, Luxembourg, Belgium, Holland, the United Kingdom, Eire, Denmark, Sweden, Finland,

[1] *World Federation*, 1939.
[2] C. K. Streit, *Union Now*, 1939.
[3] W. Ivor Jennings, *A Federation for Western Europe*, 1940.

Norway and Iceland. With the extension of the democratic system to the other States in Europe, they might of course be admitted. Defence, foreign policy, commerce and inter-State trade would be the main federal subjects.

It is unnecessary to mention other proposals of a similar nature. They all agree in advocating a federal union of nations. A federal union means that, in respect of the subjects transferred to the federal authority, the citizens of each member-State will have to obey a Government other than their own — a Government in which no doubt they will have *some*, but not the *sole*, voice in determining policy. Federation essentially means a division of powers and double allegiance. It means, in effect, nothing less than the surrender by the nation-State of part of its sovereignty. The minimum federal subjects, all our writers are agreed, are defence and foreign affairs; other common affairs may or may not be transferred to the federal authority.

The case for federal union is in theory unassailable — that the insecurity men live under cannot be ended without abolishing war and ensuring world peace; and world peace can be ensured only by establishing world government. This view is proved by the facts of history, positive and negative — the history of how individuals have been able to provide for their security through government, and the history of how States have been unable to provide for national security without a common Government. In early societies the individual relied upon his own strength for security. At a later stage, he sought the help of neighbours; but his security did not become assured until a police force was permanently established, and the force at the command of the individual correspondingly reduced. The overwhelming force at the command of the State is used to give security to all alike, to see that no one takes the law into his own hands. Disputes between individuals are referred to a common court and enforced by a common Executive.

Nations have been passing through a similar evolution. At first each nation had to rely on its individual strength, then they tried alliances only to provoke stronger counter-alliances. The League of Nations foundered on the rock of national sovereignty. It is indeed possible to argue that but for a series of accidents — the absence of the United States of America, the absence of an Anglo-American guarantee to France, a vindictive peace—the League might have been stronger; but its fundamental weakness remained : it was not an agency of government. It had no money-raising or coercive power; and it is a lesson of history that a single, effective, acceptable authority throughout the whole area

in which the peace is to be kept is a *sine qua non*. The League
method cannot prevent war, because it cannot do justice when
justice conflicts with sovereignty and because it leaves war as the
ultimate instrument of international policy. The obvious remedy is
to have a common coercive authority to enforce decisions on certain
matters of common interest; that authority will also, through its
court, declare where justice lies in disputes between States.

There is, secondly, the economic argument. Ever since the
Industrial Revolution, the countries of the world have become
more than ever economically interdependent. Interdependence is
a reality; the existence of separate States is a historical accident.
The sovereign State has therefore become an anachronism. What
concerns all must be decided by all. Nationalism must be equated
with right.

Thirdly, the changes in the technique of war and the increased
power of the means of destruction, particularly through the use
of the atomic bomb, emphasize the necessity for preventing war.
The only alternative to it is the destruction of civilization.

And, finally, while its practicability (in the sense of the people
concerned being persuaded to attempt it) may be debated, there
is no doubt that if by some miracle it is brought into existence,
it is possible to work it. The history of federal Governments
everywhere is conclusive evidence.

But can the peoples concerned be persuaded to agree to join a
federal union? While, for the reasons given above, federalism may
well be the ultimate objective, it does not seem practicable in the
immediate present. A federal union must take into account not only
the hopes but the experience of mankind. The necessary conditions
hardly exist as yet. Lord Bryce has said that the permanence
of an institution depends not merely on the material interests that
support it, but on its conformity with the deep-seated sentiment
of the men for whom it has been made. It is futile to contend
that there is anywhere, even in democratic countries, anything
more than a superficial, and therefore deceptive, sentiment in
favour of a super-State. Nations are still unprepared for a sacrifice of their sovereignty.

§7 THE UNITED NATIONS

It is against this background that we must judge the value of
the United Nations Organization, which came into existence on
24 October 1945, when twenty-nine States signified their acceptance of the United Nations Charter framed at San Francisco.

The basic features of the new scheme are as follows: Any peace-loving State may become a member of the Organization. It has six main organs : a General Assembly, a Security Council, an Economic and Social Council, a Trusteeship Council, an International Court of Justice, and a Secretariat.

(*i*) *The General Assembly* consists of not more than five representatives from each member-State ; each State has, however, only one vote. Its functions are primarily to promote international co-operation in economic, social, cultural, educational and medical fields ; to assist in the realization of human rights and fundamental freedoms for all, without distinction of race, sex, language or religion, and, in this connexion, to establish a Commission on Human Rights ; to promote higher standards of living, full employment and conditions of economic and social progress and development; to promote the development and codification of international law ; to deal with colonial trusteeships for non-strategic areas and to recommend measures for the peaceful adjustment of any situation likely to impair the general welfare or friendly relations among nations—subject to the important limitations that the Assembly is prohibited from making recommendations on its own initiative on any matter relating to the maintenance of international peace and security, which is being dealt with by the Security Council, and that any questions on which action is necessary should be referred to the Security Council by the General Assembly either before or after discussion.[1]

The Assembly elects (*a*) the ten non-permanent members of the Security Council ; (*b*) the twenty-seven members of the Economic and Social Council ; (*c*) some members of the Trusteeship Council ;[2] and (*d*) the Secretary-General (on the recommendation of the Security Council).

The admission of new members of the Organization, and their suspension and dismissal, are also made by the Assembly upon the recommendation of the Security Council.

(*ii*) *The Security Council* of fifteen (enlarged in 1965) consists of two classes of members : the five permanent and the ten non-permanent. Permanent members are from China, France, the Union of Soviet Socialist Republics, the United Kingdom and the United States. The ten non-permanent members are elected by the Assembly for two years ;[3] a retiring member is not eligible for immediate re-election.

---

[1] See pp. 160, 164-65 below.　　　[2] See p. 161 below.
[3] The non-permanent members in January 1970 were Burundi, Columbia, Finland, Nepal, Nicaragua, Poland, Sierra Leone, Spain, Syria and Zambia.

In the context of security, the Security Council is the most important body in the new Organization. Within the Security Council effective influence is wielded by the permanent members. The Charter specifically confers on the Security Council primary responsibility for the maintenance of international security ; all members of the Organization are asked to obligate themselves to accept the decisions of the Security Council and to carry them out. It is the function of the Security Council to investigate any dispute or any situation the continuance of which might lead to international friction or give rise to a dispute ; to call upon States to settle their disputes by negotiation, mediation, conciliation, arbitration or judicial settlement or other peaceful means of their own choice ; to recommend to States appropriate procedures or methods of adjustment of disputes likely to endanger the maintenance of international security ; to determine whether any situation threatens peace or involves a breach of the peace, and to take any measures necessary to maintain or restore international peace ; to take diplomatic, economic and other measures to give effect to its decisions, and to employ air, naval or land forces to maintain or restore international peace, if measures short of force prove inadequate. (It is to be made clear to the Security Council from whom and when it would obtain the military forces that might be needed to check aggression, for agreements governing the number and type of forces and the nature of the facilities and assistance to be provided are to be negotiated between the Security Council and the members of the United Nations. The Security Council could call upon some or all members to make available the forces, facilities or assistance thus agreed upon, including national air force contingents which member-States would hold *immediately* available to enable urgent military measures to be taken by the Organization.) The admission of new States to the Organization and their expulsion from it and the suspension of their rights can only be made on the recommendation of the Security Council. Further, as mentioned earlier, the General Assembly is prohibited from making recommendations on its own initiative on any matter relating to the maintenance of international peace and security which is being dealt with by the Security Council, and any questions on which action is necessary should be referred to the Security Council by the General Assembly either before or after discussion.[1]

The emphasis, within the Security Council, on its permanent members is indicated by the requirements that (*a*) the concurring

---

[1] See pp. 164-65 below for recent modifications.

votes of permanent members are required for all vital decisions of the Security Council affecting security; (*b*) the Military Staff Committee, which is to assist the Security Council in its military functions, should be composed of the Chiefs of Staff of the permanent members of the Council or their representatives.

(*iii*) *The Economic and Social Council* now consists of twenty-seven members of the United Nations elected by the General Assembly; members serve for nine years, one-third retiring triennially.

This Council may (*a*) make or initiate studies and reports with respect to international, economic, social, cultural, educational, health, and related matters, and make recommendations on any such matters to the Assembly and to the members of the United Nations; (*b*) make recommendations for the purpose of promoting respect for, and observance of, human rights and fundamental freedoms for all; (*c*) prepare draft conventions, for submission to the General Assembly, on matters falling within its competence; (*d*) call international conferences on economic and social matters; and (*e*) co-ordinate the activities of specialized agencies such as the Food and Agriculture Organization.

(*iv*) *The Trusteeship Council* is composed of the following members of the United Nations :

(*a*) Those administering trust territories.[1]

(*b*) Those States among France, China, the U.S.S.R., the United Kingdom and the United States of America which are not administering trust territories.

(*c*) As many other members elected for three-year terms by the Assembly as may be necessary to ensure that the total number of members of the Trusteeship Council is equally divided between those members of the United Nations which administer trust territories and those which do not.

The primary function of the Trusteeship Council is to see to the attainment in non-strategic areas of the objectives of the trusteeship system, which are primarily

' to promote the political, economic, social and educational advancement of the inhabitants of the trust territories and their progressive development towards self-government or independence as may be appropriate to the particular circumstances of each

---

[1] Trust territories are territories placed under the international trusteeship system (*a*) voluntarily by States responsible for their administration; or (*b*) detached from enemy States as a result of the last war and placed in that category; or (*c*) now held under mandate and placed under the trusteeship system by means of agreements.

territory and its peoples and the freely expressed wishes of the peoples concerned '.

(v) *The International Court of Justice.* The purposes of the United Nations Charter include the adjustment or settlement of international disputes ' in conformity with the principles of justice and international law '. The International Court of Justice (consisting of fifteen judges elected by the General Assembly and the Security Council meeting separately — a candidate being declared elected on securing a majority of the votes of both the Assembly and the Security Council) is the instrument of the United Nations to effect this purpose in the case of justiciable disputes referred to the Court by the parties. The judges are elected for a term of nine years : they may be re-elected. Where disputes are referred to the Court, or where member-States accept the compulsory jurisdiction of the Court in certain categories of cases, its decisions are, of course, binding upon the parties. Moreover, under the Charter, all members of the United Nations undertake to comply with the decisions of the Court. Where a party to a case decided by the Court fails to comply with its decision, the matter may be brought to the attention of the Security Council for appropriate action.

(vi) *The Secretariat* comprises a Secretary-General and such staff as the Organization may require. The Secretary-General is the chief administrative officer of the Organization, and is appointed by the General Assembly upon the recommendation of the Security Council.[1] The staff is appointed by the Secretary-General under regulations established by the General Assembly.

§8 DIFFICULTIES AND WEAKNESSES OF THE U.N.

The history of the U.N. since 1945, and more especially the Korean crisis of 1950, has brought into relief some difficulties and weaknesses in the present organization for collective security. It is clear that the fear of a possible recurrence of war has not disappeared. Nations are spending on armaments the money and the energy which they should spend on economic development and the provision of social services. Confidence in the ability of the United Nations to provide security, it is clear, has not yet been created though, it may be added, the fact that sixteen member-States were prepared to support the United Nations to stop

---

[1] Dr Trygve Lie (Norway) took office on 2 February 1946 as the first Secretary-General of the United Nations Organization; Mr Dag Hammarskjoeld (Sweden) succeeded him. U Thant (Burma), Secretary-General since 3 November, served from 1961 to 1972. He was succeeded by Kurt Waldheim (Austria).

aggression by North Korea against South Korea and in defence of collective security (1950-1953) and that Britain and France deferred in December 1956 to the United Nations in withdrawing from the Suez war which they had started earlier during the year should help to create greater confidence in the United Nations.[1]

The reasons for this state of affairs are simple. At the time when the Charter was framed in 1945, it was hoped that co-operation between the Soviet Union and the United States, which found such striking expression during the war, would be continued ; but that was not to be. Instead, soon after the war, differences began to develop about Korea, Germany, Japan, the control of atomic energy — and indeed on every political issue of importance. Two blocks gradually emerged, and every crucial question came to be considered from the point of view of its relation to the blocks, and not from the point of view of the United Nations as a whole.

The consequence of such a political climate on the system of collective security provided for in the Charter was disastrous : the machinery essential for it could not be properly built up. Articles 43, 45, 46 and 47 of the Charter are fundamental to that system According to these, the Security Council, with the assistance of the Military Staff Committee, was to negotiate with member-nations agreements for making available to it, at its call, armed forces, assistance and the facilities necessary for maintaining international peace and security. But, because of the political differences referred to earlier, and mutual suspicion, the Military Staff Committee could not function, and no agreements with member-nations could be worked out.

Article 27, paragraph 3, which contained the famous principle of unanimity of the permanent members — that decisions of the Security Council on matters other than procedural 'shall be made by an affirmative vote of seven members, including the concurring votes of the permanent members' (with certain exceptions in respect of the pacific settlement of disputes) — has been found to be a limiting factor. In defence of the veto, it must be said that it was included in the Charter because it was the expression of the valid principle that power must be linked to responsibility, and, further, continuing unanimity of purpose among the Big Five

---

[1] Other notable successes of the United Nations in getting disputes settled may be listed: A truce has been arranged in Kashmir (1948), and in the Suez Canal (1973), an agreement between the Dutch and the Indonesians was brought about, providing the basis for the establishment of a Indonesian State (1949); the dispute over West Irian between the Dutch and the Indonesians has also been settled without war (1962) and the Congo has been unified and its independence assured (1960-63).

was the very foundation of the Organization. Any other course was too academic : if the Big Five split, the Organization would be divided in any case and the members would act as they liked. What was necessary then was to maintain the unity of the United Nations, and to depend on that unity to lay the foundations of a lasting peace.

But, as it is, the existence of the veto not only prevents the proper building up of a system of collective security; it has also prevented the Organization from becoming as universal as it could be. The admission of such nations as Vietnam and the Republic of Korea, for instance, has been blocked by the veto, with the result that some are still outside the Organization.

It is not our purpose to examine the differences between the factions or to judge who is right and who is wrong. In the context of collective security, what is significant is the inability of the Security Council to act effectively; each party accuses the other of expansionist ambitions, and there is mutual suspicion. As against this, the people of the world are anxious to avoid war, and if we read public opinion aright they would like to see the United Nations established more effectively as an instrument for collective security.

§9 IMPROVEMENT OF THE U.N. MACHINERY

How then can this be done?

We must at this stage go back to first principles. Power held in reserve has always played an important part in international politics; the United Nations can be an effective instrument of collective security only if the statesmen of the powerful nations are prepared to use the power of their States on its behalf.

Granted this, how can the machinery be improved?

The United Nations should have reliable means of information on preparations for aggression and on aggression itself when it takes place ; it must be capable of taking quick and effective action ; and the action must be backed up by power. Since the Security Council, which is charged by the Charter with primary responsibility for all this, has been, so to say, paralysed, the Assembly, which also has some responsibility, ought clearly to move in the matter. According to the Charter, however, the Assembly can only make recommendations; it cannot take binding action. Article 11 clearly states that any question relating to the maintenance of international peace and security on which action is necessary shall be referred to the Security Council by the General Assembly, either before or after discussion. The Soviet delegation has made much of this restriction and suggested that only a general conference summoned under Article 109 to review the Charter could legally vest in the Assembly such functions as were proposed to be transferred to it under ' a united action for peace ' resolution which was introduced in the Political Committee by seven nations on 9 October 1950. The essentials of that resolution, which was ultimately adopted by the Assembly with modifications on 3 November 1950, are :

(*i*) If the Security Council, because of lack of unanimity among the permanent members, fails to exercise its primary responsibility for the maintenance of international peace and security in the face of a threat to peace, a breach of the peace or act of aggression, the General Assembly should immediately consider the matter, in regular or emergency session, and make appropriate recommendations to members for collective measures. including, when necessary, the use of armed forces. (The General Assembly is authorized to meet in special emergency session within twenty-four hours at the request of any seven members of the Security Council.)

(*ii*) A Peace Observation Commission should be established to observe and report on the situation in any area where there is international tension likely to endanger international peace and security. On the invitation or with the consent of the State into whose territory the Commission would go, the General Assembly could utilize the Peace Observation Commission if the Security Council failed to exercise its functions under the Charter in connexion with the matter in question.

(*iii*) Member-States should be invited to survey their resources in order to determine what assistance they can render in support of any recommendation of the Security Council or the General Assembly for the restoration of international peace and security. Each member-State should be invited to maintain within its national armed forces elements which can promptly be made available to the United Nations on the recommendation of the Security Council or the General Assembly, without prejudice to the use of such elements for self-defence.

(*iv*) A Collective Measures Committee should study and report to the Security Council and the General Assembly, not later than 1 September 1951, on methods which can be used and resources, including armed forces, which can be made available to the United Nations by member-States for the maintenance of international peace.

(*v*) Members should be urged to intensify individual and collective efforts to achieve conditions of economic stability and social progress, particularly through the development of under-developed countries and areas.

Is this a usurpation by the Assembly of a power conferred by the Charter on the Security Council? We think not. First, the Assembly has been given some responsibility for the maintenance of international peace. Second, this is only a recommendation and, clearly, the Assembly can recommend. A recommendation has, of course, no binding force as, for instance, a decision by the Security Council would have ; that means that the effectiveness of the resolution depends upon how far member-States are prepared to co-operate with the Assembly in checking aggression.

Perhaps another point may be made clear. It is difficult under the Charter to think of a war sponsored by the United Nations against a permanent member of the Security Council if any one of them is an aggressor, since each can invoke the veto in the Security Council against any preventive or enforcing action ; and an Assembly resolution cannot substantially alter the fundamental position of the Big Five under the Charter.

From the point of improved machinery for collective security, it is worth while also to explore the improved use of regional arrangements (contemplated in Articles 52-4 of the Charter) for co-operation between countries and with the United Nations ; they may be useful for localizing conflicts and ensuring peace, if pro-perly set up and organized. A small expert committee, it is sug-gested, may be established to study the problem in all its aspects.

§10 AID TO UNDER-DEVELOPED COUNTRIES

The importance of the economic development of under-developed countries as an aid in promoting contentment and peace hardly needs elaboration; the 'united action for peace' resolution passed by the Assembly specifically urged member-States to intensify individual and collective efforts to achieve conditions of economic stability and social progress — particularly by aiding under-developed countries and areas. There is no space here to discuss the ways and means of such aid; it is sufficient to draw attention to the *Report of the Fourth Session of the Sub-Commission on Economic Development*. Under-developed areas need for their economic development capital equipment and finance as well as technical assistance; and in both these respects the methods which have been tried and found suitable in the industrialized countries of the West must be considerably modified to suit the under-developed countries.

The Sub-Commission referred to above recommended (regarding finance) that international lending institutions should follow *flexible* policies in making external loans, paying due regard to the circumstances in each case and to the basic objective to be achieved. The Chairman of the Commission suggested setting up a bold new organization under the ægis of the United Nations to promote the economic development of the under-developed countries. 'The new organ,' he said, 'would work in co-operation with the International Bank and other organs of the United Nations, but it would be charged with responsibility for economic development. It should not be merely a planning or advisory organ but should have finance at its disposal.'

An International Finance Corporation has recently been established as an affiliate of the International Bank for Reconstruction and Development to facilitate the supply of Capital to underdeveloped countries ; towards the end of 1958, the General Assembly also approved establishment of a Special Fund as an expansion of the existing technical assistance and development activities of the United Nations and the specialized agencies in fields essential to the integrated technical, economic and social development of underdeveloped areas.

Regarding technical assistance, and assistance for economic development in general, the United Nations has now recognized the wholesome principle that 'it must be organically related to the economy' of the country which asks for the assistance. Besides,

'the services rendered by the United Nations must be of the kind desired by the Government of the requesting country. They must be designed to meet its needs, must be in the form that it desires and must be designed to strengthen its national economy and promote its political and economic independence. Such principles preclude the arbitrary imposition of schemes devised by foreigners to achieve the political or economic subjugation or exploitation of peoples of less highly developed countries.'[1]

The greater the help rendered to under-developed countries on the principles stated above, the better the chances for providing conditions under which collective security can be maintained.

---

[1] Dr H. L. Keenlevside in *United Nations Bulletin*, Vol. IX, No. 8.

§11 THE CREATION OF GOODWILL

Finally, to promote collective security, the development of certain national and individual attitudes will be helpful.

At the national level, what is important to realize is that the communist and democratic ideologies, together with the institutions they imply, must learn to exist side by side in the world ; for the one ideology to try to wipe out the other is undesirable and impracticable. In concrete terms this means that the Governments of the countries concerned should cease abusing the social systems and ideologies with which they are not in sympathy ; it means the sincere acceptance of the principle of co-existence and the removal of suspicions by promoting freer intercourse between the countries ; disarmament by stages is clearly indicated ; the promotion by Governments of racial harmony and equality among their citizens, for racial disharmony, wherever it exists, is a potent source of international friction ; the shedding of the last vestiges of imperialism by the countries which still cling to their colonies, through the gradual and orderly transfer of power to the peoples concerned in the manner adopted by Britain ; and the recognition by all countries concerned that communism in China has come to stay—all these things will help to produce a political climate in which the attitudes necessary to support collective security can grow.

At the individual level, the relevant attitude to be cultivated consists of two elements : (*i*) the attitude of ' live and let live ', a sense of tolerance and charity, a recognition that a diversity of cultures, by their very diversity, contributes to the increase of human happiness ; and (*ii*) non-violence, that is, the recognition that the warlike attitude is not something inherent in men, but rather that men are by nature social and can live together in neighbourly friendliness and can settle their disputes by peaceful means. These attitudes in the individual, which education can do much to cultivate, indeed go to the root of the problem of collective security.

§12 A WORLD PEACE AUTHORITY

Finally mention must be made of an important proposal (made by Grenville Clark and Louis B. Sohn [1]) which is gaining increasing acceptance among the peoples of the world, viz. the creation

[1] G. Clark and L. B. Sohn. *World Peace Through World Law*, Harvard University Press, 1962.

of a World Peace Authority which would be a *supra-national* body
(as distinguished from an *international* body like the United
Nations in which sovereignty still rests with member nations).

The main presuppositions and features of the proposal may be
summarized thus :

1. General and complete disarmament is an essential precondition for world peace and stability. Experience has shown that it
is virtually impossible to agree upon any plan of any consequence
for merely partial disarmament, since one nation or another is
almost certain to claim, and with some justification, that the particular proposed reduction would put it at a disadvantage ;

2. The world should accept an enforceable universal law against
the use or threat of use of force in international relations. The
acceptance of an enforceable universal law of the kind suggested
implies in turn the acceptance of three other essentials :

(a) the establishment of ' an adequate ' world police force in
order that, after complete disarmament has been accomplished,
the means will exist to deter or apprehend violation of the world
law forbidding national armaments and international violence ;

(b) the setting up of alternative, peaceful means to deal with
all disputes between nations, viz. the International Court of Justice
to decide those disputes which are capable of adjudication through
the application of legal principles and the World Equity Tribunal
to deal with those disputes which cannot be satisfactorily settled
on the basis of applicable legal principles ; and

(c) the setting up of (*i*) a world legislature with carefully
limited yet adequate power to vote the annual budgets of the
world peace authority ' . . . to enact appropriate penalties for violation of the world law and other essential regulations concerning disarmament and the maintenance of peace, and to keep a
watchful eye on the other organs and agencies of the peace authority ; (*ii*) a world executive, free from any crippling veto . . .
to direct and control the world inspection service and the world
police force and to exercise other essential executive functions '
in the limited area of war prevention ; and (*iii*) an effective world
revenue system to support these supranational institutions on a
reliable and continuing basis ;

3. It is essential to set up some kind of World Development
authority to reduce the dangerous disparities in wealth between
the developed and the under-developed nations, for economic
inequalities are a sure source of revolutions and international
tensions.

The proposed peace authority, it may be added, would have
carefully defined powers under limited world law — it would

operate only in the area of maintaining peace ; all other powers would be reserved to the nations and their peoples.

Whether the proposed peace authority is established through an amendment of the Charter of the United Nations or as an entirely new organization by universal or nearly universal treaty is a question of method and the choice largely depends on the practicability of either. What is important to observe, in conclusion, is that some such radical step seems necessary to create the foundations of a durable peace. The common man's impatience with living in a system of ' balance of terror ' may be expected, Clark and Sohn believe, to develop the political climate in which such a radical proposal will be universally accepted.

SELECT BIBLIOGRAPHY

Aims, Methods and Activity of the League of Nations, The Secretariat of the League of Nations, 1935

N. ANGEL, *The Great Illusion*, Heinemann, 2nd ed., 1933

A. APPADORAI, *The Use of Force in International Relations*, Asia Publishing House, 1958

W. ARNOLD-FORSTER, *Charters of the Peace*, Gollancz, 1944

J. BRYCE, *International Relations*, Macmillan, 1922

A. L. BURNS AND N. HEATHCOTE, *Peace Keeping by U.N. Forces*, Pall Mall Press, London, 1963

C. D. BURNS, *Political Ideals*, Oxford, 4th ed., 1929

E. H. CARR, *The Twenty Years' Crisis*, 1919-1939, Macmillan 2nd ed., 1946

—, *Nationalism and After*, Macmillan, 1945

G. CLARKE AND L. B. SOHN, *World Peace Through World Law*, Harvard University Press, 1962

A. COBBAN, *National Self-Determination*, Oxford, 2nd ed., 1948

C. M. EICHELBERGER, *U. N., The first Ten Years*, Harper, 1955

H. V. EVATT, *The United Nations*, Cumberlege, 1948

Everyman's United Nations, The United Nations, 6th ed., 1959

W. FRIEDMANN, *An Introduction to World Politics*, Macmillan, 2nd ed., 1952

L. M. GOODRICH AND A. P. SIMONS, *Tte United Nations and the Maintenance of International Peace*, Brookings Institution, 1955

L. M. GOODRICH, *The United Nations*, Thomas Y. Crowell Company, New York, 1962

J. MACLAURIN, *The United Nations and Power Politics*, Allen & Unwin, 1951

H. S. MORRISON AND OTHERS, *The League and the Future of the Collective System*, Allen & Unwin, 1937

R. Muir, *Nationalism and Internationalism*, Constable, 1919

P. J. Noel-Baker, *The League of Nations at Work*, Nisbet, 1926

F. L. Schuman, *International Politics*, McGraw-Hill, 5th ed., 1953

C. I. Streit, *Union Now*, Cape, 1939

E. L. Woodward, *Some Political Consequences of the Atomic Bomb*, Oxford, 1945

A. Zimmern (Editor), *Modern Political Doctrines*, Part III, Oxford, 1939

Part Two

POLITICAL ORGANIZATION

BOOK I. A HISTORY OF GOVERNMENT

CHAPTER XII

THE GREEK CITY-STATE

§1 INTRODUCTORY

THE history of political development shows that two types of States have existed, the primary external difference between which is one of size : the city-State and the country-State. The former was the prevailing form of political organization and reached its greatest development in ancient Greece and Italy (e.g. Athens, Sparta, Corinth, Rome) though it was found also in medieval Europe (e.g. Venice and Florence). The country-State was found in the ancient and the medieval world as well, but it has attained its best development in modern history.

The city-State thus demands our first attention because chronologically it comes first, and has left its mark on history for all time, both on political theory and on political organization. It is true that the differences of scale in area and population and a different outlook on life produced by industrialism and modern methods of transport, finance and capitalist enterprise have produced fundamental changes in the modern State ; but reflection shows that we have a great deal to learn from the city-State. The fundamental questions in Politics remain much the same : What are the purposes for which the State exists ? What are the means of realizing them ? What are the limits of political control ? And in answering them with reference to the modern State, the political experience of the city-State and the philosophy based on such experience are invaluable.

§2 CHARACTERISTICS OF THE CITY-STATE

The Greeks called their State *polis*, ' a word which may have originally meant no more than a fortified position on a hill to which the inhabitants of the surrounding country could fly for refuge on the approach of an enemy '; but in time it came to mean essentially a State in which the life of the people — political, intellectual, and religious — was focussed on the central city. The city-State was, therefore, an organized society of men dwelling in a walled town, the hearth and home of the political society, and with a surrounding territory not too large to allow all its free inhabitants habitually to assemble within the city walls to discharge the duties of citizenship.

Two ideas were integral to it : it loved independence ; it was small. The independence of each city was the one cardinal principle on which Greek politics was based. No Greek would willingly merge his city in any larger aggregate. For this reason, ancient Greeks never succeeded in forming one single Greek State. This had its defects : city quarrelled with city, the quarrels ultimately leading to their collapse when a powerful State arose in the north under Philip of Macedon. The Greeks knew their weakness, but clung to their ideal. The attachment of the Greeks to their small States is explained partly by geography. Greece is a land of mountains and small valleys ; the mountain ranges do not run in straight lines but, roughly speaking, rectangularly, dividing the land into little square boxes. Greece was, therefore, well adapted to be a country of separate communities. But geography cannot explain everything. This is shown by the fact that there were no mountains between Thebes and Plataea or between Argos and Corinth, yet the ideal of the small independent city-State persisted in those parts of Greece as well. A second reason may be sought in the independent spirit of the people. We shall perhaps be nearer the truth if, following De Coulanges,[1] we ascribe the separatist tendency to the religious belief of the people, the belief that the gods of one city rejected the homage and prayers of any one who did not belong to their city. Because the worship of one city was not followed by the men of another, the laws too must necessarily differ, for law in early days was intimately connected with religion. Each city had its own money which was marked with its religious emblem. Isolation was the law of the city. One result of this was that in every city the citizens were a closely restricted body. Birth within the city alone could normally qualify one for citizenship ; to admit a stranger was to invite the risk that the purity of the sacrifices might be affected. Strangers were therefore admitted only under special conditions, care being taken to see that the admission had a measure of popular support.

The city-State was of necessity small : of necessity, because the concentration of political, social and intellectual life at one central city (which was the political ideal of the Greeks) was possible only when the State was small. The city must be capable of being taken in at a glance both by eye and mind. According

[1] F. de Coulanges, *The Ancient City*, p. 270.

to Aristotle, the State should have more than ten thousand and less than one hundred thousand citizens. It should be large enough to be self-sufficing, but not so large as to prevent unity of interest and feeling among its members. The larger the territory, the less truly would the inhabitants realize their membership of the city community. Besides, they would be apt to develop interests of their own apart from their interests as members of the State. Plato's ideal State is that which approaches most nearly to the condition of the individual : if a part of the body suffers, the whole body feels the hurt and sympathizes all together with the part affected. This ideal was possible of realization only if the State was small. To be a citizen of a State did not merely imply, in the Greek view, the payment of taxes and the possession of a vote : ' it implied a direct and active co-operation in all the functions of civil and military life. A citizen was normally a soldier, judge and member of the governing assembly ; and all his public duties, he performed not by deputy, but in person ; the gods of the city were his gods, its festivals he must attend '. The city-State of the Greeks was therefore a community of persons who knew one another ; it was not only politically self-governed, it facilitated also a large measure of social discussion.

There is a third characteristic which is connected at once with the independence and the small size of the city-State : its all-inclusiveness, to which we have already referred.[1] Before the claims of the State, all other human relationships took a secondary place.

§3   CITY-STATE AND MODERN STATE COMPARED

We have noticed three characteristics of the ancient city-State : its love of independence verging on separatism, its small size, and the all-inclusive sphere of its activity. The modern State too loves independence, but the attachment to the laws and institutions of one's own State leading to the dislike of those of the stranger is not characteristic of it, except perhaps in the aggressively national State. The general acceptance by modern States of international law is the best proof of this difference. There are also a number of resemblances in the political and economic institutions and religion of many modern States, these resemblances being partly due to conscious imitation.

The modern State is a country-State, larger in size than the city-State. It does not, unlike the ancient *polis*, give undue prominence to the capital city as the centre, the heart and life of the

[1] See above, p. 95 ; for illustrations see §10 below.

nation. The citizens of Attica called themselves Athenians, after Athens, the capital city; this is an index to the fact that the citizens of the whole State identified themselves with the central city. The citizens of India are not known as Delhians, or of Britain, Londoners. The citizen, according to Aristotle, must be capable of ruling and being ruled; the small size of the city-State made it possible for its citizens to realize this ideal in a larger measure than is possible for the citizens of the modern State. The size of the ancient State explains also the difference between ancient and modern democracy: where democracy existed in the ancient world public authority was directly exercised by its holders; the citizens appeared in large popular assemblies and directly decided important public affairs. Modern democracy is representative. Incidentally we may note that the institution of slavery existed in the ancient world; this to some extent facilitated the working of direct democracy by providing the citizens with the necessary leisure, the slaves looking after agriculture, manufacture and household service. In the modern State, slavery has generally been abolished.

And, thirdly, unlike the ancient State, the modern State recognizes (though with considerable variations both in theory and practice) limits to political control. In the city-State, 'man had only full rights *qua* citizen. Among the Greeks, private and public law were not yet distinguished. The Romans separated them in principle but their private law still remained completely dependent on the will of the people and the State. Individual freedom as against the State was not yet recognized.'[1] But in the modern State, man has his rights as a person which are rather recognized than created by the State, and private law is sharply distinguished from public law. 'The free person is not absorbed in the State, but develops himself independently, and exercises his rights, not according to the will of the sovereign State, but according to his own.'[2]

These three differences apart (the differences arising from the characteristics of the city-State and the modern State), we must also note that the social, economic and political problems which a modern State has to face are much more complex than those which the city-State had to face. The complexity of these problems arises partly from the difference in size of territory and population (e.g. the adjustment of the claims of ethnic and linguistic minorities for equal or more than equal treatment, economic development, the relations between the Central Govern-

[1] Bluntschli, *The Theory of the State*, p. 59.   [2] ibid.

ment and local authorities); it arises partly also from the development of technology in recent years especially in the fields of transport, communications and the mechanization of warfare. This last development has especially made the adjustment of the relations between States an important field of State activity.[1]

§4 ITS MERITS AND DEFECTS

The great merit of the city-State as a form of social and political organization was that it enabled a measure of unity to be achieved, hardly possible in the large modern State. Its small size and homogeneity made for social consolidation and integration. It could realize in a large measure the force of those natural and artificial ties which give strength and cohesion to a State, viz. common race, language, religion, historic association, law and custom. The unity of the State enhanced the citizens' feeling of patriotism; their attachment to their State was indeed remarkable. It was said of the Athenians : 'They spend their bodies, as mere external tools, in the city's service and count their minds as most truly their own when employed on her behalf.' Their citizenship was a dedication to the service of the State, an identification of the interests of the individual with those of the State. Above all, with Freeman,[2] we may add that such a system as this calls forth the powers of man to their very highest point ; there has never been another political society in the world in which the average of the individual citizen stood as high as it did under Athenian democracy in the days of its greatness. Truly may it be said that the Greeks proved for the State how

> In small proportions we just beauties see ;
> And in short measures, life may perfect be.[3]

The city-State had its defects. The institution of slavery, which was the foundation of the city-economy, was obviously one. Secondly, the small size of the State, the source of many of its merits, was also a source of difficulties. At a certain stage in the development of the State, when *stasis*[4] or internal feud appeared, it was all the more bitter because the two extreme sections of the people, the rich and the poor, lived within the compass of a small area. Externally, it was a bar to the expansion of the State :

[1] See ch. XI.
[2] E. A. Freeman, *Comparative Politics*, p. 93.
[3] Ben Jonson, *Ode*.
[4] See below, ch. xiii, §9.

if it expanded either by becoming an imperial State or by becoming part of a federal State, it lost its true character and tended to decay. It was also too weak to defend itself against more powerful country-States, which generally had greater resources and a larger population. And, thirdly, its conception of the relation between the State and the individual was not altogether satisfactory; it did not recognize, as we must, that there are limits to political control.

§5 ORIGIN OF THE CITY-STATE

Before the rise of the city, the Greeks lived in village communities. The village community was a group of families whose numbers were, or believed themselves to have been, descended from a common ancestor, and they bore his name. They participated in a common worship; the land which they cultivated was held in common by all the families in the village; and the village was ruled by a headman, the head of that household which was considered as being nearest of kin to the original ancestor from whom they traced their descent. The headman was also usually advised by a council of the heads of families.

That the city was formed out of village communities has been accepted by scholars : according to Freeman,[1] it hardly needs proof. And if evidence is needed, we can give it threefold. First, the political speculation of Greek thinkers assumed that the city-State had been built on the village community. Thus Aristotle defines the State as the union of families and villages having for an end a perfect and self-sufficing life. Secondly, traces of such communities were found in historical times in some of the less developed parts of Greece, e.g. in Aetolia. Thirdly, the city in its developed state contained survivals of the life of the village community in its *gens* or clan.[2]

The fusion of the village communities into a city-State was sometimes brought about by compulsion by powerful kings. Sometimes it was voluntary. The greater protection which the walled city provided against enemies was a powerful incentive : a hill fort would thus be a convenient nucleus for the growth of the city; Athens, for instance, gathered round the holy rock of Athena later known as the Acropolis. The provision of improved facilities for trade or manufacture when a number of people were gathered together in one place was another incentive. Briefly

---

[1] op. cit., p. 86.
[2] W. W. Fowler, *The City-States of the Greeks and Romans*, pp. 36ff.

'they went to find efficiency'. They discovered, in the fine phrase of Aristotle, that though they could live out in the country, they could 'live well' only in the city. Doubtless, there were difficulties to be overcome. One of the foremost was, as De Coulanges has insisted, that of persuading the communities to forsake their separate individual worships and accept the new common worship. Thus when Theseus tried to unite the twelve groups which later coalesced into Athens, he had first to persuade them to adopt the worship of Athena; every community preserved its ancient worship but also adopted the one common worship.

The city is thus explained. To understand the *city-State*, however, we need to take into account other factors as well. For the significant fact about the city-State was not city life, but that the small State refused to merge itself in a larger whole, and embraced the entire life of man in community, religion and law, morals and art, culture and science, all focussed on a single city. Three reasons explain this, as we have noticed in a previous discussion,[1] viz. the lie of the land, the independent spirit of the Greeks and their religious beliefs.

§6 THE GOVERNMENT OF SPARTA

In this short history of government, it is not necessary to sketch the constitutions of all city-States; it is sufficient to give an outline of the system of government in two important States (Sparta and Athens), and give a brief résumé of the general features of Greek constitutional development.

Sparta, in the south of Greece, was formed by the union of five villages, and soon became the dominant State in that part of the land. The original Spartan constitution consisted of three elements, kings, a Council of Elders, and an Assembly of the people ; of these, the kings had the greatest power. In time, the power of the kings declined, and that of the Council and the people increased. In the fifth century B.C., the developed Spartan constitution was as follows :

There were two kings of equal power. Kingship was hereditary, but in a singular way, for the king was succeeded not by his eldest son, but by the first son born after his accession to the throne. It was partly because there were two kings, the one to check the other, that kingship was not abolished in Sparta.

The functions of the kings were threefold. They were heads of the State religion, and in that capacity made sacrifices to the

---

[1] See above. p. 176.

gods on behalf of the community. They were the supreme commanders of the army, and in the battlefield they had unlimited power of life and death. Two of the officers, known as the ephors, however, accompanied the kings to the field, not to share the command but to assist in negotiations after a victory or a defeat. The kings also had certain judicial powers, which were in fact connected with the exercise of their religious functions : they decided who was to marry an heiress whose father had died without betrothing her (to secure the maintenance and transmission of the family worship) ; they had jurisdiction in case of adoption and judged matters concerning public roads. (This was connected with religion because, in the ancient world, the boundary stone was sacred, and questions about the demarcation of property would depend largely on religious tradition.)

Next came the Council of Elders or the Gerousia, composed of the two kings, and twenty-eight other members elected by the people for life from members of the nobility over sixty years of age. As a deliberative body, it discussed and prepared the business for the Assembly ; as an administrative body, most matters of routine administration were within its competence ; as a court of justice, it tried criminal cases.

The Assembly (Apella) consisted of all citizens of pure birth, who had passed their thirtieth year and submitted to the discipline of the State.[1] Normally it met once a month ; extra sessions could be summoned at such other times as the ephors, who presided over it, thought fit. The election of all officers and members of the Council was in its hands. It also decided (without, however, any discussion) questions of war and peace, and of disputed succession to the throne.

The board of five ephors was chosen by public vote every year Any Spartan citizen was eligible for this office. They summoned and presided over the Assembly. They sat with the Council (perhaps presided over it) and brought all important business before it ; shared its criminal jurisdiction and, as its executive officers, carried out its decrees. They had civil jurisdiction. To them ' the kings were entirely subordinate. Upon their approach, the kings rose. Yearly the kings took an oath to observe the constitution, and then the ephors promised to uphold their throne. They were allowed to fine and imprison the kings.' As has been noticed earlier, two of them accompanied the kings upon all campaigns. They were in charge of the relations of Sparta with foreign powers. They were also responsible for the strict

[1] Described in §7.

maintenance of the order and discipline of the State. In their management was the secret police, whereby the surrounding masses of hostile peoples were kept in awe.

It is difficult to place this constitution under one of the usual categories — monarchy, aristocracy or democracy.

'Historically,' says Greenidge,[1] 'Sparta is a balance of the three numerical elements of sovereignty : the nobles limit the king, and the demos the nobility, and all three are found finally together in a condition of stable equilibrium. But analytically we should be inclined to recognize only two elements, and to pronounce the constitution a dynastic oligarchy of a mild type modified by a strong democratic element.'

The dynastic element is found in the power of the Gerousia ; it is mild because the members of the body are elected by the people. The democratic elements are obviously the Assembly and the ephors. All citizens are members of the Assembly ; it chooses the Elders and ephors and ratifies, or not, the Council's acts. The ephors are annually elected, and as elected officers exercise vast powers.

§7 STATE AND INDIVIDUAL IN SPARTA

It has been said in a previous section that the subordination of the individual to the State was a characteristic of all Greek States ; nowhere perhaps was the idea so fully carried out as in Sparta. The citizens lived under a lifelong iron discipline, which was almost military in its nature. The discipline indeed began with birth. As soon as a child was born, it was visited by Spartan elders, to examine whether it was in any way deformed or obviously unhealthy.

'If so, the child must not be allowed to grow up " a feeble wielder of the lance " or to be the mother of children inheriting perhaps her own weakness. It was therefore immediately after birth exposed halfway up the side of Mount Taygetus, and allowed to die almost before it had begun to live.'

If the child was normal, it was given back to its parents to be brought up by them, subject, however, to regulations prescribed by the State in the interests of its health and strength.

At the age of seven years, the male child was taken from its parents and was, through life, subjected to a severe discipline

[1] A. H. Greenidge, *A Handbook of Greek Constitutional History*, p. 107.

under the care of the State.[1] Throughout his life, as boy, youth, and man, the Spartan citizen lived habitually in public, always either himself under drill, gymnastic and military, or a critic and spectator of others ; always under the fetters and observances of a rule partly military, partly monastic, a stranger to the privacy of home, seeing his wife, during the first years after marriage, only by stealth, and maintaining little intimate relationship with his children. The supervision not only of his fellow citizens, but also of authorized censors or captains nominated by the State, was perpetually on him : his day was passed in public exercises and meals, his nights in the public barrack to which he belonged. Besides military drill, he also became subject to severe bodily discipline of other kinds, calculated to impart strength, activity and endurance. To manifest a daring and pugnacious spirit, to sustain the greatest bodily torture unmoved, to endure hunger and thirst, heat, cold, and fatigue, to tread the worst ground barefoot, to wear the same garment winter and summer, to suppress external manifestations of feeling, and to exhibit in public, when action was not called for, a bearing shy, silent and motionless as a statue — all these were the virtues of the accomplished Spartan youth. Besides the various descriptions of gymnastic contests, youths were instructed in the choric dances employed during festivals of the gods, which helped to give them regulated and harmonious movements. Hunting was encouraged as a means of accustoming them to fatigue and privation. The nourishment supplied to the youthful Spartans was purposely kept insufficient, but they were allowed to make up the deficiency not only by hunting but by stealing whatever they could lay hands upon, provided they could do so without being detected in the act : in which latter case, they were severely chastised !

The Spartan was not only compelled to concentrate his attention on military excellence, but was completely cut off from all commercial pursuits and even from agriculture. The accumulation of wealth was severely discouraged, and the possession of gold or silver punished with a fine.

§8 THE CONSTITUTION OF ATHENS

The early history of Athens resembles that of most other Greek States in the general fact that a monarchy, limited in some ways by the powers of a Council of nobles and of an Assembly of the people, passed into an aristocracy, which in turn gave place to

---

[1] G. Grote, *History of Greece*, Vol. II, pp. 297ff. This paragraph in the text is largely based on the sketch given by Grote.

a democracy. When the Government had become fully democratic in the days of Pericles (c. 500-429 B.C.) its main institutions were :

(i) *The Assembly* (*Ecclesia*). All citizens above a certain
age, probably above twenty,[1] were eligible to attend it. Normally,
it met forty times a year ; extraordinary sessions were also held
when necessary. In order to ensure the attendance of as many
citizens as possible, it was ordered that at the time of the
Assembly meetings the shops should be kept closed. A member
of the Council of Five Hundred, chosen by lot, presided over the
meeting. Any citizen was at liberty to address it. The Assembly
decided every important matter concerning the State ; from its
decisions there was no appeal.

(ii) *The Council of Five Hundred* (*Boulé*). The members
of this body were chosen by lot from citizens over thirty years
of age, fifty being chosen from each of the ten tribes into which
the population of Athens was divided. We have it on competent
authority that the office was not felt as a burden imposed on the
citizens ; ' the candidates presented themselves voluntarily, and
competition for membership was keen, since the functions of the
post were dignified and important, and the services well paid.'
The Council prepared all business for the Ecclesia, and it had
to see that the decisions of the Ecclesia were properly carried
out. Briefly, it was the permanent Government of Athens ;
unlike the Assembly it sat throughout the year. For convenience,
it was divided by tribes into committees of fifty members each,
each presiding tribe sitting in turn for a tenth of the year. The
chairman was chosen by lot from the presiding tribe for one day.
It looked after the routine administration of the State such as
superintending the building of ships and the construction of
public works, controlling the details of expenditure, looking to
the upkeep of the cavalry and poor-relief, conducting negotiations
with foreign States, etc.

(iii) *The Areopagus*. This was a council mainly composed
of men who were or had once been archons (executive officers).
All the members sat for life. At one time it was a political
power, but at the time of Pericles it had only some criminal
jurisdiction and a general power of religious supervision.

(iv) *The officers*. Nearly 95% of the offices, including
those of judges, finance officers, auditors of public accounts,

---

[1] A. J. Grant, *Greece in the Age of Pericles*, p. 146. Greenidge, however, says that all citizens over *eighteen* years of age could attend. See
Greenidge, op. cit., p. 169.

commissioners of roads, commissioners of weights and measures and keepers of the State gaol, were filled by lot. The incumbents held office for one year ; and, Aristotle tells us, except in the case of the Council of Five Hundred, no one might hold office a second time. The lot secured absolute political equality ; but in order to prevent the occupation of office by wholly unworthy and incompetent men, two safeguards were provided. First, an examination of the candidate was held after the lot had fallen upon him, but before he entered on the duties of his post. Second, each official had to undergo an examination when he laid down his office. Incapacity and dishonesty could then be punished.

Further, the Athenians realized that there were some functions which required more than mere common sense and general ability, e.g. commanding the army and looking to the water supply of the city. Obviously such posts could not be held adequately by men chosen by lot. Generals and commissioners of springs were therefore chosen by election.

(v) *The popular jury court* (*Heliaea*). This was composed nominally [1] of six thousand Athenian citizens over thirty years of age, chosen by lot at the beginning of each year. These six thousand were again divided by lot into ten sections of five hundred each, thus leaving a reserve of one thousand. When there was a case to be heard, lot was cast to decide which of the juries was to hear it. Service in the jury court was paid, but was not compulsory. It must be mentioned, too, that petty cases were decided without reference to these jury courts, by arbitrators who were selected by lot from citizens sixty or more years of age.

The account given above shows that the government of Athens in the fifth century B.C. was a full-blown democracy : sovereignty lay with the people themselves, and there was political equality. This equality was not in name only ; the institutions of government were such as to ensure its realization in practice ; the system of lot, the short tenure of office and payment for public service [2] were particularly useful in providing opportunity for government service for rich and poor alike.

---

[1] Greenidge (op. cit., p. 175) has pointed out that the traditional six thousand, if not an exaggeration, was probably a nominal number on account of the extreme improbability of so many duly-qualified citizens serving in the same year.

[2] In the days of Pericles, there was no payment for attendance at the Assembly ; this was introduced later, about the beginning of the fourth century B.C.

§9 ATHENIAN AND MODERN DEMOCRACY

By democracy we mean that form of government in which the ruling power of a State is legally vested not in any particular class or classes but in the members of a community as a whole. In this sense the constitution of Athens was clearly democratic : so are the constitutions of modern India and the United States of America. But there are important differences between ancient and modern democracy.

Modern democracy is representative, indirect ; the people govern through representatives periodically elected by them. The ordinary citizen's part in government is limited. Periodically he may vote to choose a member of Parliament from his constituency. If he has the necessary qualifications, he has the right to stand as a candidate for election and to apply for executive and judicial posts ; but in practice only a very small proportion of citizens can ever hope to be elected to the Legislature, or chosen for executive or judicial office. He has the right to criticize the Government and influence public opinion, through freedom of speech, press and association ; the effectiveness of his criticism obviously depends upon his ability and resources. In some countries, like Switzerland and the United States of America, the citizen has opportunities of ' direct legislation ' through the referendum and the initiative. The referendum is the submission of a measure passed by the Legislature to popular vote for final sanction ; the initiative is an arrangement by which a prescribed number or proportion of the people may initiate the proposal for a law to be later confirmed by popular vote. More direct part in government is taken by the people in the smaller cantons of Switzerland and the townships of New England in the U.S.A., where the qualified citizens meet to decide important issues ; but this participation is in municipal affairs, and not in those of the central Government.

Ancient democracy was direct, primary. When the Athenians called their constitution a democracy, ' they meant literally what the word itself expressed — that the people itself undertook the work of government '. Their Assembly, in which every citizen could take part, was the sovereign body in the State to decide national affairs, great and small. The opportunity for the citizen to take part in the executive and judicial administration of the State was considerable. Unlike in modern times, there was no permanent bureaucracy or Judiciary who looked to the executive and the judicial work ; these were undertaken for short

periods by ordinary citizens. The systems of lot and election,
payment, and short tenure of office ensured equal opportunity
for all. On the authority of Aristotle it has been reckoned[1]
that, excluding those employed on military duties, there were
' ten thousand officials in a State whose total number of citizens
certainly did not amount to much more than twice that number.'
In practice, therefore, every Athenian citizen probably held an
official post of some sort once in his life ; very many must have
held such posts many times. Citizenship was rightly defined as
the capacity to rule and be ruled.

It need hardly be added that it is impossible to apply the
principles and methods of ancient democracy to modern conditions : the ancient city-State was small, it was a slave-owning
democracy, and its individual life was less complex than the
modern. But the ancient conception of citizenship may be usefully assimilated by citizens in modern States so that they may
take an intelligent and active part in the problems of the State
and make their citizenship a dedication to the service of the
State.

§10 RIGHTS AND DUTIES OF CITIZENSHIP IN ATHENS

Rights in the legal sense are privileges or immunities upheld
by the State ; duties are obligations. Besides the usual civil
rights, such as the right to life, personal freedom, property,
contract, etc., the Athenian citizen in the days of Pericles had, as
we have seen, a number of political rights which enabled him
to have an effective share in his Government : the right to attend
meetings of the Assembly, to debate and vote ; the right to have
his name included in the lists for offices in the State to which
the system of lot applied ; the right to take part in the election
to certain offices, and the right to be paid for service to the State.
The short tenure of most of these offices enabled the citizens to
enjoy their rights in ' widest commonalty '. Truly citizenship was
the capacity not only to be ruled but to rule.

' An Athenian citizen,' said Pericles in his famous funeral
oration, ' does not neglect the State because he takes care of his

---

[1] A. J. Grant, op. cit., pp. 150-1 ; Aristotle, *On the Constitution of Athens*
(tr. E. Poste), pp. 42-3. Compare W. W. Fowler (op. cit., pp. 166-8),
who arrives at a total of 1,900 officials out of an adult male population
of about 30,000. Fowler, however, does not take into account the jurymen
and others included by Aristotle in arriving at his total number.

own household ; and even those of us who are engaged in business have a very fair idea of politics. We alone regard a man who takes no interest in public affairs, not as a harmless but as a useless character ; and if few of us are originators, we are all sound judges of policy.'

The effective performance of these civic duties was of course helped by the institution of slavery and the small size of the State ; in particular the latter facilitated a large measure of social discussion. Athens believed in the utility of discussing public questions. Again to quote Pericles :

'The great impediment to action is, in our opinion, not discussion, but the want of that knowledge which is gained by discussion preparatory to action. For we have a peculiar power of thinking before we act and of acting too, whereas other men are courageous from ignorance but hesitate upon reflection.'

Regarding duties, it is perhaps sufficient to state that generally, as according to the Athenian conception the State was all-inclusive, there was no limit to the *possible* interference by the Government with the life of the individual, i.e. to the imposition of duties on him. The citizen could be required to devote himself entirely to the State ; the whole was more important than the part.

'A State confers a greater benefit upon its private citizens when as a whole commonwealth it is successful, than when it prospers as regards the individual but fails as a community. For even though a man flourishes in his own private affairs, yet if his country goes to ruin he perishes with her all the same ; but if he is in evil fortune and his country in good fortune, he is far more likely to come through safely.' [1]

The specific duties of the Athenian citizen were :
(*i*) *Religious*. He must believe in the gods of the city, be present at the purification ceremony and have his name enrolled in the census, take part in the festivals of the national gods, and in the common meal, if selected for the purpose by lot.
(*ii*) *Private*. He must marry,[2] the law forbidding men to remain single. He could not take more than three changes of clothing on a journey.[3]

---

[1] Thucydides, *Works* (translated by C. F. Smith), Vol. I, p. 363.
[2] De Coulanges, op. cit., p. 293.
[3] ibid., p. 294.

(*iii*) *Political.* At a time when discords were frequent, the Athenian law permitted nc one to remain neutral; he must take sides. He had to serve as arbitrator, if selected for that post by lot.

(*iv*) *Financial.* It would appear that property taxes under democracy were imposed from about 429 B.C.[1] The heaviest burden of taxation fell upon the richer citizens, who were required to expend large sums in the performance of public services called liturgies, e.g. the training of a dramatic chorus for the religious festivals and the keeping of a warship in commission for a campaign.

(*v*) *Military.* All citizens had to serve in one or another branch of the army. The cavalry was recruited from the richer classes, who could afford to keep horses. All other men fit for service were enrolled in the classes as they came of age. They served from the age of fifteen to sixty.

§11 GREEK CONSTITUTIONAL DEVELOPMENT

Monarchy

The earliest form of government in the city-State of Greece[2] was monarchy. The king was believed by the people to derive his descent from the gods; kingship passed from father to son. The king was accorded various privileges and honours: a royal domain, the seat of honour at feasts and a choice share of booty taken in war and of food offered at sacrifices. He was priest, judge, and leader in war. He sacrificed to the gods on behalf of the people, as every father of a family did for his household. He decided disputes between families or members of families; his decisions were unquestioningly accepted by the people.

Besides the king, there were a Council of Elders, composed of the heads of clans, and an Assembly of the people. The Council was normally consulted by the king, though he was not bound to follow its advice. All freemen had the right to be present in the Assembly and to take part in the acclamation with which the proposals of the king and the Council were greeted. There was no general discussion, the king and the elders alone having the right to speak. The effective power of the Council and of the Assembly no doubt depended on the personality of

---

[1] R. J. Bonner, *Aspects of Athenian Democracy*, p. 95.
[2] Examples of Greek city-States, besides Sparta and Athens, are Corinth, Argos, Megara, Thebes.

the king, according as to whether he was of a character to need their help or dispense with it.

By the middle of the eighth century B.C., monarchy everywhere began to decline. The increasing power of the nobles and the tendency to arbitrary government by the kings contributed to this decline. The small size of the city-State was another factor of some importance : in a small State, the mistakes and vices of the king were easily noticed and became the subject of criticism ; criticism led to discontent and discontent grew into opposition. Further, 'the small size of the city rendered a bond of unity superfluous and the symbol unimpressive'.

Aristocracy

Monarchy gave place to aristocracy [1] — literally, the rule of the best ; in effect, government by the few nobles. The mode of transition differed from State to State. At Corinth, it is said that in 745 B.C. the members of the royal family, two hundred in number, deposed king Aristomenes and took the control of the Government into their own hands, electing one of their own number every year to act as president and discharge the functions of king. At Athens, on the other hand, Aristotle tells us that the Government was controlled by a permanent council of nobles, and its details were managed by nine archons selected annually by the Council. We may, however, observe some common features of the aristocracies : the concentration of power in a few privileged and wealthy nobles, and the distribution of the functions of administration, including religious duties, among a certain number of men elected by the nobles.

Aristocracies played a valuable role in the political development of Greece. They worked out the idea of public duty, the idea ' that the mind and the body alike of each individual should be cultivated to the utmost benefit of the State '. The honourable pride of noble descent led the nobles to cherish the idea, and set an example, of unselfish devotion to the State. Secondly, they planted Greek cities in distant lands and thus helped in the process of Greek expansion. Thirdly, they helped in elaborating

---

[1] It is perhaps worth observing that other causes besides the decline of monarchy helped the rise of aristocracies. (i) The limitation of the numbers of fully qualified citizens by the exclusion of the conquered from political power in States founded on conquest, such as Sparta ; (ii) inequality of wealth and (iii) the importance attached to cavalry in warfare in this period. This last factor meant that only the rich could afford horses and cavalry equipment, and their military superiority was transferred to the sphere of politics.

the political machinery of the States.[1] This was indeed inevitable, for new machinery had to be created to replace the monarchical part of the older constitutions which had disappeared. The new ruling class had perforce to create new magistracies, determine the term of their office and the limits of their power. And, lastly, under them the idea of law began to take a clearer shape in men's minds, and the traditions which had guided usage began to assume the form of laws embodied in written codes.[2]

Oligarchy

Aristocracy tended towards oligarchy, i.e. the selfish rule of the wealthy few. It is not so much a new form of government as the perversion of an old one. The perversion was apparent when privilege and exclusiveness began to be used for the oppression of the common people. The nobles alone knew the secrets of religion and the rules of law; they not only used them to their advantage but began to despise the commoners. They monopolized the ownership of land or encroached on common rights; oppressed the smaller cultivators; harassed the debtors to whom they had lent money on the security of their persons and, in general, made themselves hated. The best proofs of this perversion of oligarchy are perhaps the oligarchic oath quoted by Aristotle [3] (' I will be adverse to the common people, and contrive all I can against them ') and, conversely, the general support given by the common people to the ' tyrants ', who championed their cause against oligarchies.

Tyranny

These ' tyrants ' make their appearance in Greece from about 600 B.C. to about 500 B.C. Invariably, they came to power by taking up the cause of the oppressed section of the people against the oligarchs, and retained it with the help of the mercenaries. Pisistratus of Athens is a typical example. About 560 B.C., he put himself at the head of the discontented poor in the State.

' One day when the market was at its fullest Pisistratus appeared riding in a chariot. The horses and car were sprinkled with blood and the owner himself was wounded. The people quickly crowded round to hear what had happened. They were told that his life had been attempted by his enemies in the opposing parties. Before they had time to recover from their

---

[1] J. B. Bury, *A History of Greece to the Death of Alexander the Great*, p. 76.
[2] ibid.
[3] *Politics*, ' Everyman Library ' edition, p. 166.

surprise, one of his friends jumped up in the crowd and proposed that, to prevent the repetition of so terrible an event, a body-guard should be given to Pisistratus to defend his person.'[1]

The bodyguard was given ; it soon increased to a small army. Pisistratus seized the Acropolis and made himself master of the State. Later, he surrounded himself with a strong body of foreign mercenaries to maintain himself in power.

Though tyrants came to power in an unconstitutional manner, by the use of force, many of them did useful service to their States. For instance, Pisistratus himself at Athens and Thrasy-bulus at Miletus took great interest in the welfare of their people ; they encouraged art and literature, promoted commerce, planted colonies and developed the navy. Above all, they overthrew the hated oligarchies and paved the way for democracies. But, nevertheless the ' tyrannis ' was generally disliked in Greece, because it went against the Greek love of freedom. ' It placed in the hands of an unconstitutional ruler arbitrary control, whether he exercised it or not, over the lives and fortunes of the citizens.' It created a slavish feeling in subjects, and encouraged flattery. From the beginning of the fifth century B.C. it gradually declined.[2]

Democracy

Tyranny was in general replaced by democracy. Democracy stresses the principle of numerical equality ; it asserts, as against monarchy and aristocracy, that the mere fact of free birth is sufficient to constitute a claim to a share in political power. Its working in ancient Greece is best illustrated in the government of Athens during the days of Pericles, to which we have already referred. It is sufficient to state here the general fact that there was a drift towards democracy in Greece from the beginning of the fifth century B.C. ; and that democracies and oligarchies ' succeeded one another alternately in most of the cities till the battle of Chaeronea, in 338 B.C., put an end to the independence of the Greeks '.

§12 THE LEGACY OF GREECE

We have earlier referred to the fact that in spite of the differences in size and outlook on life between the Greek city-State and the

---

[1] Alice Zimmern, *Greek History*, p. 89.
[2] We cannot regard tyranny as a stage through which the Greek polity universally passed : we find it existed in Athens, Sicyon, Megara, Corinth, Miletus ; but not in Boeotia, Sparta, Elis.

modern State, the latter has had much to learn from the former. The most valuable of these contributions, as has been well said,[1] is that the Greeks set up the first *Rechts-staat* of history, a State in which the laws held sway : 'The Greeks endowed law with all the attributes of majesty and placed it above the ruler and even above the people.' The civilized modern State has made the supremacy of law, as distinguished from the caprice of an individual, part of its tradition ; to the extent that a departure is attempted from his fundamental principle, as for instance, in the Nazi State, there may be said to be a return to barbarism.

Secondly, the Greeks have left the moderns the results of their experiments in the art of government ; these experiments were varied and rich indeed. They tried monarchy, aristocracy, oligarchy, tyranny and democracy ; they tried the unitary State and the federal. After all, there is no new type of government left to invent, so that ' all that men can do is to ring the changes upon those which exist ' ; and in this task the history of the Greek State is at once a guide and a warning. Of particular interest in this regard is the analysis of different forms of government, an account of their strength and weakness, left us by the Greek thinkers, Plato and Aristotle. Plato has, for instance, shown that ignorance, injustice, and political selfishness are the great defects of the democracy with which he was familiar : the greatest problem of modern democracy is how to overcome these same defects. By his insistence on true knowledge as the qualification for rulers, Plato also teaches us the lesson that good leadership in the State is at least as important as the ballot-box for its well-being.

In the field of political ideals, again, the modern State has quite a lot to learn from the ancient State and its thinkers. The purpose of the State is to develop the good life ; there is no distinction between public and private morality, for, if the State itself is immoral, it cannot make its citizens moral ; citizenship is the capacity to rule and to be ruled ; true politics can be built up only on the study of human nature as it is, and not on a fanciful conception of what man and the world ought to be ; revolutions are caused by the craving of men for equality, and their best preventives are the encouragement of the middle classes in the State and ' education in the spirit of the constitution '. These are political lessons which mankind can forget only at their peril.

[1] Ruthnaswamy, op. cit., p. 34 ; and Gierke cited therein.

SELECT BIBLIOGRAPHY

R. J. BONNER, *Aspects of Athenian Democracy*, University of California Press, 1933

J. B. BURY, *A History of Greece to the Death of Alexander the Great*, Macmillan, 1914

F. DE COULANGES, *The Ancient City*, Simpkin Marshall, 1916

W. W. FOWLER, *The City-State of the Greeks and Romans*, ch. i to vi, Macmillan, 1921

E. A. FREEMAN, *Comparative Politics*, lecture II, Macmillan, 1873

A. H. J. GREENIDGE, *A Handbook of Greek Constitutional History*, Macmillan, 1920

B. E. HAMMOND, *The Political Institutions of the Ancient Greeks*, Clay, 1895

H. SIDGWICK, *The Development of European Polity*, lectures II. IV to IX, and XII, Macmillan, 1903

W. W. WILSON, *The State*, ch. ii, Heath, 1899

CHAPTER XIII

THE GOVERNMENT OF ROME

§1 MONARCHY

ROME made her appearance in history as a monarchic city-State; she achieved her greatness as a republic; in the period of her decline she was imperial and despotic.

The royal period lasted from the foundation of Rome (about 753 B.C.) to 510 B.C. At the head of the State was the king or rex. The method of electing the king shows that Roman kingship was a compound of three elements. The king was at once the hereditary and patriarchal chief of the people, the chief priest of the community, and the elected ruler of the State. On the death of a king, the sovereignty of the State reverted to the Council of Elders; they nominated a temporary king (*interrex*), who held office for 5 days; he nominated another elder with whom lay the actual designation of the new king. Finally, the choice to kingship was approved by the assembled people, and the vote of the people was ratified by the approval of the gods, as given in the ceremony of inauguration. Once elected, the king ruled for life. He was the sole ruler and his powers were expressed by the word 'imperium'. The imperium of the rex was technically unlimited, both in peace and in war. He was supreme judge, high priest and commander-in-chief in war. All officials were appointed by him. There were, however, two customary limitations to the king's absolutism. He was expected to consult the Council of Elders (the Senate) and, probably, to follow their advice; and he had to submit to the people for their final decision cases involving capital punishment.

By the side of the king stood the Senate of about 300 members selected by the king for life. It was their privilege to appoint the interrex on the death of a king; they were consulted in the choice of the new king, and their sanction was necessary to ratify the vote of the assembled freemen. But they were not supreme, for the choice of the king needed ratification by the community; and the king was not bound to accept the advice they tendered.

The free citizens voted by 'curiae' in the Assembly of the

people, and hence its name : the Comitia Curiata. The curiae were religious as well as political groups which had developed a close corporate life, each with its peculiar worship, place of worship, priests and festivals. There were thirty such curiae in Rome. A majority of the members of a curia decided its vote and the decision of the Assembly was determined by the majority of the groups. The Assembly met at the summons and under the presidency of the king or of the interrex. It has the right to elect the king, but, as we have seen, this right was limited to the acceptance or rejection of the man named by the interrex. The Comitia Curiata could also hear capital cases if submitted to it by the king. It was also summoned to witness religious rites, the making of wills and adoptions.

During this monarchial period, political rights were given only to one part of the community, the patricians ; the remainder, without political rights, were known as the plebeians. Under the later kings, the pressure from the plebeians for some share in the government became strong and led to the organization of a new Assembly, the Comitia Centuriata, in which both the patricians and the plebeians had a place. The name was derived from the century,[1] which was the unit of voting in the Assembly. The purely patrician body, the Comitia Curiata, however, continued to exist.

In 510 B.C., Tarquin the Proud, the last of the kings was expelled from the State and the republican era began.

§2 GROWTH OF THE REPUBLIC (510-287 B.C.)

On the abolition of kingship, the power of the king, both civil and military, was vested in two annually-elected officers, the consuls. Besides the short term of the consulate, its dual character was another check on the power of the consuls, for one consul could forbid what his colleague had enjoined. Further, a consul was compelled to allow an appeal to the people against a sentence which affected the life or status of a citizen.

Rome had become a republic in the sense that monarchy had been abolished, and the monarch's power transferred to elected heads ; but the institution of the Republic did not, as yet, mean that the people had equal political power. The plebeians were subject to three kinds of disabilities, political, economic, and

---

[1] The century is most likely a military term used to denote a small division in the army which nominally contained about 100 men.

social. They, being poorer than the patricians, were always a
minority in the Comitia Centuriata;[1] they could not hold political
office; and, besides the patricians had entire control of the
administration of the law, which was unwritten. The law of debt
was harsh; and the public land and pastures were allotted only
to patricians. The plebeians could not contract legally valid
marriages with patricians.

The plebeians naturally desired to have these disabilities
removed and to acquire political, economic, and social equality
with the patricians. The patricians tried to retain their privileges
as long as they could, but, on account of pressure from the
plebeians, were forced to give them up one by one. The first
success of the plebeians was the institution of the office of the
tribune in 494 B.C. to protect them against oppression by patrician magistrates. In the same year a new Assembly, called the
Concilium Plebis, composed exclusively of plebeians, came into
being. The Concilium Plebis and the tribune became the instruments through which the plebeians carried on their struggle for
equality with the patricians. From 456 B.C. the public lands of
the State were given to plebeians as well as to patricians. The
laws of the State were codified in the Twelve Tables (451 B.C.).
It was declared in 449 B.C. that laws passed by the Concilium
Plebis were binding on the whole people, if confirmed by the
Comitia Centuriata. Four years later intermarriage between the
two 'orders' was legalized. The offices of consul, dictator, and
praetor (judge) were thrown open to plebeians in 367 B.C.,
356 B.C., and 377 B.C., respectively. In 339 B.C. it was ordered
that one censor must be a plebeian. Finally in 287 B.C., the laws
passed by the Concilium Plebis were declared to be binding on
all the people without ratification by any other authority. With
the establishment of political equality between the two classes,
which this law marks, the 'struggle between the orders' was,
at last, over.

[1] The predominance of wealthy men in the Comitia Centuriata (Assembly of the Centuries) is evident from the following table:

CLASS	PROPERTY	QUALIFICATION	CENTURIES
First Class ..	100,000	*asses liberales* (copper pounds)	80
Second Class ..	75,000	,,	20
Third Class ..	50,000	,,	20
Fourth Class ..	25,000	,,	20
Fifth Class ..	11,000	,,	30

One vote was given to each century, and the First Class, though least
numerous, was divided into 80 centuries. See A. H. Allcroft and W. F.
Masom, *Tutorial History of Rome*, 4th ed., p. 78.

§3 CONSTITUTION IN THE THIRD CENTURY B.C.

We may now sketch briefly the republican constitution of Rome after the 'struggle between the orders' was over.

Executive officials

(*i*) Two consuls were elected annually by the Comitia Centuriata. They took command abroad, represented the State in dealings with other States, punished those who withstood authority, summoned and presided over the Senate, had power to issue proclamations and were the head of the civil administration.

(*ii*) Six praetors were elected annually by the Comitia Centuriata. Two of them acted as judges at the capitals; four were sent out to administer the provinces of Rome, such as Sicily and Sardinia.

(*iii*) Two censors were elected by the Comitia Centuriata for eighteen months. They had charge of finance, revised the census and framed the list of senators.

(*iv*) Four aediles were elected annually. Two were known as the curule aediles, and were elected annually by the Comitia Tributa from among the patricians and the plebeians in alternate years. The other two were elected from the plebeians annually by the Concilium Plebis. They acted as assistants to the consuls in the administration of the city, took charge of public records, public buildings, and water-supply, regulated markets and performed the police functions.

(*v*) Eight quaestors were elected annually by the Comitia Tributa and acted as paymasters of troops, and were guardians and collectors of revenue.

(*vi*) Ten tribunes were elected annually from among the plebeians. Their original and primary function was to protect those members of their 'order' who appealed to them personally for help against arbitrary acts or unjust sentences on the part of the magistrates. To enable them to perform this function adequately, the tribunes were given (*a*) the power to veto (*intercessio*) any order of a magistrate (except the dictator) which they thought was against the interests of their 'order'; (*b*) the right of using force (*coercitio*); and (*c*) the right of arresting anyone who withstood them (*prehensio*). It is no exaggeration to say that through the use of these powers the tribunate became a guardian of the whole State against the illegal proceedings of magistrates. In addition to these powers, the tribunes also had the power of eliciting resolutions from the Concilium Plebis and of acting with them in initiating legislation.

The Assemblies

There were four assemblies in Rome. The Comitia Curiata (in which the people voted by curiae) was the oldest but the least important at this time. The main constitutional function reserved to it was to pass formally the *lex curiata* which was necessary to enable the magistrates to exercise their powers. The Comitia Centuriata (in which the people voted by centuries) elected consuls, censors and praetors; enacted laws; had the exclusive right to declare war and heard cases involving the death penalty. The Comitia Tributa was yet another assembly. Here the people voted by tribes, of which there were thirty-five. It elected the quaestors and the curule aediles; shared with the Centuriata the power of legislation; and the curule aediles conducted before it certain classes of cases, e.g. those involving the charge of usury. The Concilium Plebis consisted of plebeians only. In this Assembly also, voting was by tribes as in the Comitia Tributa. It elected tribunes and two aediles; passed laws and heard appeals against fines imposed by a tribune or a plebeian aedile.

The Senate

The Senate consisted of 300 members, the list being revised by the censors once every five years. The censors were expected 'to choose every most excellent citizen of any rank'; all ex-magistrates were usually included in it. In theory it was only the advisory body to the consuls, it could meet only if summoned, and could not command magistrates to take any course of action. In practice, it was very powerful; indeed the most powerful body in the State. It exercised the power of previous deliberation on matters which had to be submitted to the people. It gave directions to the magistrates on the conduct of their administrative duties. It claimed the right of suspending a magistrate from his office, of exempting individuals from the operation of the law, and even of declaring martial law. It pointed out flaws in legislative enactments and in effect revised them. Briefly, the assemblies and the magistrates deferred to the Senate in matters which they were authorized to decide independently.

This predominance of the Senate is explained by several factors It was composed of the best men in the State. Its members had a long tenure of office. Those two features of the Senate were in striking contrast to the relatively inexperienced character of the magistrates with their annual tenure. The nature of the business which the Roman Government had to transact in an era of wars, conquests and expansion also contributed to the Senate's ascendancy, for it demanded men of experience and cool wisdom to direct the destinies of the State; the magistrates and the people were only too willing to be led by the superior wisdom of the Senate. Finally, the character of the Roman citizens was a helpful factor. They were mostly farmers, who were content to elect magistrates and express their opinions occasionally on projects of legislation; unlike the Athenians, they had neither the desire nor the ability to take a more active part in government.

This constitution was in theory democratic : the people meeting in their assemblies were sovereign in legislation; they decided on peace and war; they periodically elected their magistrates. Polybius, the historian of Rome (204-122 B.C.), after describing the several parts of the constitution, preferred to describe it as one 'in which the elements of monarchy, aristocracy, and democracy were all to be found, acting and reacting on each other in a perfectly happy and harmonious combination'. Our survey, however, would rather substantiate the verdict of Fowler[1] that it 'was neither a democracy, nor a mixed constitution, nor a government of the best men in the State, but an *oligarchy* — the most compact and powerful oligarchy that the world has ever yet seen '. The key to the understanding of the constitution lies in the power of the Senate.

§4 CHECKS AND BALANCES

The republican constitution that we have just described is remarkable for its system of checks and balances. The disposition of power was made in such a way that, while the different agencies of government were assigned definite powers, they formed mutual checks and so were prevented from abusing their powers. Let us illustrate.

The consuls, as we have noticed, had wide powers which were succinctly summed up in the word 'imperium'. But there were several limitations to their power. They held office only for one year. They were expected to consult the Senate. Important matters affecting the welfare of the State had to be decided by the people. Cases involving capital punishment had similarly to be decided by the people. The tribunes could veto their acts. They could be tried for their mistakes after they had laid down their office. Above all, the collegiate nature of the consulate itself was a check. It was, however, characteristic of the system of checks and balances that the veto of the colleague was also limited. It had to be pronounced in person; the power could be exercised only against a magistrate and not against an assembly,

[1] *The City-State of the Greeks and Romans*, p. 220.

it could not be resorted to on the battlefield and must be directed against a matter partially advanced toward completion. The tribunes, like the consuls, had important powers ; but they too were checked by the collegiate character and the short term of their office ; their veto, like that of the consul, had to be exercised in person and at the moment when the contemplated action was being taken.

The principle of checks and balances applied not only to executive officers, but to the Senate and the assemblies as well. Thus the Senate, with all its wide powers in practice, was in theory only an advisory body ; its advice could be rejected. It could meet only if summoned by the magistrates. The assemblies had, as we have seen, legislative, elective and judicial powers ; but they too were in some ways limited : these bodies could meet only if summoned ; there were several assemblies performing different functions and their power of discussion was not great.

§5 THE FALL OF THE REPUBLIC

From about the middle of the second century B.C. we notice in Rome a tendency for republican institutions to fall into disrepute. The Republic had rested on four clear principles : divided authority ; a short tenure of office for magistrates ; the final decision of important matters of state by the people ; and the refusal to give unlimited military powers to any magistrates within the city, the exercise of imperium within the city being limited by the right of appeal and by the tribunician veto. But time and again, from 133 B.C., wide executive authority was concentrated in the hands of a single man specially designated by the vote of the people : Marius was consul six times, from 107 B.C. to 100 B.C. ; Pompey was consul twice, in 70 B.C. and in 55 B.C., and pro-consul and consul in 52 B.C. ; Julius Caesar was made dictator for an indefinite period from 48 B.C., was consul for five years, and was invested with other wide powers such as those of making war and peace and appointing governors to the provinces. The brilliant achievements of these men apparently justified the departure from the accepted republican principles. But, in reality, it was fraught with grave danger to the Republic. For, with the support of the army at their command and with their prestige as successful generals, these men were able to impose their will on the populace at home and transform the Republic into an effective despotism. This trend of events is clearly noticeable during the time of Julius Caesar, but becomes most marked during the principate of Augustus. The primary cause of this transformation of the Republic into the Empire was undoubtedly that by this time Rome had by conquest become mistress of vast dominions. Necessarily the governors sent to rule the distant parts of the Empire enjoyed wide discretion, and were practically independent of the home government. Briefly, the form of government adapted to a city-State was found inadequate for the task of imperial rule.

The principate of Augustus lasted from 27 B.C. to A.D. 14 ; it was so called because Augustus was first citizen, *princeps civium*. The principate was founded on the concentration in a single person of the essence of powers extracted from the chief republican magistrates, supplemented by a few special prerogatives. The two chief bases of the power of Augustus were :

(*i*) The pro-consular imperium This carried with it the command of the army and the fleet, and power over the most important provinces. It was essentially a military command, and normally it could confer no power within Rome. Augustus, however, was allowed to exercise it within the walls of Rome ; he could therefore rule the provinces without leaving Rome. Besides, his pro-consular command was declared to be superior to that of other pro-consuls.

(*ii*) The tribunician power. In virtue of this he could control the magistrates and the Senate and exercise an unlimited power of veto. Both these powers he held virtually for life. Besides, though technically he was not consul, he was granted equal rights with the consul of convening the Senate and introducing business, of nominating candidates for election by the people and of issuing valid ordinances. He was also placed on a level with the consul in outward rank. These arrangements preserved the forms of the Republic, while they recognized the authority of the man who was the effective master of the State.

The Senate not only continued to exist but was nominally given added power. Half the Roman provinces, the more settled ones, were given over to its administration. It was given jurisdiction over important political cases within the city and appellate jurisdiction over cases from provinces. With it rested the formal choice of the princeps ; it enacted laws on domestic matters. So great was the appearance of its power that the new government is sometimes described as a ' dyarchy ', i.e. a system of dual control by the princeps and the Senate. This was true only in appearance, for what the Senate did it did with the permission of the princeps.

The popular assemblies remained, but shorn of much of their former power. They were hardly used as courts of appeal ; popular legislation almost ceased. The only power that remained to them was that of electing the officers of the State. Even here their importance was limited in two ways : the princeps ' recommended ' candidates for their choice, and the officials appointed by the princeps tended to override consuls, praetors and others.

The constitution under Augustus may properly be described as ' an absolute monarchy disguised by the forms of a commonwealth ',[1] though Augustus himself might say, ' I stood before all others in dignity but, of actual power I possessed no more than my colleagues in each several magistracy '. The office of princeps really abrogated the four republican principles we mentioned earlier : divided control, short term of office, popular power and the dissociation within the city of Rome itself of the military from the civil power.

From the time of Augustus, Rome was, therefore, an Empire. This continued, with various vicissitudes, till about A.D. 476. from which date the medieval period may be said to begin.

§6 THE GOVERNMENT OF THE EMPIRE

By the time of Augustus, Rome had to manage a vast Empire including Macedonia and Greece, part of Africa, Spain, Sicily, Sardinia and Corsica. To govern this Empire, the Romans invented no new system ; they adapted their constitution to cover the administration of the provinces.

The subject communities of Rome were grouped as provinces. A province meant properly the ' department ' or ' sphere of command ' assigned to a Roman magistrate. It was in fact an aggregate of States or communities with diverse rank and status, constituted as a *provincia*. The *provincia* of Sicily, for instance, contained 68 such communities. Some of these communities were technically free States, not subject to the control of the provincial governor, permitted to follow their own laws and free from liability to pay tribute. Their main obligations were to follow Rome in her foreign policy and to supply her with military contingents. Others were tributary States subject to the jurisdiction of the governor.

The governor was responsible for the administration of the province. His duties were to defend it from foreign attack, to

[1] E. Gibbon, *The History of the Decline and Fall of the Roman Empire*, Vol. I. ch. iii.

watch over the conduct and policy of the people subject to his charge and to decide, or remit to Rome for decision, cases involving loss of life. From 146 B.C. down to the later years of the Republic, the Senate drew up a set of regulations for each new province which the governor was expected to observe ; a commission of ten was also sent to each province to co-operate with the governor in putting them into execution, and in arranging such details as seemed necessary. This body of regulations formed the *lex provinciae,* or the constitution of the province. Money, troops, and subordinate officials were provided by vote of the Senate. The general system of taxation was to collect a tenth of the produce of the land ; those who had no land paid a poll-tax. There were, further, indirect taxes such as port dues. Direct taxes were collected by the local authorities and paid to the governor's financial assistant ; the land-tax and indirect taxes were sold to tax farmers who paid a fixed sum to the State for the right of collecting them.

The Roman provincial system had several defects. The most serious of these was the freedom of the governors from all effective control, notwithstanding the checks that were provided. The governor after resignation was liable to prosecution. ' But the courts were distant, the routes difficult, and the alien plaintiff must seek justice from the defendant's friends and accomplices.' The result of this was the practical irresponsibility of the governor, general extortion from the provincials, and maladministration. ' The Roman governor in his arrogant behaviour and general tyranny,' says T. M. Taylor, ' resembled rather a Persian satrap than a republican magistrate.' [1] These defects were only aggravated by the existence of annual commands, the absence of an organized civil service and of some central authority at home not interested in provincial misrule, which might be expected to enforce responsibility on the governors. The governing class in Rome was rather interested in exploiting the provinces for their own profit. ' Even the population of the capital at home got their share of the spoil in the frequent distributions of corn and money.' [2]

Under the Empire, a conscious attempt was made to reform the system. The governors were kept at their posts for longer terms. They were paid regular salaries and forbidden plunder. An estimate was made of the resources of the Empire, and the burden of taxation was apportioned according to capacity. The

---

[1] *A Constitutional and Political History of Rome,* p. 202.
[2] H. F. Pelham, *Outlines of Roman History,* p. 170.

system of farming the State dues was ended. The middleman gave place to the official and the official was taught to act as the servant of the State. Communications were improved, and served as an important unifying agency. An efficient civil service was developed.

§7 RIGHTS AND DUTIES OF ROMAN CITIZENSHIP

The normal mode of acquisition of citizenship was of course birth of Roman parents. Exceptional modes were the conferment of citizenship by the State on foreigners and the freeing of slaves.

The rights of a citizen under the developed Republic are usually divided into two kinds — private and public. The private rights were *jus commercium* and *jus connubium*.[1] The first is ' the legal capacity to acquire full rights in every kind of property, to effect its acquisition, and to transfer it by the most binding forms, and to defend the acquired right in one's own person by Roman process of law '. The second is ' the right to conclude a marriage which is regarded as fully valid by the State, and which, therefore, gives rise to the *patria potestas*'.[2] The public rights were those which enabled the citizens to have a share in government, viz. the rights of voting in the assemblies, of standing as a candidate for the various elective offices of the State, such as those of consul and praetor, and of serving as a fully-equipped soldier in the legions.

The Roman citizen, says Fowler,[3] was the most highly privileged person in the civilized world of that day. The great prize of his citizenship was not so much the possession of public rights as ' the legal protection of his person and his property wherever he might be in the Empire '. No one could maltreat his person with impunity. He could do business everywhere with the certainty that his sales, purchases, and contracts would be recognized and defended by Roman law ; the non-citizen had no such guarantees for his transactions. ' To live a life of security and prosperity you must be a Roman citizen.'

The citizen also had certain duties which he owed to the State. These were, obedience to law apart, twofold. (*i*) Payment of tribute. This was levied on all property, and was a fixed amount, viz. one-tenth per cent. According to Taylor,[4] this is said to

---

[1] Greenidge, *Roman Public Life*, pp. 35-6 and 136.
[2] The power or authority of the head of a family over those depending on him, especially parental authority.
[3] *Rome*, pp. 132-3.   [4] op. cit., p. 192

have been abolished by the patricians after the overthrow of the monarchy as a concession to the poor citizens, but was soon revived. After the introduction of the principle of making the soldiers' pay a direct charge on the treasury, it was only levied in time of necessity, when other sources of revenue did not suffice ; it was regarded as a loan and was repaid when the treasury was full. When the revenues from the provinces had increased, the tribute was dropped. It was not levied after 167 B.C.

(*ii*) *Military service.* The normal duration of service was, in the republican period, sixteen or at the most twenty yearly campaigns [1] for the foot-soldier, and ten campaigns for the knight. This duty incidentally implied another : the presence of the citizen at the census for registration.

There was another class of citizen recognized by Roman law, viz. the partial citizen. He possessed the private but not the public rights ; he was also subject to the duties of Roman citizenship. This status was conferred by Rome on the citizens of some towns which it conquered.

§8   THE LEGACY OF ROME

The great service that Rome rendered to political development and the political education of the world was that it passed large masses of savage and semi-savage tribes through the yoke of political discipline and taught them the way of life of the State. ' Rome was,' it has been well said by C. D. Burns, ' the political teacher and organizer of the peoples of three continents ', and thereby Rome has bequeathed the ideal of law and order.

The Roman love of order and unity was so strong that the men of the Middle Ages were obsessed by the notion of the political unity of the world in the face of the most disintegrating forces. This idea took definite shape in the conception of the Holy Roman Empire. And, according to C. F. Strong,[2] this Roman love of unity is the basis of the persistent dream among moderns of the ultimate establishment of some international or super-national authority for the prevention of war.

In the field of political organization, the contributions of Rome have mainly been the mixed constitution and the principle of checks and balances embodied in that constitution and expounded by her famous historian, Polybius. In the Roman constitution,

---

[1] Greenidge, op. cit., p. 138.
[2] *Modern Political Constitutions*, p. 22.

as we have seen, the consuls represented the monarchic element, the Senate, the aristocratic and the assemblies, the democratic. Each one of these exercised some check on the others, no one being able to act effectively without the consent of all. Thus an elaborate system of checks and balances was created. Polybius was among the first writers to perceive the advantages of a mixed constitution and of checks and balances in the organization of government.

Above all, the distinctive gift of Rome to civilization has been her system of law, which is now the basis of the legal systems of many European countries. The foundations of Roman law, as we have seen, may be traced to the Republic ; it was, however, under the Empire that it developed into a logical system. This apart, the distinctive contributions of Rome in the sphere of law have been twofold. First, in the words of MacIver,[1] it was Rome that liberated the universality of law, and ' first embodied in one comprehensive and unified code the distinctive order of the State '. Before Rome, the protection of the law had been a political privilege, fully available only to the citizen body. The stranger required a citizen-patron before he could enjoy the guarantee of law. The idea that law has a common application to all persons within a political territory had been alien to the Greeks and was worked out by Rome. This she did by developing what is known as *jus gentium,* i.e. ' the law which all men everywhere obey ', evolved by the Roman praetors out of principles presumed to be the common basis of justice for aliens and Romans alike. Secondly, the Roman conception of the law of nature [2] has been of great value. According to Cicero, the law of nature is but

' right reason, which is in accordance with nature, applies to all men, and is unchangeable and eternal. By its commands this law summons men to the performance of their duties ; by its prohibitions it restrains them from doing wrong.'

The value of this conception in later days has been great : it has helped to keep before the mental vision a type of perfect law to which human law is expected to approximate ; to sweep away ideas and institutions which have become obsolete, e.g. slavery ; to advance the cause of freedom against arbitrary rule ; to develop the doctrine of equality, as all men were declared by

[1] *The Modern State,* pp. 103-95.
[2] The Romans did not invent it ; it can be traced to the Greeks.

nature to be equal ; and to inspire jurists in the seventeenth
century (e.g. Grotius) to lay the foundations of international law.

§9 DECAY OF THE CITY-STATE

The history of ancient city-States shows that their decay was
brought about by three causes : internal quarrels ; inability to
withstand attack by powerful country-States ; and expansion. It
is interesting to reflect that all these are related in some ways to
the small size of the State, as will be seen in the sequel.

The internal dissensions within the Greek city-States became
marked in the fifth century B.C. In the oligarchic cities, the
richer and ruling class oppressed the Demos,[1] and got rid of the
most dangerous of its leaders ; in the democratic States, the
Demos exiled the few rich. This second point is illustrated by
the events which took place in Naxos. The Demos of Naxos
sent a number of its oligarchic party into exile in 501 B.C. ; the
exiles went to Miletus and asked help of its ruler, Aristagoras.
He asked for aid from the Persian satrap.[2] This is a story which
is constantly repeated in various forms during the fifth and fourth
centuries B.C. : ' Greeks, quarrelling among themselves, allow the
common enemy to be called in.' The primary reasons for these
internal feuds [3] were inequality and jealousy.

' The cause of all these evils,' wrote Thucydides,[4] ' was the
love of power, originating in avarice and ambition, and the party-
spirit which is engendered by them when men are fairly embarked
in a contest. For the leaders on either side used specious names,
the one party professing to uphold the constitutional equality of
the many, the other the wisdom of an aristocracy, while they
made the public interests, to which in name only they were
devoted, in reality their prize. Striving in every way to overcome
each other, they committed the most monstrous crimes ; yet even
these were surpassed by the magnitude of their revenges, which
they pursued to the very uttermost, neither party observing any
definite limits either of justice or public expediency, but both
alike making the caprice of the moment their law.'

Aristotle is inclined to emphasize the desire for equality as
the root cause : ' Upon the whole,' says he, ' those who aim after

---

[1] The common people.
[2] Fowler, *The City-State of the Greeks and Romans*, pp. 248-9.
[3] Technically called *stasis*.
[4] *Works* (trans. B. Jowett), Vol. I, pp. 243-4.

an equality are the cause of seditions.'[1] The effect of inequality
was aggravated by the small size of the State, because the comfort
of the few, as contrasted with the suffering of the many, was
more manifest when ' the rich man daily met the poor man and
scorned him ; the poor man daily saw the rich man and hated
him '.

The inability to withstand attack by powerful country-States
is directly related to the size of the city-State, and is best illustrated
from Greece. The Macedonians were a people devoted to
military pursuits, inhabiting a large territory to the north of
Greece and united under a strong military genius. To resist such
a people as the Macedonians, says Hammond, the Greeks would
have to do the impossible :

' to unlearn in a moment all the maxims of jealous precaution
against rival cities by which they had regulated their conduct, to
give up the practice of politics in miniature and understand at
once what was needed in politics on a larger scale.'

As it was, their jealousy prevented united resistance and, after
the battle of Chaeronea in 338 B.C., Greece lay at the mercy of
Philip, King of Macedonia.

The last cause is the expansion of the city-State, such as took
place when Rome became an Empire. Not only did she deprive
many cities of their independence, and therefore, of their statehood, but she herself lost the compactness so essential to a
city-State.

SELECT BIBLIOGRAPHY

F. F. ABBOT, *A History and Description of Roman Political
Institutions*, Ginn, 1901

W. W. FOWLER, *The City-State of the Greeks and Romans*,
Macmillan, 1921

A. H. J. GREENIDGE, *Roman Public Life*, Macmillan, 1922

W. E. HEITLAND, *A Short History of the Roman Republic*,
Cambridge, 1911

W. W. HOW and H. D. LEIGH, *A History of Rome*, Longmans,
1907

B. JOWETT (Tr.), *Thucydides*, Vol. I, Oxford, 2nd ed., 1900

H. F. PELHAM, *Outlines of Roman History*, Rivington, 1922

T. M. TAYLOR, *A Constitutional and Political History of Rome*,
Methuen, 1911

[1] *Politics* (Everyman Library edition), p. 143.

CHAPTER XIV

MEDIEVAL EUROPEAN POLITY

§1 FEUDALISM: ITS MEANING

THE most outstanding feature of medieval Europe, from A.D. 476 to A.D. 1500, was feudalism, the name given to the form of society and government which then prevailed, and which attained its most perfect development in the eleventh, twelfth and thirteenth centuries.[1] Its essential characteristics were : (*i*) the holding of land by a vassal from a lord ; (*ii*) the existence of a close personal bond between the lord and the vassal ; and (*iii*) the full or partial rights of sovereignty which the holder of an estate had over those living on it. An estate of this nature, whether big or small, was called a fief or feud ; hence the term feudalism.

According to feudal theory, the kings of the earth were vassals of the emperor,[2] who was God's vassal. They received their dominions as fiefs to be held on conditions of loyalty to their lord. Each king, in turn, parcelled out his kingdom into a certain number of large divisions, each of which he granted to a single man, who promised in general to be faithful to him and to serve him. So long as he fulfilled his duties, he continued to hold the lands, and his heirs after him, on the same terms. In the same way, the tenants-in-chief of the king divided their land among vassals on like conditions ; these vassals, among others, and so on down through any number of stages.

The king, on receiving his fief, was entrusted with sovereignty over all persons living upon it ; he became their law-maker, their commander, and their judge.

'Then, when he parcelled out his fief among his great men, he invested them, within the limits of the fiefs granted, with all his own sovereign rights. Each vassal became a virtual sovereign in his own domain. And when these great vassals subdivided their fiefs and granted parcels to others, they in turn invested

---

[1] Examples of feudalism could be found in medieval India, China and Japan as well.
[2] See §4 below.

their vassals with more or less of those powers of sovereignty with which they themselves had been clothed.'[1]

The key to the understanding of feudal society is thus to be found in the relation of the vassal to his lord. The vassal owed his lord fidelity ; this was promised by him at the ceremony of homage :

' The vassal came before his lord, bareheaded and unarmed, and declared on his knees that he became his " man ". The lord then kissed him and raised him from his knees. Then the vassal swore fidelity (fealty) to his lord.'

Among other obligations of the vassal to his lord were military service, normally limited to forty days a year ; rent for his land and house ; work at the lord's fields for a certain number of days in the year ; aids on such occasions as the knighting of the lord's eldest son, the marriage of his daughter, the ransoming of his person if he were made a prisoner of war ; relief, or the payment made when a new heir succeeded to the fief ; fines upon alienation paid when the land was alienated by the vassal to another ; lodging and hospitality to the lord and his followers on his journeys or hunting expeditions ; and attendance at the lord's court. If a vassal died without heirs his property reverted to the lord. If he were guilty of treason, the lord might claim his possession by forfeiture.

The one great duty of the lord to his vassal was to protect him : to avenge his vassal's wrongs, to defend his rights and to secure him justice in all matters. This was very important at a time when there was general insecurity.

§2 THE POLITICAL CONCEPTIONS OF FEUDALISM

The most important assumption underlying feudalism was that the individual's relation to land tended to determine his political rights and duties.

' The public duties and obligations which ordinarily the citizen owes to the State,' says Adams,[2] ' are turned into private and

---

[1] P. V. N. Myers, *Medieval and Modern History*, p. 76. Myers notes that the holders of small fiefs were not allowed to exercise the more important functions of sovereignty. Thus though in France in the tenth century there were about 70,000 fief-holders, only between 100 to 200 had the right to coin money, levy taxes, make laws, and administer their own justice.

[2] G. B. Adams, *Civilization during the Middle Ages*, p. 195.

personal services which he owes to his lord in return for land which he has received from him. The State no longer depends upon its citizens, as citizens, for the fulfilment of public duties, but it depends upon a certain few to perform specified duties, which they owe as vassals of the king, and these, in turn depend upon their vassals for services, which will enable them to meet their own obligations towards the king.'

The landless man, in fact, had no privileges as a citizen : he had to find a lord if he wanted protection and a place in the social system. He therefore entered the service of some large landowner, in some capacity or other, and obtained protection ; in return he fulfilled certain specific obligations. This brought about 'the substitution of personal loyalty to a superior for the tie of common citizenship '.

In this basic conception is implied another : the fusion of governmental rights with land tenure, i.e. the landlord had some important governmental rights over the freeman residing on his land. He could decide property titles, make military levies, coin money, levy taxes and hold his own independent courts of justice. Indeed from this point of view feudalism may rightly be defined as 'the identification of landed property with sovereignty '. Sovereignty, indeed, of this petty parcelled kind had become a private hereditary possession, an item in the family assets.

Thirdly, the State was disintegrated. It no longer acted, as a whole, but in semi-independent parts. The central authority did not act directly upon all individuals alike throughout a common territory. Feudalism was, indeed, the negation of central government and administration. The king controlled directly only his immediate vassals ; other men, lower down in the series could be reached from above only through *their* immediate lords. Authority filtered down to the lower grades of society through the higher. Feudalism was a system ' not of general obedience to common law, but of personal obedience and subordination founded upon landownership '. A community in which important governmental powers were held by large landowners, and in which the central government was weak, was very imperfectly orderly in practice.

§3 MERITS AND DEFECTS

With all its imperfections, feudalism has rendered inestimable service to the European polity. The political unity and the way of life of the State, built up laboriously by Rome in western Europe, were threatened with complete destruction in consequence of the barbarian invasions which caused the downfall of her Empire. At such a time, by welding together the strong sentiment of personal loyalty and the stable attachments connected with the possession of land, feudalism gave some order and avoided total chaos ; it provided ' a temporary scaffolding or framework of order on which a truer national life could grow .

Secondly, it fostered among the big landlords self-reliance and love of personal independence.

Turbulent, violent, and ungovernable as was the feudal aristocracy of Europe,' says Myers, ' it performed the grand service of keeping alive during the later medieval period the spirit of liberty. The feudal lords would not allow themselves to be dealt with arrogantly by their king ; they stood on their rights as freemen.'[1]

As against a royal tyranny, exceeding the bounds of law, the greater lords could oppose a military power greater than the king's.

' By God, Sir Constable,' says Edward I of England, ' thou shalt fight in France with me or hang.'   ' By God, Sir King,' is the reply, ' I will neither fight nor hang.'   The barons in England prevented kings from becoming too despotic and tyrannical, as may be seen from the history of King John's reign ; at a time when the yeoman and the burgher had not become bold enough to resist the monarch, this was a real service to the cause of freedom.

The defect, however, of the feudal system was, as may be seen from the foregoing discussion, ' the confusion of public and private rights ', which was yet essential to it.   It also rendered difficult the formation of strong national Governments, as a country was split up into a vast number of practically independent principalities.   Briefly, it was liable to the disease of anarchy ; indeed where the private ownership of land by a feudal chief was the basis of social order, anarchy was, we may say, inevitable. Adams' remark that ' the feudal system was confusion roughly organized ' sums up its true place in the evolution of European polity.

[1] op. cit., pp. 86-7.

§4 TWO UNIFYING FORCES

The Church

The separatist and disintegrating tendencies of feudalism were in striking contrast to the magnificent medieval ideal of the *Respublica Christiana,* in which churchmanship was co-extensive with citizenship — a universal Christian society, living under one principle of life, and divinely ordained to be governed by two authorities, the spiritual and the temporal (the Catholic Church and the Holy Roman Empire) in accordance with divine and natural law. On account of the weakness of this ideal in its application to the actual problems of government (i.e. on account of the absence of the means for deciding what functions pertained to the religious and what to the secular arm), quarrels took place between the Church and the Empire. We are not concerned here with their quarrels, but rather with their services as unifying influences.

The Church had internal unity. Its officials were definitely connected by the use of one language and general agreement as to the nature of the world and the duties of man. Their customs and traditions, even apart from religious ritual, were the same. The Church recognized no boundaries, whether of baronies or of States, as limits to its own spiritual sovereignty. Its lesson was brotherhood, and that lesson, though often neglected, was never completely lost sight of or forgotten. Its influence was exerted on the side of one who proved himself capable of creating larger wholes of political authority. Its laws were not diverse, but always the same and reached the people through the administration of ecclesiastical courts. The Church, says Ernest Barker,[1] enthroning itself over Christian society, makes a great and gallant attempt to unify all life, in all its reaches, political, social, economic and intellectual. Politically, it attempts to rebuke and correct kings for internal misgovernment, as when they falsify coinage, and for external misdoing, as when they break treaties. Socially, it controls the life of the family by the law of marriage, which it administers, and the life of the individual, by its system of penance ; economically, it seeks to regulate commerce and industry by enforcing just prices and prohibiting usury, as it seeks to control the economic motive in general by its conception of property as a trust held for the general benefit and by its inculcation of charity ; intellectually, it develops a single culture in the univer-

---

[1] E. Barker, in *The Social and Political Ideas of some Great Mediaeval Thinkers* (ed. F. J. C. Hearnshaw), p. 15.

sities which are its organs, and in the last resort it enforces that culture by the persecution of heresy and by excommunication ; for ' if you were excommunicated by the authorities of the Church you lost all legal and political rights '. Truly may it be said that the Church was the State in the Middle Ages.

The Holy Roman Empire

Like the unity of the Church, the idea of one universal temporal State was preserved through the institution known as the Holy Roman Empire. The Empire came into existence when Charles the Great, King of the Franks (A.D. 768-814), succeeded in bringing together under his sword the territory now included in Germany, Switzerland, Hungary, most of Italy, France and Belgium. It was on Christmas Day 800 that he was crowned by the Pope as emperor of Rome. With various vicissitudes, the Empire continued to exist till 1806, when Francis II resigned the imperial dignity. For the larger part of its history, it was an Empire only in name ; in effect it was not more than the sovereignty of Germany and Italy vested in a Germanic prince ; but it at least kept alive the ideal of the unity of Christendom.

Essentially, as Bryce has pointed out in a classic analysis,[1] the Holy Roman Church and the Holy Roman Empire were one and the same thing, the universal Christian society in two aspects : as divine and eternal it had for its head the Pope, to whom souls had been entrusted ; as human and temporal, the emperor, commissioned to rule men's bodies and acts. To the position of the emperor, we are told, three duties were attached. He who held it must typify spiritual unity, must preserve peace and must be a fountain of all law and justice, by which alone among imperfect men peace is preserved and restored. Placed in the midst of Europe, the emperor was to bind its people into one body, reminding them of their common faith, their common blood and their common interest in each other's welfare. He settled disputes between warring States, and represented the common interest of Christendom in such matters of moment as the crusades. To him the princes of Europe were bound to render obedience ; he could punish offenders against the public order of Christendom.

' And that he might be the peace-maker, he must be the expounder of justice, and the author of its concrete embodiment, the positive law ; chief legislator and supreme judge of appeal, the one and only source of all legitimate authority.'

[1] *The Holy Roman Empire*, ch. vii.

The Holy Roman Empire has been described by Frantz as the keystone of the arch of the whole temporal order of the Middle Ages ; yet ' it was not a coercive authority that the German emperor, the head of the Holy Roman Empire, exercised over the rest of Europe ; it was rather a moral authority '. It was characteristic, too, of the men of the Middle Ages that, demanding the existence of an emperor, they cared little who he was or how he was chosen, so long as he had been duly inaugurated. And they were not shocked by the contrast between unbounded rights and actual helplessness, for at no time in the world's history has theory, professing all the while to control practice, been so utterly divorced from it.[1]

§5 MEDIEVAL CITY-STATES

From the eleventh century to the fourteenth, there was, throughout Europe, a marked rise of towns to prominence. The growth of trade and industry had made them wealthy ; they now demanded self-government. Towns developed in England, France, the Netherlands, Germany, and Italy ; they acquired most power in Germany and Italy, where the central government was weakest. In Italy, indeed, they were virtually independent little city-States of the ancient Greek type.

Everywhere the principal cause of the growth of towns was the facility they offered to industry and commerce and, consequently, to the increase of wealth. Being walled towns, fortified and organized for defence, they also provided greater security than the neighbouring country — an important consideration in those days of general insecurity. The urban populations were interested in developing their trade and industry. They found, however, that they could not succeed in their endeavour unless they first got rid of their vexatious obligations to the feudal lord in whose domain they were situated : their liability to satisfy uncertain and inconvenient demands for money, to submit themselves to multiple jurisdictions and to the inconveniences arising from the unfree status of many of the artisans who had originally been slaves. They began to demand conditions under which, as Fisher put it bluntly, money could safely be made. In broad outline, they claimed :

' to be permitted to compound for their own farm or taxes, to be permitted to make their own by-laws, to be relieved of onerous

---

[1] Bryce, op. cit.

feudal servitudes, to have their civil suits tried in their own courts and within their own walls, to be able to select their own officers, and that serfs resident for a year and a day within a town or borough should be regarded as free.' [1]

What they wanted, in short, was a more or less extensive degree of political autonomy and local self-government.

The movement for emancipation is everywhere marked by the demand for a charter from the overlord — be he baron, prelate, prince or emperor — embodying the liberties claimed. In some cases, this was obtained by a monetary transaction, as at London ; elsewhere through a revolutionary process, as at Laon and Beauvais in northern France and Milan in Italy ; and in others, by a peaceful process of permitted growth', as at Tournai and St Omer in Flanders.

From the charters that have come down to us, it is clear that the freedom conferred on towns varied enormously. There is no need for our purpose to take account of the differences in detail. Broadly speaking, two kinds of chartered town are found.[2] The first and larger class includes communities enjoying certain privileges under the rule of feudal lords. A smaller class consists of those which are not only privileged but 'free'; that is, self-governing bodies corporate. Often the one class shades off into the other.

The burgesses of the first type of city (e.g. St Riquier and Breteuil) are found to enjoy the following privileges : a free status, the freedom of the land with the right freely to transfer it, convey it, mortgage it, and make it serve as security for capital ; the town-peace 'protected by special pains and penalties ' ; the right of trade ; commutation for a fixed money-rent of their servile dues and obligations, such as that of furnishing the feudal lord with lodging and subsistence during his tours, taking up arms at his summons, using the common ovens, mills, etc. ; the right to collect market-tolls ; commercial jurisdiction ; a monopoly of certain staple industries in the town and neighbourhoc ᴵ and rights of pre-emption over all imported wares.

It is to the second type of medieval city that the term ' city-State ' is more appropriate, for in addition to the privileges mentioned above, they enjoyed self-government The charter secured by the city of St Omer in 1127, for instance, recognized[3] the city

[1] H. Pirenne, *Medieval Cities*, pp. 176-7.
[2] H. W. C. Davis, *Mediaeval Europe*, p. 218.
[3] Pirenne, op. cit., pp. 197-8.

as a distinct legal territory, provided with a special law common to all inhabitants with special courts and a full communal autonomy. Its inhabitants were given the right to be tried by magistrates recruited, and often elected, from their midst. In Italy, in the south of France, and in parts of Germany, these magistrates were called ' consuls '; in the Netherlands and in northern France, *échevins* or aldermen ; and elsewhere, *jures* or jurors. Cities of this class were administered by councils, each with a president at the head, known in France and England as the mayor and in Germany as the burgomaster, who represented the city in negotiations with the lord, the king or with other cities. In some of the cities, a mass-meeting was held to elect the magistrates and councils, to vote taxes, audit accounts and decide on all questions of importance. The self-governing city may best be described as ' a commercial and industrial commune living in the shelter of a fortified *enceinte* and enjoying a law, an administration and a jurisprudence of exception which made of it a collective privileged personality '.[1]

In the general evolution of cities, only one other important feature remains to be noticed. It was generally a guild of merchants that led the agitation to secure the liberties of cities and, indeed, in the initial stages, monopolized the government of the city, ' craftsmen ' being excluded from the class of ' freemen ' of the town. In time, the craftsmen — the weavers, the spinners, the bakers and the rest — formed guilds of their own on the model of merchant guilds. In some cities there were upwards of fifty of these associations.[2]

' No sooner had these plebeian societies grown strong,' says Myers,[3] ' than, in many of the continental (i.e. European) cities they entered into a bitter struggle with the patrician merchant guild for a share in the municipal government or for participation in its trade monopoly...It lasted for two centuries and more... and during all this time filled the towns with strenuous confusion. The outcome, speaking in general terms, was the triumph of the craftsmen.'

Finally, a tendency towards a new kind of oligarchy within the crafts began to develop,[4] the master-artisans being privileged as against the ' journeymen ', and the wealthier among the master-

---

[1] ibid., p. 220.
[2] Myers, op. cit., p. 154.
[3] ibid.
[4] Sidgwick. *The Development of European Polity*, pp. 239-41.

artisans themselves acquiring a leading position as contrasted with the poorer among them.

The lines of evolution of medieval cities may be summarized thus : the city works itself free from the political system of the surrounding country ; the merchants take the lead ; then the crafts rise to equality ; finally, an oligarchy of master-artisans, and of the richer among them, develops within the crafts.

§6 IN ITALY

We have already said (in §5) that it was in Italy that the medieval cities acquired the greatest power and influence. Towards the close of the thirteenth century there were about two hundred of them[1] in northern and central Italy — self-governing little city-Republics, with just a nominal dependence upon Pope or emperor. Doubtless, their power is explained by two causes : their rich trade with the East and the absence, especially in contrast to the position in England and France, of an effective central power.

By the eleventh century, many of the cities had been granted, de Sismondi tells us,[2] not only the right of raising fortifications, but also that of assembling the citizens to concert together the means of their common defence. This meeting of all the men of the city-State capable of bearing arms was called a Parliament. It elected annually two consuls charged with the administration of justice at home and the command of the army abroad. It also appointed a secret council, called the Consilio di Credenza, to assist the Government, besides a grand council of the people, who prepared the decisions to be submitted to the Parliament. The Consilio di Credenza was at the same time charged with the administration of the finances, consisting chiefly of entrance duties collected at the gates of the city and voluntary contributions asked of the citizens in moments of danger.

The cities had acquired their freedom and a republican constitution, but, as O. J. Thatcher remarks, this did not ensure law and order.

' They were engaged in constant feuds with each other. Only members of the ruling guilds had a share in the Government, and the class distinctions among the inhabitants formed a large disturbing element. The higher and the lower nobility and the rich

[1] Myers, op. cit., p. 157.
[2] *A History of the Italian Republics*, pp. 20-1.

merchants struggled for authority and disregarded the rights of the industrial classes.'[1]

There were not only internal feuds ; it often happened that the conflicting interests of cities led to fierce struggles between them, ending only with the ruin of one of the rivals, as in the contest between Florence and Pisa or between Venice and Genoa. The issue was further complicated by the fact that some cities called in the aid of the emperor (and were called Ghibelline) while others joined with the Pope (and were called Guelph). The constant wars and the strife of parties had their inevitable result : the gradual decline of democratic institutions. The first step in this process was the adoption, by many cities in the latter half of the twelfth century and in the thirteenth, of an institution known as the Podestá, a ' stranger knight, chosen from some other city, and invested with the highest executive power '.[2] His primary function was to repress anarchy within the city ; he also had to direct military expeditions. The armed force of the city was placed at his disposal for both objects. The Podestá, it must be noticed, was an addition to the normal democratic institutions of the cities. Milan appointed its first annual Podestá in 1186 ; Genoa, in 1190. The second stage in the decline of the republican institutions of the cities is the rise of the tyrants, ' many of whom by their crimes rendered themselves as odious as the worst of the tyrants who usurped supreme power in the cities of ancient Hellas '. The Podestá was apparently inadequate to meet the dangers from within and from without, so despots came to power : Azzo VI at Ferrara (1209), Romano at Verona (1225) and Sforza at Milan (1450). Sidgwick notes the interesting fact that ' though the Tyrannus often is established by violence, he mostly goes through the form of election ',[3] a make-believe adopted by dictators in modern times as well.

Comparison with Greek city-States [4]

This survey of medieval Italian city-States shows that in some respects their origin and development were not unlike those of the ancient Greek city-States. Both owed their origin to their military advantage and the facilities for trade and industry they offered ;

[1] Thatcher, *A Short History of Mediaeval Europe*, pp. 223-4.
[2] Sidgwick, op. cit., p. 273 ; this reference also gives the rules which regulated the office.
[3] op. cit., p. 275.
[4] ibid. See lecture XIX for an elaboration of the points discussed in the two following paragraphs.

both showed a concentrated political life and patriotism, especially in the early years of their history ; in both, in the later years of their history, we find stasis. In their constitutional development, we note some striking similarities. In both, in the initial stages, the administration is in the hands of the few, while some important decisions are brought before an assembly of the people (the ' Agora ' in Greece and the ' Parlamento ' in Italy) ; dissensions arise and there is a drift to democracy, and, later still, in times of disorder, there is the rule of the despot. Finally in both cases, as Sidgwick shows,[1] civilization, with the habits of peaceful industry and the luxury thereby obtained, makes the citizens in course of time personally disinclined for war, which they carry cn more and more by means of mercenaries. This, together with their incapacity to form a stable union, leads to their ultimate defeat, when they are brought face to face with the larger country-States in their neighbourhood.

There are, however, important differences. In ancient city-States, mechanical labour was servile ; in medieval times it was free. In the former, the internal quarrels were between the rich and the poor ; in the latter, first, between the feudal nobility and the merchants, and later, between the merchants and the artisans. Again, Italian democracy was more partial than the Greek, for it never effectively included all the *free* native inhabitants of the town, but only a certain number of organized trades and crafts ; it was also more imperfectly developed, as the Italian Demos never attempted actually to govern like the Greek.[2] And, finally, the Greek tyrant almost always began and ended as an unconstitutional ruler ; in the Italian cities, the rule of the despot was to a much greater extent regularized by formal election and regarded as legitimate by general sentiment.[3]

§7 MEDIEVAL PARLIAMENTS

Before we pass on to the modern period, we must consider a significant political invention of the Middle Ages, viz. representative parliaments. It was apparently in the twelfth century, according to Jenks, that the rulers of western Europe began dealing with the deputies of their subject-communities on the matter of taxation, no longer by individual or local action but as a whole, by summons to a central Assembly or Parliament. Clearly, these parliaments owed their origin to the pecuniary needs of kings who found them convenient instruments with which to satisfy their

---

[1] ibid.   [2] ibid.   [3] ibid.

needs ; later, however, they began to criticize and control kings, and demanded and secured important powers in the government of the State.

Illustrations of medieval parliaments may be given from England, Spain, France, and Sweden. In 1295 Edward I of England summoned to the ' Model Parliament ' the lay and spiritual peers, the representatives of the lower clergy, two knights from each shire, and a varying number of members, generally two, from each town and borough. The composition of the assembly is noteworthy because in the England of those days there were only three important occupations — that of the agriculturist, of the trader, and of the priest. They were all represented in the Model Parliament : the landed interest by the lay peers and the knights of the shire ; trade and industry by the borough members ; and the Church by the spiritual peers and the representatives of the lower clergy. In Aragon (one of the medieval Spanish kingdoms) the Cortes (Parliament) was composed of four estates : the higher nobility, the knights, the clergy, and the towns and universities. To the States-General summoned by Philip IV of France in 1302 were called all tenants-in-chief, as well as representatives of cathedral chapters, monasteries, and of the burghers or inhabitants of towns. In fact the only class unrepresented was the peasantry, and it was probably presumed that the landowners spoke for the whole agricultural interests. In Sweden, until less than a century ago, the Riksdag was divided into four estates : nobles, priests, burgesses, and peasants, each of which sat and deliberated apart from the rest.

Medieval parliaments were parliaments of ' estates ', i.e. representative of special classes or interests such as the nobility, the clergy, etc., rather than representative of the people as a whole. They reflected in their composition all but one (i.e. the last) of the classes of medieval society, the noble, the knight, the priest, the burgess and the serf. For a long time the deputies of each estate were separately summoned, and, indeed, often sat in different chambers and voted separately (in Sweden till 1866). Thus it came about that in the place of single- or double-chambered assemblies, such as we are familiar with, there were sometimes three and four chambers. Further, as Jenks says, the State required not merely representatives of individuals acting haphazard, but representatives of *communities*, which could be held bound by the promises of their spokesmen — the shire, the borough, the diocese, the cathedral chapter. These bodies, though not corporations in the technical sense, were all *communities*, having property which could be seized or at least members who could be held responsible. Strangely enough, liability, not privilege. was the basis of parliamentary representation.[1] It is noteworthy, too, that the medieval representative was a delegate, i.e. one whose duty was to declare the will of those whom he represented; he had no right to use his independent judgement.

The modern Parliament is generally bicameral; it is also *national* in character. Parliament, Burke has said, is a *deliberative* assembly of *one* nation, with *one* interest, that of the whole; where not local purposes, not local prejudices, ought to guide but the general good resulting from the general reason of the whole. It is generally elected from mixed territorial constituencies, consisting of men who follow different occupations; the representative, too, is not bound by the mandate of his constituency. His duty is to consult with the representatives of other parts of the country and to devise the measures best adapted for securing the interests of the whole community; he is not, unlike his medieval counterpart, ' an agent commissioned to watch over the separate, independent, and possibly conflicting interests of his principal '.

There is also some difference in the nature of the functions performed by parliaments then and now. The medieval Parliament was scarcely a Legislature in our sense of the word, for legislation of a permanent and general kind was an occasional expedient. Its chief function, after the voting of supplies, was to criticize and complain. Today, Parliament has become enormously more important; it not only passes general laws but in some States controls the Executive. A seat in it is, therefore, eagerly sought after, with the result that elections are contested. It is interesting to reflect that not only were elections not contested in medieval times, but sometimes the royal officials in their eagerness to secure some representative had to lay hold on those whom they considered to be suitable persons and pack them off to Parliament![2]

§8 THE CONTRIBUTIONS OF THE MIDDLE AGES

The Middle Ages, says Barker,[3] are not dead. They live among us, and are contemporary with us, in many institutions of our life and many modes of our thought.

First in importance among the legacies from the period is the conception that the purpose of the political organization is ethical,

---

[1] Jenks, *A History of Politics*, p. 128.
[2] Jenks, op. cit., p. 130.
[3] op. cit., p. 11.

i.e. to maintain justice and righteousness. This is reiterated again and again by the writers of the Middle Ages.[1] The ruler is God's minister for the punishment of the wicked and the reward of the good. This may appear to some as too obvious to require statement and to others as too indefinite to be of much profit. Nevertheless the ideal is worth emphasis, for ' it is exactly the pursuit of justice which distinguishes a rational and moral society from a stupid anarchy '.

Closely related to this is a second legacy : the principle of the supremacy of law as the concrete embodiment of justice. Positive law was to embody in itself those ultimate principles of justice by which the men of the Middle Ages believed the whole universe was ordered. The law, so conceived, was supreme over every member of the community including the king : Bracton said that the king was under God and the law.

A third valuable idea which is expressed emphatically in the political literature of the time is that of the reciprocal obligations of the ruler and the ruled : the king was to maintain justice and the subjects to observe the law. This was indeed the meaning of the mutual oaths at the ceremony of coronation. It followed that a ruler who had broken his contract could be deposed ; John of Salisbury in the twelfth century even speaks of the lawfulness of slaying the tyrant. The conclusion was also deduced, that subject to the final authority of justice and the divine and natural laws, it was the community which was supreme — the community which included the king, the nobles and the people. This was the principle out of which the representative system grew. The development of representative institutions is, clearly, one of the most significant contributions of the Middle Ages to modern times.

A fourth idea is the clear recognition by men that there are aspects of the moral and spiritual life which the coercive machinery of State cannot adequately represent. This is indeed the principle which lay behind the development of the conception of the independence of the Church. That this principle was not known in ancient times has been indicated earlier ; its significance in enabling the individual to develop a free personality hardly needs elaboration.

In many other ways, the Middle Ages have influenced modern politics ; it is sufficient to mention here how the influence of the conception of the Holy Roman Empire has helped in the establishment of some international body as the arbitrator in disputes

---

[1] R. W. and A. J. Carlyle, *A History of Mediaeval Political Theory in the West.* Vol. III, p. 181.

between States, and how the influence of the guilds and municipal institutions has inspired the pluralistic doctrines of our time.

§9 TRANSITION TO MODERN HISTORY

The close of the fifteenth century may be said to mark the transition from medieval to modern history. By this time, strong, centralized national governments had been established in England, France, and Spain ; feudalism as a governmental system had declined, the cities had lost their freedom, and the power of the kings had grown. The medieval conception of a universal Empire supported by a universal Church gradually broke down under the stress of circumstances. Two of these — the Renaissance and the maritime discoveries — are relevant to the context and may be briefly noticed here.

The Renaissance was a revival of learning in Europe, a new intellectual and artistic movement. It brought with it a secular, inquiring, critical, and self-reliant spirit. It also resulted in the revival of the study of Political Science and of Roman law. The general political effect was to increase the authority of kings, for it was a fundamental doctrine of the Roman jurists (whose books were read in the medieval period) that *all* governmental power, the *imperium,* was vested in the ruler. Indirectly, the Renaissance also helped the disappearance of the medieval conception of society embodied in the Holy Roman Empire.

' It was not that the Renaissance exerted any direct political influence either against the Empire or for it. Men were too busy upon statues and coins and manuscripts to care what befell popes or emperors. It acted rather by silently withdrawing the whole system of doctrines upon which the Empire had rested, and thus leaving it, since it had previously no support but that of opinion, without any support at all.' [1]

The maritime discoveries [2] of the age contributed to the same result in a different way. The discovery of America, combined with the acquisition of greater knowledge concerning India and the Far East, forced even the most reluctant to realize that the

[1] Bryce, op. cit., pp. 360-1.
[2] 1492 Columbus discovered America.
    1497 Vasco da Gama opened the Cape route to the East.
    1497 Cabot discovered Newfoundland.
    1500 Cabral discovered Brazil.
    1519-22 Magellan sailed round the world.

world was a good deal larger than had previously been believed possible. And when in addition there appeared Copernicus with proof that there was not one universe but there were many, the question was asked: How could the rule of mankind have been entrusted by Divine Providence to pope and emperor when there were not only other continents in this world, but whole universes in space, which had never heard of either of them? [1] The maritime discoveries, besides, strengthened the power of the monarch; for men were eager for peace and order, which a strong king alone could give, so that they might take advantage of the opportunities for material wealth now offered by colonization and the rise of colonial empires. The external development of the area over which the national monarch ruled also reacted on the degree of authority which he exercised within his dominions. 'Every extension of sway intensified his dignity and power and lifted him far higher above his subjects' (Pollard).

SELECT BIBLIOGRAPHY

G. B. ADAMS, *Civilization during the Middle Ages*, Scribners, 1922

J. BRYCE, *The Holy Roman Empire*, Macmillan, 1922

H. W. C. DAVIS, *Medieval Europe*, 'Home University Library', Oxford, 1954

J. C. L. DE SISMONDI, *A History of the Italian Republics*, 'Everyman Library', Dent

E. EMERTON, *Mediaeval Europe* (814-1300), Ginn, 1894

E. JENKS, *A History of Politics*, Dent, 1900

P. V. N. MYERS, *Mediaeval and Modern History*, Ginn, 2nd ed., 1927

C. N. PARKINSON, *The Evolution of Political Thought*, ch. vii, London, 1958

H. PIRENNE, *Medieval Cities*, Princeton, 1925

H. SIDGWICK, *The Development of European Polity*, Macmillan, 1903

J. R. TANNER and OTHERS, *The Cambridge Mediaeval History*, Vol. VII, Cambridge, 1932

O. J. THATCHER, *A Short History of Mediaeval Europe*, Flood and Vincent, 1897

[1] C. Petrie, *The History of Government*, p. 69.

CHAPTER XV

THE MODERN PERIOD

§1 THE RISE OF ABSOLUTE MONARCHY

GENERALLY speaking, the three centuries in the history of Europe which followed the discovery of America are an era of absolute hereditary monarchy, there being no established constitutional authority which could effectively check the kings or call them to account. The Tudor kings of England (1485-1603), Louis XIV of France (1643-1715), Frederick the Great of Prussia (1740-86), Catherine the Great of Russia (1762-96) and Joseph II of Austria (1780-90) are the leading examples of the despots of the period.

It is sufficient in this context to indicate the main causes of this development. Two of these have already been mentioned, viz. the revival of the study of Roman law during the period of the Renaissance and the maritime discoveries. A third is the discovery of gunpowder in the fourteenth century. 'It hastened the downfall of feudalism by rendering the yeoman foot-soldier equal to the armour-clad knight.' It made all men of the same height, as Carlyle put it. It also became the practice now for rulers to keep a standing army of mercenaries which was both more serviceable and more reliable than the feudal levy supplied by the proud barons for short periods. The developments of cities and the formation of a citizen class also promoted royal power by placing within its reach materials for a permanent military force and the means of sustaining it. Such an army, carefully drilled, paid, always available and directly under his command, gave the king a new and superior force which the barons could not resist.

A fourth cause is the Reformation. From the religious point of view the outcome of the Reformation in the sixteenth century was, very broadly stated, the separation of North Germany, Denmark, Norway, Sweden, England and parts of Switzerland and of the Netherlands from the Roman Catholic Church. France, Spain, Italy, South Germany, Poland, Bohemia, Hungary and Ireland for the most part adhered to the ancient Church.

Politically it brought about, in the first half of the sixteenth century, *the development of absolute monarchy in a territorial State*. The medieval world, as we have seen, conceived of Christendom as one society, which they called the Holy Roman Empire. But Protestantism limited the society to a territorial State. It placed all ecclesiastical authority under the control of the godly prince, who was omnipotent in his own domain. It brought about the unification of all powers within the State, the concentration of all coercive authority in the hands of the civil ruler and the inculcation of the duty of non-resistance to the prince. By the confiscation of church lands, the appropriation of powers formerly exercised by the Pope, and the establishment of effective control over the local clergy, the kings

' were enriched in purse, exalted in public opinion, and simultaneously freed from the fear of being hampered in their absolutist policies by an independent ecclesiastical organization '.

Even in Catholic countries, Hayes tells us, the monarchs took advantage of the Pope's difficulties to wring from him such concessions as resulted in subordinating the Church to the Crown. The main change the Reformation brought about, therefore, was a change from a world empire to a territorial State, from ecclesiastical to civil predominance.[1]

It is interesting to reflect that the political thought of the period supported absolutism in more than one way. Machiavelli[2] freed the ruler from the limitations imposed by public morality ; he argued that the State was an end in itself, existed for its own sake, lived its own life, aimed at its own preservation and advantage, and was not bound by the obligations which should determine the actions of private persons. Hobbes, we have seen, supported absolutism by the social contract theory.[3] Above all, the divine right theory was worked out elaborately during this period and proved the most useful support to royal absolutism. The essentials of the theory are : monarchy is a divinely ordained institution ; hereditary right is indefeasible ; kings are accountable to God alone ; and non-resistance and passive obedience are enjoined by God. The nation is a great family with the king as its divinely-appointed head. The duty of the king is to govern like a father ; of the people, to obey their king as children obey

[1] According to G. P. Gooch, if the absolute State was the child and heir of the Reformation, democracy was its residuary legatee.
[2] *The Prince*, 1513.
[3] *Leviathan*, 1651.

their parents. Even if a king is wicked, argues king James 1 of England,[1] it means God has sent him as a punishment for people's sins, and it is unlawful to shake off the burden which God has laid upon them. Patience, earnest prayer and amendment of their lives are the only lawful means to move God to relieve them of that heavy curse !

§2 THE FRENCH REVOLUTION

Monarchical absolutism received a death-blow at the end of the eighteenth century from the French Revolution (1789). This was a revolt of the French people against absolute monarchy and class privilege. Chief among its causes were the abuses and extravagances of the French monarchy, the unjust privileges enjoyed by the nobility and higher clergy, the discontent of the growing middle class in society, the revolutionary character of French philosophy and literature (of Rousseau and Voltaire) and the influence of the American Revolution (1775-83).

It has rightly been said that the dominant forces at work in the social and political history of Europe in the nineteenth century were the ideas or principles inherited from the French Revolution. These are mainly three : equality, popular sovereignty, and nationality.

(i) *Equality.* In the Declaration of the Rights of Man drawn up by the Revolutionaries (1789) the doctrine of equality is proclaimed with religious fervour. 'Men are born, and always continue, free and equal in respect of their rights.' This meant primarily that all men were equal before the law, and signified the abolition of privilege, the end of serfdom, and the destruction of the feudal system. 'It involved the aspiration of affording every man an equal chance with every other man in the pursuit of life and happiness.' The Code Napoléon embodied this principle and wherever it was set up — in the Netherlands, in the West German States, in part of Poland, in Switzerland, in Italy — it exerted the same levelling influence that it had in France. And ever since 1789, the ideal of equality has been at work emancipating and elevating the hitherto unfree and downtrodden orders of society, and removing civil, religious and racial disabilities from disqualified classes in the State.

(ii) *Popular sovereignty.* The declaration referred to above stated this principle categorically. The nation is essentially the source of sovereignty ; nor can any individual or any body of

---

[1] In his book, *The Trew Law of Free Monarchies* (1603).

men be entitled to any authority which is not expressly derived
from it. The law is an expression of the will of the community.
All citizens have a right to concur, either personally or through
their representatives, in its formation. The influence of this
principle in politics may be seen in the wide adoption, not only
in Europe but in America and in the East, of the democratic form
of government in place of autocratic monarchy. It is an unconscious admission of the value of the democratic principle that even
where dictatorships have been established, they are disguised
beneath the forms of democracy.

(*iii*) *Nationality*. This principle, as we have seen earlier,
requires that every people, who feel they are one, shall be free
to choose their own form of government and to manage their
affairs in their own way. The French Revolution brought about
a revival of the nationalist sentiment in three ways.[1] First, the
great wars which followed the Revolution roused and inflamed
the national spirit in the French, united and inspired by the sense
that they were a people with a mission. Secondly, Napoleon made
conscious appeals to the national sentiment not only in France
but in Poland and in Italy. And, above all, the struggle for
liberation from the French yoke in Spain, Austria, Germany and
Russia gave the national idea an intensity such as it had never
known before and made the cause of national freedom appear
the most sacred of causes. The importance of nationalism hardly
needs elaboration ; it has been at once a unifying and a disruptive
force : dismembered nations striving for unity, and composite
nations striving for separation. It has also been, throughout the
modern era, a fruitful cause of wars : subject nations fighting for
freedom and triumphant nations aspiring after domination.

§3   THE INDUSTRIAL REVOLUTION

Beginning in England in the second half of the eighteenth
century as a succession of mechanical inventions, the Industrial
Revolution spread in due course to Belgium, France and other
parts of western Europe. In the economic sphere, it substituted
machine production for hand production. The small-scale production of goods in private homes was supplanted by mass
production in factories. It brought about a migration ' from farm
to factory, from country to city, from agriculture to industry ',
and brought into relief the capitalistic system of industry, the two

[1] Ramsay Muir, *Nationalism and Internationalism*, pp. 71-2.

social classes, the bourgeoisie and the proletariat, being sharply differentiated in function and interests.

Its political results

(*i*) It destroyed for ever the preponderant weight of the agricultural classes in the community and brought into being a new middle class, composed of factory owners, industrial capitalists, and the industrial middle class generally, who year by year became more insistent in their demand for political recognition.

(*ii*) It furthered the movement towards democracy.

' It has done this largely by developing city life . . . City life fosters democracy. Through daily contact with one another, through exchange of ideas, through increased opportunities for collective action, the dwellers of the city become less conservative than country people and more ready to engage in political activities.' [1]

In this way, the Industrial Revolution gave a fillip to the development of government by the people.

(*iii*) By prompting a policy of economic protection, it has intensified the nationalist feeling. For the only way by which a country not industrialized could hope to compete with the industrially advanced countries was to raise a tariff wall to nurse those industries which had a reasonable chance of withstanding foreign competition.

(*iv*) Paradoxically, it has also intensified international rivalries. The Industrial Revolution has, clearly, made the world interdependent in respect of raw materials and markets. The optimum utilization of the world's resources demands the fullest international co-operation. But the nationalist feeling, coupled with the competition among the leading industrialized nations for raw materials and markets, has resulted in the prevention of that co-operation and in the intensification of international rivalries.

(*v*) The concentration of large masses of people in the cities has taught the working classes the power of organization and agitation, political and economic. Through such means as the general strike, labour threatens to bring a government to its knees.

(*vi*) The result of the Industrial Revolution on governmental policy was, in the first instance, to encourage economic liberalism or *laissez-faire*. The new manufacturers wanted freedom of trade, freedom of contract, freedom of competition and free operation of the ' laws ' of supply and demand, in order that they might

[1]Myers, *Mediaeval and Modern History*, pp. 580-1.

be free to take the maximum advantage of the new inventions and increase their wealth. But very soon it was found that *laissez-faire* led to social misery ; an increase in the activities of the State was clearly demanded to protect the home manufacturer, the worker, the consumer and the investor, in order, briefly, to moralize competition.

(*vii*) And, lastly, the unequal distribution of wealth in society, accentuated by modern industrial capitalism, has led to influential theories of social and political reconstruction, such as modern socialism and communism.

§4 THE RISE OF DEMOCRACY

The hundred and twenty-five years between the French Revolution (1789) and the outbreak of the Great War (1914) are remarkable in the history of government for two developments, viz. the rise of democracy and the rise of nationalism.

At the end of the eighteenth century, democratic institutions of some sort could be found only in Britain, France, Holland, Switzerland and the United States of America. By about 1914, there was hardly a country in Europe which did not possess a constitution of a more or less popular nature. Not only in Europe but in Australia and several States of South America and Asia a more or less democratic constitution was established. Representative parliaments, elected on an extended suffrage, and the responsibility of the Executive, in varying degrees and forms, to the Legislature and the people, are its main manifestations. In some States, like Britain and Holland, the transformation was accomplished by peaceful and evolutionary methods ; elsewhere, as in Austria and Italy, a revolution was necessary before the liberal principles could be accepted. Some States, like Belgium and Britain, preferred to retain a constitutional monarch along with popular institutions ; others, like China and France, preferred republicanism. Switzerland went to the length of giving the people the power of direct legislation through the referendum and the initiative.

This development may be traced to four factors :

(*i*) *Social, economic and political conditions favouring the rise of popular government.* We have seen that the Industrial Revolution, in the latter half of the eighteenth century and in the nineteenth, furthered the movement towards democracy through the development of the middle classes and the impetus it gave to city life. ' The opportunity to unite, which urban and factory

life presented, brought with it a new consciousness of power ',
and the demand for political recognition. Moreover, the Revolution brought to the forefront social problems — such as the
concentration of population in towns, low wages, irregularity of
employment, and the threat to the health of the nation — with
which the earlier monarchic and aristocratic governments were
powerless to deal. The advance of popular education and the
wider diffusion of knowledge made possible the extension of the
franchise. Moreover, the parliamentary system itself worked
towards a widening of the electorate, ' since politicians sought
the championship of an ever-increasing body of supporters '.

(*ii*) *Abstract theory.* Rousseau's ideal of democracy became
a source of inspiration to the nations of Europe. The documents
of the American and French Revolutions, based on the writings
of Locke and Rousseau, proclaimed that men are born free and
equal and that government depends on the consent of the governed. The Utilitarians also ' pronounced democracy to be the only
rational form of government, since the majority, if supreme,
would necessarily promote the happiness of the major part of the
community '.[1] Mill, as we have seen, argued that democracy was
also the safest form of government.

(*iii*) *Misgovernment.* The incompetence and the vices of kings
also helped the rise of democracy. Thus Portugal, before it
became a Republic, was ruled by King Carlos I (1889-1908).
The revolution, which ended in the overthrow of the monarchy,
was the outcome of the vices, incompetence and unpopularity of
the king, combined with the factious strife of parties, the troubled
conditions of the country, and the corruption and inefficiency of
the Government. The king, we are told, was licentious and
extravagant and cared little for the interests of his people. Financial crises frequently occurred. The king often governed the
country by ministerial decrees. Republican parties soon sprang
up ; in 1908 the king and the crown prince were murdered ; and
in 1910 the Republic was proclaimed.

(*iv*) *Imitation.* Imitation has always been a contributory
factor in political development, particularly in the shaping of
constitutions. According to Sidgwick,[2] we must allow a large
place for it, even when we have no direct proof of it.

' In modern Europe,' says he, ' we cannot say that modern
parliamentary government, in the form of constitutional monarchy,

---

[1] A. F. Hattersley, *A Short History of Democracy*, p. 165.
[2] *The Development of European Polity*, pp. 20-1.

is an independent result of similar tendencies of development in Italy, Belgium, Spain and the Scandinavian kingdoms, where it is now[1] established; it is obvious to the most superficial student of history that the similarity now existing among forms of government in these different countries is largely due to imitation. direct or indirect, of England.'

Similarly, the constitution of the U.S.A. supplied a model for the rest of America.

§5   THE DEVELOPMENT OF NATIONALISM

The second great development in Politics since the French Revolution has been the rise of nationalism.

The political ideal of the Middle Ages was universality. England was the first country to develop a strong feeling of nationalism and to attain the full stature of organized and conscious nationhood. The English attempt in the early fifteenth century to dominate France roused the national spirit in that country. Various causes led to a similar awakening in Spain and Portugal, and, by the opening of the modern age, these two countries had emerged as fully consolidated nation-States. The sixteenth century saw the Danish and Swedish peoples also similarly organized.

But the political principle of nationalism, viz. that every people who constitute a nationality have a right to independent Statehood is primarily a development of the latter half of the eighteenth and nineteenth centuries. The history of this development falls into three periods.

(*i*) 1772-1820. The partition of Poland (1772) is the first great landmark in this history. The territory of Poland was divided, much against the desire of the Poles themselves, among the rulers of Prussia, Russia and Austria — an act which may best be characterized as ' downright robbery '. The Poles were left ' as a soul wandering in search of a body in which to begin life over again '. As Lord Acton justly remarked, this most revolutionary act of the old absolutism awakened the theory of nationality in Europe.

Soon after came the French Revolution (1789) and the subjection of a large part of Europe to Napoleon. In Russia, Germany, Italy, and Spain, however, his policy soon provoked popular and spontaneous resistance — an index of the emergence of the

[1] In 1903.

national spirit. Indeed this awakening finally brought about the downfall of Napoleon. The statesmen who met at the Congress of Vienna at the close of the Napoleonic wars (1815), however. ignored this principle in the reorganization of Europe. ' New States were formed, existing States were yoked together, and others were divided, in flagrant disregard of the rights of nationalities.' Thus thirty-nine sovereign princes and free cities were recognized in Germany, though bound together into a loose confederation ; Venice, Lombardy and Eastern Bavaria were yoked to Austria, and the Austrian Empire made a strange mixture of races, languages and religions : Bohemians, Hungarians, Italians, Poles, Serbians, and Roumanians, held together only by their subjection to the emperor ; Italy was divided into a number of States, such as Naples, Tuscany, Savoy, etc. ; Belgium was united to Holland ; and Norway to Sweden.

(ii) 1820-78. This period saw the rise of two nation-States of the first rank in central Europe, Italy and Germany ; four smaller ones in eastern Europe, Greece, Serbia, Roumania, and Monte-negro ; and two in western Europe, Belgium and Holland.

We have seen that the Congress of Vienna did not recognize the national sentiment in Italy, the country being split up among many small States, some of them also being placed under Austrian domination. The nationalist feeling was, however, kept alive by leaders like Mazzini (1805-72), Garibaldi (1807-82) and Cavour (1810-61) ; many nationalist risings took place against Austrian tyranny, until in 1871 Italian unity was achieved under Victor Emmanuel II. The struggle for Italian unity had a profound influence on Germany. The first step towards German unity was taken by the creation of what is known as the Customs Union (1828-36), a sort of commercial arrangement binding the member-States to adopt among themselves the policy of free trade. It taught the people to think of a more perfect national union. It was during the regime of Bismarck [1] (1862-90), however, that German national unity was achieved. Bismarck was the chief minister of Emperor William I of Prussia. He reformed and strengthened the Prussian army, successfully fought three wars (with Denmark 1864, Austria 1866, and France 1870-1), and, in 1871, united all the German States into the German Empire under William I.

In central Europe, nationalism was the integration of petty kindred States into two strong nation-States ; in eastern Europe. it was rather the disruption of huge polyglot empires. For all

[1] Born 1815, died 1898.

the extensive lands and all the diverse nationalities of eastern Europe were comprised in three imperial sovereignties — the Russian, the Austrian and the Turkish. In the period under reference, only the nationalities comprised under the last (and not all of them) were able to achieve their independence. The Greeks were the first to revolt against the Turkish yoke. They had the sympathy of a large part of Christian Europe on their side ; with this help they were able to attain their independence in 1827. Roumania, Serbia and Montenegro similarly revolted ; they were aided by Russia, and their independence had to be recognized by Turkey in 1878.

Very early in the period (1831), the Belgians secured their independence from the Dutch, with whom they had been unwillingly united sixteen years earlier by the Congress of Vienna.

(*iii*) *Since* 1900. The separation of Norway and Sweden took place in 1905. In 1908, taking advantage of political disturbances in Turkey, Bulgaria declared her complete independence from that power. The Great War (1914-18) led to a large extension of the national principle. The large empires of Germany, Russia, and Austria-Hungary were dismembered and, six small new States, Poland, Lithuania, Latvia, Estonia, Finland and Czechoslovakia, were created. By this dismemberment, Germany, Austria, Hungary, and Turkey were also transformed into strictly national states.

'All together, where there had been twenty-one sovereign States in 1914 (including four extensive empires), there were twenty-seven in 1920, and almost all of the twenty-seven were national.'

§6 THE FIRST WORLD WAR (1914-18)

Besides the fillip that the first world war gave to nationalism it was productive of other results : (*i*) the establishment of the League of Nations ; (*ii*) the evolution of the mandate system ; (*iii*) the extension of democracy and republicanism ; and (*iv*) the later rise of dictatorships.

(*i*) The principles underlying the League of Nations have been discussed elsewhere.[1] Here it is sufficient to say that its foundation was largely due to the realization by the men of the time that a concerted effort must be made to avoid the calamity of another world war and to promote international co-operation.

---

[1] See above, ch. xi, §14.

(*ii*) The establishment of the mandate system must, in principle, be taken to be an advance in the government of colonies and backward peoples. The territories taken by the Allies from the Germans and the Turks were not said to be 'conquered' but mandated by the Allied and Associated Powers ; and the annexing States as mandatories were obliged at fixed intervals to give an account of their stewardship to a League Commission. The idea was that the 'civilized' nations were to be trustees for the 'backward' peoples, until such time as the latter were able to govern themselves. 'The crudity of conquest was thus draped on the veil of morality.'[1]

(*iii*) The immediate aftermath of the World War seemed to confirm Woodrow Wilson's contention that the war had been waged by the United States and the Allies to make the world safe for democracy.[2]

'For, with the exception of Russia, where the Tsarist regime was supplanted by a communist dictatorship, all the Great Powers and most of the lesser ones adopted or elaborated democratic forms of government. And with the extension of democracy was associated a new vogue of republicanism.'

Germany, Austria and Russia ceased to be monarchical and became republican. The newly-created States of central Europe — Poland, Lithuania, Latvia, Estonia, Finland and Czechoslovakia — were republican. Thoroughly democratic institutions were evolved by popularly elected assemblies in Germany (1919), Austria (1928), Czechoslovakia (1920), Poland (1921), Yugoslavia (1921), Turkey (1921), Estonia (1921), Latvia (1922), Lithuania (1922), Roumania (1923), etc.[3] Three features of this extension of democracy are noticeable : the adoption by several States of the British system of ministerial responsibility,[4] and of methods for the representation of minorities such as proportional representation,[5] and the enfranchisement of women. The last 'seemed an appropriate recognition of the significant role which women had played in the World War and were playing in industrialized society'.

(*iv*) Curiously enough, although the War resulted, immediately, in an extension of the principles of democracy, it later

[1] H. A. L. Fisher, *A History of Europe*, p. 1174.
[2] C. J. H. Hayes, *A Political and Cultural History of Modern Europe*, Vol. II, pp. 888-9.
[3] ibid.
[4] See below, pp. 256-57.
[5] See below, ch. xxx, §5.

led to the rise of dictatorships. This is dealt with in the next section.

§7 REACTION AGAINST DEMOCRACY

The period 1918-39 saw a reaction against democracy in Europe and elsewhere, and the rise of dictatorship in a number of States. Thus the revolution of 1917 led to the Bolshevik dictatorships in Russia. Turkey, though nominally democratic and republican, was practically under the dictatorship of Mustafa Kemal (later Atatürk) from 1921 until his death in 1938.

In Italy, a liberal Government was overthrown and the Fascist dictatorship set up in 1922. Thereafter, dictators were established in Spain (1923), Chile (1927), Greece (1928), Brazil (1930), Dominican Republic (1930), Argentine (1931), Guatemala (1931), Portugal (1932), Uruguay (1933), Austria (1933), Germany (1933), Mexico (1934) and France (1940).

These dictatorships had certain features in common. Wherever they were established, there was a clouding, especially among the middle classes, of the liberal and democratic conscience. The belief in the utility of responsible cabinets, representative assemblies and democratic electorates declined. And so did that strong belief in civil liberty and peaceful persuasion which had been a distinctive feature of the nineteenth century. It was not regarded as the mark of a civilized polity that every citizen should be able to think as he liked, to speak as he liked and to vote as he liked. Dictatorships make the maximum use of force in government. They employ the secret police on a large scale — the Ogpu in Russia, the Gestapo in Germany — to discover and put down opposition. Their principle is ' no opposition to the party in power, and no opposition within the party '. They therefore refuse to tolerate organized minorities and insist on a State monopoly of those forces — the press, the radio, the film, etc. — which mould public opinion. Several of the dictatorships referred to above took on a violently nationalistic colour ; they expressed themselves through constitutional forms : Hitler was constitutionally the president and Chancellor of the German Republic ; Mussolini was Prime Minister to the King of Italy.

Causes

The primary cause of the growth of dictatorships (the Russian excepted) was a certain dissatisfaction with democracy and parliamentary institutions. This reaction against democracy is itself traceable to four causes.

(*i*) *The first World War*. The mere fact of the outbreak and the continuance of the war, and the sufferings which followed, helped to shake men's faith in democratic principles. Men had thought that democracy and peace were synonymous, but the events of August 1914 destroyed this illusion.[1] Again, the war left a legacy of misery and depression in nearly every country. Men looked for a better and happier world after the war ; the world that did result was not only not better, but worse. It was freely contended that parliaments were bankrupt and that democratic civilization had outlived its usefulness. Further, during the war-period there was everywhere a strengthening of the Executive at the expense of the Legislature and a considerable curtailment of personal liberty ; the ordinary citizen did as he was bid, and the habit endured.[2]

(*ii*) *The weakness of democratic governments*. Even apart from the war, the faith in democratic principles was undermined by the inability of democracy to solve adequately the problems which it had to face.

Edward Benes ably summarizes[3] the deficiencies and weaknesses of the democratic governments in the inter-war years thus :

'The deficiencies, weaknesses and of course great mistakes of the individual democracies, which it was apparently impossible to avoid, are the third category of facts which played a specially important role in the downfall of European democracies. There were the excuses of the party system, its mistakes and exaggerations ; the slowness and inefficiency of democratic methods of work and leadership during times of crises and at moments when quick actions and quick decisions were necessary ; the partiality, corruption and incapacity of bureaucracy, subjugated very often to the exaggerated party spirit ; the deficiencies, mediocrity and mistakes of the democratic leaders.'

This was particularly true of Germany and Italy. In both these countries, the democratic institutions were charged with incompetence and indecisiveness. The necessity for a strong government, for centralized and unlimited authority, was stressed on every hand. In Germany, the inflation of 1923 resulted in untold miseries. Again, from 1929, following close upon the financial crash in New York and the consequent withdrawal of American money from Germany, there was a serious economic

---

[1] Petrie, *The History of Government*, pp. 163-4.   [2] ibid.
[3] Benes, *Democracy Today and Tomorrow*, London, 1939, p. 61.

crisis. The budget was unbalanced ; six millions were unemployed ; and the cult of communism gained ground. The humiliations consequent on defeat in the war added to the resentment of the people against their Government. The revolution in Germany accomplished by Hitler and his National Socialist party was, therefore, an extraordinary psychological phenomenon.

' The dread of communism, the hatred of Jews and profiteers, the desire once again to be feared abroad, the need of a Government stronger, more progressive, and more sanguine than the Republic, which would repudiate the Peace Treaties and once more launch Germany on the course of ambition and honour, all contributed to make Hitlerism possible.' [1]

In Italy, much the same state of affairs existed. She was disgusted with the hollowness of her victory. The territories ceded to her by the Peace Treaties were not as many as she had been led to expect ; at home, there was privation instead of the expected prosperity. The high cost of living, unemployment and bad trade added to the unpopularity of the Government. Riots occurred in several parts of the country. The trend towards communism, encouraged by the success of the Bolshevik revolution in Russia, alarmed the industrialists and the middle class who feared the destruction of their property. Mussolini, supported by the Fascists, demanded and secured control of the Government by his march on Rome (1922).

(*iii*) *The lack of democratic traditions.* It must be admitted, too, that those countries in which dictatorships were established, like Italy and Germany, lacked democratic traditions which alone could have enabled them to preserve democracy.

(*iv*) *The personal factor.* The rise of dictatorships, in reaction against democracy, must in part be attributed to the rise of strong men, like Hitler and Mussolini, who, at a time of emergency, provided the leadership for which the masses were longing.

The Russian instance, we have said, is an exception : it is so only in the sense that that dictatorship was not a reaction against democracy but against hereditary autocracy. Otherwise much the same reasoning applies. The inefficiency and corruption of the Tsarist Government, the military reverses, and the suffering consequent on the war, led to discontent and the spread of revolutionary ideas. Lenin, the strongest personality of the age and

---

[1] Fisher, op. cit., pp. 1204-5.

a disciple of Marx, captured the government (1917) and established the dictatorship of the proletariat.

Comparison with ancient dictatorships

The rise of dictatorships in recent times naturally reminds the student of government of a similar development in ancient Greece and Rome. The Greek tyrants, we have seen, came to power to deal with an emergency. They championed the cause of those who were discontented with oligarchy. They meant their office to be permanent. They helped to destroy oligarchy and prepare the way for democracy. Nevertheless, they were regarded as irregular and unconstitutional by Greek sentiment.

Like the tyrants of Greece, the Roman dictator came to power to deal with an emergency. But, unlike the tyrant, the Roman dictator was, in the great days of the Republic, a constitutional official, appointed by legal process and exercising his authority in accordance with legal conventions. He was expected to lay down his office as soon as the special business for which he had been appointed was accomplished, and in no case could his tenure exceed six months.

Modern dictatorships are not all of one type : the Soviet dictatorship of the proletariat, for instance, differs from its fascist Italian counterpart. But in origin they are essentially like the Greek *tyrannis* in that they came into existence in an irregular manner (in Russia by a revolution, in Italy by the Fascist march on Rome), though, later, they expressed themselves through constitutional forms. Again, the methods they adopted to maintain their power recall the prescriptions outlined by Aristotle (and adopted by ancient tyrants) for the preservation of tyranny : the tyrant should lop off all those who are too high ; he must put to death men of spirit ; he should endeavour to know what each of his subjects says or does, and should employ spies ; he should also endeavour to engage his subjects in a war so that they may have something to do and be always in want of a leader. They agree in four other respects : the dictators came to power by championing the cause of the discontented ; they depended on force ; they meant their office to be permanent ; they helped to bring some order out of chaos. But they differed from the Greek tyrants, at least in Germany and Italy, in that (*a*) they helped to destroy the prevailing democratic forms of government, and (*b*) with the aid of modern methods of propaganda, they were able to mould public opinion according to their will and to manufacture consent.

Dictatorship versus Democracy

No realist can ignore the services rendered by dictators to their peoples. They successfully faced problems with which preceding régimes were afraid to deal, provided employment to the unemployed, increased industrial production, promoted literacy and public health, and raised the prestige of their respective countries — though only for a short time — in international politics. The following summary of the achievements of the Spanish dictator Rivera is typical :

'For the first time in their history the Spanish trains ran punctually. New railways were laid down, and a system of fine motor roads took the place of the traditional mule-tracks of Spain. Commerce and industry prospered under the dictator ... Agriculture flourished ... Labour unrest was mitigated.' [1]

But dictatorship, as a form of government, has many evils. Men towering above their fellows in wisdom, foresight, and capacity to rule are difficult to find.[2] Even if one dictator is wise and capable, his successors may not be. Dictators may deteriorate. 'All power corrupts,' said Lord Acton, 'and absolute power corrupts absolutely.' Further, dictatorship tends to attack the essential character of the modern State as a *Rechts-staat,* i.e. one based on the rule of law [3] as distinguished from the rule of arbitrary power. It also repudiates liberty. In such a State, as has been well said, there are no human rights but only State rights. It stresses the cult of violence. Force is a necessity in an imperfect world as the guardian of right ; but if it is not embodied in law, it becomes dangerous.[4] The cult of violence involves dangers without as well as within ; for fascist dictators do not believe in pacifism, and war becomes more likely. Mussolini once said that he believed neither in the possibility nor the *utility* of perpetual peace.

A democratic system is to be preferred because of the importance which it attaches to human personality. The democratic method is to reach decisions by discussion, argument, and persuasion. In a dictatorship, violence takes the place of argument. Democracy does not believe in the suppression of thought ; dictatorship not only believes in it but also in creating a likemindedness. Dictatorship, therefore, eliminates the best from

[1] J. H. Jackson, *Europe Since the War*, p. 98.
[2] G. P. Gooch, *Dictatorship in Theory and Practice*. pp. 35-40.
[3] ibid.   [4] ibid.

public life, the critical minds as well as the creative brains.
Further, it depends on a person rather than on a principle ; it
depends on the intelligence, the capacity and resourcefulness of
a single individual, and it is unsafe to entrust to the hands of
a single individual the destinies of a country. By its very nature,
therefore, dictatorship can never be a permanent or desirable
substitute for democracy.

§8 THE PERIOD SINCE 1939

The second World War broke out on 1 September 1939 and
ended on 2 September 1945. It is perhaps yet too early to estimate the ultim. consequences of this, the most disastrous war in
history, on gc iment and society ; some of the more immediate
and obvious resu..s may, however, be mentioned. The immediate
consequences of the war in Europe were the collapse of Germany
— the nation which had been the strongest European State in
1939 had become a divided and occupied country — the growth
in power of the Soviet Union and the sovietization of half of
Europe. The political and economic woes which Europe faced
as a result of the war led to such a fundamental change as ' to
lead students of history to speak of " the passing of the European
age " '.[1] Power from Europe has shifted to east and west — the
Soviet Union and the U.S.A. In Asia, the collapse of the Japanese Empire and the growth of nationalist movements led to the
establishment of several independent states — India, Pakistan,
Ceylon, Burma, Indonesia, Malaya, Cambodia and Laos. The
decline of the British, French and Belgian Empires encouraged
by the national movements stimulated by the World War, led to
the creation of several new independent States in Africa, e.g.
Nigeria, Ghana, Guinea, and the Congo. The new State of Israel
came into being largely through the good offices of the United
Nations.

With the collapse of the dictatorships involved in the war,
fascism suffered a mortal blow ; but dictatorship itself appeared
in a number of States during and after the war, e.g. Roumania
(1940), Yugoslavia (1944), the Argentine (1946), Paraguay
(1947), Thailand (1947), Peru (1948), Communist China
(1949), Venezuela (1952), Egypt (1952), Cuba (1952), Colombia (1953), Pakistan (1958) and Burma (1961). At the
same time it will be correct to say that the common man's faith

---

[1] E. Fischer, *The Passing of the European Age*, Harvard University Press,
2nd ed., 1948.

in democracy has increased, one proof is that several of the dictatorships prefer to be in the garb of democracy. But, he has begun to demand, naturally, that democracy should discover the institutions by means of which freedom from want ' may be not merely an aspiration but an established fact. Socialism too has become more ' respectable ' : Socialist Russia's great contribution to the winning of the war has been underlined in the consciousness of the average man.

In the international sphere, the fillip given to the establishment of an international organization, more powerful than the League of Nations and less limited by the theory of national sovereignty, has been noticed elsewhere.

Finally, in the conditions created by the discovery of the atomic and hydrogen bombs the theory of self-determination and notions of the value of small States in political organization are being radically revised.

SELECT BIBLIOGRAPHY

R. L. BUELL AND OTHERS, *New Governments in Europe*, Nelson, 1937

G. A. CRAIG, *Europe Since 1815*, ch. 29 and 30, Holt, Rinehart and Winston, 1961

H. A. L. FISHER, *A History of Europe*, Eyre and Spottiswoode, 3rd ed., 1952

G. P. GOOCH, *Dictatorship in Theory and Practice*, Watts, 1935

A. F. HATTERSLEY, *A Short History of Democracy*, Cambridge, 1930

C. J. H. HAYES, *A Political and Cultural History of Modern Europe*, 2 Vols., Macmillan, 1932-9

J. H. JACKSON, *Europe Since the War*, Gollancz, 1933

M. MACLAUGHLIN, *Newest Europe*, Longmans, 1931

J. A. R. MARRIOTT, *Dictatorship and Democracy*, Oxford, 1935

R. MUIR, *Nationalism and Internationalism*, Constable, 1919

C. N. PARKINSON, *The Evolution of Political Thought*, Parts III and IV, London, 1958

C. PETRIE, *The History of Government*, Methuen, 1929

H. SIDGWICK, *The Development of European Polity*, Macmillan, 1903

BOOK II. MODERN CONSTITUTIONS

CHAPTER XVI

THE GOVERNMENT OF THE UNITED KINGDOM[1]

§1 INTRODUCTORY

WE have surveyed briefly the history of government, and now proceed to a study of the systems of government in force today in some of the important States.

A few words in explanation of the order of treatment will be useful.

In this chapter and the following, is outlined the system of government in Britain and France; both these are *unitary* States. Unitarianism, Dicey has said, is the habitual exercise of supreme legislative authority by one central power. It is contrasted with federalism, which involves the division of governmental powers within the State between one central authority and a number of local or ' state ' authorities, the former passing laws and administering them in respect of *some* matters, like defence and foreign affairs, and the latter, in respect of *other* matters of a more local nature, like education and agriculture. The United States of America, Canada, Australia, Switzerland, Pakistan and India are *federal* States; these and South Africa (usually classed as a union) are taken up for study in chapters XVIII, XIX, XX, XXI, XXII and XXIII.

Chapter XXIV deals with Nazi Germany and Fascist Italy, both unitary. They are placed together as they belong to the *totalitarian* type of States. The difference between the totalitarian and the democratic type of state is that a democracy makes a distinction between state and society, while a totalitarian state does not. The final chapter in Book II, viz., chapter XXV deals with the Constitution of the Union of the Soviet Socialist

---

[1] The term ' Britain ' is used in this chapter and elsewhere to indicate the United Kingdom, as that term is shorter and commonly used and understood.

Republic.[1] This last is a federal state but is in a class by itself being a Socialist State, considered by its authorities, as being in the transition to communism.

§2 THE CONSTITUTION OF BRITAIN

We consider the government of Britain first, primarily for the reason that British political institutions have had a profound influence on shaping the governmental systems of other countries, and therefore an acquaintance with them helps to a clear understanding of those systems.

Let us ask ourselves a preliminary question : What is meant by the term ' the constitution of Britain ' ? A constitution, in general terms, is the body of rules which directly or indirectly affect the distribution or the exercise of the sovereign power in the State. It is, in a classic definition, the collection of principles according to which the powers of the Government, the rights of the governed and the relations between the two are adjusted. The constitution of India, for instance, is found in the Constitution Act passed in 1949 by the Constituent Assembly of India ; that Act contains the most important of the rules which affect the distribution and the exercise of sovereign power in India—the rules relating to the powers of the President and the Cabinet, the Governors, the composition and powers of the central and state Legislatures, etc. Britain has no such document containing all or the most important of the rules relating to her constitution. Several of these rules are found scattered through a number of charters and petitions like the Great Charter (1215)[2] and the Petition of Right (1628),[3] statutes like the Parliament Act of 1911,[4] and judicial decisions like the decision in Wilkes' case[5] (1763) ; some indeed are unwritten usages or constitutional conventions.[6] Whether we can call such a constitution as this

---

[1] Hereafter referred to as the Soviet Union, for brevity.

[2] The Great Charter guaranteed the liberties of the English Church. and. among other things, provided that ' no freeman shall be taken or imprisoned...save by the lawful judgement of his peers or by the law of the land ', and that no scutage or aid shall be imposed in our kingdom except by the common council of our kingdom ' except for certain specified purposes.

[3] The Petition of Right declared that taxes could not be levied without the consent of Parliament, that Englishmen could not be imprisoned without cause shown and trial given ; and that soldiers and sailors could not be billeted on private householders without their consent.

[4] See below, §6.   [5] See below, §13.

[6] See below, §16.

an unwritten one is a debatable point, to which we shall refer later.[1] It is sufficient here to stress the fact that the constitution of Britain is derived from several sources ; it is a composite of charters, statutes, judicial decisions and usages.

This constitution can be amended in the same way as ordinary laws are passed and amended.[2] Thus a law relating to the Crown, like the Act of Settlement (1701), is passed by Parliament and assented to by the sovereign, in the same way as an education or a public health Act is put on the statute book. Such a constitution, which does not require any special procedure or body for making constitutional laws, is known as a *flexible* constitution, in contrast to a rigid one which provides a special procedure for the purpose.

We shall now consider, in order, the Executive, the Legislature and the Judiciary of Britain.

§3 THE CROWN: ITS POSITION AND POWERS

The supreme executive authority in the State is vested in the Crown.

The Crown is a hereditary institution which Parliament regulates by rules of succession. Under the terms of the preamble to the Statute of Westminster (1931), ' any alteration in the law touching the succession to the throne or the royal style and titles ' requires the assent of the Parliaments of all the Dominions as well as the Parliament of the United Kingdom.[3] The succession

---

[1] See below, ch. xxviii, §1.

[2] There is a slight difference in respect of one law. The Parliament Acts, which enable the House of Commons to overrule the House of Lords after a delay of one year, specifically except laws extending the maximum duration of Parliament. Such a law therefore needs the consent of the House of Lords as well as of the House of Commons. W. J. Jennings, *The British Constitution*, p. 10.

[3] In April 1949, at a meeting of Commonwealth Prime Ministers held in London to consider the status of India in the Commonwealth association, it was stated that the king was the ' symbol of the free association of its independent member-nations and as such the Head of the Commonwealth '.

The following forms of the queen's title have been agreed upon for use in each Commonwealth country :

United Kingdom.—' Elizabeth the Second, by the Grace of God of the United Kingdom of Great Britain and Northern Ireland and of Her other Realms and Territories Queen, Head of the Commonwealth, Defender of the Faith.'

Canada.—' Elizabeth the Second, by the Grace of God of the United Kingdom, Canada and her other Realms and Territories Queen, Head of the Commonwealth, Defender of the Faith.'

is now governed by the Act of Settlement (1701). Briefly this provided that in default of heirs of the then reigning king, William, and of his expected successor, Anne, the Crown, together with all its prerogatives, should ' be, remain, and continue to the most excellent Princess Sophia,[1] and the heirs of her body, being Protestants '. Within the reigning family, the throne passes according to the principle of primogeniture, ' elder sons being always preferred to younger, and male heirs to female.' Provision has been made by Parliament for the setting up of a regency for the performance of the king's duties in the event of his absence, infancy, insanity, ill health, or unfitness to rule.

The sovereign must not only be a Protestant, but may not marry a Catholic. He (or she) is required to take a coronation oath to the effect ' that he is a faithful Protestant and that he will, according to the true intent of the enactments which secure the Protestant succession to the throne of the realm, uphold and maintain the said enactments to the best of his powers.'[2]

He is not answerable to any court of law, and cannot be arrested. At the beginning of his reign, he is voted a ' civil list ', i.e. a yearly allowance from the public funds for his personal and court expenses.[3]

The most important powers of the Crown are :

(*i*) It enforces national laws ; appoints and removes officers and directs the work of administration ; manages the country's

---

Australia.—' Elizabeth the Second, by the Grace of God of the United Kingdom, Australia and her other Realms and Territories Queen, Head of the Commonwealth, Defender of the Faith.'

New Zealand.—' Elizabeth the Second, by the Grace of God of the United Kingdom, New Zealand and her other Realms and Territories Queen, Head of the Commonwealth, Defender of the Faith.'

South Africa.—' Elizabeth the Second, Queen of South Africa and of her other Realms and Territories, Head of the Commonwealth.'

Pakistan.—' Elizabeth the Second, Queen of the United Kingdom and of her other Realms and Territories, Head of the Commonwealth.'

Ceylon.—' Elizabeth the Second, Queen of Ceylon and of her other Realms and Territories, Head of the Commonwealth.'

The Republic of India, while not owing allegiance to the Crown, remains a full member of the Commonwealth and acknowledges the Sovereign as Head of the Commonwealth. Now Pakistan too is a Republic and South Africa has left the Commonwealth.

[1] A grand-daughter of James I (1603-25). The present queen, Elizabeth II, is the eleventh in succession from George I (Sophia's son) who, in accordance with the Act, succeeded Anne in 1714. According to the Abdication Act 1936, the issue, if any, of King Edward VIII, and the descendants of that issue shall not have any right to the succession.

[2] F. A. Ogg, *European Governments and Politics*, p. 53.

[3] King George VI was allowed £410,000 a year, with exemption from income-tax ; Queen Elizabeth, £455,000.

foreign relations and makes treaties, and conducts its dealings with the colonies, Dominions, and dependencies; and holds supreme command over the armed establishments.

(*ii*) It summons Parliament, and prorogues and dissolves it; a speech 'from the throne' is read at the opening of a new Parliament; every law requires the assent of the Crown; orders-in-council are passed in its name.

(*iii*) It is the fountain of justice and, in that capacity appoints judges, 'and wields the power of pardon and reprieve, subject only to the restriction that no pardon may be granted in cases in which a penalty has been imposed for a civil wrong or by impeachment'.

(*iv*) It is the head of the Established Churches; as the head of the Anglican Church in England, it appoints the bishops and archbishops; as head of the Church of Scotland, its function, as A. B. Keith pointed out,[1] is insignificant.

(*v*) Finally, it is the 'fountain of honour'; titles are awarded, as for instance the Honours Lists published at the New Year and on the sovereign's birthday, in the name of the sovereign.

The 'Crown' and the 'sovereign'

The Crown has, however, to be distinguished from the sovereign; according to Gladstone,[2] this distinction is most vital to the practice of the British constitution and to right judgement upon it. The term 'sovereign' refers to the king or queen as an individual; the term 'Crown' to kingship as an institution and means, as we have seen, the supreme executive authority in the State. The king as an individual does not on his own initiative exercise the powers of the Crown; he exercises them on the advice of his ministers who are chosen from, and are responsible to, the Parliament representing the people. There was a time in the history of Britain when the king did himself exercise the powers; but the gradual evolution of democracy has made it necessary for him to be a nominal ruler. The king reigns, but does not govern.

'There is not a moment in the king's life, from his accession to his demise,' said Gladstone, 'during which there is not someone responsible to Parliament for his public conduct, and there can be no exercise of the Crown's authority for which it must not find some minister willing to make himself responsible.'

---

[1] *The King and the Imperial Crown*, no. 371-3.
[2] *Gleanings of Past Years*, Vol. I, p. 234.

Thus when he summons, prorogues or dissolves Parliament, or reads a ' king's speech ', or declares peace or war, or appoints to the highest executive offices of State, everyone knows that he does not act on his own responsibility.

It will, however, be a grave error to conclude, as the foregoing account might suggest, that the sovereign as a person has no influence on the affairs of State. That great authority, Gladstone, has said that the substance of the change that has occurred in the position of the monarchy since the end of the seventeenth century has been a ' beneficial substitution of *influence* for *power* '.[1] The whole authority of the State periodically returns into the royal hands whenever a ministry is changed. During the interval between the retirement of one Government and the appointment of another, the king (or queen) is the depositary of power.[2] ' Moreover, it is his personal duty to decide which of the leaders of the majority in Parliament shall be entrusted with the premiership. The right to commission a particular statesman to form a ministry remains, though it is conditioned by the fact that the sovereign's field of choice is narrowly restricted.' [3] Again, in the determination of policy and in administration, the sovereign has, in Bagehot's oft-quoted words, three rights : the right to be consulted, the right to encourage, the right to warn. And a king of great sense and sagacity, Bagehot adds, would want no others.

' He would find that his having no others would enable him to use these with singular effect. He would say to his minister. " The responsibility of these measures is upon you. Whatever you think best must be done. Whatever you think best shall have my full and effectual support. *But* you will observe that for this reason and that reason what you propose to do is bad ; for this reason and that reason what you do not propose is better. I do not oppose, it is my duty not to oppose ; but observe that I *warn* ".' [4]

It ought to be emphasized that the right of the sovereign to be consulted is an important one ; it is on record that more than one sovereign insisted on this right. The classic example is that of Queen Victoria :

[1] op. cit., p. 38 ; italics ours.
[2] S. Low, *The Governance of England*, p. 263.
[3] ibid.
[4] W. Bagehot, *The English Constitution*, ch. iii.

'She requires,' states one of her memoranda,[1] '(1), that he (Lord Palmerston) will distinctly state what he proposes in a given case, in order that the queen may know as distinctly to *what* she is giving her royal sanction ; (2) having *once given* her sanction to a measure, that it be not arbitrarily altered or modified by the minister. . . . She expects to be kept informed of what passes between him and the Foreign Ministers before important decisions are taken, based upon that intercourse ; to receive the foreign Dispatches in good time, and to have the drafts for her approval sent to her in sufficient time to make herself acquainted with their contents before they must be sent off.'

The warning given by a monarch cannot be lightly ignored by a minister, for it must be remembered that the former speaks from the vantage ground of an exalted station and a relatively greater experience. 'A king,' said Peel, 'after a reign of ten years, ought to know much more of the working of the machine of government than any other man in the country.' The monarch has one further advantage over his (or her) ministers : he (or she) is in a position to rise above parties and partisanship, for his (or her) personal fortunes are hardly affected by party politics. Undoubtedly, we may add, a good deal of the effective influence of the monarch depends upon his (or her) personality and the attention he (or she) devotes to affairs of State.

§4 THE SERVICES OF MONARCHY

Monarchy has endured in Britain for several reasons. First, the British are essentially conservative by temperament ; they hardly like to give up an institution which has been with them for ages. Secondly, little is gained by abolishing monarchy. The institution costs the nation but a fraction of one per cent of the annual budget. Further, the tradition is now well established that the king does not govern, but only reigns ; and, therefore, the existence of monarchy does not act as a brake on the popular will ; monarchy has now definitely become 'constitutional'. And even if kingship is abolished, some titular head, independent of electoral influences, would seem to be necessary in the place of the king. Thirdly, and above all, monarchy performs some distinct services to the nation : the presence of the king helps to give some continuity to executive policy. The traditions which sur-

---

[1] *Letters of Queen Victoria.* 1st Series, Vol. II, p. 315 : Queen Victoria to Lord John Russell, 12 August, 1850.

round a monarchy of long continuance help to inspire the actual
heads of the Government with a sense of responsibility and dignity.
The king or queen acts as a useful counsellor to the real political
heads of the State. He or she is the symbol of Commonwealth
unity, especially necessary after the passing of the Statute of Westminster (1931), which made the Dominions practically autonomous, and after India decided to become a Republic in 1949-50 ;
the British Parliament and the British cabinet have no powers to
interfere in the affairs of the Dominions or India. He or she is
also the head of British society, and is expected to set standards
of social life. The queen and other members of the royal family
visit many parts of the United Kingdom every year, and their
presence at the inauguration of scientific, artistic, industrial and
charitable works of national importance ensures nation-wide
interest and support. They also pay State visits to foreign
governments and undertake tours in other countries of the
Commonwealth, thereby contributing to better understanding
between United Kingdom and other nations, both within and
outside the Commonwealth.

§5 THE CABINET

The cabinet is the real, as distinguished from the nominal, Executive in Britain. It has been defined as a body of royal advisers
chosen by the prime minister in the name of the Crown with the
tacit approval of the House of Commons. It is, in Bagehot's
phrase, a *hyphen* which joins, a *buckle* which fastens, the legislative part of the State to the executive part of the State. Its
importance in the British political system is indicated in such
descriptions of it as ' the keystone of the political arch ' (Lowell)
and ' the steering-wheel of the ship of State ' (Ramsay Muir).

The cabinet must be distinguished from the Privy Council and
the ministry. It is a much smaller body than the Privy Council.
All members of the cabinet (about 20) are members of the Privy
Council, but all members of the Privy Council (about 294)
obviously are not members of the cabinet. The practice is for all
members of the incoming cabinet to be appointed to the Privy
Council, unless they are already Privy Councillors ; and they remain Privy Councillors for life.

It is also smaller than the ministry. The strength of the ministry
varies from Government to Government. For instance the Labour
Government of 1945 had a strength of 77, that of 1950 had 68,
the 1951 Conservative Government 63, the 1954 Conservative

Government 80 and the Conservative Government in 1971, 75.[1] The ministry consists of all the Crown officials who have seats in Parliament, are responsible to the House of Commons, and hold office so long as they command the confidence of the working majority in that body ; the cabinet consists only of some twenty of these. All cabinet members are ministers, but not all ministers are cabinet members. Further, the two differ in their functions : the ministry, unlike the cabinet, does not meet as a body for the transaction of business, for it has no collective functions in respect of the determination of policy or of administration. The function of a non-cabinet minister is to be in charge of a particular portfolio of government ; that of a cabinet minister, in addition, is to help in determining, along with his colleagues, the general policy of the Government in all departments and to control administration.

The choice of the ministers to be included in the cabinet depends on the prime minister. The first Secretary of State (a new appointment in 1962), the Chancellor of the Exchequer, important Secretaries of State such as those in charge of foreign affairs, the Home Office and Commonwealth Relations and the ministers of Defence and Labour are invariably members of the cabinet ; the others are included or not according to the wishes of the prime minister.

The formal appointment of the members of the cabinet is, of course, made by the sovereign. The usual step in its formation is for the sovereign, on the resignation of one cabinet, to send for the leader of that political party which controls a majority in the House of Commons and ask him to ' form the ministry '. If no single party commands a majority (as happened in 1924 and 1929), he invites the leader of that party, who can, either through a coalition or otherwise, assure himself of a majority or of sufficient support to undertake the responsibility of government. This leader is designated prime minister ; he suggests to the sovereign the names of the other members of the cabinet, and of other ministers. Technically he has a free hand in his choice ; in practice, he has to take into account the need for maintaining party solidarity and the claims of senior men in the party who have once served as ministers and are available for service ; for recog-

[1] According to Keesing's *Contemporary Archives*, the 77 ministers were distributed as follows : The cabinet, 20 ; other ministers of cabinet rank, 14 ; junior ministers, 43. The 68 ministers appointed in 1950 included 18 cabinet ministers, 20 non-cabinet ministers and 30 junior ministers. The 1954 ministry included 18 cabinet ministers, 20 non-cabinet ministers and 42 other ministers (*Vacher's Parliamentary Companion*, July-August 1954).

nizing ability among the younger men ; for represcnting social, economic, and religious groups in the cabinet ; for satisfying regional claims ; for including members from both Houses of Parliament ; and, above all, for getting together a team of really able men, including a variety of talents, who will work together under his leadership. The task is not easy ; Disraeli considered it ' a work of great time, great labour, and great responsibility '. Having got together his list, the prime minister submits it to the sovereign, who approves of it. Every minister of the Crown must be a Member of Parliament,[1] of one House or the other ; if he is not one at the time of appointment, he has to become one, either by being made a peer, or by a ' safe constituency ' being made available to him. The prime minister, it must be added, also assigns to each minister his individual portfolio, in consultation with him and with others.

The functions of a cabinet are succinctly set out in the *Report of the Machinery of Government Committee* (1918) as (*i*) the final determination of the policy to be submitted to Parliament ; (*ii*) the supreme control of the national Executive in accordance with the policy prescribed by Parliament ; and (*iii*) the continuous co-ordination and delimitation of the authorities of the several departments of State.

The first involves the preparation and approval of the legislative programme for each session of Parliament. Government measures are introduced, explained and defended on the floor of Parliament by members of the cabinet. The cabinet thus supplies an effective leadership to Parliament in legislation. It also approves of the ' king's (or queen's) speech ', determines its attitude to the bills introduced by private members of Parliament, and discusses the annual budget before it is introduced in Parliament. The second involves the determination of how the executive authority vested in the Crown—in respect of appointments, foreign affairs, etc.—shall be exercised. The third involves a general control and the co-ordination of the work of the several departments of the Government.

Since 1916, there has been a cabinet secretariat to help the cabinet in the performance of its functions. Its duties are :[2]

(*i*) To circulate the memoranda and other documents required for the business of the cabinet and its committees.

---

[1] This is a well-settled convention. There have been occasional exceptions. For example, Mr Gladstone once held office out of Parliament for some months in 1845-6.

[2] W. I. Jennings, *Cabinet Government*, p. 227.

(*ii*) To compile under the direction of the prime minister the agenda of the cabinet, and under the direction of the chairman, the agenda of a cabinet committee.

(*iii*) To issue summons of meetings of the cabinet and its committees.

(*iv*) To take down and circulate the conclusions of the cabinet and its committees and to prepare the reports of cabinet committees.

(*v*) To keep, subject to the instructions of the cabinet, the cabinet papers and conclusions.

The political characteristics of the cabinet may now be summarized : [1]

(*i*) *The exclusion of the monarch.* The sovereign does not attend the meetings of the cabinet. This practice dates from 1714 and arose from the circumstance that George I, the then reigning king, did not know the English language. The importance of this practice is, in the words of J. A. R. Marriott, that so long as the sovereign sat at the Council-board, some degree of political responsibility attached to him ; but the irresponsibility of the sovereign is a condition precedent to the complete responsibility of his servants.

(*ii*) *The close correspondence between the cabinet and the parliamentary majority for the time being.* This is secured, as we have seen, (*a*) by the practice of asking the leader of that party which has a majority in Parliament to form the cabinet ; and (*b*) by the rule that every minister of the Crown must be a member of one or other House of Parliament.

(*iii*) *The political homogeneity of the cabinet.* This indeed follows from (*ii*) above. It means that the members of the cabinet hold the same political opinions : the differences among them, if any, are expected to be resolved by mutual discussion, and are not, at any rate, made known to the public. From 1931 to 1945 there was a ' national ' Government, consisting of members drawn from three different parties ; but this did not substantially violate the principle of political homogeneity, for, in so far as the members thereof tacitly agreed to work on the principle of collective responsibility, explained below, some degree of political homogeneity was inevitable.

(*iv*) *Political responsibility to the House of Commons.* The members of the cabinet ' are answerable to the House for every policy that they embark upon, and for every action that they

---

[1] This analysis to some extent follows J. A. R. Marriott's in his excellent study, *English Political Institutions*, ch. iv.

take '; they hold their office only so long as they command the confidence of the House of Commons ; when they cease to have it, by convention they resign. It follows that the policy which they adopt must be acceptable to the House. The House can indicate its want of confidence by rejecting a bill introduced by a minister ; passing a non-official bill opposed by the cabinet ; refusing supply ; reducing the salaries of ministers and, finally, by a vote of ' want of confidence '. It hardly needs to be added that the principle of ministerial responsibility to the House of Commons is the means of assuring that government is in tune with public opinion.

This responsibility is, further, collective. This means in the oft-quoted words of Morley,[1] that

' as a general rule every important piece of departmental policy is taken to commit the entire cabinet, and its members stand or fall together. The Chancellor of the Exchequer may be driven from office by a bad dispatch from the Foreign Office, and an excellent Home Secretary may suffer from the blunders of a stupid Minister of War. The cabinet is a unit—a unit as regards the sovereign, and a unit as regards the Legislature. Its views are laid before the sovereign and before Parliament, as if they were the views of one man. It gives its advice as a single whole, both in the royal closet, and in the hereditary or the representative chamber. . . . The first mark of the cabinet, as that institution is now understood, is united and indivisible responsibility.'

For all that passes in the cabinet, each member of it who does not resign is absolutely and irretrievably responsible, and has no right afterwards to say that he agreed in one case to a compromise, while in another he was persuaded by his colleagues.[2]

We must perhaps add, for the sake of avoiding confusion, that the ministers are, in addition to being *politically* responsible to the House of Commons, *in law* responsible to the Crown, for the Crown appoints and dismisses them ; they are further, in common with other officers of government and according to the principle of ' the rule of law ', liable before a court of law in case any act of theirs is illegal.

(*v*) *The ascendancy of the prime minister.* The prime minister is, in the words of Morley, the keystone of the cabinet arch.

---

[1] *Life of Walpole*, 1913, pp. 155-6.
[2] *Life of Robert. Marquis of Salisbury*, Vol. II. pp. 219-20, cited by Jennings, op. cit., p. 217.

' Although in cabinet all its members stand on an equal footing, speak with equal voice, and, on the rare occasions when a division is taken, are counted on the fraternal principle of one man, one vote, yet the head of the cabinet is *primus inter pares*, and occupies a position which, so long as it lasts, is one of exceptional and peculiar authority.' [1]

An enumeration of the prime minister's most important functions [2] proves the correctness of Morley's estimate. With the sovereign's consent, he appoints and dismisses ministers and exercises a wide patronage including under this head making recommendations to the sovereign for appointment (*i*) of archbishops and bishops of the Church of England, (*ii*) to high judicial offices such as the Lord Chief Justice, (*iii*) to various royal and statutory commissions, and recommendations for the award of many civil honours and distinctions. He presides over the meetings of the cabinet ; is consulted by other ministers on the major problems of their departments ; settles disputes between departments ; controls the cabinet secretariat, and is generally responsible for seeing that departments carry out cabinet decisions. Often he is leader of the House of Commons. He is leader of his own parliamentary party, and invariably of his party outside. He is in communication with the prime ministers of the Dominions. He is the confidential adviser of the Crown and the ordinary channel of communication between the Crown and the cabinet. The power of the prime minister is indeed great. As Sidney Low says, backed by a stable, substantial majority in Parliament, his range of political action is scarcely limited. An English prime minister, with his majority secure in Parliament, can alter the laws, he can impose taxation and repeal it, and he can direct all the forces of the State. The one condition is that he must keep his majority.

Finally it is necessary to mention that the prime minister's power is largely due to the fact that indirectly he is the nominee of the political sovereign of the State, the electorate. He is returned to power as the leader of a party, whose policy has been explained to the nation at the general election and approved by them.

[1] *Life of Walpole*, p. 157.
[2] See Jennings, op. cit., pp. 153-4.

§6 THE HOUSE OF LORDS

The Queen-in-Parliament, i.e. the Queen, the House of Lords, and the House of Commons, constitutes the law-making body in Britain.

The House of Lords is largely based on the hereditary principle. It consists of just over 900 members, the number varying through deaths and the creation of new peerages. These fall into four categories:

(*i*) *Hereditary peers.* About nine-tenths of the members of the House are hereditary peers. It may be mentioned that peerages are created by the Crown, and descend to the eldest male member of the family ; the other members of the family are commoners. A peerage could not, till recently, be either alienated or transferred to another nor surrendered to the Crown.[1] The Peerage Act of July 1963, however, permits any one who has succeeded to a peerage (or who, in future, does succeed to a peerage) the opportunity to disclaim the peerage for his lifetime and so renounce for himself—but not for his successors—the rights and privileges of peerage, and at the same time removes his disqualifications to sit in the House of Commons and to vote in parliamentary elections.

(*ii*) *Peers of Scotland.* When Scotland was united with England (1707), by the Act of Union there was in existence a Scottish peerage, with 154 members. They were given the right of electing 16 of their number to represent them in the House of Lords for the duration of each Parliament ; by the Peerage Act of July 1963, the system of representation of the peers of Scotland was abolished and full rights of admission were given to all peers and peeresses of Scotland.

(*iii*) *Life peers.* The life Peerages Act 1958 has empowered the Queen to confer on any person, including women, a peerage for life carrying the right to sit and vote in the House of Lords. Ten barons for life and four baronesses for life have been created under the Act.

(*iv*) *Lords of appeal in ordinary.* There are nine of them,

[1] W. R. Anson, *The Law and Custom of the Constitution*, Vol. 1, p. 210.

appointed for life. The reason for introducing this element was to enable the House to fulfil adequately its judicial functions, noted below. They are chosen from among distinguished jurists and, unlike other members of the House, are paid an annual salary.

(v) *The Lords Spiritual.* The two archbishops, and twenty-four bishops of the Anglican Church (normally the bishops of London, Durham and Winchester and twenty-one other peers chosen in order of seniority), sit in the House by virtue of the writs of summons issued to them.

Persons under twenty-one years of age, aliens, bankrupts, and persons serving a sentence on conviction of felony or treason, are ineligible to sit in the House of Lords.

Of its organization and procedure, the essential features are the following. The Lord Chancellor, a member of the cabinet, and invariably a member of the House of Lords, is the presiding officer. Three members constitute a quorum, though in order to pass a legislative measure at least thirty members must be present. Normally the sessions of the House of Lords are coincident with those of the House of Commons, though the days and the hours of sitting are not always the same. There are several committees in the House of Lords, as in the House of Commons ; it is not necessary to refer to them because, on account of the smaller attendance in the House, invariably bills, after two readings, are debated in Committee of the Whole House before being read a third time. If the House makes amendments to a bill which comes from the Commons, the measure goes back to them for concurrence.

The powers of the House of Lords are threefold : judicial, legislative, and deliberative.

It is the supreme court of appeal for cases in the United Kingdom of Great Britain and Northern Ireland and a court of impeachment for the trial of important officers of the Crown. Impeachments have long been out of use (the last one was in 1805); there is no need for them as the principle of ministerial responsibility is now well established. The function of the House as the highest court of appeal is merely a historical survival. Actually, the House as a whole takes no part in the work, which is left to those of its members who have held high judicial offices together with the law-lords. As Ramsay Muir has noted, ' the law court which is called " the House of Lords " is in reality quite distinct from the legislative assembly of that name.'

The legislative powers of the House were until 1911 equal to those of the House of Commons in respect of ordinary bills and somewhat inferior in respect of money bills, i.e. the Lords could initiate ordinary bills, and amend and reject those which came from the House of Commons ; and, in theory at any rate, they had the power to amend and reject money bills, though this power was rarely used. This position was radically altered by the Parliament Act of 1911. This Act was ' provoked ' by the rejection by the Lords of the finance bill of 1909, providing for a tax on increase in land values ; a constitutional crisis ensued, and resulted in the passing of the Parliament Act.

(*i*) It provided that money bills, if passed by the House of Commons, should become law one month after such passage, even though the Lords should withhold their concurrence. The term ' money bill ' is so defined as to include measures relating not only to taxation but also to appropriations, loans, and audits ; and the Speaker of the House of Commons is given the absolute power to decide whether a given measure is or is not a money bill within the meaning of the Act.

(*ii*) Public bills, other than money bills or a bill containing any provision to extend the maximum duration of Parliament beyond five years, may become law without the consent of the Lords provided (*a*) that they have been passed by the Commons in three successive sessions of the same or consecutive Parliaments and (*b*) that two years have elapsed between the date of the second reading of the bill in the first of those sessions and the date on which it passes the House of Commons in the third of those sessions.

Briefly, the Parliament Act reduced the House of Lords to a definitely subordinate position. It deprived it practically of all powers in regard to money bills and limited its powers over general legislation to a suspensive veto of two years. It is, however, worth mentioning that the House could still, through its power to delay, exercise considerable power in respect of non-financial bills. The Labour Government, pledged to carry out progressive socialistic legislation, found this power inconvenient and irritating and therefore introduced a bill which became law in 1949 by which the delaying power of the Lords in respect of ordinary bills would operate only for one year. Legislation apart, the House of Lords is a ventilating chamber ; it may discuss any problem of public importance, social, economic and political.

It may be noted that, as indicated in an earlier section, a law extending the maximum duration of Parliament needs the consent of the House of Lords as well as of the House of Commons.

§7 IS THE HOUSE OF LORDS
A SATISFACTORY SECOND CHAMBER?

The tests of a good second chamber are twofold. (*i*) It must be composed differently from the first so that it may not be a mere duplication of a popularly elected first chamber ; it must thereby help to bring to the work of legislation and deliberation men with additional qualifications, and, if possible, superior to those of the members of the other chamber. (*ii*) While it should help to revise the laws passed in the other chamber, it must not be a rival to it or be an obstruction.

Judged by these standards, the House of Lords has, clearly, both merits and defects. It is differently composed from the popularly elected House of Commons. The members of the House, too, are men of considerable ability. Says a competent authority :

' It is doubtful whether, by and large, the actual working House of Lords is surpassed in its resources of intelligence, integrity, and public spirit by the House of Commons. Industry, finance, agriculture, science, literature, religion—all are represented there. Spiritual and intellectual as well as material forces find expression. The country is served from the red leather benches by men who have built up its prosperity, administered its great dependencies, risen to its highest positions in law, diplomacy, war, statecraft, and learning.' [1]

Even its worst critics admit that the debates in the House of Lords reach a very high level ; a discussion of colonial problems, for instance, in which such distinguished proconsuls as Curzon, Cromer (the maker of modern Egypt) and Milner (sometime Governor-General of South Africa) took part must indeed have been worth listening to.[2]

The functions allotted to the House cannot also be considered unsatisfactory, as they are more or less the functions envisaged for an ideal second chamber for Britain by an authoritative conference presided over by Lord Bryce (1918) :

(*i*) The examination and revision of bills brought from the House of Commons, a function which has become more needed since, on many occasions during the last thirty years, the House of Commons has been obliged to act under special rules limiting debate.

[1] Ogg, op. cit., p. 196.
[2] See, W. B. Munro, *The Government of Europe*, p. 153.

(*ii*) The initiation of bills dealing with subjects of a practically non-controversial character which may have an easier passage through the House of Commons if they have been fully discussed and put into a well-considered shape before being submitted to it.

(*iii*) The interposition of as much delay (and no more) in the passing of a bill into law as may be needed to enable the opinion of the nation to be adequately expressed upon it. This would be especially needed as regards bills which affect the fundamentals of the constitution or introduce new principles of legislation, or raise issues whereon the opinion of the country may appear to be almost equally divided.

(*iv*) Full and free discussion of large and important questions, such as those of foreign policy, at moments when the House of Commons may happen to be so much occupied that it cannot find sufficient time for them. Such discussions may often be all the more useful if conducted in an assembly whose debates and division do not involve the fate of the executive Government.

According to W. B. Munro,[1] the House appears to be doing its work fairly well on the whole.

' It examines and revises non-financial measures. It insists, when the occasion arises, that ample time be given for a full public discussion of such bills before they become part of the law of the land. It compels sober second thought and gives opportunity for passions to subside.'

Further, it is an admirable arena for the discussion of many important public questions, especially those which lie, or ought to lie, outside the domain of party politics ; its discussions, as we have noted, often reach a high level. Above all, it has ceased to be a rival or an obstruction to the will of the elected House.

What, then, explains the dissatisfaction with the House of Lords which we find in political discussions ? The reasons are really threefold. First, a predominantly hereditary body is an indefensible anachronism in a democratic State ; it symbolizes privileges not justifiable on a rational basis. The idea of a hereditary legislator is as absurd as the idea of a hereditary poet laureate or a hereditary mathematician. There has also been a serious suspicion that peerages have been bestowed not in recognition of merit or service to the community, but as a reward for contribution to party funds, that they have been practically sold for cash. The matter was so serious that it had to be investigated

[1] op. cit., pp. 151-2.

by a royal commission in 1922. Second, the composition of the House is overwhelmingly conservative in character, which means that when a Conservative Government is in office the Opposition is naturally weak and that when a Labour Government is in power, the ministerial representatives in the House are over-burdened in their effort to carry the House with the Government. Third, there is no doubt that the general attitude of the House of Lords has been conservative ; it appears to the public mind as the guardian of vested interests and a brake on progressive legislation. The classic instance of this attitude was the pronounced opposition of the Lords to the extension of the suffrage in 1832 ; it was overcome only by a threat from the Crown that a number of peers sufficient to swamp the opposition would be created. That is why H. J. Laski declares, that if there is to be a second chamber at all in a democratic State, the House of Lords, *when a Conservative Government is in office*, is perhaps as good a second chamber as there is in the world.[1]

This dissatisfaction has led to various proposals [2] for the reform of the House on more democratic and progressive lines. It is impossible to discuss them in this brief survey ; it is sufficient to say that several of them contemplate a reduction in the number of hereditary peers, and the addition of an elected element for the purpose of obviating the most common reproach, viz. that it 'represents nobody but itself, and it enjoys the full confidence of its constituents'. This, in its turn, raises other difficulties, e.g. that such a reformed House of Lords, more representative and possessing more talents, may demand greater powers and come into conflict with the House of Commons. There is considerable truth in the remark [3] that the strength of the present House of Lords, paradoxical as it may seem, arises from its weakness ; that the case for its abolition loses its force because the Lords are too weak to oppose the will of the popular House. But the position will be altered with a reformed House claiming increased powers. Whatever the future of the House of Lords may be, even as it is constituted and functions at present it is not without its uses. Says Bagehot :

---

[1] *Parliamentary Government in England*, p. 114 ; italics ours.

[2] See Marriott, *Second Chambers*, ch. xiii, for a convenient summary of these proposals. The proposal to have a House of 300 members, one half of them being hereditary peers elected by their fellows and the other half House of Commons nominees chosen for the value of their public services, has been canvassed for some time ; it is doubtful, however, if it is likely to be accepted in the near future.

[3] Munro, op. cit., p. 151.

' With a perfect lower House it is certain that an upper House would be scarcely of any value. If we had an ideal House of Commons perfectly representing the nation, always moderate, never passionate, abounding in men of leisure, never omitting the slow and steady forms necessary for good consideration, it is certain that we should not need a higher chamber. . . . But though beside an ideal House of Commons the Lords will be unnecessary, and therefore pernicious, beside the actual House a revising and leisured Legislature is extremely useful, if not quite necessary.'[1]

§8 THE HOUSE OF COMMONS

The House of Commons, the lower House, is an elected body consisting of 635 members,[2] the basis of representation being on the average one member for every 57,000 of the population. Successive measures dealing with representation have brought the House of Commons nearer to the principle of ' one man, one vote '. The Representation of the People Act, 1949, abolished plural voting, that is, the additional university and business vote, and made changes in the boundaries of the constituencies. All constituencies were made single-member. Out of a population of 55 million there is an electorate of some 35 million. Election to the House of Commons is decided by secret ballot in which British subjects (except members of the House of Lords) and citizens of the Irish Republic are entitled to vote (although voting is not compulsory) provided that they are 18 years old or over and are not subject to any legal incapacity to vote. The following persons may not vote: peers, infants (persons under 18 years of age), aliens, persons of unsound mind, felons serving a sentence of more than 12 months[3] and persons convicted within the previous five years of corrupt or illegal practices in connexion with an election.

Those eligible to vote in any constituency are those who are on the register of electors for the constituency and are resident there on a date fixed by statute. Electors normally vote in person at polling stations especially established for the purpose, although members of the armed forces, Crown servants of the United Kingdom employed overseas, and the wives of such

---

[1] *The English Constitution*, ch. iv.
[2] 516 for England, 36 for Wales, 71 for Scotland and 12 for Northern Ireland.
[3] A person sentenced for a misdemeanour may vote unless prevented by his punishment.

persons if resident overseas with their husbands may vote by proxy. Voting by post, or in certain cases by proxy, may also be allowed if the voter cannot attend in person for such reasons as physical incapacity or the nature of his work. Any person, male or female, who is a British subject of 21 years of age or over and is not otherwise disqualified, may be elected to the House of Commons. Categories of persons disqualified for election include peers (other than certain Irish peers), clergy of the Church of England, the Church of Scotland, the Church of Ireland, and the Roman Catholic Church, undischarged bankrupts, and those expressly precluded under the House of Commons Disqualification Act, 1957 (for instance, holders of judicial offices, civil servants, members of the regular armed forces and the police forces, members of the legislature of any country or territory outside the Commonwealth, and holders of other public offices listed in the Act).[1]

The House is elected for five years, but may be dissolved earlier by the Crown.

The powers of the House may be discussed under five heads :

(*i*) *Legislative.* In theory, the power of the Commons to pass laws for the United Kingdom and the colonies (barring the Dominions) is almost unlimited. The checks on this power provided by the constitution are the veto power of the Crown, and the suspensive veto of the Lords according to the terms of the Parliament Act of 1949. The former, according to the custom of the constitution, is not used ; the latter is ineffective. Further, the Judiciary has no power in Britain to declare the laws passed by Parliament unconstitutional.[2] Though in theory the power of the House of Commons to pass laws is thus great, in practice the cabinet, as is explained elsewhere,[3] has a large measure of influence in guiding legislation ; so that, in practice, we may say that ' new laws are made by the ministry with the acquiescence of the majority and the vehement dissent of the minority in the House of Commons '.

(*ii*) *Control of the Executive.* In theory, the Commons can dismiss the virtual Executive, i.e. the cabinet. For the cabinet is, as we have seen, a committee of the Legislature ; and the Commons can force it to resign, by its power (*a*) to pass a resolution of ' no confidence ' in the Government, (*b*) to reject a proposal which the Government considers so vital to its policy that it has made it a ' matter of confidence ' thus forcing the

---

[1] *Britain* 1973: *An Official Handbook*, p. 34.
[2] See below, §12.   [3] See below, §9.

Government to resign, and (c) to refuse supply. In practice, however, as is argued later,[1] the cabinet is scarcely ever turned out of office by the commons, *whatever it does*.[2] But through debates on matters of general policy, questions, and in committee, and the practice of moving the adjournment of the House (which is permitted only if the matter is deemed by the Speaker to be definite, urgent, of public importance, and to be the responsibility of the Government, and if supported by a specified number of members) the executive policy is criticized by members of the House.

(*iii*) *Control of finance.* As the guardian of national finance, the House has to determine the sources from which, and the conditions under which, the national revenues shall be raised ; to grant the money for expenditure ; to criticize the manner in which the funds are spent ; and to see that the accounts of the spending authorities are properly scrutinized and audited. These powers of the House are secured through certain rules and practices : no taxes may be imposed without the consent of the House ; no public money may be spent without similar authority ; ministers are constantly subject to interrogation on the floor of Parliament concerning the spending of public money ; and the accounts are audited by a committee of the House, viz. the Committee on Public Accounts. The method of financial control is treated at length elsewhere ;[3] it will be shown that the cabinet has in practice a predominant voice in settling the details of finance.

(*iv*) *The ventilation of grievances.* It is a function of the House to call attention to abuses and to demand the redress of public grievances. This is done through the practice of asking questions and through general debates.

(*v*) *Selective function.* The House is a place where men are tested for practical statesmanship. It is a training ground for public men where ' they have the opportunity of showing their mettle and displaying those qualities of mind and character, which distinguish the sheep from the shepherd, and the rulers from the ruled.'[4] The knowledge that those who show marked ability in the debates of the House have a reasonable chance of being chosen for the cabinet acts as a spur to good work on the part of members. This statement is subject to one important qualification, that under modern conditions of parliamentary life the private member has steadily decreasing opportunities for useful work and ' for showing his mettle ' ; the autocracy of the

---

[1] See below, §9.
[2] Low, op. cit., p. 81.   [3] See below, §11.   [4] Low, op. cit., p. 95.

cabinet is an inhibition. Further, in modern days, a man may well make his mark in public life outside the House and so qualify himself for responsible work.

These are the fivefold functions which the House of Commons is expected to perform : to make laws, to control the Executive, to be the guardian of the national finances, to ventilate grievances and indirectly to help sift the abler members from the less able. In practice, the initiative in law-making and in finance and the responsibility for both have definitely shifted to the cabinet ; and the control exercised over that cabinet is in normal circumstances a myth. Therefore, the functions effectively performed by the House in p.actice are to secure a Government which enjoys its confidence and to maintain it in power; to criticize that Government when things go wrong, and compel it to satisfy public opinion in the way it does things ; and, finally, to ventilate grievances. The growing complexity of modern government prevents the House from doing anything else.

§9   RELATION OF CABINET TO COMMONS

The cabinet in Britain is a parliamentary Executive, consisting of members chosen from the Legislature, and dependent for the continuance of its term of office on the confidence of the House of Commons. But, in practice, the parliamentary system has made the cabinet of the day autocratic for the following reasons.

(i) *The legislative initiative of the cabinet.* The cabinet initiates its measures and submits them to the Legislature. While it is true that private members of Parliament also have the right of introducing bills,[1] facts show that about 85% of the statutes passed are introduced by the Government.[2] So in the preparation of most bills which become law, the cabinet has influence.

(ii) *Rules of procedure.* The rules of procedure for conducting the business of the House of Commons favour the cabinet at the expense of the private members of the House. For one thing nearly seven-eighths of the time of the House is given over to

[1] Private members are members of the House who are neither office holders in the Government nor opposition leaders. They have the right of moving for leave to introduce Bills after question time under the 'Ten Minute Rule', i.e., the Standing Order which allows a brief speech proposing and another opposing the introduction of the Bill before the House decides whether or not to grant leave.

[2] In the years 1931-5, 219 bills were passed ; of these 183 were Government bills and 36 private members'.

Government business.[1] The Government has other advantages too ; under Standing Order 1(8), the session for the day can be lengthened to enable the Government's business to go on ; sometimes (as in 1928-9 and 1931-2), the House resolves after debate on a motion proposed by a minister to take the whole or some part of the private members' time. Again, Standing Order 57(3) of 1954 says that in all but one of the committees, Government bills shall have precedence.

(*iii*) *The working of the party system and the cabinet's power of dissolution.* Members of the House are grouped together in parties, the members being generally expected to vote with their party. The cabinet is chosen from the party having a majority in the House. The members of the majority party are interested in supporting the cabinet generally, not only because some may expect favours at the hands of the Government, but because the *risk* and *cost* attending a defeat of the Government are great. For, if the cabinet is defeated in the Commons, it can, instead of resigning, advise the Queen to dissolve the House, and a general election must be held. As Bagehot [2] acutely pointed out, the cabinet is a creature, but unlike other creatures, it has the power of destroying its creators. This makes an important difference. ' A member of Parliament, however insignificant,' says Ivor Jennings,[3] ' likes his seat, or he would not be there.' A dissolution is distasteful to him, because he has to pay a substantial sum to secure re-election, perhaps as much as £1,000. ' He has to spend an unpleasant fortnight or three weeks. Above all, he may have little certainty of being re-elected.' Further, in addition to personal discomfiture, his opposition to his Government majority may after all be helping the Opposition, which he detests more, to come to power. It is therefore rarely that a Government supporter votes against the Government. The last majority Government to be ejected by a vote of the House was the Liberal Government of 1895.[4]

(*iv*) *Financial control.* In matters of finance the dominance of the cabinet is practically complete. The province of private members is, as we shall see later,[5] limited to proposals for the reduction of expenditure proposed by the cabinet. Their criticism is ineffective, and proposals for reduction are rarely carried.

[1] See *Standing Orders of the House of Commons*, Part I, Public Business. No. 4.
[2] *The English Constitution*, ch. i.
[3] *Parliament*, p. 122.
[4] Jennings, op. cit., p. 120.
[5] See below, §10.

(*v*) *Increased State intervention.* Another factor, which has contributed to cabinet domination, is the reliance all round upon State assistance and State regulation, with their necessary corollary, planning.[1] Instead of being the body to resist the demands of the Crown for supplies until grievances have been redressed, the Commons today press for the redress of grievances by State subsidies. The result is that legislation of this character is necessarily complex, and cannot readily be amended in vital particulars, even if the Commons wished to do so, without wrecking the policy which it seeks to translate into laws.

(*vi*) *Other reasons.* The conditions of parliamentary life are not calculated to enable the Commons to control the cabinet effectively. Lord Rosebery has pointed out that the theoretical accountability of the cabinet is normally and regularly in abeyance for half the year : ' During the whole of the parliamentary recess, we have not the slightest idea of what our rulers are doing, or planning, or negotiating, except in so far as light is afforded by the independent investigations of the press.' [2] It is difficult, moreover, for a body of men who pay fitful attention to public affairs to supervise other men who have in their hands the conduct of these affairs all the time.

' The members of the House of Commons,' says Sidney Low,[3] ' are occupied in various ways ; they have many things to interest them during the short London season ; and though they may have every desire to do their political work properly, the circumstances are much against them. Half the House is taken up with business, and the other half with amusement. As the session goes on, and the weather grows warmer, and London society plunges into its summer rush of brief excitement, many members find it difficult to devote their energies steadily to their " parliamentary duties ".'

That the parliamentary system tends to make the cabinet autocratic is a fact ; it is however, ' an autocracy exerted with the utmost publicity, under a constant fire of criticism, and tempered by the force of public opinion, the risk of a want of confidence, and the prospects of the next election.' [4] The cabinet has its finger always on the pulse of the House of Commons, and espe-

---

[1] E. C. S. Wade, in his introduction to Dicey, *Introduction to the Study of the Law of the Constitution* (9th ed.), p. cxx.
[2] Rosebery, quoted by Low, in *The Governance of England*, p. 83.
[3] ibid.
[4] A. L. Lowell, *The Government of England*, Vol. I, p. 355.

cially of its own majority there ; meetings of the party are attended by Government members and these meetings help the Government to keep in touch with the views of the party members on important questions. The cabinet is also ever on the watch for expressions of public feeling outside.

§10 THE PROCESS OF LAW-MAKING

Bills may be introduced in Parliament by ministers or by private members. The former are called Government bills ; the latter, private members' bills. Again, bills may be either public or private. A public bill is one which affects the general interest and concerns the whole people, or at any rate a large section of them, e.g. the Compulsory Education Bill.[1] A private bill (which is not the same as a private member's bill) is one whose object is ' to alter the law relating to some particular locality, or to confer rights on or relieve from liability some particular person or body of persons ', e.g. one authorizing the compulsory purchase of land by a railway company, or authorizing a municipality to construct tram-lines within the municipality.

The main stages in the passing of a public bill into law are :

(*i*) *First reading.* The bill is presented, and its title read aloud by the clerk at the table of the House. Normally, no opposition is made ; the bill is deemed to have been read a first time, and is printed.

(*ii*) *Second reading.* The member in charge of the bill moves ' that the bill be now read a second time '. At this stage, there is a discussion on the principles of the bill ; if a member strays into its details, the Speaker of the House (i.e. the presiding officer) has power to pull him up.

(*iii*) *Committee stage.* If the principles of the bill are approved by the House at the second reading, it is referred to one or other of the committees (as explained below) for detailed discussion, amendment and report.

(*iv*) *The report stage.* The committee's report, embodying the suggestions of the committee to improve the bill, is presented, and any member may move amendments.[2]

(*v*) *Third reading.* On third reading only verbal amendments may be made. The bill is passed or rejected.

(*vi*) *Consideration by the House of Lords.* If the bill is

---

[1] Money bills are also public bills ; they are considered separately in §11.
[2] Subject to the Standing Orders of the House.

passed, it is sent up to the House of Lords, where it passes through more or less similar stages.[1]

(*vii*) Finally, the bill is presented to the sovereign for his assent. This assent may be given by him in person, or he may issue a commission authorizing certain commissioners to ' declare and notify his royal assent ' on his behalf. The latter is now the normal practice and is but a picturesque formality.[2]

Private bills follow a procedure in some respects different from that used for public bills. First, a petition, with the bill attached to it, must be presented. An official known as 'the examiner of petitions for private bills ' goes through the bill to see whether certain formalities in connexion with such bills have been observed by its promoters ; e.g. they must notify their intention to promote the bill by newspaper advertisements and gazette notices, and give individual notices to owners, lessees, occupiers of lands and houses, or others affected by the bill, so that the affected parties may have an opportunity to petition against the bill or any part of it. If the necessary conditions are not satisfied, a reference may be made to the Committee on Standing Orders to say whether the non-compliance may be overlooked. If the examiner's report is favourable, the bill is presented, and it is read a first and a second time. If there is no opposition at this stage, it is referred to a committee on unopposed bills ; if there is opposition, it goes to a private bill committee, normally of four members, in which the procedure is quasi-judicial, with counsel and witnesses to be heard. Then the bill follows the usual course followed by public bills.

The committee system

There are in the House of Commons five kinds of committees : sessional committees, standing committees, select committees, committees of the whole House, and private bill committees.

The sessional committees are chosen by the House for an entire session, each for a specific work, e.g. the committee of selection (to select members to the standing committees and the private bill committees) and the committee on Standing Orders.

Standing Committees are appointed by the House when necessary for the consideration of Public Bills, and, in the case of the Scottish and Welsh Grand Committees, other business committed to them. With the exception of the Scottish Standing and Grand

---

[1] Also see above. §6.
[2] See C. Ilbert, *Parliament*, pp. 75-6.

Committees [1] (which deal with Public Bills and other matters relating to Scotland), and the Welsh Grand Committee [2] (which considers the annual report for Wales and certain selected subjects for debate), each standing committee consists of from sixteen to fifty members nominated by the Committee of Selection and, as far as possible, reflecting in its composition the strength of the parties in the House.[3] The chairmen of committees are chosen by a 'chairman's panel for standing committees' named by the committee of selection. They are not committees for any definite subjects or branches of legislation but may consider any public bill referred to them by the Speaker. The procedure of a standing committee is generally similar to that of a committee of the whole House briefly indicated below.

The select committees (including joint select committees of both Houses) are appointed to inquire into and report to the House on special matters. Some of these, such as the Select Committee on Statutory Investments and on the nationalized industries, tend to be reappointed each season ; some are set up automatically by standing order such as the Committee of Public Accounts and the Estimates Committee ; others are set up as and when required.

As a rule, they consist of fifteen members, each chosen by the House on the motion of a member. It is provided,[4] however, that ' any member intending to propose that certain members be members of a select committee shall give notice of the names of the members whom he intends to propose to be members of the committee, and shall endeavour to ascertain previously whether each such member will give his attendance on the committee. Each committee chooses its chairman. The committee has power to send for persons, papers, and records.[5] It ceases to exist as soon as its work is done.

Committees of the whole House differ from *the House* in the following respects : The Speaker leaves the chair and his place

---

[1] The Scottish Standing Committee consists of thirty members nominated from Scottish Constituencies with up to twenty other nominated members ; in its plenary form it is known as the Scottish Grand Committee, with all members of the Scottish constituencies and not more than fifty others.
[2] The Welsh Grand Committee consists of 36 members for constituencies in Wales and Monmouthshire, with up to 25 other nominated members selected in order to make the balance of parties in the committee approximate to that in the whole House.
[3] *Britain 1973, An Official Handbook*, p. 39.
[4] Standing Order (Public Business) 67 (1).
[5] ibid., 61.

is taken by a chairman who is appointed in each new Parliament ; the mace is placed under the Table to indicate that the House, as a House, has adjourned. The function of a Committee of the Whole House is to consider Bills in detail, clause by clause, after their Second Reading ; the rules of procedure are less rigid than in the House. Money bills are not referred to standing committees but only to committees of the whole House, viz., the Committees of Supply and of Ways and Means.

Private bill committees consist of four members each, chosen by the committee of selection ; the procedure in these committees, as already indicated, is quasi-judicial.

§11 .CONTROL OF THE HOUSE OVER FINANCE

In a previous section [§8 (iii)] it has been noticed that the House of Commons has a fourfold function in respect of finance, viz. to determine the taxes, to make appropriations, to scrutinize accounts and to criticize the manner in which the national funds are spent. It remains to consider how the House performs these functions.

The function of the House in respect of finance begins only after the budget is presented to it by the Government sometime towards the end of February or early in March. It must, however, be remembered that the preparation of the budget involves much time and work for the Government. The budget is prepared by the Treasury (with the Chancellor of the Exchequer as its head) in consultation with, and on the basis of estimates supplied by, the various departments of government, and discussed in the cabinet before it is presented. In considering the Estimates submitted by departments, the Treasury has to look at the proposals for expenditure in relation to prospective national resources and to weigh the advantages of administrative proposals against the monetary and economic cost, taking into account current Government policy ; to decide the relative merits of expenditure proposed by different departments ; and to eliminate overlapping and uneconomic or wasteful expenditure.

It is his statutory function (a) to ensure that all expenditure is properly incurred, e.g. that no payments are made which go beyond any relevant statutory authority and (b) to audit departmental accounts and submit a report to Parliament. On presentation, the House resolves itself into a committee of the whole House 'in supply' (the Committee of Supply) to discuss the estimates of expenditure,[1] and into a committee of the whole House 'in ways and means' (the Committee of Ways and Means) to discuss proposals for raising funds. The resolutions of the Committees of Supply and of Ways and Means are reported to the House ; and on the basis of these resolutions, the Appropriation Act and the Finance Act are passed by the House authorising expenditure and taxation respectively. Every payment of money has further to be authorized by the Comptroller and Auditor-General, an officer holding office on good behaviour, and removable by the Crown on an address from both Houses of Parliament. Finally a select committee of the House, called the Committee on Public Accounts, scrutinizes the annual accounts and the reports on them made by the Comptroller and Auditor-General and makes a report to the House ; in order that its work may be effective this committee is usually presided over by a leading member of the Opposition. Question time in the House and debates also provide opportunities for private members to criticize the manner in which the money is spent.

Properly to grasp the nature of the financial control exercised by the House, two or three things have to be added.

First, as normally the Appropriation Act is passed only about the end of July (although the financial year begins on 1 April), the necessary permission for expenditure during these four months is granted by 'votes on account'.[2]

Secondly, some items of expenditure, such as the interest on the national debt, the royal civil list, and the salaries of judges, do not require an annual vote of Parliament, but are said to be charged on the Consolidated Fund, i.e. the fund to the account of the Government in the Bank of England.

Thirdly, it is a well-established principle that the House does not make appropriations save at the request of the Crown. As E. May puts it : [3] 'The Crown demands money, the Commons grant it, and the Lords assent to the grant : but the Commons do not vote money unless it be required by the Crown ', i.e. the pro-

---

[1] Early in 1971 the Expenditure Committee of the House was created, replacing the earlier existing Estimates Committee to consider public expenditure and its reports will provide further information on which the debates can draw. *Britain* 1973, *An Official Handbook*, pp. 202-3.

[2] There are some exceptions to this ; see Jennings, *Parliament*, p. 313.

[3] *Parliamentary Practice* (13th ed.), p. 446.

posal for the expenditure of public money must come from a minister of the Crown. Private members have only the right to propose a reduction ; they can neither propose a new item, nor suggest an increase in an existing item.

This rule is laid down by a Standing Order of the House.[1] By the practice of the House, a similar principle also applies to the imposition of taxes.

'The principle,' says May, 'that the sanctions of the Crown must be given to every grant of money drawn from the public revenue applies equally to the taxation levied to provide that revenue. No motion can therefore be made to impose a tax save by a minister of the Crown, unless such tax be in substitution, by way of equivalent, for taxation at that moment submitted to the consideration of Parliament ; nor can the amount of a tax proposed on behalf of the Crown be augmented, nor any alteration made in the area of imposition. In like manner, no increase can be considered either of an existing, or of new or temporary tax for the service of the year, except on the initiative of a minister, acting on behalf of the Crown.'[2]

From the foregoing account, it will be seen that the House controls the *raising of funds* through the discussion in the Committee of Ways and Means and the Finance Act ; and the *appropriation of money* through the discussion in the Committee of Supply, the Appropriation Act, and the authorization by the Comptroller and Auditor-General, an officer responsible to Parliament. Its *scrutiny of accounts* is done through the Committee on Public Accounts. It *criticizes the manner in which the money is spent* through questions and in debates.

The British financial procedure has some merits : it guarantees a financial programme which has been prepared as a unit and for which full responsibility is taken by one authority, the cabinet. The rule that proposals for taxation and expenditure must originate from the Crown is a healthy one in so far as it prevents the undue influence of localism in appropriations. The fact that proposals for income and expenditure are considered by the same body of persons, though sitting under two different names, helps to relate income to expenditure. Finally, ministers have the opportunity to defend their proposals on the floor of the House.

The control of the House has in recent times become more effective than it was, say, half a century ago, because of the

---

functioning of the Estimates and Public Accounts Committees. But it cannot be considered wholly effective. The committees of the whole House are too large, and have too little time, to discuss the estimates effectively ; the details of the budget are often not intelligible to the average member. Party solidarity, moreover, coupled with the cabinet's power to dissolve the House or its threat to regard as a vote of no-confidence any attempt by the House to reduce the budget, render the power of the Commons illusory. Finally, the indifference of the average member to financial questions makes its control a farce.

'Who is not familiar,' asks Sidney Low, ' with the farce of a debate on the Army or the Navy in committee ?...The bulk of the House—busy, fatigued, bored and idle—is out at dinner, or on the terrace, or in the smoking-room ; its members will come and vote if required, but otherwise will know no more of the debate than the newspaper-readers who will glance languidly the next morning over the array of unintelligible figures and obscure technicalities....'[1]

The fact is, as Lowell puts it,[2] in matters of finance as in legislation, the English system approximates more and more to a condition where the cabinet initiates everything, frames its own policy, submits that policy to a searching criticism in the House, and adopts such suggestions as it deems best ; but where the House, after all this has been done, must accept the acts and proposals of the Government as they stand or pass a vote of censure, and take the chance of a change of ministry or a dissolution.

§12 THE JUDICIARY

The judicial system of Britain comprises the following courts for criminal cases : the justices of the peace or magistrates, quarter sessions, assizes, the court of criminal appeal, and the House of Lords ; for civil cases, county courts, the High Court, the Court of Appeal, and the House of Lords.

Judges are appointed by the Crown ; they hold office during good behaviour, those of the highest courts being removable by the Crown, only on an address presented by both Houses of

---

[1] *The Governance of England*, p. 91.
[2] A. L. Lowell, *The Government of England*, Vol. 1, p. 327.

Parliament.[1] Their salaries cannot be reduced during their term of office. These provisions are meant to secure the independence of the Judiciary from the Executive.

Relation to the Legislature

Judges in Britain, unlike in the U.S.A., cannot entertain any question as to the competence of the Legislature to enact a given law. Supposing Parliament passes a law that Englishmen may be imprisoned without trial ; a judge may dislike it, and even consider it as being against the spirit of the constitution ; but he has no right to question its validity or declare it unconstitutional.

On the other hand, the Legislature can, by an amendment of the law, virtually override the decision of the courts. For instance, Parliament enacted the Trade Disputes Act in 1906 because it did not like the judicial decision in the Taff Vale case (1901). That decision was that the Trade Union as a body was bound to suffer for the mistakes of the officers of the union in the conduct of a strike. Parliament thought that such a decision would be a hindrance to the healthy growth of the Trade Union movement, which they considered necessary for social progress. So they passed the Trade Disputes Act, according to which the Trade Union was declared not responsible for the mistakes of its officers.

Relation to the Executive

Judges of all ranks are appointed by the Executive, but those of the highest courts are not liable to be removed except by the special procedure indicated earlier in this section. Judges of the lower ranks do not enjoy the same immunity by law, but they do in practice.

All officials are subject to the jurisdiction of the ordinary courts[2] for acts done in their official character. This implies the right of the subject, however humble, to seek redress for injury in the ordinary courts. This right forms part of the principle known as 'the rule of law'.

§13 THE RULE OF LAW

According to Dicey, who was the first to give it a clear analysis.[3] 'the rule of law' means three things :

---

[1] Since 1701 only once has such an address been moved, and that was against a judge convicted of misappropriation of funds, in 1830.

[2] See below, however, pp. 279-82.

[3] *Law of the Constitution*, Part II.

(*i*) No man is punishable, or can be lawfully made to suffer in body or goods, except for a distinct breach of law, established in the ordinary legal manner before the ordinary courts of the land. It means the supremacy or predominance of regular law, as opposed to the influence of arbitrary power.

(*ii*) No man is above the ordinary law, i.e. there is one law for all. In this sense ' the rule of law ' excludes the idea of any exemption of officials or others from the duty of obedience to the law which governs other citizens, or from the jurisdiction of the ordinary tribunals. This is in contrast to the system of administrative law prevailing in France and other European countries. The idea there is that disputes involving the Government or its servants are beyond the sphere of the ordinary courts and must be dealt with by special and more or less official bodies.

' With us,' says Dicey, ' every official, from the prime minister down to a constable or a collector of taxes, is under the same responsibility for every act done without legal justification as any other citizen. The *Reports* abound with cases in which officials have been brought before the courts, and made, in their personal capacity, liable to punishment, or to the payment of damages for acts done in their official character but in excess of their lawful authority.' [1]

One instance may be cited. In 1763, Wilkes, the editor of a paper called *The North Briton*, criticized the king's speech of the year as ' the most abandoned instance of ministerial effrontery ever attempted to be imposed upon mankind '. Lord Halifax, the Secretary of State, issued a *general warrant* for the apprehension of the authors, printers and publishers of *The North Briton* together with their papers ; the execution of which was personally superintended by Wood, the Under-Secretary. Under this warrant forty-nine persons were arrested including the editor, Wilkes, and the printer, named Leach, but including also many perfectly innocent persons. Wilkes brought an action against Lord Halifax and Mr Wood and was awarded £4,000 damages from the former, and £800 from the latter; it was decided that general warrants were illegal.

The importance of this, the distinctive aspect of the rule of law, cannot be exaggerated. As Maitland points out,[2] it ensures ministerial responsibility in the legal sense. Strictly speaking, ministers are not responsible to Parliament ; neither House, nor the two Houses together, has any legal power to dismiss one of

[1] ibid., p. 193.
[2] *The Constitutional History of England*, p. 484.

the king's ministers. But in all strictness the ministers are responsible before the courts of law, and before the ordinary courts of law. They can be sued or prosecuted there even for the highest acts of State.

(*iii*) The general principles of the constitution, e.g. the right to personal liberty, the right of public meeting and freedom from trespass, are in England the result of judicial decisions determining the rights of private persons in particular cases brought before the courts, whereas in other countries they are laid down, and seem to have their source, in a written constitution. For instance, the freedom from arrest by a *general* warrant has always been inherent in the common law of the land; it was but established by the decision in Wilkes' case. But in other countries, such fundamental rights are included as part of a constitutional declaration of rights. This is defective, according to Dicey, because the idea readily occurs that the rights are capable of being suspended or taken away; but where, as in England, the rights of individuals are thought to be inherent in the law of the land, it is felt that they cannot be taken away without a revolution in the habits of the people.

Limitations to 'the rule of law'

It is now agreed on all hands[1] that Dicey's analysis is defective; in particular, it tended unduly to exaggerate the merits of 'the rule of law'. It is now seen that the rule of law, as it prevails in Britain, is subject to one limitation.

With the extension of governmental activities into new fields such as education, public health, town-planning, the protection of the unemployed, etc., it has become common to entrust to executive authorities judicial duties which, if the rule of law prevailed without exception, would be entrusted to the ordinary courts. Thus the Roads Act, 1920, gives to the Minister of Transport power to decide appeals from the refusal of licences to run omnibuses. The Board of Education decides appeals about

[1] Wade, op. cit., pp. lxvii-xcv; Jennings, *The Law and the Constitution*, ch. ii; W. A. Robson, *Justice and Administrative Law*. Until 1947, there was another important limitation: the Crown could not be made liable in tort. This inequality has largely been corrected by the Crown Proceedings Act of 1947. This Act provides that 'the Crown shall be subject to all those liabilities in tort to which, if it were a private person of full age and capacity, it would be subject:—(a) in respect of torts committed by its servants or agents...'

Tort means the breach of a duty imposed by law whereby some person acquires a right of action for damages. See *Public Administration*, Vol. XXVIII, p. 41.

the opening of new schools. An appeal against an order of a County Council lies not to the courts but to the Minister of Health. Similarly, the District Auditor, the National Health Insurance Tribunals, the Unemployment Insurance Tribunals, and the Board of Trade exercise some judicial or quasi-judicial duties. This is a kind of administrative law, the jurisdiction of a judicial nature exercised by administrative agencies over the rights and property of citizens and corporate bodies.[1] There has been a substantial growth in the number of tribunals (there are over 2,000 in existence) and in the range of their activities during the past fifteen years.

The primary reason[2] for the growth of such administrative law is the extension of social legislation in the interests of the health, safety and general welfare of the community as a whole (public health, education, housing, etc.). For this necessitates a technique of adjudication better fitted to respond to the social requirements of the time than the elaborate and costly system of enforcement provided by litigation in the courts of law. In practically every field to which public administration has extended, new standards have had to be set up and maintained, e.g. the standard of a house reasonably fit for human occupation, the standard of capacity for work from the unemployed, etc. As W. A. Robson says, for the task of hammering out new standards in fields such as these, the courts of law would doubtless have been among the first to acknowledge their own manifest unsuitability. Expert knowledge is necessary ; and this can be provided by administrative courts. For instance, an Unemployment Insurance Tribunal can be manned by representatives of workers and of employers. Further, the mere volume of work involved by certain kinds of social legislation would have imposed an intolerable strain on the ordinary courts. Finally, there has also been a desire to provide a system of adjudication at once cheap and rapid.

While administrative law, as developed in Britain, does have these advantages, its working, according to competent observers, has also revealed some defects. These are summarized by Lord Hewart[3] in one phrase, ' administrative lawlessness '. Comparing the position in Britain with that in France, he points out that administrative law in that country, though different from ordinary law, is still law, i.e. it satisfies the requirements of a truly judicial

---

[1] Robson, op. cit., ch. i.
[2] ibid., ch. vi.
[3] *The New Despotism*, p. 43.

procedure : publicity, oral hearing, the taking of evidence, known and impartial judges, and reasoned judgement. In Britain, on the contrary, there is a lack of system ; and the essentials of judicial procedure are not always observed. Hence there is a possibility of arbitrariness, with its consequent danger to the liberty of the individual.

§14 POLITICAL PARTIES

The working of government in Britain, it must now be clear, is very largely conditioned by the existence and activity of parties. A political party is an organized group of citizens who hold similar political opinions and who work to get control of the Government in order that the policies in which they are interested may be carried into effect. There are now two major parties in Britain, the Conservative and the Labour ; there is also the Liberal party, which has a long tradition but at present little strength in Parliament.

The origins of the British parties may be traced to the days of Queen Elizabeth I (1558-1603). Towards the end of her reign, ' the Puritans, opposed to the intolerance and the extreme prerogative of the Queen's government, exerted themselves to gain seats in Parliament, where their representatives acted as an organized party in arresting the royal grant of monopolies '.[1] Clear party lines arose in the Stuart period (1603-1714).

The dividing line was primarily constitutional, i.e., whether arbitrary government by the kings or government limited by Parliament was to prevail. Those who supported the former were known as the Cavaliers ; those who supported the latter, as the Roundheads. There was also the religious issue. Those who supported the Church of England tended to form themselves into one group ; the Nonconformists, into another. In general, the king's supporters were good Churchmen ; the supporters of Parliament were for the most part Nonconformists. In the reign of Charles II (1660-85) the names of *Tory* and *Whig*[2] were applied to these two parties.

The Revolution of 1688 and the Hanoverian succession to the throne in 1714 were a triumph for the principles of the Whig party. There was, therefore, a change in the position of parties, the Whigs now supporting the new dynasty, which admitted the

[1] S. Leacock, *Elements of Political Science*, pp. 314-15.
[2] For the origin of these terms see R. Lodge, *The History of England from the Restoration to the Death of William III* (1660-1702), p. 170.

claim of Parliament to have a greater voice in the affairs of the nation, and the Tories being in the opposition.

Later, during the reign of George III, the names Liberals (Whigs) and Conservatives (Tories) came into use, the former being considered generally in favour of reform, and the latter generally in favour of the established order.

From the Revolution onwards was gradually established the practice of kings choosing their ministers from the party which commanded a majority in Parliament. This gradual development of the parliamentary system is very important in the history of British parties, for, as A. L. Lowell has shown, that system is based upon party, and by the law of its nature tends to accentuate party.

The last important landmark in the history of British parties is the formation of the Labour Party in the present century. The origin of the party may be traced to 1899 when the Trade Union Congress of the year instructed its parliamentary committee to invite all co-operative, socialistic, Trade Union and allied organizations in England and Wales to unite in calling a special convention to devise ways and means for securing the return of an increased number of Labour members to the next Parliament. The convention met in 1900 ; out of this arose the Labour Representation Committee, renamed the Labour Party in 1906.

Party organization

The nature of party organization depends on the functions which parties are called upon to perform. These functions are to fight the elections to Parliament, and, since the advent of the Labour Party, also to local bodies ; to raise funds for the purpose ; to distribute party literature ; to choose candidates for elections, and to canvass support for them by arranging meetings, taking voters to the polling booths, etc. ; to do what is needful in Parliament (according as a party is in power or in opposition); and to see that certain policies are accepted and carried out by the Government.

To perform these functions, each party has a threefold organization :

(*i*) The local party committee in each parliamentary constituency. This works in harmony with the central office and with the Member of Parliament for the district where one is returned from the party.

(*ii*) The parliamentary party. This consists of all members of the party who are actually in Parliament, with an elected leader.

In the Conservative and Liberal parties, the formulation of the policy of the party both in the country and in Parliament is largely left to the parliamentary party. Each party maintains a central office, ' with paid officials engaged in research, propaganda, and electioneering ', to act as the link with the constituency party organizations. The chief whip of the party, in addition to helping to raise funds for it, scrutinizes its parliamentary candidates ; and ' as far as possible he must get constituencies to adopt candidates whom the central office suggests to them '.[1]

(*iii*) A national organization. The Liberal Party has the National Liberal Federation ; the Conservative Party, the National Union of Conservative and Unionist Associations ; and the Labour Party, the Annual Conference. In its annual conference, each party draws up its ' platform ' and takes stock of its position in the country and devises ways and means to improve it.

Party principles

' There are, perhaps, two main tenets,' wrote Edward Marjoribanks,[2] the protection of property and the maintenance of the British Empire under the Crown, for which modern English Conservatism stands. . . . For the Conservative the safe possession of property is, after the protection of life itself, the distinguishing mark of civilized society, and one of the first duties of the State is to ensure it.'

The Conservatives believe that the present social order, resting as it does on private ownership and control of the means of production, ' is organically sound ' ; the defects which exist must be removed, but without affecting the basic structure of society ; as Sir Robert Peel said in 1834, Conservatives were ready to provide the correction of proved abuses and the redress of real grievances based on ' a careful review of institutions '. They do not believe in economic equality. Their belief in the maintenance of the British Empire made them suggest that the establishment of self-government in dependent areas need not be hastened ; it must be added that there is no desire on the part of Conservatives to undo the work of conferring on dependent territories Dominion Status or independence followed in recent years. Further, they believe in tariffs and the protection of home industries. They support the claims of the Established Church, the Crown and the House

[1] R. L. Buell (Editor), *Democratic Governments in Europe*, p. 104.
[2] *The Life of Lord Carson*, p. 364.

of Lords. It is natural that the party derives its main support from the Church, and from the wealthy people. The landlords and the commercial and industrial interests are broadly Conservative.

The Labour Party is avowedly socialistic and believes in the public ownership and control of the means of production. A few extremists apart, the party in general believes in evolutionary socialism, i.e. in using the democratic State to attain the goal of socialism and in retaining it after the goal is attained. Socialism, indeed, is the next step in democracy. Gradualness and parliamentary methods—these are the fundamental principles accepted by the bulk of the party. To start with, work, wages, education, leisure, and insurance against unemployment, sickness, and old age must be guaranteed to all ; the progressive principle in taxation must be further extended ; public utilities and natural monopolies must be nationalized ; and, later, perhaps, land and all forms of industrial capital. In the international sphere, they are inclined to support all proposals calculated to ensure collective security.[1] It need hardly be added that the party derives its main support from the working classes although many ' intellectuals ' also support it.

The party platforms of the Conservative and Labour parties in the 1951 elections are instructive in this connexion. In foreign affairs, the Labour Party would do all to secure peace ; Britain must play her full part in strengthening collective defence : ' We have had grievous disappointments, particularly with the Soviet Union. But we shall persevere ; ' the nation had to be strong and so had the Commonwealth, but peace could not be preserved by arms alone ; more aid must be given to backward countries. In domestic policy, they promised (i) full employment, increased production to bring down the cost of living and the building up of a just society ; (ii) to take steps to abolish pay differences between men and women in the public services ; (iii) limitation of dividends ; (iv) increased taxes on a ' small minority who own great fortunes and forge unearned incomes ' ; (v) measures to prevent large capital gains ; (vi) an attack on monopolies and combines which restricted production and kept prices and profits too high ; (vii) the extension and strengthening of price controls ; (viii) to stimulate production and expand imports ; (ix) to start

---

[1] In respect of Colonies the Labour Party would appear to be in favour of supporting measures designed to establish self-government more quickly than the Conservative Party would approve. It must be added, however, that the difference in this respect has not been striking, especially during the past few years : the Conservatives have swung a little to the left, Labour a little to the right.

public enterprises wherever this served the national interest ; and (x) to stop all excess profits. While dividends would be limited and the rich taxed more heavily, Labour promised reduced taxation on wages, moderate incomes and moderate inheritances as soon as tax reductions became possible. They urged the election motto : ' Forward with Labour or backward with the Tories.' [1]

The Conservative Party in its election manifesto said that if returned to power, it would try to restore Britain to world leadership and economic recovery. They saw the possibility of an agreement with a friendly Russia which would ' open to all the toiling millions of the world an era of moral and material advance undreamed of hitherto among men '. On the domestic front they would scrap iron and steel nationalization,[2] retain coal nationalization (already brought about by the Labour Government) but stop all further proposals for state ownership ; revise existing taxation on profits and give relief to firms ploughing their profits back to renew plant ; discipline monopolies and fight restrictive practices on both sides of industry ; aim to build 300,000 houses a year ; keep Britain's food subsidies but later revise the system so that family allowance increases and food subsidies were confined only to those really in need of them.

In substance, while the Labour and the Conservative parties have accepted the Welfare State as the goal of domestic policy, Labour would stress equality, Conservatism justice.

The Liberal Party in general supports a policy of social reform and amelioration, urges economy in national expenditure and a freeing of trade from tariffs. It

' urges State regulation rather than nationalization or State management, though (like the Labour Party) it wishes the Gov-

---

[1] See for later views of the Labour Party on economic and social questions the policy statements on Personal freedom, Housing, Taxation, Pensions, Public ownership and Colonial Affairs published by the Party between June 1956 and September 1957 summarized in Keesing's *Contemporary Archives*, 23-30 November 1957. There is no substantial change in the policy. A slight change—towards caution in taking up public ownership in the traditional manner—could be seen in the following two recommendations : (i) While there was no general case for subsidies to nationalized industries as such, they should not be expected to jeopardize financial stability by providing uneconomic services when a private industry in similar circumstances would be given a subsidy and (ii) While the next Labour Government would renationalize the steel and long-distance road haulage industries, the document *Towards Equality* also suggested State acquisition of shares in some of the large industrial firms as a new method of public ownership and control.

[2] This election promise was carried out by the Iron and Steel Act 1953 passed on 14th May, 1953.

ernment to control banks, investments, transport, and electric
power, and to regulate the coal industry. Its agricultural policy
is to secure a more efficient use of land through the provision
of small holdings and allotments. . . . The "Liberal Way" is
in essence a middle way between the "State Capitalism" of the
Conservatives and the socialism of Labour.'[1]

The party draws its strength from the professional and commercial classes, the small independent farmers, about one half
of the middle class, and some working men. Since the advent of
Labour to prominence, the Liberals have greatly declined in
strength and importance in English politics.

§15 LOCAL GOVERNMENT IN ENGLAND AND WALES[2]

Local government is government by popularly elected bodies
cnarged with administration and executive duties in matters concerning the inhabitants of a particular district or place.
For purposes of local government, England and Wales are
divided into County boroughs and Counties. Counties (outside
London) are further divided into three types of County district :
non-County boroughs, urban districts and rural districts. Rural
districts are themselves sub-divided into parishes. (Special arrangements have, however, been made for London which has its own
system.) Each local authority division is administered by a
different Council, though the Councils within the county (excepting county boroughs) are subject to certain kinds of supervision
by the County Council. Thus in England and Wales, in 1973
there were 58 County Councils, 83 County Borough Councils, 259
non-County Borough Councils, 522 Urban District Councils, 470
Rural District Councils and over 10,000 Parish Councils.[3]
Local Councils comprise a number of elected Councillors
(unpaid), presided over by a Chairman ; the normal term of
office of a Councillor is three years. Any person (including a
member of the House of Lords) is entitled to vote at a local
government election provided that he or she is 18 years of age
or over on the qualifying date, is a British subject or a citizen

[1] Buell, op. cit., p. 256.
[2] The system of local government is not identical in all parts of the
United Kingdom (e.g. there are slight differences between the systems in
England and in Scotland) This section gives a brief account of the
system in England and Wales.
[3] See Britain 1973, An Official Handbook, p. 68.

of the Irish Republic, is not subject to any legal incapacity and is registered as a local government elector for the area for which the election is held. In England and Wales a person qualifies for registration as a local government elector if, on the qualifying date, for the register (compiled annually) he or she is resident in the area or occupies as owner or tenant any ratable land or premises in the area of a yearly value of not less than £10.

The borough is the oldest local government unit in the country ; the incorporation of a township by means of a charter from the Crown (which was the manner in which a borough came into existence) was a special and highly valued privilege. Boroughs are divided into quarter-sessions boroughs and non-quarter-sessions boroughs, i.e. those which have a court of quarter-sessions presided over by a Recorder (judicial officer appointed by the Crown) and those which have not ; the latter are still subject to the sole jurisdiction of the Justices of the county in which the borough is situate. A county borough area does not form part of the county in which the borough is situate, i.e. it enjoys all the powers of municipal boroughs and also all the powers of County Councils in addition ; and very bitter are the struggles between county borough and county, when by means of a private Act of Parliament a county borough seeks to extend its boundaries and annex part of the county area.

The chairman of the borough council is the Mayor, a very ancient and honourable office. In some of the larger cities, he is by prescription known as the Lord Mayor ; and the Crown, as the fountain of honour, has of late years directed that in the case of certain of the larger towns, the Mayor should also be so called. All other local authorities have a chairman only.

The county council has 56 to 140 members, the strength varying according to the population of the county. The council elects its chairman. Its powers include education, the police, town (and country) planning, the provision of board and shelter for those who need it, the care of children who lack parental care, certain powers as to health and housing, and certain powers of supervision over districts, parishes and boroughs. The executive work is done by officials appointed and controlled by the council, holding office usually on good behaviour and not dismissible on political grounds.

Urban and rural district councils owe their origin to the public health legislation of the early part of Queen Victoria's reign, but have developed greatly in importance since then. Their powers include matters relating to public health, water supply, minor roads, bridges and housing. The main executive officers are the clerk, treasurer, engineer, sanitary inspector and medical officer.

Parish councils (and, in small parishes, parish meetings) date from the Local Government Act of 1894. Their main powers are in regard to the maintenance of the public right of way, the management of parish property, the alteration of boundaries, burial grounds, public libraries and recreation grounds. There are generally two executive officers : a paid clerk and an unpaid treasurer.

The present tendency is to give more and more local government powers to the larger authorities, i.e. the county and county borough councils ; thus recently these have displaced the smaller authorities in the fields of education and town and country planning, though the county councils are authorized to delegate certain of their powers to the smaller authorities in certain cases. There is also a movement towards making the areas of the counties larger, by combining some of the smaller ones. This is discernible more especially in the proposals of the Royal Commission on Greater London (published in 1960) including one that the primary units of local government in the area should be Greater London Boroughs with a population range of 100,000 to 250,000 and in the reports (so far published) of the Local Government Commission for England and the Local Government Commission for Wales which also envisage substantially larger and therefore fewer administrative units. On the other hand the counties and county boroughs have recently lost considerable powers to the central Government ; thus as part of the scheme for the ' National Health Service ' they have lost their powers as to hospitals and lunacy, and the central Government has also taken over the relief of the destitute, so far as this is done in money, and the treatment of vagrancy.

Control by the central Government

Local self-government does not mean that the local bodies are free from all control by the central Government. That Government has the power to see that a fair standard of administration is maintained. Central control is exercised primarily in three ways.[1]

(i) *Legislative.* Parliament controls local authorities through Acts of Parliament which require or permit elected local councils to implement policies prescribed and defined in those Acts.

[1] See J. A. R. Marriott, *The Mechanism of the Modern State*, Vol II, pp. 376 ff.

(*ii*) *Administrative.* The responsibility for a fair standard of efficiency in local government is insisted upon, and secured by such means as inspections, inquiries, the issue of advisory circulars, the audit of accounts, co-operation, and financial assistance in approved schemes, the withholding of grants where unsatisfactory administration is proved, and the insistence on the possession of defined qualifications by certain officers. This control is to some extent diffused, i.e. vested in several central departments such as Health, Home, Education, Transport, and Trade, though the Ministry of Housing and Local Government is the main link between local authorities and the central Government. In general the control is exercised by co-operation, advice and warning rather than by disciplinary action.

(*iii*) *Judicial.* The responsibility of the public official to law, implied in ' the rule of law ', applies to local government as well.

The main principles of English local government may be summarized thus. It is democratic, as may be seen from the existence of representative councils, elected chairmen, and a wide suffrage. While it is democratic, it is also recognized that essential local work has to be done by paid employees (appointed and paid by the councils) and, therefore, certain posts (for instance, the clerk, the treasurer and the medical officer of health) are compulsory in almost all councils. The system is a co-ordinated whole, the authority of the larger body over the smaller being definitely recognized. It is decentralized, local bodies being given the maximum amount of independence by the central authority consistent with the maintenance of a fair standard of administration, the initiative, within defined limits, in policy-making and in the spending of money resting with them. Finally, there is a tradition of honest and efficient local administration.

§16 CONVENTIONS OF THE CONSTITUTION

At the beginning of this chapter, reference was made to the fact that the ' constitution ' of Britain consists partly of laws, and partly of conventions or usages. These latter need some elaboration as there are two broad differences between laws and conventions.

(*i*) Laws are enforceable through a court of law ; conventions are not. There is no formal method of determining when conventions are broken ' and to set in motion the train of consequences, which this breach should bring '. Thus if a voter is denied the privilege of voting, he can enforce his right through a court of law. But if the sovereign chooses to exercise his veto over laws and thus break a long-established usage, a law court cannot question him.

(*ii*) Laws are more or less precisely formulated ; it is usually nobody's business to formulate conventions, with the result that, at any particular time, differences of opinion may arise about a convention which is said to be ' established '. Thus ever since Stanley Baldwin was summoned to form the ministry in 1923, it has been, according to many, a convention that the Prime Minister must be a member of the House of Commons ; but one cannot say that this is yet ' established ' : if the sovereign sends for a leading member of the House of Lords to form a ministry there may be a substantial body of opinion to support him.

The following are some of the most important conventions of the constitution :

The sovereign does not veto a bill passed by Parliament. The Crown can create a sufficient number of new peers to overcome the opposition of the House of Lords.

The party which for the time being commands a majority in the House of Commons has a right in general to have its leaders placed in office. The most influential of these leaders ought to be the Premier. Ministers are collectively responsible to Parliament. They resign office when they have ceased to command the confidence of the Commons. A cabinet may appeal to the country once by means of a dissolution.

When the House of Lords acts as a court of appeal, no peer who is not a law-lord takes part in the discussions of the House.

Parliament should be summoned at least once a year. A bill must be read three times in the House of Commons before it is sent up to the other House.

An officer of the Crown is tried in the same court as an ordinary citizen.

The Prime Minister of a Dominion advises the Queen direct as to the choice of the Crown's representative in that Dominion. The Governments of the Commonwealth consult one another in matters relating to their foreign policy.

The sanction behind the conventions is threefold : (*i*) Public opinion. If, for instance, a cabinet which clearly does not command the confidence of Parliament remains in office, public opinion condemns its action, and practically compels it to submit its resignation. (*ii*) The desire of the governing class to carry on the traditions of constitutional government and ' to keep the intricate machinery of the ship of State in working order '. (iii) Indirectly the breach of *some* conventions may bring the offender into conflict with the courts and the law of the land. This is true particularly of those usages which regulate the relations between the cabinet and the House of Commons. Thus if Parliament were not summoned every year, the Finance Act would lapse ; the Government, in order to carry on the administration, would have to ask for taxes, which the citizen would legally be at liberty to refuse to pay. He might sue the officer responsible in a court of law.

Value of conventions

Conventions play an important part in the working of the constitution. In the classic words of Dicey, many of them ' are rules for determining the *mode* in which the discretionary powers of the Crown ought to be exercised '. The discretionary powers of the Crown are those powers for which it need not get specific parliamentary sanction ; they are to be used in such a way as ultimately to give effect to the will of that power which is the true political sovereign, viz. the electorate. Thus the sovereign, in exercising his power to appoint ministers, asks the leader of that party which commands a majority in the House to advise him in the matter. He can dissolve Parliament even before its legal term is over ; he exercises this power in order to test whether the House is truly representative of the electorate, and so on.

Further, they enable the constitution to bend without breaking, to adjust itself to changing needs without a complete overhauling. Thus the convention that the sovereign does not veto the laws is an adjustment of monarchy to the needs of a democratic age ; monarchy is retained without prejudice to the supremacy of the popular will.

And, lastly, they help the constitution to work smoothly. The usages regarding the cabinet system help the Legislature and the Administration to work in unison ; those regarding the relations of Britain with the Dominions help to retain the Dominions in the Commonwealth without loss to their self-respect.

SELECT BIBLIOGRAPHY

W. R. ANSON, *The Law and Custom of the Constitution*, 2 vols., 5th ed. and 4th ed., Oxford, 1922 and 1935

W. BAGEHOT, *The English Constitution*, 'World's Classics' No. 330, Oxford

S. D. BAILEY, *British Parliamentary Democracy*, George G. Harrap, 1958

Britain. An Official Handbook, prepared by the Central Office of Information, London, 1973

G. M. CARTER, *Government of the United Kingdom*, New York, Harcourt Brace Jovanovich, 3rd ed., 1972

A. V. DICEY, *Introduction to the Study of the Law of the Constitution*, Macmillan, 9th ed., 1939

SIR EDWARD FELLOWES and T. G. B. COCKS (Editors), *Sir Thomas Erskine May's Treatise on the Law, Privileges, Proceedings and Usage of Parliament*, Butterworth, 16th ed., 1957

H. H. HANSON and H. V. WISEMAN, *Parliament at Work*, Stevens & Sons, 1962

C. ILBERI, *Parliament*, 'Home University Library', Oxford, 3rd ed., 1948

W. IVOR JENNINGS, *Cabinet Government*, Cambridge, 2nd ed., 1951

——, *The Law and the Constitution*, University of London Press, 2nd ed., 1938

——, *The British Constitution*, Cambridge, 5th ed., 1971

——, *Parliament*, Cambridge, 1939.

A. B. KEITH, *The King and the Imperial Crown*, Longmans, 1936

H. J. LASKI, *Parliamentary Government in England*, Allen & Unwin, 1938

S. LOW, *The Governance of England*, Benn, 1922

A. L. LOWELL, *The Government of England*, 2 vols., Macmillan, 1921

J. A. R. MARRIOT, *English Political Institutions*, Oxford, 4th ed., 1938

G. C. MOODIE, *Government of Great Britain* London, Methuen, 3rd ed., 1971

H. MORRISON, *Government and Parliament*: a Survey from the Inside, Oxford, 1954

R. MUIR, *How Britain is Governed*, Constable, 1940

F. A. OGG, *English Government and Politics*, Macmillan, 2nd ed., 1936

——, *European Governments and Politics*, Macmillan, 1939

W. A. ROBSON, *Justice and Administrative Law*, Macmillan, 2nd ed., 1947

Research Board (Ed.), *How Britain is Governed*, Delhi, Research, 1972

CHAPTER XVII

THE FRENCH REPUBLIC

§1 INTRODUCTORY

FRANCE today is governed by a Constitution adopted on 28 September 1958 by a vote of all adult inhabitants of France (including Algeria) and the French Union in a national referendum; the decision to hold the constitutional referendum on 28 September was taken by General de Gaulle's Government on 6 August 1958; nation-wide propaganda was conducted for and against the Constitution by 23 approved political parties and groups; and, in the result, the Constitution as submitted to the voters by the Government, was approved by an overwhelming majority.[1]

An outline of the Constitution is given in §4 and some comments based on its working are added, it being too early to describe its working in detail.

To understand the significance of the provisions of the new Constitution—of the Fifth Republic, it seems essential to give a very brief resumé of the political vicissitudes in France since 1789 (§2) and a somewhat fuller description (§3) of the institutions of the Third Republic (1875-1940), the experience of which must largely explain the important changes in the political system brought about by the present Constitution. This apart, a study of the political institutions of the Third Republic is still of interest to the student of Politics as illustrating, among other things, the working of parliamentary government under a multiple-party system, administrative jurisprudence and centralized local administration.

§2 FRANCE SINCE 1789

The remarkable fact—in the politics of France since the French Revolution of 1789—is that there has hardly been what Finer has called a political consensus: an ability to agree on the fundamentals of her political system. This is specially in contrast with

---

[1] Guinea was the only territory to show a majority of 'no' votes; on the declaration of the results of the voting, Guinea ceased to be part of the French Community and became independent.

the continuity of constitutional development in Britain, as well as with the stability of the Constitution of the U.S.A., which has continued with a few amendments since 1787. Three years after absolute monarchy was overthrown by the Revolution of 1789, the First Republic was proclaimed on 10 August 1792. This Republic lasted nominally as a Republic till 1804—nominally because during most of the period it was in essence a dictatorship. The First Republic gave place in 1804 to the First Empire with Napoleon Bonaparte as its head ; this Empire lasted till 1815. Then followed the Restoration (till 1830), the July Monarchy (1830-48), the Second Republic (1848-52) and the Second Empire (1852-70). Some stability was attained during 1870-1940, the period of the Third Republic, which was indeed the régime which lasted longest during the last one hundred and eighty years ; the sovereignty of the people also found its fullest expression during this period. These two features of the Third Republic also led to the wide acceptance of the parliamentary republic by public opinion. Military defeat at the hands of Germany led to the collapse of the Republic in 1940 when Marshal Petain was invested, temporarily, with dictatorial powers. A new Constitution was drawn up and became effective in 1946 ushering the Fourth Republic. Dissatisfaction with the working of the régime led to the rise of de Gaulle, whose Government prepared the draft of a new Constitution, which, as has been said above, was approved by the people at a national referendum on 28 September 1958. Approved by more than 80 per cent of the voters, the Fifth Republic came into existence on the day the Constitution was printed in the Journal Officiel, 4 October 1958.

§3 THE CONSTITUTION OF THE THIRD REPUBLIC

Amendment to the Constitution

France, like Britain, is a unitary State. The constitution was technically a rigid one requiring, as it did, a procedure for its amendment different from the one adopted for passing ordinary laws. The procedure for amendment was, however, exceedingly simple :

' The chambers shall have the right, by separate resolutions taken in each by an absolute majority of votes, either upon their own initiative or upon the request of the President of the Republic, to declare a revision of the constitutional laws necessary. After each of the two chambers shall have come to this decision they shall meet together in National Assembly to proceed with the revision. The acts effecting revision of the constitutional laws, in whole or in part, shall be passed by an absolute majority of the members composing the National Assembly.'[1]

The National Assembly was required to meet at Versailles. The absolute majority (mentioned above) was interpreted to mean half plus one of the legal number of members without deducting vacancies caused by resignation, death or otherwise. It will be seen that the right of each chamber to refuse to declare a revision of the constitution necessary amounted to a veto on any constitutional amendment that was desired by the other.

Could the National Assembly make *any* amendment to the constitution? A constitutional law of 1884 declared that 'the republican form of government shall not be made the subject of a proposed revision.' Authorities on the subject, however, are not agreed on the import of this law;[2] the sound view seems to be that this was not binding on the National Assembly, for what the National Assembly had enacted it could at a later time repeal. Moreover, the *real* sanction behind a constitutional amendment resides in public opinion. When that opinion, as expressed through the National Assembly, demanded that the republican form of government itself be made the subject of revision, the constitutional prohibition of 1884 would naturally be brushed aside.

The President

The head of the State was the President elected by an absolute majority of the votes of the Senate (or Upper House) and the Chamber of Deputies (or Lower House) sitting together as the National Assembly. Any Frenchman who enjoyed full civil and political rights, and who did not belong to the royal or imperial houses, could be elected to the Presidentship. The Assembly to elect the President met at Versailles and was presided over by the President of the State. If no candidate obtained an absolute majority of votes, the President announced a second ballot, and so on, if needful, until a choice was made. The President was elected for seven years and was eligible for re-election.

The President was removable from office before his legal term was over if found guilty of high treason. The charge was preferred by the Chamber of Deputies before the Senate. The Senate

---

[1] The constitutional law of 25 February 1875.
[2] See R. Poincaré, *How France is Governed*, pp. 162-3, and E. M. Sait, *Government and Politics of France*, pp. 27-8.

could not only dismiss him from office if he was found guilty, but could inflict any sentence laid down by the penal laws.

In his position and powers, the French President was much like the English king. He was, in the words of Duguit, 'a constitutional king for seven years', the titular head of the Executive, nominally vested with large powers, but enjoined to exercise them on the advice of ministers who were, as in England, responsible to an elected Legislature.

As the executive head of the State, he appointed to all civil and military positions (and, by implication, had power to dismiss the officers), and watched over the execution of the laws. He had the prerogative of mercy, i.e. the right to give a criminal a complete or partial remission of his punishment or commute it to a lighter penalty. He presided over national solemnities;[1] i.e. as Poincaré puts it, at all official ceremonies he personified both France and the Republic. He received the diplomatic agents of foreign powers, negotiated and ratified treaties and, with the consent of the two chambers, declared war. It was not necessary to communicate the terms of treaties if the 'interest and safety of the State' required them to be kept secret; but treaties of peace and commerce, and treaties which involved the finances of the State or the persons and property of Frenchmen residing abroad, had to be submitted to the chambers for approval; and no cession or exchange or annexation of territory could take place except by virtue of a law.[2] Finally, as commander-in-chief, he controlled the armed forces.

As regards legislation, the President's powers were :

(*i*) He summoned and dissolved the Parliament ; but, in the performance of this duty, the constitution gave him but little latitude. If he did not summon it sooner, it had to meet at the latest on the second Tuesday in January. He could prorogue it, but only after its session had lasted for five months. He could adjourn it, but not more than twice during the regular annual session nor for a longer period than one month in each case. He could dissolve the Chamber of Deputies before its legal term was over, but only with the consent of the Senate. He could convene a special session of Parliament, but was bound to convene it only when an absolute majority of the members of each chamber demanded it.

(*ii*) He could send messages to Parliament.

(*iii*) He could initiate legislation.

[1] The law of 25 February 1875.
[2] Sait, op. cit., pp. 42-3.

(*iv*) He had, over any bill, a suspensive veto (the power to send a bill back for the reconsideration of the chambers) which the chambers could override by a majority.

(*v*) He had the power to issue ordinances, i.e. a power delegated by the constitution or the Legislature to fill in the details of laws which were couched in general terms.

These were the powers vested in the President by the constitution but, as has been noticed already, he could exercise them only on the advice of ministers. The constitution specifically said : 'Every act of the President must be countersigned by a minister.' As has been humorously remarked, the only document which did not require such countersignature was the President's letter of resignation! It is easy to conclude from this, as indeed some writers have done, that the President was an automaton, exercising no influence on the politics of the State.[1] This, however, is a superficial view. The sounder view would appear to be that the *influence*, as distinguished from the *power*, which a President wielded depended essentially on his personality. It is true that the last word on matters of policy was with ministers, for the reason that power ultimately settles where responsibility resides. Nevertheless, the President had some influence. He had some discretion in the choice of a new Prime Minister, for in the French Parliament there were many groups and it was not always clear which leader was in a position to command a majority. Besides, he was in regular and frequent contact with his ministers. 'And while his intervention in affairs is normally limited to the giving of advice,' says W. L. Middleton, 'that advice comes from a man who, in most cases is destined to survive the cabinet he is addressing. His knowledge of the work of previous Governments and his acquaintance with the points of all important questions give weight to everything he says.'[2] Briefly, while the President could not command, he could advise ; whether his advice was taken depended very much on the personal factor, and upon the nature of the advice tendered.

The Council of Ministers

The Council of Ministers was the *real*, as distinguished from the *normal*, Executive. There was no limit fixed by the constitution to the number of ministers ; normally there were from twelve

---

[1] The Abbé Lantaigne, for instance, is said to have remarked of the Presidentship that it was ' an office with the sole virtue of impotence '!
[2] *The French Political System*, p. 195.

to fifteen. It was not necessary that they should be chosen from Parliament, but usually they were.[1] The process of forming a ministry was similar to that prevailing in Britain : the President called upon the person (whether a member of the Senate or of the Chamber of Deputies or of neither) who he thought could command the confidence of a majority in Parliament. Only such a person could be summoned to form the ministry, for the constitution specifically stated that 'the ministers shall be collectively responsible to the chambers for the general policy of the Government, and individually for their personal acts'. As has been stated earlier, under the conditions of French politics it was not always easy for the President to select the leader who could command the necessary confidence. He therefore consulted those who seemed to him best qualified to advise him, and notably the presidents of the two chambers. Having decided upon the person, and with his permission, the President appointed him the President of Council (with the countersignature of the President of Council retiring),[2] and appointed the other ministers on the recommendation, and with the countersignature, of the new President of Council.

The Council of Ministers met, as a rule, twice a week under the presidency of the President of the Republic, and once under the presidency of the President of Council. According to Poincaré to the two former sessions only did the expression 'Council of Ministers' apply ; 'the meeting which is held in the absence of the President of the Republic is known as a Cabinet Council. The Council of Ministers deals with the more important business, the Cabinet Council with current questions of internal politics.' It need hardly be added that, as ministers took collective responsibility for the administration, everything which really concerned the activity of the Government was discussed and decided at these meetings.

In relation to the Legislature, the Council of Ministers in France held essentially the same position as the cabinet holds in Britain. They introduced bills in Parliament and defended them ; introduced the budget ; answered questions addressed to them regarding the administration and, in general, supplied the necessary leadership to the Legislature ; and resigned when they had ceased to command its confidence. There were, however, some differences of detail between conditions in France and in England.

---

[1] Thus in the Rochebonet cabinet of 1877, and in the Millerand cabinet of 1920, there were ministers without seats in Parliament.
[2] Poincaré, op. cit., p. 193.

(*i*) Ministers in France had the right of entry in the two chambers and 'must be heard when they demand a hearing'.[1]

(*ii*) The constitution provided that the ministers were to be *collectively* responsible to the *chambers* for the general policy of the Government and individually for their personal acts. The responsibility of ministers of Parliament was thus in France a matter of constitutional law, not one of convention as in Britain. Further, the constitutional provision really implied two differences from the position in Britain. It meant, first, that, unlike in Britain, it was possible for the chambers to compel the resignation of one minister without such resignation involving the resignation of the whole ministry; and, secondly, that both the chambers of Parliament had equal power to make and unmake cabinets. If this constitutional provision were literally adhered to, immense difficulties were inevitable in the working of government. Individual responsibility hardly seems consistent with the character of parliamentary government, as it suggests divided counsel and conflicting views within the cabinet.[2] The equal power of the two chambers to hold the ministers responsible to them was bound to result in a deadlock between the two chambers themselves. The working of the constitution, however, shows that these difficulties were avoided by the development of conventions which more or less approximated the French system to the English. The tendency was to substitute corporate for individual responsibility,[3] and for the Chamber of Deputies to have the greater power—though there are instances, notably that of 1896,[4] in which the Senate forced a united and vigorous cabinet to resign.

More important than these differences of detail between the British and French cabinets were the major differences in their practical working.

(*i*) Ministers in France were invariably chosen from several parliamentary groups, no one of them being able to command a majority. As a consequence, the ministry lacked that homogeneity which under normal conditions was (and continues to be) the outstanding feature of the British cabinet. For the same reason the French cabinet was not able to dominate the Legislature as the English cabinet does. On the contrary, the French Legislature was much more powerful than its English counterpart. This result

[1] Constitutional law of 16 July 1875.
[2] Sait, op. cit., pp. 79-80.
[3] Sait, op. cit.
[4] ibid., pp. 79-83. 'In 1896 the Senate . . . took an aggressive attitude and boldly insisted on its right to force the Bourgeois Cabinet out, though that cabinet had the confidence of the Chamber of Deputies.'

was helped by a convention. The President's power to dissolve the Chamber of Deputies (with the consent of the Senate) had fallen into disuse, while the power of the cabinet to dissolve the House of Commons before its legal term is over has been a powerful factor in explaining cabinet autocracy in Britain.[1]

(*ii*) French cabinets were generally shortlived. It has been reckoned that their average life scarcely exceeded ten months. In the half century from 1875-1925 France had more than fifty cabinets, England only a dozen. Their fall was generally brought about (unlike in England) by the Legislature and not by the electorate. This was also due to the two causes mentioned above, that ministries were coalitions and that the cabinet had no power to advise the dissolution of the chamber. The disadvantages to government arising from the instability of the Executive are well known : long-term planning by a Government assured of a reasonably long period of office, so necessary under modern conditions, becomes difficult ; legislation suffers ;[2] administration also suffers, for 'Parliament, having subordinated the ministers, insists upon administering itself' ; and the supervision over the executive departments suffers on account of the frequent change of ministers. France suffered from these facts ; the results would have been much worse if every change of cabinet had meant a new set of men coming into office ; that was not so in France, for in each reconstructed cabinet some of the former ministers often held over.

(*iii*) The Prime Minister in France (the President of Council) was not so powerful as the British Prime Minister ; he had often to coax the members to join his cabinet, and having done this he was not in a position to treat them as subordinates.

The Senate

The Legislature consisted of two Houses : the Senate and the Chamber of Deputies.

The Senate consisted of 314 elected members, of not less than forty years of age. Senators served for nine years, one-third retiring triennially. The selection was made by an electoral college formed in the chief town of each Department (i.e. district). This electoral college was made up of four elements :

(*i*) The members who represented the Department in the Chamber of Deputies.

---

[1] See ch. xvi, §9 above.

[2] Sait, op. cit., points out that down to 1914 eight different income-tax bills were shaped in committee and debated by the Chamber without being enacted into law.

(*ii*) The members of the General Council of the Department.

(*iii*) The councillors of arrondissements (divisions of the districts).

(*iv*) The delegates of the municipal councils of the communes (towns and villages).[1]

Such a mode of election is known as indirect election, for the senators were not elected directly by the primary voters, but all their electors were so elected or were in turn the delegates of those so elected. The result was that, as Poincaré says, the whole nation did indirectly participate in the formation of the Senate. The composition of the Senate was noteworthy in that, by prescribing a special method of election for its members, by giving them a mandate of nine years, and by stipulating that they must have attained the respectable age of forty, the authors of the constitution not only showed their anxiety to differentiate the upper from the lower chamber as clearly as possible, but also wanted to make it a conservative body, which might be effectively used as a brake on political passions.

The powers of the Senate were :

(*i*) Its consent was necessary for the President of the Republic to dissolve the Chamber of Deputies. This power was of no importance in practice, for after 1877 (when alone it was used) it was never employed. President MacMahon dissolved the Chamber in that year in order to keep a reactionary ministry in power. But the country refused to uphold the President's action and ultimately forced him to resign.

(*ii*) It served as a court of impeachment 'for the trial of the President of the Republic, or the ministers, or to take cognizance of assaults on the security of the State'.

(*iii*) It shared with the Chamber of Deputies the power of legislation. According to the letter of the constitution, its power of law-making was equal to that of the Chamber except in one respect, viz. money bills had first to be introduced in, and passed by the Chamber of Deputies. In practice, however, the Senate rarely rejected money bills, while it continued to offer amendments ; but the Senate gave way when the Chamber had voted upon the budget a second time. In respect of non-financial measures, however, its equal authority was not seriously questioned.

(*iv*) Finally, in regard to the control of the Executive, its power was, according to the constitution, equal to that of the Chamber

---

[1] It ought to be noticed that these communal delegates form a large majority of the electoral college, and hence the Senate has been called the 'Grand Council of the Communes of France'.

of Deputies. As a rule, however, the Senate did not decide the fate of the ministers, and hence could not control their policy.

Thus the Senate in practice became decidedly less influential than the lower House. According to a high French authority, Barthélemy, it inherited from preceding upper Houses the privilege of being ignored—and this, in spite of the fact that the personnel of the Senate was by common consent superior to that of the Chamber of Deputies. The primary reason for this was of course that it was not as representative a body as the directly elected lower House. It will be wrong, however, to conclude that the Senate was reduced to impotence. It scrutinized, revised, and delayed when necessary. Indeed, it is noteworthy that this very subordinate position of the Senate enabled it to receive high praise from a reputed authority on European governments as approaching 'the ideal of what a second chamber ought to be'.[1] For, 'an ideal second chamber should bend very slowly to the gusts of public opinion, but it should never fail to bend when the wind sets definitely in a given direction'. It must serve as a brake, but not too tight a brake, upon the process of legislation. And this function the French Senate fulfilled admirably.

The Chamber of Deputies

The Chamber of Deputies, the lower House, was composed of 618 elected members, 599 of them being from single-member constituencies. The right to vote was given to all French citizens, of the male sex, of twenty-one years and above, who had not been deprived of their civil and political rights and who had resided in a constituency for six months.[2] Any voter, twenty-five years of age, was eligible to stand as a candidate for election, provided he did not belong to a family which had reigned in France; there were also many public offices which were incompatible with membership in the Chamber, e.g. that of a prefect.

The term of the Chamber was four years, unless it was dissolved sooner by the President with the consent of the Senate. It has been noticed earlier that, after 1877, the Chamber was never dissolved before its legal term was over.

Its functions were more or less similar to those of the House of Commons in Britain; it passed laws subject to the Senate's

---

[1] W. B. Munro, *The Governments of Europe*, pp. 470-1.

[2] Or the citizen had to show that, notwithstanding residence elsewhere, the commune was his place of true domicile or he must have paid direct taxes there for a period of five years, this being taken as evidence of local interest.

power of amendment and rejection and subject to the President's
suspensive veto; it controlled finance, subject, again, to the
Senate's power of amendment and rejection; it controlled the
Executive; it ventilated grievances; it had power to impeach the
President and the ministers; and, in conjunction with the Senate,
it helped to elect the President of the Republic and to amend the
constitution of the State. Compared with the House of Commons,
however, it may be noticed that the Chamber of Deputies was
theoretically less powerful to the extent that the French Senate
was legally more powerful than the English House of Lords. In
practice, however, it was considerably more powerful not only
because its will is deferred to by the Senate but because it was
able to control the cabinet more effectively than the House of
Commons is able to control its cabinet.

Law-making and financial control

The law-making procedure in the Chamber of Deputies was in
essentials similar to that in the House of Commons. Bills could
be introduced by ministers or private members; in practice most
bills were introduced by ministers. On introduction, the bill was
referred to a committee.

The Chamber had twenty such standing committees, each one
specializing in a given field, such as foreign affairs, agriculture,
finance, labour, etc. Each consisted of forty-four members (55
in the case of the finance committee) elected for one year by the
groups in proportion to their number. No one could be a member of more than two of these committees. In addition to these
regular committees, there were other committees consisting of
thirty-three members each which were appointed for four years,
e.g. the committees on devastated areas and on beverages.
Besides, special committees were appointed from time to time to
investigate particular questions, e.g. the one appointed for the
preparation of the Peace Treaty in 1918.[1]

It is noteworthy that bills were referred to committees in the
French Chamber before their principles were discussed and
approved by the whole House. This method had the advantage
that the committee concerned was free to amend and shape the
bill referred to it without being 'tied' by limitations. On the
other hand, it had the disadvantage that the labours of the committee might be wasted, as the Chamber might reject the bill on
the ground that it was opposed to its principles. The committee

[1] R. L. Buell (ed.), *Democratic Governments in Europe*, pp. 414-5.

appointed a reporter to present its report on the bill and defend it on the floor of the House. (Compare this with the practice in the House of Commons, where a minister is in charge of a government bill.) A discussion then ensued on the bill as a whole. A vote was then taken, and if the essential principles of the bill were approved by the House, the bill was then discussed clause by clause ; amendments were moved, and finally the bill was passed or rejected. Deputies were allowed to vote by proxy with the result that sometimes more votes were cast than there were members in the Chamber! The bill then went to the Senate and, if passed by it, to the President for his signature.

The budget system in France was also in essentials the same as the British one, with the following differences. After the budget was presented to the Chamber, it was referred to the budget committee of forty-four members—not to a committee of the whole House. The committee was free to insert, strike out, reduce or increase any item. The reporter [1] of the budget committee, not the minister of finance, was in charge of the measure in the Chamber. The Chamber, like the committee, could on its own initiative insert new items or increase the amount for any item presented ; it was not necessary that the demand should come from the President. Though this was the theoretical position, it is noteworthy that in the pre-war years the French practice in this matter was approximating to the English system, i.e. changes were made in the budget, both in committee and the Chamber, with moderation and with the approval of the Government. It was being realized more and more that, otherwise, not only did the budget lose all unity but the way was open for the undue influence of local interests in the expenditure of public money.

Control of the Executive

That the Chamber had great power over the cabinet has been indicated elsewhere. The most important causes of this power were, undoubtedly, first, that the cabinet was normally unable to command the stable support of a homogeneous party; and, second, that it was, by convention, denied the power (wielded by the English cabinet) to dissolve the House before its legal term was over. The Chamber felt free, especially because the reporter of a committee—not the concerned minister—was in charge of a bill, to mutilate important Government bills. Its control over finance gave the cabinet much less freedom than they required in

[1] The *rapporteur* in France is not merely a reporter ; he is more like the Chairman of a Committee and in some cases its Secretary.

the formulation of policy. Further, the permanent committees of the Chamber, having specialized in particular subjects, tended to become intimately acquainted with departmental business and to interfere in its conduct. They summoned officials and subjected their actions and proposals to severe criticism; the minister found himself checked in countless ways and hampered in his freedom of action. Besides, the French parliamentary procedure allowed what was known as 'the interpellation' in addition to questions addressed to ministers regarding the administration of their departments. An interpellation is a question which may be followed by a discussion and a vote. If the vote turned against the Government, they could be compelled to resign. The interpellation is a vicious institution.[1] It put the cabinet in a position of great disadvantage, for it permitted an adverse vote on the cabinet on a matter of secondary importance, taken hastily or under excitement. To secure the proper stability of a ministry, such adverse votes ought to be taken only on measures of really great importance, or on questions that involve the whole policy and conduct of the Administration. The reverse was true of the French system of interpellations.

The Judicial System

The most remarkable feature of the French judicial system was that there were *two* great regular sets of courts, the ordinary and the administrative. Broadly speaking, the former tried disputes between private citizens; the latter, those in which one of the parties was a public official.

Organization

The ordinary courts had Justices of the Peace at the bottom of the ladder. Above them came the district courts, the courts of appeal, the courts of assize and, at the top, the Court of Cassation. Judges were appointed by the President of the Republic on the advice of the Minister of Justice. The Judges of all except the lowest and the highest courts held office during good behaviour, i.e. they could not be removed by the Executive and were answerable for their conduct to the Court of Cassation alone. Justices of the Peace and judges of the Court of Cassation were, however, liable to be removed by the Executive; by convention, however, they were hardly, if ever, removed for political reasons.

[1] A. L. Lowell, *Governments and Parties in Continental Europe*, Vol. I, pp. 120-3.

The principal administrative courts were the twenty-two inter-departmental or regional councils of the prefecture, each serving from two to seven departments [1] and the Council of State. The former were the lowest administrative tribunals and consisted of a president and four councillors each, appointed by the Minister of the Interior. This Council of State was the highest administrative court. This Council had varied functions, including that of advising ministers regarding the issue of statutory 'orders. One of its sections, composed of 39 members appointed by the President of the Republic on the advice of the Council of Ministers, acted as the highest administrative court hearing appeals from regional councils and having original jurisdiction in a defined class of cases.

If disputes arose between the Court of Cassation and the Council of State, they were decided by a Court of Conflicts. This court consisted of the Minister of Justice as president, three judges of the Court of Cassation, three of the Council of State and two other persons chosen by the foregoing seven.

We may now consider in some detail the relation of French courts to the Legislature, and the French system of administrative jurisprudence.

Relation of courts to the Legislature

In view of the fact that the constitution of France, like that of the U.S.A. and unlike that of Britain, was a written and rigid one, it might be expected that the French courts, like the American, would have the power to inquire into the constitutionality of a law. As it was, however, the Court of Cassation held that it had no power to do so. The reasons were twofold. First, unlike the U.S.A., France was (and is) not a federal State. It is unnecessary for the courts in a unitary State to act as the guardian of the constitution, because there is no division of powers between two sets of authorities to be protected against mutual encroachment. And, secondly, the French courts did not derive their authority from the constitution ; they were the creation of the Legislature ; and so, if the courts dared to declare a law unconstitutional, the Legislature by a law could check it. The French practice thus resembled the British in this regard.

Administrative jurisprudence

Administrative law has been defined by Dicey as 'the body of rules which regulate the relations of the Administration or the

---

[1] In addition, the Department of the Seine has a council of its own.

administrative authority towards private citizens'. It is that portion of French law which determined (*i*) the position and liabilities of all State officials, (*ii*) the civil rights and liabilities of
private individuals in their dealings with officials as representatives
of the State, and (*iii*) the procedure by which these rights and
duties were enforced. This law differed considerably from the
law which governed the relation of one private citizen to another;
and it was administered by tribunals different from the ordinary
ones.

Poincaré illustrates the meaning of administrative law by two
telling examples.[1] Let us suppose, he says, that the Administration of Direct Taxes taxed a citizen too highly. The tax-payer
received his schedule and found upon it an unjustifiable increase,
against which he wished to protest; he must address himself to
the Council of the Prefecture.[2] Again,

'a railway has been built in front of my door; my house was
not required; I have not been expropriated; but an enormous
embankment blocks the view from my windows; I can no longer
see well within doors; my property has lost the greater part of
its value. I protest. Here again is an administrative action whose
results must be estimated. I cannot take my claim to the civil
court, but I can submit it to the Council of the Prefecture'.[3]

The system of administrative law is based, according to Dicey,
on two leading principles :

(*i*) Government and every servant of the Government possess,
as representatives of the nation, a whole body of special rights,
privileges or prerogatives as against private citizens, and the extent
of these rights, privileges or prerogatives is to be determined on
principles different from the considerations which fix the legal
rights and duties of one citizen towards another.

(*ii*) It is necessary to maintain the separation of powers between
the Legislature, the Executive and the Judiciary. The English
people interpreted this doctrine to mean that the ordinary judges
ought to be irremovable by, and thus independent of, the Executive; the French, that the Government and its officials ought to
be independent of, and to a great extent free from, the jurisdiction of the ordinary courts, to be free to act for the public weal
without let or hindrance from the latter. A statute of 1790 gave

---

[1] Poincaré, op. cit., p. 271.
[2] The Councils of the Prefecture have since been replaced by regional
councils as explained earlier.
[3] Now to the regional council.

effect to this maxim by providing that the judges should not interfere in any way with the work of administrative authorities or proceed against the officers of the Government on account of their official acts. The principle laid down here was observed thereafter.

Which system is better—the rule of law or administrative law? Englishmen, nurtured on the principles taught by Dicey, still regard the rule of law as the corner-stone of their liberty. It is now generally recognized, however, that Dicey unduly exaggerated the merits of the rule of law and the defects of administrative law. In theory, it is true, there is always the danger that justice may not be secured in administrative courts if governmental policy demands a certain decision. Further, individual rights may be sacrificed when the Administration is both the offender and the judge of the offence. In the light of French experience, however, it is not true to say that under administrative law there cannot be liberty. On the contrary, Frenchmen consider administrative law essential to their liberty. There is no ground for any suspicion of partiality on the part of the administrative courts in favour of the official': if anything, the complaint is the other way about. The Council of States as the highest administrative tribunal established traditions of impartiality which left no room for doubt on the matter. Litigation in administrative courts was also cheap and executed rapidly; and the procedure was simple. Further, administrative tribunals could be manned by individuals possessing special experience or training in particular fields. Above all, the private citizen in France often got better *real* redress from his administrative courts than the Englishman from his ordinary courts, because if a plaintiff received an award of damages under the French system, the judgement was against the Government and enforceable, whereas an award rendered under the English system is only against the offending official personally, from which, as likely as not, it is impossible to obtain actual redress.[1] This explains the remark of Goodnow[2] (a high authority) that the administrative courts were more favourable to private rights than the ordinary courts.

Political parties

There were several political groups in France ; this fact is the key to the understanding of French politics. It explains the

[1] Ogg, *English Government and Politics*, p. 612.
[2] F. J. Goodnow, *Comparative Administrative Law*, Vol. II, pp. 220-1, 231.

short-lived, weak, coalition cabinets ; the dominance of the Legislature over the Executive ; and the practical necessity under
which cabinets were placed to win votes by granting favours to
individual deputies. Briefly, the parliamentary system in France
did not work smoothly because of her multiple-party system.

The French party system is not easily intelligible.

' It would be of little use to try to analyse the precise purpose
of each of the twenty or more groups [1] which revolve so kaleido-
scopically in the Chamber and the Senate, for many of them have
none. They change not only from one election to another, but
they come and go even within the life of one Chamber. The
group labels are not the same in the Senate and in the Chamber.
The labels under which elections are fought are often quite
different from the labels adopted by groups in the Chamber.
There are some important parties in the country which are not
represented at all in the Chamber.' [2]

But underneath this seeming confusion, a certain ' pattern of
politics' could be discerned. Following Valeur [3] we may group
French parties according to four main tendencies : conservatism,
liberalism, radicalism and socialism.

The conservatives enlisted among their supporters two main
sections of the people : the clericals and the rich aristocracy.
Naturally they viewed with sympathy the claims of the Church
and favoured the restoration of property taken from it. They
liked to strengthen the army and the navy and to allow industry
greater freedom from State control. To this school of thought
belonged the National Republican Party.

Conservatives who accepted the principle that the Church
should keep out of politics may be called liberals. [4] Clericalism
was a strong force in French politics ; the liberals were those who
did not countenance any interference on the part of the Church
with the government of the country. The Democratic Alliance
Party was, broadly speaking, liberal in its outlook. [5]

The radicals may best be described as those who continued
the tradition of the French Revolution. They believed in the

[1] In the Chamber of Deputies as it stood in 1939 no fewer than 17 groups
were officially recognized.
[2] D. Thomson, *The Democratic Ideal in France and England*, pp. 57-8.
[3] In Buell, op. cit., pp. 465ff.
[4] Valeur in Buell, op. cit., p. 470.
[5] According to Ogg (op. cit., p. 545), the Radical Socialist Party is the
true liberal party of France.

principles of liberty, equality and fraternity; they were ardent nationalists, democrats and individualists. They were anti-clerical, viewing with disfavour the interference of the Church in politics. Briefly, they distrusted authority and hated privilege which could not be justified by considerations of social good. To this group belonged the Radical Socialists.

And lastly the socialists. They were themselves divided into several groups, the United Socialists, the Republican Socialists, and the Communists. It is noteworthy that the majority of French socialists rejected the Marxist philosophy of communism. They, broadly speaking, advocated collectivism : the nationalization of key industries, the increase of taxation on the wealthier classes, and progressive labour legislation such as the forty-hour week law. In general they also advocated woman suffrage, and supported the policy of disarmament among the nations. At the extreme left were the Communists.

Causes of the large number of parties in France

The existence of numerous parties in France was due to two main causes : the temperament of the Frenchman, and the lack of continuity in French history since the French Revolution.

Compared with the Anglo-Saxon, the Frenchman is theoretical rather than practical in politics.[1]

'He is inclined to pursue an ideal, striving to realize his conception of a perfect form of society, and is reluctant to give up any part of it for the sake of attaining so much as lies within his reach. Such a tendency naturally gives rise to a number of groups, each with a separate ideal, and each unwilling to make the sacrifice that is necessary for a fusion into a great party.'

He is also strongly individualist, desiring rather to follow his own bent of mind than to follow others. Party organization in France was therefore extremely flexible : the parties indeed were described as 'groups of elected representatives who bear some distinctive label, who may or may not be supported by regular organizations among the voters, who may or may not be pledged to some definite programme, and who may or may not be subject to party discipline'.

Secondly, France had a turbulent history[2] during the nineteenth century, so much that she became a byword for social

[1] Lowell, op. cit., Vol. I, p. 105.
[2] Thomson, op. cit., pp. 26-7.

instability and political fickleness. From 1791 to 1870 she devised for herself no less than eleven complete constitutions, none of which was destined to remain in force for any length of time. From the Bourbon monarchy of the *ancien régime*, she passed to the Republic of 1793, and thence, by turbulent stages, to the Empire of Bonaparte. Between 1815 and 1870 'she passed from the Bourbon Monarchy of Louis XVIII and Charles X and the bourgeois monarchy of Louis Philippe to the Second Republic of 1848, and thence to the Second Empire of Napoleon III in 1852'. The Second Empire collapsed on 4 September 1870, and after five years of deadlock, the Third Republic was finally established in 1875. This want of continuity in French history is connected with the group system in this way: Frenchmen have been unable to evolve a political consensus, to use a phrase of Lowell's, so necessary for the development of strong parties. Parties in Britain and America primarily differ in the methods of conducting government, on the fundamentals of which men agree. If that agreement on fundamentals itself is lacking, parties cannot grow properly, because 'irreconcilables' become numerous and they become disturbing factors in the evolution of political life, and of parliamentary government itself. Thus

'every form of government that has existed in France has its partisans, who are irreconcilable under every other; while the great mass of the middle classes and the peasants have no strong political convictions, and are ready to support any Government that maintains order.'[1]

Local Government

The most important feature of local government in France was its centralization. As has been well said, the minister of the interior at Paris just pressed a button—the prefects, sub-prefects, and mayors did the rest. All the wires ran to Paris.[2] This centralization (with its corollary, uniformity) is a contrast to the decentralized character of English local government. The principle accepted in England, that a local area has the right to conduct its affairs in its own way without being hindered by a rigid and paternal supervision of central authorities (except in

---

[1] Lowell (op. cit., pp. 108ff.) gives three other causes for the existence of numerous parties in France: the method of electing deputies, the system of communities in the chambers and the practice of interpellations. It may be asked whether some of these, at any rate, were not rather *consequences* than *causes*; in any case they must be considered of secondary importance.
[2] Munro, op. cit., p. 567.

so far as such supervision is clearly demanded by the general
interest and necessary to prevent gross inefficiency), was foreign
to the French system.

The main local areas of France were the Departments, the
arrondissements, and the communes.

There were ninety Departments. The executive head of the
Department was a prefect appointed and removable by the President of the Republic on the advice of the Minister of the Interior.
He occupied a dual position. As the agent of the Central Government, he was responsible for the enforcement of the national laws
within his Department on such matters as education, sanitation,
agriculture, highways, the public domain, taxation and police. He
appointed a host of officials such as inspectors and menders of
highways, tax-collectors, postmasters, and the teaching staff of
the public primary schools. In the same capacity he controlled
the sub-prefects and mayors (the heads of administration in
smaller local areas, who were also agents of the Central Government for many purposes) and had power to annul the orders of
the municipal councils. In carrying out these duties, the prefect
was bound by detailed instructions from the Central Government.
The prefect was also the executive head of his Department. As
such, he initiated all business for the consideration of the general
council of the Department, prepared a budget for local expenditure, appointed the employees of the Department and executed
the resolutions of the council. In his dealings with the council, he
was master rather than servant; for his tenure was dependent
not upon it but upon the Minister of the Interior.

The general council of the Department consisted of members
elected for six years on manhood suffrage, one from each canton
within the Department. The president was elected by the council.
The council normally met twice a year; its sessions were public.
In general its competence was limited to affairs that were deemed
to have a strictly local interest—poor relief, public buildings,
highways, bridges, traffic, and the like. Even so, as Poincaré
noted, its sessions were important and interesting.

'One after another the councillors submit reports to the assembly. What a number and what a variety of questions! A
bridge is to be built on a departmental highway; a concession
is required for a railway of local importance; a main highway
requires to be classified as such; a court of law or a prison is in
need of repairs; an idiot asylum needs a bathing-hall; agricultural societies require bounties; there are friendly societies to be
controlled, receipts to be collected, credit accounts to be opened,

taxes to be settled. Report follows upon report with bewildering rapidity . . . From time to time the assembly grows warm in respect of some question of fishery, hunting, or netting birds; from time to time also it is aroused by some political question.'[1]

The effective power of the council was, however, limited in four ways : (a) The prefect, who was its executive authority, was' not appointed by or responsible to it. (b) There were national laws on matters within its jurisdiction, which it could not disregard. (c) Its decisions could be overruled by the central authorities at Paris. (d) It was dependent on the prefect's initiative.

The Departments were divided into arrondissements; each was a Department in miniature, with a sub-prefect and an elective council made up of one member from each canton[2] within the arrondissement. It was, however, a mere administrative district 'without corporate personality, with no property, revenues, or expenses of its own'; and neither the sub-prefect nor the council had any real power.

And, finally, the smallest area of local government was the commune (a town or a parish). Every commune had a municipal council of from 10 to 36 members elected for six years on manhood suffrage. The council held four ordinary sessions every year; the sessions were public. It regulated by its deliberations the affairs of the commune. Its resolutions were of executive force by themselves, subject to three limitations :[3] (i) certain municipal proceedings were subjected to the approval of the prefect; (ii) others, of greater importance, to the approval of the Government; (iii) others, more important still, to the approbation of the chambers. It elected its mayor, the executive head of the commune, but it had no power to remove him. The mayor occupied a dual position : he was the agent of the Central Government, in matters relating to the police, public health, finance, etc.; he also drew up and signed, before legal witnesses, the deeds relating to marriages, birth, and deaths. He was also the executive of the commune, and, as such, carried out the resolutions of the municipal council in local matters like sanitation, protection against fire, the maintenance of order, and the protection of rural property. He could 'prescribe the watering of the roads, the removal of mud, snow, filth, and the sweeping of the pavements'; in this way he could forbid the straying of dogs, the shaking of

---

[1] Poincaré, op. cit., p. 69.
[2] A French canton consists of several communes.
[3] Poincaré, op. cit., p. 47.

rugs out of the window, the excessive speed of motor-cars, and what not. In a word he watched over the life, health, tranquility, and even the slumber of those in his administration.

In carrying out many of his duties, the mayor was bound to obey the orders of the prefect (the head of the Department); he could be suspended from office for a month by the prefect, or for three months by the Minister of the Interior and could be removed from office by the President of the Republic.

The spirit of French local government is best expressed thus : all authority in the State was deemed originally to be in the Central Government, with local government existing rather for the convenience of the Central Government than for the training of the people of the locality to manage their own local affairs.

§4 THE CONSTITUTION OF 1958

Sovereignty

It is explicitly stated in the Constitution that France is an indivisible, secular, democratic and social republic. It assures equality before the law of all citizens without distinction of origin, race or religion. Its principle is government of the people, by the people, and for the people. National sovereignty resides in the people ; the people exercise their sovereignty through their representatives and through the referendum. Suffrage is universal, equal and secret. All French citizens of both sexes who have reached their majority and who possess their civil and political rights have the right to vote under the conditions prescribed by law.

The Executive

(i) *The President.* The President of the Republic is the head of the State, and the head of the Community.[1] He is elected for seven years by an Electoral College, consisting of the members of Parliament, of the (departmental) General Councils and of the Assemblies of the overseas territories, as well as the elected representatives of the municipal councils.[2] The total membership

---

[1] See below, p. 321.
[2] Details concerning the number of elected representatives of the Municipal Councils are given in the Constitution : broadly speaking, the number is distributed in proportion to the population. In 1958 these local representatives included 31,401 mayors, 3,149 general councillors, 32,524 vice-mayors and municipal councillors from the middle-size and large communes, and 8,541 additional delegates for the larger communes.

fluctuates around 80,000. It is provided also that the President is elected by an absolute majority on the first ballot ; if this is not obtained, the President is elected on a second ballot by a relative majority.

The Constitution clearly states that the President can be indicted only for high treason before the High Court of Justice, consisting of members of Parliament elected in equal numbers by the National Assembly and by the Senate. Before the President is so indicted, the two Houses have to pass identical motions in an open vote and by an absolute majority of their respective memberships.

The President is not meant by the Constitution to be a mere figurehead, a Constitutional ruler to act only on the advice of the Cabinet (as he was under the Third Republic). Article 5 of the Constitution gives him important functions :

'The President of the Republic ensures respect for the Constitution. By his arbitration he assures the regular functioning of the public authorities, as well as the continuity of the State. He is the guarantor of national independence, of the integrity of the national territory, and of respect for Community agreements and for treaties.'

To enable the President to fulfil these functions, he is given important powers to be exercised by him at his own discretion, i.e., in the exercise of these powers, he is not required to act on the advice of his ministers :

He nominates the Prime Minister ; presides over the Council of Ministers (Cabinet); he may, on the proposal of the government during parliamentary sessions in a joint proposal of the two Assemblies (of Parliament), submit to a referendum any Bill dealing with the organization of public powers, containing approval of a Community agreement,[1] or providing for authorization to ratify a treaty which, though not contrary to the Constitution, might affect the functioning of (the country's) institutions and he may, after *consulting* the Prime Minister and the Presidents of the Assemblies, order the dissolution of the National Assembly provided it has been in existence for one year. Further, he is authorized to take such measures as he thinks necessary 'when the institutions of the Republic, the independence of the nation, the integrity of its territory, or the execution of its international commitments are gravely and immediately threatened and the

[1] See below, p. 321.

regular functioning of the public authorities is interrupted'; he is required only to *consult* the Prime Minister, the Presidents of the Assemblies and the Constitutional Council [1] and is not bound to accept their advice. He sends messages to Parliament which are not debated. He is authorized to refer to the Constitutional Council an international commitment—before it is ratified or approved—for its opinion whether it is in accordance with the Constitution; if the Council declares, on such reference, that the commitment contains a provision contrary to the Constitution, it can be ratified or approved only after the revision of the Constitution. He may refer Bills 'before their promulgation' to the Constitutional Council to enable the Council to decide whether they are in conformity with the Constitution. He nominates three members to the Constitutional Council.

All acts of the President other than those specified above— such as promulgation of laws, sending them to the Parliament for reconsideration, approving ordinances and decrees adopted by the Council of Ministers, making all civil and military State appointments, accrediting of ambassadors and envoys to foreign powers, acts in his capacity as Chief of the Armed Forces and exercising the right of pardon—are to be countersigned by the Prime Minister *and*, in each individual case, by the responsible minister.

Briefly, he has powers of his own and powers which he shares with the premier. In particular reference may be made to the President's power to dissolve the National Assembly which can be used by him not only to end a conflict between the Assembly and the Cabinet but also eventually to settle a conflict between himself and a prime minister backed by the Assembly.

It should be clear from the foregoing summary, that the President of the Fifth Republic is more powerful than the President under the Third Republic; his position may be said to be midway between the constitutional monarch of Britain and the President of the United States of America.[2]

(*ii*) *The Council of Ministers* (Cabinet). The French Cabinet is, in its essential character, a Parliamentary executive of the British type, in the sense that it is responsible to the Lower House and can hold office only so long as it commands the confidence of that body; further, like the British Cabinet, the French Cabinet can also introduce Bills in Parliament and its members have also to answer questions addressed to them by members of Parliament, but there are several important differences as may be seen from the following summary of the constitutional provisions:

[1] See below, p. 320.   [2] See ch. xviii, §3 below.

It has been noted earlier that the President of the Republic selects the Prime Minister; he also nominates and dismisses the other members of the Council of Ministers but on the recommendation of the Prime Minister. It is, however, added that membership of the Government is not compatible with the exercise of any parliamentary mandate, with the result that a member of Parliament must resign his membership on being chosen a Minister. It has also been noted earlier that the President of the Republic presides over the Cabinet, though in exceptional cases, by virtue of a specific assignment, the Prime Minister may deputize for the President. The members of the Cabinet may attend both Houses of Parliament and must be heard at their request. Bills may be initiated by the Prime Minister (as well as by members of Parliament); as mentioned earlier, Ministers must also answer questions addressed to them; one session a week is reserved for questions by members of Parliament and answers by the Government. The Constitution also specifically states that the Prime Minister must tender the resignation of the Government to the President when the National Assembly (the Lower House) adopts a motion of censure, or when it does not approve the programme or a declaration of general policy of the Government.

The French Cabinet resembles the British Cabinet in its accountability to the Lower House, in the close relations between the Cabinet and Parliament, and in the ascendancy of the Prime Minister. It differs from the British Cabinet in so far as it is limited by the wide powers allowed by the Constitution to the President and in the fact that Ministers, though they may be chosen from Parliament, are not members of Parliament during their term as Ministers.

The working of the Constitution of the Fifth Republic in its first years of existence would support the view that the personality and popular support for the President (de Gaulle) has helped him to have effective power. The approval of de Gaulle by the electorate by a near 80 per cent majority and his prestige as the one who had saved the country from a likely *coup d' état* gave him that support, and during these years executive leadership has come from the President, not from the premier or the cabinet.[1]

Parliament

Parliament consists of two Houses, the Senate and the National Assembly.

---

[1] J. A. Laponce, *The Government of the Fifth Republic*, pp. 204ff.

The Senate is elected by indirect suffrage, being envisaged as
representing the local authorities and territorial assemblies of the
Republic. The details of the number of members from these bodies
and mode of election, and the period for which they are to be
elected are to be determined by an organic law.[1] The Senate is
definitely inferior in power to the National Assembly. While Bills
may be introduced in either House, and every Bill is examined
successively in the two Houses with a view to get an identical text
approved by both, three provisions in the Constitution definitely
make the National Assembly the more powerful House : (i) All
financial Bills must be first submitted to the National Assembly ;
(ii) in case of disagreement between the two Houses, a joint
committee attempts to reconcile the differences ; if the joint Committee cannot agree upon a common version of the Bill under
discussion, the Government after a new reading by the Senate and
the National Assembly, can request the National Assembly to give
a final decision and (iii) the Cabinet is required to resign on a
vote of censure or disapproval of the programme or policy of the
Cabinet by the National Assembly.

The National Assembly is directly elected by adult suffrage.
The duration of the Assembly is regulated by law ; the President
may, however, as already stated, after consulting the Prime Minister and the Presidents of the Assemblies, order the dissolution of
the Assembly before its term is over provided it has been in existence one year. The powers of the National Assembly have been
indicated in our discussion of the powers of the President and the
Senate : briefly, Parliament comprising the two Houses is authorized to declare war, approve treaties of stated categories (such
as peace treaties, commercial treaties, treaties relating to international organizations, etc.), pass laws, and authorize taxes, and
appropriations ; in so far as the final decision, in case of a disagreement with the Senate, is left to the National Assembly, clearly,
it is the more powerful of the two Houses. Moreover, as already
indicated, the Government is responsible to it and not to the Senate.
The direct election of members of the National Assembly gives it
a more democratic character and must account for the greater
power given to it.

[1] A decree-law promulgated on 14 October 1958 fixed the number of
Senators at 301 (255 from metropolitian France, 33 from Algeria and the
Sahara and the remainder from overseas departments and territories);
Senators would hold their seats for nine years ; one-third of the Senate's
members would be elected at three-yearly intervals.

The Constitutional Council

The Constitutional Council consists of (a) nine members, three nominated by the President of the Republic, three by the President of the National Assembly and three by the President of the Senate for a period of nine years; one-third of the membership of the Council will be renewed every three years and (b) former Presidents of the Republic *ex-officio* for life.

The primary function of the Council, as its name suggests, is tc decide whether organic laws are in conformity with the Constitution. It is laid down that such laws before their promulgaticn must be submitted to the Council for its decision. For the same purpose, Bills also may be referred to it, before their publication, by the President of the Republic; the President of the National Assembly or the President of the Senate. Further, the Council supervises the election of the President, decides on disputed elections of deputies and senators and supervises the procedure of a referendum and announces its results.

Judicial Authority

The Constitution declares that the President of the Republic is the guarantor of judicial independence and authority. He is assisted by the Superior Council of the judiciary consisting of the Minister of Justice and nine others nominated by the President; the Council is presided over by the President of the Republic. The Council presents nominations for judges of the Supreme Court and for the senior presiding judge of the Courts of Appeal; gives its opinions on nominations of other judges by the Minister of Justice and is also consulted on questions of pardon.

Judges on their appointment hold office for life.

Amendment of the Constitution

France has a rigid constitution : the procedure for amending the Constitution in France is different from that for passing ordinary law.

The President of the Republic, on the proposal of the Prime Minister, *or* the members of Parliament may take the initiative for amending the Constitution. An amending bill must first be voted by the two Houses of Parliament in identical terms, and later also be approved by referendum.

A referendum, however, is unnecessary if the President refers the amending Bill to a joint session of the two Houses of Parliament and the Bill is passed by a majority of three-fifths of votes cast.

The Constitution adds that (*i*) the Republican form of government is not subject to revision—how far this is binding on successive Presidents of the Republic, members of Parliament or the Constitutional Council cannot be stated with certainty and (*ii*) no amending procedure can be commenced or continued if it is prejudicial to the integrity of the national territory.

The Community

The Constitution of 1958 provides for the association of autonomous member-States (in the French Oversea territories) and the French Republic in the Community. This, in some ways, unique institution is in the process of evolution; we shall first outline the position as envisaged in the Constitution and then describe some changes which have been made since 1958.

The French Republic and other autonomous member-States (in the French Oversea territories) who decide of their own free will to stay in the Community—together form the community. The Constitution declares that the competence of the Community includes foreign policy, defence, currency and common financial policy as well as common policy regarding strategic raw materials ; other specified matters are also included in the competence of the community (unless excluded by special agreement), viz., control of justice, higher education, the general organization of external and common transport and telecommunications.

The President of the Republic is also President of the Community; as he is also the President of the Community, the member-States of the Community participate in his election. The main organs of the Community are an Executive Council, a Senate and a Court of Arbitration.

The Executive Council consists of the Prime Minister of the Republic, the Heads of Government of each of the member-States and the Ministers responsible for the common affairs of the Community. The President of the Republic presides over the Executive Council.

The Senate consists of delegates elected by the Parliament of the Republic and the Legislative Assemblies of other member-States. It deliberates on common economic and financial policy before member-States pass laws on those matters and takes binding decisions on those spheres delegated to it by the Legislative Assemblies of the members of the Community.

The Court of Arbitration (its composition is to be decided by an organic law) decides on disputes between members of the Community.

The Republic or the Community may conclude agreements with States desiring association with the Republic or the Community.

In 1959 there were twelve autonomous States. Public opinion in several of them began to swing towards political independence, the Community of 1958 being considered only a transitional stage towards complete independence. In June 1960, the Mali federation (Sudan and Senegal) and Madagascar obtained international sovereignty, while remaining within the Community [1] and others followed suit. The Community devised in 1958 was modified to meet the new situation : 'the Executive Council, the Senate and the Arbitration Court will continue under either their old or new names. But instead of being advisors to the President of the Community they will become international consultative agencies . . . from various sovereign nations'. The Community thus became 'a means of facilitating France's granting independence to her former colonies . . . while maintaining with them as many cultural, economic and political ties as possible'.

Noteworthy features of the Fifth Republic especially as compared with the Third Republic

One of the persistent criticisms of the Third Republic (and of the Fourth Republic) has been the instability of the Cabinets,[2] with its possible results on continuity of policy, and the ability of the Government of the day to plan useful social and economic reforms. This instability was a result primarily of two factors, the multiplicity of parties and the consciousness of members of Parliament that once elected they could be certain of retaining their seats for the duration of Parliament ; the British Cabinet's

---

[1] J. A. Laponce, *The Government of the Fifth Republic*, pp. 314-16. See also ch. xxii, §10 below.

[2] Reference must be made to the view of M. Duverger (*The French Political System*, p. 186) that the Cabinet instability in France does not mean *political* instability : the fall of a government does not bring great change, first, because most of the defeated ministers generally reappear in the succeeding cabinet, second, because the senior civil service is remarkably stable, and, third, because the new Ministry generally executes the same policy as its predecessor. The fundamental defect of French politics, according to the same author is, immobility. It is our view that, while there is much substance in Duverger's analysis, the immobility which he diagnoses as the central defect has been there partly because of the instability of cabinets : a Government conscious of its stable existence should be in a better position to plan essential social changes and carry them out. Whether the new Constitution will help to achieve greater stability of the Cabinet and whether, as a result of it, lesser immobility in Society will be attained will be watched with great interest by students of French institutions.

power to advise the Sovereign to dissolve Parliament earlier was not available to the French Cabinet. The new Constitution removes this defect and should help to make the French Cabinet more stable. Second, the collective responsibility of the Cabinet is emphasized in the new Constitution by the provision requiring the Prime Minister to tender resignation of the Government on a vote of censure by the National Assembly, or disapproval of its policy or programme ; in the Third Republic, the collective responsibility of the Cabinet was not so sharply specified. A third noticeable feature is the higher status of the President, which according to the present writer is a clear improvement, at any rate, in the circumstances of France. The position and powers of the Constitutional Council are a useful innovation,[1] perhaps worthy of adoption by some other unitary States. Fourth, the student will note the enfranchisement of women (this was true also of the Fourth Republic) and the institution of the Referendum for constitutional amendments as making France more democratic. And, lastly, the potentialities of the Community as a useful device to balance the necessary autonomy and the essential interdependence in a Community of nations (formerly under imperial rule) will be watched with interest by the student of Politics.

In 1969, President de Gaulle proposed a bill designed to bring about a major constitutional revision, comprising reform of the Senate and of regional administration, as well as consequential changes in arrangements for future constitutional amendment and further interim appointment of a President in the event of a necessity arising from death or resignation. A referendum was held on 27 April 1969, which posed three questions before the voters : whether they wanted a reorganization of the nation (referring to changes in regional administration referred to above), whether they wanted a transformed senate to be merged with the Economic and Social Council, whether they wished the law of presidential succession to be amended so that the Premier would become interim President in the event of the President's death or disability. The referendum asked a fourth question, however — one that was not written into it, but which was on the minds of all the electorate. The French were asked if they wished to retain de Gaulle as President of the republic by voting affirmatively in the referendum, or if they wished to communicate to him their desire that he resign from office by voting negatively. In the referendum de Gaulle was defeated and he withdrew from France until the termination of the pending presidential election. In June 1969, President Pompidou[2] succeeded General de Gaulle, bringing the end of the de Gaulle era in French politics.

---

[1] There was a Constitutional Committee under the Fourth Republic with somewhat similar powers.

[2] President Pompidou passed away early in April 1974.

SELECT BIBLIOGRAPHY

R. L. BUELL (Editor), *Democratic Governments in Europe*, Nelson, 1935

P. CAMPBELL and B. CHAPMAN, *The Constitution of the Fifth Republic*, Blackwell, 1958

G. M. CARTER, *Government of France*, New York, Harcourt Brace Jovanovich, 2nd ed., 1972

M. DUVERGER, *The French Political System*, (translated by Barbara and Robert Nork), The University of Chicago Press, 1958

N. L. HILL, H. W. STOKE and C. J. SCHNEIDER, *The Background of European Governments*, Rinehart, 3rd ed., 1951

India Quarterly, July 1946

J. A. LAPONCE, *The Government of the Fifth Republic*, French Political Parties and the Constitution, University of California Press, 1961

A. L. LOWELL, *Governments and Parties in Continental Europe*, Longmans, 1919

— —, *Greater European Governments*, Harvard, 1925

H. LÜTHY, *The State of France*, Secker and Warburg, 1955

P. MAILLAUD, *France*, Oxford, 2nd ed., 1945

W. L. MIDDLETON, *The French Political System*, Benn, 1932

K. MUNRO, *France Yesterday and Today*, Royal Institute of International Affairs, 1945

W. B. MUNRO, *The Governments of Europe*, Macmillan, 1938

F. A. OGG, *The Rise of Dictatorship in France*, Macmillan, 1941

Y. PETIT-DUTAILLIS and M. MULLA, *The Evolution of French Democracy*, Thacker, 1946

D. PICKLES, ' Constitutional Revision in France ' in *Parliamentary Affairs*, Vol. VIII, No. 2

— —, *The Fifth French Republic*, Methuen, 2nd ed., 1962

R. POINCARE', *How France is Governed*, translated by B. Miall, Unwin, 1919

E. M. SAIT, *Government and Politics of France*, Harrap, 1926

W. R. SHARP, *The Government of the French Republic*, Van Nostrand, 1939

G. R. TAYLOR, *The Fourth Republic of France : Constitution and Political Parties*, Royal Institute of International Affairs, 1951

The American Political Science Review, June 1941

D. THOMSON, *Democracy in France : The Third and Fourth Republics*; Oxford, 2nd ed., 1952

G. WRIGHT, *The Reshaping of French Democracy*, Methuen, 1950

CHAPTER XVIII

THE UNITED STATES OF AMERICA

§1 THE CONSTITUTION AND ITS AMENDMENT

THE U.S.A. is a federal State, a union of 50 states.

The constitution of the U.S.A. was made by a convention of the original American states (thirteen in number), held at Philadelphia in 1787 under the presidency of George Washington ; and, having been accepted by the required number of nine states, came into effect on the first Wednesday in March (4 March) 1789. More states were admitted into the federation later, by the method provided for in the constitution for the admission of new states.[1]

An amendment to the constitution may be proposed, as has been noted elsewhere,[2] by a two-thirds vote in each House of Congress or by a convention called by Congress upon the application of the Legislatures of two-thirds of the states. The amendments proposed by either body must be ratified by the Legislatures of three-quarters of the states or by conventions in three-quarters of the states. Congress determines which method of ratification shall be used in each specific case. No state, however, may, without its consent, be deprived of its equal suffrage in the Senate.

An analysis of this method shows that, since either method of proposing amendments may be combined with either method of ratification, a total of four methods is possible. Actually, however, only two of the four methods possible have been used to bring about the twenty-two amendments so far ratified :

(*i*) Proposal by a two-thirds vote in each House of Congress and ratification by three-quarters of the state Legislatures.

(*ii*) Proposal by a two-thirds vote in each House of Congress and ratification by conventions in three-quarters of the states.

Three criticisms of the amending process are usually offered. (*i*) It is too slow and difficult. This is proved by the fact that during the hundred and seventy-five and odd years that have elapsed since the adoption of the constitution, only twenty- five amendments have become law. A constitution must adjust itself to changing times ; but the American constitution is unable effectively

---

[1] Article IV, section 3 (i). [2] Article V ; see above, p. 54.

to do so with the aid of the procedure prescribed for amending it (with the result that the judiciary has partly supplied the corrective). For instance, in 1924 Congress proposed an amendment that it ' shall have power to limit, regulate, and prohibit the labour of persons under eighteen years of age '; it has not yet been ratified by the required number of states.[1]   (*ii*) Others think it is too easy and cite the speedy ratification of the eighteenth amendment, which introduced prohibition in 1918-19, in support of their view. (*iii*) Another issue is whether the amending body could effectively alter the representation of a state in the Senate. The issue is not at present a live one; it is sufficient to say that such a change implies the breaking of a pledge given to the small states at the time when the constitution was framed, and it is not likely that it will be seriously proposed. American opinion in general is, however, inclined to support Madison's view that the method of amendment guards ' equally against that extreme facility which would render the constitution too mutable and that extreme difficulty which might perpetuate discovered faults '.

§2 DIVISION OF POWERS

In a federal State, there must be a divison of powers between the Centre and the units. In the U.S.A. the constitution (*i*) enumerates the powers of the Centre ; (*ii*) prohibits the Centre from doing certain things ; (*iii*) prohibits the states from doing certain things and (*iv*) leaves the residue, i.e. the powers not delegated to the Centre or prohibited to the states, to the states (or to the people).

(*i*) Congress is given power to levy and collect taxes, duties, imposts and excises, to pay the debts and provide for the common defence and general welfare of the United States ; to borrow money on the credit of the United States ; to declare war ; to raise and support armies and to maintain a navy ; to regulate commerce with foreign nations and among the several states ; to establish a uniform rule of naturalization and uniform laws on the subject of bankruptcy ; to coin money and regulate the value thereof, and fix the standard of weights and measures ; to establish post offices ; to legislate for the national capital and the small district in which it is situated, i.e. for the city of Washington and the District of Columbia in which it stands ; to make all needful rules and regulations respecting the territory or other property belonging to the United States ; and generally to make all laws which shall be

---

[1] The process of ratification had not been completed even by 1960.

necessary and proper for carrying into execution the foregoing powers.

(*ii*) The powers prohibited to the Centre are that it may not suspend the privilege of the writ of habeas corpus 'unless when in cases of rebellion or invasion the public safety may require it'; may not pass a bill of attainder to *ex post facto* law; may not impose any tax or duty on articles exported from any state; may give no preference 'by any regulation of commerce or revenue to the ports of one state over those of another'; and may make no law respecting an establishment of religion or prohibiting the free exercise thereof, or abridging the freedom of speech, or of the press, or the right of the people peaceably to assemble and to petition the Government for a redress of grievances. The Constitutional provisions[1] further prohibit unreasonable searches and general warrants; require serious crime to be tried on indictment found by a grand jury; forbid any person to 'be subject for the same offence to be twice put in jeopardy of life or limb', to be compelled in any criminal case to be a witness against himself, or to be deprived of life, liberty, or property without due process of law.

(*iii*) The prohibitions on the states are that no state may enter into any treaty, alliance or confederation; coin money; utter bills' of credit; make anything but gold and silver coin a tender in payment of debts; or pass any bill of attainder, *ex post facto* law, or any law impairing the obligation of contracts. Further, they are forbidden, without the consent of Congress, to levy imposts of duties on imports or exports 'except what may be absolutely necessary for executing its inspection laws', or any duty of tonnage. to 'keep troops or ships of war in time of peace, enter into any agreement or compact with another state, or with a foreign power, or engage in war, unless actually invaded or in such imminent danger as will not admit of delay'; to permit slavery; and to deny the franchise on account of 'race, colour, or previous condition of servitude' or of sex. Finally, no state 'shall make or enforce any law which shall abridge the privileges or immunities of citizens of the United States; nor shall any state deprive any person of life, liberty or property without due process of law, nor deny to any person within its jurisdiction the equal protection of law'.

(*iv*) *Residuary powers.* 'The powers not delegated to the United States by the constitution, nor prohibited by it to the states, are reserved to the states respectively, or to the people.'[2]

[1] Amendments IV and V of the Constitution.
[2] Amendment X.

It may be added, finally, that the Federal Government has certain obligations to the states. (*i*) It must respect their territorial integrity ; Congress is directed by the constitution to see that no new state is ' formed or erected within the jurisdiction of any other state ; nor any state... formed by the junction of two or more states or parts of states, without the consent of the Legislatures of the states concerned '. (*ii*) It must protect them against invasion, and, on application from their Legislature or from the Executive (when the Legislature cannot be convened), against domestic violence. (*iii*) It must guarantee to every state a republican form of government.

§3 THE PRESIDENT

The President is the head of the Executive in the U.S.A. He is elected for four years. Originally there was no limit set by the constitution to the number of times a President might be re-elected ; since 26 February 1951, however, an amendment to the constitution has come into force limiting Presidents of the U.S.A. to two terms of office :[1] ' No person shall be elected to the office of President more than twice, and no person who held the office of President, or acted as President, for more than two years of a term to which some other person was elected President, shall be elected to the office of President more than once.'

Any natural-born American citizen, at least thirty-five years of age and ' fourteen years a resident within the United States ', may stand for election.

The election of the President is by an electoral College formed for the purpose. The constitution says that the number of electors chosen in each state shall be equal to the number of members of the House of Representatives and of the Senate for that state ; in other words, equal to the state's representation in Congress. The electors shall meet in their respective states and vote by ballot for President and Vice-President.

' The person having the greatest number of votes for President shall be the President, if such number be a majority of the whole number of electors appointed ; and if no person have such majority, then from the persons having the highest numbers not exceeding three on the list of those voted for as President, the House of Representatives shall choose immediately, by ballot, the President.'

[1] President Truman, however, was specially exempted from this rule.

A similar provision is laid down for the choice of the Vice-President; with the difference that if no candidate secures an absolute majority of votes, the Senate shall choose the Vice-President, 'from the two highest numbers on the list'.

The theory of the constitution is clear : the President must be chosen by the best men of the country untrammelled by any party ties or engagements, ' on the sole ground of their judgement of the personal fitness of the leading men in the country '. The makers of the constitution thought that it would be as unnatural to make the people judges of the candidate for the chief magistracy as it would be to refer a trial of colours to a blind man. Indeed ' one of the principal aims of the founders of the American Republic was to make the New World safe against democracy '. In practice, however, the aims of the constitution-makers have hardly been realized. It is a part of the unwritten constitution that the electors shall cast their votes in accordance with the popular vote that elected them.[1] No penalty would attach if an elector should deviate, but we have it on good authority[2] ' that no elector, since Plumer of New Hampshire did so in the second election of Monroe,[3] has deviated from his instructions '. The various parties hold their national conventions long before the date fixed for the Presidential election and select their candidate. When the voters vote for the electors, therefore, they know also, in effect, for which Presidential candidate they are voting, so that, as soon as the popular vote is counted, not only are the electors known but also the in-coming President. The meeting of the electors afterwards is a mere form.

The President may be removed from office before his legal term is over on impeachment for and conviction of treason, bribery, or other high crimes and misdemeanours. The House of Representatives adopts by resolution articles of impeachment charging the person concerned with certain high crimes, and enumerates his particular offences, and chooses leaders to direct the prosecution before the Senate, which acts as High Court. The Chief Justice of the Supreme Court presides. A two-thirds vote of the members present is necessary for a conviction. The penalty may not extend further than the removal of the offender from office, and disqualification to hold and enjoy any office of honour, trust, or profit under the United States ; but ' the party convicted shall, nevertheless, be liable and subject to indictment, trial

[1] Since the sixties of the last century, in every state (with exceptions for brief periods), the electors have been chosen by popular election, though the constitution does not prescribe it.

[2] W. R. West, *American Government*, p. 134. [3] 1820.

judgement and punishment, according to law'. So far only one President, Andrew Johnson, has been impeached (1868) ; he was however, acquitted.

His powers

The powers of the President may be discussed under three heads, executive, legislative and judicial.

(*i*) *Executive*. The President is the head of the national administration. It is his duty to see that the 'constitution, laws, and treaties of the United States and judicial decisions rendered by the federal courts are duly enforced throughout the country. In the fulfilment of this duty, he may direct the heads of departments and their subordinates in the discharge of the functions' vested in them by the acts of Congress.' The department of foreign affairs is more especially subject to his control. As administrative head, the President appoints a large number of federal officers with the advice and consent of the Senate ; Congress may, however, by law vest the appointment of inferior officers in the President alone, in the courts of law, or in the heads of departments. It is now a convention that the Senate does not normally refuse its consent to the President's choice of heads of the departments who act as his principal advisers. The Senate's consent is not necessary for the removal of officers by the President. The President is the commander-in-chief of the army and the navy. The conduct of foreign affairs is in his hands ; but a treaty made by him requires the ratification of two-thirds of the Senate. Finally, though the power to declare war belongs to Congress as a whole ' clearly executive action may bring negotitation 'to such a pass as to make war almost inevitable.'

(*ii*) *Legislative*. To grasp clearly the function of the President in relation to legislation, it is necessary to recall the fact that the American Executive is non-parliamentary, i.e. is neither chosen by or from the Legislature nor removable by it. Further, the President or his advisers do not have (either by law or custom) the right to be present in Congress and take part in its deliberations, and therfore they are not in a position directly to provide the initiative and guidance in law-making so largely and effectively provided in the British Parliament by its cabinet. Nor has the President the right to summon (except for extraordinary sessions) or dissolve Congress. It must not, however, be thought that therefore the President's share in legislation is unimportant. As a leading authority has put it :[1]

[1] H. L. McBain, *The Living Constitution*, p. 116.

' We elect the President as a leader of legislation. We hold him accountable for what he succeeds in getting Congress to do and in preventing Congress from doing. Once in office, except for considerations of the patronage, which is politics rather than executive business, the time and thought of the President and his cabinet are devoted far more largely to legislative than to executive matters. This is true even when Congress is not in session.'

He exercises his influence in legislation in the following ways : (*a*) He may summon extraordinary sessions of Congress. (*b*) He may send messages to Congress (or deliver them in person as Wilson did effectively), giving information on the state of the Union and recommending for consideration such measures as he may judge necessary and expedient. Wilson, it is said, was extraordinarily successful in securing action upon the proposals conveyed in his messages. (*c*) He may ask a member of Congress to embody his ideas on a certain subject in a bill, and set the party machinery in motion to get it accepted. The effectiveness of this depends primarily on whether the party to which the President belongs commands a majority in Congress. (*d*) He may *veto* a bill, i.e. refuse his consent to a bill passed by Congress. This must be done within ten days (Sundays excepted) after the bill has been submitted to him. If he does, it must, in order to become law, again be passed in each House by a two-thirds majority. This is an effective power to prevent hasty and unwise legislation and has been frequently used—indeed about as many as six hundred times. In certain circumstances, this limited or suspensive veto may become an absolute veto, i.e. without a chance for Congress to repass the vetoed bill by the required majority. This happens when Congress adjourns before the ten days (allowed for the President to study the bill) are up, and the President refuses to sign the bill. This is termed a ' pocket veto '. (*e*) He has the ordinance power, i.e. the power exercised under congressional authority to supplement general legislation with detailed rules that have the effect of law.

(*iii*) *Judicial.* The President has the power to grant reprieves [1] and pardons for offences against the United States, except in cases of impeachment.

The cabinet

The constitution does not mention a cabinet for the purpose of collectively formulating the policy of the nation ; it authorizes

---

[1] A reprieve is a stay in the execution of a sentence.

the President only to ' require the opinion, in writing, of the principal officer in each of the executive departments, upon any subject relating to the duties of their respective offices '. By convention, however, from 1791, it has been usual for the President to summon meetings of the heads of the executive departments (normally twice a week) for the discussion of important governmental matters. The proceedings are informal and confidential. Cabinet discussions are useful in clarifying views and helping the President to make up his mind ; but he is not bound by any decisions arrived at ; his responsibility remains single and undivided. President Lincoln is reported to have said ' Seven nays, one aye —the ayes have it ', when he found in a cabinet consultation that all members were against him.

The Presidency of the U.S.A. is one of the greatest political offices of the world. Its occupant has become—with perhaps one exception—the most powerful head of a government known to our day. His public pronouncements and actions are watched with the greatest interest throughout the world. Unlike the King of England and the President of France (in part), his power is real, being exercised on his own responsibility. As Sir Henry Maine has aptly said, the King of England reigns but does not govern ; the French President neither reigns nor governs ; the American President governs, though (not being a king) he does not reign. The people look up to him for leadership.

' The nation as a whole,' Wilson has said,[1] ' has chosen him (the President), and is conscious that it has no other political spokesman. His is the only national voice in affairs Let him once win the admiration and confidence of the country, and no other single force can withstand him, no combination of forces will easily overpower him. His position takes the imagination of the country. He is the representative of no constituency, but of the whole people. When he speaks in his true character, he speaks for no special interest. If he rightly interpret the national thought and boldly insist upon it, he is irresistible ; and the country never feels the zest of action so much as when its President is of such insight and calibre. Its instinct is for unified action, and it craves a single leader.'

§4 THE SENATE

Congress is the Legislature of the United States. It consists of two bodies, the Senate and the House of Representatives.

---

[1] W. Wilson, *Constitutional Government in the United States*, p. 68.

The Senate is composed of 100 members, two senators from each state, chosen by popular vote for six years. 'The electors in each state shall have the qualifications requisite for electors of the most numerous branch of the state Legislatures.' One-third of the Senators retire every two years. Senators can be, and often are, re-elected. 'No person shall be a senator who shall not have attained to the age of thirty years, and been nine years a citizen of the United States, and who shall not, when elected, be an inhabitant of that state for which he shall be chosen.'[1] Further, during their tenure, senators may not hold any office under the United States.

The Senate is a powerful body and exercises a very real influence in national affairs, such as is perhaps exercised by no other second chamber in the world. (*i*) It has equal powers with the House of Representatives in ordinary legislation. (*ii*) In respect of money bills, its powers are, according to the constitution, inferior to those of the lower House only in one respect, viz. it cannot initiate bills for raising revenue ; by custom, appropriation bills also originate in the lower House. But the Senate is free to amend and reject any money bill. (*iii*) Its consent (by a two-thirds majority) is necessary for treaties. How important this power is may be seen from one instance. When President Wilson returned from Europe to his country after having signed the Covenant of the League of Nations on behalf of the U.S.A. (1918-19), the Senate refused to ratify his action. This refusal had important consequences on international relations ; the League failed to acquire the strength which otherwise it might have acquired. (*iv*) Its consent is necessary for appointments by the President (except for the power of appointing inferior officers vested by Congress in the President alone). (*v*) It has the power to try all impeachments. Judgement in cases of impeachment shall not, however, extend beyond removal from office and disqualification from holding and enjoying any office of honour, trust or profit under the United States.

Among the Senate's other powers are that it shares with the House of Representatives the powers to propose amendments to the constitution and the power to admit new states to the Union. If in a Vice-Presidential election no candidate secures an absolute majority, the Senate has to choose the Vice-President from among the two candidates who have secured the largest number of votes. It is the judge of the elections, returns and qualifications of its own members.

[1] Article I, section 3

That the Senate of the U.S.A. is one of the most powerful second chambers is admitted on all hands. What are the causes of its power? First, compared with other second chambers, like the British House of Lords and the French Senate (under the Third Republic), it is a small body and therefore more effective. Second, it is an elected body; this fact gives it authority and vitality. Thirdly, it has some special powers in respect of treaties, appointments and impeachments, not possessed by the House of Representatives. Fourthly, it is considered the guardian of the rights of the states as states, because of the equal representation given in it to large and small states alike (unlike in the lower House). It is true, H. J. Laski has shown, that party lines tend to override state boundaries in the discussions and voting in the Senate; but, nevertheless, the Senate continues to enjoy in popular imagination the dignity arising from its federal character. And, finally, its personnel is distinctly better than that of the House of Representatives. For one thing, the fact that it has never been renewed at any one time to the extent of more than a third of its membership gives it a tradition of experience and dignity; further, the best Americans, it would seem, prefer to be in the Senate, rather than in the lower House. The contrast drawn by de Tocqueville a hundred years ago between the Senate and the House of Representatives substantially holds good today as well:

'On entering the House of Representatives of Washington, one is struck by the vulgar demeanour of that great assembly. Often there is not a distinguished man in the whole number. Its members are almost all obscure individuals. . . At a few yards' distance from this spot is the door of the Senate, which contains within a small space a large proportion of the celebrated men of America. Scarcely an individual is to be perceived in it who does not recall the idea of an active and illustrious career; the Senate is composed of eloquent advocates, distinguished generals, wise magistrates, and statesmen of note, whose language would at all times do honour to the most remarkable parliamentary debates of Europe.' [1]

§5 THE HOUSE OF REPRESENTATIVES

The House of Representatives is composed of 436 members, elected for two years and apportioned among the several states according to their population. This is in contrast to the Senate

[1] de Tocqueville, *Democracy in America*, Vol. I (Alfred A. Knopf, 1948), p. 204.

in which every state has equal representation.   The constitution
lays down that the number of representatives shall not exceed one
for every thirty thousand,[1] but that each state shall have at least
one representative.   Members are elected for the most part from
single-member constituencies.

There is no uniform suffrage law for the House of Representatives (or for the Senate).   The constitution provides that the
voters in each state shall have the qualifications requisite for
electors of the most numerous branch of the state Legislature ;
and the right to vote shall not be denied or abridged by the
United States or by any state on account of race, colour, or previous condition of servitude, or on account of sex.   Within these
limits each state regulates the suffrage as it thinks best.

A representative must be twenty-five years or over ; he must
have been a citizen for at least seven years ; he cannot, while
a member of the House, hold any ' office under the United States ' ;
and he must be an inhabitant of that state in which he is chosen.
By convention, the representative must also be a resident of the
district which he represents.

As in the House of Commons and in the Chamber of Deputies
the effective work of the House of Representatives is done through
its committees.   The committee system saves time and conduces
to effective discussion.   There are nineteen standing committees
in the House, each devoted to one specific subject, such as Appropriations, Ways and Means, Armed Services, Foreign Relations,
Agriculture, etc.   These committees consist of from two to thirty-
five members (the standard number being twenty-one) elected
by the House when it first meets after the General Election.
Committees are always elected on a party basis, and the majority
party sees to it that it has a safe majority on each committee.[2]
The chairmen of the committees are also elected by the House.[3]
Their position is an important one, for as the Executive has no
place in the House, most bills are usually introduced by them ;
they also pilot them through the House.

---

[1] This means that each member of this House of Representatives must
represent at least 30,000 persons. Inasmuch as the membership of the
House is now 436, the number of persons each represents varies from
State to State. New York State has the largest number of representatives
—43, which is one for 344,888 persons according to the 1950 census ; but
New Hampshire, which has two, has one for each 266,621.

[2] Committees, however, are not always divided between the two parties
in exact proportion to their strength in the House. Thus in 1939, though
the Republicans constituted only a small minority in the House, they had
a substantial majority on each committee. (West, op. cit., p. 96).

[3] Invariably, the Senior member, in terms of service, on the majority
side of the Committee, is elected Chairman.

In addition to standing committees, the House has its committees of the whole House, at which the Speaker of the House does not preside, but someone named by him. Discussions at these committees are more informal than in the whole House.

Its powers

The House has equal powers with the Senate in ordinary legislation. It has the sole initiative in taxation bills, and has the sole power of impeachment. It shares with the Senate the power to propose amendments to the constitution, and to admit new states into the Union. If in a Presidential election no candidate secures an absolute majority, the House has to choose the President by ballot ' from the persons having the highest numbers not exceeding three on the list of those voted for as President '. It is judge of the elections, returns, and qualifications of its own members.

§6 LAW-MAKING AND FINANCIAL CONTROL

Law-making

The process of law-making in the U.S.A. is in some respects similar to that employed in Britain and France. Bills are given three readings in one House, referred to committees, reported, debated, considered by the other House and sent to the Executive head for his signature. But there are important differences arising primarily from the fact that the Executive is a non-parliamentary one.

Let us follow the passage of a public bill introduced in the House of Representatives. ' Introduction ' simply means that a member deposits a copy of the bill on the clerk's table or hands it to the Speaker. (Important bills are usually introduced in the names of chairmen of committees.) The first ' reading ' is, strictly speaking, no ' reading ' at all ; the bill is deemed to be read by having its title printed in the *Journal* and in the *Congressional Record*. The bill is then referred to the appropriate committee. If the committee so decides there may be public hearings on the bill, persons interested being invited or allowed to appear before the committee to have their say. Then it may report the bill to the House favourably without any change, report it amended. report it unfavourably, or not report it at all. If reported, the bill comes up for a second reading, when it is debated, amendments are offered, and a vote is taken. If the vote is affirmative, the bill must in theory be printed before being read a third time. ' As a matter of fact,' W. R. West tells us, ' the House usually assumes that the bill is engrossed[1] and proceeds immediately to the third reading, which is usually by title. However, if some member insists upon a reading in full, the third reading may be delayed until the bill actually has been engrossed, after which it is read in full.' Then comes the final vote on the bill. ' If the result is favourable, it goes to the Senate, and, after a more or less similar procedure there, to the President. If the House and the Senate cannot agree on the bill, an effort is made to settle their differences by means of a ' committee of conference,' i.e. a committee of from three to nine members appointed by each Chamber to explore points of agreement.

Some differences are noticeable between the law-making procedure outlined above and that of the British Parliament. (*i*) All bills here are introduced by private members ; in the British Parliament, most bills are introduced by cabinet members. (*ii*) The members of the Executive are not present in Congress to guide it in legislation. (*iii*) The bills are referred to committees before their principles are discussed and approved by the respective Chambers. This method has the advantage that it allows the committees greater freedom than is otherwise possible to shape the bill properly ; its disadvantage is that after all the labours of the committee, the bill may be rejected by the Chamber on the ground that its principles are not acceptable. (*iv*) There is a larger number of standing committees for the consideration of bills than in the British Parliament, though each individual committee has fewer members ; and each committee is devoted to a special subject. (*v*) The Senate in the U.S.A. has greater power than the British House of Lords to amend and reject bills. (*vi*) The President has a suspensive veto, which may in certain circumstances be an absolute veto.

Financial control

The Director of the Bureau of the Budget, an official working under the control of the President, prepares the budget more or less on the English plan with estimates of the appropriations necessary for the different departments of Government and a statement of probable revenues. The budget is submitted to Congress on the responsibility of the President. It is considered by two committees of the House of Representatives, viz. the committee on ways and means and the committee on appropriations. These committees report to the House, and later the House debates and passes the Finance Bill and the Appropriation Bill. The bills

---

[1] i.e. printed.

are then sent to the Senate, and, with any amendments agreed to by the House, to the President.

Two general features are noteworthy : (*i*) There is a lack of unified responsibility in matters of finance, because, though the President submits a unified plan, it is mutilated both in committees and in the Chambers. This is partly because the members of the cabinet and the Director of the Bureau of the Budget are not admitted to the floor of the House though they can be invited or summoned to the committees to justify and explain their proposals, and partly because the members both in committees and in the Chambers have the freedom (as not true in the British Parliament) not only to reduce items of expenditure and revenue but to propose increases, or even new items, (*ii*) The Senate has much greater power than the British House of Lords to modify revenue and appropriation bills.

The control of Congress over the national finance is effective — perhaps too effective.

§7 THE JUDICIARY

The judicial system of the U.S.A. is divided into two distinct series of courts : state courts and the federal courts.

The state courts are set up under the state constitutions, and normally concern themselves with cases which involve the adjudication of rights claimed under the state constitutions and the state laws. Judges of the state courts are usually elected by the people for short terms.

The federal Judiciary consists of a Supreme Court, 11 circuit courts of appeal, 84 district courts,[1] a court of claims and a court of customs. The Supreme Court has original jurisdiction in all cases affecting ambassadors, other public ministers and consuls, and those in which a state is a party ; in other cases in respect of which the federal courts are assigned jurisdiction, it has appellate jurisdiction ' with such exceptions and under such regulations as Congress shall make '. Judges are appointed by the President, with the advice and consent of the Senate, and serve during good behaviour. They are removable by impeachment. Their salaries may not be diminished during their continuance in office.

The jurisdiction of the federal courts, as defined in the constitution,[2] relates to two types of cases : (*i*) those which concern

---

[1] *United States Government Organization Manual*, 1950-51, p. 49.
[2] Article III.

certain *matters,* and (*ii*) those which concern certain *parties.*

(*i*) The first cover all cases in law and equity arising under the national (as distinct from a state) constitution, the laws of the United States, and the treaties made under their authority, and all cases of admiralty and maritime jurisdiction.

(*ii*) The second cover all cases affecting ambassadors and other public ministers and consuls ; controversies to which the United States is a party ; controversies between two or more states ; ' between citizens of different states ; between citizens of the same state claiming lands under grants of different states, and between a state or the citizens thereof, and foreign States, citizens, or subjects '.

The constitution, however, does not say that the cases referred to in (*ii*) above can be tried *only* by the federal courts. Congress determines by law the *exclusive* jurisdiction of the federal courts, and in all matters not exclusively assigned to them, the state courts have concurrent jurisdiction. If a state court exercises jurisdiction in such matters, however, the parties concerned have the right of appeal to the federal courts.

Relation to the Executive

(*i*) The President appoints the federal judges with the consent of the Senate, but he has no power to remove them, since they may be removed only by impeachment. The constitution explicitly says that they serve during good behaviour ; their salaries also, fixed at the time of their appointment, may not be diminished during their continuance in office.

(*ii*) Federal executive officers are liable, as in Britain, to be tried in federal courts on the principle of the rule of law.

Relation to the Legislature

(*i*) Congress has power to settle the *exclusive* jurisdiction of the federal courts. So far, it has given them exclusive jurisdiction in all suits to which the U.S.A. is a party ; in all suits between two states or between a state and a foreign nation ; in certain suits arising under the national constitution and national laws such as those relating to patents, copyright and bankruptcy ; and in suits against ambassadors or other public ministers (or their servants), and against consuls or vice-consuls.

(*ii*) Congress has power to establish federal courts inferior to the Supreme Court.

(*iii*) The consent of the Senate is necessary for the appointment of judges.

(*iv*) Judges may be removed by impeachment initiated by the House of Representatives before the Senate sitting as a court of impeachment.

(*v*) The importance of the Judiciary in the U.S.A. arises from the fact that the U.S.A. is a federal State, and there is therefore a division of powers between the states and the Centre. The constitution stands above ordinary laws, and the Judiciary is its guardian. If a law passed by a state Legislature or by the Congress is against the terms of the constitution, it is null and void, and the Judiciary has, as the guardian of the constitution, the power to declare such laws unconstitutional.

We may illustrate. (*a*) *A state law declared unconstitutional.* In 1791 Congress authorized the establishment of the Bank of the United States, in the face of violent opposition from certain sections of the states. Under its charter, the bank was entitled to operate throughout the Union, by means of branches, and it opened a branch at Baltimore in the state of Maryland. In 1818, the Legislature of Maryland imposed a stamp tax on the circulating notes of all banks or branches thereof located in the state and not chartered by it. The Baltimore branch of the federal bank refused to pay the tax. The state sued the cashier of the bank, McCulloch. The Maryland court upheld the law and ordered McCulloch to pay, whereupon the case was taken to the Supreme Court on appeal.[1] The contention on behalf of the state was that the federal Legislature had no power, according to the constitution, to start a bank. The Supreme Court declared that, according to a clause in the constitution (empowering Congress to collect taxes, to borrow money, etc., and to take the necessary steps to put this power into execution), Congress had an *implied* power to start the bank, and, thereof, the state law (the effect of which would have been to drive out the federal bank) was illegal and against the constitution. Chief Justice Marshall said :

'Let the end be legitimate, let it be within the scope of the constitution, and all means which are appropriate, which are plainly adapted to that end, and which are not prohibited, but consistent with the letter and spirit of the constitution, are constitutional.'

(*b*) *A federal law declared unconstitutional.* In 1916, Congress, with a view to restrict child labour in factories, prohibited

[1] McCulloch *v.* Maryland (1819).

inter-state trade in goods made by child labour. It relied upon a
clause in the constitution which gave it power to regulate inter-
state trade. But this particular law interfered with industry, a
matter within the jurisdiction of the state ; the Supreme Court
felt that it was not proper for Congress to use the commerce power
for the purpose of regulating industry, and so declared the law
unconstitutional.[1] Again in 1919, Congress tried to restrict
child labour in factories by resorting to its taxing power, but
the Supreme Court declared that law also null and void. In
1935 the National Industrial Recovery Act passed by Congress
in 1933 was declared unconstitutional in so far as it referred to
industries within the states.[2]

The power of the Supreme Court to declare laws unconstitutional has been used not only to protect the rights of the states
and of the Centre against mutual encroachment but also to protect the rights given to citizens by the constitution, and to protect
the rights of one department of government against encroachment
by another. One example of each will suffice.

(i) The city of San Francisco, acting under a Californian law,
passed in 1876 an ordinance directing that every male imprisoned
in the country gaol should immediately on his arrival have his
hair clipped to a uniform length of one inch from the scalp.

' The sheriff, having, under this ordinance, cut off the queue of
a Chinese prisoner, Ho Ah Kow, was sued for damages by the
prisoner, and the court, holding that the ordinance had been
passed with a special view to the injury of the Chinese, who then
considered the preservation of their queue to be a matter of
honour, and that it operated unequally and oppressively upon
them, in contravention of the fourteenth amendment to the constitution of the United States, declared the ordinance invalid, and
gave judgement against the sheriff.' [3]

(ii) A law passed by Congress in 1876 provided that ' postmasters of the first, second, and third class shall be appointed
and may be removed by and with the advice and consent of the

---

[1] Hammer v. Dagenhart (1918). It is interesting to note that a later
judgement — in United States v. Darby (1941) — reverses the decision in
Hammer v. Dagenhart. The Court in 1941 held that the commerce power
was complete in itself and acknowledged no limitations other than are
prescribed in the constitution. 'The motives and purposes which lead Congress to regulate inter-state commerce are matters for legislative judgement
upon the exercise of which the constitution places no restriction and over
which the Courts are given no control.'

[2] Schechter Poultry Corporation v. U.S. (1935).

[3] Bryce, The American Commonwealth, Vol. I, p. 330.

Senate, and shall hold their offices for four years unless sooner removed or suspended according to law'. In 1920 President Wilson, without consulting the Senate, removed from office Myers, first-class postmaster at Portland, whom he had appointed in 1917 for four years. Myers prosecuted the case first in the court of claims, and later in the Supreme Court. The Court upheld the President's unfettered power of removal, and declared the law (which had made the Senate's consent necessary for removal from office) unconstitutional.[1]

In recent years the most significant decisions of the Supreme Court have been in the realm of protection of individual rights and elimination of racial segregation in schools and other public places. The Court ruled unanimously in 1954 that segregation of children in public schools was unconstitutional. It thus rejected the doctrine of 'separate but equal facilities' which had been propounded by the Court itself in 1896 and which had become the basis for various state laws aimed at enforcing segregation. The Court declared that even if equal physical facilities were provided, segregation on the basis of race would deny equality of educational opportunities to Negro children.[2]

In 1964 the Court ruled on another significant issue—the disparity in the number of eligible voters among Congressional districts. In Westbury v. Saunders it laid down that 'as nearly as practicable' Congressional districts must have an equal number of eligible voters. The decision is likely to have far-reaching effects in the distribution of political power between urban and non-urban areas in the United States, adding considerably to the strength of the former.

The Supreme Court has served two useful purposes in the government of the U.S.A.

(*i*) It has acted, as illustrated above, as the guardian of the constitution, to protect the rights of the states against invasion by the Centre and vice versa, the rights of individuals against invasion by the Centre and the states, and the rights of the Executive against invasion by the Legislature.

(*ii*) It has permitted the constitution to develop by adapting the provisions of an eighteenth-century constitution to meet the vastly different conditions and needs of later years (the adaptation is incomplete, but that is primarily the work of the body responsible for amending the constitution) ; and, incidentally, helped to increase the powers of the Centre by laying down the doctrine of

---

[1] Myers v. U.S. (1926).
[2] *Keesing's Contemporary Archives*, (May 29-June 5, 1954), 13593.

implied powers. Thus the power to charter a federal bank pro-
ceeded from such powers as the power to collect taxes, to borrow
money and to regulate the value thereof. The power to issue
paper money was derived from the power to borrow money, and
to regulate the value thereof, and other such powers. The constitution lays down that Congress shall have the power to regulate
commerce with foreign nations and among the several states.
'The Supreme Court upheld as within the scope of this clause
acts passed by Congress pertaining to the regulation of inter-state
and foreign commerce by steamboat, by railway, by telegraphy,
by airplane, and by radio. These means of communication were
unheard of in 1787.'[1] Not only can the national Government
regulate commerce, but it has the right to engage in inter-state
commerce and to create and control companies for the construction and operation of highways, bridges, canals and railways.
Indeed, judicial construction, more than any other single factor,
has been responsible for the enormous increase in the power of
the national Government today.

§8 THE PARTY SYSTEM

The earliest party division in the U.S.A. was between the
Federalists and the Jeffersonian Republicans; the former were
in favour of making the Federal Government strong by interpreting the constitution liberally in its favour, the latter were
champions of state rights. Till 1800, the Federalists had the
upper hand, though Washington (the first President) himself was
not a party man and indeed denounced all parties. With the
election of Jefferson (the leader of the Republicans) to the Presidency in 1800, the Republicans came to power; the Federalists
gradually declined in importance, and by 1816 had ceased to
exist. From 1816-30 there were no definitely marked national
parties; so the period is generally known as the 'era of good
feeling', but was really 'an era of particularly bad feeling, based
on personal rivalries',[2] small groups following the lead of men
like Adams, Clay, Jackson and Calhoun. In the forties a realign-
ment of parties into Whigs and Democrats is noticeable. The
former stood for protection in industry, the establishment of a
national bank and a generally positive policy of social improvement by State action. The latter stood for extreme individualism
and the extension of the suffrage. In the fifties and sixties, the
issue of slavery overshadowed all other questions. The Democratic

---

[1] West, op. cit., p. 63.
[2] West, op. cit., pp. 439-40.

party, with its main base of strength in the agrarian Southern states, was confronted by a new political grouping — the Republican party — that opposed slavery and espoused an economic programme beneficial to the East and the Mid-West. The Civil War (1861-5) resulted in the abolition of slavery. The two parties, the Republicans and the Democrats, however, continued to exist,[1] but their evolution during the past sixty years 'has rather taken the form of consolidation of party structure than a collective adherence to any single principle or policy'. Each party draws up its platform according to circumstances and chiefly with an eye to political success. There is a difference rather in emphasis on certain ways of doing than in fundamentals.

Thus the Democratic Party platform in 1952 advocated a strong national defence programme and supported collective security measures in Europe, Asia and in the Americas to stem Soviet expansion. The platform expressed support to 'the victims of Soviet imperialism' and pledged economic aid to under-developed nations in Asia. It endorsed measures for securing 'real, effective disarmament' and proclaimed that world peace was the 'greatest of all our goals'. The Republican programme differed but little from the one outlined above, except that it used strong language to condemn the 'corruption, incompetence, and disloyalty in public office' of the Democrats. The Republican platform singled out American policy in the Far East for special criticism and asserted that the 'Asia Last' policy of the Democrats had resulted in a great accession of strength to Communism in that continent.

The divergence between the two Parties is perhaps a little more marked in respect of internal policy, though here also there is a large measure of agreement. Thus under the administration of F. D. Roosevelt, the Democrats envisaged a more active role for the Federal Government than the Republicans. While the Democrats have stressed the need for governmental action to promote social welfare, the Republicans have argued that such 'intervention' will hamper private enterprise. Republicans are also more inclined to lay stress on reduction of expenditure and budget balancing than Democrats. The 1952 platforms reveal the same general trend : a difference in emphasis relating to issues of domestic policy. Thus both Parties supported social security measures, though the Democratic proposals were a little more comprehensive than those of the Republicans. Both supported the

---

[1] There have also been other minor parties like the Prohibition party, the Populists, the Socialists, etc.

principle of price supports for agricultural commodities, but Republicans charged that their opponents were seeking 'to control the farmer and to socialize agriculture'. While they professed solicitude for the welfare of the working man, the two Parties were sharply divided on the Taft-Hartley Act (1947) which had placed certain curbs on trade unions. Republicans favoured the retention of the Act with minor amendments while Democrats demanded that it should be repealed outright. While Democrats pointed with pride to the positive role of the Federal Government in promoting welfare, the Republicans alleged that for twenty years the Democratic Administration had 'praised free enterprise while actually wrecking it'. The Republican platform alleged that the 'wanton extravagance and inflationary policies of the Administration in power have cut the value of the dollar in half and imposed the most confiscatory taxes in our history'. It demanded a reduction of expenditure and of taxes and the balancing of the national budget. The Democratic platform, on the other hand, asserted that while proposals for tax relief, especially for people with low incomes, should be examined, it would be dangerous to indulge in 'reckless promises'.[1]

Eight years later, in 1960, the Republican Party sought the mandate of the voters on the basis of what it described as the solid achievements gained under the leadership of President Dwight Eisenhower; the Democratic Party charged that American prestige abroad had slumped precipitously while social advance at home had made no significant progress. Both the Parties spoke of the challenge of the communist world and their willingness to negotiate with the Soviet Union without sacrificing principles. Both claimed to be equally firm in their determination to oppose the seating of the People's Republic of China in the United Nations; their adherence to the principles of the U.N. Charter; and their avowal of support for America's allies. The Democrats placed somewhat greater emphasis than the Republicans on economic assistance to the underdeveloped countries; the Republicans were a little more assertive in proclaiming the value of 'firmness' in dealing with the challenge of 'world communism.'

In the domestic field both the parties expressed their solicitude for the Negroes, the aged, the wage-earners and the farmers. The Democratic platform pledged its support to an 'Economic Bill of Rights,' and expressed its hope of creating a sense of national purpose and setting a higher standard of public behaviour.

[1] *Annals* of the American Academy of Political and Social Sciences, CCLXXXIII (September, 1952), pp. 161-86.

The party system in the U.S.A. is instructive to the student of Politics mainly for its thoroughgoing organization. This is explained by two sets of causes, general and particular. The general causes are that parties fulfil some necessary functions in public life and enable democracy to work. Out of the several social problems which call for solution, they select what they consider the most urgent, work out solutions and present them to the electorate ; serve as agencies of political education ; select candidates : and establish a continuing and collective responsibility. The causes particular to the U.S.A. are threefold : (*i*) the frequent popular elections in the country not only to the Legislature but to administrative and judicial posts ; (*ii*) the gap between the Executive and the Legislature ; (*iii*) the large extent of territory to be covered. The more thorough the organization the greater the chances for parties to succeed in the elections, and the greater the opportunity for the winning party in the Presidential election to influence the Legislature to carry out its programme.

Party Organization and the Direct Primary

American political parties have four major levels of organization. At the bottom of the pyramid stands the ' precinct committeeman ' who organizes party activities in the ' precinct '—the smallest voting district with a designated polling booth where qualified resident voters exercise their franchise in all elections. The precinct committeeman is the connecting link between the party organization and the voters and has been described as ' the indispensable cog in the wheel '. Above the precinct committee are the county, state and national committees of the party. The national committee is not the supreme policy-making body of the party : that responsibility is vested in the national convention which meets during each Presidential-election year. The ' national chairman ', as the presiding officer of the national committee is known, is not the principal leader of the party. He only symbolizes the organization of his party.

American party organizations are not as cohesive and disciplined as for instance their British counterparts except during the time of elections.[1] As a result considerable differences of opinion might exist even on important matters of public policy among various levels of the party organization in a state or between a state organization and the national organization. Well-knit party organizations are most commonly found at the country and city

---

[1] Austin Ranney and Willmoore Kendall, *Democracy and the American Party System*, p. 223.

levels and it is there that 'bosses' have occasionally made their appearance. The 'boss' or party leader and the 'ring', i.e. the select friends and followers of the 'boss', formed a sort of oligarchic ruling group in the city. There have been instances of fraud, force, and intimidation employed by certain 'bosses' to perpetuate their political power. But the qualities of individual 'bosses' and the ways by which they attained and held power have varied widely. In the final analysis the power of the 'boss' or any political leader depends on the support of the voters.

Strenuous attempts have been made during recent decades in the United States to put an end to abuses in the election system. In order to guard against the hand-picking of candidates by a 'boss' or a 'caucus' of leaders of a dominant faction, the device of direct primary elections has been introduced for nominations to most elective offices. Primaries are thus elections in which members of a particular party decide on who should be the nominees of the party for various elective offices. The primary elections are governed not by party regulations but by state law ; they are administered by public officials. All citizens who satisfy the legal requirements can participate in the primary regardless of whether they are considered as loyal party members by the 'boss' or the party organization. There are, however, wide variations among states in respect of such legal requirements governing the right to vote in a primary. Primaries are usually held about two or three months before the general election. The winner of the primary is the candidate who secures the largest vote and he thus becomes the official candidate of the party even if he is disowned by leaders of the party organization.

It has been argued that the system of primary elections weakens party responsibility since the party organization is deprived of a decisive voice in the nomination of candidates. Usually, however, the party organization is sufficiently strong and entrenched to bring about the nomination of men of its choice. Occasionally there are revolts against the 'bosses' and aroused voters can use the primary to rout the handpicked men of the party organization.

A number of states provide for a Presidential primary for the election of delegates to the national convention of a party. The state laws relating to such primaries show wide variations.

§9 HOW THE CONSTITUTION HAS DEVELOPED

The constitution of the U.S.A. has now been outlined ; it remains to summarize the various factors that have contributed to its development to its present form from the original of 1787. These are set out under the four following heads.

(*i*) *Formal amendment.* The method of amendment provided by the constitution has already been described. Of the twenty-two amendments effected through this process the most important are : (*a*) the inclusion in the constitution of a list of fundamental rights of individuals, such as freedom of religion, of speech and of the press, and the rights of the people peaceably to assemble, to keep and bear arms, to be secure in their persons, houses, papers and the like and to trial by jury ; (*b*) the abolition of slavery ; (*c*) the direct election of senators ; and (*d*) the adoption of woman suffrage.

(*ii*) *Judicial interpretation.*[1] This has helped the constitution to adjust itself more or less to changing conditions, and virtually widened the actual powers of the Centre, carrying them beyond what the framers could have foreseen.

(*iii*) *Usages.* As in Britain, constitutional usages have played an important part in developing the constitution. Thus the constitution provides that the President shall be elected by the electoral college : the intention of the constitution-makers clearly was that the electors should have discretion in voting for the President. In practice, the electors vote according to their ' mandate ' ; so the election is in effect direct. Other usages are : (*a*) Cabinet ministers are prevented from speaking or being present on the floor of either House of Congress, but the embargo does not extend to their appearance before the committees of Congress. (*b*) The initiative in appointments is taken by the President and not by the Senate. (*c*) Normally the Senate does not refuse consent to the President's choice of the personnel of his cabinet. (*d*) If the senators from the state in which the office lies agree to an appointment made by the President, the Senate confirms it ; otherwise not., (*e*) Appropriation bills also usually originate in the House of Representatives. (*f*) Usage prohibits anyone from seeking to represent in Congress a ' district ' in which he does not reside.

The general tendency of the body of usage that has grown up has been in the direction of a greater and more direct popular control of the Government, to make the American political system more democratic than it was at the beginning or than it was originally intended or expected to be.[2] The leading example, of course, is the revolutionary change made in the system of electing the

---

[1] See above, §7 for illustrations.
[2] H. W. Horwill, *The Usages of the American Constitution*, p. 201.

President both in the restriction of the choice of presidential
electors to the method of popular vote and in the forfeiture by
the electors themselves of the power to do anything more than
register the popular will. Some conventions, like the one permitting heads of departments to appear before the committees of
Congress, have served to fill the gap between the Legislature and
the Executive.

(iv) *Development by law.* The constitution has left many details
to be worked out by the state Legislatures and by Congress. Thus
the method by which members of Congress are nominated and
the qualifications of voters are left to be decided by the laws of
the various states. The structure of the subordinate federal courts
and the organization of the various executive departments, and
the succession to the Presidency in case of ' removal, death, resignation, or inability, both of the President and Vice-President '—
these are regulated by the laws of Congress.

SELECT BIBLIOGRAPHY

M. S. AMOS, *Lectures on the American Constitution.* Longmans,
1938

S. K. BAILEY, H. D. SAMUEL and S. BALDWIN, *Government in
America*, Henry Holt, 1957

D. W. BROGAN, *The American Political System*, Hamish Hamilton, 1943

——, *An Introduction to American Politics*, Hamish Hamilton,
1954

J. BRYCE, *The American Commonwealth*, Macmillan, 1888

——, *Modern Democracies*, Vol. II, Macmillan, 1929

E. S. CORWIN, *The Twilight of the Supreme Court*, Yale, 1934

M. C. CUMMINGS and D. WISE, *Democracy under Pressure: An
Introduction to the American Political System*, New York,
Harcourt Brace Jovanovich, 1971

P. GOODMAN, Ed., *American Constitution*, New York, John Wiley,
1970

H. J. LASKI, *The American Presidency*, Allen & Unwin, 1940

W. B. MUNRO, *The Government of the United States*, Macmillan,
6th ed., 1947

F. A. OGG and P. O. RAY, *Introduction to American Government*, Appleton, 6th ed., 1938

AUSTIN RANNEY and WILLMORE KENDALL, *Democracy and the
American Party System*, Harcourt, Brace, 1956

C. WARREN, *The Supreme Court in United States History*, 2 Vols.,
Little, Brown, and Company, 2nd ed., 1937

W. R. WEST, *American Government*, Pitman, 1939

CHAPTER XIX

CANADA AND AUSTRALIA

§1 CANADA[1]

CANADA was founded in 1608 as a French colony. The colony passed by conquest under British rule in 1760 though, it was formally ceded to Britain only in 1763 by the Treaty of Paris. Its present constitution dates from 1867 when the British North America Act[2] was passed, uniting the then existing four provinces[3] into a federation. The number of provinces has since increased to ten, the latest province to join the Federation being Newfoundland (31 March 1949).

Until 1949 the constitution could be amended by the King in Parliament of Britain on an address presented by both Houses of the Parliament of Canada to His Majesty the King. By convention the Imperial Parliament did not refuse to make an amendment which was supported by a substantial body of opinion in Canada. Where, however, an amendment proposed by the Parliament of Canada was opposed by one or more of the provincial Legislatures, the position was one of extreme delicacy and the chances were that imperial legislation would be refused. An amendment adopted in 1907 to vary the then existing state of subsidies received by the provinces from the Federal Government

---

[1] It is interesting to reflect that in both official usage and common parlance, Canada was often referred to as the Dominion of Canada. As K. C. Wheare points out (*The Constitutional Structure of the Commonwealth*, p. 14), that term has now fallen into disuse. In 1947 new letters patent were issued constituting the office of Governor-General and in them the word 'Canada' replaces 'Dominion of Canada' or 'Dominion' where they had occured in the former letters patent. See also ch. xxiii below.

[2] This Act is referred to as the Constitution for the sake of brevity; it is the Constitution in the sense that it is 'the Supreme law of the Dominion, and therefore its provisions must control all government bodies in Canada-Dominion, provincial and municipal' (R. M. Dawson). A full understanding of the Constitution needs reference (in addition to the Act) to conventions, principles of the Common Law as defined by the Court; British and Canadian Acts of Parliament and Orders-in-Council; judicial interpretations of the written constitution and other laws.

[3] The two provinces called Upper and Lower Canada were from 1840-1867 joined under a single administration.

was based on the assent of all the provinces ; this precedent was held to be binding.[1]

During the autumn of 1949, in response to an address made by Canada's twenty-first Parliament, the Parliament of the United Kingdom amended the British North America Act to vest in the Parliament of Canada the power to make amendments to the constitution of Canada except as regards matters specified in the amendment (such as matters within the classes of subjects assigned exclusively to the Legislatures of the provinces, the rights and privileges secured to the Legislature or the Government of a province, and the use of the English or the French Language).

The question of ' transporting to Canada ' the amendment of the British North America Act has been under discussion in several conferences of the eleven Governments (recently in 1960 and 1961). Some ideas are clear. The role of the British Parliament in the amending process is a formal one, as action is taken on any request from the Canadian authorities and it is agreed that the amending power should rest within Canada. But there is as yet no agreement on how to bring it to Canada or how to amend the constitution if it is to be amended in Canada. Amendment by the Parliament of Canada with the unanimous consent of the provinces for such fundamental subjects as the use of the English or French language ; and with the consent of the legislatures of at least two-thirds of the provinces representing at least fifty per cent of the population of Canada for less fundamental subjects seems to have fair support ; but as yet, no firm conclusions have been agreed upon regarding the entire question of transferring the amending process to Canada.[2]

The principle of the division of powers in Canada between the Federation and the units is, broadly speaking, the opposite of that adopted in the U.S.A. ; i.e. the powers of the provinces are enumerated, and the residue is left with the Dominion. A general provision in the constitution, however, provides that matters of a purely local nature are within the sphere of provincial legislation and the Provincial Governments have in fact been able, as a result of judicial interpretation, to exercise this power. Twenty-nine powers are specifically enumerated as being outside the scope of such legislation, i.e. as being beyond all doubt matters central.

[1] See A. B. Keith, *The Constitutional Law of the British Dominions*, p. 109.
[2] See R. M. Dawson, *The Government of Canada*, new edition, revised by Norman Ward, p. 136.

Among the important federal subjects are trade and commerce ;
postal service ; the militia, naval and military services, and
defence ; navigation and shipping ; currency and coinage ; banking ;
naturalization and the treatment of aliens ; marriage and divorce ;
criminal law and procedure. To the provinces are assigned, among
other things, the amendment of their constitutions (except as
regards the office of Lieutenant-Governor) ; municipal institutions,
hospitals, asylums and like bodies ; local works and undertakings
(with exceptions) ; property and civil rights in the province and
the administration of justice. Both the Federation and the provinces can pass laws dealing with agriculture and immigration ;
but the federal law will prevail over that of a province in case the
two clash.

The Executive

The executive powers of government are vested in the Queen
of Canada, whose title, so far as Canada is concerned, is :

' Elizabeth the Second, by the grace of God of the United
Kingdom, Canada and her other realms and territories Queen,
Head of the Commonwealth, Defender of the Faith.'

The functions of the Crown are carried partly by the Queen
herself, but, for the most part, by the Governor-General. In such
matters as declarations of war and neutrality, conclusion of peace,
ratification of treaties, and appointments of envoys and pleni-
potentiaries the Queen exercises her prerogative powers on the
advice of her Canadian Ministers. She may also award titles of
honour, but in accordance with Canadian wishes no such awards
have been made for a generation.

The Governor-General is appointed by the Queen as her
personal representative upon the advice of the Canadian Prime
Minister, who countersigns his Commission of Appointment.
Until 1952, in order to preclude accusations of political bias, the
Governor-General was chosen from distinguished figures in the
public life of the United Kingdom. Since that time he has been
a Canadian. Traditionally, he serves for five years, but his term
of office may be extended, as was the case with the first Canadian
appointee, Mr Vincent Massey. Although, in accordance with
the Letters Patent of 1947, the Governor-General is empowered
to perform any function that the Sovereign might perform, his
real powers, like the Queen's, are sharply limited by convention.
' His history, like that of his illustrious prototype, has been a

steady, unsensational, rather reluctant progress from virtual dictatorship to virtual impotence.'[1] He summons, prorogues, and
dissolves Parliament, delivers the opening Śpeech from the Throne,
and gives his assent to bills passed by Parliament. Legally, he may
withhold assent from such bills or reserve them for the Sovereign's
pleasure, but constitutionally this power is obsolete. The Governor-
General may disallow provincial bills upon the advice of his
Ministers. He appoints Lieutenant-Governors, Senators, and Judges, is Commander-in-Chief of the Canadian Armed Services, and
exercises the power of pardon, always on the advice of his Ministers. As the Cabinet, they are a Committee of the Queen's Privy
Council for Canada. The Governor-General has a discretionary
power in selecting a Prime Minister, but his choice must have
the support of a majority of the House of Commons. His Ministers
must keep him informed on government matters. Like the Queen,
he retains three rights '. . . the right to be consulated, the right to
encourage, the right to warn '. The Governor-General has many
ceremonial duties, including the reception of diplomatic envoys
and the entertainment of heads of states. His public addresses
during his tours of the country are necessarily confined, as one
holder of the office has said, to ' Governor-Generalities '.

The Governor-General is not a viceroy. This fact is of some
significance from the legal point of view ; he is liable to the courts
both civilly and criminally for any acts done in his private or
his public capacity if these acts are illegal. [2]

The real Executive of the State is a cabinet of ministers chosen,
as in Britain, from the party which commands a majority in the
elected House of Parliament. Appointments are formally made
by the Governor-General on the recommendation of the prime
minister ; by convention, representation is given in the cabinet,
as far as possible, to all the provinces. The Canadian cabinet
resembles the British cabinet in all essential particulars — the
exclusion of the Governor-General from its meetings, political
homogeneity, joint responsibility, responsibility to Parliament and
the ascendancy of the prime minister. In addition to their executive duties, the ministers, like their British counterparts, have
important work in connexion with legislation. They initiate most
of the important bills in the Legislature and supply effective
guidance and leadership to it.

---

[1] Robert MacGregor Dawson (Ed.), *Constitutional Issues in Canada
1900-1931* (Toronto, 1937), p. 65.
[2] Keith, *The Dominions as Sovereign States*, p. 214.

The Legislature

The Parliament of Canada consists of the Queen represented by the Governor-General, the Senate, and the House of Commons.

The Senate of Canada, like that of Italy, is a nominated body. It consists of 102 members nominated for life by the Governor-General on the advice of the cabinet. The 102 members are distributed as follows :— Ontario, 24 ; Quebec, 24 ; the Atlantic Provinces 30 ; [1] and the Western Provinces, 24. [2] The Governor-General may add [3] five or ten members (representing equally the five divisions of Canada) in order primarily to overcome deadlocks between the two chambers. It is noteworthy that, unlike the U.S.A. and Swiss upper Houses, the Canadian Senate does not accord equal representation to the component units of the federation. A senator must have attained the age of thirty years. He must be a Canadian citizen (natural-born or naturalized) and resident within the province for which he is appointed. Finally, he must possess land or tenements worth 4,000 dollars, and own property exceeding by the same amount his debts and liabilities. Appointments are, as a rule, made on purely party lines.

According to law, the Senate has equal powers with the lower House in ordinary laws, and somewhat inferior powers in regard to financial bills, these having to originate in the lower House. It may apparently amend and reject the latter class of bills. [4] The actual influence exercised by it naturally varies with the Government in power.

' The purely partisan character of the Senate has resulted in the rule that it accepts the legislation of the party without serious dissent, and that it attacks, when there is a change of regime, the legislation sent up to it with a vigour which dies away as the members, usually old, die off and are replaced by nominees of the new Government.' [5]

It is clear, moreover, that, being a nominated chamber, it lacks the authority which a popular chamber may claim ; indeed, it has been doubted [6] whether it commands even its own confidence !

---

[1] Nova Scotia, 10 ; New Brunswick, 10 ; Prince Edward Island, 4 ; Newfoundland, 6.

[2] Manitoba, Alberta, Saskatchewan and British Columbia, 6 each.

[3] If, on the recommendation of the Governor-General, the sovereign thinks fit to direct.

[4] See however W. P. M. Kennedy, *The Constitution of Canada*, p. 385 ; ' Theoretically it may reject a finance bill, but can make no amendments to it. '

[5] Keith, *The Dominions as Sovereign States*, p. 299.

[6] Laski, *A Grammar of Politics*, p. 329.

The lower House, the House of Commons, is composed of 264 elected members. Originally, the basis taken for computing the number of members was that the number of representatives of Quebec was fixed at 65 and that of every other province at ' such a number of members as will bear the same proportion to the number of its population (ascertained by the census) as the number 65 bears to the population of Quebec so ascertained. ' This basis was abolished in 1946. The present system is far too complex to be summarized,[1] but it resulted in the following distribution in the election of 1968:

Ontario	88
Quebec	74
British Columbia	23
Saskatchewan	13
Alberta	19
Manitoba	13
Nova Scotia	11
New Brunswick	10
Newfoundland	7
Prince Edward Island	4
Yukon Territory	1
North-West Territory	1

The right to vote is given to all Canadian citizens of British subjects of either sex who have attained the age of 21 years and have been resident in Canada for a year prior to the election. The Government is at present (1971) actively considering the proposal to lower the age of franchise to 18 years. They must vote in the polling division where they resided at the time the writs for the election were issued. Certain classes of citizens are disqualified for the franchise, such as judges, electoral returning officers, convicts, the insane, Doukhobors exempt from military service who are disqualified by a provincial law from voting in the province in question, and persons disqualified ' for corrupt and illegal practices '. The term of the House is five years, unless it is sooner dissolved by the Governor-General.

The Canadian House of Commons performs more or less the same functions as its British counterpart: it passes laws, controls finance, controls the Executive, gives expression to public grievances and needs, and serves as an arena wherein future leaders may distinguish themselves. It is (at any rate in theory) not so powerful as the English House in so far as it is limited by a written constitution; by the possibility that the laws passed by it may be declared *ultra vires*; and by matters reserved for the provinces, on which it cannot legislate.

---

[1] For details see R. M. Dawson, *The Government of Canada*, p. 365 and *The International Year Book and Statesmen's Who's Who*, 1972, p. 117.

The Judiciary

Power has been given to the Federal Government [1] to provide for the constitution, maintenance and organization of a general court of appeal for Canada, and for the establishment of any additional courts for the better administration of the laws of Canada. As it is, however, there are only two federal courts, the Supreme Court (established in 1875) and the court of exchequer and admiralty. All other courts in the land are provincial courts, which, however, may hear disputes relating to federal as well as provincial law.

Judges of the superior, district and country courts (with a few exceptions) are appointed by the Governor-General ; normally, they are selected from the bar of the province concerned. Their salaries, allowances and pensions are fixed and provided by the Parliament of Canada. The constitution also states that the judges of the superior courts shall hold office during good behaviour, but may be removed by the Governor-General on an address of the Senate and the House of Commons.

The Supreme Court of Canada is in some respects more powerful than the Supreme Court of the U.S.A., for it can hear appeals from provincial courts on purely provincial law. [2] But it is somewhat less powerful than that Court as its power to interpret the constitution is reduced by the fact that the Governor-General of Canada is vested with the power of disallowing provincial bills. [3]

Canada and the Commonwealth

The question must be discussed at this stage whether the fact that Canada is a member of the Commonwealth (she is described as a Dominion in Section 1 of the Statute of Westminster 1931) imposes any limitations on her independence, i.e. freedom of decision and action with respect to internal and external affairs. The answer is a clear ' no '. The Parliament of Canada is free to pass any laws she likes. Such laws cannot be declared *ultra vires* on account of repugnancy to laws passed by the British Parliament. Further, that Parliament may not pass laws applicable to Canada

[1] Section 101.

[2] Till 1933 appeals in criminal and civil cases could go to the Privy Council in London ; but since 1933 appeals to the Privy Council in criminal cases have not been permitted, nor in civil matters since 1949.

[3] It should be added that the Federal Government is unlikely to use the power of disallowance to disallow provincial legislation which the courts are likely to find *ultra vires.*

except with her consent. This legislative freedom is expressly recognized by the following clauses of the Study of Westminster.

2(1) The Colonial Laws Validity Act 1865 [1] should not apply to any law made after the commencement of this Act by the Parliament of a Dominion.

(2) No law and no provision of any law made after the commencement of this Act by the Parliament of a Dominion shall be void or inoperative on the ground that it is repugnant to the law of England, or to the provisions of any existing or future Act of the Parliament of the United Kingdom, or to any order, rule or regulation made under any such Act, and the powers of the Parliament of a Dominion shall include the power to repeal or amend any such Act, order, rule or regulation in so far as the same is part of the law of the Dominion.

(3) It is hereby declared and enacted that the Parliament of a Dominion has full power to make laws having extra-territorial operations.

(4) No Act of Parliament of the United Kingdom passed after the commencement of this Act should extend, or be deemed to extend, to a Dominion as a part of the law of that Dominion, unless it is expressly declared in that Act that Dominion has requested, and consented to, the enactment thereof.

Canada is also free to administer her own laws and have them interpreted by her courts without interference from, or being subject to, Britain.

There are some laws and conventions which appear to impose limitations on her internal sovereignty ; but they are not limitations, for she is at perfect liberty to abolish them if she chose. (i) The Governor-General of Canada is appointed and removed by the sovereign of Britain ; this is no restriction on Canada's sovereignty : The appointment is made by the Queen as Head of the State in Canada and not as Head of the State in Britain — when she ascended the throne in 1952, she was proclaimed in Canada as ' Elizabeth the Second, by the Grace of God, of Great Britain, Ireland and the British Dominions beyond the seas, Queen Defender of the Faith, Supreme Liege Lady in and over Canada ' — and, further, she appoints him on the advice of the Canadian Government. (ii) The Governor-General may reserve a Canadian bill for the consideration of Her Majesty [2], but both the reservation, and the decision as to its fate if reserved, must

---

[1] This Act provided that any colonial legislation which was repugnant to an imperial Act applicable to the Colony was to that extent void and inoperative.

[2] British North America Act 1867, sections 55 and 57.

be exercised in accordance with the advice of the Canadian. Government. It was placed on record at the Imperial Conference of 1930 that 'His Majesty's Government in the United Kingdom will not advise His Majesty the King to give the Governor-General any instructions to reserve Bills presented to him for assent.' (iii) The sovereign may disallow Canadian bills. Not only has disallowance been long a dead letter, but when the sovereign disallows a Canadian bill, she must disallow it on the advice of the Canadian Government. There is one seeming exception to this : The Colonial Stock Act of 1900 had provided that the British Treasury might lay down conditions under which Colonial stocks would be admitted as trustee securities in the United Kingdom. The third of these conditions laid down by the Treasury [1] was that the country concerned must place on record a formal expression of its opinion that legislation which appeared to the government of the United Kingdom to alter any of the provisions affecting such trustee stock to the injury of the stock holders, or to depart from the original contract, might properly be disallowed. This is intended to facilitate Canada's borrowing in the London market and is not a serious derogation of sovereignty. (iv) Canada has no power to amend her Constitution in certain matters (as has been discussed earlier) but this is because of the inability of the federation and the provinces to agree on a method of amending the Constitution without the intervention of the British Parliament. (v) The Sovereign has the prerogatives of mercy and of honour ; it is open to the Canadian Parliament to regulate or cancel them. (vi) From a strictly legal point of view, it may be argued that the imperial Parliament which removed the restrictions on Dominion legislation by passing the Statute of Westminster (being a sovereign body) is free to reimpose them ; the argument is purely academic.

External Relations

As in the sphere of internal affairs, so in the sphere of external relations, there are no legal restrictions on Canada's freedom. It is now settled doctrine that 'each Commonwealth Government is the final judge of what its policy in any matter should be, and of the extent to which it should cooperate with the other governments in the conduct of external affairs. This follows naturally from the fact that each Government is responsible to its Parliament for the policies that it pursues and for the manner in which it applies them.'

[1] K. C. Wheare, *The Constitutional Structure of the Commonwealth*, p. 38.

Canada is a member of the United Nations and is eligible for membership of its Security Council. She is represented in foreign states through her own ministers. In 1942 Canada signed an agreement with the U.S.S.R. providing for an exchange of consular representatives between the two countries. She can make such treaties as she likes with foreign states and have them signed by her own representatives ; she insisted on this right in 1923 in the matter of the Halibut Fishery Treaty with the U.S.A. She has the right to renounce obligations in respect of treaties to which she was not a party ; none of the Dominions, for instance, accepted the obligations imposed by the Locarno Pact of 1925 which had been negotiated and signed by Britain and in the negotiations leading to which the Dominions had not been parties.[1]

The most difficult question in respect of foreign policy is that of war and neutrality. Can Canada remain neutral in a war to which Britain is a party ? The question arises because

' It is legally impossible for Great Britain to be at war without the whole of the Empire, including the Dominions, being at war too, and it is legally impossible for any Dominion to be at war without Great Britain at war. It is only the King who can legally make a declaration of war and the King cannot be partly at war and partly at peace.'[2]

It is, however, agreed that no Dominion need take steps to aid the Commonwealth in any war which has not been brought about by its own action ; that the sovereign in committing a Dominion to a war must take its consent[3] ; and that provision must be made for associating the Dominions in the body which takes final decisions in the conduct of the war, so that they may be heard in the formulation and direction of policy.

§2 THE COMMONWEALTH OF AUSTRALIA

Australia is a federal State composed of six states. The present constitution is based primarily on the Commonwealth of Australia Constitution Act, passed by the British Parliament in 1900.

---

[1] *The British Empire*, p. 217.

[2] Salant, *An Outline of the Constitutional Laws of the British Empire*, p. 31.

[3] It is significant that, at the outbreak of war in 1939, the South African Parliament discussed the question of remaining neutral, though the resolution in favour of neutrality was defeated. Eire remained neutral, and, what is more, her neutrality was recognized by both Britain and Germany. These points suggest the thought that neutrality is legally possible.

Prior to the passing of that Act, Australia consisted of six provinces, New South Wales, Tasmania, Victoria, Queensland, South Australia and Western Australia, each with its own government and following its own policy in regard to economic and political matters. The absence of a common fiscal policy led to grave inconveniences. This, together with the need for a common defence policy, gave rise in the latter half of the nineteenth century to a movement in favour of the establishment of a common government, and led to the passing of the Commonwealth of Australia Act.[1]

This constitution is, as in other federal States, a rigid one. An amendment passed by an absolute majority of each House of Parliament must be submitted in each state to the electors qualified to vote for the election of members to the House of Representatives.[2] (If any such law is passed by one House and rejected by the other and is passed a second time by the initiating House after an interval of three months, the Governor-General *may* refer the law to the electors of the House of Representatives.) If then it is accepted by a majority of the electors in a majority of states and by a majority of the total number of voters, it becomes law. Amendments which propose to diminish the proportionate representation of any state in either House of Parliament or the minimum number of representatives of a state in the House of Representatives, or to alter the territorial limits of any state, shall not, however, become law unless the majority of the electors voting in that state approve them.

The principle followed in Australia in respect of the division of powers between the Federal Government and the states resembles in the main that followed in Switzerland and the U.S.A. (*i*) The powers of the Federal Government are enumerated (some being exclusively federal and others concurrent) ; (*ii*) the residue is left with the states ; and (*iii*) there are some prohibitions on the Federal Government and on the states.

The *exclusive* powers of the Federal Government include the power ' to make laws for the peace, order, and good government of the Commonwealth with respect to the seat of government '. Other matters declared to be exclusively federal are naval and military affairs, and coinage.[3] The *concurrent* subjects include foreign and inter-state trade ; postal, telegraphic, telephonic, and other like services ; census and statistics ; banking and insurance,

---

[1] The Act came into effect from 1 January 1901.
[2] The lower House of the Commonwealth Parliament.
[3] Sections 114 and 115.

other than state banking and state insurance ; weights and measures ; bills of exchange ; copyrights ; naturalization ; marriage and divorce ; immigration and emigration ; social services ; and conciliation and arbitration for the prevention and settlement of industrial disputes extending beyond the limits of any one state. As elsewhere, when any law of a state is inconsistent with any law of the Commonwealth on a concurrent subject, the latter prevails.

Examples of prohibitions on the Commonwealth are that it shall not, by any law or regulation of trade, commerce, or revenue give preference to one state over another ; it shall not abridge the right of a state or its residents to the reasonable use of the waters of its rivers for conservation or irrigation. Prohibitions on the states include the issuing of coinage and the raising of military or naval forces.

The Executive

The executive government is carried on in the name of the Queen. The functions of the Crown are performed, as in Canada, partly by the Queen herself and partly by the Governor-General, both acting on the advice of ministers responsible to the Australian Parliament.

The Governor-General occupies the same position and exercises more or less the same powers as his counterpart in Canada, the only differences in law being the following : The appointment and dismissal of all officers of the executive government (except the ministers) in Australia are vested in the Governor-General in Council, whereas in Canada they are vested in the Governor-General. The Governor-General of Australia has no power to appoint the Governors of the states, their appointment being vested in the Queen. Finally, he has no power to veto the laws passed by the Legislatures of the states.

The ministry resembles in all essentials that of Canada. Ministers are styled Ministers of State and appointed to the Federal Executive Council, which, however, may contain other Executive Councillors called honorary ministers. [1]

The Legislature

The Parliament of the Commonwealth consists of the Queen represented by the Governor-General, the Senate, and the House of Representatives.

[1] E. Salant, *An Outline of the Constitutional Laws of the British Empire*, p. 49.

The Senate is constituted, as in the U.S.A. and Switzerland, on a truly federal basis. It consists of 60 members, ten from each component state. Members are elected (on the basis of universal suffrage [1]) by the whole of each state voting as an undivided constituency on the system of preferential voting.[2] Any person over the age of twenty-one, if a natural-born subject or naturalized for at least five years, who has resided within the Commonwealth for three years, is eligible for election. The term of the Senate is six years, one-half retiring every three years.[3]

It has equal powers with the House of Representatives except with regard to money bills, which may originate only in the latter body. The Senate also has no power to amend a money bill; it may, however, reject it, or, if unwilling to take this extreme step which may provoke a first-class political crisis, return it to the House of Representatives with suggestions of amendment for its consideration. To overcome deadlocks between the two Houses it is provided [4] that if a bill is rejected twice (with an interval of three months) by the Senate, the Governor-General may dissolve both the Houses simultaneously; and if the newly elected Houses also disagree, the bill may be laid before a joint session; an absolute majority of the total number of both Houses decides the issue. Though the law is silent on the relative powers of the Senate and the House of Representatives in respect of the control of the Executive, it has been well established by usage that the ministry is responsible to the lower House; the Senate does not attempt to turn it out.

In estimating the utility of the Senate in the constitution from its record of work, it is sufficient to say that it has not fulfilled the expectations of its founders. It was intended to be a body of talented legislators which could not only revise the laws passed by the lower House, but which might, on acount of its federal basis, guard the rights of the smaller states against invasion by the larger. But it has not been able to attract talent, the better sort of politician preferring the more powerful lower House; and state-loyalties have rarely influenced its deliberations or divisions. Moreover, up to 1919 it hardly served as a moderating influence

---

[1] There is no uniform franchise law for the whole Commonwealth; but the existing provisions in practice amount to universal suffrage with some exceptions.

[2] A system of voting in which the voter is allowed to mark his preferences for candidates; see below, ch. xxx, for an explanation.

[3] In case of prolonged disagreement with the House of Representatives, it, together with the House of Representatives, may be dissolved, and an entirely new Senate may be elected.

[4] This provision has been used only once, in 1914.

in ordinary legislation, the Labour Party having had considerable strength in it. Since that date it has been more active in this direction.

The House of Representatives consists of 124 elected members,[1] the number of seats being allocated to the various states periodically on the basis of population. The constitutional provisions are that the number of members shall be as nearly as practicable twice the number of senators, and no state may have less than five. The total number is distributed, for the most part, in single-member constituencies. The rules governing the qualifications of the voters and the members are as for the Senate. Compulsory voting was introduced in 1925. The term is three years, unless the House is dissolved earlier by the Governor-General.

Its functions, broadly speaking, correspond to those of the House of Commons in Britain, with three important restrictions. (*i*) Australia has a written constitution, which is obviously a limitation on its powers. (*ii*) In Australia, a federal State, the House can consider legislation only in respect of the subjects allotted to the Commonwealth whether exclusively to itself or concurrently with the states. (*iii*) Its powers in respect of constitutional amendment are limited. It is also limited, more than the House of Commons is, by the upper Chamber, which has greater powers as compared with the House of Lords.

The Judiciary

The judicial power of the Commonwealth is vested in the High Court of Australia and in such other federal courts as the Parliament creates or invests with federal jurisdiction. Judges are appointed by the Governor-General in Council. Their salaries are fixed and may not be diminished during their continuance in office. They may be removed from office on the ground of proved misbehaviour or incapacity, but even then only on an address to the Governor-General from both Houses of Parliament in the same session.

The High Court, in the main, occupies the same position in Australia as a guardian of the constitution as the Supreme Court does in the U.S.A. There are two differences. (*i*) Appeals may

---

[1] One member, representing the Northern Territory, has no vote except on certain specified matters; in 1948, representation of the Australian Capital territory was provided for under similar conditions. See Keith, *The Dominions as Sovereign States*, p. 288 and n. 1; and *The Statesman's Year-Book, 1963*, p. 310.

be carried (subject to specified conditions [1]) from its decisions
to the Judicial Committee of the Privy Council, whereas there is
no appeal from the decisions of the Supreme Court of the U.S.A.
(*ii*) The High Court may hear appeals from the Supreme Courts
of the states on purely state law ; the Supreme Court of the U.S.A.
cannot entertain such appeals.

Comparison with Canada

This survey leaves little doubt that Australia is more truly
federal than Canada. The residuary powers here are with the
units, not with the Centre ; the Governors of states are not
appointed by the Governor-General of the Commonwealth ; the
laws passed by states cannot be vetoed by the Governor-General ;
the upper House of the Legislature has a more truly federal
basis with equality of representation for the units, and in practice
enjoys greater powers than the Senate of Canada ; the Judiciary is
more truly federal in the sense that it has larger powers of interpretation than its Canadian counterpart ; and, lastly, the states
have a definite place given to them in the amendment of the
constitution the consent of a majority of states being required
for such amendment.

The explanation of this difference is twofold. (*i*) Canada was
originally a unitary State, converted into a federation by the
component provinces being made autonomous units of the new
federation, and the federal constitution was ' to a great extent
drafted by men who were in favour of a legislative union '.[2] The
Australian federation was formed by the union of originally
independent units and was drafted by men who believed as much
in ' state rights' as in the utility of a common government.
(*ii*) The atmosphere in which the Canadian federal scheme was
mooted (1864-7) was such as to incline its authors towards
centralization. The civil war in America (1861-5) was fresh
in the minds of all and had made many doubt the wisdom of
emphasizing ' state rights ' ; and it was thought necessary, in order
to prevent the disruption of the State, to strengthen the Centre
as against the provinces.

Australia and the Commonwealth

What we have said earlier on Canada and the Commonwealth
applies to Australia as well ; there is no need to repeat the details.

---

[1] Section 74. One of the conditions is that the High Court has the right
to permit or refuse to permit appeals in cases involving the interpretation
of the constitution.
[2] H. E. Egerton, *Federations and Unions within the British Empire*, p. 39.

Like Canada, Australia is also mentioned in the Statute of Westminster (1931) as a Dominion; like Canada, Australia has complete freedom of decision and action with respect to internal and external affairs. Like Canada, Australia has the Queen of Britain as the head of the State. The proclamation issued on 29 May 1953 gives the following title :

Elizabeth the Second, by the Grace of God, of the United Kingdom, Australia and Her other Realms and Territories, Queen, Head of the Commonwealth, Defender of the Faith.

There is a Governor-General, as we have noted earlier, appointed by the Queen on the advice of the Australian Government ; he has the power of reservation at his discretion, in particular the Australian Constitution provides that Bills must be reserved which limit the matters on which the judicial committee of the Privy Council may be asked to grant special leave to appeal from the High Court of Australia. The Queen has the power of disallowance. Neither the power of reservation nor of disallowance is a restriction, as we have seen in respect of Canada, on account of the legislative freedom given to the Australian Parliament by the Statute of Westminster. The same is true of other apparent limitations.

What we have said earlier in respect of Canada's freedom in external affairs applies equally to Australia.

SELECT BIBLIOGRAPHY

A. BRADY, *Democracy in the Dominions*: a Comparative Study in Institutions, Oxford, 2nd ed., 1952

J. BRYCE, *Modern Democracies*, Vol. I, ch. xxxiii to xxxvii and Vol. II, ch. xlvi to lii, Macmillan, 1923

R. M. DAWSON, *The Government of Canada*, revised by Norman Ward, Toronto, 4th ed., 1963

H. E. EGERTON, *Federations and Unions within the British Empire*, Oxford, 2nd ed., 1924

S. ENCEL, *Cabinet Government in Australia*, Melbourne, 1962

J. E. S. FAWCETT, *The British Commonwealth in International Law*, Stevens, 1963

A. B. KEITH, *The Constitutional Law of the British Dominions*, Macmillan, 1933

——, *The Dominions as Sovereign States*, Macmillan, 1938

W. P. M. KENNEDY, *The Constitution of Canada*, Oxford, 2nd ed., 1938

D. KERR, *The Law of the Australian Constitution*, The Law Book Co. of Australasia, Sydney, 1925

G. S. KNOWLES, *The Commonwealth of Australia Constitution Act* (as altered to 1 July 1936), The Government Printer, Canberra, 1936

J. R. MALLORY, *Structure of Canadian Government*, Macmillan, Toronto, 1971

J. D. B. MILLER, *Australian Government and Politics* : An Introductory Survey, Duckworth, 1954

G. V. PORTUS (Editor), *Studies in the Australian Constitution*, Angus and Robertson, 1933

V. R. RIDDELL, *The Constitution of Canada in its Historical and Practical Working*, Oxford, 1917

E. SALANT, *An Outline of the Constitutional Laws of the British Empire*, Sweet and Maxwell, 1934

The British Empire : A Report on its Structure and Problems, by a Study Group of Members of the Royal Institute of International Affairs, Oxford, 1938

The Constitutions of all Countries, Vol. I, *The British Empire*, H. M. Stationery Office, 1938

P. G. WALKER, *The Commonwealth*, Secker & Warburg, 1962

K. C. WHEARE, *The Statute of Westminster and Dominion Status*, Oxford, 5th ed., 1953

——, *The Constitutional Structure of the Commonwealth*, Oxford, 1961

CHAPTER XX

SWITZERLAND

§1 INTRODUCTORY

SWITZERLAND is a small federal State of 22 cantons [1] with about four million people. Her political institutions deserve study because they have 'demonstrated the possibility of close cooperation between people who at one time were independent of each other politically and who today are widely divided by language and religion'. About 71 per cent speak German, 21 per cent French, and about 6 per cent Italian. By religion about 57 per cent are Protestant, nearly 41 per cent Catholic, and 0.5 per cent Jews. The Swiss system of government is a 'real democracy in operation', to use Bonjour's significant phrase ; Switzerland has a greater variety of institutions based on democratic principles than any other country.

The modern history of Switzerland begins with its recognition as an independent and sovereign State by the Treaty of Westphalia (1648). At that time, and for two centuries later, it was a confederation, a league of States, with no strong central authority. A civil war which broke out in 1848 between the Catholic and Protestant cantons induced the Swiss people to transform their confederation into a strong federation, though they still call their State 'the Swiss Confederation'. The constitution of 1848 was revised in 1874, and the constitution of that year, modified later in some respects, is the one under which Switzerland is governed today.

The constitution is a rigid one but there are two methods of amending it.[2]

(*i*) If both Houses of the Legislature agree on a particular amendment, it must be submitted to the voters, and becomes law

---

[1] Or more correctly 19 cantons and 6 half-cantons. 'Each of the half-cantons has a government of its own as complete as that of any of the whole cantons. It counts for only half as much as a whole canton, however, in a constitutional referendum, and sends but one representative to the upper House of the Federal Legislature, whereas each of the whole cantons sends two.' (R. C. Brooks, *Government and Politics of Switzerland*, p. 53.)

[2] Chapter iii of the constitution (Articles 118-23).

if approved not only by a majority of the citizens voting but also by a majority of the cantons, i.e. by a majority of voters in a majority of cantons. This method is known as the obligatory referendum.

(*ii*) If 50,000 citizens desire a certain amendment, they may send up the proposal in general terms, or in the form of a bill complete in all details, by means of an initiative petition.

When an initiative demand is couched in general terms (unformulated initiative), the Federal Assembly, if it approves of it, will proceed to undertake the revision in the sense indicated in the demand, and will submit it for adoption or rejection by the people and the cantons. If, on the contrary, it does not approve, the question whether there shall be a revision or not must be submitted to the vote of the people. If a majority of the Swiss citizens taking part in the vote pronounce in the affirmative, the Federal Assembly will proceed to undertake the revision in conformity with the decision of the people.

When a demand is presented in the form of a bill complete in all details (the formulated initiative), the Federal Authority must submit it for the approval of the people and the cantons. If the Federal Assembly does not approve of it, however, it may frame a bill of its own or recommend to the people the rejection of the bill proposed, and submit to them its own bill, or proposal for rejection, at the same time as the bill presented by popular initiative.

To become law the bill must be accepted by a majority of voters and a majority of cantons.

§2 DIVISION OF POWERS

The division of powers in Switzerland between the Centre and the units resembles that in the U.S.A. in its essential feature : the powers not vested in the Centre and not prohibited to the units belong to the units. 'The cantons are sovereign so far as their sovereignty is not limited by the Federal Constitution ; and, as such, they exercise all the rights which are not delegated to the Federal Power.' [1]

The federal powers are partly exclusive and partly concurrent. Among the former are the right to declare war and conclude peace, and to make alliances and treaties with foreign States (subject to the proviso that the cantons retain the right to conclude treaties with foreign States in respect of matters of public

---

[1] Article 3 of the constitution.

economy and police and border relations) ; military instruction
and the arming of troops ; the policing of embankments and
forests ; the utilization of water-power ; aerial navigation ; customs
duties ; posts and telegraphs ; roads and bridges in the maintenance of which the ' Confederation ' is concerned ; railways ; coinage ; issuing bank-notes and other fiduciary money ; weights and
measures ; and the manufacture and sale of gunpowder. Among
the powers which the Federal Authority may exercise in common
with the cantons are : civil and criminal law ; the regulation of
fishing and hunting ; the regulation of industry and insurance ; the
control of the press ; and the encouragement of education. ' When
the Federal Government exercises a concurrent power, its statutes
prevail over those of a canton.'

There are some prohibitions on the Federal Authority as well
as on the cantons, e.g. no person may be compelled to become a
member of any religious association, submit to any religious instruction, perform any act of religion, or incur any penalties of
any kind whatsoever by reason of his religious opinions ; no
impediment to marriage may be based upon grounds of religious
belief, the poverty of either party, their conduct, or any other consideration of a police nature ; the sentence of death may not be
pronounced for any political offence. Examples of prohibitions
imposed on the cantons alone are that no canton may expel from
its territory any citizen of the cantons nor deprive him of his rights
as a native or burgher ; subject to any stamp duty or registration
duty documents which are liable to Federal stamp duty or which
have been exempted therefrom ; attack other cantons in the event
of difference arising between it and them. Among other noteworthy
restrictions are (*i*) cantons must submit all new constitutions
or modifications to existing constitutions, to the federal government for its approval, (*ii*) all separate alliances and treaties of a
political character between cantons are forbidden and (*iii*) no
canton or half-canton may without the permission of the federal
government, maintain a standing force of more than 300 troops.

While the division of powers in Switzerland is thus similar
to that in the U.S.A. in its essential features, it differs in three
respects. *First*, the sphere of the Federal Authority and that of
the cantons are not, as they are in the United States, separated
into water-tight compartments, especially in the field of administration. There are certain departments of the administration which
have been entirely centralized and in which the Federal Authority enjoys the sole control of officials ; the collection of customs
duties, the management of the telegraphs, the telephone service,

and the post offices are examples. In others — such as civil law
— the Federal Authority legislates, but the cantons organize the
courts, determine legal procedure and appoint judges. For the
execution of many Federal laws, the Federal Authority makes use
of the administrative machinery of the cantons, which is to this
extent placed in a subordinate position in relation to that Autho-
r·*y. Such is the case, for instance, in the execution of military laws.
Second, the Federal Government in Switzerland is vested with
greater powers than that in the U.S.A. Not only has it a larger
number of legislative powers than the latter, it has wider powers
in respect of the guarantee of cantonal constitutions, the preservation of the rights of the people, and the like. Thus the constitution provides that the ' Confederation ' guarantees to the cantons
their territory, their sovereignty within specified limits, their
constitutions, the liberties and rights of their people, the constitutional rights of the citizens, and the rights and powers conferred
by the people on the authorities. As a condition of the guarantee,
the Federal Authority may demand that the cantonal constitutions
contain no provisions contrary to those of the Federal constitution, that they assure the exercise of political rights according to
republican — representative or democratic — forms of government, and that they have been accepted by, and are susceptible
to amendment at the demand of, the absolute majority of the
people. Further, in case of differences arising between cantons,
the cantons must submit to the decision of the Federal Authority ; in case of disturbances within the canton, the Government
of the canton has to notify the Federal Executive, which is authorized to take the necessary steps to restore order. And *third,* the
cantons in Switzerland do not enjoy the same security against
invasion of their powers by the Federal Legislature as the states
in the U.S.A. because the Swiss Federal Court has no power,
unlike its counterpart in the U.S.A., to declare any Federal law
unconstitutional.

§3 THE EXECUTIVE, THE LEGISLATURE
AND THE JUDICIARY

The Executive

The supreme executive power of the Federation is vested in a
Federal Council composed of seven members elected for four
years by the two chambers of the Federal Assembly (the Federal
Legislature) in joint session. The constitution does not require
that the members should be chosen from the Assembly, any Swiss

citizen who is entitled to vote being eligible for the Federal Council ; in practice, the Assembly chooses the Federal Councillors from its own ranks. According to constitutional law, no two members of the Federal Council can be chosen from the same canton ; and, according to convention, not more than five are chosen from the German-speaking cantons.

The Federal Assembly annually elects the President and the Vice-President of the Federal Council. It is provided in the constitution that the President shall not be elected President or Vice-President for the ensuing year ; and by custom the Vice-President one year is always elected President in the subsequent year, so that the office passes by rotation among the members of the Council. During his year of office, the President of the Council is President of the Swiss Confederation. He has, however, no more power than the other councillors, and is not more responsible than they are for the course of the Government. 'He is simply the chairman of the executive committee of the nation, and as such he tries to keep himself informed of what his colleagues are doing, and performs the ceremonial duties of the titular head of the State.' [1]

The powers of the Federal Council may be described under three heads : executive, legislative and judicial. As head of the administration it ensures the observance of federal laws and the maintenance of peace and order ; has general charge of foreign affairs and 'ensures the external safety of Switzerland and the maintenance of its independence and neutrality' ; administers the finances of the federation, prepares the budget and submits accounts of receipts and expenditure ; makes such appointments as are not entrusted to the Federal Assembly, Federal Tribunal, or other authority ; supervises the conduct of business by all federal employees ; and enforces the guarantee of the cantonal constitutions.

Its members have the right to speak, but not to vote, in both Houses of the Federal Assembly, and also the right to table motions on the subject under consideration. They are subject to interpellation in either House. The Federal Council has the right of introducing bills into the Federal Assembly. 'As a matter of fact most of the important measures of federal legislation, including the budget, are drawn up by the Federal Council, either upon its own motion or upon request by the Houses.'

Its judicial duties relate to some cases arising out of administrative law. Originally it served as the chief administrative court

[1] L. Lowell, *Greater European Government*, p. 319.

of the State ; but, latterly, much of its administrative jurisdiction has been transferred to the Federal Court.

The Swiss Executive is remarkable for three features. *First,* it is a collegiate, a plural, executive. It has no prime minister. The President does not select his colleagues, and has no authority over them. *Second,* it is at once a parliamentary and a non-parliamentary Executive. It is parliamentary in so far as (*i*) its members are chosen by, and in practice from, the Legislature ; (*ii*) its members have the right of being present in the Legislature, taking part in its discussions and introducing bills ; (*iii*) it carries out the will of the Legislature. It is worthy of note that the responsibility of the Executive to the Legislature is enforced in different ways in Switzerland and in Britain. In Britain, the cabinet resigns if a bill introduced by it is defeated in Parliament, or if a bill introduced by a private member is passed by Parliament against its opposition. In Switzerland, members of the Federal Council are not expected to resign because a bill introduced by them, however important it may be, has failed of passage in the Federal Assembly.[1] They simply drop the matter, or remodel the bill to meet the criticism which has caused its defeat. It is a non-parliamentary Executive because (*i*) its members are not members of the Legislature ; indeed, when chosen Federal Councillors they resign their seats in the Federal Assembly and (*ii*) their term of office is fixed ; the Federal Assembly has no power to dismiss them out of hand. The Swiss Executive, therefore, combines the merits of both types of Executive, viz. responsibility and stability. *Third,* it is not based upon a party majority in the legislative bodies ;[2] its members ' are elected not only from different party groups but from party groups fundamentally opposed to each other '. Its non-partisan character makes it possible for the Council to be virtually a permanent body. While it is elected afresh every four years the old members are often re-elected it they are willing to serve. Some members of the Council have held office as long as thirty-two years.[3] If it be asked, how they are able to work together without much friction, the explanation lies in the political sense of the Swiss, in their ability to understand and practise compromise in politics.

The Swiss Executive has indeed earned the admiration of many competent observers. The opinion of Bryce [4] is typical.

---

[1] Brooks, op. cit., p. 127.
[2] ibid., p. 127.   [3] ibid., p. 106.
[4] *Modern Democracies,* Vol. I, pp. 398-9.

' It provides ', says he, ' a body which is able not only to influence and advise the ruling Assembly without lessening its responsibility to the citizens, but which, because it is non-partisan, can mediate, should need arise, between contending parties, adjusting difficulties and arranging compromises in a spirit of conciliation. It enables proved administrative talent to be kept in the service of the nation, irrespective of the personal opinions of the Councillors upon the particular issues which may for the moment divide parties ... It secures continuity in policy and permits traditions to be formed.'

We may add that the Council's small size enables it to act quickly and efficiently; besides, most members are chosen originally from the leadership of their parties in parliament thus reflecting long terms of service at various levels of government and experience in assuming responsibility.

The Legislature

The Federal Assembly is a bicameral body, composed of the Council of States (the upper Chamber) and the National Council (the lower Chamber).

The Council of States is composed of 44 members, two from each full canton and one from each half-canton. The method of choice and the term of office of the members are decided by the cantons. As a matter of fact, in all but four cantons, the members are elected by the people ; in the exceptional four cantons they are elected by the cantonal Legislatures. Their terms of office are four years in eighteen and a half cantons, three in three, and one in one.[1] The membership of the Council of States is usually quite stable, as most deputies are re-elected for as long as they wish to serve. According to competent observers,[2] the calibre of the individual deputy is also high. Almost half of the membership of the Council of States in 1960 were recipients of doctorates.

The National Council consists of 196[3] members, elected for four years by proportional representation.   Every lay Swiss citizen who has reached the age of twenty years, and who is not excluded from the rights of active citizenship by the laws of the canton in which he is domiciled, has the right to take part in

[1] G. A. Codding, *The Federal Government of Switzerland,* p. 72.
[2] ibid., p. 73.
[3] ibid., p. 75 ; the maximum is 200.
[4] There are some cantons which return only one member each ; in these there is, of course, no proportional representation.

elections. Each canton elects a member for every twenty-four thousand inhabitants[1]; but no canton, however small its population, is without at least one representative. Every Swiss citizen entitled to vote is eligible for membership of the National Council.

Until 1971 women were denied the right to vote at federal elections. This disability was removed after a Government-sponsored amendment of the Federal Constitution was accepted by the male electorate of Switzerland on 7 February 1971. The woman suffrage movement had been active in Switzerland for many years. On the federal level, two motions introduced into the legislature in 1918 to grant women the same civic rights as men were ignored. ' Although the Federal Council accepted a postulate in December, 1945, calling for a partial revision of the Constitution "in order to express publicly the confidence we have in our Swiss Women", the Council of States refused, in 1951, to permit the Federal Council to draw up a constitutional amendment for submission to the people.'[2] On 13 June 1958, however, the Swiss Federal legislature agreed that it was desirable to grant political rights to women; and on 1 February 1959 a constitutional amendment to give the voting right to the women was submitted to the male electorate. The proposal was turned down. At the cantonal level there was more success for the movement. In 1959 by referenda, two cantons, Varid and Neuchatel, agreed to give women the right to vote, and in 1960 Geneva followed suit.[3]

This disability of women had led one writer to remark, ' Switzerland can be labelled as one of the least democratic of modern democratic systems.'[4] With the final success of the feminist movement, however, this one blot on the democratic character of the Swiss Constitution has been removed.

The two Chambers have absolutely equal powers, at any rate in theory. No measure can be enacted which has not been approved by both. This is a unique feature. The two Houses have managed to work together without excessive friction. In fact seldom does one House seriously attempt to overthrow the decisions of the other on matters of national importance.

The constitution states explicitly that, subject to the rights reserved to the people and to the cantons, the supreme power of

---

[1] A fraction of this number greater than 12,000 is counted as 24,000.
[2] G. A. Codding, *The Federal Government of Switzerland*, p. 58.
[3] ibid., p. 59.
[4] ibid., p. 155.

the Confederation shall be exercised by the Federal Assembly. This is a significant fact ; it means that the Legislature is supreme so long as it retains the confidence of the people. Its decisions are not subject to any executive or judicial veto. It passes laws on federal matters and revises the constitution (subject to the powers reserved to the people). Its consent is necessary for treaties with foreign States, for the declaration of war and the conclusion of peace. The enactment of the annual budget, the approval of State accounts and decrees authorizing loans are included among its powers. It is vested with a general supervision of federal administration and of the Federal Court. It decides conflicts of jurisdiction between the federal authorities. Finally, it elects the Federal Council, the Federal Tribunal, the Chancellor, and the Commander-in-Chief of the federal army. In respect of other offices also, the Legislature may be vested by federal legislation with the right of election or confirmation.

The two chambers meet separately for all purposes except for electing the officers mentioned, exercising the right of pardon, and pronouncing on conflicts of jurisdiction when they meet in joint session.

The working of the constitution during the last fifty years has led authorities [1] to conclude that the Swiss Parliament as a body does not enjoy the prestige that the framers of the Constitution of 1848 thought it should have. The reasons are two-fold. (*i*) The Swiss legislature has to work with the knowledge that almost any fundamental law that it passes may be subject to a legislative referendum (explained in the next section). This naturally creates an atmosphere of doubt or indecision. (*ii*) The federal executive has risen in importance. ' Consequently,' according to Codding, ' the legislature has been reduced to a certain extent to the position of an advisory body with the electorate exercising the real decision-making power.'

The Judiciary

The constitution provides for the establishment of a Federal Tribunal, the *Bundesgericht,* for the administration of justice in federal matters. Judges are elected by the Federal Assembly. Any Swiss citizen eligible for election to the National Council may be elected a member of the tribunal, provided he is not a member of the Legislature or holder of any other office simultaneously. The number of judges and the organization of the court

[1] G. A. Codding, op. cit., p. 84.

are determined by law. At present there are 26 judges and 12 alternates. Their term of office is six years ; by custom the members of the tribunal are re-elected as long as they care to serve. The jurisdiction of the tribunal covers all civil suits between the Confederation and the cantons or between the cantons themselves. It also covers all suits brought by an individual or corporation against the Confederation, and suits between a canton and an individual or corporation, if either party demands it and if the matter in dispute reaches the degree of importance to be prescribed by federal legislation. The Federal Assembly also has power to enlarge the jurisdiction of the tribunal ; this power has been used so freely by the Assembly that the Tribunal has now a large appellate jurisdiction in civil suits brought up from cantonal courts. Finally, it now functions also as an administrative court.

The Swiss Federal Tribunal is, however, less powerful than the Supreme Court of the U.S.A. because it has no power to declare federal laws unconstitutional. The constitution expressly says [1] that the Federal Tribunal shall administer laws passed by the Federal Assembly and such decrees of that Assembly as are of general application. Clearly, this means that the cantons have no safeguard against encroachment on their powers by the Federal Government. The danger is lessened by the fact that the methods of popular legislation prevalent in Switzerland provide ample facilities for a majority of the cantons to prevent a federal law from coming into effect.

§4 THE REFERENDUM AND THE INITIATIVE

Of the many democratic institutions in Switzerland, the one that most deserves study is the popular voting upon laws by means of the referendum and the initiative. The referendum consists of the submission to the people, for approval or rejection, of a law passed by the Legislature. The initiative is the right of private citizens to bring forward a proposal of a constitutional or legislative character for the decision of the whole people.

The referendum is of two kinds, compulsory and optional. It is compulsory when every law passed by the Legislature must be submitted for the approval of the people ; optional when a bill passed by the Legislature need be referred to the people only on demand by a prescribed number of people. In the Federation, the referendum, we have seen, is compulsory in respect of constitutional laws. It is optional in respect of ordinary laws : ' federal

[1] Article 113.

laws are submitted for acceptance or rejection by the people if a demand be made by 30,000 ... citizens or by eight cantons. Federal decrees which are of *general effect* and *are not urgent* are likewise submitted on demands.' [1] The interpretation of what is of a general nature and what is urgent is left to the Legislature. The optional referendum also exists in respect of treaties. 'International treaties concluded for an unlimited duration or for more than fifteen years shall also be submitted to the people for acceptance or rejection if demanded by 30,000 Swiss citizens entitled to vote or eight cantons '. This was used as late as 1958 when the citizens approved an Italian treaty relating to the use of part of the Swiss National Park for a hydro-electric project. In the cantons, the compulsory form of referendum has been gradually prevailing over the optional. It is in use in all the cantons for amendments to the constitution and in several for the adoption of ordinary laws as well. The referendum (whether compulsory or optional) is used in all cantons, except one, for the adoption of ordinary laws.

The initative, as has been noted earlier, is in use in the Federation for constitutional laws in two forms, the formulated and the unformulated ; it is not used in the Federation is respect of ordinary laws. It is in use in all cantons, for constitutional laws and for ordinary legislation. [2]

The machinery of the referendum and the initiative in Switzerland is roughly as follows. In the case of the compulsory referendum, the procedure is simple. Once or twice a year, sometimes more, the people are called upon to vote by secret ballot in their communes upon the proposals adopted in the interval by the Federal Assembly or the cantonal Legislature. With the optional referendum some preliminary formalities are necessary. Within a period of from one to twelve months (90 days in respect of Federal laws) citizens who desire the rejection of a law must collect the number of signatures required by law (in some cantons as few as 500, in the Federation as many as 30,000). The date for the popular voting is then fixed, normally allowing a sufficient interval to permit the supporters and opponents of the proposals under reference to place their arguments before the people. If the vote is against it, the matter is referred by the Executive to the Legislature. This body, after examining the correctness of the returns, passes a resolution declaring its act to be void. The

[1] Article 89 ; italics ours.
[2] G. A. Codding, *The Federal Government of Switzerland*, p. 67 : ' All cantons have provisions in their constitutions for the popular initiative of laws.'

procedure for the initiative petition is much the same as for the optional referendum, except that here the signatures are obtained for a new law, not for cancelling a law passed by the Legislature. Invariably, too, opportunity is afforded to the Legislature to express its opinion on the proposed law, and to suggest counter-proposals, if it so desires.

If we take into account the referendum and the initiative relating to federal matters only, from 1848 to 1960 the Swiss people were called to the polls some two hundred times to express their opinion on some piece of constitutional or ordinary legislation : that is, an average of about 1.7 times a year.[1] In cantonal matters, these methods have been used oftener. The experience of their working shows[2] that, in general, (i) there has been an increasing use of the institutions of direct democracy : the average number of popular votes between 1848 and 1874 was 0.4 times a year, whereas since 1935, it increased to 2.8 times a year. (ii) The degree of participation naturally varies according to the interest of the electorate in the issue before them. Codding reckons that during 1950 to 1960 the average turnout was 50.4 per cent, rising to a maximum of 66·7 per cent on the referendum relating to the right of women to vote. (iii) Proposals made under the initiative are less accepted than those emanating from the Legislature. Almost 90 per cent of all such proposals have been turned down, whereas about 67 per cent of all legislative proposals have been accepted in referendum. (iv) The proportion of the people who vote at a referendum is less than that for ordinary elections, suggesting that people are more willing and qualified to choose between men than between laws. Finally (vi) the people show a tendency to reject radical measures ; a good example is the rejection in 1922 of an initiative proposal to impose a special tax on property in excess of 80,000 francs.[3]

Finally, from all accounts, it is clear that the referendum and the initiative have come to stay in Switzerland, the Swiss being on the whole satisfied with their experiments in direct democracy. Defects indeed there are : occasionally, influenced by local rivalries, the people use the referendum and the initiative as instruments of a narrow conservatism or demagogy. But, nevertheless, on the whole they are valued, particularly as useful agencies of civic education and as the surest methods of discovering the real wishes of the people ; they are excellent barometers of the political

[1] G. A. Codding, op. cit., p. 65.
[2] See Rappard, op. cit., p. 71 ff. and G. A. Codding, op. cit., p. 65 ff.
[3] *American Political Science Review*, 1923, p. 445.

atmosphere. Foreign students of the Swiss constitution also agree
that the methods of popular legislation have worked successfully in
Switzerland, the Swiss people being well qualified by intelligence
and knowledge of public affairs, their non-partisan and independent spirit and their conservative nature, to profit by them.[1]
It is indeed the excellence of individual character that has made
Switzerland the envy and pattern of modern domocracies.

' Survey the countries of the world,' writes Dubs ; [2] ' you may
find elsewhere greater political achievements, but assuredly in no
country will you meet so many good citizens of independent
opinions and sound practical judgement ; nowhere so great a
number of public men who succeed in fulfilling their functions in
minor spheres with dignity and skill ; nowhere so large a proportion of persons who, outside their daily round, interest themselves
so keenly in the welfare and in the difficulties of their fellow
citizens.'

SELECT BIBLIOGRAPHY

F. Bonjour, *Real Democracy in Operation*, Allen & Unwin, 1920
R. C. Brooks, *Government and Politics of Switzerland*, Harrap,
1920
J. Bryce, *Modern Democracies*, Vol. I, Macmillan, 1923
G. A. Codding Jr., *The Federal Government of Switzerland*,
Allen & Unwin, 1961
C. Hughes, *The Federal Constitution of Switzerland*, Oxford,
1954
A. L. Lowell, *Greater European Governments*, Harvard, 1926
W. E. Rappard, *The Government of Switzerland*, Van Nostrand,
1936
J. M. Vincent, *Government in Switzerland*, Macmillan, 1900

[1] Bryce, op. cit., Vol. I, pp. 448-53.
[2] In his *Manual de Droit Public*, cited by Bonjour in *Real Democracy in Operation*, p. 17.

CHAPTER XXI

PAKISTAN

§1 THE BACKGROUND

PAKISTAN came into being as an independent State on 14 August 1947 as a result of the partition of territories which constituted British India into two independent States—India and Pakistan. The Constituent Assembly of Pakistan was inaugurated on 14 August 1947 ; but owing to the preoccupations of the new State with urgent problems of refugee rehabilitation, law and order. etc., the task of constitution-making was seriously undertaken only in 1949. Two controversial questions—one relating to the role of Islam in the new State and the other concerning the position of East Pakistan in the federation—proved to be the major hurdles in constitution-making ; the general background of political instability and frequent changes of government further added to the delay in framing a constitution. In October 1954. the Constituent Assembly of Pakistan was reconstituted and a final draft was introduced in the Assembly on 9 January 1956. The Constitution became effective on 23 March 1956 and was valid until abrogated by the President (Iskander Mirza) on 7 October 1958. The 1956 Constitution of Pakistan was based on the parliamentary democratic principle and envisaged a Cabinet form of government. A National Assembly elected on the basis of adult franchise. a Cabinet commanding a majority in the Assembly, a nominal head of the State, a set of justiciable fundamental rights and the Cabinet system of government in the two constituent units of Pakistan were the major features of the Constitution.

The Constitution was abrogated by the President on the ground that it had not worked in Pakistan in the way it was meant to be worked. The following passages from an authoritative study on Field Marshal Ayub Khan reveal the official thinking on the subject:

' So, to all intents and purposes, the people at the helm of affairs in Pakistan and their associates abroad liked to believe that democracy was practised 'in the country. The truth is that nothing was more untrue. Had the politicians been responsible to the people and had they any conception of democracy, the will of the people would have been sought and their welfare should have been the goal.

'Had general elections been held, a large majority of those politicians, who were thoroughly unpopular with the masses and knew it, would have lost their seats. Elections would have brought an end to their political careers and with it the termination of their lucrative jobs. In order to put off the general elections indefinitely, they had been conspiring among themselves to create confusion, to divert the attention of the people to irrelevant issues.

'We did have a Constitution, but we were not working according to it.'[1]

An academic view may also be cited:

'The troubles in Pakistan did not arise because the Constitution was unworkable or too elaborate. The sole cause of the malaise was that the spirit of the provisions was violated by selfish and self-seeking men. They respected neither the principle underlying the Constitution nor the well-understood conventions of democratic government. The ills of Pakistan were caused by men, not institutions.'[2]

To follow the developments: President Mirza, with the support of the then Commander-in-Chief, General Mohammad Ayub Khan, declared Martial Law and established a military dictatorship over the country. The uneasy coalition between the two men did not, however, last long; within a matter of weeks, Mirza was exiled and Ayub Khan took over as the sole ruler of the country as President and Chief Martial Law Administrator.

As early as 8 October 1958 Ayub Khan had announced that the ultimate aim of the new regime was to restore democracy 'but of the type that people can understand and work'. As a first step in that direction, he introduced his system of basic democracies, local units of government, to serve as training ground for democracy. The President's (Election and Constitution) Order 1960 provided that, as soon as possible after the general elections under the Basic Democracies Order 1959, the elected members of the local Councils should, by secret ballot, declare whether or not they had confidence in the President. If the

---

[1] Colonel Mohammad Ahmad, *My Chief*, Longmans, 1960, pp. 95-96.
[2] Dr I. H. Qureshi, in R. Braibanti and J. J. Spengler (Ed.), *Tradition, Values and Socio-Economic Development*, Duke University Press, 1961, p. 242.

majority voted in the affirmative, the President would be deemed to have authority to take the necessary steps to make a new Constitution and to have been elected for the first term of office under the new Constitution.[1] In February 1960, Ayub Khan received the vote of confidence. On 17 February 1960, President Ayub Khan announced the setting up of an 11-member Constitution Commission to make recommendations regarding the future Constitution of Pakistan. The Commission was asked to examine the 'progressive failure' of parliamentary democracy in Pakistan and to consider how best the recurrence of political instability could be prevented. The terms of reference of the Commission stated *inter alia*:

'And having taken into account the genius of the people, the general standard of education and of political judgement in the country, the present state of a sense of nationhood, the prime need for sustained development and the effect of the Constitutional and administrative changes brought into being in recent months, to submit constitutional proposals in the form of a report advising how best the following ends may be secured:

'"A democracy adaptable to changing circumstances and based on Islamic principles of justice, equality and tolerance, consolidation of national unity and a stable system of government."'

The Constitution Commission examined the replies to its questionnaire and interviewed some 565 persons before submitting its recommendations on 6 May 1961. The President of Pakistan, after taking into account the recommendations of the Commission, promulgated the Constitution on 1 March 1962.

The Constitution as proclaimed on 1 March 1962 was entitled the Constitution of the Republic of Pakistan, and Article I said:

'The State of Pakistan shall be a Republic under the name of the *Republic of Pakistan*.' (Italics ours.)

The Constitution (First Amendment) Act 1963 amended the italicized words above to read 'Islamic Republic of Pakistan'.

The Law Minister in introducing the Amendment Bill explained the significance of the change as follows:

'We should not also forget that there is a constitutional obligation placed on us not to encourage things which are prohibited by Islam nor to assist things which would lead us to renounce Islam. The combined effect of all these things indicated

---

[1] *The Indian Year-book of International Affairs*, Vol. XI, p. 138.

the essential character of our State. Therefore, it would be expedient if we call the State by the name of " Islamic Republic of Pakistan ".

' This change which is sought to be brought—firstly I want to emphasize on this point—is not repugnant to the provisions of the Constitution. Secondly, the change, which is sought to be brought in this respect, would harmonize the Constitution more and more in accordance with the essential character of our people, and the character of the Constitution and the character of the people both point out to this that the name of the State ought to be " Islamic Republic ".

' Why there is such a desire, many people would ask. What is there in a name ? I think if the people could create a State, it is brought against the heaviest odds and if the people could give a new State of nationalism by defining " nationalism " they ought to be proud to incorporate in the name of the State the ideology which has inspired the State. The essential character of our people in regard to the supreme entity should be incorporated in the name of the State and that change, I think, would meet with the general concurrence of the people and I believe there cannot be two opinions on this point in this country that the essential character of our people is Islamic and the ideologies which inspired the State were to preserve the values which go to make up Islam.'

In order that Muslims were enabled to lead their lives in accordance with the teachings of Islam, provision was made in the Constitution for the setting up of an

' Advisory Council of Islamic ideology." This body will consist of eminent men in theology, law, economics, administration, etc. and will be supported by the Islamic Research Centre. Wherever in doubt, Legislatures and the President will consult this body to make sure that laws conform to the teachings and requirements of Islam.'

The first amendment referred to above instructed the Council also to examine all laws in force immediately before the Amendment (1963), with a view to bringing them into conformity with the teachings and requirements of Islam as set out in the Holy Quran and Sunnah.

We need not describe the structure of government as outlined in the Constitution of 1962, as that Constitution was superseded by the one adopted by the National Assembly of Pakistan on 10 April 1973. It is adequate to say that, under that Constitution, (*i*) Pakistan was a federal State of two Provinces, West Pakistan and East Pakistan ; (*ii*) the Executive was of a Presidential type, being modelled more or less on the American Presidency (the President was a real, and not only a nominal, Executive) ; (*iii*) the Central Legislature consisted of the President and one House known as the National Assembly of Pakistan. Under the scheme of Basic Democracies mentioned earlier, the National Assembly was elected by an electoral college of some 80,000 electors elected on the basis of adult suffrage. As the theory of the Constitution was that the President was finally responsible to the country for administration, the National Assembly had not much control over the Executive ; it could pass laws, and pass the Annual Budget, but its effective power was limited by the powers of the President. There was a Supreme Court as head of the judiciary. Political parties, though banned early in 1962, were later legally permitted and members of the opposition parties in the National Assembly enjoyed freedom to debate government policies.

Following a wave of unrest during February / March 1969 in Pakistan, President Ayub Khan resigned on 25 March and handed over power to the army under the leadership of Major-General Yahya Khan, who immediately proclaimed Martial Law throughout the country and appointed himself the Chief Martial Law Administrator. Soon after he became President, he stated that he would relinquish power to a civilian government, which would be allowed to draw up a constitution, as soon as law and order was restored. The elections for a new National Assembly for drafting the constitution were held in late 1970, in which two political parties, one led by Z. A. Bhutto and the other by Sheikh Mujibur Rahman emerged victorious in West Pakistan and East Pakistan respectively.

The proposed transfer of power to a civilian government could not, however, be effected as, even before the Constituent Assembly could meet, differences of opinion between the leaders of the two wings of Pakistan developed, especially on the question of autonomy for the constituent units of the proposed federation. It is sufficient to say that the leaders of East Pakistan announced on 26 March 1971 the formation of an independent ' Bangla Desh ' (later ' Bangladesh ') and that Yahya Khan decided to use force to crush the freedom (secessionist) movement. Yahya Khan, as the world now knows, failed in his efforts to crush the freedom fighters who continued their war of liberation with great determination.

Events moved rapidly. The Government of Pakistan declared war on India on 4 December 1971; this resulted in a decisive defeat for Pakistan on 17 December and the successful liberation of Bangladesh. Widespread popular indignation at Yahya Khan's conduct of his country's affairs, resulting in the loss of East Pakistan, led to his removal from power and the rise of Bhutto to the Presidency. Bhutto successfully secured popular support and had a Constitution drafted and adopted by the National Assembly of Pakistan on 10 April 1973; this constitution was authenticated by the President of the National Assembly on 12 April 1973.

§2 THE CONSTITUTION OF 1973

The Republic and Its Territories

Pakistan is a Federal State known as the Islamic Republic of Pakistan. The secession of East Pakistan from Pakistan (and its formation into the independent State of Bangladesh) left its mark on the enumeration of the territories of Pakistan. They include the provinces of Baluchistan, the North-West Frontier, the Panjab and Sind, the Islambad Capital Territory, the federally administered tribal areas and such States and Territories as might be included in Pakistan by accession or otherwise. Islam is the State religion.

Fundamental Rights and Principles of Policy

Part II of the Constitution enumerates the fundamental rights of the citizen. In our study of the Indian Constitution,[1] we have explained the concept of fundamental rights. The fundamental rights enumerated in the Pakistani Constitution are more or less similar to, though not identical with, the rights which were included in the Constitution of 1962; security of person; safeguards as to arrest and detention; freedom of movement; protection against retrospective punishment, double punishment and self-incrimination; freedom of assembly, association, trade, business or profession and speech; freedom to profess religion and to manage religious institutions; the right to acquire, hold and dispose of property, equality before law and non-discrimination in respect of access to public places and preservation of language, script and culture.

[1] See Chapter XXIII.

The object of the provision of fundamental rights in the
Indian Constitution applies equally to the Constitution of Pakistan
and is specifically stated in Article 2 thus[1]

' The State shall not make any law which takes away or
abridges the rights conferred by the Constitution, and any law
made in contravention of this clause shall, to the extent of such
contravention, be void It need not be added that the rights are
not absolute, for, the exercise of these rights by the citizen is
subject to any reasonable restraints imposed by law in the
interests of public order, the integrity, security or defence of the
State, friendly relations with foreign states, decency and morality.

One interesting provision in the Constitution regarding fundamental rights must be mentioned.   Article 2, to which reference
has been made above, specifically states in one of its sections[2]
that the provisions of this Article shall not apply to any law
relating to members of the Armed Forces, or of the police, or of
such other forces as are charged with the maintenance of public
order, for the purpose of ensuring the proper discharge of their
duties or the maintenance of discipline among them. The exact
import of the provision is not clear ; time will no doubt show
any lacunae in it which distinguishes the members of the public
services engaged in the maintenance of public order from the
members of the public services engaged in other work in respect
of their rights as individuals.

The principles of policy, which are also included in Part II of
the Constitution, are distinguished from fundamental rights in that,
while the violation of fundamental rights by law or executive
action is liable to be questioned in a court of law, ' the validity
of an action or of a law shall not be called in question on the
ground that it is not in accordance with the Principles of Policy,
and no action shall lie against the State, any organ of authority
of the State or any person on such ground.'[3] The principles include,
among others, the following: maintenance of an Islamic way of
life, promotion of local government institutions, discouragement
of parochial or other prejudices, full participation of women in
national life, protection of the family, protection of minorities,
promotion of social justice and promotion of the social and
economic well-being of the people.

[1] Article 8, section (2).
[2] Section 3.
[3] Article 30, section (2).

The Federation

We have already noted that Pakistan is a federal State with four provinces as its units. The division of powers in the federation follows, in some respects, the division in the Indian Constitution, viz., the Federation or the Centre is given both exclusive and concurrent powers; but the division of powers is unlike that in the Indian Constitution in so far as the powers of the Provinces are not enumerated. The Constitution states that a Provincial Assembly shall, and Parliament shall not, have power to make laws with respect to any matter not enumerated in either the Federal Legislative list or the concurrent legislative list. This also means that the residuary power is, unlike in the Indian Constitution, with the units and not with the Centre. Mention must also be made of the provision in the Constitution regarding inconsistency between federal and provincial laws: if any provision of an Act of a Provincial Assembly is repugnant to any provision of an Act of Parliament which Parliament is competent to enact or to any provision of an existing law with respect to any of the matters enumerated in the concurrent legislative list, the Act of Parliament, whether passed before or after the Act of the Provincial Assembly, or, as the case may be, the existing law, shall prevail and the Act of the Provincial Assembly shall, to the extent of the repugnancy, be void. Provision is also made in the Constitution for legislation by the Centre for two or more Provinces in matters not enumerated in the federal list or concurrent list.

The exclusive powers given to the Centre are enumerated under 67 heads and include the defence of the federation in peace or war; the military, naval and air forces; external affairs, nationality, citizenship and naturalization; posts and telegraphs; nuclear energy; trade and commerce with foreign countries and so on. The concurrent powers are enumerated under 47 heads and include criminal law, criminal procedure, civil procedure, marriage and divorce, arbitration, arms, fire-arms and ammunition, drugs and medicine, environmental pollution, population planning and social welfare and so on.

On the administrative relations between the Federation and the provinces, the powers which may be exercised by the Federation in relation to one or more Provinces appear important enough to be mentioned here:

First, the Federal government has been empowered, with the consent of the government of a Province, to entrust, either conditionally or unconditionally to the government or its officers functions in relation to any matter to which the executive authority of the Federation extends. *Vice versa*, it is also open to the government of a Province, with the consent of the Federal government, to entrust (either conditionally or unconditionally) to the Federal government or to its officers functions in relation to any matter to which the executive authority of the Province extends.

Secondly, the executive authority of every Province has to be so exercised as not to impede or prejudice the exercise of the executive authority of the Federation, and the executive authority of the Federation extends to the giving of such directions to a Province as may appear to the government to be necessary for that purpose. Besides, directions may be issued to a Province as to the manner in which the executive authority thereof is to be exercised for the purpose of preventing any grave menace to the peace or tranquillity or economic life of Pakistan or any part thereof.

The Executive

The executive in Pakistan is a parliamentary one, i.e., while the executive authority is exercised in the name of the President, the effective power is with the Prime Minister and Federal Ministers, who are chosen from Parliament and are responsible to it.

The President, the head of State, is elected by the members of Parliament, at a joint sitting of both Houses. Only a Muslim who is qualified to be elected as a member of the National Assembly (i.e. the Lower House of Parliament) and is not less than forty-five years of age is qualified to be elected as President. He holds office for five years and may be re-elected; but no person shall hold that office for more than two consecutive terms. He may be removed from office by Parliament at a joint sitting of both Houses by a two-third majority of the Parliament on the ground of physical or mental incapacity or on a charge of violating the Constitution or gross misconduct.

The President has, according to the Constitution, several powers. As already stated, he is the head of State. He appoints the Prime Minister, the Chief Justice of the Supreme Court, and on his advice other judges of the Supreme Court; the judges

of the High Court ;[1] Governors ; the Chief Election Commissioner
and the Auditor-General of Pakistan. He summons and prorogues
either House of Parliament and dissolves the National Assembly.
He may address either House of Parliament or a joint sitting
of both Houses. A Bill passed by Parliament requires his assent
to become law.[2] He may issue a Proclamation of Emergency
on account of war or internal disorder ; in case of failure of the
Constitution in a Province, he may issue a Proclamation assuming
to himself, or direct the Governor of a Province to assume
on behalf of the President, all or any of the functions of the
government of the Province ; if he is satisfied that a situation
has arisen whereby the economic life, financial stability or credit
of Pakistan or any part thereof is threatened, he may after
consultation with the governors of the Provinces or (as the case
may be, the governor of the Province concerned) by Proclamation
make a declaration to that effect. He has power to grant pardon.

While these are the powers vested in the President by the
Constitution, the Constitution also lays down the two basic
principles of the parliamentary type of Executive : first, in the
performance of his functions, the President shall act on and in
accordance with the advice of the Prime Minister and his advice
shall be binding on him ; and, second, the Prime Minister and the
Federal Ministers shall be collectively responsible to the National
Assembly. Even in the selection of the Prime Minister (unlike
the Constitutions like those of Britain, India and France) the
President has no choice, for it is laid down that the Prime
Minister shall be elected by the votes of the majority of the total
membership of the National Assembly and that the person so
elected shall be called upon by the President to assume the
office of Prime Minister. But the Federal Ministers are appointed
by the Prime Minister and hold office during his pleasure. While,
therefore, the President is, clearly, a titular head of State,
the Constitution lays down that the Prime Minister shall keep the
President informed on matters of internal and foreign policy and
on all legislative proposals the Federal Government intends to
bring before Parliament. It is presumed that, since the President

---

[1] A Judge of the High Court is appointed by the President after
consultation with the Chief Justice of Pakistan; with the Governor
concerned; and except either the appointment is that of the Chief Justice,
but the Chief Justice of the High Court. Article 183 (1).

[2] The President shall assent to a Bill within seven days after it has
been presented to him for his assent, and if the President fails to do so,
he shall be deemed to have assented to the Bill at the expiration of the
said period. Article 75.

has to be kept informed, he may advise the Prime Minister of his own views on matters on which he is informed, though, clearly, his advice is not binding on the Prime Minister.

Enough has been said to indicate that the Executive in Pakistan follows more or less the British model of parliamentary government: the effective executive power is with the Prime Minister, the Prime Minister and other Federal Ministers are chosen from Parliament, and they are collectively responsible to the National Assembly. It ought, however, to be mentioned that in law the Prime Minister of Pakistan has more powers than the British Prime Minister: the Constitution clearly lays down that the Prime Minister shall be the chief executive of the Federation;[1] he appoints other Ministers and they may be removed by him. Further, a motion of no-confidence may be passed against the Prime Minister by the National Assembly. The only political condition of the power of the Prime Minister is that he must keep the majority of the National Assembly on his side.

The Legislature

Parliament is the legislature of the Federation.

Parliament consists of two Houses, the National Assembly and the Senate.

The National Assembly consists of two hundred members elected by 'direct and free vote', for a period of five years; there shall be ten additional seats reserved for women. Members are elected by citizens of Pakistan who are not less than eighteen years of age[2] whose names appear on the electoral roll and who are not declared by a competent court to be of unsound mind.

The duration of the National Assembly is five years, unless it is dissolved earlier.

The Senate consists of sixty-three members, fourteen elected by the members of each Provincial Assembly, ten by the members from the Federally Administered Tribal Areas and two chosen from the Federal Capital in such manner as the President may, by order, prescribe.

The Senate shall not be subject to dissolution but the term of

---

[1] Article 90.

[2] For the first general elections to the National Assembly or a by-election had before the holding of the second general election only persons who are not less than twenty-one years of age shall be entitled to vote. Article 51.

office of its members shall be four years, one half of them retiring every two years.[1]

The Parliament elects the President; makes laws; controls the finances of the nation and controls the Executive; its powers (except for the election of the President) are more or less similar to those of the British Parliament. There are, however, two main limitations not applicable to the British Parliament. First, as there is a written Constitution in Pakistan, the powers of the Pakistani Parliament are limited by the provisions of the Constitution; and second, as Pakistan is a Federal State, the legislative powers of Parliament are limited to those (exclusive and concurrent) which are enumerated in the Constitution as being vested in it.

Of the two Houses, the National Assembly has, clearly, greater power. We have earlier stated that the Prime Minister and the Federal Ministers shall be collectively responsible to the National Assembly—and not to Parliament as a whole. It follows that a resolution for a vote of no-confidence may be passed against the Prime Minister by the National Assembly.

In respect of legislative powers of the National Assembly and of the Senate, a distinction is made between (i) Money Bills and other Bills and (ii) Bills with respect to any matter in Part I of the Federal Legislature list and Bills relating to any matter in Part II of the Federal Legislature list and Concurrent Legislature list.[2]

(i) The Senate has no power with regard to Money Bills: 'A Money Bills shall originate in the National Assembly and after it has been passed by the Assembly it shall, without being transmitted to the Senate, be presented to the President for assent.'

(ii) With regard to a Bill with respect to Part I of the Federal Legislative list, it originates in the National Assembly, which is then, being passed by it, transmitted to the Senate for its consideration. If it is passed with amendments or is rejected by the Senate, it shall be reconsidered by the National Assembly and if the Bill is again passed by the National Assembly, with or without amendment, it shall be presented to the President for assent.

[1] See for exceptions Art. 59.
[2] It may be stated briefly that Part I of the Federal Legislature list contains 59 items, Part II of the Federal Legislature list 8 items and the Concurrent Legislature list 47 items. For details see Fourth Schedule of the Constitution.

A Bill relating to Part II of the Federal Legislative list or the Concurrent list may originate in either House, and be considered by both Houses independently and differences between the two are settled by a vote in the joint sitting of both Houses.

The Judiciary

Article 175 of the Constitution states that there shall be a Supreme Court of Pakistan, a High Court for each Province[1] and such other Courts as may be established by law.

The Chief Justice of Pakistan, as stated earlier, is appointed by the President and other judges are appointed by the President after consultation with the Chief Justice. A somewhat novel provision is made in the Constitution regarding the removal of judges for misconduct or physical or mental incapacity. It will be remembered that the practice in several Constitutions (e.g. India, Bangladesh) is that Parliament by a special majority has the power to remove judges in such cases. The Pakistan Constitution provides for a Supreme Judicial Council[2] which has the power to enquire into the capacity and conduct of a Supreme Court Judge or a High Court Judge when the President refers the matter to the Council; and if the Council advises the President that a Judge should be removed from office, the President may remove him from office. In so far as a judicial inquiry is provided to consider the conduct or capacity of a judge, the provision must be considered a salutary one; but in so far as an enquiry, to be instituted by the President (which means the President acting on the advice of the Prime Minister) not only on information received by the President from the Supreme Judicial Council but *from any other source*,[3] it is not certain if political influence will not be brought to bear on the institution of such proceedings.

The Supreme Court has original and appellate jurisdiction: original, in any dispute between the Federal government and one or more Provincial governments or between one Provincial government and one or more other Provincial governments; appellate, to hear and determine appeals from the judgements, decrees final orders or sentences of a High Court as specified in the Constitution.[4]

---

[1] Article 192, however, provides that any two Provinces may, with the consent of the President, agree that there shall be a common High Court for the two Provinces.
[2] For the constitution of the Council, see Article 209.
[3] Italics ours.
[4] See Article 18.5 for details.

The importance of the Supreme Court in a Federal State with a written Constitution (which Pakistan is) need not be elaborated. It is guarantor of the Constitution which has important provisions relating to the division of powers between the Federation and the Provinces and to the fundamental rights of the citizen.

The Provinces

On the structure of governments in the Provinces, little need be said except that, broadly speaking, the Provinces have the same form of parliamentary executive as in the Federation. The governor is the head of the Province; the legislature in the Provinces is unicameral, not bicameral as it is in the Federal government.

Islamic Provisions under the Constitution

As Pakistan is an Islamic Republic, it is but natural that there are special provisions in the Constitution to ensure that ' Pakistan would be ' as the preamble to the Constitution states, ' a democratic state based on Islamic principles of justice ' and that ' the Muslims shall be enabled to order their lives in the individual and collective spheres in accordance with the teachings and requirements of Islam '. We have already referred to the requirement in the Constitution that only Muslim citizens of Pakistan shall hold the office of the President and the Prime Minister. Other relevant provisions are the following: all existing laws shall be brought in conformity with the injunctions of Islam as laid down in the Holy Quran and Sunnah and no law shall be enacted which is repugnant to such injunctions (Art. 227). A Council of Islamic ideology shall be constituted of eight to fifteen members with the following functions: to make recommendations to Parliament and the Provincial Assemblies as to the ways and means of enabling and encouraging the Muslims of Pakistan to order their lives individually and collectively in all respects in accordance with the principles of Islam; to advise a House, Provincial Assembly, the President or Governor on any question referred to the Council as to whether a proposed law is or is not repugnant to 'the injunctions of Islam; to make recommendations as to the measures for bringing existing laws into conformity with the injunctions of Islam, and to compile in a suitable form for the guidance of Parliament and the Provincial Assemblies, such injunctions of Islam as can be given legislative effect.

Amendment of the Constitution

The Constitution may be amended by an Act of Parliament.

It is laid down that (*i*) a Bill to amend the Constitution shall originate in the National Assembly; (*ii*) when a Bill is approved by the National Assembly by a majority of not less than two-thirds of its total membership, it shall be transmitted to the Senate ; (*iii*) if the Bill is also passed by the Senate by a majority of the total membership of the Senate it shall be presented to the President for his assent ; (*iv*) if the Bill is passed by the Senate with amendments, it shall be re-considered by the National Assembly, and if the Bill is amended by the Senate is passed by the Assembly by the votes of not less than two-thirds of the total membership of the Assembly it shall be presented to the President for his assent ; (*v*) if the Bill is not passed by the Senate within ninety days of its receiving the Bill, it shall be deemed to have been rejected by the Senate ; and (*vi*) a Bill to amend the Constitution which would have the effect of altering the limits of a Province shall not be passed by the National Assembly unless it has been approved by a resolution of the Provincial Assembly of that Province passed by the votes of not less than two-thirds of the total membership of that Assembly.

From this brief sketch of the Constitution, it will be seen that, after twenty-six years of independence, and after experimenting with two Constitutions, Pakistan has settled down to a democratic form of government on the British model, and special provisions are included in the Constitution to enable the Muslims of Pakistan to order their lives in accordance with the teachings of Islam. Political parties are legally recognized. The Prime Minister is the centre of power in the State, and, if he can continue to command the majority in the National Assembly there are few Prime Ministers in the world who have as much political power as he has according to the Constitution.

SELECT BIBLIOGRAPHY

Pakistan Review, April 1962.

Colonel Mohammad Ahmed, *My Chief*, Longmans, 1960.

The Constitution of the Islamic Republic of Pakistan 1973 (Lahore, Pakistan Legal Publications, 1973).

CHAPTER XXII

BANGLADESH

§1 THE BACKGROUND

REFERENCE has been made earlier (*i*) to the announcement by the leaders of East Pakistan on 26 March, 1970, of the formation of an independent Bangladesh, when differences of opinion between the leaders of the two wings of Pakistan on the question of autonomy for East Pakistan could not be resolved; and (*ii*) to the decision of Yahya Khan to use force to crush the freedom struggle.

The reasons for the demand for autonomy, which the leaders of East Pakistan made on the eve of national liberation, are not relevant to our study of the Constitution of Bangladesh ; they will be read as part of the political history of Pakistan and Bangladesh. But some indication of the essential cause for the secession of East Pakistan from Pakistan is worth mention if only because the preamble to the present constitution contains a reference to nationalism and democracy among the ideals which inspired the national liberation struggle, as the following paragraph states :

'Pledging that the high ideals of nationalism, socialism, democracy and secularism, which inspired our heroic people to dedicate themselves to, and our brave martyrs to sacrifice their lives in, the national liberation struggle, shall be the fundamental principles of the Constitution.'

A study of the political developments in Pakistan from 1947 to 1971 makes it clear that the people of East Pakistan had begun to feel that they were being exploited by West Pakistan, and that there was no attempt at establishing real democracy in the country. In 1971 the population of East Pakistan was about 75 million, whereas that cf West Pakistan was about 60 million, i.e., East Pakistan had a majority in the whole state, with more than 50% of the population. But it had not received its due share in decision-making in the government of Pakistan ; no truly democratic Constitution had been evolved for the whole state. From 1958 to 1969, effective power lay with the military régime (Ayub Khan ruled from 1958 to March 1969), supported by the army, the bureaucracy and the feudal and the business aristocracy. It has been pointed out by scholars that all senior military members of the administration were West Pakistanis, and of the senior officers in the Central Services 87% were West Pakistanis in 1960.[1] East Pakistan's share in the army was some 10%, with very few Bengalis in senior positions such as that of the Lieutenant-General. Economic disparities between the two wings were widening; by 1969-70, the per capita income of West Pakistan was 61% higher than in the East. The economic development of East Pakistan received a low priority and its foreign trade earnings were diverted to finance imports for West Pakistan. In cultural matters, the claims of East Pakistan were neglected. It is relevant to note that Ayub Khan admitted awareness of the discontent in Pakistan in his broadcast of 21 February 1969 that the 'people of East Pakistan believe that in the present system they are not equal partners and also they do not have full control over the affairs of the province'. The reference to nationalism and democracy in the preamble mentioned above can now be understood.

To continue our account of the background of the Constitution. The war of liberation ended, as we have noted earlier, on 17 December 1971; the process of recognition of the new State was completed with Pakistan's recognition of Bangladesh on 22 February 1974. After the announcement on 26 March 1971 of an independent Bangladesh, a Revolutionary government was established with Sheikh Mujibur Rahman, the leader of the Bengali Nationalist Movement, as its President. Early in January 1972, after he returned from a Pakistani prison and took charge of his office as President, Mujibur Rahman promulgated the Provisional Constitution Order which provided that 'whereas it is the manifest aspiration of the people of Bangladesh that a parliamentary democracy shall function in Bangladesh, there shall be a cabinet of ministers, with the Prime Minister as the head'; 'the President shall, in exercise of his functions, act in accordance with the advice of the Prime Minister'; 'the President shall commission as Prime Minister a member of the Constituent Assembly' and all ministers shall be appointed by the President 'on the advice of the Prime Minister'. Justice Abu Sayeed Choudhury, a former High Court Judge and Vice-Chancellor of Dacca University, became the new President of the Republic, and Mujibur Rahman took over as the Prime Minister of Bangladesh.

[1] A. Rahman, *East and West Pakistan*: A Problem in Political Economy of Regional Planning, Occasional Paper No. 20, Harvard University, Centre for International Affairs, 1968.

The first step towards framing a new Constitution was taken when the Bangladesh Constituent Assembly Order was pro-mulgated by the President on 23 March 1972. It provided for the formation of a Constituent Assembly consisting of the members who had been elected from Bangladesh (East Pakistan at the time of election) to the then Pakistan National Assembly and the East Pakistan Provincial Assembly in the elections held in 1970 and 1971. The Assembly consisting of 430 members held its first sittings on 10 and 11 April and elected a 34-member Constitution Drafting Committee with instructions to the Com-mittee to submit its report to the Assembly by 10 June 1972. The Committee invited ' from any institution or person interested to send proposals in writing for the consideration of the com-mittee during the preparation of the draft Constitution '. Some memoranda were received and considered by the Committee. The Committee approved the text of the Constitution Bill on 11 October The next day, the Law Minister introduced the Constitution Bill in the Constituent Assembly; after discussion, the Constitution was adopted by the Constituent Assembly on 4 November 1972 unanimously. It was authenticated by the Speaker of the Constituent Assembly on 14 December 1972 and was published for general information on the same day. It is noteworthy that the political consensus prevailing in the newly independent State on the broad framework of the State helped the unanimous passing of the Constitution, and in the relatively short period of 24 days (from its introduction to its final passage). The popularity of the ruling Awami League Party and the charisma of its leader, Mujibur Rahman, no doubt helped both the unanimous passing and the quick acceptance of the Consti-tution.

§ 2   THE CONSTITUTION

Objectives and general features

Bangladesh is a unitary State, an independent and sovereign Republic to be known as the People's Republic of Bangladesh.

The preamble mentioned the objective of the Constitution: ' to realize through the democratic process a socialist society, free from exploitation—a society in which the rule of law, fundamental human rights and freedom, equality and justice, political, economic and social, will be secured for all citizens . We shall endeavour to show, after we analyse the Constitution, how it seeks to realize the objective.

On the general features of the Constitution, the main aspects to be noted here—these will become clear as we analyse the Constitution in the following pages—are: it includes a list of principles of State policy and fundamental rights and mentions in addition to the rights of citizens their duties as well; and provides for a parliamentary executive responsible to the legislature, adult suffrage, direct election and single electoral roll for each constituency and the rule of law.

Fundamental Principles of State Policy and Fundamental Rights

The fundamental principles of State policy, included in Part II of the Constitution, are fundamental in the sense that they are guidelines to the State in the making of laws and in the interpretation of the Constitution and the laws; it is expressly stated that they shall not be judicially enforceable.

The principles may be summarized under four heads: nationalism, secularism, democracy and socialism.

The Bengali nation, the Constitution states, derives its identity from its language and culture; the unity and solidarity of the nation must be maintained: The Constitution makes special mention of measures to conserve the cultural traditions and heritage of the people and to foster and improve the national language, literature and the arts that *all* sections of the people are afforded the opportunity to contribute towards the enrichment of the national culture. It should be obvious, too, that, while these measures are necessary, the maintenance of the unity and solidarity of the nation is primarily a function of making socialism, democracy and secularism real and effective; to these we now turn.

A socialist economic system shall be established with a view to ensuring the attainment of a just and egalitarian society, free from the exploitation of man by man. To this end, a number of principles are included in Part II: Ownership by the State on behalf of the people of the key sectors of the economy, co-operative ownership; private ownership within such limits as may be prescribed by law; emancipation of peasants and workers; and the responsibility of the State to provide conditions for the securing to the people the basic necessities of life including food and clothing and to ensure the right to guaranteed employment with reasonable wages and the right to social security ; raising of the level of public health and morality and equality of opportunity.

Democracy is fundamental: human rights and freedoms and respect for the dignity and worth of the human person shall be guaranteed and effective participation by the people through their elected representatives in administration at all levels must be ensured. Free and compulsory education must be provided to all children to such stage as may be determined by law, and illiteracy must be removed within such time as may be determined by law.

The principle of secularism shall be realized: communalism in all its forms must be eliminated, no religion shall be granted political status by the State and there must be no discrimination against or persecution of persons practising a particular religion.

Before we take up fundamental rights mention must be made of an interesting Article in the Constitution relating to the duties of citizens: 'It shall be the duty of every citizen to observe the Constitution and the laws, to maintain discipline, to perform public duties and to protect public property.' It is adequate to say that no greater principle will contribute to the maintenance of the unity and solidarity of the nation than the fulfilment of duties by the citizens as mentioned in this Article.

On fundamental rights the Constitutional provisions are more or less similar to those in other Constitutions studied in this book (Pakistan, India): equality before law, equality of opportunity and public employment, right to protection of law, protection of right to life and personal liberty, freedom of movement, freedom of assembly, freedom of association, freedom of thought and conscience and speech, freedom of occupation, freedom of religion and the right to property. Three general aspects of these rights may be indicated here. First, they are judicially enforceable ; secondly, all laws inconsistent with the fundamental rights shall be void to the extent of the inconsistency and thirdly, the exercise of most of the rights is subject to reasonable restrictions imposed by law. For instance freedom of speech and expression and freedom of the press are guaranteed to every citizen 'subject to any reasonable restrictions imposed by law in the interests of the security of the State, friendly relations with foreign States, public order, decency or morality, or in relation to contempt of court, defamation or incitement to an offence' It need not be added that the Court has the right to judge the reasonableness of the restrictions imposed by law, and therein lies the constitutional guarantee of the rights.

The Executive

Bangladesh has a parliamentary executive, somewhat on the model of the British system, with two differences, (*i*) the conventions which regulate the relations between the Executive and the Legislature are, in Bangladesh, written into the Constitution and (*ii*) Bangladesh has a President as the head of the State instead of a monarch.

The President is the head of the State. Only one who is qualified for election as a member of Parliament and not less than thiry-five years of age is qualified for election as President. He is elected by members of Parliament in accordance with the procedure prescribed in the Constitution, the essence of which is that he is elected by secret ballot at a special session of Parliament convened for the purpose. The President holds office for five years ; he may be elected for a second term of five years but not for a third term. Before his term is over, the President may be removed from office by a two-thirds majority in Parliament for physical or mental incapacity ; he may be impeached by Parliament on a charge of violating the Constitution or of grave misconduct, the majority in Pariament for removal being two-thirds.

The President has, constitutionally, a number of powers. He is the head of the Executive. He appoints the Prime Minister and, on his advice, other Ministers. He appoints the chief officials of the State. He appoints the judges of the Supreme Court. He summons, prorogues and dissolves Parliament. He addresses the members of Parliament and may send messages to Parliament. He has a suspensory veto over laws passed by Parliament. The supreme command of the defence services of Bangladesh is vested in him. He has the prerogative of mercy. These are his nominal powers ; except in case of appointment of the Prime Minister, the President must act in accordance with the wishes of the Prime Minister.[1]

The Cabinet is the real, as distinguished from the nominal, Executive ; the Prime Minister is its head. Ministers must invariably be chosen from Parliament ; a Minister, who at the time of his appointment is not a member of Parliament, shall cease to be a Minister unless elected as a member of Parliament within

[1] Article 48: 3.

a period of six months from the date of his appointment. The
Prime Minister is appointed by the President ; other Ministers
are appointed by the President on the advice of the Prime
Minister. The constitutional provision that ' the executive power
of th: Republic shall, in accordance with this Constitution, be
exercised by or on the authority of the Prime Minister '[2] ensures
the ascendancy of the Prime Minister in the Cabinet and in the
country. The Cabinet is collectively responsible to Parliament,[2]
but the Prime Minister can advice the President to dissolve
Parliament even if he ceases to retain the support of the majority
and his advice is binding on the President.[3] As we have pointed
out in our study of the British Constitution, few members of
Parliament would like to take the risk of losing their seats which
a dissolution may involve ; there is every inducement, therefore.
for members of the ruling party to support the Government
in power. Add to this the provision that a member of
Parliament loses his seat if he resigns or votes against his party
in Parliament.[4] This provision has been, as pointed out by
a competent writer,[5] deliberately incorporated in the Constitution
to prevent members from crossing the floor of the House
and thus ensuring party discipline essential for the success
of parliamentary government ; it must be added that the same
party discipline helps the Prime Minister as leader of the
majority party to ensure his ascendancy in the Cabinet, in the
party and in Parliament.

The Legislature

The legislative powers of the Republic are vested in
Parliament known as the House of the Nation. It consists of 300
members chosen from single territorial constituencies by direct
election by citizens of eighteen years or above (for a temporary
period of ten years from 1972 fifteen seats are reserved exclusively for women). A citizen of Bangladesh, who has attained
the age of twenty-five years is qualified to be elected as a
member of Parliament (subject to the usual disqualifications such
as being of unsound mind, an undischarged insolvent, a prisoner
who has undergone a sentence of not less than two years for a
criminal offence, unless a period of five years has elapsed since
his release, etc.)

[1] Article 55 (2).
[2] Article 55 (3).
[3] Article 57 (2).
[4] Article 70.
[5] Abul Fazl Huq, in *Pacific Affairs*, vol. 43, p. 71.

Parliament's powers include the powers of law-making and financial control, and control of the executive, much the same as in Britain. There is no need to repeat the same here. We need only add that (*i*) the procedure for making laws and controlling the finances is not in all respects similar, though in essentials its holds good ; (*ii*) Parliament's power of law-making in Bangladesh is not limited, as the British Parliament's is, even by the limited powers vested in a second chamber, as there is no second chamber in Bangladesh. On the other hand, the head of State, unlike in Britain, has a suspensory veto over laws passed by Parliament, i.e., when a Bill is presented to the President, after being passed by Parliament for his signature, he may return the Bill or any particular provision of it to be reconsidered ; if the Bill is again passed by Parliament with or without amendments, it shall be presented to the President for his assent, whereupon the President shall assent to the Bill ; (*iii*) the power of Parliament in Bangladesh is limited by the Constitution, whereas the British Parliament is legally sovereign.

The Judiciary

The Supreme Court (with two Divisions, the Appellate Division and the High Court Division) is the highest court in the land. Its judges, as has already been noted, are appointed by the President, the Chief Justice on the advice of the Prime Minister and the other judges on the advice of the Chief Justice. The independence of the Judiciary from the Executive is ensured by the following provisions of the Constitution:—A judge shall not be removed from his office except by an order passed by the President pursuant to a resolution of Parliament supported by a majority of not less than two-thirds of the total number of members of Parliament on the ground of proved misbehaviour or incapacity.[1] A person who has held office as a judge shall not after his retirement or removal therefrom shall be eligible for any appointment in the service of the Republic.[2] The remuneration payable to the judges of the Supreme Court is charged upon the consolidated fund which is not submitted to the vote of Parliament.[3] Finally an express provision says that the State shall ensure the separation of the judiciary from the executive organs of the State.[4]

[1] Article 96 (1).
[2] Article 99.
[3] Articles 88 (*b*) and 89.
[4] Article 22.

Amendment of the Constitution

Any provision of the Constitution may be amended by Parliament subject to two requirements: (*i*) the title of the Bill must expressly state that it will amend or repeal a provision of the Constitution and (*ii*) it must be passed by the votes of not less than two-thirds of the total number of members of Parliament. Technically, the Constitution is a rigid one in so far as a procedure different from the one used for passing ordinary laws, is prescribed for amendment of the Constitution. The procedure itself cannot, however, be considered a complex one which would make it, as in the USA, difficult to amend the Constitution.

Democracy and Socialism

Earlier in this section we mentioned the objective of the Constitution as the realization of a socialist society through the democratic process. We may conclude this section by raising the question: are the constitutional provisions adequate to realize the objective?

It appears to the present writer that, so far as Constitutional provisions go, the objective is adequately taken care of. The essence of a socialist society is indicated as an egalitarian society free from exploitation. As we have indicated earlier, the Constitution enjoins on the State ' to attain through planned economic growth, a constant increase of productive forces and a steady improvement in the material and cultural standards of living of the people with a view to securing to its citizens ' the basic necessities of life, including food, clothing, shelter, education and medical care, the right to work at a reasonable wage ; the right to reasonable rest, recreation and leisure and the right to social security in times of unemployment, illness or disablement, widowhood, old age, etc. The State is also enjoined to endeavour to ensure equality of opportunity. Above all, it is provided that the State may nationalize private property paying or not paying compensation, a clearly socialistic provision, and this provision may not be challenged in any court of law.

The democratic process is, again, fully provided for. We recall that a State may, in the political sense, be termed a democracy if it provides institutions for the expression and, in the last analysis, the supremacy of the popular will on basic questions of social direction and policy. The Bangladesh Constitution does provide for such institutions—adult suffrage, elected Parliament, with power to control the executive, make laws and control the finances: local self-government and an independent judiciary. Besides, through the constitutional recognition of freedom of speech and press, as well as the right of assembly, dissent is legally recognized. Discrimination on grounds of religion, race, caste, sex or birth is unconstitutional. Equality of opportunity of public employment is written into the Constitution as a fundamental right and is implemented through an independent Public Service Commission.

So far as constitutional provisions go, democracy and socialism are, in the opinion of the present author, fully safeguarded. How far they are implemented in practice depends upon the mores of the people, tolerance, and the attitude of give and take. For, all the institutions of man are merely so many expressions of his mind. ' It matters little what other gifts a people may possess ', Lord Balfour has said, ' if they are wanting in those which, from this point of view, are most important: if, for example, they have no capacity for grading their loyalties, as well as for being moved by them. if they have no natural inclination to liberty and no natural respect for law ; if they lack good humour and tolerate foul play ; if they know not how to compromise and when ; if they have not that distrust of extreme conclusions which is sometimes misdescribed as want of logic, if corruption does not repel them ; and if their divisions are profound.' Further, the habit of taking an intelligent interest in public affairs, being critical of government, independent thought, tolerance and the subordinaton of private interest to public good must become widespread.

It can reasonably be hoped that the people of Bangladesh, who have fought so courageously and unitedly to wrest freedom from unwilling hands, will be able to develop these habits of mind and to achieve socialism through the democratic process which is the objective of the Constitution.

SELECT BIBLIOGRAPHY

Bangladesh Documents (New Delhi, Ministry of External Affairs, no date)

The Constitution of the People's Republic of Bangladesh.

Abul Fazl Huq, ' Constitution-making in Pakistan ', in *Pacific Affairs*, Vol. 46, No. 1, Spring 1973.

CHAPTER XXIII

INDIA

§1. EVOLUTION OF THE INDIAN CONSTITUTION

THE year 1892 is an important landmark in the political and constitutional development of British India. The period before that date witnessed the gradual establishment of British power and of *ordered* government ; the period from 1892 to 1947, the realization of *self*-government.

The outlines of the first period are, briefly, as follows. The East India Company, mainly a commercial concern at its foundation, came gradually to acquire territorial power. Successive charters gave it political authority. The battle of Plassey (1757) brought in its wake the assumption of the diwani [1] by the Company, and a system of dyarchy in Bengal, i.e. a system of dual control by the Company and the Nawab of Bengal. The Regulating Act of 1773, Pitt's India Act of 1784, and the various Charter Acts (1813-53) extended the control of Parliament over the Company's possessions in India. Finally, the Mutiny of 1857-8 resulted in the establishment of direct rule by the English Crown and the organization of an efficient bureaucracy.

Legally, the king in Parliament was the supreme law-making authority for British India ; and the Secretary of State, representing the Crown, was charged with the superintendence, direction and control of all acts, operations, and concerns which related to the government or the revenues of India. The Governor-General, as the head of the administration in India, was required to pay due obedience to the orders of the Secretary of State ; when he protested, as Lord Mayo did in 1870, he was reminded of his subordinate position.

' The Government established in India,' so runs a dispatch of the Secretary of State that year, ' [is from the nature of the case] subordinate to the Imperial Government at home. And no Government can be subordinate, unless it is within the power of

---

[1] This covered the whole of the financial administration and the civil government.

the superior Government to order what is to be done or left undone, and to enforce on its officers. through the ordinary constitutional means, obedience to its directions as to the use which they are to make of official position and power in furtherance of the policy which has been finally decided upon by the advisers of the Crown.'

The Governor-General was assisted by an Executive Council.

In its turn, the Central Government strictly controlled the provinces ; whether from the administrative, the financial or the legislative point of view, the concentration of authority at the Centre was a cardinal feature of the constitution. Every local Government was required to obey the orders of the Governor-General in Council, and to keep him constantly and diligently informed of its proceedings and of all matters which ought in its opinion to be reported to him, or as to which he required information ; and it was under his superintendence, direction and control in all matters relating to the government of its province. The governmental system was in theory ' one and indivisible '.

From 1892

The period from 1892 is best described as one which saw the growth and realization of self-government. The evolution of self-government in India has two aspects. On the one hand, it involves the demand by Indians for the government of the country by and for themselves — the nationalistic idea ; and, on the other, the demand for the sharing of political power by an increasing number of people — the democratic idea. The two are often combined and in practice are indistinguishable.

The stages in this evolution may easily be marked. The Indian National Congress held its first meeting in 1885, and demanded *inter alia* the presence of elected members in the Legislative Councils, the right to discuss the budget and ask questions, and the reference to a standing committee of the House of Commons of issues between the Councils and the Governments. Bradlaugh introduced in the House of Commons a Home Rule Bill for India, at the request of the Congress. Ultimately the maximum concession then deemed possible and wise by the Government took shape in an Act of 1892, which recognized, though only indirectly and inadequately, the principle of election to both the central and the local Legislatures. The demand for the Indianization of the Services was made and gradually conceded.

The Minto-Morley Reforms of 1909 form the next important landmark. They increased the representative element in the Legislative Councils — with a non-official majority in those of the provinces — and extended their powers ; but they cannot justly be described as embodying any new policy. They were essentially of an evolutionary character ; the change they introduced was one of degree and not of kind, the object being to associate the people with the Government in the decision of public questions to a greater extent than before. Lord Morley himself emphatically repudiated the idea that the Act of 1909 was in any sense a step towards parliamentary government. It is symptomatic of the moderate character of the political demands then made that the Congress welcomed the Reforms and G. K. Gokhale spoke of their ' generous and fair nature '.

Soon, however, disillusionment came ; the fatal weakness of the Reforms revealed itself ; they brought in an element of challenge and obstruction — influence without responsibility. The Great War (1914-18) provided an opportunity for a striking manifestation of India's loyalty and co-operation. The announcement of 20 August 1917 in Parliament was almost an inevitable result. The gradual development of self-governing institutions with a view to the progressive realization of responsible government was officially declared to be the goal of British policy in India ; and the Reforms which followed embodied that principle.

The Act of 1919 introduced several changes in the constitution of India, as regards both the central and the provincial Governments. The central Legislature was made bicameral ; in both the chambers, the Council of State and the Legislative Assembly, there was a majority of elected members. It also received additional powers to influence and criticize the Government. The most important change in the government of the provinces was the introduction of the system known as dyarchy. Its essence is a division of the Executive into the Reserved Half and the Transferred Half, the former responsible, through the Secretary of State for India, to the British Parliament and electorate for the administration of *certain* matters of government, the latter responsible, through the Legislative Council, to an Indian electorate for the administration of certain *other* subjects. Dyarchy was worked in different provinces until 1937, with varying degrees of success.

Meanwhile steps were taken, with the appointment of the Indian Statutory Commission in 1927, to make a new constitution for

India. That Commission reported in 1930. Three Round Table Conferences were summoned at London in 1930, 1931 and 1932, to discuss proposals for the making of the new constitution; and, in the light of their discussions, a White Paper was issued by the Government in 1933 laying down definite proposals for reform, which were to be submitted to a joint select committee of Parliament for examination and report. The Committee was accordingly appointed, and their Report was made the basis of the Government of India Act, 1935.

The Act of 1935 so far as it related to the Provinces was brought into operation in 1937. Negotiations were in progress to secure the assent of a sufficient number of states — necessary for inaugurating the Federation of India contemplated in the Act — when the war broke out in 1939. Events moved fast. Indian leaders resented India being made a party to the war without India's consent; popular ministries resigned in eight (Congress-majority) provinces; the Muslim League took the opportunity to declare that the Muslims had suffered grievously at the hands of the 'Hindu-Congress' Administrations, that Muslims and Hindus were two nations and that the only satisfactory way for the peaceful governance of the country was the partition of India into two sovereign States, one Muslim and the other Hindu; Britain suffered a series of reverses at the hands of Japan, being compelled to evacuate Burma and Malaya, and there was, in the early days of 1942, even fear of a Japanese invasion of India. To secure the willing and active co-operation of India at that crisis, the British Cabinet sent Sir Stafford Cripps to India with fresh proposals for the governance of the country, but they did not find favour with Indian leaders. A 'Quit India' resolution, passed by the Congress in the latter part of the year, crystallized the general desire in India for independence; the Muslim League agitation for Pakistan grew in intensity, and when with the close of the war fresh elections were held in 1946, it was evident that the League demand for partition had support from the majority of Muslims, though not from all.

It was in these circumstances that the Labour Government, which had been returned to power in August 1945, decided in March 1946 to send a Cabinet Delegation to India with the Secretary of State for India at its head to settle the Indian constitutional problem and to use 'their utmost endeavours to help her to attain her freedom as speedily and fully as possible'. On 16 May, the Mission put forward the following proposals with the full approval of His Majesty's Government.

(*i*) There should be a Union of India embracing both British India and the states, which should deal with the following subjects : Foreign Affairs, Defence, and Communications ; and should have the powers necessary to raise the finances required for the above subjects.

(*ii*) The Union should have an Executive and a Legislature constituted from British Indian and states representatives. Any question raising a major communal issue in the Legislature should require for its decision a majority of the representatives present and voting of each of the two major communities, as well as a majority of all the members present and voting.

(*iii*) All subjects other than the Union subjects and all residuary powers should vest in the provinces.

(*iv*) The states would retain all subjects and powers other than those ceded to the Union.

(*v*) Provinces should be free to form Groups with Executives and Legislatures, and each Group could determine the provincial subjects to be taken in common.

Initially, Baluchistan, the North-West Frontier Province, the Punjab and Sind might form one Group, Bengal and Assam a second, and the remaining Provinces a third.

It was provided, however, that after the first elections under the new constitution, provinces would be free to leave the group into which they had been provisionally placed.

(*vi*) The constitutions of the Union and of the Groups should contain a provision whereby any province could, by a majority vote of its Legislative Assembly, call for a reconsideration of the terms of the constitution after an initial period of 10 years and at 10-yearly intervals thereafter.

(*vii*) To work out a constitution on the basis of these broad principles, the Viceroy would summon a Constituent Assembly at New Delhi consisting of representatives of British India elected by the members of the provincial Legislatures in such a way that as nearly as possible for each one million of the population there would be one representative and that the proportion between the representatives of the main communities would be on the same basis. Later, representatives from the Indian states — their number being determined on the same proportion — would join the Assembly.

(*viii*) There would be a special Advisory Committee consisting of all important interests including minorities to formulate fundamental and minority rights and to recommend their inclusion in the Union, Group and provincial constitutions.

(*ix*) During the making of the constitution, the administration would be carried on by an Interim Government having the support of the political parties. It would be a purely Indian Government except for its head, the Governor-General.

The proposals seemed for a time to find favour with the main political parties, but differences of opinion soon manifested themselves over the interpretation of some of the proposals with the result that ultimately they had to be given up.

In the meantime a Constituent Assembly of the kind proposed by the Cabinet Mission was elected and it held its first session on 9 December 1946; the Muslim League, however, boycotted it. Subsequent negotiations of the Viceroy with political leaders made it clear that the partition of India was the only lasting solution of the Indian problem; accordingly the British Government made a statement on 3 June 1947 providing for the partition of India in the event of a clear majority of the Muslim Majority Areas of Bengal, and the Punjab and Sind and British Baluchistan voting for it. The vote which was taken later favoured partition, and accordingly India was divided into two independent States, India (or Bharat) and Pakistan; and Britain transferred her power to these two States with effect from 15 August 1947. The legal basis of this transfer of power is the India Independence Act passed on 18 July 1947 by the British Parliament.

That Act declared that as from 15 August 1947, two independent Dominions were to be set up in India, to be known respectively as India and Pakistan; demarcated the territories of the two Dominions and provided for the determination of the boundaries of the provinces of Bengal, the Punjab and some of the disputed areas in Assam by a Boundary Commission; stated in unambiguous terms that His Majesty's Government in the United Kingdom had thereafter no responsibility in respect of the government of any of the territories which immediately before 15 August 1947 were included in British India; and added that the suzerainty which His Majesty had been exercising over the Indian States (some 600 in number) by virtue of treaties, agreements and usage lapsed from the date, making them therefore legally independent.

From the date of the transfer of power, the legislative powers were to be exercised by the Constituent Assembly already in existence; and except in so far as other provisions were made by the Constituent Assembly, the governance of the country was to be carried on as nearly as possible in accordance with the

Government of India Act, 1935, and the Orders in Council made thereunder — with such modifications as might be made by orders of the Governor-General.

Legally and in practice, therefore, from 15 August 1947 India as a Dominion was completely free to shape her own policy, both domestic and foreign, like any other Dominion, i.e. the Indian Legislature and the Indian Government enjoying the confidence of that Legislature were free to carry on the governance of the country without any interference from Britain. India was free also to make any constitution which suited her conditions, and free to decide whether she would continue to be a Dominion in the Commonwealth or an independent State outside the Commonwealth. And India took full advantage of her newly won freedom. At the beginning, for some months immediately after partition, the Government was preoccupied with communal troubles which unfortunately followed the large-scale migrations of people from Pakistan to India and vice versa ; but as soon as these troubles had been got over, the Government initiated and carried out policies both at home and abroad in accordance with what they thought was best for India. They selected delegations to international conferences, and laid down their foreign policy without control or interference from any other country. It took, however, more than two years to frame a new constitution, and until that was framed, the country continued to be governed in accordance with the Act of 1935 with certain adaptations and modifications authorized by the Governor-General to bring that Act into line with the new status of India, and with the altered situation arising from partition. It need hardly be added that the Governor-General acted on the advice of the Ministers.

The Constituent Assembly referred to earlier considered various aspects of the Constitution for several months and agreed upon general principles in regard to them ; they then appointed a committee to prepare a draft of the Constitution on the basis of the general principles approved by them ; discussed the draft article by article ; and finally adopted it with important modifications on 26 November 1949. The Constitution came into force on 26 January 1950.

§2 THE CONSTITUTION OF 1950
DIVISION OF POWERS

India is declared in the Constitution to be a Union of states.

The aim of the Constitution is stated clearly in the preamble. The aim is to constitute India as a sovereign democratic Republic and, further, to secure to all citizens of India social, economic and political justice ; liberty of thought, expression, belief, faith and worship ; equality of status and of opportunity ; and to promote among all fraternity, assuring the dignity of the individual and the unity of the nation.

The constitution follows the modern practice in laying down certain fundamental rights ; the State shall not deny to any person equality before the Law or the equal protection of the laws, subject to the right of the State to make any special provision for the advancement of any socially and educationally backward classes of citizens or the Scheduled Castes and Tribes ; the State shall not discriminate against any citizen on grounds only of religion, race, caste or sex ; there shall be equality of opportunity to all citizens in matters of employment under the State ; the practice of untouchability in any form is forbidden. Subject to the right of the State to impose by law reasonable restrictions in the interests of the security of the State, friendly relations with foreign States, public order, decency or morality or in relation to contempt of court, defamation or incitement to an offence, all citizens shall have the right to freedom of speech and expression, to assemble peaceably and without arms, to form associations or unions, to move freely throughout and reside in any part of the territory of India, to acquire, hold and dispose of property ; subject to the right of the State to prescribe the professional or technical qualifications necessary for carrying on any occupation, trade or business and to the right of the State to carry on any trade, industry or business by itself or through a Corporation owned or controlled by the State, all citizens have the right to practise any profession, or to carry on any occupation, trade, industry or business ; no person shall be convicted of any offence except for violation of a law in force at the time of the commission of the act charged as an offence ; no person shall be deprived of his life or personal liberty except according to procedure established by law ; subject to public order, morality and health, all persons are equally entitled to freedom of conscience and the right freely to profess, practise and propagate religion ; every religious denomination shall have the right to establish and maintain institutions for religious and charitable purposes, to manage its own affairs in matters of religion and to own and acquire property ; any section of the citizens residing in the territory of India having a distinct language, script and culture of its own shall have the right to conserve the same ; and all minorities, whether based on religion, community or language, shall have the right to establish and administer educational institutions of their choice. Subject to the saving of certain laws providing for the acquisition of estates by the states and of certain other categories of social welfare legislation affecting property rights, no person shall be deprived of his property save by authority of law and without payment of an amount[1] which may be fixed by law: the amount to be paid has been left to be determined by the legislature and it will not be open to the courts to go into the question whether the amount fixed is adequate or not. The right to move the Supreme Court for the enforcement of fundamental rights has been guaranteed under the Constitution.

In addition to these rights, which are justiciable, i.e. enforceable through resort to courts if violated, the constitution, following the constitution of Eire, also lays down certain directive principles of state policy, which are not enforceable by any court but are nevertheless fundamental in the governance of the country, and it is the duty of the State to apply these principles in making laws. The State is to direct its policy towards securing that the citizens, men and women equally, have the right to an adequate means of livelihood ; that the ownership and control of the material resources of the community are so distributed as best to subserve the common good ; that there is equal pay for equal work for both men and women ; that the level of nutrition and the standard of living of the people is raised and public health improved ; that the right to work, to education and to public assistance in case of unemployment, old age, sickness and disablement, and just and humane conditions of work including a living wage and necessary leisure are provided ; and that international peace and security are promoted by maintaining just and honourable relations between nations, by fostering respect for international law and treaty obligations, and by encouraging settlement of international disputes by arbitration.

Though India has been described in the constitution as a Union of states the constitution is federal in its structure.

Before the scheme of reorganization of the component units of the Union came into force on 1 November 1956, the units of the Union, which were called states, were 27 in number and were classified into three categories, namely, Part A states, Part B

---

[1] The word in Article 31 originally was compensation. Following a judicial pronouncement, the word 'compensation' was substituted by 'amount'.

states and Part C states, and the territory of India comprised the territories of those states and the territory specified in Part D of the First Schedule to the Constitution, i.e. the Andaman and Nicobar Islands. As from 1 November 1956, when the Constitution (Seventh Amendment) Act, 1956 came into force, the component units of the Union had been reduced to 20 in number and they had been classified into two categories, namely, states and Union territories. The Union by 1974 consisted of 21 states and 10 Union territories and the territory of India now comprises the territories of those states and the Union territories.

The division of legislative powers is as follows :

97 subjects are listed as Union subjects. The most important of these are defence, naval, military and air forces, foreign affairs, war and peace, trade and commerce with foreign countries, emigration and immigration, posts and telegraphs, maritime shipping and navigation, Union railways, currency and foreign exchange, census, industries the control of which by the Union is declared by Parliament to be expedient in the public interest, inter-state migration and inter-state commerce.

65 subjects are enumerated as being within the sphere of the states, including public order, the administration of justice (except the Supreme Court), police, prisons, libraries, local government, public health and sanitation, education, communications (with exceptions), agriculture, forests, trade and commerce within the state development of industries (with exceptions), relief of the disabled and unemployable, and land revenue.

47 subjects are concurrent, including criminal law and procedure, civil procedure, marriage and divorce, newspapers, factories, welfare of labour, trade unions, industrial and labour disputes, and economic and social planning.

The residuary power (i.e. subjects not enumerated in the three lists referred to above) is to be with the Union.

In respect of subjects on which both the Union and the states have power to make law, a law made by the Union shall prevail in case of conflict with the state law. If, however, there is conflict between the law made by the state legislature on a concurrent subject and an earlier law made by Parliament on the same subject, the law made by the state legislature shall prevail notwithstanding such conflict if the state law has been reserved for the consideration of the President and has received his assent.

The Union Executive. The head of the Union is a President elected for five years by the members of an electoral college consisting of the elected members of both Houses of Parliament and the elected members of the Legislative Assemblies of the states ; he may stand for re-election. The election is to be in accordance with the system of proportional representation by means of the single transferable vote and by secret ballot. To be eligible for such election, a person must be a citizen of India, not less than 35 years of age, and be qualified for election as a member of the House of the People.

A President may be removed from office before his term of office is over by impeachment for violation of the Constitution. The charge may be preferred by either House of Parliament if supported by not less than two-thirds of the total membership of the House ; the other House shall then have the charge investigated, and if on such investigation a resolution sustaining the charge is passed by that House, supported by not less than two-thirds of the total membership of the House, the President is removed from office.

The President appoints the Prime Minister, and, on his advice, other ministers. All executive action of the Government of India is to be taken in the name of the President. He makes rules for the more convenient transaction of the business of the Government of India and for the allocation among ministers of such business. He must be informed of all the decisions of the Council of Ministers relating to the administration of the Union and of all proposals for legislation ; he may call for such information relating to the administration and proposals for legislation as he may think necessary, and he may ask the Prime Minister to submit for the consideration of the Council of Ministers any matter on which a decision has been taken by a minister but which has not been considered by the Council. When a bill is passed by both Houses of Parliament, it has to be sent for his assent ; he may return bills other than money bills for their reconsideration. When the two Houses cannot agree on the provisions of a bill, he may summon them to a joint sitting. When Parliament is not in session, he may promulgate ordinances. When a bill is reserved by the Governor of a state for his consideration, he may assent to it or withhold his assent, or he may direct the Governor to return it (provided it is not a money bill) to the Legislature for reconsideration. In a grave emergency when the security of India is threatened, he may issue a Proclamation of Emergency, with important consequences mentioned below.[1] He appoints the judges of the Supreme Court and High Courts. The President is also the Supreme Commander of the Defence Forces.

While the President has these legal powers he is intended by the Constitution to be a constitutional head, i.e., to be guided by the advice of his Council of Ministers. These ministers, it is laid down, shall be chosen from members of Parliament (or must be elected to the Paliament within six months). While individually they hold office during the pleasure of the President, they are collectively responsible to the House of the People.[2] The Constitution specifically adds that the Council of Ministers shall be collectively responsible to the House of the People. It is clear that the Union executive is a parliamentary executive of the the British type.

Parliament. The Union Legislature, termed Parliament, is bicameral, the two House being known as the Council of States (Rajya Sabha) and the House of the People (Lok Sabha).

The Council of States is to consist of not more than 250 members of whom 12 are to be nominated by the President from persons having special knowledge or practical experience in such matters as literature, science, art and social service, and the rest are to be filled by representatives of the states and of the Union territories. It is provided that the representatives of each state shall be elected by the elected members of the Legislative Assembly of the state and those of the Union territories shall be chosen in such manner as Parliament may by law prescribe. The duration of the House is six years, one-third retiring at the end of every two years. The membership of the Council, as constituted at present is 243. Of these 231 represent the States and Union territories, of whom 230 are indirectly elected and one representing the Union territory of Arunachala Pradesh, is nominated by the President. Twelve members, specialists as mentioned earlier, are nominated by the President.[3]

The House of the People now consists of five hundred and twenty-four members. Of these 506 are chosen by direct election from territorial constituencies in the 21 states and 15 from eight Union territories. One member is nominated by the President to represent the Union territory of Arunachala Pradesh and two members are nominated by him to represent the Anglo-Indians.[4]

[1] §5.   [2] See Article 75 (2) (3).
[3] *India* 1973, pp. 24-25.   [4] *ibid.*

The duration of the House of the People shall normally be five years unless it is dissolved sooner. Election is on the basis of adult suffrage; and, for a period of ten years, seats are reserved for the Scheduled Castes and the Scheduled Tribes, roughly in proportion to their population strength. It is also provided that the President may nominate not more than two members of the Anglo-Indian community to the House of the People if he is of opinion that that community is not adequately represented in the House.

Regarding the relation between the two Houses of the Legislature, the position is as follows: ordinary bills may be introduced in either House, and can become law only if approved by both Houses. Irreconcilable differences of opinion between the two are resolved by a vote taken at a joint sitting of both Houses. Money bills and other financial bills may be introduced only in the House of the People. In the case of money bills, the Council of States has only a suspensive veto of 14 days; at the end of this period, notwithstanding the veto of the Council of States, they are presented to the President for his assent.

The Supreme Court is the highest Court in the land. It consists of the Chief Justice of India and, until Parliament by law prescribes a larger number, not more than seven other judges appointed by the President. At present the Supreme Court consists of fourteen judges including the Chief Justice. In the appointment of a judge other than the Chief Justice, the Chief Justice of India shall always be consulted. A judge holds office until he attains the age of sixty-five years; he may, however, be removed from office before the term is over by an order of the President if an address by each House of Parliament, supported by a majority of the total membership of that House and not less than two-thirds of the members of that House present and voting, has been presented to the President for such removal on the ground of proved misbehaviour or incapacity. The privileges and allowances of a judge and his rights in respect of leave of absence or pension cannot be varied to his disadvantage after his appointment.

The jurisdiction of the Court is partly original and partly appellate. It has exclusive original jurisdiction in any dispute between the Government of India and one or more states, between the Government of India and any state or states, on one side and one or more other states on the other, or between two or more states, in so far as the dispute involves any question on which the existence or extent of a legal right depends. In addition, article 32 of the Constitution gives an extensive original jurisdiction to the Supreme Court in regard to the enforcement of fundamental rights. It is empowered to issue directions or orders or writs such as those of *habeas corpus*. whichever may be appropriate to enforce them. It has appellate jurisdiction in (*a*) a civil, criminal or other proceeding if the High Court of a state certifies that the case involves a substantial question of law as to the interpretation of the Constitution, or if the Supreme Court gives special leave appeal, and (b) in civil cases if the High Court of a state certifies that the amount involved is not less than twenty thousand rupees or that the case is a fit one for appeal to the Supreme Court (with some restrictions). It is also provided that the Supreme Court may, in its discretion, grant special leave to appeal from any judgement, decree. determination. order, or sentence in any cause or matter passed or made by any court or tribunal in India (excepting a court or tribunal constituted under any law relating to the Armed Forces). There is also conferred on the Supreme Court criminal appellate jurisdiction in a limited class of cases. The Supreme Court has also some advisory functions on a reference made to it by the President under Articles 143 and 317 of the Constitution.

§4 THE STATE GOVERNMENT

(*i*) *The states.* The states are made up of the three categories of states which were the component units of the Union prior to 1 November 1956 when the scheme of States Reorganization came into force, namely, Part A states (which were former Governors' provinces) Part B States (which were former Indian states or unions of such states) and some of the Part C states (which were either former Indian states or unions of such states or former Chief Commissioners' provinces).

The Indian Union today consists of 21 states and 102 Union territories.[1] The following are the 21 states:

Andhra Pradesh, Assam, Bihar, Gujarat, Haryana, Himachal Pradesh, Jammu and Kashmir, Kerala, Madhya Pradesh, Maharashtra, Manipur, Meghalaya, Karnataka, Nagaland, Orissa, Punjab, Rajasthan, Tamil Nadu, Tripura, Uttar Pradesh and West Bengal.

The state Executive. The executive power of the state is vested in a Governor[2] appointed by the President for five years. Only a cirizen of India who has completed the age of thirty-five years is eligible to be a Governor. The Governor holds office during the pleasure of the President.

On the Union Territories see pp. 415 ff.
[2] Under Article 153 of the Constitution as amended by the Constitution (Seventh Amendment) Act, 1956, it is permissible to appoint the same person as Governor for two or more states.

The Governor appoints the Chief Minister, and, on the advice of the Chief Minister, appoints the other ministers. The Chief Minister would normally be the person who is likely to command a stable majority in the Legislature. While individually the ministers hold office during the pleasure of the Governor, the Council of Ministers, it is stated specifically, shall be collectively responsible to the Legislative Assembly of the state. ; The Governor appoints the Advocate-General ; all executive action of the Government of a state is to be taken in the name of the Governor ; all decisions of the Council of Ministers relating to administration, and proposals for legislation, have to be communicated to him ; he may call for any information relating to administration and proposals for legislation ; he has the right to nominate to the Legislative Council (in those states where one exists) one-sixth of the total number of its members ; he summons the Legislature and may dissolve the Legislative Assembly ; he may address the Legislature or send messages to it ; his assent is necessary for a bill to become law, and, instead of giving his assent, he may ask the Legislature to reconsider a bill, if it is not a money bill, or may reserve a bill for the consideration of the President ; when the Legislature is not in session, he may promulgate ordinances having validity for a limited period.

These are among the legal powers of the Governor. It is obvious, however, that essentially his position is, like that of the President, that of a constitutional head.[1] He is to act on the advice of the Council of Ministers already referred to, and this Council of Ministers with a Chief Minister at its head is in all essentials like the Cabinet of Britain, and of the Union of India — a parliamentary Executive. The Constitution (Seventh Amendment) Act, 1956 has, however, made certain special provisions for investing the Governors of Andhra Pradesh, Punjab[2] and Bombay[3] with special responsibility with respect to certain matters.[4]

The state Legislature. The constitution envisages the possibility of some states having a bicameral legislature, and others a unicameral one.

Where there are two Houses, one is known as the Legislative

---

[1] The Governor of Assam has some discretionary functions under para 9(2) & 18(3) of the 6th Schedule.

[2] Since reorganized. See p. 408 n.

[3] Since divided into Maharashtra and Gujarat.

[4] See Article 371.

Council and the other the Legislative Assembly, and where there is only one House, it is called the Legislative Assembly.

The number of members of the Legislative Council of a state, it is stated, shall not exceed one-third of the total number of members in the Legislative Assembly of that state and shall in no case be less than forty. Of the total number, one-third shall be elected by electorates consisting of members of municipalities, district boards and such other local authorities in the state as Parliament may by law specify ; one-twelfth shall be elected by graduates of three years standing ; one-twelfth by teachers of educational institutions of certain categories ; one-third by the Legislative Assembly of the state ; and the remainder shall be nominated by the Governor. One-third of the total number of members shall retire on the expiration of every second year.

The Legislative Assembly is directly elected on the basis of adult suffrage, with reservations for Scheduled Castes and Scheduled Tribes as in the Union House of the People, the reservation being provided only for the first ten years. The duration of the Assembly shall normally be five years unless it is sooner dissolved. The number of members shall not be less than sixty nor more than five hundred.

Where two chambers exist, their relative powers are as follows : ordinary bills may be introduced in either chamber, and the consent of both is necessary before a bill can be presented to the Governor for his assent. If, however, within three months, the Legislative Council does not pass a bill in the form desired by the Assembly, the bill may be again passed by the Assembly, and transmitted to the Council, and it shall be deemed to have been passed by both the Houses after the expiry of one month notwithstanding the fact that it has not been agreed to by the Council. Money bills and other financial bills can be introduced only in the Legislative Assembly. In the case of Money bills, the Legislative Council has only a suspensive veto of 14 days, after which period they are presented to the Governor for assent.

The state Judiciary. Judges of a High Court are to be appointed by the President after consultation with the Chief Justice of India and the Governor of the State. In the appointment of a Judge, other than the Chief Justice, the Chief Justice of the High Court concerned is also to be consulted. As regards conditions of service and mode of dismissal, the provisions closely follow those which have already been discussed in relation to the Supreme Court ; it is provided, however, that a judge of a High Court shall hold office until he attains the age of sixty-two years.

Regarding the jurisdiction of High Courts it is provided that, until altered by any law made by the appropriate Legislature, it shall be the same as immediately before the commencement of the constitution, with the modification that they shall have also original jurisdiction in respect of any matter concerning the revenue and its collection.

Every High Court, it is provided, shall have superintendence over all courts and tribunals throughout the territory in relation to which it exercises jurisdiction other than those constituted under any law relating to the Armed Force.

Powers have been conferred on the High Courts to issue writs within their respective jurisdictions not only to any person or authority but also to Government for the enforcement of fundamental rights and for other purposes. The High Courts have been also given power to take over cases from subordinate courts involving questions of the interpretation of the constitution.

Former Indian states. As has already been stated, before 1 November 1956 when the scheme of reorganization of the component units of the Indian Union came into force, there were certain units of the Union known as Part B states which were former Indian states or Unions of such states. They were eight in number :

Hyderabad, Jammu and Kashmir, Madhya Bharat, Mysore, Patiala and East Punjab States Union, Rajasthan, Saurashtra, and Travancore-Cochin.

The Indian states had a semi-independent status under the British régime. In view of the unique constitutional position held by these states, it will be useful briefly to explain their status before 15 August 1947.

Position of Indian states before 15 August 1947

In 1940 there were some 600 Indian states. They varied considerably in area, population and revenue. They agreed, however, in three respects : They were not British territory, their subjects were not British subjects, and in general they were under a system of personal rule, the supreme power in each state being vested in a Ruling Chief. Many progressive states — Mysore, Cochin and Travancore among them — had all the essentials of a developed system of administration such as a distinction between the privy purse and the state revenues, and an independent judiciary. Some states had gone further and followed a policy of associating their people with the government. Nearly forty states had Legislative Councils with power to pass resolutions and laws, and to ask questions, though in nearly every case the Executive was vested with power to override the wishes of the Councils. A few had gone further, and introduced partial responsibility of the Executive to the Legislature : in Cochin and Rajkot, through a system of dyarchy ; in Mysore, by including two members of the Legislature in the Council of Ministers which worked on the principle of joint responsibility.

Paramountcy

The British Crown as Paramount Power had certain rights and obligations in relation to the states. These rights and obligations were generally summed up in the term 'paramountcy'. Paramountcy was based upon the treaties, engagements, and *sanads* which the Paramount Power had at various times entered into with the states, supplemented by usage and by decisions of the Political Department of the Government of India on matters pertaining to the states. The activities of the Paramount Power may be enumerated under three heads.[1]

(a) *External affairs.* The states surrendered the exercise of all their rights of external sovereignty to the Crown : they had no international life. They could not make peace or war or negotiate or communicate with foreign states. They could not cede, sell, exchange or part with their territories to other states without the approval of the Paramount Power, nor without that approval could they settle interstatal disputes.

This statement of the position, it ought to be explained, does not mean that 'treaties with foreign (non-Indian) states concluded by the British Crown are *proprio vigore* binding on the Indian states without their concurrence'.[2] They became binding on the states only if they had been concluded with the previous consent or express authority of the states themselves. This position was accepted by the Government of India when the issue was raised in connexion with the Geneva Dangerous Drugs Convention and Opium Agreement of 1925.[3]

---

[1] See the *Report of the Indian States Committee*, 1928-9.
[2] D. K. Sen, *The Indian States, their Status, Rights and Obligations*, p. 118-19.
[3] ibid.

' To attempt to enforce any policy of suppressing or restricting the cultivation of opium in Indian states apart from any arrangement which may be entered into under Treaty obligations would mean interference in their internal administration such as the Government of India have no power to exercise either by prescriptive or by Treaty rights.'[1]

(*b*) *Defence and protection.* The Paramount Power was responsible for the defence of the Indian states and had the final voice in all matters connected with defence, including establishments, war material, communications, etc. It defended them against both external and internal enemies.

(*c*) *Internal affairs.* The succession of a ruler was not valid without the recognition of the Paramount Power ; that Power had the right to settle disputed successions and to secure religious toleration. Further, it had rights in regard to railways, posts and telegraphs. It had the right to prevent gross misrule. In regard to constitutional reforms in the states, it is clear, according to authoritative statements made in Parliament,[2] that while the Paramount Power did not obstruct proposals for constitutional advance initiated by the Rulers it had also ' no intention of bringing any form of pressure to bear upon them to initiate constitutional changes '.

The Indian States Committee said that it was impossible to define paramountcy. ' Paramountcy must remain paramount,' they said, ' it must fulfil its obligations, defining or adapting itself according to the shifting necessities of the time and the progressive development of the states.'[3]

Were the states sovereign ? The answer is that they had no external sovereignty, while they had varying degrees of internal sovereignty. A letter[4] from Lord Reading, as Viceroy, to the Nizam of Hyderabad sums up the position adopted by the Paramount Power, though only grudgingly accepted by the states.

' The sovereignty of the British Crown is supreme in India, and, therefore, no ruler of an Indian state can justifiably claim to negotiate with the British Government on an equal footing. Its supremacy is not based only upon the Treaties and Engagements

[1] Memorandum of the Government of India to the League of Nations Opium Advisory Committee, quoted by Sen, op. cit., p. 119.
[2] 21 February 1938, 6 April 1939, 16 December 1939.
[3] *Report* (1929).
[4] 27 March 1926. See Appendix to the *Report of the Indian States Committee*, 1928-9.

but exists independently of them, and quite apart from its prerogative in matters relating to foreign powers and policies, it is the right and duty of the British Government, while scrupulously respecting all Treaties and Engagements with the Indian states, to preserve peace and good order throughout India. . . .

' Where imperial interests are concerned or the general welfare of the people of a state is seriously and grievously affected by the action of its Government, it is with the Paramount Power that the ultimate responsibility for taking remedial action, if necessary, must lie. The varying degrees of internal sovereignty which the rulers enjoy are all subject to the due exercise by the Paramount Power of this responsibility.'

1947-1950

The transfer of power from Britain to India coupled with the partition of the country naturally brought about fundamental changes in the position. The British Government when transferring power to India made it clear that they would not transfer paramountcy over the states to India, with the result that legally the states became independent. The compelling force of circumstances, however, made it evident that it was in the interests both of the states and the Dominion of India that the states in the territory should accede to the Dominion. As it happened, largely due to the initiative taken by the States Ministry of the Government of India and the willing co-operation extended by the rulers of the states concerned, the large majority of states preferred to be integrated with the territory of India, losing their separate identity ; some decided to merge themselves with the neighbouring states so that a bigger political unit resulted from such merger, and a few, being big enough by themselves, retained their individuality.

In the result the eight states mentioned above became component units of the Indian Union at the commencement of the Constitution and they [1] were in all essentials similar in their governmental function to the Part A states which were former Governor's provinces. The only important difference was that the Rajpramukh — that is, the Chief Prince recognized by the President for purposes of the Constitution — occupied the position held by the Governor in respect of the Part A states.

---

[1] The position of the state of Jammu and Kashmir is slightly different — see Article 370 of the Constitution.

On the abolition of the constitutional distinction between Part A and Part B states, as from 1 November 1956, the institution of Rajpramukh was abolished and of the 8 states mentioned above some continued to remain separate units (states) of the Indian Union and some were merged in the new units (states) established under the reorganization scheme.

(*ii*) *Union territories.* The Union territories which roughly correspond in status to the former Chief Commissioners' provinces are made up of some of the erstwhile Part C states, the territory previously specified in Part D of the First Schedule to the Constitution and certain other areas.

The Union territories are the following :

Andaman and Nicobar Islands, Arunachala Pradesh, Chandigarh Dadra and Nagar Haveli, Delhi, Goa, Daman and Diu, the Laccadive, Minicoy and Amindivi Islands, Mizoram and Pondicherry.

The governmental structure of the Union territories is different from that of the states mentioned in (i) above. It is provided in the Constitution that every Union territory is to be administered by the President acting, to such extent as he thinks fit. through an administrator appointed by him. The President may appoint the Governor of a state as the administrator of an adjoining Union territory and where a Governor is so appointed he shall exercise his functions as such administrator independently of his Council of Ministers.

The Administrators of Delhi, Goa, Daman and Diu, Mizoram and Pondicherry are designated as Lt.-Governors while the administrators of Andaman and Nicobar Islands, Arunachala Pradesh and Chandigarh are designate as Chief Commissioners The Lt.-Governor of Goa, Daman and Diu is concurrently the Administrator of Dadra and Nagar Haveli. The Laccadive, Minicoy and Amindivi Islands have a separate administrator.

Under the Government of Union Territories Act, 1963. legislative assemblies and Councils of Ministers have been constituted in Goa, Daman and Diu, Mizoram and Pondicherry. The Delhi Administration Act, 1966, provides for a Metropolitan Council and an Executive Council for the Union territory of Delhi; Arunachala Pradesh has a Pradesh Council and the administrator may appoint not more than five members of this Council as Counsellors whom he may consult on matters relating to the administration of the territory.

The Legislative Assemblies in the Union territories may make laws with respect to matters in the state field, namely, those enumerated in List II or List III in the Seventh Schedule in so, far as they are applicable in relation to Union territories. Parliament can also make laws with respect to such matters for the Union territories.

The Metropolitan Council in Delhi has the right to discuss and make recommendations about matters in so far as they relate to Delhi.

§5 THE UNION AND THE STATES

The essential principle of a federation applies to India as to other federal states, viz., that in respect of subjects which are allotted by the constitution to the states, the states have power to pass laws and administer them. This principle is, however. subject to important qualifications, as follows.

Legislative

(*a*) The Constitution authorizes the Governor of a state to reserve a bill for the consideration of the President. This means that when the Legislature of a state has passed a bill, instead of assenting to or withholding his assent to it, he may reserve it for the consideration of the President of the Union — who, it follows, may or may not agree with the wishes of the states legislature. It may, however, be argued that the power of the President in this respect can operate only when the Governor of the state, acting on the advice of his ministers who are responsible to the legislature, has reserved it for the consideration of the President, and, therefore, this provision cannot be considered an imposition from above.

The Constitution, however, makes it obligatory for the Governor to reserve for the consideration of the President any bill which in his opinion would, if it became law, so derogate from the powers of the High Court as to affect its independence. This must be considered a salutary provision, the very existence of which should prevent the legislature of the state from attempting to interfere with the administration of justice.

The Constitution has also provided that any law made by a legislature of a state for the compulsory acquisition of property for public purposes shall not have effect unless it is reserved for the consideration of the President and has received his assent — vide article 31(3).

(*b*) The previous sanction or instructions of the President is necessary for the introduction of certain type of bills into the state legislature and for promulgating certain types of ordinances.[1]

(c) Notwithstanding the division of powers, the Union Parliament has power to make any law for implementing any treaty or agreement with other countries, even though the subject of the treaty or agreement may fall in the state list. Thus the power to make laws to implement an International Convention relating to some aspect of public health is with the Union Parliament, although public health is a subject in the state list. This power was, however, given to the Union to obviate the difficulties that have arisen in other federations like Canada — where the Centre had not been provided with such a power.

(d) The Union Parliament has power to legislate on a specified state subject[2]. (i) if the legislatures of two or more states pass resolutions to the effect that the matter should be regulated so far as those states are concerned by law of Parliament or (ii) if the Council of States declares by a resolution supported by not less than two-thirds of the members present and voting that it is necessary or expedient in the national interest that Parliament should make such a law. This second provision has been necessitated by the consideration that a subject which is normally appropriate for state legislation may, in certain exceptional circumstances—e.g. the subject of Agriculture during a period of widespread agricultural depression in several parts of India—assume national importance requiring legislation on a national scale.

(e) If the President is satisfied that a grave emergency exists whereby the security of India is threatened whether by war, external aggression, or internal disturbance, he may make a Proclamation to the effect and thereupon, among other consequences, the Union Parliament is empowered to make laws even in respect of the matters enumerated in the state list.

Administrative

It is laid down that the executive power of every state must be so exercised as to ensure compliance with the laws made by Parliament, and so as not to impede or prejudice the executive power of the Union, and the executive power of the Union shall extend to the giving of such directions to a state as may appear to the Government of India to be necessary for these purposes.

[1] e.g. Articles 304 and 213.   [2] Articles 252 and 249.

Moreover, (*i*) tne executive power of the Union includes the giving of directions to a state as to the construction and maintenance of means of communication declared to be of national or military importance and as to the measures to be taken for protection of the railways within the state ; (*ii*) with the consent of the Government of a state, the President of the Union may entrust to that Government functions in relation to any matter to which the executive power of the Union extends ; (*iii*) in emergency, the executive power of the Union extends to the giving of directions to any state as to the manner in which its executive power is to be exercised ; and (*iv*) in case of the failure of the normal constitutional machinery in the states, the President of the Union may assume to himself all or any of the executive functions of the government of the state.

Besides the legislative and administrative powers of the Union in relation to the states indicated above, we must note that by means of grants-in-aid to such states as Parliament may determine to be in need of assistance, the Union is in a position powerfully to influence the policy of the states ; that Governors are appointed by the President ; and above all the Union is charged with the duty of protecting every state against external aggression and internal disturbance and of ensuring that the government of every state is carried on in accordance with the provisions of the constitution. If the President on a report from the Governor or otherwise is satisfied that a situation has arisen in which the administration of the state cannot be carried on in accordance with the normal provisions of the constitution, the President may by Proclamation [1] assume to himself all or any of the functions of the government of the state and declare that the powers of the legislature of the state shall be exercisable by or under the authority of Parliament.

Taking all these facts into consideration, critics of the constitution point out that there is over-centralization, and that the federation is only nominal, the government being in fact a unitary one. This criticism, while it has some force, is not quite true. The real position may be stated thus : India was originally a unitary state, and, by devolution from the Centre, the provinces

---

[1] Any such Proclamation requires the approval of Parliament within two months from the date of issue. No such Proclamation can be continued in force for more than six months without the further approval of Parliament. Nor can any Proclamation be continued in force for a period of more than three years.

became more and more autonomous. The Indian states were also effectively under the control of the Government of India whatever be their theoretical position. The relation between the Union and the states under the constitution, therefore, bears the marks of history and experience. Moreover, the overwhelming power of the Centre can and will be brought into play only in emergency and not in normal times. Above all, the social and economic and political conditions of the modern world—large-scale industry, the increasing interdependence of countries, increasing insecurity and the total nature of war—together with the experience of other federations supports the view that everywhere, whatever the letter of the constitution, the Centre does in fact exercise an increasing measure of control over the units, certainly in emergencies, and to a lesser extent in normal times ; and the people everywhere have come to appreciate the need for greater uniformity in essential matters, without unduly curtailing the scope for diversity and experiment which is the great advantage of a federation.

§6 THE ADMINISTRATIVE SYSTEM:
THE STRUCTURE OF ADMINISTRATION

Administration may be defined as the execution, in non-judicial matters, of the law or will of the State as expressed by the competent authority.

In a normal federal State, there are two distinct administrative authorities, the Federal and the state, the Federal Government controlling the administration of the subjects allotted by the constitution to the Federal Authority, the states controlling the administration of the subjects allotted or reserved by the constitution to the states. In the United States, for instance, the regulation of commerce with foreign States is a federal subject ; the Federal Government administers this subject, implementing the laws passed by Congress in regard to this item, appointing officers and controlling them. Education is a subject assigned by the constitution to the sphere of the states ; the state Governments in the fifty states administer this subject in their respective states, implementing the laws passed by the state legislatures in regard to education and the appointment and control of officers.

The statement given above with reference to administration in a normal federal State does not mean—and it has nowhere been the practice—that there is (or should be) a complete separation between the Federal and the state administrative systems although the points of contact and liaison between the two necessarily vary with each federal State. As is illustrated below with reference to India, the appointment of federal officers in certain key posts in the administration of the states, the giving of directions to state governments to ensure that the state administration does not impede or prejudice the executive power of the Union, and the entrusting to state governments of functions in relation to any matter to which the executive power of the Federation extends are some of the ways in which liaison between the state and the Federal Government is established in the field of administrative advantage.

(a) The states

The District. It should be evident that, in a large country like India, the efficiency of administration demands that the whole country should be subdivided into smaller units and that the administrative authority should be distributed amongst subordinate officers, who should, of course, be subject to supervision and control.

Apart from a few exceptions such as the capital cities of states, 'every inch of soil' in India forms part of a district, and at the head of every district there is an officer known in some states (e.g. Madras) as the Collector and in others (e.g. East Punjab) as the Deputy Commissioner.

The Collector, as the chief executive authority in the district, is primarily responsible for the maintenance of law and order and the criminal administration of the district, and for this purpose the police force is under his control and direction. Where the separation of the Executive and the Judiciary has not yet been effected, as magistrate he exercises general supervision over the inferior courts. As Collector, he is the head of the revenue organization. This dual capacity of the Collector gives him a high status in the eyes of the people and thus great influence. ' In areas where there is no permanent revenue settlement, he can at any time be in touch through his revenue subordinates with every inch of his territory. This organization in the first place serves its peculiar purpose of collecting the revenue and of keeping the peace. But because it is so close-knit, so well established and so thoroughly understood by the people, it simultaneously discharges easily and efficiently an immense number of other duties. It deals with the registration, alteration, and partition of holdings ; the settlement of disputes ; the management of indebted estates ; loans to agriculturists ; and, above all, famine relief. Because it controls revenue, which depends on agriculture, the supreme interest of the people, it naturally serves also as the general administration staff....Several other specialized services exist with staffs of their own...but in varying degrees the District Officer influences the policy in all these matters, and he is always there in the background to lend his support, or, if need be, to mediate between specialized service and the people.' [1]

The Collector wields large powers of patronage ; he is responsible for making a vast number of minor appointments, for instance, of village headmen and accountants, of revenue officials and office clerks. It is true that on account of the setting up of specialized departments in fields like public health, agriculture, engineering, etc., each district has its body of district heads of departments, each of whom looks to his own state departmental chief—the Inspector-General of Prisons or Jails, the Surgeon-General, the Chief Conservator of Forests, the Chief Engineer or the Registrar of Co-operative Societies—for control. But except in matters of pure routine, the Collector must be informed of almost every activity in all these departments, because it must impinge at some point upon the operation of the primary government agency in his district.

The district in most parts of the country (Assam being the only exception) has a District Board, which, as an administrative authority, has limited powers in regard to education, public health, sanitation, medical relief and public works including roads and bridges. The members of the District Board are elected on adult suffrage and almost everywhere the Chairman is an elected member. While possessing little control over the details of administration, the state Government holds the ultimate power of superseding, suspending or abolishing a District Board. The proper organization of the District Board with a view to seeing that it has the necessary powers, including financial, to carry out the responsibilities which are by law vested in it is one of the major problems facing the state Governments : on the one hand the state Governments have to see that the springs of local self-

---

[1] Indian Statutory Commission Report, Vol. I, 1930. The statements made in this extract are as true today as they were in 1930.

government are preserved and on the other they have to ensure that (*i*) the District Boards have the necessary trained administrative staff free from political control in the discharge of their duties, and (*ii*) the essential supervisory control is retained in the state Governments and the prestige of the District Collector as their agent is retained.

The Subdivision and the Taluk. The district is further split up into smaller divisions. The officers in charge of these subdivisions are known variously as Sub-Collector, Assistant Collector or Deputy Collector. The general revenue and magisterial charge of the subdivision is vested in the subdivisional officer subject to the control of the Collector.

The subdivision has many taluks (or tahsils) each of which has at its head an officer known as the Tahsildar (or Mamlatdar). It is sufficient to say that he is to the taluk what the Collector is to the district, though in a lesser measure ; he has revenue and magisterial powers and has to supervise the administration within the taluk.

Corresponding to the District Board in the district there is in the taluk (though not in some states, e.g. East Punjab and Uttar Pradesh) a Taluk Board, a minor self-government authority. It is a subordinate agency of the District Board composed, in the main, of elected members and, as a rule, chooses its own Chairman.

The Village. Finally comes the village, which is the basis of the administrative system. According to the 1951 census, 82.7 per cent or nearly five-sixths of the people live in villages and there are about 558,089 of them. The village officers include the headman (called the *patel*) responsible for the collection of revenue and the maintenance of peace in the village ; the village accountant (*karnam* or *talati*) responsible for the keeping of village accounts and registers of holdings and records of land revenue ; the village watchman (the *talyari*) and the irrigation canal controller (the *nirganti*).

The Village Panchayat [1] which exists in most villages in the country is an elected body with jurisdiction over a village or group of villages ; the primary function is to look after such matters as wells and sanitation ; it is sometimes entrusted with

---

[1] Originally it meant a body composed generally of five leading men of the village.

the care of minor roads and irrigation, the management of schools and dispensaries, forests and irrigation works. In the plans for development of the villages under the Five Year Plan, especially under the Community Projects programme, the Village Panchayats have an important part to play.

Local self-government in urban areas. Mention has been made above of local self-governing authorities in rural areas—the District Board, the Taluk Board and the Village Panchayat—which are important in administration ; a word may be added here of local self-government in urban areas

The unit of local self-government in urban areas is the municipality. There are some 800 municipalities varying in size from cities like Amritsar with some 4 lakh inhabitants to small towns with a few thousand. In every town all or nearly all Councillors of the municipality are elected on adult suffrage ; most elect their own Chairman ; some have paid executive officers in charge of municipal administration. The functions of municipal councils include the administration of education, public health, sanitation, medical relief, water supply, lighting, and roads and bridges : as in the case of rural authorities, the state Government has powers of supervision including the ultimate power of supersession, suspension or abolition of a municipal council.

The big cities—Calcutta, Bombay and Madras, and a few others—fall in a special category : they have corporations constituted each under its separate statute and vested with larger powers and privileges than municipal councils ; they enjoy a considerable measure of freedom in the administration of the city's affairs, though, inevitably, certain powers of control in relation to appointments, contracts, the raising of loans and the audit of accounts are reserved to the state Governments.

The Secretariat and the Heads of Departments at the Capital. To co-ordinate and control the district and other local authorities and to be in charge of state administration we have the Secretariat and the Heads of Departments.

At the Secretariat the Ministers have their offices. The Secretariat is an important adjunct of state administration partly because of the large part the Minute, the Note and the Report play in the administration. ' Armies of clerks people the rabbit-warrens of the Secretariat, receiving and despatching correspondence, submitting notes, furnishing information, starting the files on their journey to Superintendent, Under-Secretary and Minister. The smooth circulation of dispatch boxes is their constant preoccupation.' The business of the Secretariat is to give advice and information, prepare questions and ripen them for the decision of the supreme executive of the province.

The Secretariat is, for the convenience of its own internal working, subdivided into departments—Home, Finance, Revenue, Development, Local Self-Government, etc.—and in charge of one or more of these departments is a Secretary to Government ; the Secretary has the necessary administrative staff — Joint Secretary, Deputy Secretary, Assistant Secretary, Assistant — to assist him in his work ; the Secretary himself is directly under the Minister in charge of the portfolio. The Secretary receives communications principally from the heads of the administrative departments [1] — the Board of Revenue, the Inspector-General of Police, the Director of Public Instruction, the Director of Agriculture, the Director of Industries, the Registrar of Co-operative Societies, the Inspector of Local Boards, etc. All the Heads of Departments are individuals except in the Board of Revenue which for histori-cal reasons and on account of the largeness and multiplicity of the questions involved is of a collegial character. The Heads of Departments are charged with the duty and responsibility of admi-nistering the affairs of their respective departments. The routine administration of the ordinary affairs of the departments is within their competence and discretion. It is only on extraordinary matters and questions of new policy that they have to go to the supreme executive by way of their Secretary and Secretariat.' [2]

(b) The Union

The Central Secretariat, which is the apex of the Union Administration, is divided into thirty Ministries, [3] a Ministry being a unit of administration of the Government of India and a Minister being in charge of such a Unit. [4]

---

[1] From this general description, the Finance and the Legal Secretary must be differentiated. They deal with no administrative departments but are concerned with the internal working of the Government.

[2] M. Rathnaswamy, in *India Quarterly*, Vol. VI. p. 35.

[3] There are in addition, some units which do not form part of any Ministry, though they form part of the administrative machinery, such as the Indian Audit and Accounts Department under the control of the Comptroller and Audit-General; the Election Commission; the Cabinet Secretariat; the Prime Minister's Secretariat; the President's Secretariat; the Union Public Service Commission; the Planning Commission.

[4] It is not essential that there should be a separate Minister for every one of the Ministries.

The names of the Ministries are indicated below

Agriculture
Atomic Energy
Cabinet Secretariat
Commerce
Communications
Posts and Telegraph Board
Culture
Defence
Education and Social Welfare
Electronics
External Affairs
Finance
Health and Family Planning
Heavy Industry
Home Affairs
Industrial Development
Information and Broadcasting

Irrigation and Power
Labour, Employment and Rehabilitation
Law, Justice and Company Affairs
Parliamentary Affairs
Petroleum and Chemicals
Planning
Railways
Science and Technology
Shipping and Transport
Space
Steel and Mines
Supply
Tourism and Civil Aviation
Works and Housing

It is unnecessary in this context to describe the functions of the Ministries in detail; in most cases the name of the Ministry is indicative of its primary functions, e.g., The Ministry of Industrial Development is concerned with the development and regulation of industries and with certain controls relating to textiles, etc., the Ministry of External Affairs with India is relations with foreign countries including the countries of the Commonwealth, the Ministry of Agriculture and the development of agriculture and so on.[1]

Organization of a Ministry. Let us take by way of illustration the Ministry of Industrial Development.[2]

The Ministry of Industrial Development consists of a Secretariat, four attached offices and eight subordinate offices.

The Secretariat staff comprises Secretary 1, Joint Secretaries 3, Officers on Special Duty 2, Development Commissioner (Small Scale Industries) 1, Textile Commissioner and ex-officio Joint

[1] It should be noted that the names of Ministries and the number of officers are often changed; as examples, however, these remain relevant. A Note in some detail on the function of the Ministries is given at the end of section 7.
[2] Since this passage was written, the Ministry of Industry has been replaced by the Ministry of Industrial Development with some variations in the pattern of internal organization. However, it still provides a good enough illustration of the general pattern of organization.

Secretary 1. Chairman (All-India Handloom Board) 1, Deputy Secretaries 7. Under Secretaries 14. Section Officers 48, Others 505. Total strength 583.

The Ministry has forty-eight Sections and six Special Sections. The four attached offices are, the office of the Economic Adviser to the Government of India, the office of the Development Commissioner, Small Scale Industries, the office of the Salt Commissioner and the All-India Handicrafts Board.

The subordinate offices include those of the Joint Registrar and Textile Commissioner, Controller of Patents, Designs and Trade Marks, and All-India Handloom Board. The distinction between the three parts of the Ministry the Secretariat, with a Secretary at the head (who is himself subject to the Minister), the attached offices and the subordinate offices is fundamental to the understanding of the nature of administration. The Secretariat is, broadly speaking, the organization which makes policy and issues instructions for implementation of policy ; the attached offices and the subordinate offices are alike in so far as their primary function is to implement the policy as laid down by the Secretariat : perhaps it may be said that the attached offices are sometimes consulted and their advice is sought by the Ministry on questions relating to the formulation of policy.

For a complete understanding of the organization of the Ministry, it must be added that the Ministry has under its control nine State undertakings (NSIC), two Boards (Central Silk Board), a Commission, viz., All-India Khadi and Village Industries Commission, a Committee, viz. Cotton Textile Fund Committee and a semi-Government Organization, viz. the Indian Standards Institution.

A detailed study of how in practice the Ministry carries on its day-to-day work (Secretariat procedure) is beyond the scope of this short section on the administrative system. A word must, however, be said about it if only to give the student some idea of what administration involves, and to enable him to understand the significance of the criticism so often levelled at the administration that it is paralysed by ' red tape '. The criticism means that the written work — the Note, the Minute and the Report and the file with the red tape — plays a disproportionate part in the disposal of official work, and causes unnecessary delay.

Normally papers that are received in the Ministry are passed on (after they are diarized or entered in a register) to Assistants ; these Assistants study the papers and examine them in the light of rules and precedents, if any, and make suggestions for their disposal. These papers are passed on to the higher officers — the Section Officers, the Under-Secretary, the Deputy Secretary, the Joint Secretary or the Secretary ; these higher officers consider the suggestions made by those below them and pass orders on them. The power to pass orders on papers is vested in the officer ; the officers at the lower level are given the power to dispose of the relatively less important cases, those above them the more important ones, and so on.

The essence of the system is 'noting' by Assistants, who have power to deal with cases but not to dispose of them, and 'decision' by officers at various levels, on the basis of the policy applicable to them as laid down by the Minister. It has a clear advantage : a detailed examination of every case in the light of rules and precedents ensures careful consideration. But inevitably it involves delay.

Under an alternative system which is in vogue in England, clerks, or clerical officers as they are called there, deal purely with routine processes, e.g. filing, record-keeping, typing, etc. Matters involving discretion or judgement and affecting matters of policy are dealt with in the first instance by officers. Papers as they are received are put up as far as possible direct to officers capable of passing final orders on them. The intention is to avoid intermediaries who cannot effectively deal with a case but can only offer an opinion.

There is no doubt that the English system is distinctly better. It effects a saving in time ; it also ensures that the examination and disposal of a paper at every stage is done by a relatively more mature mind, and this affects quality. In the Indian system, it is inevitable that the first examination by an Assistant should colour the final disposal, as, naturally, the suggestions made by the Assistant, in the large majority of cases, form the basis of consideration at higher levels ; the higher officers are not bound by them, but in quite a number of cases they save the effort of thinking, especially when a higher officer has so much to do.

So far as the present writer is aware, the benefits of the English system are known to Indian administrators and a beginning has been made in adapting it to Indian conditions ; but the shortage of trained administrative personnel at the officer level makes a change-over to the new system necessarily slow.

It should also be added that the personal interview, the conference and the telephone are now playing an important role in breaking the rather slow and conservative methods of ' red tape ', and that the existence of a class of highly trained and efficient officers at the higher rungs of the ladder, though not as numerous as is desirable, does give a quality to the Central administration which is distinctly praiseworthy and gives hope that the small mind and the rule of precedent will not be allowed to hinder the development of administration in the right direction.

§7 THE ADMINISTRATIVE SYSTEM: THE PUBLIC SERVICES

The term ' Public Services ' refers to the personnel employed by Government on both the civil and the military side of the administration. Article 311 of the Constitution distinguishes five categories of persons on the civil side of the administration :

> a person who is a member of a civil service of the Union ;
> a person who is a member of an all-India service ;
> a person who is a member of a civil service of a state :
> a person who holds a civil post under the Union ;
> a person who holds a civil post under a state.

It should be explained for the sake of clarity that (*i*) the persons mentioned in all these five categories are sometimes generally referred to as civil servants ; and (*ii*) the expression ' persons holding civil posts ' includes all the personnel, whether permanent or temporary, employed in the civil administration of the Union or a state, who have not been incorporated into a ' service ' of the Union or of the state concerned.

An analysis of the Article referred to above also focusses attention on one aspect of the structure of Civil Services in the Indian federation : while, as in other federal States, the Union and the states have their separate public services to administer their respective affairs, in addition, there are certain services, viz. the all-India services, common to the Union and the states. Article 312 states that if the Council of States has declared by a resolution supported by not less than two-thirds of the members present and voting that it is necessary or expedient in the national interest to do so, Parliament may by law provide for the creation of one or more all-India services common to the Union and the states. At present there are two all-India services, the Indian

Administrative Service and the Indian Police Service. Dr Ambed-
kar explained to the Constituent Assembly the *raison d' être*
of this probably unique arrangement thus :

' It is recognized that in every country there are certain posts
in its administrative set-up which might be called strategic from
the point of view of maintaining the standard of administration
... There can be no doubt that the standard of administration
depends upon the calibre of the civil servants who are appointed
to these strategic posts. The Constitution provides that, without
depriving the states of their right to form their own civil services,
there shall be an all-India service recruited on all-India basis
with common qualifications, with uniform scale of pay, and
members of which alone could be appointed to these strategic
posts throughout the Union.'

Clearly the existence of one or more all-India services, whose
members man the key posts in the Union and state administrations, will help the cohesion of the federation, and is, in the
present author's judgement, a desirable feature in the context
of the Indian federation.

From the analysis given above, it also follows that the Services
under the legislative control of the Union comprise three classes :
(*i*) all-India services ; (*ii*) civil services of the Union other than
the all-India services, such as the Indian Foreign Service, the
Indian Customs Service, the Indian Audit and Accounts Service
and the Central Secretariat Service, and (*iii*) defence services,
i.e. members of the Army, Navy and Air Force.

Recruitment and conditions of service

The detailed regulation of the recruitment and conditions of
service of civil servants in connexion with the affairs of the Union
is left by the Constitution, subject to the general provisions made
by it, to the Union Parliament, and in connexion with the affairs
of any state, to the state legislature ; until such regulation by the
Union Parliament or the state legislature, as the case may be, it
is left to the President — or the Governor of the state — to make
the regulations.

The Constitution itself lays down the broad principles and
prescribes the general method relating to the recruitment and
conditions of service. These may be summarized under two
heads : (*i*) the Public Service Commissions, and (*ii*) Security of

The Public Service Commission. Consultation with independent Public Service Commissions established under the Constitution is obligatory (*i*) on all matters relating to methods of recruitment to civil services and for civil posts, (*ii*) on the principles to be followed in making appointments to civil services and posts, and in making promotions and transfers from one service to another, and on the suitability of candidates for such appointments, promotions or transfers, and (*iii*) on all disciplinary matters affecting a person serving under the Government of India or the Government of a state in a civil capacity, including memorials or petitions relating to such matters.

It is the duty of the Union and the state Public Service Commissions to conduct examinations for appointments to the services of the Union and the services of the state respectively.

The importance of these provisions in the Constitution relating to recruitment and conditions of service of civil servants may be stated thus : the Governments of the Union and the states need for their services the best talent which is available in the country and willing to join them ; competition through examinations gives a reasonable inducement for talent to take up Government service and ensures that those who do well in them can get in. Besides, the fact that the principles of making appointments, giving promotions, and effecting transfers are laid down and that disciplinary matters affecting Government servants are decided after consultation with an independent body is a further inducement for potential entrants to Government service and essential to the ensuring of efficiency and morale.

The independent Public Service Commission referred to above has been recognized in modern States as the best agency for advising Government on recruitment to the civil services and advising them on matters relating to the conditions of their service. The independence of their members, as will be indicated presently with reference to the Public Service Commissions in India, is generally secured by giving them a fixed tenure of office and by making their removal conditional upon an enquiry, and order, by the highest judicial authority in the land.

The Indian Constitution makes the following provisions :

(*i*) There shall be a Public Service Commission for the Union and a Public Service Commission for each state, it being provided that, by agreement, two or more states may have a joint Commission.

(*ii*) The Chairman and the members of a Public Service Commission shall be appointed, in the case of the Union Commission or a joint Commission, by the President and, in the case of a state Commission, by the Governor of the state. It is provided that, as nearly as may be, one-half of the members of every Public Service Commission shall be appointed from among persons who have at the dates of their respective appointments held office for at least ten years either under the Government of India or under the Government of a state.

(*iii*) A member of a Public Service Commission shall hold office for a term of six years from the date on which he enters upon his office or until he attains, in the case of the Union Commission the age of sixty-five years, and in the case of a state Commission or a joint Commission the age of sixty years, whichever is earlier.

(*iv*) The Chairman or any other member of a Public Service Commission shall only be removed from his office by order of the President on the ground of misbehaviour after the Supreme Court has, on enquiry, reported affirmatively. The President has also been authorized to remove the Chairman or any other member on grounds of insolvency, infirmity of mind or body and being engaged in any other paid employment.

(*v*) The Chairman of the Union Public Service Commission shall be ineligible for further employment either under the Government of India or under the Government of a state ; other members of the Union Public Service Commission and the Chairman and members of the state Public Service Commissions, while declared eligible for stated positions in Public Service Commissions, are declared ineligible for any other employment under the Government of India or under the Government of a state.

These provisions are designed, and should be adequate, to ensure that members of the Public Service Commissions are recruited from among experienced and competent persons, and to give them that independence from the Government of the day which is so essential to ensure confidence in their impartiality.

Security of Tenure. The Constitution provides that every person who is a member of a defence service or of a civil service of the Union or an all-India service, or holds any post connected with defence or any civil post under the Union, holds office during the pleasure of the President, and every person who is a member of a civil service of a state or holds any civil post under a state holds office during the pleasure of the Governor of the state. But no person who is a member of a civil service of the Union or an all-India service or a civil service of a state or holds a civil post under the Union or a state shall be dismissed or removed by an authority subordinate to that by which he was appointed ; and no such person shall be dismissed or removed or reduced in rank until he has been given a reasonable opportunity of showing cause against the action proposed to be taken in regard to him. There are some exceptions to this last clause, such, for instance, as that a person may not be given an opportunity of showing cause against the action proposed to be taken where he is dismissed or removed or reduced in rank on the ground of conduct which has led to his conviction on a criminal charge, or where the President or Governor, as the case may be, is satisfied that in the interest of the security of the state it is not expedient to give to that person such an opportunity, but these exceptions do not detract from the reasonable security which is due to a civil servant.

The conditions of service are regulated by the Government Servants' Conduct Rules : it is sufficient to say that once a candidate has been recruited to the services, granted reasonable efficiency and good behaviour, he is certain of keeping his place until the age of retirement ; he has reasonable chances of promotion based on the principle of seniority coupled with efficiency ; in cases of proved incompetence or neglect of duty, he is liable to be punished, even by dismissal. He must also as a civil servant abstain from party politics and faithfully carry out the orders of his superiors ; he must also observe strict official secrecy.

It will be useful to cite the following rules from the Government Servants' Conduct Rules, framed under the Government of India Act, 1919 (which are, in their substance, still in force) in order to know precisely the political rights and duties of Government servants.[1]

'Taking part in politics and elections : (1) (*i*) No Government servant shall take part in, or subscribe in aid of, or assist in any way, any political movement in India, or any political movement relating to Indian affairs.

[1] So far as Central Government servants are concerned, these have been recently revised.

'Explanation : the expression "political movement" includes any movement or activities tending directly or indirectly to excite disaffection against, or to embarrass, the Government as by law established, or to promote feelings of hatred or enmity between different classes of His Majesty's subjects, or to disturb the public peace.

(*ii*) 'No Government servant shall permit any person dependent on him for maintenance or under his care or control to take part in, or in any way assist, any movement or activity which is, or tends directly or indirectly to be, subversive of Government as by law established in India.

'Explanation : a Government servant shall be deemed to have permitted a person to take part in or assist a movement or activity within the meaning of Cl. (*ii*) if he has not taken every possible precaution, and done everything in his power to prevent any person so acting or if, when he knows or has reason to suspect that such person is so acting, he does not at once inform the local Government or the officer to whom he is subordinate.

(2) 'A whole-time Government servant shall not canvass or otherwise interfere or use his influence in connexion with, or take part in, any election to a legislative body whether in India or elsewhere :

'Provided that a Government servant who is qualified to vote at such election may exercise his right to vote, but if he does so, shall give no indication of the manner in which he proposes to vote or has voted.

(3) 'A Government servant who issues an address to electors or in any other manner publicly announces himself or allows himself to be publicly announced as a candidate or prospective candidate for election to a legislative body shall be deemed, for the purpose of sub-rule (2), to take part in an election to such body.

(4) 'Save in the case of a whole-time Government servant who, with the permission, if any, required under any law or order for the time being in force, is a candidate for election to a Municipal Committee, District Board or other local body, the provisions of sub-rules (2) and (3) shall apply in the case of an election to any such Committee, Board or body.'

§8 AMENDMENT OF THE CONSTITUTION

An amendment of the constitution may be initiated by the introduction of a bill for the purpose in either House of Parliament, and when the bill is passed in each House by a majority of the total membership of that House and by a majority of not less than two-thirds of the members of that House present and voting, it is to be presented to the President for his assent and, on his assent being given, it will become law.

If, however, the amendment seeks to make any change in the distribution of legislative powers as between the Union and the states, the representation of states in Parliament or the powers of the Supreme Court or other subjects specified in the proviso to Article 368, the amendment sought to be made has to be ratified by the legislatures of not less than one-half of the states.

A limited constituent power is also given to the legislatures of the states to initiate amendments regarding the number of Houses of the legislatures. Such an amendment becomes law if a bill making such amendment is afterwards enacted by Parliament.

It will be noticed that this method of amendment is not so difficult as the methods provided in the constitutions of Australia, Switzerland, or the U.S.A., nor so easy as the method in the U.S.S.R. By providing that there must be a majority of the total membership of each House and also a majority of not less than two-thirds of the members of each House present and voting, it ensures that more than ordinary attention is given to the amendment of the constitution ; and by making the consent of a proportion of the units essential for a change, among other matters, in the distribution of legislative powers, the representation of states in Parliament and the powers of the Supreme Court, it ensures that the vital interests of the units receive due attention ; on the whole the method of amendment strikes a middle ground between easy amendment and extreme rigidity and must be considered satisfactory. The relative ease with which twenty-five amendments to the Constitution have been made since its adoption on 26 November 1949 — two of them [1] effecting important changes in fundamental rights — show that it is not too difficult to make amendments to the constitution so long as the party which has a majority at the Centre has also a majority in most states.

[1] For one of them see p. 413

§9 GENERAL ASPECTS

(*i*) *The position of minorities.* One of the tests of a good constitution is whether or not it affords sufficient protection to racial, religious and linguistic groups in the pursuit of those cultural and communal interests which mark them out as special groups within the body politic and which indeed afford variety and colour to society but which are not detrimental to it. Besides, such of those groups as are backward in their general, educational and economic development relatively to the other communities should be given reasonable assurance that they will have their due share in the legislative and administrative set-up in the state. As is well known, this problem of the protection of minorities loomed large in Indian political discussions throughout this century ; and it will be interesting to observe how the constitution has dealt with this vital subject.

So far as the religious and cultural interests are concerned, their inclusion as fundamental rights which are justiciable gives ample protection : the right of all persons to freedom of conscience and to profess, practise and propagate religion ; of every religious denomination to establish and maintain institutions for religious and charitable purposes, to manage its own affairs in matters of religion and to own and acquire property ; of linguistic and cultural groups to conserve their language, script and culture ; and of all minorities whether based on religion or language, to establish and administer educational institutions of their choice.

Regarding the legislature, it is satisfactory to note that before the constitution was finally adopted, it was decided, with the consent of the communities concerned, to do away with the separate electorates and reservation of seats for Muslims, Indian Christians and Sikhs which, according to nationalist opinion, had largely contributed to the growth of the separatist tendency in the country. In the first draft of the constitution, indeed, though separate electorates were not provided, the reservation of seats for the three communities was conceded for a transitional period of ten years ; the desire, however, for launching the new republic on a genuinely democratic and secular basis proved strong enough to do away with reservation of seats as well.

Only in respect of three classes, viz. the Scheduled Castes, the Anglo-Indian community and the Scheduled Tribes, was it deemed necessary to insert special provisions which may be considered as political safeguards. The more important of these are the following : Seats are reserved in the House of the People, and in the Legislative Assemblies of the states, for Scheduled Castes and Scheduled Tribes, more or less on a population basis. The President is authorized to nominate two members of the Anglo-Indian community to the House of the People if he is of opinion that that community is inadequately represented, and the Governor of a state may similarly nominate as many members of the community to the Legislative Assembly as he considers appropriate for securing their representation. But these provisions regarding reservation and nomination which were to cease to have effect on the expiration of ten years from the commencement of the constitution have been given a new lease of life by an additional ten years by the Constitution (Eighth Amendment) Act, 1960. The claims of the members of the Scheduled Castes and the Scheduled Tribes are to be taken into consideration, consistently with the maintenance of efficiency, in the making of appointments to the Union and state services. Provision is made for the first ten years to see that the special position occupied by the Anglo-Indian community in the railway, customs, postal and telegraph services is not suddenly disturbed and that the special educational grants made for the benefit of that community are also not suddenly withdrawn. A special officer has been appointed by the President to investigate all matters relating to the safeguards provided for the Scheduled Castes and Scheduled Tribes under the constitution and to report to the President upon the working of those safeguards. The Constitution also provides for the appointment of a Commission to investigate the conditions of backward classes and to suggest ways and means of improving their social and economic conditions. A Commission was appointed by the President for this purpose in 1953 and it has presented its report to the President.

By the Constitution (Seventh Amendment) Act, 1956, the right of the children belonging to linguistic minority groups to receive instruction in their mother tongue at the primary stage of education has been recognized and the President has been empowered to issue such directions to any state as he considers necessary for securing the provision of adequate facilities for such instruction. A special officer for linguistic minorities has been appointed by the President to investigate all matters relating to the safeguards provided for linguistic minorities under the constitution and report to the President on those matters.

(*ii*) *Democratic aspect.* The democratic features of the constitution are obvious : adult suffrage, elections to the Union House

of the People and the State Assembly once in every five years ;
election of the President of the Union ; constitutional safeguards
for freedom of speech, expression and association ; the attempts
to attain a reasonable measure of social and economic equality
by the provision of certain fundamental rights in respect of
abolition of untouchability, equality of opportunity in matters
of employment and the provision of educational facilities and the
like. At the same time, it is noteworthy that the constitution
has not adopted such democratic devices as the referendum,
initiative and recall, which prevail in Switzerland and the
American states : in the present state of educational and political
development of the country, it was rightly felt that they would
be more a hindrance than a help to the expression of the real
will of the people in legislation and administration.

(*iii*) *Membership of the Commonwealth.* India became a Republic on 26 January 1950 with an elected President as the head
of the State. No account of the constitution can, however, be
complete without mentioning one more significant feature —
which is, incidentally, found nowhere in the Constitution Act,
viz. India's membership of the Commonwealth. An official
statement issued at the conclusion of the Conference of the
Commonwealth Prime Ministers in London on 27 April 1949
said :

' The Governments of the United Kingdom, Canada, Australia,
New Zealand, South Africa, India, Pakistan, and Ceylon, whose
countries are united as members of the British Commonwealth
of Nations and owe a common allegiance to the Crown, which is
also the symbol of their free association, have considered the
impending constitutional changes in India.

' The Government of India have informed the other Governments of the Commonwealth of the intention of the Indian people
that under the new constitution which is about to be adopted
India shall become a sovereign independent Republic. The
Government of India have, however, declared and affirmed India's
desire to continue her full membership of the Commonwealth of
Nations and her acceptance of the King as the symbol of the
free association of its independent member nations and as such
the Head of the Commonwealth.

' The Governments of the other countries of the Commonwealth, the basis of whose membership of the Commonwealth is
not hereby changed, accept and recognize India's continuing
membership in accordance with the terms of this declaration.

' Accordingly the United Kingdom, Canada, Australia, New Zealand, South Africa, India, Pakistan and Ceylon hereby declare that they remain united as free and equal members of the Commonwealth of Nations, freely co-operating in the pursuit of peace, liberty and progress.'

The Constituent Assembly of India endorsed this decision on 17 May 1949 when it resolved ' that this Assembly do hereby ratify the declaration, agreed to by the Prime Minister of India, on the continued membership of India in the Commonwealth of Nations as set out in the official statement issued at the conclusion of the Conference of the Commonwealth Prime Ministers in London on 27 April 1949 '

How is it possible to find room within the Commonwealth for a State with a republican constitution ? B. N. Rau, Adviser to the Constituent Assembly, explains this by a simple analogy : [1]

The various member States of the United Nations are completely sovereign and independent ; yet they find it possible to recognize certain organizational authorities for the purpose of working together. In just the same way the members of the Commonwealth can, without impairing their sovereignty or independence in any way, recognize His Majesty as the head of the Commonwealth association. The King is thus the symbol of free association for all members and not a link of subordination for any. Accordingly, the Government of India has declared and affirmed not only India's desire to remain within the Commonwealth but also " her acceptance of the King as the symbol of the free association of its independent member nations and as such the Head of the Commonwealth ". The declaration thus preserves the dignity of the King without impairing India's sovereign status.'

§10 INDIA, MEMBER OF THE COMMONWEALTH

At present (1975) the total membership of the Commonwealth is thirty-one. Besides the United Kingdom, Canada, Australia, Sri Lanka, and India, these are: New Zealand (1948),[2] Malaysia (1957), Ghana (1957), Nigeria (1960), Sierra Leone (1961), Cyprus (1961), Uganda (1962), Trinidad and Tobago (1962), Jamaica (1962), Kenya (1963), Tanzania (1964), Malawi (1964).

---

[1] *India Quarterly*, Vol. V, No. 4, p. 295.

[2] The dates indicate when these states became independent.

Malta (1964), Zambia (1964), The Gambia (1965), Singapore (1965), Guyana (1966), Botswana (1966), Lesotho (1966), Barbados (1966), Mauritius (1968), Nauru (1968), Swaziland (1968), Tongo (1970), Fiji (1970) and Bangladesh (1972).

The Commonwealth is a unique form of political association; in this section an attempt is made, briefly, to indicate the differences and similarities among members of the Commonwealth as well as the bonds which keep them as members of it.

Differences

An onlooker from outside the Commonwealth will perhaps be struck more by the differences among its members than by the similarities and common ideal in which they share. Here is a voluntary association of eighteen independent States; including the dependent territories of its members (only some, e.g. the United Kingdom have dependent territories), it occupies approximately one quarter of the world's land surface and contains, again approximately, one quarter of the world's population. They come from all continents; vary widely in size, population and racial composition, language, industrial development and national income, and the influence which they have on international affairs. In their political institutions, too, there are variations. The United Kingdom, Canada, Australia, New Zealand, Sri Lanka, Sierra Leone, Kenya, Trinidad and Tobago, and Jamaica are monarchies owing allegiance to the Queen of the United Kingdom; Malaysia is also a monarchy owing allegiance to an indigenous monarch; India, Bangladesh, Ghana, Nigeria, Tanganyika, Cyprus and Zanzibar are Republics with a President as the head of the State; Uganda has a President as head of State, but has not declared herself a Republic.[1]

It follows too that those member States which owe allegiance to the Queen of the United Kingdom are legally and constitutionally (as explained in respect of Canada and Australia by way of illustration — though the precise links vary from member to member) more closely linked to the United Kingdom than the Republic members of the Commonwealth. Several are unitary States, e.g. the United Kingdom, Ghana and New Zealand; others are federal, e.g. Canada and Australia; India, though a federation in constitutional law, is described in her constitution, as a Union of States.

---

[1] Of the more recent members, Malta, the Gambia, Guyana and Barbados are monarchies in which the Queen is represented by a Governor-General; Malawi, Zambia, Singapore and Botswana are Republics; Lesotho has an indigenous monarch. Kenya is now a Republic.

Similarities

These differences apart, the members of the Commonwealth are similar in two respects, viz. (*i*) their independence and freedom to follow internal and external policies which they themselves decide upon ; and (*ii*) their recognition of the Queen of the United Kingdom as Head of the Commonwealth.

(*i*) *Independence* :   All members of the Commonwealth — monarchies and republics — are perfectly free to follow the policies, domestic and foreign which they like to follow. Members differ in power and potential ; but they are equal in status. They are in no way subordinate one to another in any aspects of their domestic or external affairs. As Wheare succinctly puts it, equality of status means no dependence ; it means independence. This independence has naturally been used by them so freely that the differences in the policies followed by them are striking.   To illustrate : India has taken to planning for a socialist pattern of society, which perhaps is unique among Commonwealth countries.   In foreign policy each nation has developed along its own lines : Australia and New Zealand are linked with the United Kingdom and Pakistan in SEATO and with the U.S.A. in the Pacific Security Pact (the ANZUS) ; Canada has economic and defence ties with the U.S.A. ; the U.K. is a member of the European Economic Community and is also tied up with Canada in the NATO ; Pakistan has obligations to Britain under the SEATO and the CENTO and the U.S.A. under her military alliance with that country ; India has preferred to follow an independent non-alignment policy. The central fact which is clear from this account can be put thus: the Commonwealth is not a super-state ; it has no central government (legislature, executive or judiciary) and every member has unfettered control over its own affairs, domestic and foreign.

(*ii*) *The Queen as Head of the Commonwealth* : We referred to the recognition by all members of the Queen of the United Kingdom as Head of the Commonwealth. This way of describing the Queen as Head of the Commonwealth was adopted in 1949 when the proposal for declaring India a Republic within the Commonwealth was accepted. It was adopted because there was a consensus of opinion that allegiance to the Crown as in a monarchy should not be insisted upon as a condition of continuance in the Commonwealth and that a Republic could co-exist with monarchy without affecting the benefits of membership for both. The Commonwealth has been an evolving institution and sound commonsense prevailed over any theoretical difficulty of allowing Republics to co-exist with Monarchies in the same political club ; the example of India has since been followed by other members, such as Pakistan and Ghana.

The Sense of belonging together

It is, however, necessary to emphasize that the title has no constitutional significance ; it is a symbolic expression testifying to the integrity of the Commonwealth ; it confers no legal rights or imposes no legal duties on the Governments or the people of member-States. The symbolic significance is, however, not to be ignored as it has its definite uses. It promotes the sense of belonging to one family. Any one who observed the remarkably friendly reception accorded to Prince Philip by Indian citizens when he visited India in 1959 and to Queen Elizabeth II when she visited India in 1961 will realize the significance of the sense of belonging to a political family. Such sense of belonging develops the idea of mutual assistance and co-operation which is all to the good in this world of tensions. And secondly, in the words of a former Secretary of State for Commonwealth Relations, Gordon Walker,

'Other countries recognize that, since the Members of the Commonwealth together form a political entity, they can confer benefits on each other that need not be extended under most-favoured nation treaties and the like to foreign countries. This is an aspect of the recognition of the Queen as Head of the Commonwealth that is often overlooked — it is the mark by which foreign countries recognize that the Members of the Commonwealth form a close association that has a certain status as such in the comity of nations.'

That members continue to be in the Commonwealth because they feel they gain by doing so is a truism. What are the tangible benefits to members by this free association ? Let us recall in this connexion a fact of history. All the members of the Commonwealth were parts of the British Empire ; entry into the Commonwealth has so far followed upon the achievement of self-government by British dependencies ; the achievement of independence does not automatically result in membership of the Commonwealth ; the practice has been that the newly independent member is admitted by agreement of all members of the Commonwealth. The desire to join, and continue in, the Commonwealth can be partly explained by a certain historical experience shared in common, though that experience has varied in details from member to member. The tradition of an efficient civil service administration, the rule of law — with legal notions derived partly from the English Common law and justice administered by permanent and independent judges trained in the law, a common political inheritance in the form of parliamentary institutions, the close economic ties and advantages especially derived from membership in the Sterling Area (Canada is not a member), trading connections, commercial methods, transport services, possible preferential advantages and collaboration to further economic growth, especially in the under-developed countries, the English language as a medium of communication as a unifying force, co-operation in defence if desired by a member — these among other things do help to bring the members together. Above all, consultation on all topics of mutual interest — which is the one moral obligation of membership — does develop a sense of belonging, which is the essence of the Commonwealth idea.

The process, and the importance, of consultation are thus explained in an official statement : There is a general understanding, affirmed at past Imperial Conferences and given formal expression in the External Affairs Agreement with Ceylon of the 11 November 1947, that Membership of the Commonwealth carries with it an obligation to inform or consult, as may be appropriate, all the other Members on any projected action which might affect their interests, especially in relation to foreign affairs, and thus to give them the opportunity of expressing their own individual views. Consultation does not affect the responsibility of the country which consults ; it is, however, its moral obligation to take the views of the country consulted fully into account. The exchange of information among members on foreign and domestic policies is a continuous process through the stream of telegrams and dispatches between capitals, the discussions of High Commissioners with members of Government, the informal meetings of Commonwealth delegations at the United Nations, the *ad hoc* conferences of ministers on matters of finance, trade, external affairs and at the apex, the periodic conferences of Prime Ministers — attendance at which is taken as the real test of full membership of the country concerned in the Commonwealth.

It is proper, however, to doubt, with Wheare,[1] about the extent to which Members of the Commonwealth carry out their obligation to communicate with and consult each other on matters of common knowledge. When the United Kingdom decided upon

[1] K. C. Wheare, *Constitutional Structure of the Commonwealth*, p. 142.

and executed the landings at Suez in 1956, it did so without effective consultation with the other Members of the Commonwealth. Nor could it be supposed that communication and consultation between India and Pakistan is as full as it is between Australia and New Zealand, or New Zealand and the United Kingdom.

SELECT BIBLIOGRAPHY

A. APPADORAI, *Dyarchy in Practice*, Oxford, 1948

——, *Constitutional Proposals of the Sapru Committee*, Padma Publications, Bombay, 1945.

G. AUSTIN, *Indian Constitution: Cornerstone of a Nation*, Oxford, 1972.

D. D. BASU, *Commentary on the Constitution of India*, 2 vols., 1955-56, S. C. Sarkar & Sons Ltd., 3rd ed., Calcutta

P. B. GAJENDRAGADKER, *Indian Parliament and the Fundamental Rights*, Eastern Law House, Calcutta, 1972

B. K. GOKHALE, *Constitution of India and Its Working*, A. R Shetti & Co., Bombay, 1972

SIR MAURICE GWYER and A. APPADORAI (Selected by), *Speeches and Documents on the Indian Constitution, 1921-47*, 2 vols., Oxford, 1957

THE INDIAN INSTITUTE OF PUBLIC ADMINISTRATION, *The Organisation of the Government of India*, Asia Publishing House, Bombay, 1958

IVOR JENNINGS, *Some Characteristics of the Indian Constitution*, Oxford, 1953

G. N. JOSHI, *The Constitution of New India*, Macmillan, 1950

A. B. KEITH, *A Constitutional History of India, 1600-1935*, Methuen, 2nd ed., 1938

Report of the Indian Statutory Commission, 2 vols., H. M. Stationery Office, 1930

Report of the Indian States Committee, 1928-9 Manager of Publications, Delhi, 1929

Report of the Joint Committee on Indian Constitutional Reform (Session 1933-4), Vol. I, Part I, H. M. Stationery Office, 1934

Report on Indian Constitutional Reforms, Superintendent, Government Printing, Calcutta, 1918

D. K. SEN, *The Indian States, their Status, Rights and Obligations*, Sweet and Maxwell, 1930

G. N. SINGH, *Landmarks in Indian Constitutional and National Development*, Vol. I, 1600-1919, Atma Ram, Delhi, 1950

The Government of India Act, 1935, Manager of Publications, Delhi, 1935

CHAPTER XXIV

THE REPUBLIC OF SOUTH AFRICA

§1 GOVERNMENTAL STRUCTURE UNDER THE LEGISLATIVE UNION

UNTIL 31 May 1961, South Africa was a legislative union of four provinces, the Cape of Good Hope, Natal, Transvaal and Orange Free State, a self-governing Dominion within the Commonwealth. On 5 October 1960 a referendum was held among the white voters (1,800,426 registered voters) to decide whether the Union should become a republic; a majority voted in favour and the Republic of South Africa Constitution Act 1961 established, with effect from 31 May 1961, the Republic consisting of four provinces, the same as in the Union mentioned above.

The decision to adopt a republican form of government in accordance with the majority vote at the referendum had nothing directly to do with the termination of the Union's membership of the Commonwealth indicated in the announcement on the evening of 15 March 1961 following a Prime Minister's Conference [1]; the latter decision was directly the result of the decision of South Africa to erect *apartheid* into a social philosophy. *Apartheid* means racial segregation; the South African view is that, as the indigenous and the European-descended people belong to different races, they must be kept apart; it involves a sense of permanent inferiority for the black man and injustice to him as he has to live and work in the areas where the white man is supreme. As Lord Hailsham said, 'what brought about the present crisis was not so much apartheid itself, as the complete inability of its advocates to admit, even to the smallest possible degree, the possibility of compromise or relaxation.'[2] A multi-racial Commonwealth cannot, consistent with its character, accept such a philosophy and hence the decision that South Africa could not continue in the Commonwealth.

---

[1] India, though a Republic, is a member of the Commonwealth. See pp. 447 and 449
[2] *The Round Table*. V. 51, p. 222.

The Constitution of the Legislative Union (before 31 May 1961)

It will be useful to sketch briefly the constitution of the Legislative Union which functioned before the Republic was established partly because it will help us in understanding the present constitution and partly because it is a type of constitution almost *sui generis* in political science ; as will be explained below, it had some federal elements, though, essentially, it had the characteristics of a unitary State.

The Executive

The executive government was carried on, as in Canada and Australia, in the name of the Queen, the functions of the Crown being performed partly by the Queen herself and partly by the Governor-General, both acting on the advice of ministers responsible to the Union Parliament.

The Governor-General occupied the same position and exercised more or less the same powers as his counterparts in Canada and Australia. As in Australia, the appointment and dismissal of all officers of the executive government (except the ministers) were by law vested in the Governor-General in Council. The Governor-General in Council had (as the Governor-General has in Canada) the power to appoint the executive heads of the provinces (here called Administrators), and to veto provincial ordinances.

The ministry was a parliamentary Executive resembling that of Canada.

The Legislature

The Legislature of the Union consisted of the Queen, represented by the Governor-General, the Senate and the House of Assembly.

The Senate consisted of 89 members, the number of Senators from each province varying according to the size of the European population in that province : this number would be calculated by adding together the number of parliamentary and provincial Council constituencies in each province and dividing the total by five to the nearest figure. Under this formula, the Orange Free State and Natal had 8 seats each, the Transvaal 27 and the Cape 22. There were 16 nominated members, nominated ' on the ground mainly of their thorough acquaintance, by their official experience or otherwise, with the reasonable wants and wishes, of the Coloured (i.e., all non-European) races in South Africa.' There were four (additional) European senators elected by natives for five years under the Representation of Natives Act, 1936[1] and two elected[2] and two nominated senators for South-West Africa. There was also one nominated Senator (under an Act of 1951) acquainted with the wants and wishes of the Coloured people of the Cape and Natal. The members elected from the provinces were elected under a system under which the majority party in each province could take all the Senate seats in that province. A senator had to be at least thirty years old, a British subject of European descent, and resident in the Union for five years. The normal term of a Senate was five years : it could be dissolved by the Governor-General earlier.

According to the law which prevailed up to 20 June 1955, the Senate had equal powers with those of the House of Assembly in respect of ordinary bills ; it could not originate or amend money bills, nor any bill so as to increase any proposed charges or burden on the people.

If a bill other than a money bill was passed by the House of Assembly in two successive sessions and was twice rejected by the Senate (or passed by it with amendments to which the House of Assembly would not agree), the Governor-General had power to convene a joint session, at which it was deemed to be passed if it secured the absolute majority of the total number of members present. Where the disagreement was on a money bill, the Governor-General could summon a joint sitting ' during the same session in which the Senate so rejects or fails to pass such bill ' (Section 63).

Under the law passed on 20 June 1955[3] the position was radically altered ; the power of the Senate was reduced to delay-

---

[1] The Asiatic Land Tenure and Indian Representation Act, 1946, made provision for two European senators to represent Indians in the provinces of Natal and Transvaal, one of them to be nominated by the Governor-General ' on the ground mainly of his thorough acquaintance . . . with the reasonable wants and wishes of Indians in the Provinces of Natal and Transvaal ', and the other to be elected by Indian voters in the two provinces. They were to have held office for a period of five years notwithstanding any earlier dissolution of the Senate. The above provisions were to have come into force on a date to be fixed by the Governor-General, but this was never done and this portion of the Act was repealed in 1948.

[2] The two elected members from South-West Africa are elected by the members of the territorial Legislative Assembly and the members of the Indian Assembly.

[3] The law which also altered the composition of the Senate to the one outlined earlier in this section, was passed because the Government in power chosen from the Nationalist party was anxious to secure the two-thirds majority in a joint session of Parliament necessary to alter the ' entrenched clauses ' of the South Africa Act and place the Cape Coloured Voters on a separate electoral roll ; they did not also brook any possible hindrance from the powers given earlier to the Senate.

ing legislation desired by the House of Assembly; it could no longer act as a brake. It provided : (*i*) That if a money Bill passed by the Assembly was rejected by the Senate, it should be submitted to the Governor-General unless the Assembly decided otherwise ; if assented to by the Governor-General, it should become an Act of Parliament in spite of the Senate's non-concurrence. (*ii*) That any other Bill passed by the Assembly but rejected by the Senate in two successive sessions, and in successive calendar years, should be presented to the Governor-General and, if he assented thereto, should become law.

The House of Assembly consisted of 163 members ; of these 150 were distributed among the provinces on the basis of population ; six were reserved for South-West Africa, three were reserved for the representation of Africans in the Cape Province and four members were chosen by the Coloured voters of the Cape and Natal.[1] The right to vote for the election of the first 150 was given to all adult whites over 21 years of age, who had not been declared mentally unsound or who had not been convicted of certain specified offences, e.g. treason, murder. The whites comprised the overwhelming bulk of the electorate : in the 1948 general election, there were 1,403,681 white voters in a total general electorate of 1,452,173. In 1948, there were also 47,329 non-European voters on the Cape common roll and 1,163 on the Natal common roll. Nearly all of these were persons of mixed race who were usually described as 'Coloureds' in South Africa. No Natal Indian or Native had the vote in 1948. No non-Europeans were or are voters on the Transvaal or Orange Free State rolls. Only Europeans had the right to vote in South-West Africa. The right to vote for the election of the three members to represent the Africans was, in the Cape of Good Hope, given to all African males who were able to read and write their name, address, and occupation, who had for twelve months occupied property worth £75 in the registration district, or who had resided for three months in the Cape and earned £50 a year.[2] Only Union nationals of European descent, who had resided five years in the Union and were qualified as registered voters were eligible for membership, including the three seats reserved for the Africans in the Cape Province. The House of Assembly sat for five years from the date of its first meeting unless dissolved earlier.[3]

---

[1] Africans in other provinces, barring a few in Natal, had no right to vote.

[2] Keith. *The Dominions as Sovereign States*, p. 289.

[3] Save for a mere handful of people of Indian origin in the Cape. the people of Indian origin in South Africa had no vote. In 1946 the Smuts

The Judiciary

The judicial system had at its apex the Supreme Court with its two Divisions : Provincial Divisions, one in each of the four provinces ; [1] and an Appellate Division. Judges were appointed by the Governor-General in Council. As elsewhere, their salaries could not be diminished during their continuance in office ; they could not be removed from office except by the Governor-General in Council on an address from both Houses of Parliament in the same session praying for such removal on the ground of misbehaviour or incapacity.

Until June 1952, the right of the Supreme Court, in its Appellate Division, to declare or nullify the constitutionality of an Act passed by the Legislature was hardly called in question. In June 1952, however, was passed the High Court of Parliament Act, which definitely vested that power in a new High Court of Parliament. The Act made the Senators and members of the House of Assembly sitting together the High Court of Parliament to which could be referred any judgements of the Appeal Court which would declare an Act of Parliament invalid.[2] The High Court of Parliament, after considering a report from a judicial Committee made up of 10 Senators and members of the House of Assembly, could confirm, vary or set aside an Appellate Court judgement. The Appellate Division of the South African Supreme Court held (on 13 November 1952) the High Court of Parliament Act invalid. Dr Malan accepted the judgement but said that he would appeal to the electorate to give the Government a mandate to take steps to place the sovereignty of Parliament beyond doubt.

In May 1955, the Union Parliament passed the Appeal Court Act which raised the number of judges in the Appellate Division of the Supreme Court from six to eleven, and also provided (a) that a quorum of five was required to hear all appeals except those involving the validity of an Act of Parliament, when the

Government passed the Asiatic Land Tenure and Indian Representation Act, Part II of which provided for one European Senator to be elected by qualified Indian voters of Natal and the Transvaal. Qualified Indian voters from Natal and the Transvaal were also to elect three members of the House of Assembly. This special communal representation was opposed by people of Indian origin as well as Europeans and never came into operation. In 1948 the Malan Government repealed Part II of the Act.

[1] There were also some Local Divisions.

[2] The High Court of Parliament Act was the answer of the Nationalist Government (led by Dr Malan) to the action of the Supreme Court in March 1952 in invalidating a law to put Coloured Voters on a separate list.

full bench of 11 judges would be required and (*b*) that the judgement of a majority of such quorums (three and six respectively) would in all cases be accepted as the judgement of the Court.

Until 1950 appeals could be taken from the Appellate Division of the Supreme Court to the Privy Council, though leave was only given in cases involving major constitutional issues.

In 1950 the Privy Council Appeals Act was passed to sever all links with the Privy Council.

The federal elements in the Union Constitution are :   (*i*) In practice, the Union Cabinet was constructed with regard to the need for representing, as far as practicable, all the provinces. (*ii*) The provinces also received recognition in the allocation of federal business. Pretoria in Transvaal was the administrative capital, Cape Town the seat of Parliament, the Bloemfontein in Orange Free State the headquarters of the Supreme Court, Appellate Division. (*iii*) Above all, there were certain matters on which under the constitution, the provincial Legislatures could make laws, 'ordinances' as they were termed. Examples are direct taxation within the province ; education other than higher education ; agriculture (subject to conditions defined by the Union Parliament); hospitals and charitable institutions, municipal institutions ; local works and undertakings within the provinces ; roads, markets, fish and game preservation ; and, generally, all matters which, in the opinion of the Governor-General in Council, are of a merely local or private nature or in respect of which the Union Parliament delegated to the provinces the power to make ordinances.

But, in spite of these, South Africa was in essence a unitary State because (*i*) though the provinces were assigned certain subjects, the Union could also legislate on them, overriding provincial ordinances, the provincial ordinances required for their validity the assent of the Governor-General in Council ; and a provincial ordinance was null and void if it was repugnant to any Act of the Union Parliament. (*ii*) The Chief Executive Officer of the province, styled the Administrator, was appointed by the Governor-General in Council ; and the conditions of appointment, tenure of office and retirement of public officers within the province could be regulated by the Union Parliament. (*iii*) With the exception of certain provisions of the Act, the Union Parliament could amend the Constitution by legislation in the same way as it could amend ordinary laws. Moreover, the exceptions themselves (amending the constitution safeguarding the Cape native franchise and providing for the equal treatment of the English and Dutch languages) were subject to amendment by the Parliament provided the amendment was passed by both Houses of Parliament sitting together, and at the third reading was agreed to by not less than two-thirds of the total number of members of both Houses. In either case, the consent of the provinces was not required for such amendment. (*iv*) Legally, it was open to the Union Parliament even to abolish the provincial legislatures or reduce their powers. It is significant that the only safeguard provided in the Act of 1909 against such drastic exercise of power (viz., that a bill proposing such an abolition or reduction should be reserved for the sovereign's pleasure) was repealed in 1934.[1]

§2 THE CONSTITUTION OF THE REPUBLIC

The head of the Republic is the State President, who is elected for a seven-year term by an electoral college consisting of the members of the Senate and the House of Assembly at a meeting specially convened for the purpose. He is not eligible for re-election unless it is expressly otherwise decided by the electoral college. He shall cease to hold office on a resolution passed by the Senate and by the House of Assembly during the same session declaring him to be removed from Office on the ground of misconduct or inability to perform efficiently the duties of his office.

The State President is Commander-in-Chief of the South African Defence Force ; may dissolve the Senate or the House of Assembly or the Senate and the House of Assembly simultaneously ; appoints Ministers and deputies to Ministers ; confers honours ; appoints, accredits and recognizes diplomatic personnel ; summons and prorogues Parliament ; may pardon or reprieve offenders ; enters into and ratifies international conventions, treaties and agreements ; may proclaim and terminate martial law, may declare war and make peace, and make appointments.

It is added in the Constitution that the executive government of the Republic in regard to any aspect of its domestic or foreign affairs is vested in the State President, acting on the advice of the Executive Council ; he is not bound to take the advice of the Executive in specified matters such as the appointment of ministers, the summoning of Parliament or the dissolution of the House of Assembly.

---

[1] The provinces were, however, consoled by the passing of Act No. 45 of 1934 under which the Parliament was not to abolish any provincial Council or abridge their powers save on the petition to the Parliament of the Council affected. Keith, op. cit., p. 68.

It will be clear that South Africa has the same type of executive as in Britain and India ; the State President is essentially a Constitutional head acting on the advice of his Executive Council consisting of Ministers chosen from Parliament and responsible to it. It is added in the constitution that a minister and a deputy minister may sit and speak, but not vote, in the House of which he is not a member.

The legislative power of the Republic is vested in the Parliament consisting of the State President, a Senate and a House of Assembly.

As has been stated earlier the State President has power to summon, prorogue and dissolve Parliament, either both Houses simultaneously or the House of Assembly alone. He may also dissolve the Senate at any time within 120 days of any dissolution of the House of Assembly or the expiry of the term of Office of a provincial Council. A session of Parliament has to be held at least once a year.

The Senate consists of 54 members, 43 elected and 11 nominated. The elected members are 14 from the Transvaal, 11 from the Cape Province, 8 from Natal, 8 from the Orange Free State and 2 from South-West Africa. The State President nominates 11 members, acting on the advice of the Executive Council, 2 from each of the four Provinces, 2 from South-West Africa and 1 from among the Coloured voters in the Cape Province. At least one of the two senators nominated by the State President from each province should be thoroughly acquainted with the interests of the Coloured population. Similarly, one of the senators nominated from South-West Africa should be selected mainly for his thorough acquaintance with the reasonable wants and wishes of the Coloured races of the Territory.

A senator must be a white South African citizen, at least 30 years of age, qualified as a voter in one of the provinces and resident for five years within the Republic. The term of a senator is five years. unless the Senate is dissolved earlier.

The House of Assembly consists of 160 members chosen in electoral divisions as follows—Cape of Good Hope. 54, Natal 18, Transvaal 73, Orange Free State 15, and South-West Africa 6.

A member of the House of Assembly must be a White South African citizen, qualified as a voter and resident for five years within the Republic. The term of the House of Assembly is five years unless sooner dissolved by the State President.

Of the two Houses, clearly, the House of Assembly is the more powerful. While ordinary bills can originate in either House, money bills can originate only in the House of Assembly ; the Senate may not also amend such bills.

Two more provisions concerning the powers of Parliament are noteworthy : (*i*) The House of Assembly may not originate or pass money bills (for taxation or appropriation) unless it has been recommended by the State President during the session ; what has been a convention in the British Parliament has been made into a constitutional law ; and (*ii*) no court of law shall be competent to enquire into or to pronounce upon the validity of any Act passed by Parliament, other than an Act which repeals or amends or purports to repeal or amend the provisions of Sections 108 and 118 (relating to English and Afrikaans being the official languages of the Republic).

The Supreme Court is the highest court of the land. It is constituted as follows : [1] (*i*) The Appellate Division, consisting of the Chief Justice and 7 judges of Appeal. It has no original jurisdiction, but is purely a Court of Appeal. (*ii*) The Provincial Divisions. In each Province there is a provincial division of the Supreme Court while in the Cape there are two such divisions possessing both original and appellate jurisdiction. (*iii*) The Local Divisions. There is a local division each in the Cape, the Transvaal and Natal exercising the same original jurisdiction within limited areas as the provincial divisions. The division in the Cape has appellate jurisdiction within its area of jurisdiction.

The judges hold office till they attain the age of 70. No judge can be removed from office except by the State President upon an address from both Houses of Parliament in the same session praying for such removal on the ground of misbehaviour or incapacity.

SELECT BIBLIOGRAPHY

R. H. BRAND, *The Union of South Africa*, Oxford, 1909
N. MANSERGH (Editor), *Documents and Speeches on British Commonwealth Affairs 1952-62*, 2 vols., Oxford, 1963
H. J. MAY, *The South African Constitution*, Juta & Co. Ltd., Cape Town, 2nd ed., 1949

[1] *The Statesman's Year Book*, 1971/1972. p. 1299.

CHAPTER XXV

NAZI GERMANY AND FASCIST ITALY

§1 TOTALITARIAN STATES

NAZI Germany and Fascist Italy are here grouped together, as they illustrate one type of State in political science, viz., the totalitarian. The concept of the totalitarian State has been explained earlier in this book ; in Mussolini's expressive phrase, ' all within the State, none outside the State, none against the State '. The governmental system in Germany and Italy in the pre-Hitler and pre-Mussolini period is also briefly sketched to provide a background for understanding the rise of Hitler and Mussolini.

§2 GERMANY: THE WEIMAR CONSTITUTION[1]

The government of Germany was from 1919 to 1945 formally based[2] on what is known as the Weimar constitution, i.e. the constitution framed at Weimar in 1919. Fundamental changes were made in that constitution after the rise of the Nazis to power, so fundamental indeed that its makers would probably not recognize their handiwork in its later modified form. Nevertheless, for a proper understanding of the Nazi structure, it is

[1] Today Germany is divided into two states, the Federal Republic of Germany with a liberal democratic and federal Constitution in the West and the German Democratic Republic in the East. The Federal Republic of Germany cannot be said to be fully sovereign, as the U.S.A., Britain and France have, according to a Convention signed in 1949, retained some rights over the state (which they had during the Occupation at the close of the Second World War) including the stationing of armed forces in Germany and the protection of their security ; nor can the German Democratic Republic be said to be sovereign as it is under Soviet control. In Italy, a new constitution has been proclaimed ; a description of it is not attempted here, as it seems to have little to contribute to political science. It seemed best, from the point of view of political science, to elucidate the essential features of government in Germany under the Republican and Nazi régimes and in Italy under the Fascists instead of attempting to describe the features of present-day Germany and Italy.

[2] F. Ermarth, *The New Germany*, p. 46. ' The Weimar constitution has never been formally abrogated. The German courts continue to apply it and refer expressly to those provisions that are still in force.'

necessary to describe the essential features of the Weimar constitution.

Under the Weimar constitution, Germany was a federal State composed of eighteen states (or, more properly, territories, *Länder*).

The constitution could be amended by legislation, but only if an amendment was passed by a two-thirds majority of the members of the Reichstag [1] present (provided too that at least two-thirds of the legal total of members were present) and by a two-thirds majority of the votes cast in the Reichsrat.[2] If the necessary majority in the Reichsrat was not reached, and within two weeks the Reichsrat demanded an appeal to the people, the amendment had to be submitted to the people and the consent of a majority of the voters was necessary. The constitution could also be amended on the initiative of one-tenth of the qualified voters, supported on a referendum, by a majority of the voters.

The constitution enumerated the powers of the Federal Government and left the residue with the states. The powers given to the Federal Government, however, were so many that the states became relatively unimportant in the federal system: The Federal Government had exclusive legislative powers on such subjects as foreign relations, colonial affairs, nationality, freedom of domicile, immigration and emigration, military organization, the monetary system, customs, and posts and telegraphs. It had concurrent powers regarding civic rights, penal law, judicial procedure, passports, poor relief, the press, associations and assemblies, population questions, public health, labour laws, commerce, weights and measures, paper money, banking and exchange, traffic in foodstuffs, luxuries and articles of daily necessity, industry and mining, insurance, navigation and railways. If there was a conflict between federal law and state law of a concurrent subject, the former prevailed. In cases of doubt the Supreme Court decided the matter. Where there was need for the issue of uniform regulations, say in respect of sanitary administration or the maintenance of public order and security, the Federal Government could pass laws on these matters. It could by legislation lay down fundamental principles governing the rights and duties of religious associations, education, the conditions of service of officials and the land laws. Finally, its taxation power was practically unlimited ; it was only required to have some consideration for the financial requirements of the

---

[1] The lower House of Parliament.
[2] The upper House of Parliament.

states. Add to this the fact that the federal laws were for the most part carried out by the state authorities, subject to the Federal Government's instructions and supervision, and the enormous power of that Government is obvious. No wonder that many competent observers considered Weimar Germany (though technically federal) to be in effect a unitary State.[1]

The Executive

The chief executive authority was vested in the President, elected by popular vote (the vote being given to men and women of twenty and over) for seven years. Any German who had completed his thirty-fifth year was eligible, and the details of the election were determined by law. The President was eligible for re-election. He could be removed from office before his term was over by impeachment before the supreme judicial court, or by a resolution of the Reichstag supported by a two-thirds majority and ratified by a popular referendum. If, however, the people did not ratify the resolution by a majority, their refusal operated to re-elect the President for a full seven-year term and the Reichstag which proposed the recall was dissolved. On paper the powers of the President were considerable : he had command over the army and the navy ; he represented the State in foreign affairs and concluded treaties with the consent of the Reichstag ; he appointed and dismissed officials, where no other system of doing so was prescribed by law ; he could make use of the armed forces to compel a state to fulfil the duties imposed on it by the constitution or the laws of the Reich ; he could take steps to restore public security and order in case they were seriously disturbed and for this purpose abrogate the fundamental rights of the people (such as personal liberty, secrecy of correspondence, freedom of speech, publication and association, and property) ; and, finally, he had power to grant pardon. But, as in France, all orders and decrees of the President required for their validity the counter-signature of the Chancellor, or a minister, who was really responsible to Parliament. In order words, the principle of ministerial responsibility made the President the nominal head of the State ; and in this respect he was like the French President and the English king.

The Government of the Reich consisted of the Chancellor and ministers. The President appointed and dismissed the Chancellor ;

[1] See A. L. Lowell, *Greater European Governments*, p. 285, and the authorities cited therein.

and on the latter's recommendation, the ministers. It was expressly provided by the constitution that the Chancellor and the ministers required the confidence of the Reichstag in the administration of their office. Any one of them had to resign ' should the confidence of the Reichstag be withdrawn by an express resolution '. Although the Chancellor laid down the general course of policy, each minister conducted the branch of administration entrusted to him and was personally responsible for it to the Reichstag. It was thus possible for the Reichstag to vote want of confidence in a single minister, as well as in the cabinet as a whole. The German Executive was thus a parliamentary one, on the model of the English and the French.

The Legislature

The Parliament was bicameral, consisting of the Reichsrat, or upper House, and the Reichstag, or lower House.

The Reichsrat had 66 members, each state sending one or more members of its ministry,[1] in the ratio of one member for every million inhabitants, with the qualification that every state had at least one representative and no state, however large, had more than two-fifths of the total number. The latter provision was obviously intended to prevent Prussia, with about three-fifths of the population of Germany, from dominating the chamber. The Reichsrat was intended to function rather as a preliminary chamber than a revisory one : bills introduced by the Government were first placed before the Reichsrat. If the Reichsrat disagreed with the Government, the Government could still introduce them in the Reichstag, but in doing so had to state the divergent opinion of the Reichsrat. Similarly, the ministry was bound to introduce in the Reichstag bills initiated by the Reichsrat, even though they were opposed to them ; but in doing so, they could place before the Reichstag their own point of view. The Reichsrat also had a suspensive veto over the bills passed by the Reichstag, because it could only delay the passing of a bill for reconsideration by the Reichstag, and, with the President concurring, have it referred to the people ; its refusal to pass a bill would not by itself prevent it from becoming law.

The Reichstag was elected by universal, equal, direct and secret suffrage, by all men and women over twenty years of age, in accordance with the principle of proportional representation. The total number of members was not fixed, but varied with the

[1] Half of the representatives of Prussia had to be appointed from among the Prussian provincial administrative authorities.

number of votes cast at the election, one representative being assigned to every 60,000 votes cast. The actual number of members has varied from 466 to 647. The term was four years, although the body could be dissolved earlier — not exceeding once for the same cause — by presidential decree. The Reichstag had power to pass laws (subject to the suspensive veto of the Reichsrat, and the power of the people to veto the laws); it could amend the constitution (subject, again, to the powers of the Reichsrat and the people already described), control the Executive, ventilate grievances, and discuss any matter of public importance. The declaration of war and the conclusion of peace, alliances and treaties with foreign States required for their validity the consent of the Reichstag.

The Judiciary

The judicial system recognized two series of courts, the ordinary and the administrative.

Judges were appointed for life and held office during good behaviour ; they could not be removed from office or transferred or retired against their will except by virtue of a judicial decision and for the reason and in the manner prescribed by law.

There was also a special tribunal (the Staatsgerichtshof) to try impeachments against the President or the ministers, and settle questions arising under the constitution (such as inter-state disputes and conflicts between the Federal Government and states).

Noteworthy features of the Weimar constitution

The Weimar constitution thus provided a full-grown democratic constitution : universal suffrage with provision for minority representation, a parliamentary Executive, popular initiative and popular veto on laws, and the direct selection of the head of the State being its essential features. There are two other features, which may be briefly mentioned.

(*i*) An elaborate bill of fundamental rights for the citizen, such as personal liberty, the secrecy of correspondence, freedom of speech, press and association, and the like. In practice this failed to give any security of the kind contemplated.

(*ii*) Workers' councils and economic councils.[1]

' The wage-earners and salaried employees are entitled to be represented in local workers' councils, organized for each establishment in the locality, as well as in district workers' councils,

[1] Article 165.

organized for each economic area, and in a national workers' council, for the purpose of looking after their social and economic interests.

'The district workers' councils and the national workers' council meet together with the representatives of the employers and with other interested classes of people in district economic councils and in a national economic council for the purpose of performing joint economic tasks and co-operating in the execution of the laws of socialization. The district economic councils and the national economic council shall be so constituted that all substantial vocational groups are represented therein according to their respective economic and social importance.

'Drafts of laws of fundamental importance relating to social and economic policy, before introduction into the Reichstag, shall be submitted by the ministry to the national economic council for consideration. The national economic council has the right itself to propose such measures, for enactment into law. If the ministry does not approve them, it shall, nevertheless, introduce them into the Reichstag together with a statement of its own position. The national economic council may have its bills presented by one of its own members before the Reichstag.'

The full complement of workers' and national economic councils contemplated by the makers of the constitution never came into existence. In 1920, however, a national economic council was established on a provincial basis, with 326 members representing various economic groups, such as agriculture, industry and commerce, and with advisory powers. The German Economic Council has inspired the creation of similar bodies in other countries in Europe and elsewhere. A suggestion to create a body on similar lines in India was made by Sir Arthur Salter in a report submitted to the Government of India in 1931 ; the suggestion, however, was not adopted.

§3 THE DICTATORSHIP OF HITLER

The primary reasons for the failure of the Weimar Republic and the rise of the dictatorship of Hitler have been explained elsewhere.[1] Contributory factors were the humiliation consequent on defeat in the Great War and the vindictive treaty of Versailles, the economic depression, the lack of a continuous democratic tradition in Germany, the inability of the democratic Governments to solve the problems which they had to face, and the dynamic

[1] See above, ch. xv, §7.

leadership of Hitler. Suffice it here to say that Hitler rose to power as the leader of the National Socialist party, which secured the largest number of seats (secured by any single party) in the Reichstag in the elections held in July 1932, and again in November of that year — though it still had no majority. On 29 January 1933, Hitler was made Chancellor. The Reichstag was dissolved, and in the elections of March of that year his party secured 288 seats out of a total of 647. Allying itself with the Nationalist Party, it had a working majority of fifty-two per cent. The new Reichstag passed on 24 March 1933 (by the required two-thirds majority for passing constitutional laws) the Enabling Act 'to end the distress of Reich and nation'. Its important provisions were :

(*i*) National laws could be enacted by the Reich cabinet as well as in accordance with the procedure established in the constitution. This applied also to the laws referred to in Article 85, paragraph 2 (the power to enact a budget) and in Article 87 (the power to borrow) of the constitution.

(*ii*) The laws enacted by the Reich cabinet could deviate from the constitution in so far as they did not affect the position of the Reichsrat and the Reichstag. The powers of the President remained untouched.

(*iii*) Treaties of the Reich with foreign States which concerned matters of national legislation did not require the consent of the bodies participating in legislation. The Reich cabinet was empowered to issue the necessary provisions of these treaties.

This is a remarkable law, for, taken together with the fact that the members of the ministry were the choice of the Chancellor, it virtually meant the concentration of all legislative power in the hands of one man, Hitler.

Under the powers vested in him by this law, Hitler rapidly transformed the structure of the German State. The independent powers vested in the states were abolished in 1934 and the State thus became unitary in character. The Legislatures in the states were dissolved, and the states were governed by high commissioners appointed by the Chancellor of the Reich, and subject to his orders. The Reichsrat, the federal upper House, had no *raison d'être* and consequently was abolished. The head of the State was styled Leader and Chancellor ; this office combined in itself the former offices of President and Chancellor. The nominal and the real heads of the State were thus combined in one person. There was a cabinet to assist the Leader ; its members were appointed and dismissed by him. The Reichstag was retained ; its members all belonged to one party, since all parties other than the National Socialist were abolished by law. There was therefore no opposition. The Reichstag seldom met ; when it did meet it did little else besides applauding a speech by Hitler. It delegated the function of law-making to the ministry by a new Enabling Act (1937); this Act was so framed as to give the ministry unrestricted power to pass any laws it thought necessary for the good of the State. The civil and judicial services of the State were reorganized to ensure that they were thoroughly loyal to the policy of the new State.

§4 NAZI GERMANY

Nazi Germany was characterized by five important features.

(i) It was totalitarian. The State was all-inclusive. It offered an answer to all questions, a solution to all problems. This feature followed from the first principle of National Socialist philosophy, that the State was an end in itself, and the individual but an instrument to enable it to realize that end. The individual, therefore, had no fundamental rights ; he had only fundamental duties.

The control of the State over the individual and the group expressed itself in several ways. Freedom of speech and association was abolished. All means of moulding public opinion — the press, the theatre, the cinema, the radio, the school and the university — were strictly controlled by the State. All trade unions, and political parties, with the exception of the National Socialist party, were destroyed. As far as possible, every form of social organization that was capable of influencing the attitude and the opinion of the members of the State, social, political and economic, was brought under a leadership which was fully in sympathy with the attitude of the dominant party. Youth associations, cultural, sports and recreational bodies, co-operative societies, were all brought under the influence of the State. In October, 1933, a Reich Chamber of Culture was set up under Dr Goebbels. This consisted of seven chambers, each dealing with some aspect of cultural life (literature, the press, the radio, the theatre, music, art, the cinema).[1] Each of these had a president and an executive board, and included professional organizations from the whole of Germany. The presidents came together from time to time and met as the Reich Advisory Board

[1] S. H. Roberts, *The House that Hitler Built*, p. 241.

of Culture.[1] Essentially the purpose of this elaborate organization was, as Goebbels said, 'the uniform moulding of the will' in the direction of National Socialism, and to put down all independent rights, criticism and opposition. It was also sought to bring the churches under control.

In respect of economic life, the Minister of Economics was empowered to carry out within his jurisdiction all measures that he considered necessary to foster the German national economy. The type of control that was thus exercised may be illustrated from the regulation of agriculture. In 1933, a sort of agricultural guild, known as the Reich Estate for Food Production, was set up, an autonomous public body with wide powers to put agriculture on a sound footing.

'Everything to do with agriculture came under its control. It could regulate production of all crops, it could alter or fix prices, it could organize distribution, it could reduce rates of mortgage, it could prevent industry making undue demands on agriculture ; and, not least, it could enforce its decisions by penalties of imprisonment, fines up to £8,000 sterling, and by forbidding guilty persons to work on the land at all. It took over all associations, co-operative bodies and trading groups in any way connected with agriculture.'[2]

(*ii*) It was a one-party State, only the National Socialist Party being legally recognized. The Party was declared by law to be 'the bearer of the idea of the German State and inseparably connected with the State'. Its emblem, the swastika, was the emblem of the State ; its leader, the head of the State. Numerous powers were 'transferred to the party organizations, such as the right of appointing municipal councillors, selecting jurors and members of the school boards, investigating public records and consulting with State authorities on practically every matter'.[3] Members of the party were accorded various privileges, such as preference in employment, reductions in railway rates, and so on. In giving high school marks, the school authorities had to take into consideration the activities of the pupils in the youth organization.[4]

(*iii*) It was a 'folk State'. This was directly related to the racial theory which lay at the root of the National-Socialist conception of the State. The theory has two elements :—(*a*) The

[1] ibid. [2] ibid., p. 193. [3] Ermarth, op. cit., p. 65.
[4] Ermarth, op. cit., pp. 67-8n., 74.

'blood' of a social group, a race, determines its total outlook and mode of thought. This is as complete a denial of other influences in the make-up of a nation's life as Marx's materialistic interpretation of history, which makes the mode of production determine everything. (*b*) The Nordic race, to which family the Germans belong, has to its credit the finest qualities of men and the greatest achievements of history. It follows, therefore, that if the nation is to be united, and keep up and improve its own record of achievements, it is essential to maintain the racial purity of the State. Members of other races, especially 'inferior' races like the Jews, should have no place in the State. The Jews were, therefore, deprived of much of their property, and of opportunity for earning a living in Germany. Marriages between citizens of German or kindred stock and Jews were also prohibited.

(*iv*) It was a 'leader State'.

'The principle which made the former Prussian army an admirable instrument of the German nation,' wrote Hitler,[1] 'will have to become the basis of our statal constitution, that is to say, full authority over his subordinates must be invested in each leader and he must be responsible to those above him.'

Frankly, German politics was based on the principle that every citizen was directly or indirectly responsible to Hitler for his life and conduct. The Government was, therefore, a dictatorship. The actions of the Leader were above criticism; they must be right. The consent of the masses was helpful, but not essential, for the continuance of the Government. Democracy was a show, and so was the theory of separation of powers. The concentration of powers in one leader was necessary for the efficacy of the State; therefore his will must be law.

(*v*) It follows that all those who opposed the will of the Leader in any way must be compelled by force to obey the Leader, or, in the alternative, be put aside in what were known as concentration camps, or otherwise denied opportunity to oppose his will.

§5 ITALY: THE CORPORATIVE STATE

The history of modern Italy begins with the completion of her national unity in 1870 due to the efforts of three great men, Cavour, Garibaldi and Mazzini. The genesis of her constitution

[1] *Mein Kampf* (tr. J. Murphy), p. 375.

may, however, be traced earlier, to the *Statuto* granted by King Albert of Sardinia to his people in 1848, and later extended to the whole of Italy, when Sardinia expanded, so to say, over the rest of Italy. The *Statuto* was of course considerably modified, especially after the Fascist Revolution of 1922. Instead of the liberal democratic constitution which it established, there was established under Mussolini an authoritarian régime in Italy, brought about, however, by a series of constitutional amendments to the *Statuto*. That document provided no special machinery for amending the constitution; it was taken for granted that it could be amended by the ordinary law-making body. It is noteworthy that Italy was one of the few States which had, at one and the same time, a ' written ' and a flexible constitution.

Italy was (and is-) a unitary State. The head of the State was the king ; the succession to the throne was vested in the House of Savoy and regulated according to Salic Law, by which only male heirs were recognized. The king, like his English counterpart, was a constitutional ruler, being bound to act on the advice of the Prime Minister.

According to the constitution (as modified up to July 1943), the Prime Minister, designated ' Head of the Government ' (Duce), was appointed by the king and was responsible to him for the policy of the Government. The Duce chose the other ministers, who were responsible to *him* ; besides, he directed and co-ordinated their activities. His consent was necessary before any business could be considered by Parliament. If either Chamber of Parliament rejected a measure, he could require it to be reconsidered after three months, without discussion, and to be voted upon by ballot. He could require that even though a bill was rejected by one chamber, it be considered and voted upon by the other. Without the consent of Parliament, he had the power to promulgate decrees having the force of law ; they had, however, to be published immediately and referred to Parliament within two years.

The Head of the Government was advised by the Fascist Grand Council. In its origin, this Council was a purely party organ ; it was later given a legal status as part of the governmental machinery. It consisted of (*i*) life members, the surviving members of the quadrumvirate who led the march on Rome in 1922 ; (*ii*) *ex officio* members, the ministers, the presidents of the Senate, of the Italian Academy, and of the various confederations,[1] and the higher officials of the Fascist party ; and

---

[1] Explained below.

(*iii*) nominated members, appointed normally for three years by the Head of the Government from among those who had rendered meritorious service to the nation or to the fascist revolution. The Head of the Government was the president of the Council. The Council had a threefold function. It appointed the chief officials of the party, including the Secretary-General. It prepared a list of people to succeed the Head of the Government in case any mishap befell him. It was an advisory body to the Crown and to the Head of the Government on matters of administration.

The Parliament consisted of two Chambers, the Senate and the Fascist and Corporative Chamber.

The Senate had 543 [1] members. With the exception of the princes of the royal blood, who were members of the Senate, its members were nominated for life by the king on the advice of the Head of the Government from specified categories of citizens These included the higher dignitaries of the Church, ministers. generals, admirals, ambassadors, the Attorney-General, members of the Royal Academy, persons who had for three years paid 3,000 lira in direct taxes and those who had in any capacity rendered meritorious services to the nation. According to the *Statuto,* the Senate had equal powers with the lower House except in one respect : it could not initiate money bills. In practice it had always been ineffective, much more so after the advent of the fascists to power, for the real power rested with the Executive and not with the Legislature.

The Fascist and Corporative Chamber met for the first time on 23 March 1939. Its composition was so closely related to the economic structure of the State based on the corporative principle that it is best explained after outlining that structure.

Corporative structure

It will be remembered that fascism as a political and economic theory did not share in the socialist belief in a class war ; on the contrary, it believed that employers and workers should continue to be partners in one social function, viz. production. The corporative structure was an attempt to translate his fascist belief into practice. It was based on the principle that employers and workers must be organized into associations approved by the State, and that through these associations their participation in national production must be regulated and controlled. Its main institutions were :

[1] On 28 October 1939.

(*i*) *Syndicates.* For every trade or occupation in a district, a syndicate of employers and one of workers could be formed and could apply for legal recognition. Only one syndicate was permitted for each category and in each district. Legal recognition was granted if the syndicate concerned satisfied certain conditions. If it was a syndicate of employers, it must consist of members employing at least 10% of the workers in some branch of trade in the district ; if it was an employees' syndicate, its members must include at least 10% of the workers in the particular trade and district. Among its objects must be not only the general furthering of the economic interests of its members ; it must also take an active part in their technical instruction and in their religious, moral, and national education, and support of charitable foundations open to them. The legally recognized syndicate was subject to State control in several ways ; e.g. the election of its president and its secretary must receive the approval of the State before they could take up their duties. It was empowered to represent legally the particular division of employers or employees for which it was formed, to levy contributions not only from members but from the whole category of employers or workers whom it represented ; to defend the interests of its members in disputes adjudicated in labour courts ; and finally, to negotiate collective labour contracts binding upon all those engaged in the trade within the area of its jurisdiction. The contracts must cover such matters as their own duration, disciplinary regulations, hours of work, weekly rest, annual holidays with pay, wages, and the treatment of workers in cases of sickness.

(*ii*) *Federations.* Syndicates of employers and syndicates of workers were grouped separately into federations to co-ordinate the activities of the syndicates, each with a council, an executive committee and a president or secretary.

(*iii*) *Confederations.* The federations were in turn organized into nine confederations. Four of these represented employers in Industry, Agriculture, Commerce, and Credit and Insurance ; four represented workers in these same fields ; the ninth represented professional men and artists. Each confederation had a national congress and a governing body.

(*iv*) *Corporations.* Up to this point the employers and workers were organized separately in parallel organizations. They were brought together in the ' corporations of category ', each consisting of an equal number of representatives from employers and workers in a particular branch of trade plus a few technical experts and members of the Fascist party. Each was presided over by someone appointed by the Head of the Government. There were twenty-two corporations covering such branches of production as fruit-growing, oil, livestock, timber, textiles, forestry, paper-making and printing, building, fisheries, water, sea and air transport, inland communications, and so on. Their function was to advise the Government on industrial questions generally, and, in particular, to help adjust disputes between capital and labour, to regulate wages, hours of labour and the conditior s of employment within their respective branches, and to promote vocational education.

(v) *The National Council of Corporations.* This consisted of the most important members (about 500) of the corporations. It served to co-ordinate the activities of the corporations in all important matters of economic policy and to settle such conflicts as arose between various branches of national economy ; for instance, between agriculture and industry.

The Fascist and Corporative Chamber

Now to resume the description of the structure of government. The Chamber consisted of some 650 members drawn from three groups : from members of the Grand Fascist Council, from the National Council of the Fascist party and from the National Council of Corporations. The Fascist and Corporative Chamber took the place of the former Chamber of Deputies (abolished in 1938). Measures approved by the Grand Fascist Council were debated in the Chamber as well as in the Senate. As has been noted earlier, a bill rejected by the Chamber could nevertheless be submitted to the Senate for its consideration. After three months, a rejected bill could be referred to it again for decision by ballot (without discussion), but no subject could be discussed by the Chamber without the previous sanction of the Head of the Government. Clearly, the Parliament of Italy merely served to confirm the decisions made by the Executive.

The Judiciary

Like most other European countries, Italy had two sets of courts, the ordinary and the administrative. The Court of Cassation was the highest ordinary court ; the Council of State was the highest administrative court.

General aspects

Italy under Mussolini was a fascist State ; it was therefore an authoritarian State. Authority was exercised for the sake of the community, but was not derived from the community. It was, further, a one-party State. The constitution was hardly democratic; only one political party was legally recognized; the Opposition hardly existed; the rights of free speech, free publication and free association were severely curtailed to suit the purposes of the State. It emphasized the power of the Executive at the expense of the Legislature. The State was totalitarian, recognizing no limits to its activity. The economic structure and the political structure of the State were inextricably connected.

The system of government outlined above is instructive to the student of Political Science as containing many novel features. The most important of these is, clearly, the corporative structure of the State. A second is the intimate connexion between the Party and the State. This connexion may be noticed in (*i*) the combination in one person of the Head of the Party and the Head of the Government; (*ii*) the appointment of the secretary of the Party by royal decree on the nomination of the Head of the Government; (*iii*) the organization and powers of the Grand Fascist Council; and (*iv*) the composition of the Fascist and Corporative Chamber. Finally, the position of the Head of the Government, his relations to the ministry and the relations of the ministry both to the Head of the Government and to the Legislature, if not unique, are not usual in modern constitutions.

SELECT BIBLIOGRAPHY

R. T. CLARK, *The Fall of the German Republic*, Allen & Unwin, 1935

F. ERMARTH, *The New Germany*, Digest Press, 1936

H. E. GOAD and M. CURREY, *The Working of a Corporate State*, Nicholson & Watson, 1933

A. GROSSER, *Western Germany*, Allen & Unwin, 1955

F. PITIGLIANI, *An Italian Corporative State*, King, 1933

S. H. ROBERTS, *The House that Hitler Built*, Methuen, 1933

C. T. SCHMIDT, *The Corporate State in Action*, Gollancz, 1939

CHAPTER XXVI

THE UNION OF SOVIET SOCIALIST REPUBLICS

§1 RUSSIA BEFORE THE REVOLUTION OF 1917

At the beginning of the present century, Russia,[1] as she was then known, was an autocracy, the Tsar being the source of all authority in the State. There were, however, liberal groups in the country clamouring for reform. Their demand became so insistent after the defeat of Russia in the Russo-Japanese war (1904-5), that the emperor Nicholas II issued a manifesto on 17 October 1905, granting to his people the fundamental civil liberties — freedom from arbitrary arrest, freedom of opinion, of the press, of assembly and organization. The manifesto also promised an extension of the franchise for elections to the State Parliament (the Duma), and announced the 'immutable rule that no law shall become effective without the approval of the State Duma and that the elected representatives of the people shall be given the opportunity to participate effectively in the control over the activities of the officers appointed by Us [the Crown] to ensure the conformity of such activities with the law'.[2] The hopes engendered by this announcement were never fulfilled ; at the beginning of the first World War (1914), Russia still remained an autocracy, the Parliament being powerless either to pass the laws it liked or to control the Executive. The administration was corrupt ; the masses were poor and illiterate, and the educated classes were completely divorced from them. The defeat of Russia in the war was a death-blow to the monarchy. The revolutionary parties in the State exploited the opportunity, and the Tsar abdicated on 2 March 1917. This was the first stage of the Russian Revolution. From March to October, a provisional government, headed by Kerensky and consisting of 'the flower of Russian Liberalism', functioned ; its authority, however, was seriously questioned by radical revolutionary groups headed by the Petrograd Soviet (Council) of Soldiers' and Workmen's Depu-

---

[1] The present name of the State, the Union of Soviet Socialist Republics was first adopted in 1922 ; Russia is one (and the most important) unit in this federation.

[2] M. T. Florinsky, *Toward an Understanding of the U.S.S.R.*, pp. 11-12

ties, deriving their inspiration from the communist philosophy of Karl Marx. In October came the second stage of the Russian Revolution when the Bolsheviks [1] (headed by Lenin) captured power and established a socialist State. They have ever since remained the masters of the State. From 1917 up to the present day the government of Russia has undergone many changes into which it is unnecessary to enter in this context. It is sufficient to outline the main features of the present constitution adopted on 5 December 1936 and as amended on 25 February 1947.

§2 THE STRUCTURE OF GOVERNMENT

The U.S.S.R. is a federal State consisting of fifteen soviet socialist republics.[2]

The constitution can be amended by decisions of the Supreme Soviet (the national Parliament), adopted by a majority of not less than two-thirds of the votes in each of its chambers. It is thus technically a rigid constitution, though the particular method of amendment cannot be considered as making it difficult to bring about constitutional changes.

The division of powers between the Union and the units follows the model of the U.S.A. in principle, the powers of the formei being enumerated and the residue being vested with the latter. The most important of the subjects decided by the Union are war and peace, foreign affairs,[3] admission of new republics into the U.S.S.R., defence, foreign trade on the basis of State monopoly, establishment of national economic plans of the U.S.S.R., administration of banks, industrial and agricultural establishments, and trading enterprises of all-Union importance, administration of transport and communications, direction of the monetary and credit system, organization of State insurance and laws regarding

---

[1] This word means 'majority' and was first used to indicate the majority of the Russian Social-Democratic Labour Party, who differed from the minority (the Mensheviks) at the Party Congress held in 1903, first over minor questions of organization and later also over important issues of social policy.

[2] D. J. R. Scott, *Russian Political Institutions*, p. 69.

[3] Mention may be made of Article 18-a of the Constitution ; each Union Republic has the right to enter into direct relations with foreign States and to conclude agreements and exchange diplomatic and consular representatives with them, and 18-b : each Union Republic has its own Republican military formations. These suggest that the units have some voice in foreign affairs, though their precise significance is not yet clear. It is evident that it was on the basis of these Articles that the U.S.S.R. demanded and secured separate representation for two of its Constituent Republics, viz. the Byelorussian Soviet Socialist Republic and the Ukrainian Soviet Socialist Republic, in the United Nations.

citizenship of the Union. Besides these, the Union may also establish fundamental principles for (*i*) the use of land as well as the exploitation of its deposits, forests and waters ; (*ii*) the maintenance of public health ; and (*iii*) labour legislation.

An interesting, and perhaps unique, feature of the position of the constituent units in the U.S.S.R. is that they have the right freely to secede from the U.S.S.R. It is doubtful if this is of any practical significance, for leaders of the Communist Party, including Stalin, have publicly expressed the view that the federation of Soviet Republics is but a transitional stage towards complete unity, and that the right of secession must be interpreted in the light of the need for strengthening the U.S.S.R.[1]

The highest executive organ of the State is the Council of Ministers elected at a joint sitting of the two chambers of the Supreme Soviet (the Parliament) and responsible to it and, between sessions of the Supreme Soviet, to its committee, the Presidium. Its powers include the direction and co-ordination of the work of the federal departments ; execution of the national economic plans ; the administration of the monetary and credit system ; the maintenance of public order, the defence of the interests of the State and of the rights of citizens ; general supervision in the sphere of relations with foreign States ; the direction of the general organization of the armed forces of the country and the setting up, when necessary, of special committees and other administrative organs to deal with economic, cultural, and military matters. It may suspend the orders and resolutions of the Councils of Ministers of the constituent republics if such orders and resolutions violate federal laws or decrees.

The Legislature of the U.S.S.R., the Supreme Soviet, consists of two Houses, the Soviet (Council) of the Union and the Soviet (Council) of Nationalities. The Soviet of the Union has 738[2] members, elected by the citizens of the Union by territorial districts on the basis of one deputy for every 300,000 of the population for a four-year term. The Soviet of Nationalities has 640[2] members, elected by the citizens of the Union by Union and Autonomous Republics, Autonomous Regions, and National Areas[3] on the basis of thirty-two deputies from each Union Republic, eleven deputies from each Autonomous Republic, five deputies from each Autonomous Region, and one deputy from

[1] Florinsky, op. cit., p. 91.
[2] 1958 figures.
[3] The Autonomous Republics, Autonomous Regions and National Areas are local divisions within the Union Republics with varying degrees of autonomy in local affairs.

each National Area also for a four-year term. The right to vote is given to all citizens, men and women, who have reached the age of eighteen, irrespective of race and nationality, religion, educational qualifications, residence, social origin, property, status, or past activity, with the exception of insane persons, and persons condemned by a court to deprivation of electoral rights. Every citizen has only one vote. Voting at elections is by secret ballot. The right to stand as a candidate for election is given to all voters who have reached the age of twenty-three. Candidates are nominated by one of the following bodies : public organizations and societies of working people ; Communist party organizations ; trade unions ; co-operatives ; youth organizations and cultural societies. The term of both Houses is four years, unless they are dissolved earlier by reason of irreconcilable differences between them.

The Supreme Soviet exercises all the powers vested in the Union, except those delegated by the constitution to other organs of that government. Normally it meets twice a year. The two Houses have equal powers : the legislative initiative belongs in an equal degree to both, and a law is considered adopted if passed by a simple majority in each House. In case of disagreement between the two bodies, a conciliation committee, consisting of an equal number of members from both Houses, is appointed to explore points of agreement ; if its decision does not satisfy one of the chambers, the question is considered a second time in the chambers, and, if differences still continue, the Supreme Soviet is dissolved and a fresh election held. At a joint sitting of both Houses, the Supreme Soviet elects the Council of Ministers, the Presidium (explained below), and the Supreme Court of the U.S.S.R. — the highest tribunal of the land.

The Presidium is an interesting innovation of the Soviet constitution. It consists of thirty-three members elected by the Supreme Soviet, and continues in office until the election of the new Presidium. Its functions are primarily administrative, but also partly legislative. It convenes two ordinary sessions of the Supreme Soviet a year, and special sessions at its discretion or on the demand of one of the constituent republics ; it dissolves the Supreme Soviet when its two chambers fail to agree, and arranges for fresh elections ; it arranges referendums on its own initiative or on demand by one of the Union Republics ; in the intervals between sessions of the Supreme Soviet it removes from office and appoints the Ministers, subject, however, to subsequent confirmation by the Supreme Soviet ; it awards titles, exercises the right of pardon, appoints and replaces the high command of the armed forces and, in the intervals between sessions of the Supreme Soviet, it declares war ; finally it has power at any time to order mobilization, ratify international treaties and appoint or recall ambassadors. It has power to interpret existing laws of the U.S.S.R., issue decrees and rescind decisions and orders of the Council of Ministers of the U.S.S.R., and of the Councils of Ministers of the constituent republics, in case they do not conform to the law. This last provision is a significant one, for, while providing against the admitted danger of allowing the Executive unfettered discretion in the making of policy, it leaves the validity of executive action to be declared, unlike in Britain and the United States, by legislative, not by judicial, decision.

The organization of the Judiciary differs somewhat from that prevalent in other States. The Supreme Court of the U.S.S.R. the highest court in the land, consists of 45 judges and 20 assessors elected by the Legislature for a term of five years. The judges of lower courts are similarly elected, by primary voters or by regional soviets, for a period of three to five years. They may, however, be recalled by the bodies that elected them or by a decision of the higher courts.[1] The judges are declared[2] to be independent, ' subordinate only to the law '. It is also noteworthy that, as in Switzerland, the Supreme Court has no power to declare the Union law unconstitutional, for the constitution says,[3] that ' in case of conflict between a law of a constituent republic and a law of the Union, the Union law shall prevail '.

Economic life

The U.S.S.R., it will be recalled, is a socialist State. The economic foundation of the U.S.S.R., the constitution declares, consists of the socialist economic system and the socialist ownership of the tools and means of production, which has been firmly established as a result of the liquidation of the capitalist economic system, the abolition of private ownership of the tools and means of production, and the abolition of the exploitation of man by man. Socialist property takes two forms : State property and the property of collective farms and co-operative organizations. The land, its deposits, waters, forest, mills, factories, mines, railways, water and air transport, banks, means of communication and State farms are State property. Public enterprises in collective farms and co-operative organizations, with their livestock and equipment and products raised or manufactured by them, form

---

[1] Florinsky, op. cit., p. 133. [2] Article 112. [3] Article 20.

the property of the collective farms and co-operative organizations.

Industry, transport, banking and trade are thus (almost wholly) State owned and controlled and are directed by a Planning Commission. Agriculture is carried on either in State farms or in collective farms.[1] A collective farm is, in form, a voluntary co-operative agricultural association of peasants, each peasant contributing to the common stock his implements, draught animals, seed and labour, and entitled to a share of the total output. Members are, however, allowed to retain for personal use a plot of land attached to the house, and as personal property their houses, small farm tools, and small livestock. The affairs of the farm are managed by an elected council. The agricultural economy of the U.S.S.R. is, it will be seen, socialistic in a somewhat different sense from that applied to her industry, for it is not for the most part directed by State officials. It is socialistic in the sense that (i) all agricultural land is owned by the State : (ii) a small part of it is cultivated as State farms ; and (iii) private enterprise and the employment by anyone of another's labour for his private profit do not exist in the other and larger part of it, viz. the collective farms. Further, the land occupied by collective farms is public property, secured to them 'without payments and without time limit, that is, for ever'.

In State-owned industries and farms, and in collective farms. the payment of wages is based on the principle 'from each according to his ability, to each according to his work'.

It is noteworthy that alongside the socialist economy, which covers more than ninety-five per cent of the production, distribution and exchange in the U.S.S.R., the law permits the small-scale enterprise of individual peasants and handicraftsmen conducted by their personal labour, provided they do not employ others for their private profit.

The right to hold personal property is not altogether abolished, being permitted in income from labour and savings deposited in State banks or invested in government bonds, houses occupied by their owners, household articles and utensils, tools, furnishings, and other personal belongings.

To what extent is the constitution democratic ?

It is sometimes claimed that the constitution of Soviet Russia is a perfect democracy. *Pro forma* the constitution is clearly

---

[1] At the end of 1955 the number of State farms stood at 5134 and the number of collective farms at 87,500 (D. J. R. Scott, op. cit., p. 201).

democratic : universal suffrage ; 'one person, one vote'; the equal eligibility of all voters to be elected (with the least number of disqualifications found in any State); direct election to both chambers ; vote by ballot ; periodical elections ; the election of the Executive by the Legislature and its responsibility to the Legislature ; the equal eligibility to administrative and judicial offices ; the election of judges and the provision for referendums provide political equality and the opportunity for all to take part in government. It is also true that the vast economic inequalities which hamper the working of democracies elsewhere have been done away with. But fundamentally and in spirit, the U.S.S.R. is not democratic, at any rate according to orthodox notions of democracy. Its affinity is rather to the totalitarian States, and this for two reasons. First, the way of life prescribed by the U.S.S.R. is near-totalitarian ; everyone feels he has to conform to the pattern of life set by the State ; this is anti-democratic. Since the death of Stalin, available evidence points to the emergence of liberal trends ; criticisms of government are heard in private conversations, though not in the Press or public meetings. To the extent that such liberal trends grow, the State will be less and less totalitarian. The ideal of democracy is to permit a larger degree of freedom to the individual to think and express himself (differently, it may be, from the opinions held by the group in control of government) in speech and action than is permitted in the U.S.S.R. Second, an alternative Government must be possible in a democracy ; under the conditions which prevail in the U.S.S.R., this is clearly impossible. For an alternative Government is possible only when an Opposition is allowed to exist, when parties which differ in their programme from the party in power are tolerated. In the U.S.S.R., only the Communist party is given some constitutional status [1] as the union of 'the most active and politically conscious citizens from the ranks of the working class and other strata of the working people,' and entitled to nominate candidates for elections. In the elections held in 1937, there was no contest at all in any of the constituencies. Apparently, elections are not entirely free ; and 'free' elections are essential to a democratic system of government. Briefly a one-party State is the antithesis of democracy.

For a balanced view, it is also useful to cite the Soviet defence of the one-party State.[2]

---

[1] Articles 126 and 141.
[2] A. D. M. Kirichenko, *Soviet State Law*, pp. 361-62.

' True, in the Soviet Union there is a one-party system, which evolved historically. But this is not a shortcoming — on the contrary, it is one of the merits of Soviet democracy in general and the Soviet electoral system in particular. There are no antagonistic classes in the Soviet Union, and, therefore, there is no basis for the existence of a diametrically opposed political parties. The interests of the workers, peasants and intellectuals are expressed and safeguarded by the Communist Party of the Soviet Union.'

Novel features of the constitution

The U.S.S.R. is, as Stalin said, ' an entirely novel socialist State, unprecedented in history '. Its novel features are : (*i*) It is a socialist State ; the socialist organization of its economic life is therefore its most important novel feature. (*ii*) The right to secede is granted by the constitution to the component units of the federation. (*iii*) The Centre is given power to amend the constitution by a two-thirds majority of its Legislature, the units having no share in the amendment. This is somewhat uncommon in federal States. (*iv*) There is a concentration of powers in the Supreme Soviet ; it elects the Executive and the Judiciary ; and the laws it passes are not subject to executive or judicial veto. The only appeal from it is by referendum to the people. (*v*) The two chambers of the Supreme Soviet have equal powers — this is found only in Switzerland among the major States. (*vi*) The composition and functions of the Presidium are unique. (*vii*) The U.S.S.R. is a one-party State. (*viii*) Unlike in most written constitutions, in the Constitution of the Soviet Union the fundamental duties are also stated[1] (in addition to the fundamental rights).

' Every citizen of the U.S.S.R. is obliged to abide by the Constitution, to observe the laws, to work according to his abilities, to maintain labour ·discipline, honestly to perform public discipline, to respect the rules of socialist intercourse, to safeguard and fortify socialist property, to serve in the Armed Forces and to defend the socialist Motherland.'

§3   COMPARISONS AND CONTRASTS

The system of government in the U.S.S.R., outlined above, has some striking resemblances with, and some differences from, the

[1] Articles 12 and 130-133 of the Constitution. See also Kirichenko, op. cit., p. 342.

system of government in Nazi Germany and Fascist Italy outlined earlier. In Hitlerite Germany as well as in Mussolini's Italy the State was totalitarian, there being no limits to the sphere of the State ; individual freedom was at a discount. Parliament was relatively unimportant ; the Executive was (whatever be the theory of the constitution) all-powerful. Further, though couched in democratic forms, they were essentially dictatorships, alternative Governments being in practice impossible and an Opposition not being tolerated. Freedom of speech and organization was restricted. Since only one party was tolerated, the party became in effect the ultimate organ of government and the direct source of public policy. A determined effort was made, through control of education and of the means which mould public opinion, to influence the attitude of the citizens so that it might be in sympathy with the dominant party. And, finally, the younger generation were encouraged to form groups fully in sympathy with the dominant party, and it was from these groups that the members of the party were recruited. The U.S.S.R. also is a one-party State ; individual freedom in a democratic atmosphere as understood in the United Kingdom and the U.S.A. is at a discount.

The differences are no less striking. Germany and Italy were fascist States ; the U.S.S.R. is a socialist State and claims that its socialism is in a transitional stage towards communism. In the former, the dictatorship arose for the preservation of class differences ; in the latter, for their destruction. Therefore, fascist dictatorships left industry for the most part under private ownership, though they subjected it to rigorous State control ; the communist State had necessarily to take the instruments of production under its ownership and control. Therefore, the latter implies radically new social values in a far more fundamental economic revolution. For, whereas fascism aimed mainly at preserving old institutions that were threatened, communism seeks to establish values that are new.[1]

SELECT BIBLIOGRAPHY

G. M. CARTER, *Government of the Soviet Union*, Harcourt Brace Jovanovich, New York, 1972

G. M. CARTER, J. C. RANNEY and J. H. HERZ, *The Government of the Soviet Union*, The World Press, Calcutta, 1954

W. H. CHAMBERLIN, *The Russian Revolution*, Macmillan, 1935

G. D. H. *and* MARGARET COLE, *A Guide to Modern Politics*, Gollanez 1934

[1] G. D. H. and Margaret Cole, *A Guide to Modern Politics*, pp 74-5.

M. T. FLORINSKY, *Toward an Understanding of the U.S.S.R.*, Macmillan, 1939

J. N. HAZARD, *The Soviet System of Government*, Rev. Ed. 4, Sterling Publishers, New Delhi, 1971

M. HINDUS, *Mother Russia*, Collins, 1943

A. DENISOV M. KIRICHENKO, *Soviet State Law*, Foreign Languages Publishing House, 1960

A. NOVE, *The Soviet Economy, An Introduction*, Allen & Unwin, 1961

J. F. NORMANO, *The Spirit of Russian Economics*, John Day, 2nd ed., 1950

B. PARES, *Russia*, Penguin Books, 1940

D J. R. SCOTT, *Russian Political Institutions*, Allen and Unwin, 1958

A. L. STRONG, *The New Soviet Constitution*, Henry Holt, 1937

BOOK III. ORGANIZATION OF GOVERNMENT

CHAPTER XXVII

THE CLASSIFICATION OF STATES

§ 1 INTRODUCTORY

IN our analysis of the subject-matter of Politics,[1] we indicated that from a study of governments in the past and in the present, we should be in a position to formulate, by an inductive process, principles regarding the organization of government, its structure and working. To this we now turn.

There is, however, one preliminary inquiry to make. There are, as our survey has shown, different types of States. A discussion of principles relating to the organization of government, to be realistic, must needs take into account the similarities and differences between States; these are best studied by a classification of States.[2]

§ 2 EARLY CLASSIFICATIONS

Aristotle was among the earliest thinkers to attempt a comprehensive classification. The basis of his classification is at once quantitative and qualitative. He takes into account the *number* of those in whom sovereign power is vested, and the *end* to which the conduct of government is directed. The supreme power in a State must necessarily be in the hands of one person, or of a few, or of the many. The one, or the few, or the many, may govern the community for the common good or for their own selfish or class interests. The first type of constitution is a *normal* one; the second, a *perverted* one. Taking these two

---

[1] See above, p. 4.
[2] Some writers like Gilchrist (*Principles of Political Science*, p. 231) prefer the term 'the classification of the forms of government' on the ground that the 'form of States' is really the form of government. When we consider the fact that States differ not only in their forms of government, but in their professed *end* (e.g. totalitarian States *v.* democratic States) and in their very *nature* (e.g. unitary *v.* federal), the term 'the classification of States' seems preferable; it has, besides, the support of writers like Hobbes and Locke, and, in recent times, Bluntschli and Marriott.

principles together, Aristotle arrived at the conclusion that six
kinds of State are possible : monarchy and its perversion, tyranny ;
aristocracy and its perversion, oligarchy ; polity and its perversion, democracy.

Two observations are necessary to help us to understand
Aristotle's account correctly. First, he used the term ' polity '
to describe the unselfish rule of the masses ; ' democracy ' was
for him a perversion. To us, the former is a somewhat unfami-
liar term, and the latter does not necessarily indicate the arbitrary
or selfish rule of the demos. Aristotle's dislike of ' democracy '
must be explained by the degeneration of Greek democracies in
his day. Second, in his definition of oligarchy and of democracy
Aristotle was not entirely logical. He defined oligarchy as the
rule of the rich in the interests of the rich, be they few or many ;
and democracy, as the rule of the poor, be they many or few,
in the interests of the poor.[1] On his own first principles, a
constitution in which the rich ruling in the interests of the rich
are in a majority should have been called a democracy ; and
one in which the poor ruling in the interests of the poor are in
a minority, an oligarchy. Aristotle was aware of this illogicality,
but after a thorough discussion,[2] he decided that the question of
numbers was accidental ; that of wealth, essential. To keep to
the facts of life is more important than to attempt a meaningless
logical precision ; Aristotle knew that normally ' there were many
poor and few rich '.

A few of the later classifications — by Polybius, Hobbes,
Locke, Montesquieu, and Rousseau — will also be briefly referred to. In all of them the influence of Aristotle may be traced.

Like Aristotle, Polybius adopted an ethical standard when
marking off one State from another. ' The rule of one may be
held to be a kingship only when his rule " is accepted voluntarily
and is directed by an appeal to reason rather than to fear and
force ". Otherwise it is a *despotism*. Nor can every oligarchy
be properly described as an aristocracy, but only where " the
power is wielded by the justest and wisest men selected on their
merits ". Similarly the rule of the many may easily become
nothing but *mob-rule* ; the honourable designation of a democracy must be reserved for a government where " reverence to
the gods, succour of parents, respect to elders, obedience to laws
are traditional and habitual ".'[3]

---

[1] *Politics*, bk. IV, ch. iv.   [2] ibid.
[3] Polybius, cited by Marriott in *The Mechanism of the Modern State*,
Vol. I, p. 26.

Hobbes is content with a threefold classification, basing it entirely on the location of sovereign power in the one, the few, or the many, and paying no heed to the ethical *differentiae* noted by Aristotle and Polybius.

' The difference of Common-wealths consisteth in the difference of the Sovereign, or the Person representative of all and every one of the Multitude.... When the Representative is one man, then is the Common-wealth a MONARCHY : when an Assembly of All that will come together ; then it is a DEMOCRACY, or Popular Common-wealth : when an Assembly of a Part only then it is called an ARISTOCRACY. Other kind of Common-wealth there can be none : for either One, or More, or All, must have the Sovereign Power (which I have shewn to be indivisible) entire.' [1]

Hobbes was aware of other names of government such as Tyranny, Oligarchy and Anarchy, but he refused to consider them as other *forms* of government. Those who were discontented under Monarchy called it Tyranny ; those who were displeased with Aristocracy called it Oligarchy ; and those who nursed grievances against Democracy called it Anarchy.

Locke substantially follows Hobbes in his classification, with some differences of detail. Thus he says, ' according as the power of making laws is placed, such is the form of the commonwealth '.[2] If the majority, in whom the whole power of the community is placed at the dawn of civil society, retain the legislative power in their own hands and execute those laws by officers of their own appointing, the form of the government is a perfect democracy ; if they put the power of making laws into the hands of a few select men and their heirs or successors, then it is an oligarchy ; if into the hands of one man, then it is a monarchy, hereditary or elective.

Montesquieu (1699-1785), the French political philosopher, held that States are of three types, the republican, the monarchic and the despotic. If all or part of the people have the sovereign power, the State is a republic, a democratic or an aristocratic one. A monarchy is the rule of a single person according to law ; a despotism, the rule of a single person arbitrarily. Montesquieu indicates the various principles animating the various forms of government, the sustaining and driving powers behind

[1] Hobbes, *Leviathan*, pp. 96-7.
[2] *Of Civil Government*, bk. II, ch. x.

them. Thus the virtue of the citizens is the principle of a republic. In a democracy, this virtue takes the shape of love of country and desire for equality. That the members of a ruling class will be moderate towards the people, maintain equality among themselves, and enforce the laws against persons of rank — this is the virtue of an aristocracy. The mainspring of monarchy is honour : the confidence or conceit of the individual and of the governing classes concerning their own special importance, a confidence which spurs men to accomplish things quite as much as virtue itself. Despotism requires neither virtue nor honour, but fear which suppresses both courage and ambition among subjects.

Rousseau, like Hobbes, is content with a numerical *differentia* : governments are monarchies, aristocracies or democracies.

Their inapplicability to modern conditions

Whatever was the value of these classifications at the time when they were formulated, it should be clear to the student of modern constitutions that they are quite inapplicable to existing political conditions. They do not help one to understand the resemblances and differences between States, which is the object of a classification. To illustrate : Under the classification adopted by Aristotle, almost every State in the preceding survey should be termed a democracy (or a polity) ; we know, however, that there are marked differences between them. Britain is a unitary State ; the U.S.A., a federal one. The U.S.A. is a federal State with a non-parliamentary Executive ; India and Australia are federal States but with parliamentary Executives. Switzerland is also federal but with an Executive which is at once both parliamentary and non-parliamentary. The inapplicability of older classifications is primarily due to the developments in political constitutionalism in recent times. The authors whom we have cited were classifying States with which they were familiar. But we have to frame a classification which is more in accordance with modern conditions.

§3 A CLASSIFICATION OF MODERN STATES

The classification outlined below is based upon the suggestions made by Bryce Marriott, Strong and Lindsay. While it applies to most modern States, it does not claim to be applicable to all. The terms used in the classification have been defined in

Part I and in Part II, Book II. Three explanations may be added.

		Basis of Division	A	B
I	1	The conception regarding the sphere of the State	Liberal[1]	Totalitarian[1] (a) communist (b) fascist
II		The nature of the political organization		
	2	The nature of the State	Unitary[2]	Federal[2]
	3	The nature of the constitution	Flexible[3]	Rigid[3]
	4	The nature of the electorate	(i) Adult suffrage[4] (ii) Single-member[4] constituency	(i) Restricted suffrage[4] (ii) Multi-member constituency[4]
	5	The nature of the Legislature	Bicameral[5] (a) elective or partially elective second chamber (b) non-elective second chamber	Unicameral[6]
	6	The nature of the Executive	Parliamentary[7]	Non-parliamentary[7]
	7	The nature of the Judiciary	The rule of law[8]	Administrative law[8]

[1] See above, ch. ix, §7.

[2] See above, ch. xvi, §1, and below, ch. xxvii. The class of States which are termed Legislative unions, e.g. South Africa before 1961, is a class by itself, neither unitary nor federal.

[3] See above, ch. xvi, §2, and below, ch. xxviii.

[4] See above. ch. xvi, §8. Restricted suffrage indicates the restriction of the right to vote to men, as in Switzerland until 1971 ; or to men and women in possession of prescribed educational or property qualifications as under the Government of India Act of 1953

[5] Consisting of two chambers.

[6] Consisting of one chamber.

[7] See above, ch. xvi, §9, and ch. xvii, §4.

[8] See above, ch. xvi, §13, and ch. xvii, §7.

(*i*) The classification is framed on two major bases. ' I. The conception regarding the sphere of the State,' whether liberal or totalitarian. This *differentia* has assumed such importance in modern times that it deserves emphasis in any scheme of classification. The life of the people in liberal States has a quality all its own, different not only in degree but in kind from that of the people in totalitarian States. As has been indicated elsewhere, totalitarian States themselves fall into two types, the communist and the fascist, the former abolishing, and the latter retaining, private capital. ' II. The nature of the political organization.' Under this heading three *differentiae* are noteworthy, viz. the nature of the State (unitary or federal) ; the nature of the constitution (flexible or rigid) ; and the structure of the Government (the electorate, the Legislature, the Executive and the Judiciary).

(*ii*) It cannot be assumed that a State which comes under A in respect of 1 comes under A also in respect of 2, 3, 4, 5, 6, and 7. Thus the U.S.A. is a Liberal State (1) ; but is not a unitary State (2) ; her constitution is not a flexible one (3) ; and her Executive is not a parliamentary one (6).

(*iii*) As we adopt in effect seven bases of classification, it is necessary to deal with each State seven times in order to place it properly. Thus :

BRITAIN : Liberal, unitary State, flexible constitution, adult suffrage and single-member constituency, bicameral Legislature with a non-elective second chamber, parliamentary Executive, and the rule of law.

THE FRENCH REPUBLIC : Liberal, unitary State, rigid constitution, adult suffrage and multi-member constituency, bicameral Legislature with an elective second chamber, parliamentary Executive, and administrative law. And so on.

The rest of the book follows the order of the principle of classification laid down in the Table under ' II. The nature of the political organization.' A chapter on ' The Separation of Powers ' has, however, been added before a consideration of the electorate, the Legislature, the Executive, and the Judiciary.

SELECT BIBLIOGRAPHY

ARISTOTLE, *Politics*, Bk. IV, ' Everyman Library ', Dent

J. BRYCE, *Studies in History and Jurisprudence,* Vol. I, Essay III, Oxford, 1901

T. HOBBES, *Leviathan*, ch. xix, ' Everyman Library ', Dent

J. Locke, *Of Civil Government*, ch. x, in *Social Contract*, 'World's Classics' No. 511, Oxford

J. A. R. Marriott, *The Mechanism of the Modern State*, Vol. I, ch. ii, Oxford, 1927

J. J. Rousseau, *The Social Contract*, Bk. III, ch. iii to viii, in *Social Contract*, 'World's Classics' No. 511, Oxford

M. Stewart, *Modern Forms of Government*, Allen & Unwin.

G. F. Strong, *Modern Political Constitutions*, ch. iii, Sidgwick & Jackson, 1930

CHAPTER XXVIII

UNITARY AND FEDERAL STATES

§1 UNITARY AND FEDERAL STATES

A UNITARY State may be defined as one organized under a single central government; and unitarianism, as the habitual exercise of supreme legislative authority by one central power.[1] Britain, France and Italy are unitary States; India has some characteristics of the unitary State, although in Constitutional Law it is a federal State.

A federal State is one in which there is a central authority that represents the whole, and acts on behalf of the whole in external affairs and in such internal affairs as are held to be of common interest; and in which there are also provincial or state authorities with powers of legislation and administration within the sphere allotted to them by the constitution.[2] It is, in the words of Hamilton, 'an association of States that forms a new one'; or, as Dicey put it, it is a political contrivance intended to reconcile national unity with the maintenance of the state rights. The U.S.A., Canada, Australia, Switzerland and the U.S.S.R. are federal States.

The distinctive feature of federation is the formal division of governmental powers by a constitution between the constituent units (states, provinces, or cantons) and the larger State which they compose. The units have power to pass laws on the subjects allotted to them and to administer and interpret them; and the Federal Authority has similar power on the subjects allotted to it. Both the units and the Federal Authority may exercise their legislative, administrative and judicial powers only within the limits set by the constitution. The supremacy of the constitution is, therefore, a second important feature of federation. The constitution of the U.S.A., for instance, explicitly declares: 'This constitution and the laws of the U.S.A. which shall be made in pursuance thereof... shall be the supreme law of the land, and the judges in every state shall be bound thereby, anything in the constitution or laws of any state to the contrary notwithstanding.' This supremacy implies that the laws passed

---

[1] See above, ch. xvi, §1.
[2] H. Samuel in *The Nineteenth Century*, No. 428, p. 676.

by any authority in the State, if contrary to the constitution, may be declared *ultra vires*; some authority, such as a Supreme Court, to interpret the constitution and decide conflicts of jurisdiction between the Centre and the units is therefore essential. It also means that neither the Federal Authority nor any unit thereof has the power to change the constitution as it likes; for then one of the two, and not the constitution, becomes supreme. In other words, a federal State has necessarily a rigid constitution. Normally, the machinery to amend the constitution is one in which both the Federal Authority and the units have a definite place. The U.S.A., Australia and Switzerland are instances of this. These then are the essential features of federation: the division of powers, the supremacy of the constitution, the existence of a court to interpret the constitution, and the rigidity of the constitution.

By contrast, in a unitary State there is no constitutional division of powers between the Centre and local territorial divisions; at any rate it is one which the Centre is not powerless to alter. The distinguishing mark of a unitary State is that all local governing authorities within the State (provinces, counties, districts) are created, their powers defined, and their form of organization determined by the Central Government. That Central Government may be limited by a superior constitution in a number of ways without affecting the unitary character of the State; but if the constitution gives powers to the local bodies independent of, and not modifiable by, the Central Government, the political system partakes of the essential nature of federation. Therefore, it is by the nature of the relationship of the Central to the local bodies that one determines whether a State is federal or unitary. Briefly, in the former, both the central and local authorities derive their power from a common source; in the latter the Central Government has authority legally to determine the powers, indeed the very existence, of the local authorities. It follows that in the unitary State, the constitution need not *necessarily* be supreme, for the Centre may have the power to modify it, as in Britain; there is no need to have an authority to decide conflicts of jurisdiction between the Centre and the local authorities; and the constitution need not *necessarily* be rigid.

§2 FEDERATION AND CONFEDERATION

A federation must be distinguished from a confederation. The League of Nations was an example of the latter. The American

Confederation, whose articles were drawn up by the Continental Congress in 1777, and which lasted from 1781 to 1789, is another. Here each one of its thirteen State-members was a sovereign body-politic. The only form of common control was exercised through the Congress, ' a body of delegates which had no power to compel the States to its will, and no power to command or to tax the individual citizens of the thirteen States.' Congress was primarily to look after foreign relations, declare and conduct war, build and equip a navy, and issue requisitions upon the States for soldiers and for funds. The working of the system for eight years proved its inadequacy, for while Congress could pass resolutions ' it had no authority to make law, in the sense of regulations backed up with a power of enforcement.' The confederation gave place to a federation. The German Confederation, as it existed from 1815 to 1866, is a third example. This was a union of 39 States, including kingdoms, free cities, and principalities. The primary aim of the union was the external and internal security of the States. The common authority was the Central Assembly called the Diet, consisting of delegates of the Governments of the States. But no central Executive was established, each State acting as the executor of the resolutions of the union. In 1866 it had to be dissolved to give place (later, in 1871) to the Federation of the German Empire.

A confederation, like a federation, is a union of States with a common recognized authority in certain matters affecting the whole, and especially in respect of external relations. But it differs from a federation in that it is a league of sovereign States (*Staatenbund* is the expressive German term, *Staaten* being plural) ; whereas federation creates a new State (*Bundesstaat*, *Staat* being singular). In the former, sovereignty rests with the component States ; in the latter, the component States give up their sovereignty in favour of the new State, sovereignty in the new State being exercised by the amending body of its constitution. It follows that while the units of a confederation have the legal right of secession, the units of a federation have not.[1] The distinction between the two forms of union is therefore fundamental, founded upon the source of ultimate authority, sovereignty.

Another difference between the two is that the common authority of a confederation deals only with the Governments of the constituent units, and not, as in a federation, directly with

[1] The U.S.S.R. is an exception. See, however, above, ch. xxv.

their individual citizens. The citizen in a confederation therefore has to obey only one Government, that of his own State ; the orders of the common authority are binding on him only in so far as they are imposed on him by the Government of his own State. The citizen in a federal State, on the other hand, has to obey two Governments, that of his state and that of the Federal Authority.

From these two differences may be deduced a third : the confederation, being a looser union than the federation, is generally less stable.

§3 CONDITIONS OF FEDERALISM

The normal method of establishing a federation has been the coming together of a number of States, formerly separate and sovereign, to establish a common government for better security. This was how the United States, Switzerland, and Australia came into existence. Sometimes it has been the other way round. In Canada, for instance, an originally unitary State was converted into a federal one by a constitution marking out the spheres of the provinces, and making each of them part of a federal State. This is a process of devolution or decentralization, designed to secure a more efficient government.

The conditions which favour the establishment and continuance of a federation are as follows :

(*i*) *The desire for union.* Obviously, unless some political units desire to unite and establish a common government for their common interests, there is no basis for federation. This desire normally arises when a number of small independent States, locally adjacent, come to feel that if they do not unite, their independence will be threatened by more powerful States. It will not arise where the separate States are so powerful as to be able to rely, for protection against foreign encroachment, on their individual strength. ' If they are,' said J. S. Mill, ' they will be apt to think that they do not gain, by union with others, the equivalent of what they sacrifice in their own liberty of action ; and consequently, whenever the policy of the (con)federation, in things reserved to its cognizance, is different from that which any one of its members would separately pursue, the internal and sectional breach will, through absence of sufficient anxiety to preserve the union, be in danger of going so far as to dissolve it.' [1] The felt need for strength in external relations

---

[1] *Representative Government*, ch. xvii.

is invariably coupled with the desire of the separate States, by conjoint action, to develop foreign trade, remove internal trade barriers and prevent internecine warfare. The thirteen American States, which joined to form the U.S.A., were eager not only to stabilize their hard-won independence of England, but also to adopt a uniform commercial policy, and generally to make the maximum use of the opportunities afforded by union to advance their general prosperity. The six colonies which federated to form the Commonwealth of Australia in 1900 'would not have done so except under the dread of danger from imperializing Powers in the Pacific, a danger not apparent until the closing years of the last century'.[1] At the same time 'there was a general feeling that an authority with wider powers than any existing before the federation was necessary for industrial and social development, and that a supreme judicial authority ought to be established to avoid the expense and delay involved in carrying cases to the Privy Council in London'.[2] These two instances also remind us that the sentiment of union is induced by community of blood, language and culture, and the similarity of political institutions. These create and keep up common sympathy among the peoples concerned and conduce to an identity of political interest without which a federation cannot come into being, or if forcibly created, cannot last long.

(*ii*) . *The desire for local independence.* While there must be a desire for union, this desire should not be so great as to result in the demand for the establishment of a unitary State. A desire among the component states for the preservation of their independence in all but essentially common matters is a precondition for this form of political organization. Federalism is a natural constitution only for a body of States which desire union and do not desire unity.[3]

(*iii*) *Geographical contiguity.* The physical contiguity of countries which are to form a federation ' is certainly a favourable, and possibly a necessary, condition for the success of federal government '. If they are widely separated, the desire for union cannot easily emerge, as the advantages to be obtained do not appear real enough to make the necessary sacrifice worth while. The proposal for a federation of the countries which form part of the British Commonwealth, which found some support in the

[1] Strong, *Modern Political Constitutions*, pp. 111-12.
[2] ibid.
[3] Dicey, *Introduction to the Study of the Law of the Constitution.*

last century, fell through partly because these countries were physically wide apart.

(*iv*) *The absence of marked inequalities among the component units.* If there is any State so much more powerful than the rest as to be capable of vying in strength with many of them combined ' it will insist on being master of the joint deliberations : if there be two, they will be irresistible when they agree ; and whenever they differ everything will be decided by a struggle for ascendancy between the rivals '.[1] The classic instance of this is the German Empire, established in 1871 ; the predominance of Prussia vitiated the federal principle.

(*v*) *Political education and legalism.* The permanence of a federation demands a capacity on the part of the people to appreciate the meaning of a double allegiance, and the ability to prevent the centrifugal principle of political action from overcoming the centripetal. It also means a developed sense of legalism, or in other words ' a general willingness to yield to the authority of the law courts ' which decide indeed what the constitution at any moment is.

§4 PROBLEMS OF FEDERAL GOVERNMENT

The federal State, differing as it does from the unitary in essential features, has to face a number of problems which the latter has not. The most important of these are :

(*i*) *A satisfactory division of powers.* The problem which all federal States have to solve is how to secure an efficient Central Government, while allowing scope for the diversities, and free play to the authorities, of the units. It is, to adopt Bryce's metaphor, to keep the centrifugal and centripetal forces in equilibrium, so that neither the planet states shall fly off into space, nor the sun of the Central Government draw them into its consuming fires. The general principle on which the division of powers should rest is fairly obvious. ' Whatever concerns the nation as a whole should be placed under the control of the national Government. All matters which are not primarily of common interest should remain in the hands of the several states.[2] Such subjects as foreign affairs, defence, the control of the armed forces, foreign trade, maritime shipping and currency, are clearly of common interest and are everywhere federal ; municipal institutions, hospitals, local public works,

[1] Mill, op. cit., ch. xvii.
[2] Dicey, op. cit., p. 143.

property and civil rights, and the administration of justice within
the state, are clearly of a local nature and are everywhere allotted
to the units.   On a number of subjects, however, the common
interests, or the purely local interest, is not quite so clear, and,
therefore, the details of the division vary under different federal
conditions.

There is a variation not only in the particular subjects which
fall within the sphere of the Centre and of the units, but also in
the way in which the division is effected. Broadly speaking, our
survey suggests, there are three such methods.

(*a*) In the U.S.A., Australia, Switzerland, Weimar Germany,
Pakistan and the U.S.S.R., the powers of the Centre are enumerated
in the Constitution ; the residue is left to the units. The
enumeration itself is not of a uniform type ; in the U.S.A., there
is one list of exclusively federal subjects allotted to the Centre,
with some prohibitions both on the Centre and on the units ; in
Australia, Switzerland, Pakistan and Weimar Germany, the Centre
has power to pass laws on an exclusively federal list as well as
on a concurrent list, Central laws in respect of concurrent subjects
prevailing over those of the units ; in the U.S.S.R. there is only
an exclusively federal list.   The device of concurrent powers is
specially noteworthy as it provides a plan by which the Centre
can step in some matters when the Government of a unit is
lazy or unprogressive and when the need for uniformity demands
its interference, while leaving the initiative in the first instance
to the units.

(*b*) In Canada, the powers of the provinces are enumerated ;
the residue is left to the Centre, though, as has been indicated
in the section on Canada, this is qualified in some ways by the
powers granted to the provinces in respect of matters of a
' merely local or private nature '.

(*c*) In the federal scheme for India, as outlined under the
Act of 1935, the powers of the Centre and of the provinces were
more or less exhaustively enumerated in three lists, the exclusively federal, the concurrent and the exclusively provincial ;
further, the residuary power as such was neither with the Centre
nor with the provinces, but was to be allotted (as and when each
specific case arose) to the Centre or to the provinces by the
Governor-General in his discretion.

A word may be added about the ' enumerated ' and the ' residuary ' powers. The object of enumerating the powers of any
authority is to limit it. Where, then, a federal constitution
enumerates the powers of the Centre, as in the U.S.A., the object

clearly is to limit its powers as against the units, and enable the latter to retain all the rest; conversely, where it enumerates the powers of the units, as in Canada, the object is to limit their powers as against the Centre. In general, therefore, it is true to say that the greater the 'reserve of powers' with the units, the more markedly federal is the State whose constitution permits such reserve to them.[1]

But three things must be emphasized. (*a*) The 'more markedly federal' nature depends not on the mere fact that the residue is allotted to the units, but on the content of that residue; it would be absurd, for instance, to consider Weimar Germany markedly federal *because* the residue was left with the states. (*b*) The idea of the residuary powers has little significance, as in the federal scheme for India referred to above, where care was taken to enumerate every conceivable power, so that very little was left as the 'reserve of powers'. (*c*) Under modern economic and social conditions, where an increasing number of problems can be met only by an authority representing the general interest, it seems the wisest policy (if it were possible) to enumerate the powers of the units and leave a large reserve of powers to the Centre.

The governmental powers must not only be satisfactorily distributed between the Centre and the units, but provision must be made to prevent either from encroaching upon a sphere allotted to the other. Here, again, federations differ in respect of the safeguards provided against this possibility, and their efficacy. The most common safeguard is the establishment of an independent court to interpret the constitution and decide conflicts of jurisdiction between the Centre and the units. The American and the Australian courts are the best instances of this; in Switzerland and in the U.S.S.R. the Supreme Court has no power to declare the federal law unconstitutional and, to that extent, the judicial safeguard is ineffective as a means of protecting the rights of the units. A second safeguard is the power given to the people, as in Switzerland, by the referendum and the initiative to decide finally on constitutional laws, the opinion of a majority of the people[2] being, as it ought to be, final. Thirdly, the constitution is made rigid, i.e. not alterable by the ordinary law-making body of the Centre or of the states.

---

[1] Strong, op. cit., p. 101.
[2] In Switzerland, as has already been noted earlier, the affirmative vote of a majority of cantons is also necessary for the passing of constitutional amendments.

Invariably, too, some part is given to both the Cen*ᵣ ᵤ* and the
units in the process of amending the constitution, the U.S.S.R.
being an exception in that it ignores the units ; again invariably,
the part assigned to the units is greater than that allotted to the
Centre. The central Legislature is given the power to *propose*
amendments in the U.S.A., Australia, and Switzerland ; the final
ratification by a majority of the units is made essential (in the
U.S.A. by three-fourths of the states). Further, some fundamental
rights of the units (as, for instance, the right to equal membership in the Senate in the U.S.A., and territorial limits in Australia) are made unalterable except with the consent of the states
affected.

(*ii*) *Protection of the smaller units against dominance by the
larger.* As the units in no federation are identical in size and
population, it is possible that the larger units may have a predominant influence in legislation on account of their larger representation in the lower House of the central Legislature (everywhere
constituted on the basis of population). Two provisions are generally adopted to prevent this evil. (*a*) In the second chamber of
the central Legislature, every unit is given equal representation
(in the U.S.A., Australia, Switzerland, and the U.S.S.R.), or a
provision is made, as in Weimar Germany, restricting the number
of members that may be sent to the second chamber by *any* unit
to less than one half of its total strength. Further, in the first
four States mentioned, the second chamber is given powers equal,
or very nearly equal, to those of the first. The constitution of
the U.S.A. goes further and gives the Senate two important powers
denied to the House of Representatives, those of consenting or
refusing its assent to appointments and treaties made by the President. (*b*) It is stated (in Australia and Switzerland) that no
amendments to the constitution may become valid until they have
been ratified not only by a majority of the whole people, but also
by a majority of the federal units. In the U.S.A. the consent of
three-fourths of the states is necessary.

(*iii*) *Organization of the relation between the Centre and the
units.* Ideally, in a federal State, the Centre and the units ought
to be mutually independent in the spheres allotted to each by
the constitution — in legislation, in administration, and in finance.
This mutual independence is indeed the distinguishing principle
of federalism and it can be truly said that the greater the independence of the units from the Centre in their defined spheres,
the more truly is the political system federal in character. In
actual practice, this ideal condition rarely obtains. Various points

of contact are established between the two, partly by law and partly by usage.

In our survey of federal States, several methods of federal control over the units sanctioned by the constitution have been noticed : the federal guarantee to every state in the U.S.A. of a republican form of government and of protection against invasion and, on the application of the state authorities, against domestic violence ; the power of the federal government in Switzerland to refuse approval to the new constitutions (or modifications to existing constitutions) of the cantons ; the power of the Governor-General in Canada to veto provincial laws and to appoint the Governors of the provinces, the control of the Governor-General in the abortive Indian federation over the Governors whenever the latter acted in their individual judgement or at their discretion ; and the administration of many federal laws through the administrative machinery of the units in Switzerland and Weimar Germany, which, to this extent, is placed in a position subordinate to the Federal Government. The last is particularly noteworthy. Experience shows that such administrative decentralization has at least two advantages : it makes the administration of federal laws more popular (being in the hands of local men) than it otherwise would be ; and, secondly, by avoiding unnecessary duplication of the administrative machinery, it secures economy.

Of the instruments of federal control over the units established by usage, the most noteworthy is the system of grants-in-aid given by the Federal Government in the U.S.A. to the states in recent years. These grants are made for the development of agricultural and vocational education, for the construction of roads, for maternity and infancy aid and so on, and in 1946 entailed congressional appropriations of nearly $743,000,000. The states are not bound to accept them, but once they accept them, they subject themselves in some degree to federal control over the activities for which the money is voted.

(*iv*) *Organization of the relation among the units.* Each state is more or less independent not only of the Centre but of other states as well. Such provisions as are included in federal constitutions to regulate their relationship are calculated to secure harmony among them in respect of certain essential matters, and to prevent any two or more of them from conspiring against the interests of the whole. Thus every state is enjoined to give full faith and credit to the public acts, records and judicial proceedings of every other state ; the citizens of every unit are declared to be entitled to the privileges and immunities of citizens of every other ;

it is required (with exceptions in certain constitutions, e.g. India) that all articles grown, produced or manufactured by any one of the units shall be admitted free into every other ; all separate alliances and treaties of a political character between the units are forbidden ; and so on.[1]

(*v*) *A satisfactory method of amendment.* The peculiar problems of federal States in regard to the amending body are that (*a*) neither the Centre nor the units by themselves should be given the power to alter the constitution, as such power is likely to affect one of the essential features of federalism, viz. the supremacy of the constitution ; and (*b*) it is desirable that in the body which is authorized to change the constitution, both the Centre and the units are given some place, and further the smaller states must be protected against dominance by the larger. How these problems are faced by the different federations has already been indicated in (*i*) and (*ii*) above.

(*vi*) *Secession.* It is possible that one or more of the units may, as the southern states of the U.S.A. did in 1861, claim the right of secession from the whole. The secessionists in the U.S.A. argued that the general government emanated from the people of the several states, forming distinct political communities and acting in their separate and sovereign capacity, and not from all the people forming one aggregate political community. ' The constitution of the United States is, in fact, a compact to which *each State is a party . . .*; the several states or parties have a right to judge of its infractions ; and in case of a deliberate, palpable, and dangerous exercise of power not delegated, have the right also, in the last resort, to interpose for arresting progress of the evil, and for maintaining, within their respective limits, the authorities, rights and liberties appertaining to them.' Those who opposed the right of secession argued that *the people of the country as a whole* were the real parties to the union, and not the states, and cited in evidence the preamble to the constitution :

---

[1] Article 118 of the constitution of Australia ; Articles I and IV of the constitution of the U.S.A. ; Articles 7 and 60 of the constitution of Switzerland ; and Article 121 of the constitution of Canada. The relevant Articles in the constitution of India are 301, 302 and 303. Article 301 lays down the general rule that trade, commerce and intercourse throughout the territory of India shall be free ; exceptions to this rule are stated in Articles 302 and 303 : thus power is conferred on Parliament by Article 302 to impose restrictions on trade, commerce and intercourse between one state and another in the interest of the public ; Article 303 stipulates that such power should not be abused by the Parliament or the State Legislature by preferring one state to another, or by making discrimination between one state and another.

' We, the people of the United States, in order to form a more
perfect union, establish justice, ensure domestic tranquillity, provide for the common defence, promote the general welfare, and
secure the blessings of liberty to ourselves and our posterity, do
ordain and establish this constitution for the United States of
America.'

Arguments apart, the issue in the U.S.A. was decided, by force of
arms, against secession. It is interesting to note that the constitution of the U.S.S.R. is unique in recognizing the legal right of
secession. Where such a right is not recognized by the constitution, it seems clear, as a matter of constitutional theory, that the
units do not have it. The only legal method for a unit to regain
its sovereignty would appear to be an amendment of the constitution permitting the unit to go out of the Union. Sovereignty in a
federal State ' lies in the body, wherever and whatever it may be,
which has power to amend the constitution. Legally speaking,
this sovereign body can entirely abolish the federation and restore
each member of it to its original independence '.[1] It is difficult,
however, to see how a federal State can prevent a determined
unit from seceding except by force of arms ; no constitutional
provisions seem adequate to meet such a situation.

§5 MERITS AND DEFECTS

The unitary State has, as compared with the federal State, two
distinct advantages.

(*i*) ' The whole problem of the organization of a government is
enormously simplified when the decision is made to establish a
unitary government.'[2]   The constitution-making body does not
have to concern itself, as it must in a federation, with the manner
in which the territory shall be divided into political divisions nor
the manner in which governmental powers shall be divided between
two authorities. The territorial distribution of power (between
the Centre and local bodies) is a matter of internal organization
to be decided by the Central Government. The prolonged discussions at the Round Table Conferences in London, which set about
drawing up a federal constitution for India, afford ample illustration of the difficulties in a federal constitution. Further the distribution of powers made by the constitution of a federal State is
modified, only by a special procedure for federal constitutions

[1] *Leacock, Elements of Political Science*, p. 228.
[2] Willoughby, *The Government of Modern States*, p. 174.

must necessarily be rigid. And it is found, notably in the U.S.A. and in Australia, that because of the difficulty of getting the amending body into operation, the changes in the constitution do not keep pace with the changes in the social and economic life of the State. For example, child labour could be abolished easily in England ; its abolition was found difficult in the U.S.A. In the unitary State also, the identical difficulty may arise when its amending body is of the same cumbrous type ; but at any rate the difficulty is not further complicated by a constitutional division of powers with its attendant traditions of state loyalty and the support of vested interests. Federalism, therefore, incidentally tends to produce conservatism. ' The difficulty of altering the constitution produces conservative sentiment, and national conservatism doubles the difficulty of altering the constitution.'[1]

(ii) A unitary State is, other things being equal, stronger than a federal one. Here, all the powers of government are concentrated in the hands of one single set of authorities. All the force of government can, therefore, ' be brought to bear directly upon the problems of administration to be solved. There can be no conflict of authority, no conflict or confusion regarding responsibility for work to be performed, no overlapping of jurisdictions, no duplication of work, plant, or organization which cannot be immediately adjusted.'[2] By contrast, in a federal State there are two sets of authorities, each limited by the powers given to the other. That is why, as Dicey said, the comparative weakness of federalism is no accident ; it is inherent in it.

' The distribution of all the powers of the State among co-ordinate authorities necessarily leads to the result that no one authority can wield the same amount of powe as under a unitarian constitution is possessed by the sovereign. A scheme again of checks and balances in which the strength ot the common government is, so to speak, pitted against that of the state governments leads, on the face of it, to a certain waste of energy. A federation therefore will always be at a disadvantage in a contest with unitarian States of equal resources.'[3]

When a question of external policy arises which interests only one part of the union, the existence of states feeling themselves specially affected is apt to have a strong and probably an unfortunate

[1] Dicey, op. cit., pp. 173-4.
[2] Willoughby, op. cit., p. 177.
[3] Dicey, op. cit., pp. 171-2 and p. 605.

influence. Another source of weakness in a federation is the divided allegiance of the citizens. This may give rise to the dissolution of the State by the rebellion or secession of states, and to division into groups and factions by the formation of separate combinations of the component states.

The great advantage of the federal State is the principle of compromise between unity and diversity which it embodies. It provides the means of uniting a number of small states into one nation under one national government, without extinguishing their separate Legislatures and Administration.[1] The argument of the preceding paragraph, that the federal government is weak as compared with a unitary one, presupposes that a choice is open between them. But the history of federations shows that often the choice is only between complete independence of the units, with the consequent weakness of all, and federalism with greater strength for every one. As Dicey truly says, ' a federal system sometimes makes it possible for different communities to be united as one State when they otherwise could not be united at all. The bond of federal union may be weak, but it may be the strongest bond which circumstances allow.' In such circumstances, federalism helps a number of small states to obtain greater strength through union while ensuring their individuality in essentially local matters. It recognizes the fact that closer union is necessary for some purposes, while separate existence is necessary to provide for diversity. It thereby prevents the rise (by force) of a despotic Central Government absorbing other powers and menacing the private liberties of the citizen ; and, by creating many local Legislatures with wide powers, relieves the national Legislature of a part of that large mass of functions which may otherwise prove too heavy for it.

There is another series of advantages which a federal State provides ; but they apply equally to unitary States which allow a large measure of decentralization. These are the advantages pertaining to local self-government on a large scale. Self-government stimulates the interest of people in the affairs of their neighbourhood, sustains local political life, educates the citizen in his daily round of civic duty, teaches him that perpetual vigilance and the sacrifice of his own time and labour are the price that must be paid for individual liberty and collective prosperity. Further it conduces to the good administration of local affairs by giving the inhabitants of each locality due means of overseeing the conduct of their daily administration.[2]

---

[1] See Bryce, *The American Commonwealth*, ch. xxx, for a good discussion of the merits of federation.   [2] ibid.

SELECT BIBLIOGRAPHY

J. Bryce, *The American Commonwealth*, Macmillan, 1910

A. V. Dicey, *Introduction to the Study of the Law of the Constitution*, ch. iii and Appendix IV, Macmillan, 9th ed., 1939

A. Hamilton, J. Jay, and J. Madison, *The Federalist*, ' Everyman Library ', Dent

D. G. Karve, *Federations*, Oxford, 1932

J. S. Mill, *Representative Government*, ch. xvii, ' World's Classics ' No. 170, Oxford

A. P. Newton, *Federal and Unified Constitutions*, Longmans, 1923

M. Venkatarangaiya, *Federalism in Government*, Andhra University, Waltair, 1935

W. F. Willoughby, *The Government of Modern States*, ch. xii and xiii, Appleton Century, 1936

K. C. Wheare, *Federal Government*, Oxford, 5th ed., 1953

CHAPTER XXIX

RIGID AND FLEXIBLE CONSTITUTIONS

§1 WRITTEN AND UNWRITTEN CONSTITUTIONS

STATES, we have said earlier, may be classified according to the nature of their constitutions, whether they are flexible or rigid. The question may be raised whether constitutions may also be classified according as to whether they are written or unwritten.

A written constitution may be described as one in which the fundamental principles concerning the organization of a government, the powers of its various agencies and the rights of the subjects, are written down in one document (or a few documents as in the French constitution of 1875). Thus the constitution of the United States of America (1789) outlines the composition of the Legislature, the Executive, and the Judiciary and their powers, and the fundamental rights of citizens ; and, besides, mentions a method for its amendment.

An unwritten constitution, by contrast, is one in which the fundamental principles of the organization and powers of a government are not codified in one document, but where many of them are followed as a matter of usage. The constitution of Britain is a good example.

' The English have left the different parts of their constitution just where the wave of history had deposited them ; they have not attempted to bring them together, to classify or complete them, or to make a consistent and coherent whole.' [1]

Of the eleven modern constitutions we have surveyed, the British constitution alone is unwritten.

It is interesting to note that, as a matter of history, written constitutions have been, relatively speaking, of recent growth. The first considerable attempts at written constitutions in modern times were made in the American colonies [2] when they became independent of Great Britain. New Hampshire, South Carolina,

---

[1] M. E. Boutmy, *Studies in Constitutional Law*, p. 7, cited by Marriott in *The Mechanism of the Modern State*, Vol. I, p. 153.

[2] Britain tried two experiments in this direction, ' the Agreement of the People ' (1649) and ' the Instrument of Government ' (1653) but neither became a permanent part of her constitution.

Virginia, Pennsylvania and Maryland among others, each adopted a written constitution in 1776 ; Georgia and New York followed suit in 1777, and Massachusetts in 1780. The U.S.A. adopted its constitution in 1789. On the continent of Europe, France set the example. After the *ancien régime* was destroyed by the Revolution of 1789, she adopted a written constitution in 1791 ; since then France has tried twelve other written constitutions and the thirteenth is now being worked. One after another, the European States followed the French example [1] and adopted written constitutions ; indeed, not only in Europe but in Asia, America, and Australia the written constitution became the rule. Further, no State which has once tried the written constitution has ever returned to the unwritten type.

The documentary constitution differs from the unwritten one not only because it is a document. It supplies a standard of reference to which the acts of the Government of the day may always be compared. And, since its framers contemplate it as the fundamental law of the nation, which ought not to be lightly changed, they almost invariably [2] make it rigid, i.e. unalterable by the ordinary law-making process ; unwritten constitutions can hardly be rigid.

While the written constitution can thus in a general way be distinguished from the unwritten one, it is hardly adequate to classify constitutions on the ground of their written or unwritten nature ; for the written or unwritten nature *as such* has not much political significance. Further, such a classification is on the whole misleading. First, it wrongly suggests the idea that the written constitutions have no unwritten elements, and vice versa. Our survey, particularly of the governments of the United States of America and Britain, makes it clear that constitutions in general contain both elements, the written and the unwritten. [3] Second, it wrongly suggests, at any rate to the layman, that the Acts of the Legislature in every State with a written constitution are void if repugnant to that constitution. Indeed, in a famous judgement, [4] Chief Justice Marshall himself expressed this view.

' Certainly all those who have framed written constitutions contemplate them as forming the fundamental paramount law of the

---

[1] e.g. Spain in 1808, 1812 and 1876 ; Bavaria in 1818 ; Italy in 1848 ; Prussia in 1850 ; Germany in 1919 ; and so on.

[2] There are written constitutions which are flexible, e.g. Italy, New Zealand and Finland.

[3] See above, ch. xvi, §§2 and 16, and ch. xviii, §9.

[4] Marbury v. Madison, 1803.

nation, and consequently the theory of *every* such government must be that an act of the Legislature, repugnant to the constitution, is void.'

As a matter of fact, this is not true. In France, under the Third Republic, the Judiciary did not claim the power to declare the Acts of the Legislature unconstitutional, primarily because the Judiciary did not owe its existence to the constitution but was itself created by an Act of the Legislature, and that Legislature could take effective steps to prevent the Judiciary from exercising any such power. The Fifth Republic of France, as indicated already, has set up a constitutional Council which has the power to decide on the constitutionality of laws. In Switzerland, the constitution itself, as we have seen,[1] specially lays down that the Federal Tribunal shall administer the laws passed by the Federal Assembly. A somewhat similar provision is found in the constitution of the U.S.S.R.[2] The Italian constitution of 1848 made no provision for its amendment; the absence of any such provision has been interpreted to mean that the Legislature can make amendments to the constitution: and no question of repugnancy arises.

§2 RIGID AND FLEXIBLE CONSTITUTIONS

A more adequate basis on which constitutions may be classified is the method for their amendment. If that method is the same as that for the passing of ordinary laws, the constitution is 'flexible'; if it is a different one, the constitution is 'rigid'. Britain and Italy[3] have flexible constitutions; all the other States in our survey have rigid constitutions.

Rigid constitutions, however, vary considerably both in the methods they provide for constitutional amendment and in the extent of difficulty they experience in adjusting themselves to changing times. Our survey suggests that rigid constitutions are, broadly, of four types.

(*i*) Those in which the Legislature may make constitutional amendments, but subject to certain restrictions not prescribed for passing ordinary laws. The constitutions of the French Republic, South Africa, and the U.S.S.R. fall under this head. The restrictions themselves are not the same everywhere. The requirement that a constitutional amendment, after it is adopted by the Legis-

---

[1] See above, ch. xx, §3.   [2] See above, ch. xxv, §2.
[3] Other States with flexible constitutions are New Zealand and Finland.

lature, has to be submitted to a referendum before it can be adopted or to a joint session of the chambers of the Legislature with a three-fifths majority for the passing of constitutional amendments, as in France ; a joint session with a two-thirds majority for the passing of *some* constitutional amendments, as in South Africa ; and a two-thirds majority in each of the two chambers of the Legislature, as in the U.S.S.R., are illustrations.

(*ii*) Those in which the final decision is with the people. Australia and Switzerland, as we have seen,[1] make the consent of a majority of the voters necessary for constitutional amendment. In both, the initiative in proposing amendments to the constitutions is taken by the Legislature ; in Switzerland, in addition, 50,000 voters may also take the initiative. The Weimar constitution, also provided for the referendum and the initiative for the passing of such amendments.

(*iii*) Those in which the final decision is with a prescribed majority of the component units of the federation. Thus Australia and Switzerland make the consent of a majority of the units essential in addition to the consent of a majority of the voters. The United States of America requires a three-fourths majority of the states. In Australia and the United States of America another restriction is added : in respect of amendments to certain essential matters, such as the changing of the territorial limits of the states in Australia, the consent of the affected state is required. The motive for prescribing restrictions of this kind (to protect the smaller units of a federation from being dominated by the larger) has been noted elsewhere. It is, however, noteworthy that *all* federations do not prescribe these conditions ; the U.S.S.R. and Canada are exceptions.

(*iv*) Those which leave the final decision in the hands of an outside authority. Canada, for instance, leaves the decision[2] to the sovereign in Parliament in Britain.

Merits and defects

The flexible constitution has clearly one advantage. In a period of great social changes, new ideas can make their way without being compelled to pass through the complicated machinery for amendment framed in an earlier period. Thus child labour in factories could be abolished easily in England ; the proposal for its abolition, made by Congress in the U.S.A. in 1924, has

---

[1] See above, ch. xix, §2 and ch. xx, §1.
[2] in certain specified matters. See, however, ch. xix, §1, for the precise position in respect of Canada.

not yet been ratified by the required number of states. As Bryce remarks,[1] flexible constitutions

' can be stretched or bent so as to meet emergencies without breaking their framework ; and when the emergency has passed, they slip back into their old form, like a tree whose outer branches have been pulled on one side to let a vehicle pass '.

That is why it has been said of the English constitution that it bends but does not break.

But the defect of a flexible constitution is that it may be in a state of perpetual flux, and may be the plaything of politicians. Because of the ease with which fundamental changes may be made, valuable rules and institutions may be abolished in a transient gust of unpopularity, and thus lose irreparably the stability given by antiquity and unbroken custom.[2] As Sidgwick recognized, this danger varies according to the manner of composition of the Legislature, but certainly it is important enough in the modern democratic State, in which the Legislature is popularly elected for short periods varying from two to five years. In any case, in a properly organized society, it is desirable to impose some restrictions on the power of the Legislature to interfere with such fundamental rights of the citizen as freedom of speech and of religion.

The advantage of a rigid constitution is that it recognizes that there are some fundamentals, be they the rights of citizens or the rules relating to the composition and powers of the agencies of government, which ought not to be lightly changed, and it ensures that adequate consideration will be given to them when it is sought to change them.

On the other hand, the rigid constitution has at least two serious defects. It is not easily adaptable, and it may break under changing conditions or emergencies. This danger is greater in a federal than in a unitary State, on account of the complication caused by the division of powers. It also varies according to the difficulty of the particular amending process ; for instance it is greater in the United States of America than in the U.S.S.R. Secondly, under a rigid constitution the Judiciary may have too much power to decide upon the constitutionality of laws. It is better not to give judges such power, for the constitution will always reflect the spirit of the time at which it was made, and the judges will,

---

[1] *Studies in History and Jurisprudence*, Vol. I, p. 162.
[2] Sidgwick, *The Elements fo Politics*, pp. 561-2.

in interpreting the constitution, be better acquainted with that spirit than with the new.[1] If, on the other hand, they try to interpret differently, to adjust the constitution to the changing times, they may be drawn into party conflict, and the confidence in their impartiality thereby be impaired.

' And from the same cause, there arises a further danger that the Legislature or the Executive may be tempted to misuse its control over the appointment and dismissal of judges in order to obtain a tribunal subservient to its wishes ; while yet the withdrawal of all control of this kind would leave the judges in too independent a position.'[2]

To avoid both these defects, the following method suggested by H. J. Laski[3] seems the best for constitutional amendment : in unitary States, let a two-thirds majority in Parliament be secured for the passing of constitutional laws; in federal States, let a constitutional law be passed by the federal Legislature by a two-thirds majority in two successive sessions, and if a majority of the states protest against any such change, let it again secure a two-thirds majority in order to become law.

SELECT BIBLIOGRAPHY

J. BRYCE, *Studies in History and Jurisprudence*, Vol. I, Essay III, Oxford, 1901

H. FINER, *The Theory and Practice of Modern Government*, Vol. I, ch. vii, Methuen, 1932

H. SIDGWICK, *The Elements of Politics*, ch. xxvii, Macmillan, 1908

C. F. STRONG, *Modern Political Constitutions*, ch. vi-vii, Sidgwick & Jackson, 1930

---

[1] Laski, *A Grammar of Politics*, p. 304.
[2] Sidgwick, *The Elements of Politics*, p. 564.
[3] Laski, op. cit., pp. 305-8.

CHAPTER XXX

THE SEPARATION OF POWERS

§1 THE THEORY OF SEPARATION OF POWERS

GOVERNMENTAL power expresses itself in three forms : legislation, administration and judicial decision. It is of prime importance to the theory of the organization of government to determine whether, and to what extent, these powers should be combined in the same persons or body of persons, or should be entrusted to three separate agencies, co-ordinate and mutually independent.

Early in the modern period Bodin,[1] the French writer, pointed out in *The Republic* (1576) that some separation was essential. The Prince, he thought, ought not to administer justice in person, but should leave such matters to independent judges.

'To be at once legislator and judge is to mingle together justice and the prerogative of mercy, adherence to the law and arbitrary departure from it : if justice is not well administered, the litigating parties are not free enough, they are crushed by the authority of the sovereign.'[2]

The theory of separation of power was, however, clearly formulated for the first time by Montesquieu in *The Spirit of Laws* (1748):

'When the legislative and executive powers are united in the same person, or in the same body of magistrates, there can be no liberty ; because apprehensions may arise, lest the same monarch or senate should enact tyrannical laws, to execute them in a tyrannical manner.

'Again, there is no liberty, if the judiciary power be not separated from the legislative and executive. Were it joined with the legislative, the life and liberty of the subject would be exposed to arbitrary control ; for the judge would be then the legislator. Were it joined to the executive power, the judge might behave with violence and oppression.

'There would be an end of everything, were the same man or the same body, whether of the nobles or of the people, to exercise

---

[1] 1530-96.
[2] Cited by Bluntschli in *The Theory of the State*, p. 517.

those three powers, that of enacting laws, that of executing the public resolutions, and of trying the causes of individuals.'[1]

Seventeen years later Blackstone, an English jurist, gave expression to similar views.

'In all tyrannical governments the supreme magistracy, or the right both of *making* and of *enforcing* the laws, is vested in one and the same man, or one and the same body of men ; and wherever these two powers are united together, there can be no public liberty. The magistrate may enact tyrannical laws, and execute them in a tyrannical manner, since he is possessed in quality of dispenser of justice with all the power which he as legislator thinks proper to give himself. . . . Were it (the judicial power) joined with the legislative, the life, liberty, and property of the subject would be in the hands of arbitrary judges, whose decisions would be then regulated only by their own opinions, and not by any fundamental principles of law ; which, though legislators may depart from, yet judges are bound to observe. Were it joined with the executive, this union might soon be an overbalance for the legislative.'[2]

And, finally, we may cite an American classic, *The Federalist* (1788), for another authoritative exposition of the theory.

'The accumulation of all powers, legislative, executive, and judiciary, in the same hands, whether of one, a few, or many, and whether hereditary, self appointed, or elective, may justly be pronounced the very definition of tyranny.'[3]

There has been some controversy[4] among students of political science whether Montesquieu, the author of the theory (and others who followed him), contemplated an absolute or only a limited separation of the three powers. There is no doubt that the sound opinion, as *The Federalist* pointed out,[5] is that he did *not* mean that the three departments ought to have no *partial agency* in, or no *control* over, the acts of each other. His meaning, as his own words import, and still more conclusively as illustrated by the example in his eye (viz. the British constitution), can

---

[1] *The Spirit of Laws*, bk. XI, ch. vi.
[2] 1765, *Commentaries on the Laws of England*, Vol. 1, pp. 146 and 269.
[3] *The Federalist*, Essay XLVII.
[4] See, e.g., G. H. Sabine, *A History of Political Theory*, p. 559.
[5] loc. cit.

amount to no more than this, that 'where the whole power of one department is exercised by the same hands which possess the *whole* power of another department, the fundamental principles of a free constitution are subverted'.

Rightly interpreted, therefore, the theory of separation of powers merely means that a different body of persons is to administer each of the three departments of government ; and that no one of them is to have a *controlling* power over either of the others. Such separation is necessary for the purpose of preserving the liberty of the individual and for avoiding tyranny.

§2 ITS APPLICATION TO MODERN GOVERNMENTS

Before we consider to what extent the legislative, the executive, and the judicial powers in modern governments are combined and separated, it is useful to have some idea of what complete separation involves. It means a Legislature elected directly by the people for a fixed term ; an Executive elected directly by the people, or indirectly by an electoral college as in the United States of America, for a fixed term and independent of the Legislature in discharging its function ; and judges similarly elected, and independent of both the Legislature and the Executive in respect of their term of office and their salary. The Legislature will not have the power of choosing, controlling, or dismissing the Executive or the Judiciary ; the Executive will not have the power of dissolving the Legislature or vetoing laws or of appointing and dismissing judges ; the judges will not have the power of declaring laws unconstitutional or of trying executive officers.

If we look into the constitutions of several States, we find that there is not a single instance in which the three departments or powers have been kept absolutely separate and distinct. Instead, we find some union and some separation. This may be illustrated from Britain, the United States of America, and the French (Third) Republic.

Britain

In Britain, the Executive forms an integral part of the Legislature, the cabinet being considered as 'the first legislative chamber.' The cabinet is chosen from the Legislature. Ministers take part in its proceedings, initiate laws, and have power to issue statutory orders. The cabinet has power to advise the dissolving of the House of Commons before its normal term of five years is over, and to recommend the creation of peers in the House of Lords. On the other hand, the Legislature has power, by refusal of supply and other methods, to terminate the term of the cabinet.

The Executive appoints the judges; and, further, it has been vested in recent times (due to the growth of administrative law) with power to try certain cases.[1] On the other hand, according to the principle of the rule of law, the judges have power to sit in judgement on the conduct of government officials.

The Legislature has power to present an address to the Crown for the removal of judges. The second chamber is also the final court of appeal for the United Kingdom of Great Britain and Northern Ireland.

But there is *some* separation of powers as well in the British constitution :

'A close study of the English Government in its practical working shows that, *organically*, the principle of the separation of powers has been carried out with a rigidity that is found in few or no other government.'[2]

The exercise of legislative power is vested in the Legislature, which is a department of government distinct from the Executive.[3] The executive power is vested in the Crown, and Parliament never attempts to deprive it of any of its executive powers nor takes to itself the function of administration.[4]

In like manner, the Judiciary has been established as a distinct and independent branch of the government. Judges hold office during good behaviour, and are not liable to be dismissed by the Executive. Their salaries are independent of annual budgetary provision, being a permanent charge on the Consolidated Fund.

The United States of America

The framers of the constitutions of the states in the United States of America consciously adopted the principle of the separation of powers. The Massachusetts constitution of 1780 explicitly declared :[5]

[1] See above, ch. xvi, §13.
[2] Willoughby, op. cit., p. 238 ; italics ours.
[3] Though members of the cabinet are chosen from Parliament, the Executive is only a part of the Legislature and not the whole of it.
[4] In the U.S.A. treaties and appointments require confirmation by the Senate for their validity ; no such rule obtains in Britain.
[5] Article XXX.

' In the government of this commonwealth, the Legislative department shall never exercise the executive and judicial powers of either of them ; the executive shall never exercise the legislative and judicial powers or either of them ; the judicial shall never exercise the legislative and executive powers or either of them to the end and it may be a government of laws and not of men.'

The popular election of executive officials and of judges so widely prevalent in the states is an attempt at a rigid application of the theory. So too the constitution of the United States of America is an essay in the theory of separation. The separation is evident in the relations between the Legislature and the Executive. Congress and the President are (the former directly and the latter indirectly) elected by the people for fixed terms ; the President and the heads of departments do not sit in Congress, or initiate laws ; and Congress cannot be dissolved by the President before it has run its term. The separation is also evident in the relation between the Executive and the Judiciary : the term of the judges is made independent of the Executive.

Yet, even here, there are many points of contact between the Legislature, the Executive, and the Judiciary. The President sends messages to Congress ; he has a suspensive veto over the laws passed by it ; and heads of departments appear before the committees of Congress. The Senate's consent is necessary for the appointments made by the President, and the treaties negotiated by him. The House of Representatives may impeach the President before the Senate. The President appoints the judges, and has the power of pardon except in cases of impeachment. Judges may sit in judgement over the conduct of government officials, and they have the power to declare laws passed by Congress unconstitutional.

The French Republic

In the government of the third French Republic, also, we find some union of powers and some separation. The participation of members of Parliament in the election of the President as members of the Electoral College, the President's suspensive veto, the cabinet system, the power of the Parliament to indict the President and the ministers before the High Court of Justice, and the President's power of pardon illustrate the former ; the existence, as elsewhere, of three distinct organs of Government to perform the work of legislation, administration and judicial decision, and the system of administrative jurisprudence, illustrate the latter.

§3 IS SEPARATION DESIRABLE AND PRACTICABLE?

Sufficient has been said to indicate that a complete separation of the Legislature, the Executive and the Judiciary is not found in any modern constitution. All constitutions recognize the fact that government is an organic whole. Therefore, the separation of powers necessary for the maintenance of liberty has to be reconciled with the need for their co-operation with, and dependence on, each other. They realize that some union of powers promotes harmony in government and some separation makes for liberty, while both are essential for efficiency. The question naturally arises as to what extent separation is desirable and practicable.

A detailed study of the proper organization of the relationship of the Legislature to the Executive, the Legislature to the Judiciary, and the Executive to the Judiciary — which allows for partial union as well as partial separation — is attempted in the chapters that follow ; [1] here it is sufficient to draw attention to two general principles. First, the principle of vesting the exercise of the three powers of government — the legislative, the executive, and the judicial — in three distinct organs, which Willoughby has called an *organic* separation of powers as distinct from a *personal* separation, is fundamental to the efficient working of government. More than one department may be under the *direction* of the same persons as regards their superior officers, as the legislative and the executive departments in Britain are directed by the cabinet ; what is essential is that each department should in the main confine itself to the work which properly belongs to it. This is merely the political application of the economic principle of division of labour ; it makes for specialization and efficiency. It is obvious, for instance, that the Legislature as a body is unfit to undertake the work of judges,[2] because it is subject to the influences of party politics, ' because its organization as well as its temper is out of accord with the judicial spirit, and because its members are not chosen for their

---

[1] See below, ch. xxxi, §1, xxxii, §§1, 2 and xxxiii, §2.
[2] It has been noted earlier that even though in Britain the House of Lords is nominally the highest court of appeal, its judicial function is in practice done by a select number of experts.

capacity or training '. And, second, no one department should have *absolute* control over the other two, for that is inimical to liberty. If, for instance, the Executive has absolute control over the Judiciary, justice cannot be impartial, and the freedom of the individual is bound to suffer. Within the limits set by these two general principles, there must be points of contact and inter-action between the three departments, so that there may be the maximum harmony and co-operation between them in the essential tasks of government.

SELECT BIBLIOGRAPHY

A. HAMILTON, J. JAY and J. MADISON, *The Federalist*, 'Every-man Library', Dent

C. L. MONTESQUIEU, *The Spirit of Laws*, Hafner, 2nd ed., 1949

W. F. WILLOUGHBY, *The Government of Modern States*, Appleton Century, 1936

CHAPTER XXXI

THE ELECTORATE

§1 SUFFRAGE

REPRESENTATIVE government as distinguished from direct democracy is based on the principle that popular *sovereignty* can exist without popular *government*. The primary means by which the people exercise their sovereignty is the vote. Those who are qualified by the law of the State to elect members of the Legislature form the electorate.

As our survey has shown, there is no uniformity in modern States regarding the constitution of the electorate. The broad distinction is between States in which the right to vote is given to all adult citizens [1] and those in which the right to vote is restricted to adults, or only those, who possess specified qualifications in respect of race, property or education. Britain, the U.S.A., Canada, Australia, Weimar Germany, India and the U.S.S.R. are instances of the former; South Africa of the latter. Everywhere, too, those who cannot or those who are obviously unfit to use the vote (such as persons of unsound mind and criminals) are disfranchised. A residence requirement, of three to six months' stay in a constituency, is also invariably insisted upon.

The point naturally arises as to the principle on which a State may decide in favour of adult or restricted suffrage; or having decided against adult suffrage, its grounds for deciding on a particular kind of restriction such as property, education, race, or sex. It was widely held by theorists in the nineteenth century that every individual had 'the inalienable and sacred right' to participate in the formation of the law and that no one could be deprived of this 'upon any pretext or in any government'. The Declaration of the Rights of Man roundly asserted:

'The law is an expression of the will of the community; *all* citizens have the right to concur, either personally or by their representatives, in its formation.'

The age at which a person is considered to be an adult for purposes of voting varies from state to state. In Great Britain, U.S.A. and Russia, it is eighteen; in Germany, twenty; in India, twenty-one; in Norway, twenty-three; in Denmark and Japan, twenty-five.

Adult suffrage may indeed be supported by several strong arguments. (*i*) It is a personal injustice to withhold from any-one, unless for the prevention of greater evils, the ordinary privilege of having his voice reckoned in the disposal of affairs in which he has the same interest as other people.[1] ' If he is compelled to pay, if he may be compelled to fight, if he is required implicitly to obey, he should legally be entitled to be told what for ; to have his consent asked, and his opinion counted at its worth.' (*ii*) Political equality is a basic principle of democracy ; any form of restricted franchise necessarily infringes the principle of equality between individuals in some degree. (*iii*) If the right to vote is denied to some, their interests may be overlooked by the Legislature. As J. S. Mill pointed out[2] :

' Rulers and ruling classes are under a necessity of considering the interests and wishes of those who have the suffrage ; but of those who are excluded, it is in their option whether they will do so or not, and, however honestly disposed, they are in general too fully occupied with things which they *must* attend to, to have much room in their thoughts for anything which they can with impunity disregard.'

These arguments have not, however, been allowed to pass unchallenged. It has been urged[3] that (*i*) where there is *prima facie* proof that those who have been excluded will not suffer by exclusion, their interests being adequately cared for by the representatives of those included, their disfranchisement is justi-fied. The political interests of wives, daughters, and sisters, for instance, are safe in the hands of husbands, fathers, and brothers, on account of the intimate relations of affection that bind the members of the family. (*ii*) The exclusion of a class is justi-fiable when that class is likely to make a dangerously bad use of the vote. The ignorant masses, according to many competent writers,[4] come under this category. Enfranchising them might, thought Macaulay, lead to one ' vast spoliation ' ; ' a few half-naked fishermen would divine with the owls and foxes the ruins of the greatest of European cities.'[5] It might, thought Sir Henry Maine, work against scientific progress.

' Universal suffrage, which today excludes free trade from the United States, would certainly have prohibited the spinning

---

[1] Mill, *Representative Government*, ch. viii.   [2] ibid.
[3] See Sidgwick, *The Elements of Politics*, p. 379.
[4] e.g. Macaulay, W. E. H. Lecky, H. S. Maine, and Sir James Stephen.
[5] Quoted by Fisher in *The Republican Tradition in Europe*, p. 274.

jenny and the power loom. It would certainly have prohibited
the threshing machine. It would have prevented the adoption
of the Gregorian calendar, and it would have restored the
Stuarts.'[1]

Sir James Stephen went so far as to remark that universal
suffrage tended to invert what he regarded as 'the true and
natural relation between wisdom and folly'.[2] The main deduction made from these counter-arguments is that suffrage should
be based in part upon education and property so that only those
who are able to read and write, and those who have some stake
in the country, should be allowed to elect representatives to the
Legislature.

These considerations suggest the thought that, while adult
suffrage is certainly the ideal, the constitution of the electorate
at any particular time is a matter to be adjusted in accordance
with the particular conditions of each State. Take, for instance,
the enfranchisement of women. As Willoughby suggests,[3] this
should be influenced largely by the attitude taken by women
themselves, the legal and social status of the women in the community concerned, and the extent and character of their education
and general training.[4] Again, the extension of the franchise,
which might be feasible and desirable in a settled community
long accustomed to the exercise of the powers of self-government,
might be impracticable and undesirable in the case of a community beginning to learn the art of self-government. The extent
of literacy is a factor to be taken into consideration. If universal
suffrage is introduced in a community, the vast majority of
whom are illiterate, multitudes may simply cast their votes as
directed by other individuals or organizations. Under such
conditions, Mill's wise saying that universal teaching must
precede universal enfranchisement must be heeded. The administrative difficulty of managing a vast electorate, of ensuring

[1] *Popular Government*, p. 36.
[2] *Liberty, Equality, Fraternity*, pp. 258-9.
[3] *The Government of Modern States*, p. 273.
[4] Mention should be made here of a *fetwa* (Koranic interpretation) issued
by the Al Azhar University in Cairo, the leading intellectual and theological
institution in the Islamic World, on 12 June 1952 pronouncing against the
right of women to vote or to sit in Parliament on the ground that (i) women's nature was 'swayed by emotions' which made them 'of instable
judgement'; voting would mean attendance by women at public meetings,
speaking in public and constant journeys which would be unseemly; and
(ii) it was inconsistent with the authority of Islamic law. *Keesing's Contemporary Archives* 1952-54, pp. 123-31.

an adequate supply of reliable and impartial returning officers and polling officers, is sometimes a major consideration, as it was in India when the electorate was extended under the constitution of 1935.

§2 MODES OF ELECTION AND OF VOTING

Should election be direct or indirect?[1] Of the (elected) legislative bodies we have studied, the French Council of the Republic and the National Assembly of Pakistan and the Senate of South Africa are indirectly elected bodies. All others are directly elected. – The system also obtains, at least in name, in respect of the election of the Presidents of the United States of America and India.

The argument for indirect election is, in theory, a strong one. The electors who are finally to choose the members of the Legislature may be expected to be more competent at their job than the citizens who elect them. Being comparatively few, they should be less moved than the demos by the gusts of popular passion ; and, therefore, their choice should be more careful and enlightened, and be made with a greater feeling of responsibility, than election by the masses themselves. This should tend to improve the quality of the Legislature.

But experience with the indirect system of election has not confirmed this deduction from abstract reasoning. The successful working of the system demands an honesty of purpose and independence, in both the primary voters and the intermediate electors, which rarely obtain. If the latter are chosen under pledges, as invariably they are, the whole meaning of indirect election is lost. Indirect election also has positive disadvantages. As the number of persons in whom the final selection is vested is comparatively small, it affords additional facilities, for intrigue and for ' every form of corruption compatible with the station in life of the electors '. The possibility of corruption is increased by the fact that, holding no permanent office or position in the public eye, the electors ' would risk nothing by a corrupt vote except what they would care little for, not to be appointed electors again '. Secondly, indirect election is decidedly inferior to direct election as a means of cultivating public spirit ; interest in public affairs is considerably less when a middleman is interposed between the voter and his representative.

[1] See Mill on this subject in *Representative Government*, ch. ix.

Secret v. public voting

Vote by ballot (or some form of secret voting) is now the universal practice. But this fact must not lead one to think that public voting was at no time prevalent or that it has no advantages. It was in use till recently in Denmark,[1] Prussia,[2] and the U.S.S.R.[3] The case for public voting is in theory unassailable : voting is a public responsibility, and, therefore, its exercise should also be public. If the suffrage is a trust, asked Mill,[4] if the public are entitled to a person's vote, are they not entitled to know his vote ? Under the system of secret voting, the voter is free from the sense of shame or public responsibility ; he may, therefore, be tempted to abuse his trust, to further his own or a class interest.

If, in spite of such a clear case, public voting has disappeared in modern States, it is because its working revealed a serious practical defect : the possibility of the coercion of the voter. If a citizen has to vote in public, he may be compelled to vote for particular persons, whose pressure he may not be able to withstand. The experience of Prussia till 1920 may be cited in proof.[5] The Government took advantage of the opportunity which public voting afforded to exert pressure upon the electors to vote for Government candidates ; and landholders and employers did likewise in respect of those who were more or less subject to their control. The result was that large numbers of voters, rather than be exposed to intimidation of this kind or to loss of their positions through having their votes known to the public, abstained from voting.

Clearly, in circumstances like these, where a *free* vote cannot be given, secret voting is preferable to public voting. But, where a community is sufficiently enlightened and its members are sufficiently courageous to withstand improper pressure, public voting is certainly desirable.

§3 THE DUTY OF A REPRESENTATIVE

There are two views concerning the essential nature of an elected representative. According to one, he is simply an agent or delegate, an ambassador, who has to vote in the Legislature according to the instructions, the mandate, of his constituents. According to the other, he is a senator, who is chosen for his

---

[1] Till 1901. [2] Till 1920. [3] Till 1936.
[4] *Representative Government*, ch. x.
[5] Garner, *Political Science and Government*, p. 585.

superior wisdom and integrity, and who is, therefore, free to use his best judgement upon the issues he is called upon to decide. The former may be called the theory of instructed representation ; [1] the latter, of uninstructed representation.

The theory of instructed representation errs in several respects. (*i*) It is impossible in practice for any member to state his total views partly because there is not the time to do so, partly because new issues are bound to arise. ' And upon those new issues he cannot, item by item, consult their considered judgement.' Nor is it possible for the constituency, on their initiative, to instruct their member in all matters that come up before the Legislature. (*ii*) It makes deliberation in Parliament ineffective, for, by assumption, the member has arrived at his final decision before Parliamentary deliberation begins. Indeed, as Burke rightly saw,[2] it would result in an absurd state of affairs in which the determination precedes discussion, in which one set of men deliberates and another decides, and where those who form the conclusion are far away from those who hear the arguments. (*iii*) It is immoral, for it demands the sacrifice of the judgement and conviction of the representative in favour of those of others. (*iv*) It may affect the quality of the Legislature. Men of superior intellect and integrity will hardly seek election to a place in which they are not free to think for themselves, and vote according to their conscience. The community is therefore the loser. (*v*) It emphasizes local interests and local opinion to the possible prejudice of common interests and of ' the general good resulting from the general reason of the whole '.

On the other hand, we should not jump to the opposite conclusion and say that the representative is a master who is always at liberty to disregard the fundamental convictions of his constituency. The right view to take is somewhat as follows : A representative is elected by a constituency to confer with representatives who come from other parts of the country as to what is best for the nation as a whole. He must be reasonably consistent in his views. Plainly, as Laski suggests, he is not entitled to get elected as a free trader and to vote at once for a protective tariff. The electors are, therefore, ' entitled to a full knowledge of the political opinions and sentiments of the candidate ; and not only entitled, but often bound, to reject one who differs from themselves on the few articles which are the

---

[1] Sometimes also called the telephone theory of representation.
[2] Speech to the electors of Bristol, on 3 November 1774. *The Works of Edmund Burke*, Vol. II, ' The World's Classics ', pp. 159-66.

foundation of their political belief '.[1] The representative must also be reasonably industrious. Burke has said that it ought to be the happiness and glory of a representative to live in the strictest union, the closest correspondence and the most unreserved communication with his constituents. Their wishes ought to have great weight with him ; their opinions, high respect ; their business, unremitted attention ; otherwise, indeed, he simply does not perform his duty. From his central position in the constituency, he has a unique opportunity to instruct his constituents and to broaden their horizon. And, finally, the representative should be allowed freedom of judgement, i.e. freedom to vote according to *his* judgement, even when it differs from that of his constituents. The whole matter is authoritatively summed up in Burke's eloquent address to the electors of Bristol.

' To deliver an opinion is the right of all men ; that of constituents is a weighty and respectable opinion, which a representative ought always to rejoice to hear ; and which he ought always most seriously to consider. But *authoritative* instructions, mandates issued, which the member is bound blindly and implicitly to obey, to vote, and to argue for, though contrary to the clearest conviction of his judgement and conscience — these are things utterly unknown to the laws of this land, and which arise from a fundamental mistake of the whole order and tenor of our constitution.

' Parliament is not a *congress* of ambassadors from different and hostile interests ; which interests each must maintain, as an agent and advocate, against other agents and advocates ; but Parliament is a *deliberative* assembly of *one* nation, with *one* interest, that of the whole ; where, not local purposes, not local prejudices, ought to guide, but the general good resulting from the general reason of the whole. You choose a member indeed, but when you have chosen him, he is not member of Bristol, but he is a member of *Parliament*.'

It is interesting to record that the Swiss constitution provides that ' members of the two Councils (the Council of States and the National Council) shall vote without instructions '.[2]

§4 SINGLE- V. MULTI-MEMBER CONSTITUENCIES

It is the practice in all countries to divide the whole territory into convenient electoral districts (single-member or

Mill, *Representative Government*, ch. xii.   [2] Article 91.

multi-member) primarily for the purpose of enabling the member to keep in touch with his constituency. Practically every State in our survey, except Germany, Italy and to some extent India, has adopted the single-member plan ; Weimar Germany had a multi-member system ; Mussolini's Italy, a corporate structure which, as has been explained, is somewhat peculiar ; and India has both single-member and multi-member constituencies.

The single-member constituency (sometimes called the district system) satisfies one important requisite of a good electoral system ; that areas which return members to the Legislature must be small enough to enable candidates to be known in a genuine way, and also to enable the finally elected member to keep in close touch with his constituents. It is simple and economical, especially for the candidates ; therefore it is more democratic because the poor candidate is not at such a disadvantage as he would be in a large constituency. It is more likely to encourage local talent than the larger multi-member constituency, because men of moderate means and position will feel more confidence where the constituency is small and their local influence counts. Further, it is clearly an advantage that more and more leaders of the community should be induced to take an active interest in the political process. Above all, the working of electoral systems throughout the world points to the fact that the single-member system tends to provide a more stable majority in a Legislature than the multi-member system, and thereby helps to form a strong Executive. The multi-member system generally coupled with provisions for minority representation, encourages the multiplication of groups [1] in a Legislature, making it difficult for any groups to command a majority, and, therefore, to work a parliamentary Executive.

The single-member system, however, is not without its defects. (*i*) Election from small districts greatly facilitates the power of the Government to control the elections, for the smaller the district the more easily can it influence a sufficient number of voters to obtain the return of Government candidates. This was the experience of France under the single-member system, and constituted one of the principal reasons which induced her, in 1919, to abandon it for a time. (*ii*) It leads to the choice of men who regard themselves as representatives of local interests rather than as representatives of the interests of the country as a whole. The experience of both France and Italy with the

---

[1] See below, §5 of this chapter.

single-member system of choosing deputies substantiates this.[1] As Gambetta once said, it made the Chamber of Deputies 'a broken mirror in which France could not recognize her own image'. (*iii*) It increases powerfully the temptation of legislative majorities to 'gerrymander' the State, that is, to construct the electoral districts in such a way as to give the majority party more representatives than its voting strength entitles it to. (*iv*) In certain conditions, it results in the return of the candidates disliked by the bulk of the constituency, thus tending to distort the representative system. This might occur when more than two candidates contest the one seat, as the following hypothetical instance shows. Suppose at an election 1,000 votes are cast, divided amongst four candidates as follows : A 280 ; B 260 : C 240 ; D 220. A is returned. But it is quite possible that A is disliked by the majority of the voters. The inadequacy of the system increases with the number of candidates. And if a number of members were returned in this way, the majority in the Legislature might well be elected by a minority of voters. Thus, in 1924, the Conservative Party in Britain secured 412 seats out of a total of 615, though they had the support of only 48% of the voters. In the Indian elections of 1951-52, the Congress Party secured 362 seats out of 489 in the Houses of the People, though they secured only 44·85% of the total votes.[2] (*v*) Finally, it is possible under this system that minorities may not be adequately represented in the Legislature. Thus in the Indian elections referred to above, the Socialist Party won only 12 seats, though they secured 10·50% of the total votes which would entitle them theoretically to some 50 seats.[3] The inadequacy varies according to the distribution of the minorities in the country. Theoretically it is possible for a minority group to be a minority in every constituency, and, therefore, to go without any representation at all. But this rarely obtains. It is significant that Gladstone, while introducing the Redistribution Bill of 1885, defended the single-member system on the ground that it provides for minority representation.

'The recommendations of this system I think are these — that it is very economical, it is very simple, and it goes a very long way towards that which many gentlemen have much at heart — namely, what is roughly termed representation of

---

[1] Garner, in *The American Political Science Review*, Vol. XVII, pp. 610 ff.
[2] *Political Quarterly*, Vol. XXXIII, p. 245.
[3] ibid.

minorities. It may be termed the representation of minorities ; it may be termed the representation of separate interests and pursuits ; but give it what name you like, there is no doubt that by means of one-member districts, you will obtain a very large diversity of representation.' [1]

Nevertheless there is the possibility that the minorities may not be represented adequately, i.e. in proportion to their voting strength. Thus in the British election of 1924, referred to above, the Liberal Party secured less than 8% of the seats though their voting strength was as high as 20% and the Labour Party, 25%, though their voting strength was about 34% of the whole.[2]

§5 THE REPRESENTATION OF MINORITIES

Minorities are of various kinds : political, national, racial, linguistic, and communal. It is an accepted proposition in Politics that the majority in a democratic State have the right to *decide* on the passing of a law ; it is equally accepted that in the *deliberation* which precedes decision, the voice of the minorities should be heard through representatives who enjoy their confidence. For law must be built on the widest acquiescence if it is to command effective obedience ; and the best way to ensure such wide acquiescence is to provide opportunities for the adequate expression of minority opinion, and for the majority to accept the reasonable wishes of minorities. Where large groups of men feel that their wishes are not taken into consideration in the framing of the laws which they are compelled to obey, the way is open for discontent and rebellion.

Among the methods which have been adopted for the adequate representation of minorities, the most important are described under the five following headings.

(*i*) *Proportional representation.* The principle underlying this system is that, in a real democracy, every section of opinion should be represented in the Legislature in proportion to its strength in the country. ' A majority of the electors would always have a majority of the representatives ; but a minority of the electors would always have a minority of the representatives.'

---

[1] Quoted in the *Report of the Royal Commission appointed to inquire into Electoral Systems*, 1910, p. 2.

[2] Conservative Party   7,451,132 votes   412 seats
Liberal Party   3,008,474 votes   46 seats
Labour Party   5,484,760 votes   151 seats

Proportional representation may be achieved by two methods : by the single transferable vote or by list system.

The essentials of the 'single transferable vote' are the multi-member constituency, the quota, the possession by the voter of only *one* vote, the marking of preferences, and the transfer of votes. The system demands multi-member constituencies ; indeed this type of constituency is essential to any form of minority representation. Further, to be elected, a candidate, instead of getting an absolute majority of votes or a plurality, needs only the quota, i.e. the total number of votes divided by the number of seats.[1] Again, it is essential to the system that, though the constituency returns more than one member, the voter has only *one* vote. He may, however, indicate his preferences for other candidates besides his first choice. Thus if there are eight candidates and only three seats to be filled, the voter may place beside the names of the candidates the numbers, 1, 2, 3, 4 etc. His vote is credited to his first choice unless it is found *either* that his first choice does not need it as he has reached his quota, or because he has secured so few votes that it cannot possibly help him to be elected. In such a case, the elector's vote is credited to his later choices. When the voting papers are counted, the first choices of the voters are first reckoned. If all the seats are not filled, owing to the fact that a sufficient number of candidates do not get the quota, the other seats are filled by reckoning the second preferences indicated in the surplus votes of the successful candidates. If a sufficient number still do not get the quota, the candidate with the lowest number of votes is eliminated, and his votes are added to others according to the preferences expressed therein, and so on, until the required number of candidates is returned.

It will be observed that every minority which is strong enough to get the quota by itself, or through the aid of other groups as expressed, say, in the second and third preferences, is assured of representation ; it will not be sure of it, if a majority of votes or plurality is insisted upon as the criterion of success in election.

This system prevails in Great Britain for the election of members for the National Assembly of the Church of England ; for Education Authorities in Scotland ; in Northern Ireland for both Houses of Parliament ; in Eire for elections to the lower House ; in South Africa for Senatorial elections and in certain

---

[1] This is only one (and perhaps the simplest) of the many ways of reckoning the quota. Another is $\dfrac{\text{total number of votes}}{\text{number of seats} + 1} + 1$.

municipalities ; in Canada for some municipal elections and in India for the election of the President of the Union.[1]

The list system also demands a multi-member constituency. Every party prepares a list of candidates for each constituency. The voter votes for the list he likes (not the candidate) ; and the seats are divided among the parties in proportion to the number of votes each list has secured. This method was once in vogue in Austria, Belgium, Czechoslovakia, Finland, Germany, Latvia, Lithuania, Poland and Yugoslavia.[2] The list system prevails in Switzerland today.[3]

The merit of proportional representation is obvious ; it ensures the representation of every group in the Legislature in proportion to its strength, so necessary to give it a sense of security in the State. Parliament will truly be a mirror of the nation, as it must be in a democracy ' which professes equality as its very root and foundation '. The single transferable vote also develops civic interest, for the system of preferences implies that the voter must give some time to consider the issues involved.

But it may justly be contended that proportional representation, ' however useful for a debating society, is useless as a means of establishing an instrument of government '. For it has been the experience of most countries which have worked it that it leads to the return of a large number of small parties. A system which makes it possible for all parties however small[4] to obtain separate representation necessarily encourages such disintegration. This, in turn, leads to the instability of the Executive by necessitating fragile coalition governments, which fall when any section of opinion is outraged. Further, legislation under such conditions is likely to lose all coherence and creative force, because it will be the result of enforced compromise to meet the wishes of several groups. The system encourages ' minority thinking ', the voters and the leaders all being encouraged to think in terms of, and to fight for, sectional interests. A Legislature elected on this basis represents a number of isolated interests ; it hardly helps to form the general will of the nation. The tie between the elector and the member is bound to be less direct and personal on account of the enlargement of the area of the constituency. In the list system, the freedom of choice

---

[1] Strong, *Modern Political Constitutions*, p. 178.

[2] A. J. Zurcher, *The Experiment with Democracy in Central Europe*, ch. v.

[3] G. A. Codding, op. cit., pp. 76-7. The system is known as the flexible list system.

[4] Provided, of course, they are able to secure the quota.

of the voter is severely curtailed as he cannot express his preference for an individual without voting for the whole party list; and *pari passu* the party organization gains in power. The single transferable vote may be puzzling to voters, and besides, being so complicated in the process of counting, may place them at the mercy of the counting authority. For these reasons, the bulk of competent opinion is against proportional representation.[1]

' To establish the system . . . is to organize disorder and emasculate the legislative power; it is to render cabinets unstable, destroy their homogeneity, and make parliamentary government impossible.'

(*ii*) *The single non-transferable vote.*[2] The distinctive element of this scheme is that each elector may exercise only one vote, no matter how many representatives are to be elected. In a constituency having 500 voters and five representatives, each voter will be given only one vote. There will therefore be 500 votes and no more. If any candidate obtains 100 votes, he will be sure of election. Thus the system ensures representation for minorities of any considerable size.

(*iii*) *The limited vote* is so called because each voter is allowed to vote only for a limited number of candidates, i.e. a number less than that of the seats to be filled. For instance in a constituency returning five members, each elector may be allowed only four votes, or less; no party can then monopolize the representation of the constituency. This system has been tried in Portugal and in some of the states of the U.S.A.

(*iv*) *The cumulative vote.* Under this system the voter is given as many votes as there are seats to be filled by the constituency; but he may spread them over several candidates or concentrate them on one. The power of accumulation enables a numerically weak party to secure some representation by the concentration of its voting power on its own candidate. This has been tried for elections to school boards in England and for electing local officers in some states of the U.S.A.

(*v*) *Communal representation* may be secured either by (*a*) separate electorates where the voters of each community vote separately for candidates of their own community, e.g. Hindus vote for Hindu candidates, Muslims for Muslim candidates, and

---

[1] H. Sidgwick, H. Finer, and H. J. Laski, among others, are against it. The late Ramsay Muir, however, was in favour of it.

[2] Also called the Japanese system because it was in use for some years in Japan.

so on ; or by (b) the reservation of seats in a joint electorate, in which case the voters may vote for candidates of communities other than their own, but the member of the community (for whom seats have been reserved) securing the highest votes among the candidates of his community will be declared elected in preference to members of other communities who might have secured a larger number of votes. Seats are reserved in this way for the Scheduled Castes within the ' general ' seats in Madras. Communal representation was introduced in India for the first time in 1909, at the request of the Muslim community.

The argument urged in favour of communal representation is, primarily, that when people are so divided by race, religion, and caste as to be unable to consider the interests of any but their own community, and when one community does not trust another, communal representation is not merely inevitably but is actually best because it appeals to those instincts which are strongest. Indeed, according to this view, it is an inevitable and even a healthy stage in the development of a non-political people. It is realistic because it takes note of actual conditions, and avoids wishful thinking. Secondly, there is the argument of *status quo* : a safeguard exists and should not be taken away without the consent of the communities concerned ; its abolition without their consent would be considered a breach of faith, a cancellation of assurances on which they have been relying for their security.

But it may be urged with equal force [1] that communal representation is fraught with the most disastrous consequences for the healthy political development of a nation. (a) As the authors of the Montagu-Chelmsford Report realized, the crucial test to which a proposal of the kind should be subjected is whether it will or will not help to carry India towards responsible government ; and they had no hesitation in stating that communal representation would not help in achieving that object. For responsible government rests on an effective sense of common interests. ' The history of self-government among the nations who developed it, and spread it through the world, is decisively against the admission by the State of any divided allegiance ; against the State's arranging its members in any way which encourages them to think of themselves primarily as citizens of any smaller unit than itself.' (b) Again, communal representation perpetuates existing class divisions. It teaches men to think as

[1] On this whole subject see the *Report on Indian Constitutional Reforms, 1918*, paras. 227-31.

partisans and not as citizens, and 'it is difficult to see how the change from this system to national representation is ever to occur'. That the authors of the joint report were correct in this judgement is proved by events since their time ; the division of India into two States is but the logical corollary of the introduction of separate electorates. (*c*) The communal system stereotypes existing relations.

' A minority which is given special representation owing to its weak and backward state is positively encouraged to settle down into a feeling of satisfied security ; it is under no inducement to educate and qualify itself to make good the ground which it has lost compared with the stronger majority. On the other hand the latter will be tempted to feel that they have done all they need do for their weaker fellow-countrymen, and that they are free to use their power for their own purposes. The give and take which is the essence of political life is lacking. There is no inducement on the one side to forbear, or to the other to exert itself.' [1]

Unqualified joint electorates are, therefore, the ideal. For a transitional period, i.e. until the minorities learn to have confidence in the reasonableness of the majority, the reservation of seats in a joint electorate may be tried with advantage as a step in promoting that confidence. The argument sometimes urged against this, that the candidate elected under this system is bound to be less communal in so far as he has to seek the votes of all communities, should in reality be considered its strong recommendation.

Separate electorates were tried in India from 1921 to 1947, and the experiment offers conclusive evidence against them as a method of ensuring minority representation. In the 1950 constitution, India has wisely discarded them in favour of joint electorates while retaining reservation of seats for the Scheduled Castes.

§6 POLITICAL PARTIES

Their merits

The representative system in the modern State is closely connected with the political party. A political party is a more or less organized group of citizens who act together as a political

[1] ibid.

unit, have distinctive aims and opinions on the leading political questions of controversy in the State, and who, by acting together as a political unit, seek to obtain control of the Government. It is based on two fundamentals of human nature : men differ in their opinions, and are gregarious ; they try to achieve by combination what they cannot achieve individually. Religious and communal loyalties, and the attachment to a dynasty or leader, also help parties to develop. Party enthusiasm is maintained by such elements of human nature as sympathy, imitation, competition and pugnacity.

Parties fulfil certain necessary functions, so necessary, indeed, that many competent thinkers consider them essential to the working of representative government. They enable men and women who think alike on public questions to unite in support of a common body of principles and policies and to work together to see that those principles and policies are adopted by the Government of the day. In the mass and without organization, the people can neither formulate principles nor agree on policy. Parties make articulate the inarticulate desires of the masses. Out of the innumerable problems which call for solution in a State, they select those which are the more urgent, study them, think out solutions and present them to the people. They act, in Lowell's phrase, as the brokers of ideas. They preserve a sense of continuity in public policy. They organize and educate the electorate, and help to carry on elections. They dramatize politics and keep the nation politically alive. They sometimes help to discover ability, although only as part compensation for the repression of other abilities. Under a two-party system, moreover, they help to maintain a keen and responsible Opposition which puts the Government on their mettle, and induces in them the strength and confidence necessary to enable them to plan long-term policies.

Their defects

The party system has serious defects, however. It lowers the moral tone and the intellectual standards of society. Adhesion to the party creed becomes the supreme political virtue. Moreover, to keep up the vigour and zeal on one's own side, one has to pretend that there is agreement on the political principles of one's party. The party leader has to make the worse seem the better reason ; he can seldom afford to speak the whole truth except perhaps to his intimate circle. The party system thus encourages hollowness and insincerity. Intellectual honesty is at a discount, for an appeal to the honour of the party is considered sufficient to silence possible opposition. Political conformity is applauded and political difference derided. The system thus puts a premium on cowardice in public life and obstructs the free course of opinion. Tact, agreeableness, flattery, ' the gift of the gab ' and other such adventitious social qualities receive undue importance ; truth, justice and reason recede into the background.

While the individual is thus silenced by the moral oppression of numbers, all those who exploit the public interests may manipulate the party as they please. The party becomes a tool for the use of private interests under cover of serving the public weal ; elections to the Legislature, which it conducts, while ostensibly national, often turn on narrow and selfish interests. That is why it is said of the House of Representatives in the U.S.A. that it represents every interest except the public interest ! Corruption becomes a fine art and incidentally drives the finer sort of men away from politics. All this criticism means that the party is in effect a *faction;* it aims at securing personal and sectional benefits rather than at carrying out a programme of public policy. Alexander Pope's definition of party as ' the madness of the many for the gain of the few ' is seen to be more realistic than its broader and more well-known formulation by Burke [1] in terms of national interest. President Ayub's criticism of parties, referred to in our chapter on Pakistan, is in some measure true of other countries as well.

A non-party democracy

Doubtless it was some such realization as this that led Rousseau to declare that any community in which parties existed was incapable of a true common will. A non-party democracy is therefore hailed by thinkers (both in the West and in the East) as the only remedy which will make representation more real and public life more honest. It has the support of America's first and greatest President. In his farewell address, Washington warned the Americans against the party spirit. The alternating domination of one faction over another, sharpened by the spirit of revenge natural to party dissension which in different ages and

[1] ' Party is a body of men united, for promoting by their joint endeavours the national interest, upon some particular principle in which they are all agreed.'—*Thoughts on the Cause of the Present Discontents.*

countries has perpetuated the most horrid enormities, is itself a frightful despotism.

'The disorders and miseries gradually incline the minds of men to seek security and repose in the absolute power of an individual; and sooner or later the chief of some prevailing faction, more able or more fortunate than his competitors, turns this despotism, to the purpose of his own elevation on the ruins of public liberty. A fire not to be quenched, it demands a uniform vigilance to prevent its burning into a flame, lest, instead to warming, it should consume.'

Attractive as a non-party democracy would appear to be, we suggest it is not practicable, even if it were desirable. If we were writing on a clean slate, it might perhaps be possible by means of a constitutional provision to prohibit party organization and party funds; but we have to deal with States where parties have come to stay. There is the initial difficulty: who is to bell the cat? If a Government in power (itself a party Government) prohibits parties, will it apply the rule to the party from which it is chosen? If it does not, the road to one-party dictatorship is clear—a possibility with which one has to reckon in this imperfect world. The fact that Ayub himself, after denouncing parties, joined a party (also referred to in our chapter on Pakistan) is suggestive.

Further, the desirability of abolishing parties is open to question; for, in spite of their defects, they perform, as we have seen, certain essential functions. In a non-party democracy, the only means for the education of the electorate are the speeches of independent candidates, discussions in the Legislature, and agitation in the press. But without the association and discipline provided by the parties, these are likely to lack a sense of unity, responsibility, and continuity. Politics will lose its 'colour' and interest. No Government in power will be able to reckon in advance the support which it can normally command, and therefore be bold enough to cope adequately with its problems. These are serious defects which a governmental system can have, and would have to be met before the non-party system could be adopted.

It is better, then, frankly to recognize the existence of parties and to regulate them. More stringent laws to root out corruption and fraud in making up the party roll and in the conduct of business at party meetings and for the prevention of bribery and undue influence at elections may go some way to improve matters.

The more active participation of upright and public-spirited citizens in party politics is essential. The more they keep out of them the more do they help to increase the evils which they hate. Further, the rigidity of parties in the Legislature has to be lessened by the provision of greater opportunities for the ' free ' vote of members.[1] Finally, we must rely on the existence of a mobile body of public opinion, ' owing no permanent allegiance to any party, and therefore able, by its instinctive reaction against extravagant movements on one side or the other, to keep the vessel on an even keel '.

§7 THE TWO-PARTY V. MULTIPLE-PARTY SYSTEM

Granted parties are tolerated, the question arises as to which system is preferable, the two-party or the multiple-party ?

The multiple-party, or group-system as it is sometimes known, has some advantages. It reflects perhaps more accurately than the two-party system the way in which the popular mind is actually divided. And further, where parties are numerous there is likely to be less of the uncritical sentiment of loyalty to party, less probability that their members will regard all questions habitually and systematically from a party point of view.

But, nevertheless, if a choice were possible, the two-party system is preferable to the multiple-party. (*i*) It gives the necessary strength and stability which enable the Government to attempt great measures. Long-term planning of policy can be successfully attempted only by a Government which is certain of a reasonably long period in office ; that certainty can be provided, if at all, only under a dual party system. (*ii*) The multiple-party system not only enfeebles the Executive, but gives a disproportionate power to self-seeking minorities ; it turns important branches of legislation into class bribery and thus lowers the tone of public life. (*iii*) The dual party system leads further to a more regular, systematic, and sober criticism of the Government than is likely under the group system. The object of the Opposition being ' to get in,' it is the business of its leaders to scrutinize the measures of the ministry carefully in order to expose all their weak points. At the same time there are strong inducements for them to abstain from attacking measures which are wisely chosen, because they expect to come to power and

[1] The Swatantra party of India is one of the few parties, known to the author, which adopts this in practice.

the blow may recoil on themselves. (*iv*) The superiority of a two-party system over a multiplicity of groups is to be found, above all, in the fact that it provides the only method by which the people at the electoral period can directly choose their government.

' It enables that government to drive its policy to the statute-book. It makes known and intelligible the results of its failure. It brings an alternative government into immediate being. The group-system always means that no government can be formed until after the people have chosen the legislative assembly.' [1]

§8 THE REFERENDUM AND THE INITIATIVE

So far the organization of the electorate has been considered; a word may be added about its powers. Its most important power, of course, is that of periodically electing its representatives to the Legislature. Can it be entrusted with any other functions in respect of legislation, administration, or judicial work?

In our survey of modern constitutions, two other ways in which the voters in some States — The French Republic, Australia, Switzerland (both in the Federal Government and in the Cantons), Germany, and the U.S.S.R. — share more directly in legislation have been noticed, viz. through the referendum and the initiative.[2] The referendum, it has been seen, is made use of in both its forms, the compulsory and the optional; it is applied to constitutional as well as to ordinary laws. The initiative is applied in some States to constitutional laws only, elsewhere to ordinary laws as well. What are the merits and defects of these methods of direct (popular) legislation?

Strictly from the point of view of democratic theory, the referendum and the initiative have some definite merits. They embody the principle of popular sovereignty better than the Legislature can; and, therefore, when a law has received the approval of the people themselves, it is likely to command more willing obedience than when it has only received the approval of the Legislature. The referendum ensures that laws opposed to the popular will are not passed; the initiative ensures that the people are not

[1] Laski, *A Grammar of Politics*, p. 314.
[2] In ch. xvii, xix, xx, xxi, xxiv and xxv. These are also in use in Eire and in the states of America. The constitutions of several of the new States created after the Great war (1914-18)—Latvia, Estonia, Lithuania, Austria and Czechoslovakia—also provided for some form of popular legislative activity. See Zurcher, op. cit., p. 93.

denied the laws they desire because of the unwillingness of the
Legislature, controlled as it sometimes is by vested interests, to
pass them. Indeed, the demand for the grant of these rights is
often made because of a belief among the people that the Legislature has failed more or less to translate the people's wishes into
laws. The referendum is particularly useful as a check on legislative bodies, where, as in Switzerland, the Executive has no veto
on the bills passed by them. Direct legislation, by means of the
referendum and the initiative, is also of high value as a means
of political education. In campaigns for the choice of legislators,
personalities necessarily play some part ; but in initiative and
referendum campaigns there is the maximum opportunity to hear
and decide solely on the basis of the facts and principles involved.
The Swiss people have repeatedly shown ability to learn and to
change their opinions upon questions submitted to them.[1]

While the referendum thus primarily serves as a check on the
Legislature and as an agency of political education, it serves other
purposes also. It is an excellent barometer of the political
atmosphere, and Legislature ought to welcome the opportunities
it affords for discovering the wishes of the people which it seeks
to represent. It also helps to resolve deadlocks between the two
chambers of the Legislature (as under the Australian constitution
and under the Weimar constitution of Germany), or between the
Legislature and the Executive (as under the constitutions of
Czechoslovakia, Lithuania and the Free City of Danzig).[2] Thirdly,
the referendum places before the voter a particular issue for
consideration, making it easier for him to give his considered
judgement, especially as contrasted with a general election campaign, in which he has, through his one vote, to elect his representative to the Legislature and simultaneously give his verdict
on an omnibus party programme raising several issues.

A study of the working of the referendum and the initiative in
those States where they have been in operation causes two reflec-
tions, however. First, the theoretical advantages referred to above
have not been realized in all States, at any rate to the same extent.
Second, direct legislation also has certain positive limitations
which considerably lessen its value as a governmental institution.
Regarding the first, it is sufficient to cite the authority of Bryce :
after a survey of modern democracies he comes to the general
conclusion that while the Swiss are well qualified by intelligence
and knowledge of public affairs and their conservative nature to

---

[1] Brooks, *The Government and Politics of Switzerland*, p. 163.
[2] Zurcher, op. cit., p. 98.

profit by the referendum and the initiative, it is more difficult to
speak in the same terms of other States. That it has done little
good, and perhaps done positive harm, would appear to be the
prevalent opinion in America.[1] The proportion of people who
vote at referenda is less than at ordinary elections ; further, where
the referendum is optional it is little resorted to. These facts
suggest the thought that people are more willing to choose
between men than between laws ; at any rate, the educative value
of the referendum in practice is not as great as was expected.
Where the initiative exists, the methods employed to get the
signatures of the people are not always fair ; also, the bills and
amendments are not skilfully drawn up.

The referendum has five positive limitations. (*i*) It tends to
weaken, if not to paralyse, the sense of responsibility under which
the Legislature does its work (as indicated in our chapter on
Switzerland); for the feeling might develop that the ultimate
responsibility for any given measure rests not upon its members,
but upon the voters ; and this in turn is likely to react on the
quality of membership of the Legislature. It is true that fear of
the popular veto may tend to make some legislators timid rather
than reckless ; [2] but timidity, it may be argued, is equally undesirable in so far as it leads to conservatism or even reaction.
(*ii*) Experience shows that the proportion who actually vote at
referenda is invariably less than fifty per cent of the qualified
voters, for people develop ' electoral fatigue '. Thus the decision
arrived at is invariably that of a minority, which is contrary to
democratic principles. The argument that since it is open to all
to vote, failure to do so must be taken to mean approval, ignores
the reasons why many people do not, in practice, turn up to vote.
If, to cure this defect, voting is made compulsory, it is found that,
in sheer disgust, voters drop blank papers in the ballot box !
(*iii*) The number of specific questions capable of decision by
mass voting is very small. What is significant in legislation is not
the acceptance or rejection of a simple principle, say of protection or free trade, but its translation into terms of a statute with
all its details, exceptions and delimitations. ' The difficulty, in
fact, which direct government involves is the final difficulty that
it is by its nature far too crude an instrument to find room for
the nice distinctions in the art of government.' [3] On many sub-

---

[1] H. Finer, *The Theory and Practice of Modern Government*, Vol. II,
p. 931.
[2] Brooks, op. cit., p. 162.
[3] Laski, op. cit., p. 322.

jects, an opinion can be formed only after long and careful examination of the points at issue ; the busy and ignorant voter hardly seems the person qualified or likely to make that examination. Indeed the referendum is an appeal from responsibility to irresponsibility, from knowledge to ignorance. This defect is much greater in respect of the initiative, for, unless under that system an examination of the initiative bills by the Legislature is made compulsory, it brings before the people bills that have not run the gauntlet of parliamentary criticism. (*iv*) Where the Executive is of the parliamentary type as in Britain, the referendum is likely to embarrass and confuse the Government.

'Unless there should occur a complete break with English political tradition, it is hardly conceivable that a ministry could with self-respect, or indeed with advantage to the country, remain in office after the rejection by the electorate of a government bill of first-rate importance. Could Mr Baldwin have retained office in 1924 if a scheme of Tariff Reform, declared by him to be essential to a solution of the problem of unemployment, had been rejected on referendum ? '[1]

Incidentally, this explains why the referendum has not been introduced in the English system of government. (*v*) Direct legislation causes delay, and complicates the process of legislation.

Some of these defects may be overcome or lessened by the adoption of certain devices. When a bill is to be submitted to the people, the voter may be supplied in advance not only with the text of the bill, but a concise statement of its purpose and a summary of its contents. The initiative may be required to be drafted by an official (or recognized) draftsman, and it may have to be signed in the presence of a public authority. And before the opinion of the people is sought, the Legislature may in every case be given an opportunity to discuss it, and, if necessary, to submit to the voters along with it a statement embodying its own views or even a counter-proposal. The small size of the electorate, the absence of wide divergences of economic and social interests and of party influences, the presence of literacy and of an independent opinion are conditions which facilitate successful popular legislation. Nevertheless, it is advisable to restrict its use, as far as possible, to simple and intelligible issues, concerning the fundamentals of the constitution, on which a direct expression of opinion by the electorate may be helpful and desirable.

[1] Marriott, *The Mechanism of the Modern State*, Vol. I, p. 462.

§9 THE PLEBISCITE AND THE RECALL

Two other political devices call for mention in this context as being connected with the powers of the electorate on legislation and other matters of political importance. They are the plebiscite and the recall.

The plebiscite, like the referendum, is a vote of the people on a matter referred to them; but unlike it, it is a vote on some important public question (rather than on a law). The political destiny of a State or part of a State or of a national minority are points on which plebiscites are taken. For example, a plebiscite was taken in 1935 in respect of the Saar in order to decide whether it should be returned to Germany. In 1942 Canada took a plebiscite on the issue of conscription for overseas service.

The recall means the 'calling back' of elected legislators, executive officers or judges before the expiration of the period for which they were elected, followed by the election of others to fill the places left vacant. This device is prevalent in many American states. In the state of Oregon, for instance, it is provided that when a prescribed percentage of electors in any electoral area have signed a petition demanding a vote on the dismissal of an elected official, a popular vote shall be held on the matter (unless the official immediately resigns), and if the vote by a majority goes against the official, he shall be dismissed and a new election shall be held for the choice of his successor for the unexpired residue of his term.[1] This procedure has been adopted by other American states and has been frequently successful,[2] though very rarely in the case of members of the Legislature. Judges may be recalled by popular vote in six states; even judicial decisions may be reversed by popular vote in the state of Colorado.

Outside the American states, there used to be provision for executive recall in Germany and Latvia. In Germany, the Reichstag could, by a two-thirds majority vote, bring before the electorate a proposal to recall the President. The Latvian President could be recalled by a specified majority of the Legislature. The constitutions of twelve German states contained provision for the recall of the Legislature or of the Executive, on a petition initiated by the electorate. In eight Swiss cantons, the people may, by a

[1] Bryce, *Modern Democracies*, Vol. II, p. 162.
[2] Strong, op. cit., p. 291.

specified majority, demand the dissolution and re-election of the cantonal Legislature before the expiration of its term.[1]

There can be no two opinions on the undesirability of the recall. It is wrong and mischievous. It asks too much of the average voter. If it is applied to the legislator there is a real danger of turning him into a mere mouthpiece of the voters' mandate, contrary to the sound principles laid down by Burke. If it is applied to the executive official, it tends to make him timid and corrupt. If it is applied to the judge (or to his decisions) it destroys the independence which is so necessary for the proper administration of justice.

SELECT BIBLIOGRAPHY

G. A. CODDING, *The Federal Government of Switzerland*, pp. 60-67, Allen & Unwin, 1961

H. FINER, *The Theory and Practice of Modern Government*, Vol. I, Part IV, Methuen, 1932

J. W. GARNER, *Political Science and Government*, ch. xix, American Book Company, 1932

C. G. HOAG and G. H. HALLETT, *Proportional Representation*, Macmillan, 1926

J. S. MILL, *Representative Government*, 'Worlds' Classics' No. 170, Oxford

M. OSTROGORSKI (Tr. F. CLARKE), *Democracy and the Organization of Political Parties*, 2 vols., Macmillan, 1902

Report on Indian Constitutional Reforms, ch. viii, Government Printing Office, Calcutta, 1918

Report of the Royal Commission appointed to inquire into Electoral Systems, 1910, H. M. Stationery Office, 1929

H. SIDGWICK, *The Elements of Politics*, ch. xx, Macmillan, 1908

W. F. WILLOUGHBY, *Principles of Legislative Organization and Administration*, The Brookings Institution, 1934

[1] Here the recall is usually applicable to the legislative body as a whole and in a few instances to the members of either House from a single electoral district. See Brooks, op. cit., p. 322.

CHAPTER XXXII

THE LEGISLATURE

§1 THE FUNCTION OF THE LEGISLATURE

LEGISLATURES in modern States, we have seen, do not all perform identical functions. Everywhere they pass laws, determine the ways of raising and spending public revenue, and discuss matters of public importance. Almost everywhere they have some part in the process of amending the constitution. They control the Executive in States where, as in Britain and Canada, the Executive is a parliamentary one. Some Legislatures, as in Switzerland and the U.S.S.R., have elective functions. The Upper Houses of some States (Britain, for instance) have judicial functions, both original and appellate. Some share in executive functions: the consent of the Senate is necessary in the U.S.A. for the appointment of officers and the making of treaties; in France, under the Third Republic, the Senate's consent was necessary for the dissolution of the lower House.[1] This variety can, of course, be explained only by the circumstances in which constitutions were framed and have developed in the respective countries. The judicial function of the House of Lords, for instance, is a historical survival, and is not of much significance, for, as we have seen, that function is in effect performed by the Lords of Appeal and the Lord Chancellor. The functions of the Senate of the United States of America in respect of appointments and treaties must be explained, partly at any rate, by the desire of the states on the establishment of the Federation to have some check on the new federal authority (to whom they were surrendering large powers); the Senate, being considered the guardian of state rights, was vested with these powers.

Practice apart, the question may be raised as to what is the proper function of a legislative body. We may discuss this under four heads: legislation, administration, finance, and the ventilation of grievances.

(i) *Legislation.* The first important function of a Legislature is, of course, to enact laws. The part that a legislative body

---

[1] The consent was necessary according to the law of the constitution, though it had, by convention, fallen into disuse for a considerable time.

(which is normally very large in size) should have, must, however, be correctly grasped. That great authority, J. S. Mill, has said : a numerous representative assembly is not fitted for the direct business of legislation, which is skilled work demanding study and experience. It is not competent to do work itself but it can cause it to be done, it is competent to determine to whom or to what sort of people this work shall be confided, and to give or withhold the national sanction when it has been done.

'Every provision of a law requires to be framed with the most accurate and long-sighted perception of its effect on all the other provisions ; and the law when made should be capable of fitting into a consistent whole with the previously existing laws. It is impossible that these conditions should be in any degree fulfilled when laws are voted clause by clause.' [1]

The mere time necessarily occupied in getting through bills renders Parliament incapable of passing any except on broad principles. Mill himself suggested that the duty of making the laws should be entrusted to a small body of experts, a Commission of Legislation, not exceeding in number the members of a cabinet. No one would wish, he added, that this body should of itself have any power to *enact* laws ; the Commission would only embody the element of intelligence in their construction ; Parliament would represent that of will. Indeed, it should be a rule that no measure can become law until expressly sanctioned by Parliament. Technical knowledge needs to be tempered by the representatives' knowledge of social needs and the desires of the public. While Mill's specific suggestion has not anywhere been adopted, it is significant that the responsibility for the initiation of new legislation in most parliamentary democracies is vested in the Executive, which avails itself of the advice of experts and of advisory bodies representing special interests.

(ii) Administration. A popular assembly is still less fitted to administer or to dictate in detail to those who have the charge of administration. Here again its proper office is that of superintendence and check : to throw the light of publicity on the Government's acts ; to censure them if found condemnable, and, if the men who compose the Government abuse their trust or fulfil it in a manner which conflicts with the deliberate sense of the nation, to expel them from office, and virtually appoint their successors.[2]

---

[1] Mill, *Representative Government*, ch. v.   [2] ibid.

(*iii*) *Finance*. In matters of finance, it should be a rule that public money cannot be raised or spent without Parliament's sanction ; but proposals for raising and spending money must come from the Executive. Further, the right of private members to propose new items of expenditure should be restricted, because this puts a premium upon particular interests instead of on the general interest, or upon the immediately apparent instead of the more essential.

(*iv*) *The ventilation of grievances*. Finally, a Legislature is a useful organ of public opinion, ' the nation's Committee of Grievances, and its Congress of Opinions ', a place where every interest and shade of opinion can have its cause presented. This is a most important function in a democracy, which has been well described as a government controlled by public opinion.

§2 BICAMERALISM

Most modern constitutions provide for a Legislature of two chambers, the lower and the upper. Among the exceptions are Greece, Turkey, two Balkan States (Yugoslavia and Bulgaria), some Canadian provinces,[1] some Swiss cantons,[2] and some Indian states.[3]

The more important arguments advanced in favour of a second chamber are the following :

(*i*) It is a safeguard against the despotism of a single chamber. Lecky and J. S. Mill are strong exponents of this view. Of all the forms of government that are possible among mankind, says the former, there is none which is likely to be worse than the government of a single omnipotent democratic chamber ; it is at least as much susceptible as an individual despot to the temptations that grow out of the possession of uncontrolled power, and it is likely to act with much less sense of responsibility and much less real deliberation. Mill expressed himself equally strongly : the same reason, he said, which induced the Romans to have two consuls makes it desirable that there should be two chambers, so that neither of them may be exposed to the corrupting influence of undivided power, even for the space of a single year.

(*ii*) A second chamber serves as a check upon hasty and ill-considered legislation. An elected Legislative Assembly, it is

---

[1] All except Quebec and Nova Scotia.
[2] With the exception of six cantons, each has a unicameral legislature. See Brooks. *The Government and Politics of Switzerland*, p. 313.
[3] Madhya Pradesh, Orissa and the Punjab.

argued, may be moved by strong passions and excitements; a second chamber, constituted differently and if possible with superior or supplementary intellectual qualifications, helps to restrain such tendencies and compels a careful, sober consideration of legislative projects. It is, as it were, an appeal from ' Philip drunk' to ' Philip sober '. It interposes a necessary delay between the introduction and the final passing of a measure, and subjects it to revision which may introduce improvements in form or substance.

(*iii*) It helps to provide adequate representation of the aristocratic element of the community. The lower House, elected as it is on a wide suffrage, is bound to reflect the views of the *masses*; the upper House serves to balance this undue preponderance, and minimizes the danger of class legislation.

(*iv*) The constitution of a second chamber is the best way of providing adequate representation to certain ' interests ' in a country, which need representation but which, for want of proper organization or other reasons, may not get such representation in the lower House. Labour, Women, Landlords and Chambers of Commerce were thus given special representation under the Government of India Act, 1935.

(*v*) A second chamber makes it possible for people of political and administrative experience and ability (who for reasons of age, finance, or health are not likely to try to enter the lower House through the arduous process of electioneering) to be brought into public life and made available for the service of the State.

(*vi*) In federal States, the second chamber affords an opportunity for giving representation to the component units of the federation *as units*, the lower House being constituted on a population basis.

(*vii*) And, lastly, it is argued, particularly by J. A. R. Marriott, that the experience of history has been in favour of two chambers. No major State, whatever its form of government, whether federal or unitary, monarchical or republican, presidential or parliamentary, constitutionally flexible or rigid, has been willing to dispense with a second chamber. And even those States, like England, which tried the unicameral experiment during a period of social disorder, went back to the orthodox pattern after a time. It is not wise to disregard the lesson of history.

Bicameralism has not, however, had the unanimous support of political thinkers. At least from the time of the Abbé Siéyès, the dilemma has been posed that if a second chamber dissents from the first, it is mischievous ; if it agrees with it, it is super-fluous.[1] Further, the opponents of bicameralism suggest that it is unnecessary to have a second legislative chamber, with its attendant delay and expense, as a safeguard against the despotism of a majority in a single chamber. Other safeguards exist and are possible, e.g. the suspensive veto of the Executive, a second vote in the same chamber after an interval, and so on. In any case, as Mill rightly said,[2] the check 'which a second chamber can apply to a democracy otherwise unchecked' is not of much value, because few will then be disposed to listen to its opinion. Again, legislation, it is argued, is not so hasty or ill-considered as is often made out ; 'almost any measure that is enacted becomes law as the result of a long process of discussion and analysis' ; the committee system is especially useful in securing the necessary care in legislation. Finally, the difficulties in the construction of a second chamber in such a way that it will not compete with the first but will at the same time be constituted differently from it and will attract talent are too great to be over-come. Even the additional argument, applied to federal States, that a second chamber embodies the federal principle, is to be discounted, for experience shows that members of the second chamber often vote on party, rather than state, lines.

§3 THE UPPER HOUSE

Disregarding the pros and cons and granting that it is decided to have a second chamber in a State, what are the considerations to be kept in view in constructing one — in respect of its com-position, duration and powers ?

The main principle is that it should be differently composed from the first so that legislative measures may receive considera-tion a second time by a body different in character from a primary representative Assembly, if possible with superior or supplementary intellectual qualifications ; otherwise there will be duplications. This differentiation is usually brought about in the following ways.

(*i*) *In the method of choice of members.* The lower House is generally a directly elected body ; the upper House is, in the

---

[1] For a modern version of the dilemma, see Laski, *A Grammar of Politics*, p. 331. The first part of the dilemma assumes, it may be added, that the will of the people is reflected in the lower House ; and that an upper House, which is nominated or hereditary, has no authority to oppose it.

[2] *Representative Government*, ch. xiii.

main, a hereditary body, as in Britain, or a nominated body, as in Canada and Italy, or an indirectly elected one, as in France, or a partly nominated and partly (indirectly) elected body, as in India.[1] The objections to the hereditary principle are obvious : the qualities required for a legislator are not handed down from father to son ; a hereditary body is, besides, an anachronism in a democratic age. Nomination has one merit : it enables men of character and ability who may not desire to contest elections to be made available for the service of the community (through nomination). A most serious objection to it is that the nomination is certain to be abused by being made on party lines ; and, further, a nominated upper House, not being representative, may not command the confidence of the people. Indirect election gives some representative character to the body so elected, and presumably gives the choice of the legislators to people more competent than the primary voters ; but it provides greater opportunity for corruption than direct election.

(*ii*) *In the tenure of membership.* In the United States of America, members of the lower House are elected for two years ; but members of the upper House for six years ; in France (under the Third Republic), the corresponding periods were four and nine years. Besides, as we have seen, the principle of partial renewal is applied to members of the upper House, one-third, for instance, retiring every two years in the United States of America and in India.

(*iii*) *In qualifications for membership.* In the United States of America, for membership of the House of Representatives, the age qualification is 25 ; but for membership of the Senate, it is 30. Differentiation may also be made by prescribing a property or educational qualification, as was done for membership of Indian Council of State.

The best method of constructing the upper House is, perhaps, the one recommended by Sidgwick in his *Elements of Politics,*[2] viz. a combination of nomination and indirect election. This gives it a differential character, makes it a partially representative body, and provides an opportunity for the nomination of the

---

[1] In the U.S.A., the U.S.S.R., Australia, and Switzerland (almost wholly) the upper House is also directly elected, but differentiations are made in other ways.

[2] pp. 476-7. H. B. Lees-Smith in his *Second Chambers in Theory and Practice,* pp. 216 ff., recommends the Norwegian system, in which the second chamber is a small body elected by the first, and roughly proportionate to the composition of the latter. Laski also commends the scheme in *A Grammar of Politics,* pp. 332-3.

best men. A small body is preferable to a large one ; two hundred ought to be the upper limit. The upper House so constituted may be given a fairly long tenure, say six years ; it could also be renewed partially, say one-third every two years. Its powers should be on the lines recommended by the Bryce Conference Committee, which we have already cited, the essential idea being that the upper House should not obstruct the will of the lower House, but should be helpful in revising the laws passed by the lower. Further, it must have power to interpose such delay in the passing of a bill into law as may be needed to enable the opinion of the nation to be adequately expressed upon it.

§4 THE LOWER HOUSE

That the lower House should be elected by the people hardly needs special mention. The organization of the electorate and the methods of election and of voting (both in theory and practice) have been discussed elsewhere.[1] The size of the House is also a matter for careful consideration. The principles are clear enough : it should not be too large to make effective deliberation possible ; it must not be too small to make the formation of reasonably small constituencies easy, for if the constituencies become very large, members cannot maintain effective contact with their electors. In fixing the actual number, the area of the State and the population must, of course, be taken into consideration ; five hundred would be a reasonable number. Regarding the tenure of the House, the principle is that it must be sufficiently long to enable members to familiarize themselves with procedure and to settle down to useful work ; a very long period may result in members losing touch with the electorate. Perhaps a period of not less than four years nor more than five is the best, subject to the qualification that the House may be dissolved earlier by the Executive when the electorate has to be consulted on an issue which was not placed before it at the general election. The functions of a body so constituted must be more or less the functions which we have discussed in §1 of this chapter. It must make the final decision in matters of legislation and finance, the initiative being with the Executive, and the revision, subject to the final sanction of the lower House, being left to the upper House. It should, besides, be the organ of public opinion on all matters of public importance. Above all, it must watch and control the Govern-

[1] See above, ch. xvi to xxv and xxix.

ment, compelling it to justify all its acts before the Legislature and before the public; and 'if the men who compose the Government abuse their trust or fulfil it in a manner which conflicts with the deliberate sense of the nation', it must have power to expel them from office, and either expressly or virtually appoint their successors. This last function it can, of course, only perform efficiently where the Executive is a parliamentary one; where a non-parliamentary Executive prevails, its function in this regard must necessarily be secondary and indirect.

SELECT BIBLIOGRAPHY

H. J. LASKI, *A Grammar of Politics*, ch. viii, Allen & Unwin, 1930

H. B. LEES-SMITH, *Second Chambers in Theory and Practice*, Allen & Unwin, 1923

J. A. R. MARRIOTT, *Second Chambers*, Oxford, 2nd ed., 1927

J. S. MILL, *Representative Government*, ch. ix-xiii, 'Worlds' Classics' No. 170, Oxford

W. F. WILLOUGHBY, *Principles of Legislative Organization and Administration*, The Brookings Institution, 1934

CHAPTER XXXIII

THE EXECUTIVE

§1 ITS FUNCTIONS

THE Executive is the second main branch of government. The term is used in a broad sense to indicate ' the aggregate or totality of all the functionaries and agencies which are concerned with the execution of the will of the State as that will has been formulated and expressed in terms of law '.[1] In this sense, it includes not only those (like the President in the U.S.A. and the cabinet in Britain) who exercise supreme control but also the host of subordinate officials, like policemen and clerks, who simply carry out orders. It is more common in political science to restrict the use of the term Executive to those whose primary duty is rather that of ' seeing that laws are enforced ' than that of ' doing the things which the laws call for '; the term ' the Civil Service ' is used to connote all other executive officials taken together.

Our survey of constitutions indicates that the functions of the Executive are not everywhere, or at all times, identical. They vary according to the type of Executive (being greater in respect of legislation in countries having a parliamentary Executive than in those having a non-parliamentary Executive), and according to the prevailing conceptions regarding the sphere of the State (being greater in totalitarian than in liberal States). An outline of the more important functions may, however, be attempted under three headings.

(i) *Legislative*. It has been noticed that while laws are everywhere passed by the Legislature, the Executive has some share, direct or indirect, in the process of legislation — recommending measures for its consideration, initiating bills, defending them in parliament, exercising a suspensive veto, etc. Besides, almost everywhere it has the power of delegated legislation, i.e. of issuing statutory orders and rules under the power vested in it by the Legislature. The power of summoning, proroguing and dissolving the Legislature (in countries where the constitution

---

[1] Garner, *Political Science and Government*, p. 677.

does not itself fix its tenure and date of meeting) is also invariably vested in the Executive.

(*ii*) *Administrative*. Three kinds [1] of administrative duties may be distinguished. The first is the direction and supervision of the execution of laws. To enable the Executive to perform this duty efficiently, it is vested with the power of appointing and removing the higher officials, directing their work, and exercising disciplinary control over them. In some States, as in the U.S.A., the appointments may be made by the Chief Executive only with the consent of one chamber of the Legislature. The second is the military power ; this includes the supreme command of the army, navy and air force, and, in some States, the power to declare war.[2]

' The command and application of the public force to execute the laws, to maintain peace, and to resist foreign invasion, are powers so obviously of an executive nature and require the exercise of qualities so peculiarly adapted to this department, that they have always been exclusively appropriated to it in every well-organized government on earth.' [3]

And the third is the power to represent the Government in its relations with other States, conduct negotiations with them, and conclude treaties. In some States, treaties require for their validity the consent of the Legislature, or one of its chambers : in the U.S.A. all treaties require for their validity the consent of the Senate ; in France the consent of the Legislature is necessary for some treaties.[4]

(*iii*) *Judicial*. In the main, this relates to the pardoning power vested in the Executive in almost every State (with or without limitations) ; [5] but it also includes in some countries, as in Britain, the quasi-judicial power of trying certain disputes between government officials and private citizens.[6]

§2　TYPES OF EXECUTIVE

Our study of constitutions, past and present, shows that there have been many different types of Executive. The executive

---

[1] Some writers would prefer to call the three duties here listed together as ' administrative ' by three separate names, ' administrative ', ' military ' and ' diplomatic '.

[2] e.g. in Britain ; in the U.S.A., Congress alone can declare war.

[3] Kent, *Commentaries*, Vol. I, p. 283.　　[4] See above, ch. xvii, §4.

[5] See above, ch. xvi, §3.　　[6] See above, ch. xvi, §13.

power was vested in two kings in Sparta ; but the kings were so far from being kings in the ordinary sense that they were not even chief magistrates. The real Executive was a Council, the College of Ephors.[1] Rome in republican days vested the executive power in two consuls of equal power ; but there were other magistrates also who 'though inferior in rank to the consuls, were still strictly co-ordinate with them, and were in no sense their agents or delegates '.[2] In the seventeenth-century European States the executive power was vested in one single hereditary monarch. In modern Britain, the real executive power is vested in a cabinet chosen from Parliament ; in the U.S.A., in a President elected by an electoral college ; in Switzerland, in a Federal Council of seven elected by the Legislature. In a short survey like this, it is impossible to compare and contrast all types with one another ; but two distinctions are pronounced in modern democratic States, and must be discussed.

Single and plural Executives

The primary difference between the single and the plural Executive (illustrated respectively by the President of the U.S.A. and the Federal Council of Switzerland) is that in the former, the final control rests with one individual, whereas in the latter, it rests with a Council. The President of the U.S.A. has his ministers, but they are strictly *his* ministers, named by him and dependent on him ; they are his advisers and agents, not his colleagues.[3] The position of the President of the Swiss Confederation, on the other hand, as has been noticed earlier,[4] is wholly different. He is simply the chairman of the Federal Council and exercises the usual powers of a chairman. The other members of that Council are his colleagues, not merely his agents or advisers ; executive acts are the acts of the Council as a body, not of the President personally.[5]

The single Executive has one clear advantage. It secures the unity, singleness of purpose, energy and promptness of decision so necessary for the success of an Executive. This consideration is of particular importance at grave crises of national existence, when unity of control is absolutely essential. A collegial Executive, on the other hand, impairs unity of control by dividing

---

[1] E. A. Freeman, *Historical Essays*, Essay XII.
[2] ibid.
[3] ibid.
[4] See above, ch. xx, §3.
[5] Freeman, op. cit.

responsibility. What a Board does, says J. S. Mill,[1] is the act of nobody for nobody can be made to answer for it.

A plural Executive, has however, its compensating advantages. It is a maxim of experience that in a multitude of counsellors there is wisdom.[2] A collegial Executive is safer than a single one. It renders more difficult the encroachment of the Executive on the liberties of the people in general. While it hinders the commonwealth from making the most of a great man, it prevents it from being dragged through the dirt by a small man.[3]

'The presidency of Washington and the presidency of Pierce are in Switzerland alike impossible.... America, with her personal chief, runs a risk which Switzerland avoids. As in all cases of risk, the more adventurous State sometimes reaps for itself advantages, and sometimes brings on itself evil, from both of which its less daring fellow is equally cut off. It may be that each system better suits the position of the nation which has adopted it.'[4]

Parliamentary and non-parliamentary Executives[5]

The second distinction is between an Executive (as in Britain) chosen from Parliament and holding office only so long as it commands the confidence of that Parliament, and another (as in the U.S.A.) chosen independently of the Legislature and holding office for a fixed term.

The parliamentary Executive has several advantages. (*i*) It ensures harmony and co-operation between the Executive and the Legislatures, which makes for efficient legislation. The Executive's experience of the administrative process is useful in making the laws passed by the Legislature more realistic than they are otherwise likely to be. In Laski's expressive phrase, Congress in America legislates in a vacuum. The divorce of the Executive from the Legislature is 'the forcible disjunction of things naturally connected'; it is indeed injurious to both.

[1] *Representative Government*, ch. xiv.
[2] ibid.
[3] ibid.
[4] Freeman, op. cit.
[5] The parliamentary Executive is also sometimes called the cabinet type of Executive: the non-parliamentary is called the fixed or presidential type. For examples and characteristics of the parliamentary type, see ch. xvi, xvii, xix: for the non-parliamentary, see ch. xviii.

' The Executive is crippled by not getting the laws it needs, and the Legislature is spoiled by having to act without responsibility : the Executive becomes unfit for its name, since it cannot execute what it decides on ; the Legislature is demoralized by liberty, by taking decisions of which others (and not itself) will suffer the effects.' [1]

(*ii*) It contributes to the efficiency of the administration by bringing the ministry into constant contact with the Opposition. The Opposition, eager to ' get in ', keeps the ministry up to a high pitch of alertness through questions and vigorous criticism. (*iii*) It makes for responsibility to popular will. An Executive, liable to lose the confidence of Parliament as the result of the exercise of arbitrary power, is careful not to be autocratic. By its very nature, it is always induced to adopt a policy which has the support of public opinion. Even so ' autocratic ' an Executive as the British cabinet always has its finger on the pulse of the House of Commons and of the larger public outside.[2] (*iv*) It provides a simple method whereby persons fitted to be members of an Executive may make known their ability ; [3] indeed, according to Laski there is no alternative method that in any degree approaches it.

But the parliamentary Executive has its defects. (*i*) Its tenure is uncertain, being liable to be upset at any moment by a breeze of popular disfavour, ' if the dominant party in the representative chamber is either small or wanting in coherence '. Cabinet government worked successfully in Britain because of the existence of two, and only two, well-organized and powerful political parties, one of which was willing and able to take up the work of government when the other laid it down ; when three parties so divided the House that no one party was able to command a majority (as happened between 1923 and 1929), it did not work well. In most other countries which have adopted the cabinet system of government, two strong parties have not developed, however ; French experience in this regard is typical. Ministries there are shortlived and uncertain of their period of office ; the uncertainty renders it difficult for them to adopt a farsighted and consistent policy. Under other conditions, where one party dominates the House, there is quite a different danger, which we have noticed in connexion with the British cabinet : [4]

---

[1] Bagehot, *The English Constitution*, ch. i.
[2] See above, ch. xvi, §9.
[3] See above, ch. xvi, §8 ; Laski, *A Grammar of Politics*, pp. 299-300.
[4] See above, ch. xvi, §9.

there is a constant temptation to members to vote, not in what they may consider the best way, but in the way that will help to keep in or turn out the ministry, and this tends to make the cabinet autocratic. (*ii*) Ministers are liable to be distracted from their executive duties by their parliamentary work. This is specially true in countries where the ministry has no stable majority ; France under the Third Republic is a typical example. Further it happens that under such conditions the ministry is unwilling to propose measures, however salutary, that are likely to be unpopular, but is merely anxious to propose measures 'whose chief merit is their vote-catching quality'. (*iii*) The choice of ministers in this system is limited to members of the dominant party in Parliament ; it is quite possible that they will not possess general administrative ability, still less the special knowledge required for particular departments.

By contrast, the great advantages of a presidential system of government are its stability and freedom from control by a fickle legislative majority. Thus the President of the U.S.A. is elected for a fixed term, and except in the case of some definite crime being judicially proved against him, he cannot be constitutionally removed before the end of that term. He is free to pursue a reasonably continuous and consistent policy ; and, with nothing either to gain or fear from Congress, is free to think only of the welfare of the people. Moreover, according to J. A. R. Marriott, there is a real gain in efficiency of administration because ministers are not distracted by the necessity of constant attendance in the Legislature, and in efficiency of legislation because the minds of legislators are concentrated upon their special functions.[1]

These advantages, however, are gained at the cost of too great an isolation of the executive and legislative branches from each other, with all the attendant disadvantages noticed above and the possibility of deadlocks between two branches of government, which ought, if possible, to be avoided. In the U.S.A., if Congress and the President do not agree, neither party has any means of getting rid of the other. The President cannot dissolve Congress and he is in no way called on to resign his own office. A similar situation would be met in Britain either by the resignation of the ministry or by the dissolution of the House of Commons.

[1] *The Mechanism of the Modern State*, Vol. II, pp. 113-14. Marriott, however, seems to discount the value of the increasing part that the American Executive plays in legislation. See above, ch. xviii, §3.

It may be, as Freeman suggests,[1] that each system is suited to the circumstances of the country where it prevails, for the great lesson of political history is that no kind of government worthy to be called government is universally good or bad in itself. Nevertheless, it is impossible to withhold admiration for the Swiss system which has the merits of both types of Executive and avoids the defects of both.

§3 THE ORGANIZATION OF THE CIVIL SERVICE

We have earlier distinguished the Civil Service from the chief Executive, the duty of the former being to obey the orders of the latter. Briefly, it is ' a professional body of officials, permanent, paid and skilled '.[2] There was a time in history, as we have noticed with reference to Athens, when civil servants were not *permanent* officials, and were recruited for the most part from ordinary citizens, with no specialized training. That is a state of things which can hardly be revived, for the problems of modern government are very complex, requiring for their efficient solution a body of men who are trained for their job and who take to government service as a vocation for life.

The importance of the Civil Service has grown with the increased activity of the State. The modern State, we have noticed earlier,[3] is not a police State, but a social service State : its functions have, therefore, increased enormously. As the scope of State activity widens, the Civil Service grows not only in numbers [4] but in power, for every extension of the area of State activity increases the points at which officials and citizens come into contact with each other. The greater the prohibitions and restrictions by Government on personal conduct, the greater, inevitably, the power of the Civil Service. The growth of delegated legislation and administrative justice, noticed earlier, must also be reckoned among the causes of the increasing importance of the Civil Service, for they increase the area of discretion vested in that service.

Three or four principles have gradually been established in the past hundred years regarding the organization of the Civil Service.

---

[1] op. cit.
[2] Finer, *The Theory and Practice of Modern Government*, Vol. II, p. 1163.
[3] See above, p. 101.
[4] From the statistics given by Herman Finer (*Theory and Practice of Modern Government*, 1949 ed., p. 760), the number of members in the Civil Service in Great Britain rose from 31,943 in 1861 to 717,000 in 1947.

(*i*) The political Executive should have little control over the appointment of permanent officials because that might lead to party patronage, favouritism and insecurity of service. Men of ability and character will not be tempted to join the Service when no guarantee of continuous livelihood exists. Further, appointment by the political Executive may lead to corruption. The time and mind of ministers will be devoted to the rewarding of the followers of a party and to the interviewing of an endless number of candidates and those who come to plead on their behalf, rather than to the formulation of policies for the promotion of social good and their efficient administration. It is now recognized that to avoid these evils, members of the public Services must be appointed by persons other than those in the cabinet and under rules which reduce to a minimum the chances of personal favouritism. A Public Service Commission, with members holding office during good behaviour, is entrusted with the duty of recruiting men to the Service by open competition (supplemented by interviews in certain cases). The fundamental principles in the conduct of the Service thus constituted are permanence in office and the dissociation of tenure of office from the changes of government caused by the cabinet system. Once a candidate has been admitted to the Service, granted efficiency and good behaviour, he should be certain of keeping his place until the age of retirement. The Executive should have the right of dismissal, to be exercised only in cases of incompetence or neglect of duty, and never for political reasons or to make room for favourites.

(*ii*) Promotion must be on the basis of seniority tempered by factors of efficiency.

(*iii*) Members of the Civil Service must abstain from party politics, and loyally carry out the orders of their chief, whichever party be in power, in so far as they are within the limits of the law. They must, further, observe strict official secrecy.

(*iv*) The minister takes the responsibility for the action of his subordinates. It is a convention that no mention should be made in Parliament of a minister's permanent subordinates, either by way of praise or criticism ; and no minister should take shelter behind the staff of his department.

In India, before the transfer of power to Indian hands in 1947, a further principle was recognized in the organization of the Civil Service, though, luckily, only to a limited extent, viz. communal representation. Thus the Government of India had laid down the rule that 12½% of all vacancies to be filled by open competition should be reserved for the Scheduled Castes. This meant that if they obtained less than the prescribed percentage in open competition, this percentage would be secured to them by means of nomination. Similarly, in connexion with posts which were filled from the open market otherwise than by competition, recruitment was made approximately in proportion to the population of the various communities : Hindus excluding Scheduled Castes 60%, Scheduled Castes $16^2/_3$%, Muslims $13^1/_3$% and other communities 10%. Such discrimination in favour of minorities is not followed in European countries. The clause usually inserted in the constitutions of these countries is to the effect that differences of race, language or religion shall not prejudice any national in admission to public employment.

The *raison d'être* of communal reservation in the Services was said to be the unequal cultural development of the communities in the State. It was based on the view that the efficiency of the public services was a function not merely of the qualifications of the entrants thereto but of the social harmony in the body politic they served. Such harmony, it was argued, could only be secured by the fair representation of the various communities in the services through reservation and the like. The principle, however, worked under two healthy safeguards ; in order to secure a fair degree of (if not the maximum) efficiency, a minimum qualification was imposed ; and communal representation was not taken into account in making promotions. If a senior found a junior promoted over him merely because he belonged to another community, there would be discontent within the Service. Such treatment would be going a long way on the road towards dividing the Service by communities ; and ' a body which is divided against itself cannot have that loyalty and *esprit de corps* which are so vital in public service '.

The policy of the Government of India in regard to communal representation in the public Service was revised in 1950 in the light of the provisions of the constitution which lay down *inter alia* that with certain exceptions no discrimination should be made in the matter of appointments to the Services under the State on grounds of race, religion, caste, etc. The exceptions are that special provisions shall be made for the Scheduled Castes and Scheduled Tribes in all Services and for Anglo-Indians in certain specified Services, as follows :

(*i*) *Scheduled Castes.* The existing reservation of $12\frac{1}{2}$% of vacancies filled by direct recruitment in favour of the Scheduled Castes will continue in the case of recruitment to posts and Services made, on an all-India basis, by open competition. Where recruitment is made otherwise than by open competition the reservation for Scheduled Castes will be $16^2/_3\%$.

(*ii*) *Scheduled Tribes*. Both in recruitment by open competition and in recruitment made otherwise than by open competition there will be reservation in favour of members of the Scheduled Tribes of 5% of the vacancies filled by direct recruitment.

(*iii*) *Anglo-Indians*. The reservations which were in force in favour of Anglo-Indians in the Railway Services, the Posts and Telegraphs Department and the Customs Department on 14 August 1947 will be continued.[1]

The orders regarding reservation of vacancies in favour of the various communities will not apply to recruitment by promotion, which will continue to be made as heretofore irrespective of communal considerations and on the basis of seniority or merit as the case may be.

In all cases, certain minimum qualifications are prescribed and the reservations are subject to the overall condition that candidates of the requisite communities, possessing the prescribed qualifications and suitable in all respects for the appointment in question, are forthcoming in sufficient numbers for the vacancies reserved for them.

§4 WHY THE POWER OF THE EXECUTIVE HAS GROWN

Before we pass on to the Judiciary, mention must be made of a remarkable trend in modern politics : the growth in the power of the Executive at the expense of the Legislature. This development is true not only of government in totalitarian States but also in democratic States. What are the reasons for this new development ?

It might, indeed, be expected that the Legislature should generally be ' the great overruling power in every free community ', for the will of the State must be expressed before it can be enforced, and that will is expressed by the Legislature. The Legislature has power over the purse, it has power to regulate matters the power over which has not been conferred on other departments ; where a parliamentary Executive exists, the tenure of the Executive is controlled by the Legislature ; and the importance of the legislative function has increased in proportion to the increase of collectivist legislation.

But in practice, the Executive tends to overshadow the Legislature for several reasons. (*i*) Modern executive business is

---

[1] Subject to certain specified conditions contained in Article 336 of the constitution.

concerned not only with the execution of laws, but also in many cases with the initiation of bills to be sanctioned by the Legislature. (*ii*) The increase of collectivist legislation, which increases the importance of the Legislature, *pari passu* increases also the importance of the Executive; for almost every law delegates to the Executive the power of enacting subsidiary legislation. (*iii*) In many States, the Executive has acquired quasi-judicial powers. (*iv*) War necessarily results in an increase in the power of the Executive; and the habit acquired in war-time tends to continue in peace-time as well. (*v*) Legislatures have everywhere been declining because of the inadequacy of the territorial basis of representation; the methods of election and the party system do not induce the best men to enter Parliament; the electorate, by demanding and acquiring powers of direct legislation, competes with the Legislature; other organizations like the Trade Union Congress and the press are similarly competing with the Legislature for power; and the Executive's control of the organs of public opinion, particularly the radio, necessarily operates to reduce the importance of the Legislature as a *free* organ for the expression of public opinion. (*vi*) In totalitarian States, the concentration of power in the Executive is part of their very philosophy. (*vii*) Finally, the nature of modern government is such that leadership, continuous and acknowledged, concentrated and co-ordinating, adequately informed and equipped, is vitally necessary.

SELECT BIBLIOGRAPHY

J. BRYCE, *Modern Democracies*, Vol. II, ch. lxvii, Macmillan, 1921

H. FINER, *The Theory and Practice of Modern Government*, Vol. II, Part VII, Methuen, 1932

E. A. FREEMAN, *Historical Essays*, Essay XII, Macmillan, 1896

F. W. GARNER, *Political Science and Government*, ch. xxii, American Book Company, 1930

F. J. GOODNOW, *Principles of Constitutional Government*, ch. x, Harpers, 1916

L. D. WHITE, *The Civil Service in the Modern State*. University of Chicago Press, 1930

— —, *Introduction to the Study of Public Administration*, Macmillan, 2nd ed., 1939

W. F. WILLOUGHBY, *Principles of Public Administration*, The Brookings Institution, 1939

Executive, and that their salaries should not be diminished during their term of office. The extent to which these encroachments are met and the methods by which they are met have been discussed elsewhere.

CHAPTER XXXIV

THE JUDICIARY

§1 ORGANIZATION OF THE JUDICIARY

'THERE is no better test of the excellence of a government than the efficiency of its judicial system',[1] for nothing more nearly touches the welfare and security of the citizen than his knowledge that he can rely on the certain, prompt, and impartial administration of justice. The judge, therefore, fulfils an onerous function in the community. His primary duty is to interpret law, to apply the existing law to individual cases, and, by so doing, to hold the scales even both between one private citizen and another, and between private citizens and members of the Government. Incidentally, however, in the process of interpretation, as we have seen, he cannot help making new law,[2] this law-making function being relatively more important in federal States than in unitary States.

The rôle of the Judiciary being so important, it is obviously essential to choose men of honesty, impartiality, independence and legal knowledge to fill the places of judges. Three methods of appointing them are in vogue, as we have seen : nomination by the Executive,[3] election by the Legislature,[4] and election by the people.[5] There is no doubt that, of the three, the first is the best. A numerous Legislature can hardly be expected to estimate efficiently the legal knowledge required for judicial decisions, and, besides, is likely to be too much influenced by political considerations. For similar reasons, the popular election of judges is also open to objection. Only in three out of the thirty-eight American states where the system prevails has it given any satisfaction.[6]

Regarding the duration of their office, it is now recognized that the preservation of judicial independence requires that judges should hold office for life,[7] independent of the pleasure of the

---

[1] Bryce, *Modern Democracies*, Vol. II, p. 421.
[2] See above, pp. 63-4.
[3] In Britain, The French Republic, the U.S.A., Canada, Australia, South Africa, Germany, Italy and India.
[4] In Switzerland and the U.S.S.R.
[5] In some Swiss cantons and American states.
[6] Ogg and Ray, *Introduction to American Government*, 8th ed., p. 874.
[7] This is sometimes expressed as 'holding office "during good behaviour",' i.e. so long as they are not guilty of any crime known to the law.

Executive, and that their salaries should not be diminished during their term of office. The extent to which these requirements are met and the methods by which they are met have been discussed elsewhere.[1]

§2 RELATION TO LEGISLATURE AND EXECUTIVE

Relation to the Legislature

What should be the relation of the Judiciary to the other departments of Government ? So far as its relation to the Legislature is concerned, three or four principles may be formulated.

(*i*) The more the Judiciary is separated from party politics, the better. This means that the Legislature must not have the power to elect judges ; and, further, it is desirable that no member of the Legislature should be eligible for a judicial office. (*ii*) The Legislature may be vested with the power of recommending the removal of judges either by the presentation of an address to the Executive as in Britain, or by impeachment as in the U.S.A. This power is necessary as an ultimate safeguard against a judge who abuses his power by receiving presents, for instance. None, not even a judge, can be entrusted with power without some guarantee against its abuse. (*iii*) The Judiciary in a unitary State (like France) need not have the power to question the validity of laws passed by the Legislature. (*iv*) In federal States, the power of the Judiciary to declare unconstitutional a law passed by the Legislatures is essential in order to maintain the supremacy of the constitution. Our survey shows that the Judiciary in India, the U.S.A. and Australia is vested with ample powers of this kind ; but we find that in Canada and Switzerland the Judiciary has considerably reduced powers.

Relation to the Executive

In organizing the relation between the Judiciary and the Executive, the most important principle clearly is that there must be a separation between the two. The separation is desirable because, as far as possible, no member of the Executive should have judicial functions (subject to the exceptions we have noted in connexion with administrative law in Britain[2]); and because, while it may

---

[1] See above, pp. 79-80, and part II, bk. II.
[2] See above, ch. xvi, §13.

have the power of appointing judges, the Executive must not have the power of dismissing them. The reason for the second restriction has been explained above. The reason for the first is that such a combination involves damage to both liberty and efficiency. To liberty, because if the two are not separated, the Executive, as judge, has to sit in judgement over its own conduct, which is obviously injurious to freedom ; to efficiency, because its members are not chosen for their capacity or training as judges.

But the Executive may be vested with two powers in relation to the Judiciary. The first is the appointment of judges. The appointment of judges by the Executive also has defects ; but alternative methods, such as popular election and election by the Legislature, are worse. The only ultimate guarantee that the best men are chosen as judges lies in a convention, supported by professional opinion, that judges must not be chosen for political or party reasons. The Executive's second power in connexion with the Judiciary is the power of pardon.

In its turn, the Judiciary may be vested with the power to review the acts of the Executive. The government officer must be answerable in a court of law for his conduct as a government servant. This is an important safeguard of liberty. It has been noticed in the discussion of modern constitutions [1] that, in general, States on the continent of Europe have established separate administrative courts for the trial of cases in which the Government or its servants are parties. The relative merits and defects of 'the rule of law' and 'administrative law' have also been examined in the same context.

§3 EXECUTIVE AND JUDICIARY IN INDIA

We have pointed out earlier that in India a number of executive officials are transferred to the judicial department, and vice versa. For example, members of the revenue staff are chosen as sub-magistrates, and sub-magistrates rejoin the revenue staff as deputy collectors. Similarly a number of executive officials perform judicial functions : collectors, who are also district magistrates ; revenue divisional officers, who are also subdivisional magistrates ; and deputy tahsildars who are also sub-magistrates. The district magistrate tries very few cases ; [2] but he exercises administrative control over the sub-magistrates who try the bulk of the criminal cases in

---

[1] See above, ch. xvi, §13 and xvii, §7.
[2] In Madras in 1926 he tried on the average one case and heard eight appeals.

the district. These magistrates have to send to the district magistrate regular statements showing the nature of the cases they have tried, the alleged offences and the results of trials, as well as copies of their judgements. The admonitions of the district magistrates regarding delays or errors in the conduct of cases or the award of punishments are communicated to the sub-magistrates subsequent to the disposal of the cases, with the intention of regulating their disposal of future cases. A district magistrate may also issue general circulars to all magistrates under his control for their instruction or guidance in dealing with cases.

The problem of the separation of executive and judicial powers thus centres in collectors, divisional officers, deputy tahsildars, and sub-magistrates.

That a man who is trying a criminal should try him in a purely judicial spirit and not be influenced by anxiety regarding promotion or prospects is admitted on all hands. This principle was indeed accepted by Sir Harvey Adamson (Home Member to the Government of India) in the Imperial Legislative Council in 1908.

' The exercise of executive control over the subordinate magistrate by whom the great bulk of criminal cases are tried is the point where the present system is defective. If the control is exercised by the officer who is responsible for the peace of the district there is the constant danger that the subordinate magistracy may be unconsciously guided by other than purely judicial considerations.'

It must be remembered too that the promotion and prospects of subordinate magistrates depend partly on the recommendation of the district magistrate as collector ; it is therefore likely that they will subordinate their own views to what they assume to be his views.

There are advantages [1] too in members of the Indian Administrative Service being shifted from executive work to judicial work, because a district judge, for instance, trained in the executive field during his earlier years, may not possess those legal attainments or the judicial frame of mind necessary for an impartial administration of justice.

Progressive opinion in India, therefore, is in favour of effecting a separation of the Executive from the Judiciary. It demands that the control of the subordinate magistracy should be trans-

---

[1] It must be admitted that the system has its advantages also.

ferred to some authority independent of the district magistrate or collector, either to the district and sessions judge or to some officer appointed as his assistant for the purpose. Further, there should be separate officers to discharge the functions of divisional officers and deputy tahsildars, on the one hand, and of first-class and second-class magistrates on the other. Sub-magistrates should be recruited from the bar and placed under the control of the High Court in the same way that district munsiffs are.

A section of opinion in India, however, still seems to fight shy of adopting these or similar proposals in the direction of separation. Apart from the additional expenditure which any scheme of bifurcation necessarily involves, it is pointed out that the existing system secures administrative efficiency. Magistrates subordinate to the district magistrate have the duty of taking preventive measures and quelling disturbances of the public peace ; there is a side of magisterial work which must be regarded as preventive rather than punitive. The argument is that in India the head of the district has to deal with riots and local outbreaks, in which case he must be able to count on the support of the subordinate magistrates. For this purpose it is very desirable that he should be the chief magistrate of the district and that he should know his men. This advantage is now secured by the fact that sub-magistrates are chosen from revenue officials and are controlled by the collector who is also district magistrate. Further, any real scheme of separation will disintegrate the whole system of district administration, which has been built up as an organic whole, both the revenue and magisterial departments being controlled by the district collector and magistrate. To transfer the magisterial powers of the collector to the district judge, or to another officer, will, it is feared, gravely lower his prestige and his value in the scheme of district administration, and lessen the opportunities available for the collector and the sub-divisional officers for keeping personal touch with the people in the district.

Progressive opinion, it may be said, has now won, as the principle of separation of the Executive from the Judiciary has now been accepted. Several states including Tamil Nadu, Uttar Pradesh and Maharashtra have now adopted schemes for the separation of the Judiciary from the Executive ; in other states where the process is not completed, proposals to effect the separation are under active consideration.

In conclusion, it is only necessary to remind the ' routine mind ' of the dictum laid down by de Tocqueville that what we call necessary institutions are no more than institutions to which we are accustomed, and that the possibilities of experiment in the social constitution are far greater than most of us imagine.

SELECT BIBLIOGRAPHY

J. BRYCE, *Modern Democracies*, Vol. II, ch. lxviii, Macmillan, 1921

F. J. GOODNOW, *Principles of Constitutional Government*. ch. xviii-xix, Harpers, 1916

H. SIDGWICK, *The Elements of Politics*, ch. xxiv, Macmillan, 1908

W. F. WILLOUGHBY, *Principles of Judicial Administration*, The Brookings Institution, 1939

INDEX

INDEX